PROBABILITY AND

MW00808779

This book addresses the role of statistics and probability in the evaluation of forensic evidence, including both theoretical issues and applications in legal contexts. It discusses what evidence is and how it can be quantified, how it should be understood, and how it is applied (and, sometimes, misapplied).

After laying out their philosophical position, the authors begin with a detailed study of the likelihood ratio. Following this grounding, they discuss applications of the likelihood ratio to forensic questions, in the abstract and in concrete cases. The analysis of DNA evidence in particular is treated in great detail. Later chapters concern Bayesian networks, frequentist approaches to evidence, the use of belief functions, and the thorny subject of database searches and familial searching. Finally, the authors provide commentary on various recommendation reports for forensic science.

Written to be accessible to a wide audience of applied mathematicians, forensic scientists, and scientifically-oriented legal scholars, this book is a must-read for all those interested in the mathematical and philosophical foundations of evidence and belief.

RONALD MEESTER is Professor in probability theory at the Vrije Universiteit Amsterdam. He is co-author of the books *Continuum Percolation* (1996), *A Natural Introduction to Probability Theory* (2003), *Random Networks for Communication* (2008), and *Wiskunde in je vingers* (in Dutch, 2015) and has written around 120 research papers on topics including percolation theory, ergodic theory, philosophy of science, and forensic probability.

KLAAS SLOOTEN works as Statistician at the Netherlands Forensic Institute and at the Vrije Universiteit Amsterdam where he is Professor by special appointment. He has published around 30 articles on forensic probability and statistics. He is interested in the mathematical, legal, and philosophical approaches to the evaluation of evidence.

PROBABILITY AND FORENSIC EVIDENCE

Theory, Philosophy, and Applications

RONALD MEESTER

Vrije Universiteit Amsterdam

KLAAS SLOOTEN

Netherlands Forensic Institute and Vrije Universiteit Amsterdam

CAMBRIDGE
UNIVERSITY PRESS

CAMBRIDGE
UNIVERSITY PRESS

University Printing House, Cambridge CB2 8BS, United Kingdom

One Liberty Plaza, 20th Floor, New York, NY 10006, USA

477 Williamstown Road, Port Melbourne, VIC 3207, Australia

314–321, 3rd Floor, Plot 3, Splendor Forum, Jasola District Centre, New Delhi – 110025, India

79 Anson Road, #06–04/06, Singapore 079906

Cambridge University Press is part of the University of Cambridge.

It furthers the University's mission by disseminating knowledge in the pursuit of
education, learning, and research at the highest international levels of excellence.

www.cambridge.org
Information on this title: www.cambridge.org/9781108428279
DOI: 10.1017/9781108596176

First published 2021

A catalogue record for this publication is available from the British Library.

ISBN 978-1-108-42827-9 Hardback
ISBN 978-1-108-44914-4 Paperback

Contents

Preface

Uncertainty is an unavoidable and essential ingredient of almost all applications of forensic science. Traces may carry information on who or what left them, by which activity they arose, and several other questions. In many cases there is no way to uniquely identify the only possible source or activity. This means that, while these forensic traces can reduce our uncertainty, they cannot be expected to eliminate it.

Probability theory and statistics are mathematical disciplines that are concerned with uncertainty in many different ways. It is, therefore, to be expected that probability theory and statistics are crucial for understanding the philosophy, theory, and practice of forensic science. This book offers an in-depth discussion about what the mathematical disciplines of probability theory and statistics can contribute to forensic science, and more specifically about the interpretation of evidence.

The diversity of the discipline of forensic science is reflected in the hugely varying nature of the subjects we treat in this book. On the one hand, there is a chapter discussing a number of concrete legal cases, and on the other hand there are chapters which are very theoretical in nature, and for which it is yet unclear whether or not their conclusions will in the future be relevant in the practice of forensic science. This is only natural. Any instance of applied mathematics can only be done in an idealized situation. If mathematics has anything to say about forensics, then it must do so with great care, realizing its limitations, and taking into account the inevitable gap between theory and practice.

At the same time, the applied mathematician should not be too modest either. Identifying correct ways of reasoning in the presence of uncertainty, for instance, is absolutely crucial for forensic science, and mathematics has a lot to say about this. Furthermore, although the details of a probabilistic model of a given situation may be somewhat unrealistic, probability theory will very often be able to draw general conclusions with many practical implications. Forensic science benefits a lot from mathematical and probabilistic modeling, but mathematics itself is also challenged by forensic science, leading to new concepts, ideas, and paradigms. Such interplay between theory and practice has been a driving force for the development of mathematics over the centuries, and the particular discipline discussed in this book is no exception.

Apart from the daily practice and the theory of forensic science, philosophy plays a very important role in this book. Probability theory and statistics alike cannot be applied or even developed without reflection about their meaning and interpretation. For instance, if we want to make an assessment about the probability that a given suspect is the donor of a particular DNA profile, or is guilty of a certain crime, then we first must come to terms with the meaning of the word "probability" here. What exactly does such a probability mean? Similarly, we must decide which statistical paradigm is suitable for our purposes, which forces us to think about what statistical evidence really is.

Philosophy is so important that we feel that we need to start with it. One cannot use concepts that are not, in one way or another, well defined and explained. Apart from the opening chapter on philosophical issues concerning the interpretation of probability, statistics, and of forensic science itself, there are many chapters and sections in the book where philosophical issues are discussed and commented upon. For instance, the reader will find philosophical positions about statistical evidence in Chapters 2 and 3, about the nature of evidence in Chapter 3, about Bayesian networks in Chapter 6, about match probabilities in Chapter 7, about the concept of being a contributor to a DNA mixture in Chapter 8, about significance tests and p-values in Chapter 9, and about an extension of probability theory in Chapter 13.

We hope that the book is found interesting and useful for mathematicians, forensic scientists, and to some extent perhaps also for legal representatives, albeit probably in different ways. We have tried to introduce the basic concepts extensively at a calm pace, with many elementary, not necessarily forensic examples. We fully acknowledge though that there are chapters and sections that will be very demanding for non-mathematicians. Our advice to such readers is to simply skip these parts, and read the "Summary and conclusions" sections at the end of each chapter. We have tried to summarize the main findings in each chapter in an accessible way for a large audience. Of course, it will often not be possible to summarize the conclusions of a full chapter in, say, one page, but in any case the "Summary and conclusions" sections mention the concepts which have been studied and discussed. Hopefully they serve a purpose for those who do not read the full text. Many a conclusion can be understood in itself, without understanding the detailed mathematics leading to it.

This book is also particularly useful as a textbook for a course. We have used it ourselves for a full-semester course, "Forensic Probability and Statistics", taught at VU University, at the MSc level of mathematics. The collected set of exercises that we have made for this course can be obtained from the authors upon request.

To improve the readability of the text, we have mostly postponed bibliographical notes to the end of each chapter. Obviously, we have made use of ideas of many of our colleagues, but we found article-style referencing in the main text not so suitable for this book. Sometimes we deviate from this habit though, for instance when we use a quote from the literature, or when the historical development of a particular subject is important for the actual content. For instance, a discussion of the so-called database controversy in Chapter 11 would be virtually impossible without an account of the various positions held by a large number of researchers in the past. Our reference policy reflects the fact that we look at forensic science from a mathematical perspective. We have included references whenever we think that they are important for our message and our approach, or when certain concepts we use are further explained there. Obviously this means that our list of references is not to be considered a complete list for forensic science at large.

Next we explain the content and composition of the book. As mentioned before, we start with our philosophical position on probability, statistics, evidence, and forensic science. After that, in Chapter 2, we introduce and study the likelihood ratio in great detail. The likelihood ratio quantifies evidence for one hypothesis relative to another one, which we believe is the fundamental notion of statistical evidence. In Chapter 3 we further investigate the nature of the likelihood ratio, and we argue that a likelihood ratio is very different from a conventional statistical parameter. Indeed, we argue that it is an epistemic concept, an expression on our knowledge of the world, rather than an expression about the world itself.

After the first three chapters, the basis of our position and approach has been laid out, and we then continue with our first applications to forensic questions. First, we do that in idealized circumstances in Chapter 4, and after that we discuss applications to a number of concrete legal cases. The last chapter in this second block of three chapters is devoted to Bayesian networks, in order to investigate their usefulness in dealing with dependencies between various pieces of evidence.

In the next two chapters, we will follow a more specific forensic path, by discussing the mathematics of forensic DNA analysis in great detail.

In the two chapters to follow we compare the evidential interpretation of the likelihood ratio to more standard frequentist notions, like p-values and Neyman–Pearson theory. Our conclusions not only touch forensic science, but also have implications for statistical evidence at large. Frequentist notions can be useful if properly understood and interpreted, but we will find that they are not suitable for statistical evidential quantifications.

After that we move our attention to database searches and familial searching, a subject that has seen considerable debate and confusion. We also discuss belief functions and their applications in forensic science. Belief functions generalize probability distributions, and there are reasons why this is sometimes useful and perhaps even necessary, since not all (lack of) knowledge can be properly described by probabilities. Finally, in the last chapter, we comment on six recommendation reports for various aspects of forensic science, and we investigate how the recommendations relate to the theory and philosophy as developed in the book.

This is not a book about technical statistical and probabilistic issues. We have tried to select those topics that we think will have lasting value, and of course we were also to some extent led by our own preferences. Concepts are more important for us than mathematical technicalities. Forensic science is a field with rapidly developing technical possibilities, and as such its needs will also change. But the concepts that we discuss in this book will remain valuable, we expect. Indeed, at all times we will need to think about what probability and statistics have to say about evidence, and this book addresses this question in great detail.

Most of this book was written during many visits of the authors to leisure park 'n Kaps in Tubbergen, in the beautiful region of Twente in the east of the Netherlands. The park offers excellent working conditions, allowing for many hours of undisturbed, concentrated work.

1

Some Philosophy of Probability, Statistics, and Forensic Science

Before we embark on our task of discussing the mathematics of probability and statistics in legal and forensic science, we need to think about how probabilistic and statistical statements could or perhaps should be interpreted and understood in this context. That is, we need to agree on a philosophical interpretation of probability and statistics suitable for our purposes. This is a very important and subtle issue. In any real life application of probability it is crucial to agree (as much as we can) about what we mean when we write down probabilistic assessments about hypotheses or events. Probabilistic statements are known for their difficult interpretation, and certainly in legal and forensic affairs, vagueness about the very meaning of such questions should be avoided. Our discussion will be rather brief and we do not claim completeness in any way. The philosophy of probability is a huge subject of which we will barely scratch the surface. Apart from a philosophical position towards probability theory and statistics, we will also spend a few words on our philosophical position about forensic science itself.

1.1 The Kolmogorov Axioms of Probability

Let us start with the basic mathematical setup of probability theory. Since our focus will be on situations in which the truth is one out of only finitely many possibilities, we can restrict ourselves to probability distributions on finite outcome spaces. If Ω is such a finite outcome space, then a probability distribution on Ω is a mapping P from all subsets of Ω to $[0, 1]$ with the properties that

$$P(\Omega) = 1 \tag{1.1}$$

and

$$P(A \cup B) = P(A) + P(B), \tag{1.2}$$

for all $A, B \subset \Omega$ such that $A \cap B = \emptyset$. The quantity $P(A)$ is supposed to represent the probability that the outcome of the experiment is an element of A.

Other properties quickly follow from this definition, and we mention some of them, without proof:

(1) $P(\emptyset) = 0$;
(2) If $A \subset B$ then $P(A) \leq P(B)$. More precisely, $P(B \backslash A) = P(B) - P(A) \geq 0$;
(3) $P(A \cup B) = P(A) + P(B) - P(A \cap B)$, for all $A, B \subset \Omega$.

These properties align with our intuitive understanding of probabilities. Indeed for (2), if A implies B then the probability of B must at least be as large as the probability of A. Property (3) can be understood when you realize that when you add up the probabilities of A and B, you have counted the contribution of the intersection twice. Hence you must subtract it from the sum to obtain the probability of the union of A and B.

It is not difficult to see that a probability measure P is determined by the probabilities of the singletons in Ω. Indeed, for all $A \subset \Omega$ we have

$$P(A) = \sum_{\omega \in A} P(\{\omega\}).$$

One of the most important ideas in probability theory is the notion of conditional probability. Given a probability measure P, the conditional probability of A given B, denoted $P(A \mid B)$ is defined (if $P(B) > 0$) by

$$P(A \mid B) = \frac{P(A \cap B)}{P(B)}. \tag{1.3}$$

This quantity is supposed to represent the new probability of A once we have learned (or supposed) that B occurs. It can be understood heuristically: when we condition on B, we restrict ourselves to only outcomes in B, hence the $P(A \cap B)$ in the numerator. But in order to make sure that the total probability is still one, we have to normalize and divide by $P(B)$. Hence, B now plays the role of Ω.

The very useful Bayes rule

$$P(A \mid B) = \frac{P(B \mid A) P(A)}{P(B)} \tag{1.4}$$

follows from applying (1.3) twice. Although mathematically elementary, the rule is very significant in forensic and legal affairs, where it is often used in the so-called *odds form*:

$$\frac{P(H_1 \mid E)}{P(H_2 \mid E)} = \frac{P(E \mid H_1)}{P(E \mid H_2)} \times \frac{P(H_1)}{P(H_2)}. \tag{1.5}$$

Here, H_1 and H_2 typically are unobserved events, often called *hypotheses*. An example of such an event is "suspect is guilty of the crime." The event E can typically be observed, and refers to certain evidence, for instance the event that the suspect has a certain DNA profile. The left-hand side is the ratio of the probabilities of the hypotheses H_1 and H_2 after we have learned about the evidence E. The fraction at the far right is the same ratio before knowing this evidence, and the remaining fraction

$$\frac{P(E \mid H_1)}{P(E \mid H_2)} \tag{1.6}$$

is called the *likelihood ratio*. We will come back to this rule and its use and interpretation extensively and in great detail in the chapters to follow, but note already at this point that we view hypotheses as events which can be assigned a probability.

A very important question to ask now, is why the axioms in (1.1) and (1.2) would be acceptable as axioms for the theory of probability. Why can probability be axiomatized this way? Without agreement on what "probability" actually means, this question will be an impossible one to answer. The axioms are abstract mathematical notions, but they are supposed to capture the bare essentials of what we would like to call "probability." The axioms would be useless if there would be no instantiations of them that correspond to some intuitive notion of probability, whatever that notion may be.

Consider the simplest example of a probability distribution, namely the situation where each outcome is assigned the same probability. Specifically, writing $|A|$ for the number of elements in the set A, one can set

$$P(A) = \frac{|A|}{|\Omega|}.$$

Clearly this P satisfies (1.1) and (1.2), and as a mathematical object P is clear. But how useful is it? How can we know that this is an applicable or useful model of what we are considering it to model? The point we want to make has been very clearly explained by Poincaré [122]:

"The definition, it will be said, is very simple. The probability of an event is the ratio of the number of cases favorable to the event to the total number of possible cases. [...] So we are compelled to define the probable by the probable. How can we know that two possible cases are equally probable? Will it be by convention? If we insert at the beginning of every problem an explicit convention, well and good! We then have nothing to do but to apply the rules of arithmetic and algebra, and we complete our calculation, when our result cannot be called into question. But if we wish to make the slightest application of this result, we must prove that our convention is legitimate, and we shall find ourselves in the presence of the very difficulty we thought we had avoided."

For example, suppose that we want to model tosses of a coin we have in our pocket. If we define $P(H) = 1/2$ and $P(T) = 1/2$, where H stands for heads and T for tails, then we assign equal probability to each, and hence also say that no other outcomes (e.g., landing on its edge) are considered possible. But how can we know, Poincaré asks, whether this is the "correct" probability, and what would that even be? Our mathematical definition of a function that we call probability is an abstract entity, and its definition sheds no light on the question on if or how we can see the probabilities as properties of physical objects.

We have not defined what probability is, outside the abstract mathematical framework above, is what Poincaré's quote above suggests. Instead, we can ask for concrete and useful instantiations of concepts that satisfy the axioms of Kolmogorov, and which also somehow align with our intuitive idea about what probability is.

One of the more powerful attempts in that direction is to interpret the probability of an event as the relative frequency of the occurrence of the event in a sequence of repetitions of the same experiment. A first natural idea when applying probability is that, if we were to repeat the same experiment many times independently, we would expect to see the outcomes having certain relative frequencies which are a property of the experiment, so that we may define their probabilities as these relative frequencies. It is useful and interesting to see how the natural axioms (1.1) and (1.2) and the equally natural definition (1.3) follow from interpreting probability in such a frequentistic way, and this is what we now first explore. We will conclude, however, that such a frequentistic interpretation does not solve the circularity dilemma of Poincaré: it will re-appear in a slightly disguised form. As such, it will not tell us what probability is in any ontological sense, but this does not prevent the notion of frequencies from being very useful in many circumstances.

1.2 The Frequentistic Interpretation

In many applications of probability theory we have a process or experiment in mind that can be repeated. To take a canonical example, when we flip a coin, we are inclined to think that the probability for heads to come up is $1/2$. And indeed, repeating the coin flip many times will often show that about half of the time heads does come up. This empirical fact can be seen as support for the statement that the probability of heads is $1/2$. Moreover, we humans have the capacity to imagine infinitely many coin flips. When we do so, we imagine that if we were able to carry out infinitely many such repetitions of the coin flip, the *relative frequency* of heads coming up would converge to $1/2$. That is, if we throw the coin k times, and k_h denotes the number of heads, we imagine that k_h/k tends to $1/2$ as k gets larger.

This kind of frequentistic reasoning leads to the standard Kolmogorov axioms of probability stated above in a very straightforward way. Indeed, when we flip the coin k times, and the number of heads among these k flips is k_h, then the relative frequency of heads is equal to k_h/k. The relative frequency of tails can be written as k_t/k, where k_t is the number of tails among the k flips. Since obviously

$$\frac{k_h}{k} + \frac{k_t}{k} = 1, \tag{1.7}$$

and this identity is preserved under taking the limit of more and more experiments, we see that we arrive at the first axiom (1.1), since heads and tails are the only possible outcomes.

To see that the *addition* of probabilities in (1.2) is also reasonable in such a context, imagine that we roll a die k times. Denoting the number of 1's and 2's (say) among the k outcomes by k_1 and k_2 respectively, then the relative frequency of seeing a 1 or a 2 is equal to the sum $(k_1 + k_2)/k$ of the original relative frequencies. As above, this then remains true in the limit as the number of experiments tends to infinity. This argument extends to any two subsets A and B of the outcome space which are disjoint, and leads to the second Kolmogorov axiom (1.2).

Hence frequentistic reasoning adheres to the axioms of probability. In fact, it might even be the case that many people accept (1.1) and (1.2) as the axioms of probability, *because* they are satisfied by limiting relative frequencies.

Relative frequencies also lead to the notion of conditional probabilities defined above in an elegant way. Indeed, suppose that we repeat a certain experiment k times (where k is large), and that on each occasion we observe whether or not the events A and B occur. The number of occurrences of an event E is denoted by k_E. Conditioning on B means that we only look at those outcomes for which B occurs, and disregard all other outcomes. In this smaller collection of trails, the fraction of the outcomes for which A occurs is $k_{A \cap B}/k_B$ which is equal to

$$\frac{k_{A \cap B}/k}{k_B/k}, \tag{1.8}$$

and this is indeed about $P(A \cap B)/P(B)$. Hence this latter expression is a very natural candidate for the conditional probability of A given B, again from the frequentistic point of view.

The question now is whether or not this notion of probability solves the circularity dilemma of Poincaré that we discussed above. The answer is no, and we explain this now.

Obviously, not all infinite sequences of coin flips have the property that the relative frequency of heads converges to $1/2$. In fact, if any toss can be heads or tails, then any infinite sequence can in principle occur. We could, for instance, only throw tails. In fact it is also not difficult to construct infinite sequences of coin flips for which the relative frequencies of heads do not converge at all; not to 1/2 and not to any other number. This being undeniably true, the reader might object that such a sequence of only tails will not occur in real life. Indeed, anyone repeatedly flipping a coin will see that the relative frequencies of heads will – after some time – be close to 1/2. But the key question now is: on what grounds are we going to differentiate between sequences that lead to the "right" probability of 1/2, and those that do not? That is, we need to worry about those sequences for which the relative frequency of heads does not converge to 1/2. These anomalous sequences have to be somehow ruled out as not being relevant. The only possible way to do this seems to be to say that such exceptional sequences rarely occur and form a very small minority compared to the collection of possible sequences.

This argument would boil down to saying that the overwhelming majority of the infinite sequences of coin flips lead to a relative frequency of 1/2 for heads, and that the exceptional sequences form a tiny minority. But now we face a problem: what do we mean by "exceptional"? How do we define that? The only way to do that is to say that such exceptional sequences essentially do not occur, but quantifying this again presupposes some notion of chance already. The circularity of Poincaré appears again, albeit in a slightly different form.

So although interpreting probability frequentistically is very useful, it does not solve our problem to the extent that it does not tell us what probability *is*. Relative frequencies form an instantiation of the axioms of probability, that much is clear. They do not define probability in any way, but at the same time, they are extremely useful in situations where repetitions of similar events play a role. For instance, casinos make a profit by relying on the calculus of probability, interpreted as relative frequencies. Casinos are not concerned at all with philosophical discussions about the nature of probability. They are concerned with making money, and for that purpose, relative frequencies are very useful.

In fact, the application story of relative frequencies gets even better. It turns out that in the standard Kolmogorov axiomatization of probability, laws of large numbers can be proven which are consistent with the empirical facts about convergence of relative frequencies. For instance, the probability that after k flips with the coin, the fraction heads deviates by more than a given $\epsilon > 0$ from 1/2 tends to zero as k tends to infinity.

For casinos, it is important to have a very precise idea about the relative frequencies: if a coin would come up heads with frequency 0.501, then this could harm the casino. They can use results such as those we just mentioned, to decide that a coin seems safe for use in the casino based on its relative frequency in a long series being sufficiently close to 0.5. On the other hand, if a coin is used for the toss at the beginning of a soccer match, then 0.501 as the long run frequency is clearly less relevant. Thinking of probabilities in terms of relative frequencies is extremely useful, and leads to a mathematical theory which is consistent with many empirical facts.

Closely related to the concept of relative frequencies in repeatable experiments, is the notion of population proportions. If we have a population of, say, 100 individuals of which 40 carry a certain characteristic, then one may claim that upon randomly choosing a population member, the probability that the chosen member has the characteristic is 40/100. The idea behind this is that proportions, like frequencies, satisfy the Kolmogorov axioms, as is easily verified. The fact that the phrase "randomly choosing a population member" already assumes some notion of probability in which each member has the same probability to be chosen, implies that the idea of proportion cannot be used to define what probability is either. It is, however, another instantiation of the axioms of Kolmogorov. Whenever we speak of a population *frequency* instead of a population proportion, we think of the fraction of an infinite population that would have a certain characteristic.

All this makes it tempting to associate probability with (at least conceptual) repeatability, or even to require repeatability for the assignment of probabilities. We next explain why we disagree with that.

1.3 The Inadequacy of Relative Frequencies in the Legal and Forensic Context

For our purposes, things may not be so easy and straightforward, for at least two reasons. First of all, we would like to make probabilistic statements about, say, the guilt of a certain suspect, or about the hypothesis that a given man is the father of a given child. These kind of probabilistic statements, if they make sense at all, cannot be interpreted in the same vein as the coin flips because every single legal or forensic situation is genuinely unique, and cannot be repeated. Repetitions of the coin flip would not make sense from a frequentistic point of view if the circumstances of different coin flips would not be essentially the same. The implicit assumption in the context of coin flips, or for that matter in any application of a frequentistic interpretation of probabilities, is that we repeat the *same* experiment many times. This, then, obviously often does not make sense in the legal context that we are interested in. No two legal cases are the same and this means that a phrase like "The probability that John Smith is the criminal" does not make sense from a frequentistic point of view. We have to give this statement another meaning, that is, we need another instantiation of probability than the frequentistic one.

Moreover, when two individuals have the same information, it need not be the case that they make the same probabilistic assessment. Their background knowledge and expertise may lead them to incorporate this information differently leading to different probabilistic assessments. As a result, the probabilistic analysis of a situation will differ among different people, and each such interpretation should therefore be interpreted subjectively, not objectively. So if we want to use the axioms of Kolmogorov described above in (1.1) and (1.2) we need to argue that such a subjective view on probabilities can be based on these very same axioms. In short, we need a subjective instantiation of probability.

In the next section we will give such an instantiation, namely *epistemic* probability, which intends to assign probabilities based on one's *information* or *knowledge*, and which also allows one to assign probabilities to events that already have taken place. Many probabilistic statements in legal and forensic cases can, and we think should, be interpreted from such an epistemic point of view. A judge will base the verdict on his or her personal conviction of the truth based on the information he or she has, not on the truth itself. This illustrates the fact that most probabilistic statements in legal and forensic affairs are genuinely epistemic in nature.

So, many probabilistic statements in legal and forensic affairs do not seem to make sense when interpreted frequentistically, especially when they relate to individual cases. This is, of course, not to say that frequentistic probability should be abandoned from forensic and legal contexts. To give but one example, it might be useful or even necessary to think about the quality of a legal system in terms of the fraction of wrong convictions. Such questions should be approached frequentistically, despite the fact that individual cases typically should not. Another example is the fact that one tends to think about DNA profiles in a frequentistic manner. If the actual population frequency of a given profile would be known to us, then one may interpret the subsequent checking of people's DNA in the same vein as flipping a coin: one postulates a fixed p representing the probability for any person to have the profile (ignoring familial relationships). That is, one may interpret this number p frequentistically.

But even this rather straightforward application is not easily possible without complications. This is due to the fact that in practice p is typically not known precisely. If we have no certainty about p, then upon checking people's DNA one by one, one may actually learn something about the unknown p, and then we are back in the epistemic context where one's probability assessment depends on the information one has. This information may in part, but not entirely, consist of a sample of the population and the relative frequency therein. We discuss this issue briefly in Section 1.6 below, and more extensively in Chapters 3 and 7.

Hence, there is at first glance a certain tension between epistemic and frequentistic interpretations of probability and this leads to rather interesting questions. For instance, is it possible to combine two different interpretations of probabilities (epistemic and frequentistic) into a single formula, like Bayes' rule (1.4)?

Does such a formula still make sense when the probabilities involved in the formula should be interpreted in different ways?

To briefly elaborate on this, suppose that in (1.4), H_1 is the hypothesis that John Smith committed a certain crime, H_2 the hypothesis that an unknown person did it, and that E is the evidence of finding a certain DNA profile at the scene of the crime, which we assume comes from the culprit, and which is identical to the profile of John Smith. The probabilities $P(H_i)$, $P(H_i \mid E)$ represent epistemic probabilities for a hypothesis to be true, while $P(E \mid H_i)$ can represent frequentistic probabilities for persons to have the relevant DNA profile. So we have two different interpretations of P within the same formula. The only way to meaningfully interpret the formula then, it seems, is to embrace a frequentistic number into one's epistemic probability. This makes sense, since there is no reason why empirical facts and observed frequencies cannot be incorporated into one's epistemic analysis. Epistemic probabilities are based on all our knowledge, and this knowledge may lead us to conclude that a frequentist interpretation is (exactly or approximately) appropriate, such as in the example with DNA profiles. In other words, it is reasonable to assume that epistemic interpretations include, but are more general than, frequentistic ones and that we should interpret Bayes' rule epistemically in situations like this. A remark to more or less the same effect was made by Cooke [38], where we read on page 108:

"Subjective probabilities can be, and often are, limiting frequencies. In particular, this happens when a subject's belief state leads him to regard the past as relevant for the future in a special way."

Let us next study epistemic probability in some more detail, and investigate how such an epistemic interpretation can adhere to the axioms of Kolmogorov (1.1) and (1.2) as well. Since we want to use classical probability calculus like Bayes' rule, such an axiomatic foundation of epistemic probability is very important for our purposes.

1.4 Epistemic Probability

As we explained in the previous section, we need a well-founded interpretation of epistemic probability suitable for our purposes. Epistemic probability allows different people to make their own probabilistic analysis of a given situation. The basic idea is that the probabilistic analysis of a situation of an agent, depends on the information (including both case specific information and general knowledge) he has, and not directly on the actual truth itself. This information can vary greatly among various people.

We saw in the previous section that the idea behind frequentistic interpretations of probability is the concept of relative frequencies. For epistemic probability interpretations, a different approach is needed. The epistemic probability of an event A of a certain agent is sometimes called the *degree of belief* this agent has in the event A. If the agent knows for sure that A does not occur, then his degree of belief in A is 0, while complete confidence in the occurrence of A implies that his belief in A is equal to 1.

Although the extremal point 0 and 1 are rather easy to interpret, the values in between are not. In fact, there is no consensus in the philosophical literature that belief comes in continuous degrees at all, but for our purposes we do assume that it does. How should we define and quantify one's degree of belief in a certain event A? One approach (but not the only one) is to ask people how much money they would be willing to pay for the bet on the occurrence of the event A which pays out 1 if A actually occurs. Since the amount of money an agent wants to bet crucially depends on her or his information (and indeed probably on many other things as well), different people will be willing to pay different amounts for the same bet. Let us therefore define the notion of degree of belief this way. Here and in the sequel we refer to the agent as "he." This is meant to include both sexes.

Definition 1.4.1 The degree of belief that an agent has in an event A is the maximal amount of money he is willing to pay for a bet which pays out 1 if A actually occurs.

Obviously the degree of belief will differ among different agents. For one thing they may have different information, and moreover, not all people are willing to take the same risks. This makes this approach a genuine subjective one. Note that it is important that we ask for the *maximal* amount an agent is willing to pay. Many people would probably be willing to pay a very small amount for a bet on an event they know (or think) occurs. The key point is to determine what they are maximally willing to pay.

If we adopt this idea, then one can also assign degrees of belief to factual things. For instance, if agent A throws a die in such a way that agent A sees the result but agent B does not, then agent B will still be able to express his degree of belief in the event that the outcome is 2. The fact that the die has already been thrown is completely irrelevant for this. Agent A, however, will have a very different degree of belief in the outcome 2, because he knows whether or not it has occurred.

If you are worried about assigning nontrivial probabilities to events that we know are either factually true or not, then you should be aware of the fact that this is precisely what needs to be done in legal and forensic circumstances. If we want to assign a probability to the event that a given individual is the donor of a certain DNA profile, then this is factually either true or not. But this is not important. What matters is what we can say about this question on the basis of the information that we have. As such the question about the origin of the DNA profile is no different than the question about what the outcome is of an already thrown die. As long as we have not obtained any knowledge on the outcome of the experiment, we are in the same epistemic position as when it has not yet been carried out. The fact that reality changes is irrelevant for our assessment as long as our knowledge about it does not change.

Why would the degrees of belief an agent assigns to the various events satisfy the Kolmogorov axioms of probability? Of course, if the agent behaves irrationally, then they need not. For instance, an irrational agent might pay 2 for a bet whose maximal payout is 1. However, a rational agent will not do that, and the amount he is willing to pay for the *sure* event Ω should be 1, at least confirming (1.1).

The second axiom (1.2) is less clear, but there are several ways to go about it. One approach is to also consider the possibility of *selling* a bet, rather than buying it. When an agent sells a bet on A for a certain price, he receives the paid amount for the bet, but he has to pay 1 to the buyer of the bet if A actually occurs. This sounds quite natural, since a bet can only be bought if someone else sells it, so buying and selling seem to go hand in hand. Note, however, that determining one's price for a bet does not necessarily imply that anything is traded at all. It can also, and typically will be, merely a thought experiment used to investigate one's personal valuation of a certain bet, and therefore one's personal belief in the corresponding event.

In principle, willingness to buy a bet for a certain price does not necessarily imply willingness to sell it for the same price. But let us for now assume that buying and selling prices agree, and that a bet on an event A simply represents a certain value. What can we deduce from such an assumption?

Consider, then, an agent who wants to buy a bet on $A \cup B$, where A and B are disjoint events. At the same time, this agent sells bets on A and B individually to other parties. Given that he sells the bet on A and the bet on B for α and β, respectively, his buying price for $A \cup B$ will be at *most* $\alpha + \beta$. Indeed, if he were to buy $A \cup B$ for more, then he would lose money with certainty, while a price of $\alpha + \beta$ will make him play even. Hence we find that the price for the bet on $A \cup B$ must be at most the sum of the individual prices. A similar argument but now for selling a bet on $A \cup B$ and buying individual bets on A and B leads to the conclusion that the price for $A \cup B$ must be at least the sum of the individual prices, and we conclude that the second axiom (1.2) also holds.

The key idea, then, is that no agent will collectively buy and sell certain bets when he knows that no matter the outcome, he will always lose money. For a proper understanding of what follows, the above discussion provides enough information. For the interested reader, we briefly elaborate by providing two characterization of probability distributions in betting terms, which reinforce the betting interpretation of probabilities. Readers who are not particularly interested in this can safely skip the rest of this section.

Let Ω denote the outcome space of the experiment as before. Suppose the agent buys and sells certain bets. Then there should be at least one outcome $\omega \in \Omega$ so that if ω occurs, then the agent does not lose money, otherwise he would always lose money. This property is called the *no sure loss* property. In the following formal definition, the agent buys the bets $A_1, \ldots, A_N$ and sells the bets $B_1, \ldots, B_M$. We use the *indicator-function* $1_E(\omega)$, which is defined to be 1 if $\omega \in E$ and 0 otherwise. Note that if the actual outcome is ω, the total net profit of this collection of bets is equal to

$$\sum_{i=1}^{N} \left(1_{A_i}(\omega) - P(A_i)\right) + \sum_{j=1}^{M} \left(P(B_j) - 1_{B_j}(\omega)\right). \tag{1.9}$$

Definition 1.4.2 Let Q be a mapping from all subsets of Ω to $[0,1]$. We say that Q satisfies the *no sure loss property* (or is *coherent*) if for all choices of $A_1, A_2, \ldots, A_N \subset \Omega$ and $B_1, B_2, \ldots, B_M \subset \Omega$, there is an $\omega \in \Omega$ such that

$$\sum_{i=1}^{N} \left(1_{A_i}(\omega) - Q(A_i)\right) + \sum_{j=1}^{M} \left(Q(B_j) - 1_{B_j}(\omega)\right) \geq 0. \tag{1.10}$$

Note that in this definition it is implicit that buying and selling prices agree. The following result says that in order for the prices an agent is willing to pay for the various events to satisfy the usual axioms of Kolmogorov, it is necessary and sufficient that the agent avoids sure loss. This seems to be a rather weak requirement, since no rational agent will make a collective bet that will cost him money for sure.

Theorem 1.4.3 *Let Q be a mapping from all subsets of Ω to $[0,1]$. Then Q is a probability distribution if and only if $Q(\Omega) = 1$ and Q satisfies the no sure loss property.*

Proof It is sufficient to show that the no sure loss property is equivalent to finite additivity. First suppose that Q has the no sure loss property, and let A and B be disjoint subsets of Ω. Choose $N = 2$, $M = 1$, $A_1 = A$, $A_2 = B$, and $B_1 = A \cup B$. Applying the no sure loss property with these choices gives that there is an $\omega \in \Omega$ such that

$$1_A(\omega) + 1_B(\omega) - P(A) - P(B) + P(A \cup B) - 1_{A \cup B}(\omega) \geq 0.$$

Since $1_A(\omega) + 1_B(\omega) - 1_{A \cup B}(\omega) = 0$, we find $P(A) + P(B) \leq P(A \cup B)$. Repeating the argument with $N = 1$, $M = 2$, $A_1 = A \cup B$, $B_1 = A$, and $B_2 = B$ gives the opposite inequality.

For the other direction, assume that Q is a probability distribution and suppose that there are sets $A_1, \ldots, A_N$ and $B_1, \ldots, B_M$ such that for all $\omega \in \Omega$, we have

$$\sum_{i=1}^{N} \left(1_{A_i}(\omega) - Q(A_i)\right) + \sum_{j=1}^{M} \left(Q(B_j) - 1_{B_j}(\omega)\right) < 0.$$

It then follows that

$$\sum_{\omega \in \Omega} Q(\{\omega\}) \left\{ \sum_{i=1}^{N} \left(1_{A_i}(\omega) - Q(A_i)\right) + \sum_{j=1}^{M} \left(Q(B_j) - 1_{B_j}(\omega)\right) \right\} < 0.$$

Since

$$\sum_{\omega \in \Omega} Q(\{\omega\}) \sum_{i=1}^{N} 1_{A_i}(\omega) = \sum_{i=1}^{N} Q(A_i)$$

and similarly for the B_j, we find that

$$0 = \sum_{i=1}^{N} Q(A_i) - \sum_{i=1}^{N} Q(A_i) + \sum_{j=1}^{M} Q(B_j) - \sum_{j=1}^{M} Q(B_j) < 0,$$

a contradiction. $\qquad\square$

We also mention a characterization of probability distributions in betting terms which only involves buying bets.

Consider two sets of collections $A_1, A_2, \ldots, A_N \subset \Omega$ and $B_1, B_2, \ldots, B_M \subset \Omega$. If it is the case that for all $\omega \in \Omega$, the number of the A_i that occur is at least as large as the number of B_j that occur, then an agent might not be willing to spend more on buying all of the B_j than on buying all of the A_i. This somewhat natural property also characterizes probability distributions, as we now show.

Theorem 1.4.4 *A function Q from the subsets of Ω to $[0, 1]$ is a probability distribution if and only if (1) $Q(\Omega) = 1$, and (2) for all $A_1, A_2, \ldots, A_N \subset \Omega$ and $B_1, B_2, \ldots, B_M \subset \Omega$ such that for all $\omega \in \Omega$,*

$$\sum_{i=1}^{N} 1_{A_i}(\omega) \geq \sum_{j=1}^{M} 1_{B_j}(\omega), \tag{1.11}$$

we have

$$\sum_{i=1}^{N} Q(A_i) \geq \sum_{j=1}^{M} Q(B_j). \tag{1.12}$$

Proof It is sufficient to show that property (2) is equivalent to finite additivity. First suppose that (2) is true. Let $A, B \subset \Omega$ be disjoint. For all $\omega \in \Omega$ we have

$$1_A(\omega) + 1_B(\omega) = 1_{A \cup B}(\omega), \tag{1.13}$$

so by (2) we find both $Q(A) + Q(B) \geq Q(A \cup B)$ and $Q(A \cup B) \geq Q(A) + Q(B)$. So Q is finitely additive.

Conversely, suppose that Q is finitely additive. Let $A_1, A_2, \ldots, A_N \subseteq \Omega$ and $B_1, B_2, \ldots, B_M \subseteq \Omega$ be such that (1.11) holds. Then

$$\sum_{i=1}^{N} Q(A_i) = \sum_{\omega \in \Omega} Q(\{\omega\}) \sum_{i=1}^{N} 1_{A_i}(\omega)$$

$$\geq \sum_{\omega \in \Omega} Q(\{\omega\}) \sum_{j=1}^{M} 1_{B_i}(\omega) \tag{1.14}$$

$$= \sum_{j=1}^{M} Q(B_j),$$

so (2) holds. □

We see that there are interpretations of epistemic probability which satisfy the axioms of Kolmogorov. This, however, is in itself not quite enough to also allow for using the *calculus* of probability, in which conditional probability plays such an important role. In the frequentistic interpretation, we not only convinced ourselves in (1.7) that relative frequencies satisfy the axioms of probability, but also that the definition of conditional probability can be suitably interpreted in the frequentistic setting, see (1.8). Therefore, in order to complete the picture, we also need such a justification for using the classical formula (1.3) within our epistemic interpretation.

Recall that $P(A)$ is the amount of money an agent is willing to pay for a bet on the occurrence of A which pays out 1 if A occurs. It seems reasonable to interpret $P(A \cap B)/P(B)$ as the amount of money the agent is willing to pay for a bet on A if he already knows that B occurs. Does this interpretation make sense?

We argue it does. If $P(A \cap B)/P(B)$ is close to 1, then apparently the agent is willing to pay almost the same amount for the bets on $A \cap B$ and B. Hence, as far as this agent is concerned $A \cap B$ and B are almost the same. A similar argument is valid for when the ratio is close to 0. More generally, if the agent has equal belief in $A_1 \cap B$ and $A_2 \cap B$, then A_1 and A_2 should reasonably have the same belief if it is now given that B occurs. Hence, the conditional belief in A given B should be proportional to $P(A \cap B)$, and therefore equal to $P(A \cap B)/P(B)$.

1.5 Problems and Anomalies

In the previous section we have shown how probability distributions can be characterized via a betting context. As such, it seems reasonable to say that there is some philosophical backup for using probability distributions to quantify degrees of belief of agents. This, however, is not to say that there are no problems with such an interpretation, and in this section we mention some of them. We will return to these issues in Chapter 13 where we explain how some of the concerns below can be dealt with when we use belief functions rather than probability distributions to quantify degrees of belief.

In order to explain which problems arise, let us consider the degree of belief of an agent in the event that the Nile is longer than the Mississippi. If the agent knows which of the two rivers is the longer one, then he will be willing to pay 1 or 0 for such a bet. If he is fairly sure that the Nile is longer, then he might be willing to pay an amount close to 1. But suppose now that the agent has absolutely no idea, or even more extreme, that he has even never heard of those two rivers. If that is the case, and we denote by A the event that the Nile is longer, then the agent will not be willing to pay a lot for the bet on A, but, and this is the crucial observation, he will not be willing to pay a lot for the bet on A^c, the complement of A, either. That is, his degree of belief $P(A)$ in A and his degree of belief $P(A^c)$ in A^c should *both* be small, and this clearly violates the Kolmogorov axioms since these axioms require that $P(A) + P(A^c) = 1$. In other words, probability in this sense need not be additive.

In fact, there are situations in which it is natural to suspend all judgment about an event A, that is, to assign $P(A) = P(A^c) = 0$. Suppose that one morning, you find a huge sealed jar of gum balls at your doorstep. On it is a little note that says: "I can sell you a bet that pays out 1 euro if the number of gum balls is even and a bet that pays out 1 euro if the number of gum balls is odd. How much are you willing to pay for either of these bets?" Without any reliable way to count the gum balls or having other evidence, you are completely ignorant about the number of gum balls being even or odd, so it is reasonable not to buy any of the two bets. Therefore, assigning $P(A) = P(A^c) = 0$ is, although not completely forced, a very reasonable thing to do. On the other hand, you would be willing to pay 1 euro for the bet that the number of gum balls is either odd or even. Hence the amount of money one is willing to pay for certain bets is not necessarily additive.

If we base epistemic probability on the Kolmogorov axioms of probability theory, one cannot withhold belief from a proposition without assigning that belief to the negation of the proposition, since $P(A) + P(A^c) = 1$. However, we have just discovered that this property is not always desirable. We can rephrase this by saying that the Kolmogorov axioms cannot distinguish between the willingness to bet on the negation of a proposition A on the one hand, and not being willing to bet on the proposition A itself. This is very relevant for applications in legal issues, where for instance, increased belief in the guilt of a suspect should perhaps not be based on the dismissal of certain exculpatory evidence.

All this suggests that the usual axioms of probability may not always be appropriate if we interpret probability as a degree of belief. This begs the question as to what goes wrong in our interpretation of epistemic probability that we gave in the previous section, which seemed to be a rather convincing way of relating epistemic probability to the axioms of probability. The answer lies in the assumption that the price for which an agent is willing to buy a certain bet is the same as the price for which an agent is willing to sell the same bet. However, there are many situations in which this will not be the case. In the bet about which of the Nile or the Mississippi is the longer river, we saw that ignorance about the answer leads to a very low buying price. But the selling price will be high, since the agent does not want to take the risk that he has to pay out if the river on which he bets turns indeed out to be the longer one. The difference between buying and selling prices arises precisely from ignorance in the case.

Note that Theorem 1.4.4 is in terms of buying bets only. Selling bets does not play a role. In what sense is this theorem problematic then? The answer to this question lies in the implicit assumption that the price of a collection of bets is the sum of the prices of all members of that collection. This seems, at first sight, quite reasonable, but the example with the Nile and the Mississippi above shows that it need not be. Indeed, an ignorant agent may not be willing to pay any positive amount for either of the individual bets on the two rivers, but would of course be willing to pay 1 for the bet that one of the two rivers is the longer one.

For a forensic example, we next briefly mention the classical *island problem*, which we study in great detail in Chapter 4. In the classical version of the island problem a crime has been committed on an island, making it a certainty that an inhabitant of the island committed it. Suppose that the island has $N + 1$ inhabitants. In the absence of any further information, the classical point of view is to use (1.5) and start by assigning prior probability $1/(N + 1)$ to each of the hypotheses H_i that the ith person committed the crime, $i = 1, \ldots, N + 1$. The idea behind this practice is that the uniform distribution, assigning equal probability to each possible outcome, should somehow represent prior ignorance: if you do not know anything, then spreading the probability mass evenly seems fair.

Of course, if you randomly select an islander in the sense that each islander has probability $1/(N + 1)$ to be chosen, then no matter what, the probability that you found the criminal is $1/(N + 1)$. However, in general it is not reasonable to regard the identification of a suspect as the result of such a process, and hence a uniform distribution may not be appropriate.

Ignorance is not the same as uniform probabilities. Every probability distribution is obtained from a particular state of knowledge. A uniform distribution may be appropriate if there is knowledge that tells us so. It is appropriate when we know that outcomes are equally likely (say, whether a child will be a boy or a girl), or when our knowledge on various possibilities does not allow to distinguish between them. In other situations, a uniform distribution may not be appropriate.

In the island problem, we do in general not have prior information pointing to any individual. We have information about the full population, but no further information on the individual level. With a uniform distribution over the population, you nevertheless make a statement about each individual. This is very relevant in legal cases since these are against individuals, not against a whole population. Ideally, if we want to reflect the lack of evidence against any individual, we would like to assign degree of belief 1 to the collection of all inhabitants and degree of belief 0 to each individual, because this would correspond precisely to our knowledge. Clearly, the Kolmogorov axioms of probability do not allow us to do so. Hence, the widespread use of the odds form (1.5) of Bayes' rule suffers from certain problems with the prior probabilities when these prior probabilities are supposed to express ignorance.

There is, however, yet another way to see that identifying ignorance with uniform distributions is problematic, in the sense that it is an ambiguous notion in general. For instance, consider a uniformly chosen point on a two-dimensional disc of radius 1. If one describes the disc by polar coordinates r and θ, then uniform means that the pair (r, θ) is chosen uniformly on the product space $[0, 1] \times [0, 2\pi)$. But if one describes the notion with respect to ordinary Cartesian coordinates, this leads to a completely different notion of uniformity. Indeed we see that he description, or parametrization, of the outcome space determines what "uniform" means, and as such, "uniform" is not a generic notion. With polar coordinates, the probability that a uniformly chosen point lies in the disc centered at the origin with radius $1/2$, is equal to $1/2$. In Cartesian coordinates, this probability is $1/4$.

We make one last remark. There are situations in which not betting on both A and A^c (that is, suspending judgment) is either not allowed or has unacceptable consequences. In these situations an agent is forced to put one price on the bet on A, meaning he should be willing to both buy and sell the bet for that price. In such scenarios, the assumption of matching buying and selling prices seems justified, and therefore the use of the Kolmogorov axioms seems unproblematic. However, in a situation where an agent is forced to buy and sell the bet on A for the same price, this price only provides a measure of how likely the agent thinks A is relative to A^c. It does not represent an agent's actual belief in A. The price for which an agent is willing to buy a bet on A only represents his or her belief in A if he is completely free in buying any bet.

The conclusion of this section must be that probability distributions are reasonable, but not the only nor necessarily the perfect candidates to describe and quantify epistemic probabilities, or degrees of belief. It is good to keep this in mind when reading through the book, but it should not prevent us working with them.

Mathematical models and scientific viewpoints are never perfect, and in many situations probabilities based on the axioms of Kolmogorov actually work quite well. In Chapter 13 we will discuss a generalization of probability distributions, namely belief functions, and apply these to some of the problems discussed in the book. This generalization, for instance, allows for the possibility of suspending all judgment, and as such it constitutes an interesting possibility that deserves to be explored. But for now we stick with classical probabilities, and in the next chapters we discuss the use of (1.5) in great detail.

1.6 An Example: DNA Profiles

There are at least two reasons to discuss the very basics of forensic DNA profiles at this point. First of all, it is convenient to be able to discuss DNA profiles in various examples before we treat them in great detail in Chapters 7 and 8. Second, DNA profiles provide a good opportunity to illustrate the difference between frequentistic and epistemic probabilities, in a genuine forensic setting.

Let us first briefly discuss some of the relevant biology. We restrict ourselves to nuclear DNA here, which resides in the nucleus of almost every cell of our body, and which is divided into chromosomes. We normally have 23 pairs of such chromosomes, one of which determines the gender: men have one X-chromosome and one Y-chromosome and women have two X-chromosomes. The other 22 pairs are called *autosomal* chromosomes. From every pair, we have received one such chromosome from each of our parents. In the discussion below we restrict our attention to such autosomal chromosomes. The DNA on these chromosomes can be thought of as a large word written in an alphabet of four letters, which are traditionally denoted by A, C, G, and T.

The DNA of different people is very similar: more than 99% of the DNA of different people is identical and can therefore not be used to differentiate between people. However, there are specific positions in our DNA at which the genetic codes are not identical for most people, and which in addition do not seem to have any effect on someone's physical appearance.

On some of these sections of the DNA, the variability consists of there being a differing number of repetitions of a small portion of a code, for example repetitions of ACAT where the number of such repetitions varies. Such a position is called a S(hort) T(andem) R(epeat) *locus* (plural loci), and the precise genetic code at such a locus differs among chromosomes. The current standard technique of forensic laboratories is not to inspect the precise genetic code, but to measure the length of the variable parts. Any such outcome of a length is then called an *allele*. An allele can therefore be denoted by a number denoting this length. (In fact, the allele number is taken to be equal to the number of repetitions of the STR motif that

Table 1.1 *Genotypes in a DNA profile.*

Locus	Allele 1	Allele 2
D10S1248	13	15
vWA	16	16
D16S1359	11	13
D2S1338	17	20
D8S1179	8	11
D21S11	29	31.2
D18S51	17	17

yields a fragment equally long as the one that was measured. For example, if the measured length is equal to the length that we get when there are eight repetitions of the STR motif, we call the fragment allele 8. On the DNA sequence level, there may turn out to be several variants that have the same length. These variants are not distinguished between when we only measure the length of the alleles.)

Since chromosomes come in pairs, everyone has two alleles at a given locus, one coming from the father, and one coming from the mother. The pair of the two alleles at a locus is called the *genotype* at that locus, and is written as an unordered pair of numbers. The genotype $(12, 15)$ is the same as the genotype $(15, 12)$, since from the genotype alone we cannot infer which allele came from which parent. The two alleles can very well be the same at a locus. In that case we say that the carrier of the DNA is *homozygous* at that locus, otherwise he or she is *heterozygous.*

We reserve the term *DNA profile* of a person for the set of the determined genotypes on various loci, sometimes called the *typed* loci. A set of loci that is investigated simultaneously is sometimes called a *kit* or a *multiplex.* (Although it is not important for the exposition which loci these kits contain, we mention here that the (nowadays superseded) SGMPlus kit contains 10 autosomal loci, the NGM kit contains 15 autosomal loci, while the PPF6C kit contains 23 autosomal loci.) Hence the DNA profile of a person consists of the genotype of the loci that are typed. In Table 1.1 we have written down some possible genotypes on seven loci.

Consider now the population frequencies of DNA profiles in a hypothetical idealized (arbitrarily large and random mating) population. For such a population, it is well known that the population frequencies of the alleles remain constant over the generations, and that the population frequency of genotype (a, b) is $2p_a p_b$ if $a \neq b$ and is p_a^2 if $a = b$, where p_x is the population relative frequency of allele x. For example, consider the first locus D10S1248 in the above table. Suppose that 10% of the alleles in the population of interest are allele 13, and that 20% are allele 15. We write this as $p_{13} = 0.1$ and $p_{15} = 0.2$. What now do we expect to be the frequency of the genotype $(13, 15)$ in the population? Since there are two ways to obtain genotype $(13, 15)$, one where the 13 comes from the father and one where the 13 comes from the mother, the fraction in the population with genotype $(13,15)$ is $2 \cdot 0.1 \cdot 0.2 = 0.04$. In other words, 4% of the population has this genotype at this locus. These arguments, heuristic as they are here, can be made more precise, as we will do in Chapter 7.

For the second locus vWA the computation is slightly different because the genotype is homozygous at this locus. In this case, both parents must have passed on 16, and the population frequency of genotype $(16, 16)$ will, via the same arguments, be p_{16}^2, where p_{16} denotes the population frequency of allele 16.

We can perform this computation for each locus separately, and for each locus this leads to a population frequency of that genotype at each locus. The population frequency of the full typed genotype, that is, of all loci simultaneously, is then not yet determined. Often, we may assume that alleles at different loci are obtained independently of each other. We can then obtain the population frequency of the whole DNA profile as the product of each of the population frequencies of the involved genotypes at the individual loci. When we now keep in mind that forensic laboratories produce genotypes at 20 or mor loci, we can conclude that the population frequency of such a profile is astronomically small, which makes it very suitable for identification purposes.

To summarize, in an ideal population the relative frequencies of the profiles factor over the loci, and the relative frequencies of a genotype (a, b) are in one formula expressed in the relative frequencies of the alleles via $(2 - \delta_{a,b}) p_a p_b$, where $\delta_{a,b} = 1$ if $a = b$ and 0 otherwise.

For evidential purposes, however, what we need to define is the *probability* that an arbitrarily chosen person has a specific DNA profile, possibly conditional on knowing profiles of other persons. If we know the population frequencies of all alleles, we can define the probability for a person to have a certain DNA profile to be the same as the population frequency of that profile as it would occur in the above discussed hypothetical ideal population. In practice, however, one typically does not know the precise population frequency of the alleles. We will need to define a subjective probability for alleles to be of the type we are interested in, based on the knowledge we have, that is, a population sample and an understanding of the biological and evolutionary processes. Then one's epistemic probability of observing a certain DNA profile in a randomly chosen person is not necessarily equal to the population frequency of the profile that would be obtained with the actual allele frequencies. Observing the profiles of randomly chosen people will change our epistemic position. If we, for instance, sample an individual who turns out to have a certain allele, then this will in general affect our probabilistic assessment of the next person also having that same allele.

Hence, this is a concrete example which illustrates that frequencies and epistemic probability are genuinely different concepts. If we describe our knowledge of the unknown population frequency by a random variable W, taking values in $[0, 1]$, then only if W concentrates at a single point do we know the population frequency, in which case the frequentist interpretation applies. Hence, the frequentist position is a special case of the epistemic one, as indicated in our discussion above in Section 1.3. We will further discuss this in Chapter 3 and in Section 7.2.

1.7 Statistics

We have explored some philosophical interpretations of probability. In this section we shed some light on our philosophical position of doing statistics in the field of forensic sciences, and this position is strongly connected to our epistemic interpretation of probability.

Our position in doing statistics in forensic science could perhaps be called "Bayesian", but let us say a few words about this position so that it is not misunderstood. Consider, for instance, a given DNA profile. This profile has a certain frequency p in a given population, but we may be uncertain about the value of p. When we assume – as we often will – that our uncertainty about p can be described by a probability distribution, we do not mean to say that the actual frequency is interpreted as a realization of a random variable. Instead, this so-called *prior distribution* tells us that our epistemic probability assessment is that p has certain values, based on the knowledge and information that we have. It is not a probabilistic assessment of the value of the population frequency itself. A probability distribution which expresses uncertainty about p is interpreted by us as our uncertainty arising from lack of knowledge. If we have full knowledge, this distribution reduces to a point mass. Knowledge and information vary among various people, so that this is a genuinely subjective notion.

Mathematically it makes no difference whether the distribution we use for a certain parameter describes the actual value of that parameter, or our uncertainty about it. One can think of the parameter either as being random, or as non-random but unknown. The problems with the interpretation of the priors are the same in the two points of view. Bayesian statistics has often been criticized because of the fact that a prior distribution has to be chosen, since what could be the ground for such a choice? Using Bayes' rule for evidential purposes has the same problem. How does one choose a prior? In fact, the choice of the prior is perhaps less relevant than often perceived, since as the number of observations increases, its effect diminishes. In forensic science, however, this argument is not useful, since asymptotics are largely irrelevant in this field.

The point is, however, that frequentist methods of quantifying statistical evidence suffer from crucial defects. We will see, first below in Section 1.7.1 and further on in Chapter 2, that statistical evidence is *relative* and should only be formulated in terms of a likelihood ratio. A proper use of this evidence will require that one formulates prior odds for the hypotheses of interest. This means that we simply have to deal with the problem of the prior. This is not a problem of the method, but of the nature of what statistical evidence actually is. Information can only be interpreted in context. We turn to statistical evidence now.

1.7.1 Statistical Evidence

Suppose we have two competing hypotheses H_1 and H_2. Few people will deny that it is among the responsibilities of statistics to make intelligent statements about H_1 and H_2 after inspecting certain data. But various different types of statements are possible, and it is of importance to distinguish carefully between them.

One possibility is that circumstances force us to make a *choice* between the two hypotheses, and to undertake appropriate action once the choice is made. However, another possibility is that we want to know how much *evidence* the data provides for either of the hypotheses H_1 and H_2. This is a very different question. Indeed, the data may be neutral as far as evidence for H_1 or H_2 is concerned, but the circumstances may force us to make a choice nevertheless. It may also be that the data support one hypothesis to some extent, but that nevertheless the action is taken that would be taken if the other one were true for reasons of risk assessment. In the decision-making context, one is in the first place concerned with choosing one of two actions, and this may involve judging whether there is evidence for either of them, but that is not the ultimate goal there.

Different goals require different statistical paradigms. As far as the decision-making interpretation is concerned, the classical Neyman–Pearson paradigm has been dominant ever since its introduction in 1933. We describe the paradigm in detail in Chapter 10, but we make some remarks already at this point. The main ingredient of the Neyman–Pearson paradigm is the likelihood ratio as in (1.6), which expresses the ratio of the probabilities of the observed data given the first and the second hypothesis respectively. The paradigm calls for choosing the first hypothesis if this ratio is sufficiently high, where "sufficiently high" is defined in some precise way that we will discuss in Chapter 10.

The Neyman–Pearson paradigm has been explicitly designed for decision making. In the words of Neyman ([114], page 258) himself:

"The problem of testing a statistical hypothesis occurs when circumstances force us to make a choice between two courses of action: either take step *A* or take step *B*."

Setting up a decision procedure using the Neyman–Pearson paradigm means that one wants to control error rates in the sense of how many wrong choices are made in the long run. However, in this book we are primarily concerned with *evidence*, not decision-making. Does the data provide evidence for a certain hypothesis? As we remarked already, this really is a very different question than having to make a choice between two competing hypotheses.

The first question, of course, is what statistical evidence *is*, and after that we should ask how it could possibly be quantified. Without attempting to give a formal definition, evidence, as a first approximation, is information that changes our opinion about, or degree of belief in a certain hypothesis. A sequence of coin flips provides evidence about the fairness of the coin, and the discovery of a DNA profile at the scene of the crime provides evidence for the hypothesis that a given person is the criminal.

When it comes down to quantifying such evidence, a very widely used idea is the so-called *p*-value. In a *p*-value procedure we consider a single hypothesis H, often a hypothesis one wants to disprove. We observe data x that we assume can be seen as a realization of a certain random variable X. We take some function $T(\cdot)$ of the observations in such a way that given H, the distribution of the random variable $T(X)$ is known, at least approximately. T is called a *test statistic*. For a given observation x we now compute the probability of the set of all outcomes y for which $T(y)$ would in some sense be at least as extreme as the observed $T(x)$ is. If the probability of this set under H is too small, then H will be rejected.

A simple example of such a *p*-value procedure is repeatedly flipping a coin with the purpose of finding out whether or not the coin is fair. Suppose we flip the coin 100 times yielding data x. Let $T(x)$ be the number of heads, whose distribution under the hypothesis of fairness is well known. Suppose we observe 60 heads. We then compute the probability, assuming that the coin is fair, of obtaining at least 60 or at most 40 heads, so by "at least as extreme" in this case, we mean deviating more from the expected number of heads (under the assumption of fairness) than the observed 60. If this probability is smaller than a previously chosen α the procedure calls for rejecting the hypothesis of fairness. We say in that case that the *p*-value procedure rejects H with *significance level α*. One often interprets this predetermined α as a quantification of the evidence against H. For instance, rejection of H under $\alpha = 0.01$ is often supposed to correspond to very strong evidence against H.

In this paradigm, one can talk about the amount of evidence for an isolated hypothesis H, and interpret the significance level α as a quantification of the evidence against H. However, as we will see, this interpretation is very problematic. This has been observed by many of our colleagues, see for instance Richard Royall [129] for a very forceful discussion. The *p*-value paradigm essentially rests on the idea that if an extreme observation is made, then either a very unlikely event has occurred, or the underlying hypothesis H is false. If the occurred event is too unlikely, then the conclusion must be that H is false. In the words of Fisher [68]:

"Belief in the [null] hypothesis as an accurate representation of the population sampled is confronted by the logical disjunction: Either the hypothesis is untrue, or the value [of the test statistic] has attained by chance an exceptionally high value."

This idea, however, is rather problematic, for at least three (connected) reasons.

First of all, the paradigm works without any prior information of H, or, for that matter, without any probabilistic assessment of H itself. This is problematic in the sense that the paradigm is, therefore, silent about the only thing that really matters to us, namely the probability that H is true given the evidence. It *cannot* speak about this probability. As such the paradigm addresses the wrong question. This point is addressed with a number of examples in Chapter 5 and in general in Chapter 9.

Second, the quote by Fisher above is not really a logical disjunction. Indeed, it is quite possible that the hypothesis is false, but that *also* the value of the test statistic is exceptionally high. If the observed value of the test statistic is high under both the hypothesis and its negation, then the disjunction reduces to a tautology. In legal affairs, we should compare the probability of the data under *all* reasonable hypotheses. If both the assumption of innocence and the assumption of guilt have the property that the observed data are extremely unlikely under them (sometimes a realistic scenario), then this paradigm obviously falls short. In such a case, it is important to investigate how the probabilities of the data under the various hypotheses *relate* to each other. That is, we then can only make a meaningful statement about evidential value of one hypothesis compared to another. This point will be discussed in great detail in Chapter 2.

Third, we note that a p-value also depends on the probabilities of data which have not been observed. It seems quite reasonable, however, to insist that the evidential value of the data with respect to a certain hypothesis H should only depend on the distribution under H of the outcomes that have actually been observed. We elaborate on this issue in Section 2.3.1.

As we will discuss in Chapter 9, the idea of quantifying evidence with p-values is in essence a frequentistic notion. But evidence is not. When we obtain certain data, p-values are silent about the probability that one of the hypotheses is true given this particular data. In fact, the whole idea of defining evidence for a given single hypothesis will turn out to be problematic. Data may support H_1 over H_2, but H_3 over H_1, so that it does not make sense to ask whether or not the data supports H_1 in isolation. In this book we will many times be led to the idea that a proper measure of evidence for a certain hypothesis can only be meaningfully defined in *comparison with another hypothesis*.

It is precisely the likelihood ratio that we briefly described above that is able to quantify this idea of evidence. Indeed the likelihood ratio compares the probability of the observed data E under two competing hypotheses H_1 and H_2, that is, it is equal to $P(E \mid H_1)/P(E \mid H_2)$. If the likelihood ratio is large, this provides evidence for the first hypothesis *relative* to the other. If it is small it provides evidence for the second hypothesis *relative* to the first. Indeed since,

$$\frac{P(H_1 \mid E)}{P(H_2 \mid E)} = \frac{P(E \mid H_1)}{P(E \mid H_2)} \times \frac{P(H_1)}{P(H_2)},$$

we see that the likelihood ratio is precisely the factor between the prior odds for H_1 and H_2 and the posterior odds after having obtained the data E.

We will develop all this carefully and in detail in Chapter 2. As such, we will use the likelihood ratio as our basic quantification of evidence for one hypothesis compared to another. This, it seems, is the only reasonable way to quantify evidence, and we will give many examples to illustrate this position.

Of course, we want a measure of evidence to be reasonable in certain ways. Evidence can point in the wrong direction, that is the nature of things – but it would be nice to have some bounds on how often it can point how strongly in the wrong direction. As we will see in Section 2.4 the likelihood ratio behaves quite well in this respect. Given all this, it may not come as a surprise that the likelihood ratio is perhaps the most important single concept in this book, and we devote a full chapter to studying its basic properties.

1.8 Forensic Science

What is a suitable philosophical foundation of forensic science itself? In forensic science one is typically interested in the source of a certain trace. Perhaps one expects, therefore, that the goal of forensic science should be to narrow down the possible sources of a trace to a single object. This is called *individualization* in the literature, and some go so far as to call individualization the essential characteristic of forensics.

One route to individualization is via the notion of *uniqueness*: one can perhaps narrow down the possible donors of, say, a DNA profile to a single individual, because DNA profiles are supposed to be unique. Or, to give an example from a actual testimony in a court case on fingerprints (People versus Gomez [33] cited in [36]):

"And we profess as fingerprint examiners that the rate of error is zero. And the reason we make this bold statement is because we know based on 100 years of research that everybody's fingerprints are unique, and in nature it is never going to repeat itself again."

A bold statement indeed, and there has been a lot of criticism on this uniqueness approach. First of all, it has been put forward that uniqueness claims are unproven. Certainly not all human beings have been tested for their DNA profile or for their finger prints, so there must be other arguments for such uniqueness claims. Perhaps, then, the testimony above rests on the assumed underlying argument that had fingerprints not been unique, surely by now a duplicate fingerprint must have been observed somewhere sometime. But well, is there anyone in the world who as access to *all* fingerprints ever recorded? And if the answer to that question is no, how can we draw the uniqueness conclusion?

Shifting to DNA profiles, it is also true that we certainly have not recorded all DNA profiles in the world. Nevertheless, it is probably true that DNA profiles are unique if we make them sufficiently large by taking more and more genetic material in consideration.

However, this is just a special case of saying that when you take two different objects, and you look at them closely enough, you will *always* find differences. This is not only true for DNA profiles, but for any two given objects in the world. If we accept this statement, then, returning to the uniqueness question concerning fingerprints that we discussed above, it must be true that no two fingerprints are really the same. Doesn't that justify the quote from the People versus Gomez case above?

The crucial point is that the uniqueness in the quote above does not refer to the possible fact that any two fingerprints will be different upon close enough inspection. The quote refers to the claimed fact that that our *methods of analysis* will always find a difference between any two fingerprints. And that is what it is all about in forensic science. The quote can only refer to the fact that the methods used have so far always found a distinction between any two fingerprints (leaving aside the fact that this claim cannot be verified). The quote, therefore, maintains an epistemic position, rather than an ontological one.

Uniqueness in the strict ontological sense, therefore, is largely irrelevant. The ontological statement or conviction that any two objects will at some scale be different, is not so important for forensic science. What matters is not the question whether two objects are the same or different; what matters is whether or not our parameters of detection are capable of detecting a possible difference. Can we *know* they are different? We need rules governing the determination that objects are classified as being the same or not. While uniqueness in itself is in fact a rather banal and useless notion, we can certainly move forward in forensic science by defining, studying, and improving methods and parameters of analysis under which certain claims of rarity can be made and defended.

So we arrive at the conclusion that also in forensic science, an epistemic interpretation is called for. An epistemic foundation of forensic science will not concentrate on the question whether two objects are the same, but whether our methods and ways of analyzing things can detect differences. Suppose, for instance, that we have some coincidental DNA match. The cause of this duplication is not exact duplication, but rather duplication under a specific set of rules for deeming profiles consistent or the same. The consequence of imposing such rules, is that we should expect some duplication in all sets of objects. "The question is," citing [36]:

"... not duplication or non-duplication, but, again, diagnosticity or selectivity: some quantified assessment of the degree of duplication under a specified set of rules for determining consistency."

This is how we will approach forensic problems in this book. We are not interested in the question whether or not one's DNA profile is unique. We are interested in probabilistic statements that help us to evaluate the evidential value of the data, and such statements will in no way depend on possible uniqueness of characteristics or traces. This position has certain consequences, and we mention one of them here.

As we saw in Section 1.6, DNA profiles have small probabilities. Suppose now that we have a population of 100,000 people. Does anything magical happen when p, the profile probability that we assign, decreases below $1/100,000$, so that (again by a good approximation) the expected number of individuals with this profile is smaller than one? The answer is no. The value of p will determine the evidential value of a match with this profile, but not because of some claim of uniqueness. It can adequately be interpreted as the level of *surprise* that we find this particular profile. The surprise will be higher, and therefore the evidence stronger, for smaller p, but $p = 1/100,000$ does not play a special role within this interpretation. The evidential value of the match has nothing to do with the population size.

Another consequence of this line of thought, is that we are not interested in a match/no match assessment of the data. We are only interested in evaluating the evidential value of the data, as expressed in the likelihood ratio. In fact, once we know the evidential value, it is no longer important whether this value was the result of a "full match" or of a "partial match," whatever that might be. The evidential value is all that matters, and probability theory and statistics have excellent ways of expressing such evidential values. This makes probability and statistics indispensable for forensic science.

1.9 Summary and Conclusions

In legal and forensic science, people make probabilistic statements. This is only natural since in this context there is typically a lot of uncertainty about what actually happened. In mathematics, uncertainty is traditionally described with probability distributions, which are axiomatized with the classical axioms of Kolmogorov. In short, the axioms confirm that the probabilities of disjoint events add up, and restrict the total probability to exactly 1. This leads to a rich mathematical theory of probabilities, but does not explain what the nature of probability *is*. If we want to meaningfully apply mathematics, we need concrete instantiations of the theory.

The most widely used instantiation is that of relative frequencies. This notion adheres to the idea that the probability of an event is the fraction of times it occurs when repeating similar experiments. Although very useful in many situations, we have concluded two things. First of all, relative frequencies cannot be used to define what probability is, even though one may think about probability in terms of such relative frequencies. Second, and more importantly for our purposes, a frequentistic interpretation of probability is of very limited use in the legal and forensic context since legal trials and forensic circumstances are unique, and not repeatable.

Hence we were led to an epistemic interpretation of probability in which probability is not associated with frequencies of events, but instead with statements about knowledge based on incomplete information. As such, this is a genuine subjective notion of probability, very suitable in our context where various agents (suspect, judge, jury, prosecutor, etc.) have certain information.

One way to express one's epistemic probability of an event A is to ask how much money one would be willing to pay maximally for the bet that pays out 1 if A occurs. We have shown that if an agent behaves rationally in the sense that he would never collectively buy and sell bets that would cost him money for sure, then the probabilities assigned by that agent satisfy the axioms of probability. This makes it possible to use the full force of the mathematical theory about probability in an epistemic context. Probability, as we interpret it in this book, is about personal assessment in the light of varying information. This makes it possible to speak about the probability, say, that a certain person committed a certain crime, while at the same time assuming that probabilistic assessments adhere to the axioms of probability.

We have noted that certain problems remain when using probability theory for epistemic purposes. Most notably, the axioms of probability imply that $P(A) + P(A^c) = 1$, so one cannot withhold probability of A without making the probability in A^c larger. This does not always comply with the notion of epistemic uncertainty, for instance when an agent has no information whatsoever about either A or A^c. The problem can also be formulated in the betting context that we just described: willingness to buy a bet on A for a certain price should not automatically imply that you also want to sell the bet for that same price. Indeed, if an agent has no information whatsoever about an event A, then the buying price will be low, but the selling price will be high. For this reason, classical probability theory is not a perfect fit with epistemic uncertainty.

Our position in statistics can be called "Bayesian" in the sense that we describe our uncertainty about hypotheses with probability distributions. We carefully distinguish between decision making and providing evidence. The first relates to the Neyman–Pearson paradigm, while the second, as we have started to argue, is best captured by a likelihood ratio. This means that our notion of evidence is always relative: data provides evidence for H_1 relative to H_2. The classical p-value procedure is briefly discussed and rejected as a measure of evidence, but we will come back to this issue in full detail in later chapters.

Finally, forensic statistics should not be concerned with the match/no match paradigm, but instead with quantification of evidence. Forensic science is not about proving that two things are identical and hence the same, but instead should be concerned with providing evidence for hypotheses based on the information that we have. A full match (whatever that may be) provides more evidence than a partial match, but the difference is not qualitative. This view of forensic science fits perfectly well with our philosophical position in probability and statistics.

1.10 Bibliographical Notes

The classical mathematical account on a subjective account of probability is the book by Bruno de Finetti [55]. Recent texts on subjective probability in the context of forensic science include [19] and [157], which also contain many other references for further reading. In [108], arguments against a subjectivist concept of probability in a forensic context are given. The book [172] by Peter Walley is a very good source for a discussion on epistemic probability in terms of buying and selling bets. He develops this theory in great detail. This book also contains several statements that parallel and overlap the statements of Theorems 1.4.3 and 1.4.4. An excellent starting point for further exploring the philosophy of statistics is Dennis Lindley in [94] who also has a lot to say about the philosophy of probability. Another very relevant text is the monograph [27] by William Briggs. The opening chapters of the classic [156] by Richard Swinburne on confirmation theory treat the philosophy around various notions of probability. A concise treatment of the philosophy of probability in connection with forensic science is the unpublished appendix [53] to [3] by Philip Dawid. For a concise and very readable account on the philosophy and epistemology of forensic science, we refer to Simon Cole [36]. This paper contains many references for further exploring this subject. Another suitable starting point is [61] in their criticism on the PCAST report. We will discuss this report in Chapter 14.

2

Evidence and the Likelihood Ratio

In this chapter we discuss the notion of statistical evidence, introduce and study the likelihood ratio in detail, and place all this in the Bayesian framework at large. We illustrate the ideas with a number of examples.

2.1 From Evidence to Likelihood Ratio

The answer to the question what statistics is about does not have an unambiguous answer. One aspect of statistics is about making decisions on the basis of certain data. On the other hand, statistics is also concerned with the question as to what evidence the data provides for a particular hypothesis. These objectives are not the same, as we argued already in Section 1.7. Indeed, forcing a choice between two competing hypotheses H_1 and H_2 is not the same as deciding whether or not the data actually provides evidence for either of them.

In this chapter we ask ourselves what statistical evidence is, and how the strength of evidence for one or multiple hypotheses should or can be quantified. For example, given certain observations, like a match between a DNA profile at the scene of a crime and the DNA profile of a certain individual, we want to know to what extent this match provides evidence for the hypothesis that this individual is the donor of the DNA profile at the scene of the crime.

So what does it mean to say that data E provides evidence in favor of or against a hypothesis H? It seems reasonable to say that E provides evidence in favor of or against H if it is the case that our assessment about whether or not H is true changes upon observing E. In order for this to make sense, we should be willing to define a "prior" assessment about the truth of H, quantified or expressed as $P(H)$. In Chapter 1 we explained why we are willing to do so.

Taking the existence of such a prior assessment for granted, we might say that E provides evidence (against or in favor of) H if

$$P(H \mid E) \neq P(H), \tag{2.1}$$

that is, if one's probability of H changes upon observing E. In writing down (2.1), we implicitly assume that a phrase like $P(H \mid E)$ actually makes sense, meaning that one can make probabilistic statements involving both H and E. We will see that this is a many situations a very natural condition.

Although (2.1) seems rather natural, the first remark we make is that it may happen that $P(H \mid E) = P(H)$. One might call E *neutral* evidence in that case. The reason that we will not use the phrase "neutral evidence" very often, is that data which is clearly irrelevant for H and has nothing to with H would still be called neutral evidence, which is a somewhat unfortunate nomenclature. We will see examples in this book where evidence that was thought to be very relevant turned out to be neutral.

We point out that with this definition of evidence, alternatives do play a role, albeit this is not completely obvious from the formulation in (2.1). To make this more clear, we write

$$P(H \mid E) = P(H) \times \frac{P(E \mid H)}{P(E)}. \tag{2.2}$$

Thus, E provides evidence for H precisely when $P(E \mid H) \neq P(E)$. It is typically possible to compute the probability of the observed data assuming that a certain well-specified hypothesis is true, so $P(E \mid H)$ is often available. But in order to compute $P(E)$ we need to know the possible alternatives for H, and how plausible these alternatives are a priori. Indeed, if besides H, the alternatives $H_1, \ldots, H_n$ are possible, then

$$P(E) = P(E \mid H)P(H) + \sum_{i=1}^{n} P(E \mid H_i)P(H_i). \tag{2.3}$$

Hence, the question whether or not E provides evidence for H depends on the alternatives that are possible besides H. If H is not true, then there must be something else that somehow gave rise to E, and (2.3) shows that in order to compute $P(E)$ we need to know what these alternatives are, and how plausible they are. So, whether or not the data supports H_1 may depend on how likely the alternatives are – see Example 2.1.2 below in which the same data does or does not support a given hypothesis, depending on the prior probabilities.

We can try to define evidence as information that changes our opinion about, or our degree of belief in, a certain hypothesis, *relative to another, competing hypothesis.* To elaborate on this, it seems natural to investigate how the probabilities of two hypotheses H_1 and H_2 change upon observing E. We then want to know how $P(H_1 \mid E)/P(H_1)$ relates to $P(H_2 \mid E)/P(H_2)$, and the factor between these rates of change determines the relative weight of the evidence for H_1 relative to H_2. That is, we want to solve for x in the equation

$$\frac{P(H_1 \mid E)}{P(H_1)} = x \times \frac{P(H_2 \mid E)}{P(H_2)}.$$

Solving this gives

$$x = \frac{P(E \mid H_1)}{P(E \mid H_2)}.$$

Note that this expression does not involve priors, and it motivates the following definition.

Definition 2.1.1 If E denotes the observed data, we define the *likelihood ratio* $LR_{H_1, H_2}(E)$ of H_1 versus H_2 as

$$LR_{H_1, H_2}(E) := \frac{P(E \mid H_1)}{P(E \mid H_2)}. \tag{2.4}$$

When no confusion is possible we write LR_{H_1, H_2} or sometimes even just LR. The likelihood ratio quantifies the evidence that the data E provides for H_1 relative to H_2. We will often slightly abuse terminology and call E itself the evidence.

We can write

$$\frac{P(H_1 \mid E)}{P(H_1)} = LR_{H_1, H_2}(E) \times \frac{P(H_2 \mid E)}{P(H_2)}, \tag{2.5}$$

or equivalently,

$$\frac{P(H_1 \mid E)}{P(H_2 \mid E)} = LR_{H_1, H_2}(E) \times \frac{P(H_1)}{P(H_2)}. \tag{2.6}$$

It is this last form (2.6) which is most widely used, and which is known as the *odds form of Bayes' rule*. The left-hand side of (2.6) is called the *posterior odds* of H_1 and H_2, whereas the fraction

$$\frac{P(H_1)}{P(H_2)}$$

is called the *prior odds*. The prior odds are seen as the ratio of the probabilities of H_1 and H_2 before taking into account the evidence E, and the posterior odds constitute the same ratio after seeing the evidence E. In words, formula (2.6) reads

$$\text{posterior odds} = \text{likelihood ratio} \times \text{prior odds}.$$

So while the likelihood ratio measures the strength of the evidence of the data for H_1 relative to H_2, we need the prior odds to transform this into the ratio of the actual posterior probabilities. The likelihood ratio merely tells us by which factor we should multiply the prior odds to obtain the posterior odds. Mixing up the likelihood ratio with the posterior odds is known as the *prosecutor's fallacy*.

We will use the likelihood ratio as our basic quantification of evidence the data E provides, always for one hypothesis compared to another. If the likelihood ratio is larger than 1, the data provides evidence for the first hypothesis *relative* to the other. If it is smaller than 1, the data provides evidence for the second hypothesis *relative* to the first. A large likelihood ratio simply says that H_1 does a much better job explaining the evidence than H_2, but it does *not* say that H_1 necessarily explains the data well. Indeed, perhaps the evidence E is very unlikely under both hypotheses. The likelihood ratio is a measure for the strength of the hypothesis H_1 *relative to* H_2. It is a genuinely comparative notion.

The likelihood ratio approach reflects that evidence for a hypothesis H_1 can only be relative, at least when we want the strength of the evidence to be independent of the prior. The idea is not to express how much evidence the data provides about a single hypothesis H_1, but rather to measure or express the strength of the evidence for H_1 relative to another hypothesis H_2.

The data gives no information about prior odds. If we have no information whatsoever about how likely we assess the hypotheses to be before seeing the data, then strong evidence (that is, a large likelihood ratio) for one hypothesis versus another does not imply that the former hypothesis is therefore more likely. We illustrate all this with an example.

Example 2.1.2 Suppose that we have a vase containing 100 balls. Each ball is either black or white. Consider the hypothesis H_1 saying that the vase contains 90 white balls and 10 black balls, versus the hypothesis H_2 which says that the vase contains 50 white and 50 black balls. Suppose we draw 10 balls with replacement. Each of the 10 drawn balls turns out to be white, and this event is denoted by E. We have $P(E \mid H_1) = (9/10)^{10}$ and $P(E \mid H_2) = (1/2)^{10}$. The corresponding likelihood ratio is easily computed to be $(9/5)^{10}$, which is roughly 357. Hence, the obtained evidence is 357 more likely under H_1 than under H_2.

Does this number 357 now mean that we should believe H_1 to be true, or at least that the probability of H_1 after seeing the evidence E is high? The answer to this question is no, and it is very important to understand this. There are at least two reasons for why the probability of H_1 need not be high after having seen the data, and we discuss these now.

First, there is equation (2.6), which implies that for the posterior probabilities, the likelihood ratio is not enough, and we need the prior probabilities as well. If the prior probability of H_1 is sufficiently low, then a large likelihood ratio does not necessarily mean that the posterior probability of H_1 is high as well. This is, of course, due to the comparative nature of the likelihood ratio.

There is, however, yet another major concern which also has to do with the comparative nature of the likelihood ratio. Although after seeing the evidence H_1 is 357 times more likely relative to H_2 than before seeing the data, it may be the case that the probability of H_1 actually *decreased* by observing E. Indeed, there could be a third hypothesis that explains the data even (much) better than H_1. For instance, consider hypothesis H_3 which says that the vase contains only white balls, and suppose that in addition, the prior probabilities for each of the three hypotheses H_1, H_2, and H_3 are undisputed and equal to $1/3$. It is now straightforward to compute $P(H_1 \mid E) = 0.258$, $P(H_2 \mid E) = 0.001$ and $P(H_3 \mid E) = 0.741$. So despite the fact that the likelihood ratio of H_1 versus H_2 is 357, the probability of H_1 has actually decreased upon observing E, and it would be wrong to say that the data supports H_1. Although H_1 explains the data much better than H_2, the third hypothesis H_3 explains it (much) better than H_1.

So whereas the data provides evidence for H_1 relative to H_2, it certainly does not provide evidence for H_1 relative to H_3. In the numerical example just given, we had $P(H_1 \mid E) < P(H_1)$. But if we take different prior probabilities, say $P(H_1) = 0.6$, $P(H_2) = 0.3$ and $P(H_3) = 0.1$, then it turns out that $P(H_1 \mid E) = 0.676$. Hence, with these priors, H_1 has become more plausible after seeing the data E. This example supports the claim that evidence is relative. The data is not interpretable as evidence in favor or against H_1 since it, simply, depends on the possible alternatives and their prior probabilities.   □

We saw in this example that it is possible that a likelihood ratio in favor of H_1 is bigger than 1 while at the same time the posterior probability of H_1 is smaller than the prior probability. There are, however, circumstances that forces the probability of H_1 to increase upon observing E.

First, if the hypothesis H is the *best* explanation of the data E, then it must be the case that $P(E \mid H)/P(E) \geq 1$ and it follows from (2.2) that the posterior probability of H will always be at least as large as the prior probability.

Second, if the two hypotheses of interest are each others complement, then it cannot happen that the likelihood ratio is larger than 1 while the actual probability of the first hypothesis goes down. This is not a surprise. In fact, if there are only two alternatives H and H^c and the likelihood ratio is larger than 1, then H is the best explanation and the previous point applies.

Finally, from (2.5) we observe the following. Suppose that $P(H_1) = \delta$. This implies that the left-hand side is at most $1/\delta$. If the likelihood ratio is larger than $1/\delta$, then it must be the case that $P(H_2 \mid E) < P(H_2)$ so that E is in absolute sense evidence against H_2. Hence the existence of *any* H_1 so that the product of its prior and the likelihood ratio of H_1 versus H_2 is at least 1, is in absolute sense evidence against H_2. If $LR_{H_1, H_2}(E) > 1$, this in itself is never enough to conclude that H_1 has become more likely. However, if the likelihood ratio is large enough, it does provide evidence *against* H_2. In words, this means that if there is an alternative H_1 for H_2 for which the combination of its plausibility and the evidence in favor of it (versus H_2) is large enough, then we must lose faith in H_2, but in general we cannot say whether it is H_1 that becomes more likely or yet another hypothesis.

2.2 Further Examples of Likelihood Ratios

In this section we give two further examples of likelihood ratios. The first perhaps appears anecdotal, but it is instructive and we will explain its forensic relevance. The second example is our first genuine forensic example, namely the basic version of the so-called *island problem*.

Example 2.2.1 Consider a deck of 52 cards, where each card has a number between 1 and 52 (inclusive). (We use numbers instead of the usual card notation for notational convenience.) The hypothesis H_n states that the deck is a normal deck of cards, where each number between 1 and 52 is used once. The hypothesis H_u states that all cards in the deck have the same (unspecified) number. Writing H_i, $i = 1, \ldots, 52$ for the hypothesis that all cards have number i, we can write

$$H_u = \bigcup_{i=1}^{52} H_i.$$

Suppose that we shuffle the deck, draw one card, and the result is the number 12. Denoting this event by E we can easily see that $LR_{H_{12}, H_n} = 52$. The observation of the number 12, therefore, is evidence in favor of H_{12} relative to H_n. This may seem unfair, since whatever card is chosen, there will be this amount of evidence that the deck is uniform with the chosen number. It seems then to be the case that the simple act of drawing of any card always is evidence against a normal deck of cards.

However, this is not quite true. The hypothesis H_{12} is an example of a so-called *data-driven* hypothesis, that is, a hypothesis that one formulates only after obtaining the evidence. Obviously, when we tailor a hypothesis around the data such that it is the best possible explanation for it, the data will tend to confirm this very hypothesis with a likelihood ratio larger than 1, as discussed in the previous section.

Instead, we can also compute LR_{H_n, H_u}, the likelihood ratio of two hypotheses which are not data driven. Clearly we have $P(E \mid H_n) = 1/52$. Furthermore, if we make the additional assumption that $P(H_i \mid H_u) = 1/52$ for all i, then we have

$$P(E \mid H_u) = \sum_{i=1}^{52} P(E \mid H_i) P(H_i \mid H_u) \qquad (2.7)$$

$$= \frac{1}{52} \sum_{i=1}^{52} P(E \mid H_i) = \frac{1}{52}. \qquad (2.8)$$

Hence it follows that $LR_{H_n, H_u}(E) = 1$, so the evidence of obtaining a 12 gives no information whatsoever about the deck being normal or uniform, as expected.

To understand the likelihood ratio of 1/52 that we obtained when comparing H_n to H_{12}, it is instructive to look at prior probabilities. If prior probabilities are meaningful and given by $P(H_n) = \pi_0$, $P(H_u) = 1 - \pi_0$ and $P(H_i) = (1 - \pi_0)/52$ for all $i = 1, \ldots, 52$, then we find, using (2.6), that

$$\frac{P(H_n \mid E)}{P(H_{12} \mid E)} = \frac{1}{52} \times \frac{\pi_0}{(1 - \pi_0)/52} = \frac{\pi_0}{1 - \pi_0}.$$

One can say that all prior probability $1 - \pi_0$ of H_u concentrates on H_{12} after drawing a 12. This is very reasonable, since after a 12 is drawn, the only way that the deck can be uniform is that it contains only cards with the number 12. The posterior probability of H_n has not changed, in accordance with our intuition.

We saw that the evidence E of drawing a card with number 12 constitutes evidence of H_{12} relative to H_n. In fact, since $P(E \mid H_{12}) = 1$, it will provide evidence for H_{12} relative to *any* alternative hypothesis, although certainly not by the same amount. For instance, it will hardly produce evidence for H_{12} compared to the hypothesis that all but one card have number 12. So again, we cannot speak of some absolute amount of evidence for H_{12} in isolation, and in order to make a meaningful evidential statement, we should always mention the alternatives.   □

Although Example 2.2.1 is anecdotal, it conveys a further important message which is extremely relevant for applications in forensic science. The evidence for H_{12} relative to H_n was quite large (52), but this was clearly the effect of choosing this particular hypothesis after seeing the data. One would not have investigated H_{12} in isolation if the drawn card had not been 12, and it is no surprise that there is strong evidence supporting a data-driven hypothesis. This, however, is compensated by the fact that the prior for H_{12} was a lot smaller than the prior for H_u, namely by, again, a factor 52. So the price we have to pay for a large likelihood ratio is a small prior, eventually leading to the same posterior probability for H_n.

A forensic analogue that we will discuss in detail in Chapter 11 is the situation in which we try to find a match of a given DNA profile (found at the scene of a crime) in a DNA database. If the profile yields a match with a certain person, then this will prompt us to consider the hypothesis that this person was the donor of the DNA profile at the scene of the crime. This is again a data-driven hypothesis with, logically, a large likelihood ratio relative to the hypothesis of innocence. However, the corresponding prior probability will be small, compensating the effect of choosing a data-driven hypothesis. The warning is the obvious one now: one should interpret a large likelihood ratio with care, taking into account the way the hypotheses were chosen. It is possible that two people who both carry out an analysis of the situation, arrive at different likelihood ratios. This need not be an indication that one of them is wrong. It is quite possible that they are both correct, but answer different questions.

Our next example is the island problem in its classic form.

Example 2.2.2 (The island problem) Our starting point is an island. On this island a crime is committed and we assume it a certainty that the criminal C is an inhabitant of the island. We denote the collection of all people on the island by X. We introduce indicator random variables Γ_x, taking value 1 if $x \in X$ has a certain characteristic Γ and 0 otherwise. We assume that the Γ_x are independent and identically Bernoulli distributed with success probability p.

Now we obtain information that Γ has been found at the scene of the crime, and we assume that we may conclude that $\Gamma_C = 1$. Suppose further that we obtain the information that a certain identified person S has Γ. What is the strength of this evidence for the hypothesis that $\{S = C\}$ relative to $\{S \neq C\}$? Writing $E_C := \{\Gamma_C = 1\}$, $G := \{S = C\}$, and $E_S := \{\Gamma_S = 1\}$, we are interested in the likelihood ratio given by

$$\frac{P(E_C, E_S \mid G)}{P(E_C, E_S \mid G^c)}. \tag{2.9}$$

In (2.9), the numerator $P(E_C, E_S \mid G)$ is equal to p. Indeed, knowing that G occurs, S and C are the same individual so the probability that this person has Γ is just p. If they are not the same person we need two individuals to have Γ, which has probability p^2. Hence the denominator in (2.9) is equal to p^2 and the likelihood ratio is $p/p^2 = 1/p$.

The choice of the likelihood ratio in (2.9), however, might be a source of debate. One could reasonably argue that the event E_S is background information, whereas the true evidence is given by the crime stain profile revealing E_C. This would lead to a situation in which we work conditionally on E_S and where the relevant likelihood ratio is given by

$$\frac{P(E_C \mid G, E_S)}{P(E_C \mid G^c, E_S)}. \tag{2.10}$$

In (2.10) the numerator $P(E_C \mid G, E_S) = 1$, since knowing that S has the characteristic, and knowing that $S = C$, it follows that E_C must occur. The denominator is p, so this likelihood ratio is equal to $1/p$ as well. The strength of the evidence is the reciprocal of p so the less frequent the characteristic is, the stronger is the evidence, as common sense requires.

If we write $\pi_S := P(G)$ for the prior probability of guilt, we obtain

$$\frac{P(G \mid E_C, E_S)}{P(G^c \mid E_C, E_S)} = \frac{1}{p} \cdot \frac{P(G \mid E_S)}{P(G^c \mid E_S)} = \frac{1}{p} \cdot \frac{\pi_S}{1 - \pi_S}. \tag{2.11}$$

Since we also have that $P(G \mid E_C, E_S) + P(G^c \mid E_C, E_S) = 1$, it now follows that the posterior probability of guilt is given by

$$P(G \mid E_C, E_S) = \frac{1}{1 + p(1 - \pi_S)/\pi_S}. \tag{2.12}$$

$\square$

We already mentioned that confusing the likelihood ratio with the posterior odds is a mistake which goes under the name *prosecutor's fallacy*. In Example 2.2.2, the prosecutor's fallacy would be to say that the odds of S being guilty versus not being guilty are equal to $1/p$, which potentially dramatically over- or underestimates the probability of guilt.

There is another way to look at the likelihood ratio and the corresponding prior and posterior odds which may help avoid the confusion that sometimes arises. We first explain this with a basic numerical example.

Consider an island with 107 inhabitants, 100 men and 7 women. Now a burglary takes place on the island. Without any further information, and assuming that every individual is a priori equally likely to be the criminal, the prior probability of the event M that a man committed the burglary is equal to $100/107$. But now the authorities find the remains of a cigarette at the scene of the crime, and they conclude that the criminal smokes. How does this change our conviction that a man committed the crime? In order to say something about this, we need to have information about the general smoking behavior of men and women. Suppose for the sake of simplicity that research has shown that 50% of the men smoke, and so does as many as 6 out of every 7 women.

We summarize all this information in Table 2.1.

Table 2.1

	smoker	non-smoker	total
men	50	50	100
women	6	1	7
total	56	51	107

The last column represents the prior odds for the hypothesis that the criminal is a man versus the hypothesis that it is a woman. Indeed, we immediately read off that the prior odds are equal to 100/7. If we now ask for the posterior odds, we ask for the probability that the criminal is a man or a woman given that the criminal smokes. Hence now it is the first column that we have to consider, since we can restrict our attention to the smoking population. We read off the posterior odds as 50/6.

So we see that the table contains all the information (and more) that we need and Bayes' rule does not seem to be needed at all. In fact, Bayes' rule is just a formal description of what we learn from the table. To reinforce this point, we can see in more detail how the prior information and the likelihood ratio of a man being the criminal versus a woman, are used to complete the table.

First we have the prior odds, which indicate how the last column of Table 2.1 should be completed. Then the two terms of the likelihood ratio (the numerator and the denominator respectively) tell us how the 100 men are to be divided into a smoking and non-smoking group, and similarly for the women. Since the probability for a man to smoke is 1/2 and for a woman 6/7, this leads to Table 2.1 from which we read off the posterior odds as being 50/6. The likelihood ratio allows us to properly distribute the totals of the last column over the other two columns row-wise, and then the posterior odds can be read off in the first column. The first column can also be used to read off the posterior probability directly: it is just 50/56.

Note that although we have set the number of islanders to 107 here, this number is essentially irrelevant. If we, say, double all numbers, the result would have been the same. This is to be expected: in Example 2.2.2 the size of the island never played a role. This number, N say, can only play a role if one relates π_S to N, for instance by taking $\pi_S = 1/N$.

A table works by virtue of the fact that we can represent probabilities as proportions in an appropriate population. The only thing that is needed is to set up a population in which all relevant probabilities can be interpreted as such fractions. Let us reconsider the basic island problem from Example 2.2.2 in this way.

Example 2.2.3 (Example 2.2.2 continued) Recall that on an island a crime is committed and we assume it a certainty that the criminal is an inhabitant of the island. We want to design a table for this problem which represents the correct probabilities. The prior probability that $S = C$ was said to be π_S, and we can achieve this by taking a population of size N, of which $\pi_S N$ have label C. Thinking of S as being drawn randomly from that population gives the correct prior probability that S has label C. Here is the first step of the table:

	Γ	not Γ	total
C			$\pi_S N$
not C			$(1 - \pi_S)N$
total			N

Then we incorporate the likelihood ratio into the table, and distribute the totals over the two rows respectively, as dictated by the likelihood ratios:

	Γ	not Γ	total
C	$\pi_S N$	0	$\pi_S N$
not C	$p(1 - \pi_S)N$	$(1 - p)(1 - \pi_S)N$	$(1 - \pi_S)N$
total	$(\pi_S + p - p\pi_S)N$	$(1 - p)(1 - \pi_S)N$	N

We can now read of the posterior probability of S being C in the first column as being equal to

$$\frac{\pi_S}{\pi_S + p - p\pi_S},$$

leading to the same answer as in (2.12).   □

Here is a final example of the use of a table.

Example 2.2.4 A breathalyser is calibrated so that, if it is used on a driver whose blood alcohol concentration exceeds the legal limit, it will read positive 99% of the time, while if the driver is below the limit, it will read negative 90% of the time. At Christmas, 10% of drivers on the road are above the legal limit. If all drivers were tested, what proportion of those testing positive would actually be above the limit?

We can take a (virtual) population of 1,000 drivers (the size does not matter, just make sure that the numbers are big enough as to avoid fractions, for convenience), and we complete the table in the usual way, starting with the prior information, which is represented by a fraction of the virtual population, and then incorporating the given conditional probabilities to distribute the numbers over the remaining columns. This leads to the following table.

	positive test	negative test	total
above limit	99	1	100
below limit	90	810	900
total	189	811	1,000

We now read off the posterior odds 99/90 for being above versus below the limit for someone with a positive test. Of course one can also read off the posterior probability for being above the limit if the test is positive: this is 99/189. □

2.2.1 Combination of Evidence

We have argued that the likelihood ratio $LR_{H_1, H_2}(E)$ is a reasonable measure for the strength of the evidence the data E provides for H_1 relative to H_2. In most cases, however, there are multiple pieces of evidence that need to be taken into account. A small computation indicates how we can in principle use the likelihood framework to deal with this.

Suppose that there are two pieces of evidence E_1 and E_2, and that we want to compute $LR_{H_1, H_2}(E_1 \cap E_2)$, the likelihood ratio corresponding to the combined evidence E_1 and E_2. We write

$$\frac{P(E_1 \cap E_2 \mid H_1)}{P(E_1 \cap E_2 \mid H_2)} = \frac{P(E_1 \mid H_1)}{P(E_1 \mid H_2)} \times \frac{P(E_2 \mid E_1, H_1)}{P(E_2 \mid E_1, H_2)}. \tag{2.13}$$

From this we see that it is in general

$$LR_{H_1, H_2}(E_1 \cap E_2) \neq LR_{H_1, H_2}(E_1) \times LR_{H_1, H_2}(E_2).$$

For equality to be true here, it is sufficient that E_1 and E_2 are *conditionally independent*, conditional on both H_1 and on H_2. Multiplying likelihood ratios for two pieces of evidence E_1 and E_2 is allowed precisely when

$$\frac{P(E_2 \mid E_1, H_1)}{P(E_2 \mid E_1, H_2)} = \frac{P(E_2 \mid H_1)}{P(E_2 \mid H_2)}.$$

The rightmost factor in (2.13) is often denoted by $LR_{H_1, H_2}(E_2 \mid E_1)$ so that (2.13) reads as

$$LR_{H_1, H_2}(E_1 \cap E_2) = LR_{H_1, H_2}(E_1) \times LR_{H_1, H_2}(E_2 \mid E_1). \tag{2.14}$$

Here is an example with combination of evidence.

Example 2.2.5 Consider again a deck of 52 cards. As before, H_n denotes the hypothesis that the deck is normal. Denote by H_t the hypothesis that the deck consists of cards with only two numbers, each of which appears on 26 cards. Suppose now that we draw two cards with replacement. Let E_1 be the event that the first card is a 12, and let E_2 be the event that the second card is a 14. It is not hard to see that $LR_{H_n, H_t}(E_1) = LR_{H_n, H_t}(E_2) = 1$, assuming that given H_t all combination of two numbers are equally likely. This is rather intuitive, since the drawing of one card should give no evidence for the deck being normal versus the deck being of the special type we considered.

However, it is not the case that $LR_{H_n, H_t}(E_1 \cap E_2) = 1$. Indeed, choosing two different cards in two consecutive drawings is more likely under H_n than under H_t. To be precise, this latter likelihood ratio is equal to 102/52, that is, roughly 2. So we cannot multiply likelihood ratios in this case. It is, therefore, not the case that E_1 and E_2 are conditionally independent given the hypotheses. This may be seen as somewhat surprising, given the fact that E_1 and E_2 are the results of independent drawings with replacement. It illustrates that the notion of conditional independence is rather tricky and easily leads to mistakes.   □

2.3 The Likelihood Ratio Meets Necessary Requirements

We have introduced and developed the likelihood ratio as a natural quantification of evidence for one hypothesis versus a second one. In this section we investigate to what extent the likelihood ratio, as a measure of evidence, satisfies a number of properties that we deem necessary for *any* quantification of evidence. Hence, the purpose of this section is twofold: we elaborate further on properties a quantification of evidence should possess, and we argue that the likelihood ratio is very satisfactory from this point of view. Classical frequentistic measures, like the *p*-value, do *not* adhere to our requirements. All this adds to the interpretation of the likelihood ratio as a measure of evidential weight.

2.3.1 Dependence on Probabilities of Observed Data Only

What characteristics should a proper measure of evidence strength possess? Recall that we want to decide to what extent the observed data provides (relative) evidence for certain given hypotheses. It seems reasonable that a proper measure of the strength of evidence the data provides should only depend on the observed data, and not on observations that might have been, but were not observed. It should in particular not depend on how the two probability distributions corresponding to the hypotheses in question spread their probability mass over these unobserved values. Whatever is unobserved should not play a role. We need to explain the data that we have obtained, and we are not concerned with how well the hypotheses could have explained something specific that did not happen.

We now carefully further argue for this position, as follows. Suppose that we consider two hypotheses H_1 and H_2, and suppose further that the observed data has the same probability under both hypotheses. Furthermore, suppose that the distribution of unobserved values differ under the two hypotheses, either by assigning different probabilities to shared outcomes, or by simply having different possible outcomes, or both. An observer, confronted with the actual data, now has no way whatsoever to distinguish between the two hypotheses H_1 and H_2. He has no way of telling whether the data comes from H_1 or from H_2, since the observed outcomes have precisely the same distribution under either of them. An example could be that we consider the observed data to be a DNA profile where the hypotheses state that it comes from a person from one or another population. It may be that while the population frequencies differ for most profiles between these populations, the profile that we have observed is equally frequent in both.

It follows that for any reasonable quantification of evidential value in which H_1 is involved, be it absolute or relative to another hypothesis H_3, replacing H_1 by H_2 should make no difference whatsoever. If a researcher quantifies the evidence for H_1 (absolute or relative), then replacing H_1 by H_2 should not make a difference for the very simple reason that the researcher will not be able to distinguish between H_1 and H_2. Hence two hypotheses whose induced distribution only differ on unobserved outcomes, should receive the same evidential value, if this evidential value is to mean anything at all.

Although we believe that this is a necessary property of any measure of strength of evidence, we do note the somewhat worrying fact that a classical *p*-value procedure to quantify evidence, as discussed in Section 1.7, does *not* comply to this constraint. Indeed, in that paradigm of hypothesis testing, one computes and uses not only the probabilities of the observed values, but also of those unobserved values that are in some sense "more extreme." For instance, suppose that you are interested in the question whether or not a certain coin is biased. In order to say something about this, you flip the coin 100 times, and obtain, say, 62 heads. In a *p*-value procedure, one computes the probability, assuming the coin is fair, that one obtains at least 62 (or, in a two-sided test which often is to be preferred, at least 62 or at most 38) heads. If this probability is very small (the first one is about 0.0104), then the hypothesis of fairness is rejected. The logic behind this, is that you simply do not believe that flipping a fair coin results in as many as 62 heads: this probability would just be too small.

However, notice that this decision does not only depend on the observed data. Indeed, it depends on the probabilities of the unobserved outcomes which are more extreme than the one observed. Within this paradigm one is forced to also take into account the probabilities of unobserved outcomes.

Likelihood ratios, on the other hand, do depend only on the probabilities the two competing hypotheses assign to observed data. A likelihood ratio simply involves the probability of the observed data under various hypotheses, and does not depend on the probability of unobserved outcomes in any way. Thus, the likelihood ratio behaves very satisfactorily with respect to this requirement.

This is not to say that the likelihood ratio does not need external information that is not provided by the data. We will see many examples of this in this book, but here is a first one. Suppose that a hypothesis H can be decomposed into $H = H' \cup H''$, where H' and H'' are disjoint. Then $P(E \mid H)$, the probability of evidence E given H cannot be computed without knowing the relative prior probabilities of H' and H''. Indeed: $P(E \mid H) = P(E \mid H')P(H' \mid H) + P(E \mid H'')P(H'' \mid H)$. That is, the probability $P(E \mid H)$ now depends on external information. Note that this was already an issue in Example 2.2.1, and we refer to Example 5.2.3 for another natural example where this happens. One may either view $P(H' \mid H)$ and $P(H'' \mid H)$ as part of the hypothesis H, or as parameters known by, say, the authority requesting the computation.

We conclude that a likelihood ratio always depends on the probabilities of observed values under the various hypotheses only, and that it may in addition depend on external information. Unobserved outcomes, however, never play a role.

2.3.2 Irrelevance of the Experimental Setup

In this section we discuss a strongly related issue, namely the way the outcomes were obtained. The experimental setup of a certain experiment might have a big effect on the possible outcomes of the experiment. The experimental setup (which must be decided upon beforehand) has an effect on the likelihood ratios that can possibly be obtained. In this sense, the experimental setup is not irrelevant for the likelihood ratio. But once the experiment has been carried out and the data has been obtained, then for the computation of the likelihood ratio, this setup is no longer relevant anymore in the sense that it is not important which outcomes could have been obtained but were not. All the researcher has to do at that point is to compute the likelihood ratio corresponding to the relevant hypotheses.

To elaborate on this claim, imagine that a researcher applies a certain stopping rule as to how many experiments he is going to perform. Such a stopping rule should only depend on the data, and not on which hypothesis is true. Let N be the random number of experiments that the researcher performs, and suppose that N is a stopping rule, that is, the occurrence of the event $\{N = n\}$ only depends on the outcomes of the first n experiments. We then compute, writing E_i for the data of the ith experiment:

$$\frac{P(N = n, E_1, \ldots, E_n \mid H_1)}{P(N = n, E_1, \ldots, E_n \mid H_2)} = \frac{P(E_1, \ldots, E_n \mid H_1)}{P(E_1, \ldots, E_n \mid H_2)} \times \frac{P(N = n \mid E_1, \ldots, E_n, H_1)}{P(N = n \mid E_1, \ldots, E_n, H_2)}. \tag{2.15}$$

The last fraction is equal to 1 by assumption, so we see that the information about N cancels, and we are left with the likelihood ratio corresponding to just the data $E_1, \ldots, E_n$. In this sense, the likelihood ratio is independent of the experimental setup, and it does not matter why we stopped after n experiments.

This is in sharp contrast to the more classical procedure in which the null hypothesis of interest is rejected as soon as the data falls in an appropriate rejection region. To define this rejection region, and to make sure that its probability under the null hypothesis is not too big, the full experimental setup must be known, of course. This can lead to situations in which the very same data leads to different evidential values as the result of a different statistical setup.

To give but one example, in the previous section we discussed the situation that 100 coin flips resulted in 62 heads. To compute the corresponding p-value, we computed the probability to see at least 62 or at most 38 heads. But from the data we have described, it is in fact impossible to say whether or not this is the correct p-value. We need to know whether the researcher had planned to perform 100 coin flips from the outset, or whether he used another stopping rule. These different experimental setups correspond to different notions of being "more extreme," and hence to different p-values. We discuss more examples of this phenomenon in Section 9.7, but here is an example of the problem.

Envision a different way to end up with 100 coin flips with 62 heads. Perhaps the researcher originally set out to flip coins until seeing 5 consecutive coin flips of the same type in a row. Perhaps this happened for the first time after 100 coin flips, among which 62 heads occurred. This would, of course, have been a very different experiment than the original one in which the researcher from the outset planned to perform 100 coin flips. In the second experiment, one can think of a researcher who rejects the null hypothesis of fairness if the number of coin flips to first see 5 similar flips in a row would be too small, say. If that is the original setup, then the corresponding p-value would be the probability, under the null hypothesis, that the number of coin flips needed for 5 similar flips in a row would be at most 100.

Clearly, this will result in a different p-value than obtained by the first researcher. However, they are based on the exact same data, and there is no reason whatsoever to think that the evidential value of this data for the null hypothesis should be different in the two experiments.

The fact that the likelihood ratio does not depend on the experimental setup once the results have been obtained does not mean that some manipulation is impossible. But this manipulation is always at the level of designing an experiment in order to make certain values of the likelihood ratio as (un)likely as possible. For instance, suppose a researcher would like to disprove a certain relation between two objects, and that he runs a series of tests. Each test is either negative, pointing towards no such relation, or positive, pointing in the opposite direction. If it so happens that the very first test is negative, then the researcher may decide to stop at that point, because he knows that the ensuing likelihood ratio will be satisfactory for him.

His peers may decide to repeat the experiment but now without the desire to disprove the relation. They may decide to perform 20 experiments, say. By doing that, they change the values of the likelihood ratios that can possibly be obtained. Once the data has been gathered, all this is no longer important anymore, and the likelihood ratio summarizes the evidential value. Intuitively it should be obvious that performing many more experiments (in the context just described) is better than performing only one, in the sense that the likelihood ratio found points in the correct direction more often than with only one experiment, and this intuition is essentially correct.

So although the likelihood ratio can be computed with the data in hand, a researcher may try to design an experiment in which the likelihood ratio is expected to be rather decisive in one or both directions. Not all experiments are equally useful. In Section 2.4 we investigate the distribution of future likelihood ratios in detail. We will see that the likelihood ratio has the pleasant property that although it (or rather the data) can be misleading, this will not happen too often (Proposition 2.4.2). Even better, even a devilish researcher who wants to reject a certain true hypothesis and is prepared to perform as many experiments as necessary to be able to do this, will with high probability *never* reach his goal, see Section 2.4.3.

2.4 The Distribution of the Likelihood Ratio

The likelihood ratio is a number that can be computed after seeing the data, provided probability distributions for the hypotheses involved are available. But in Section 2.3.2 we already implicitly discussed the idea that we can also view a likelihood ratio as a *random variable*. Indeed, suppose that we choose the data E randomly, with the distribution that we have chosen for H_1. When we do that, we can interpret the likelihood ratio corresponding to this observation, that is, $LR_{H_1, H_2}(E)$, as a realization of a random variable. Indeed, computing the likelihood ratio corresponding to E simply boils down to mapping the outcome E of the random draw to a non-negative number in a well-defined way.

There are several different notations possible for this construction, all of which appear in the literature. Assuming that we are dealing with discrete outcome spaces, one may introduce the probability distributions P_{H_1} and P_{H_2} on the outcome space of the data, describing the probabilities of choosing E when the distributions for H_1 or H_2 are used, respectively. A formula like $P_{H_2}(LR_{H_1, H_2} = x)$, then refers to the probability of finding a likelihood ratio of x when we sample E according to the distribution corresponding to H_2.

Alternatively, one may introduce the notation $\mathcal{H}$ for a random variable which is distributed as drawings under hypothesis H. In this notation, one may write $P(LR_{H_1, H_2}(\mathcal{H}_2) = x)$ for the same probability as above.

However, the most widely used way of writing this down is to write

$$P(LR_{H_1, H_2} = x \mid H_2) \tag{2.16}$$

for the probability that LR_{H_1, H_2} takes the value x under H_2, again implicitly assuming that H_2 leads to a probability distribution on the outcome space.

Although we think that the first two notations have certain advantages over the third, we will use the notation in (2.16), mainly because this notation is most common in the field. Whenever we use it, the reader should keep in mind that although the notation suggests that we simply condition on a hypothesis being true, what we in fact mean is that we use the *distribution* that corresponds to the hypothesis.

We finally remark that one can also investigate the likelihood ratio corresponding to H_1 and H_2, assuming that we draw data under the assumption that a third hypothesis H_3 is true. Statements of that type then for instance involve $P(LR_{H_1, H_2} = x \mid H_3)$, and this is also well defined.

2.4.1 Basic Properties of the Likelihood Ratio Distribution

We start by an elementary but very useful relation between the distribution of the likelihood ratio under H_1 and H_2, respectively.

Proposition 2.4.1 *We have*

$$P(LR = x \mid H_1) = x P(LR = x \mid H_2), \text{ for all } 0 \le x < \infty. \tag{2.17}$$

Before we prove this proposition, we pay special attention to the extreme cases $x = 0$ and $x = \infty$. If H_1 is true, then the numerator of the likelihood ratio cannot be equal to 0, so $P(LR = 0 \mid H_1) = 0$ and the identity in (2.17) is correct. On the other hand, since the denominator of the likelihood ratio cannot be 0 under H_2 we have $P(LR = \infty \mid H_2) = 0$ and the right-hand side of (2.17) is not defined for $x = \infty$ since $0 \cdot \infty$ is not defined. Hence we must exclude $x = \infty$ in the statement of the proposition.

Proof of Proposition 2.4.1 Let

$$\mathcal{E}_x = \{E : P(E \mid H_1)/P(E \mid H_2) = x\}$$

be the set of all pieces of evidence for which we obtain a likelihood ratio equal to x. Then

$$P(LR = x \mid H_1) = \sum_{E \in \mathcal{E}_x} P(E \mid H_1) = \sum_{E \in \mathcal{E}_x} x P(E \mid H_2) = x P(LR = x \mid H_2),$$

which is what we needed to show. Note that it is the second equality in which we use that $x < \infty$. $\square$

It now follows that

$$\text{if } P(LR = x \mid H_2) > 0, \text{ then } \frac{P(LR = x \mid H_1)}{P(LR = x \mid H_2)} = x, \tag{2.18}$$

which we can summarize as "the likelihood ratio of the likelihood ratio is the likelihood ratio." This property reinforces the fact that for discriminating between H_1 and H_2 on the basis of evidence E, it is sufficient to know the likelihood ratio corresponding to E. This follows, of course, already from Bayes' rule, since this rule tells us that to go from prior to posterior odds, only the likelihood ratio of the observed data is important, not the observed data itself. This can also be concluded from (2.18), since it says that if we interpret the likelihood ratio as our evidence (instead of the original data), then the likelihood ratio that we get is the same as the original likelihood ratio.

Since, as already remarked before, $P(LR = \infty \mid H_2) = 0$ we can, for all $k = 0, 1, 2, \ldots$, write

$$E(LR^{k+1} \mid H_2) = \sum_{0 \le x < \infty} x^{k+1} P(LR = x \mid H_2)$$

$$= \sum_{0 \le x < \infty} x^k P(LR = x \mid H_1) \tag{2.19}$$

$$\le E(LR^k \mid H_1), \tag{2.20}$$

with equality if

$$P(LR = \infty \mid H_1) = 0. \tag{2.21}$$

It is easy to see that (2.21) is equivalent to

$$P(E \mid H_1) > 0 \Rightarrow P(E \mid H_2) > 0 \text{ for all } E. \tag{2.22}$$

In words, (2.22) says that if H_1 is able to explain E, so is H_2, and in the sequel we assume that this condition is satisfied.

Assuming (2.22), we thus have

$$E(LR^{k+1} \mid H_2) = E(LR^k \mid H_1).$$

Taking $k = 0$ leads to the remarkable property that

$$E(LR \mid H_2) = 1. \tag{2.23}$$

Taking $k = 1$ leads to

$$E(LR \mid H_1) = E(LR^2 \mid H_2) \ge (E(LR \mid H_2))^2 = 1. \tag{2.24}$$

To see that condition (2.22) is really necessary for these conclusions, we consider Example 2.2.1 once more. When we look at H_n versus H_{12}, then the drawing of one card gives $E(LR \mid H_{12}) = 1/52$, which is therefore not equal to 1. This is due to the fact that condition (2.22) is not satisfied since an outcome different from 12 is explainable by H_n but not by H_{12}.

Property (2.24) is quite intuitive since you may expect supporting evidence for H_1 if H_1 is in fact true. Reasonable as this may sound, (2.23) states that the corresponding statement is not correct when H_2 is in fact true. In words, (2.23) says that the average likelihood ratio in favor of the first hypothesis compared to a second hypothesis is 1, if in reality the second hypothesis is true. That is, the average likelihood ratio does not discriminate at all between the hypotheses. This property does not mean that a comparison is on average useless, but it does mean that whatever H_1 is, from time to time evidence generated by H_2 will give evidence in favor of H_1. Perhaps the most remarkable thing about (2.23) is that the expectation is independent of what the hypotheses are.

We can also assume the converse of (2.22), that is,

$$P(E \mid H_2) > 0 \Rightarrow P(E \mid H_1) > 0. \qquad (2.25)$$

If this is true then we can prove in the same way as above that

$$E(LR^{-1} \mid H_1) = 1.$$

Without (2.25) we would obtain $E(LR^{-1} \mid H_1) \le 1$.

2.4.2 Misleading Evidence

We have seen that the average likelihood ratio in favor of H_1, if the evidence is in fact coming from H_2, is equal to one. Thus, there must be possibilities for evidence in favor of the wrong hypothesis H_1, sufficiently many for the average likelihood ratio to be unity. Similarly, it may also be possible that we get a likelihood ratio in favor of H_1 if H_2 is in fact true. In both cases, we would get evidence that strengthens our belief in a hypothesis that is not the one that generated our data. We have called such evidence misleading evidence. A natural question is, how often evidence can be misleading, and in particular how strongly misleading it can be how often.

Our next statement gives a bound on $P(LR \ge x \mid H_2)$ for $x > 0$. It shows that when H_2 is in fact true, the likelihood ratio cannot be too big too often.

Proposition 2.4.2 *(a) For all $x > 0$ we have*

$$P(LR \ge x \mid H_2) = P(LR \ge x \mid H_1)E(LR^{-1} \mid H_1, LR \ge x)$$
$$\le 1/x.$$

(b) For all $x \geq 0$ we have

$$P(LR \leq x \mid H_1) = P(LR \leq x \mid H_2)E(LR \mid H_2, LR \leq x)$$

$$\leq x.$$

Proof (a) We have

$$P(LR \geq x \mid H_2) = \sum_{y \geq x} P(LR = y \mid H_2)$$

$$= \sum_{y \geq x} \frac{1}{y} P(LR = y \mid H_1)$$

$$= \sum_{y \geq x} \frac{1}{y} P(LR = y \mid H_1, LR \geq x)P(LR \geq x \mid H_1)$$

$$= P(LR \geq x \mid H_1)E(LR^{-1} \mid H_1, LR \geq x)$$

$$\leq 1/x.$$

The statement in (b) is proved similarly.   □

Proposition 2.4.2 is particularly useful in practice for estimating $P(LR \geq x \mid H_2)$, especially for large x. Indeed, in many cases the exact distribution of the likelihood ratio and hence the probabilities that the likelihood ratio exceeds some threshold, are hard to compute explicitly. If we want to estimate $P(LR \geq x \mid H_2)$ directly from a random sample of likelihood ratios obtained under H_2 then a sample size (far) greater than x will be needed, in view of the fact that $P(LR \geq x \mid H_2) \leq 1/x$. This easily becomes computationally prohibitive.

However, in view of Proposition 2.4.2 the required estimate can also be obtained from a sample of likelihood ratios obtained under H_1. Explicitly, suppose we have a sample of N such likelihood ratios, denoted by $r_1, \ldots, r_N$. Since we can estimate $E(LR^{-1} \mid H_1, LR \geq x)$ by

$$\left(\sum_{i=1}^{N} 1_{r_i \geq x} \right)^{-1} \sum_{i=1}^{N} \left(1_{r_i \geq x} \frac{1}{r_i} \right),$$

and $P(LR \geq x \mid H_1)$ by

$$\frac{1}{N} \sum_{i=1}^{N} 1_{r_i \geq x},$$

we can use Proposition 2.4.2 to estimate $P(LR \geq x \mid H_2)$ by the product of these two expressions, that is, by

$$\frac{1}{N} \sum_{i=1}^{N} 1_{r_i \geq x} \frac{1}{r_i}.$$

This technique is a special case of the more general approach of *importance sampling*, where an auxiliary distribution is used to generate an event of interest (in this case, a sufficiently large likelihood ratio) that does not occur very often under the distribution that we aim to study. By sampling from the auxiliary distribution and then correcting for the fact that we have obtained the events of interest "too easily," we can arrive at an unbiased estimate of the probability of interest at a much reduced computational cost.

Proposition 2.4.2 states that misleading evidence in either direction cannot be strongly misleading too often. The probabilities $P(LR < 1 \mid H_2)$ or $P(LR > 1 \mid H_1)$ may be large but most, if not all, of that misleading evidence must be weakly misleading. We will encounter (for example in Section 7.6.5) likelihood ratio distributions such that the probability $P(LR > 1 \mid H_1)$ is small, even if $E(LR \mid H_1)$ is large.

The fact that a likelihood ratio need not point in the "right" direction may be perceived as problematic, especially when one would consider such likelihood ratios as erroneous in the same sense as for classical statistical error probabilities. We stress already here that this rests on a misconception of the concept of error, and in Chapter 10 we will extensively discuss this. At this point, we again note that the likelihood ratio simply cannot be erroneous. Provided, of course, the probabilistic models used for its calculation describe the actual mechanism of obtaining data, the likelihood ratio tells us which of the two mechanisms explains these data better, and how much better.

Error rates apply to decisions taken in the course of a procedure, and represent a relative proportion in a long and hypothetical series of cases. In other words, error rates are probabilities that are *predictive*. Likelihood ratios are not probabilities, but a ratio of two of them: they tell us how to best *explain* what has happened.

If we make predictions that are often wrong, then we need not attach much value to our predictions. But this is not what likelihood ratios do. They provide explanations, and Proposition 2.4.2 says that it cannot happen that a wrong explanation is x times better than the true explanation more than one in x times.

2.4.3 Behavior Under Repeated Experiments

Suppose we are in a context in which repeatable experiments make sense. As we explained in Chapter 1, in many applications in forensic and legal matters this is not the case. Nevertheless, one can imagine a situation in which a malicious researcher wants to find evidence for hypothesis H_1 over his rival's hypothesis H_2 which happens to be correct. He does so by repeating the experiment many times, until the totality of the observations so far has a likelihood ratio exceeding x in favor of H_1. What is the probability that he will *ever* succeed? Perhaps surprisingly, this probability is also bounded above by $1/x$. We can see this as follows.

Let $X = (X_1, X_2, \ldots)$ be the vector of the random observations of the researcher and write $LR_n := LR_{H_1, H_2}(X_1, \ldots, X_n)$, that is, the likelihood ratio after n experiments. Note that LR_n is again a random variable now, not a fixed number. Let $N = \min\{n : LR_n \geq x\}$ be the first time the likelihood ratio is at least x, where $N = \infty$ if this never happens. Then

$$P(N < \infty \mid H_2) = \sum_{n=1}^{\infty} P(N = n \mid H_2). \tag{2.26}$$

The occurrence of the event $\{N = n\}$ only depends on $(X_1, \ldots, X_n)$. Let C_n denote the set of outcomes $(x_1, \ldots, x_n)$ of $(X_1, \ldots, X_n)$ for which $N = n$ occurs, and denote by A_n the event that $(X_1, \ldots, X_n) \in C_n$. Note that the events A_n, $n = 1, 2, \ldots$ are pairwise disjoint.

By the very definition of C_n and by Proposition 2.4.2, each $(x_1, \ldots, x_n) \in C_n$ is at least x times as likely under H_1 than under H_2. Hence we find

$$\sum_{n=1}^{\infty} P(N = n \mid H_2) = \sum_{n=1}^{\infty} P(A_n \mid H_2)$$

$$\leq \frac{1}{x} \sum_{n=1}^{\infty} P(A_n \mid H_1)$$

$$\leq \frac{1}{x},$$

since the events A_n are mutually disjoint.

Finally, we remark that it is also the case that if H_2 is true, then LR_n converges to zero as n tends to infinity, with probability one (assuming that H_1 and H_2 are not identical). Indeed, since

$$LR_n = \prod_{i=1}^{n} \frac{P(X_i \mid H_1)}{P(X_i \mid H_2)},$$

it suffices (by taking logarithms) to show that

$$P\left(\sum_{i=1}^{n} \log\left(\frac{P(X_i \mid H_1)}{P(X_i \mid H_2)}\right) \to -\infty \mid H_2\right) = 1. \tag{2.27}$$

Since $f(x) = \log(x)$ is a concave function, we have by Jensen's inequality that

$$E(\log(LR) \mid H_2) \leq \log(E(LR \mid H_2)) = 0, \tag{2.28}$$

in view of (2.23). If H_1 and H_2 do not specify the same distribution, then we have in fact strict inequality here, and then (2.27) follows from the usual law of large numbers for independent and identically distributed random variables.

2.4.4 Asymmetry of the Likelihood Ratio Distributions

At first sight, one might expect, perhaps from the arbitrariness of the choice of which hypothesis should be H_1 and which one H_2, some aspects of symmetry. For example, one might expect that the evidence is potentially equally discriminating in favor of H_1 as it can be in favor of H_2. This, however, is not the case.

To see this, imagine that there are two mechanisms that produce data and we wonder which one has produced the data that we have. It is perfectly conceivable that the first mechanism only rarely produces data that are unusual for the second mechanism, and usually produces data that are also usual for the second mechanism. In that case, data that come from the second mechanism will never be strongly discernible. Data produced by the first one are discernible if they are of the type that is unusual for the second mechanism. Thus, the likelihood ratio when applied to data from the first mechanism will sometimes, but rarely, be large, and usually slightly point towards the hypothesis that, in fact, did not generate the data.

This example shows that there can be no general properties of likelihood ratios that express symmetry in its distribution with regard to the distribution if H_1 and H_2 are true. The distributions are related to each other via (2.18).

If one takes many independently obtained pieces of evidence which all are identically distributed, then one would expect limiting behavior that is controlled by the central limit theorem. However, this cannot apply to the likelihood ratio itself, as the likelihood ratio for the independent pieces of evidence is obtained by multiplication. Taking logarithms, the resulting $\log(LR)$ become additive, and then the central limit theorem applies. One may therefore expect that the $\log(LR)$ distribution, in the limit where more and more evidence is obtained, converges to a normal distribution. This must hold both for the distribution if H_1 is true, but also for the one where H_2 is true.

The following result says three things. First, if we assume that $\log(LR \mid H_1)$ is normally distributed, the distribution $\log(LR \mid H_2)$ must also be normal. Second, despite the possible asymmetry in the distributions of the likelihood ratio under H_1 or H_2 respectively, it says that when we consider many (conditionally independent) pieces of evidence, the expected logarithm of the likelihood ratios under H_1 and H_2 are each others inverse. Apparently, adding up many pieces of evidence overrules the potential asymmetry. Finally, it says that for $\log(LR)$ the variances are determined by the means.

Proposition 2.4.3 *If* $\log(LR \mid H_1)$ *is* $N(\mu, \sigma^2)$ *distributed, then* $2\mu = \sigma^2$ *and* $\log(LR \mid H_2)$ *is* $N(-\mu, \sigma^2)$ *distributed.*

Proof Let $f_i(x)$ be the probability density of the $\log(LR)$ distribution under H_i. Then $f_1(x)/f_2(x) = \exp(x)$, by (the continuous version of) (2.18). By assumption, f_1 has a $N(\mu, \sigma^2)$ density. But then f_2 must satisfy

$$f_2(x) = \frac{1}{\sigma\sqrt{2\pi}} \exp\left(-\frac{(x-\mu)^2}{2\sigma^2} - x\right).$$

The expression in the exponent of this density is equal to

$$-\frac{(x-\mu)^2 + 2\sigma^2 x}{2\sigma^2} = -\frac{(x - (\mu - \sigma^2))^2 + 2\mu\sigma^2 - \sigma^4}{2\sigma^2}.$$

Since f_2 is a density, it follows that $2\mu\sigma^2 = \sigma^4$, hence $2\mu = \sigma^2$. Thus f_2 is the density of a normal distribution with mean $-\mu$ and variance σ^2. □

This proposition tells us that, as we gather more independent evidence and the distribution of $\log(LR)$ resembles a normal distribution more and more, it is not possible that the log-likelihood ratio concentrates around its mean, since the variance grows linearly with the expectation. It is perhaps remarkable that for the likelihood ratio itself, the variance also grows linearly with the expectation: we have $\mathrm{Var}(LR \mid H_2) = E(LR \mid H_1) - 1$, as (2.24) shows.

2.4.5 The Weight of the Evidence

The average likelihood ratio that we discussed in Section 2.4.1 is not so easy to interpret, being a weighted sum of numbers that play a multiplicative role: the likelihood ratio transforms prior into posterior odds by multiplication. On a logarithmic scale, the likelihood ratio will transform the logarithm of the prior odds into the logarithm of the posterior odds by addition. Taking the average of additive factors perhaps makes more sense, as it informs us about the average shift in log-odds the evidence will bring about. Therefore it seems natural to judge the utility of the likelihood ratio by looking at the logarithmic scale. Indeed, in Section 2.4.3 and Section 2.4.4 we already saw that the logarithm of the likelihood ratio is a natural quantity to consider.

It turns out that indeed if we look on a logarithmic scale, we get somewhat better behavior, in a sense that we explain now. We have

$$E(\log(LR) \mid H_2) = \sum_{x \geq 0} \log(x) P(LR = x \mid H_2), \tag{2.29}$$

where the sum is over all x that can be taken by LR, and where any base is allowed for the logarithm. If $P(LR = 0 \mid H_2) > 0$ this expression is equal to $-\infty$. Otherwise we already noted in (2.28) that by Jensen's inequality we have

$$E(\log(LR) \mid H_2) \leq \log(E(LR \mid H_2)) = 0. \tag{2.30}$$

For likelihood ratios encountered when H_1 is true, we have

$$E(\log(LR) \mid H_1) = \sum_{x>0} \log(x) P(LR = x \mid H_1)$$

$$= \sum_{x>0} x \log(x) P(LR = x \mid H_2)$$

$$\geq E(LR \mid H_2) \log(E(LR \mid H_2)) = 0, \tag{2.31}$$

where we have used that $f(x) = x \log(x)$ is a convex function and hence again by Jensen's inequality, $E(f(X)) \geq f(E(X))$ for any random variable X. The inequalities (2.30) and (2.31) together are rather satisfactory, since they express that on average, the logarithm of the likelihood ratio has the desired sign.

The quantity $\log(LR)$ is called the *weight of evidence*. In many ways, it is more natural to consider the weight of evidence than the likelihood ratio itself. For instance, if independent pieces of evidence are considered then the weight of evidence becomes additive.

It is interesting to see how the logarithm of a likelihood ratio comes into play when interpreting numerical values of likelihood ratios, as follows. In Example 2.1.2 we came across a likelihood ratio of 357. Is this a large number? The unavoidable subjective element in the evaluation of such numbers can perhaps be dealt with when one compares the numerical value of a certain likelihood ratio to a canonical experiment which may serve as a benchmark. Here is a suggestion along these lines which reflects the use of a logarithmic scale.

Consider two urns, one containing only white balls, and the other containing an equal number of white and black balls. We choose one urn and draw a succession of balls from it, with replacement. We have two hypotheses about the contents of the chosen urn $- H_1$ saying all white versus H_2 saying half white and half black $-$ and our evidence consists of the colors of the chosen balls.

Suppose now that you draw five balls and they are all white. The likelihood ratio of H_1 versus H_2 corresponding to this outcome is 32. A likelihood ratio of 357 as occurring in Example 2.1.2 corresponds to drawing between 8 and 9 white balls in a row. So the strength of the evidence corresponding to a likelihood ratio of 357 is the same as the strength of the evidence of H_1 (all white) versus H_2 (half white, half black) when we draw about 8 or 9 white balls in a row. Without translating this into a verbal statement, it may be useful to compare the outcome to such a canonical experiment because it can serve as a benchmark for interpreting the numerical value of a likelihood ratio. But it is not a benchmark for the posterior odds, since we have given no information about which vase is a priori more likely.

The canonical experiment of the white and black balls further suggests that the logarithm of the likelihood ratio is a quantity of some interest. Indeed, the number of white balls that must be chosen in order for the likelihood ratio to reach a certain level L is $\log_2(L)$. It is not unreasonable to say that when the logarithm of the likelihood ratio is 2α, the evidence is twice as strong as when the logarithm of the likelihood ratio is equal to α, since the evidence corresponds to twice as many white balls chosen. A likelihood ratio which is twice as large cannot be so interpreted at all.

As a further example where the weight of the evidence behaves better than the likelihood ratio itself, consider the question whether or not the evidence has the tendency to favor the true hypothesis that actually generated it more strongly than any other hypothesis. Of course this cannot be true for every item of evidence on its own: we have already seen that we may get misleading evidence. A natural question therefore is whether the likelihood ratio in favor of H^* versus H_2 will *on average* support H^* most strongly when $H^* = H_1$, where H_1 denotes the true hypothesis.

It is easy to see that this is not true, and we will give an example in Section 7.6.4: for genetic data from parents and children, on average the likelihood ratio in favor of being monozygotic twins (versus unrelated) is larger than the average likelihood ratio in favor of the true relationship, being parents and children, versus unrelated.

However, if we instead consider $\log(LR)$, the weight of the evidence, then we do have this property. Indeed, we have, for any H^*, H_1, and H_2 that

$$E(\log(LR_{H^*, H_2}) \mid H_1) = E(\log(LR_{H^*, H_1}) \mid H_1) + E(\log(LR_{H_1, H_2}) \mid H_1)$$
$$\leq E(\log(LR_{H_1, H_2}) \mid H_1), \tag{2.32}$$

where the inequality follows from (2.30). The inequality is strict when H^* and H_1 do not specify the same distribution. Note that the first step can always be taken, since any evidence produced by H_1 cannot have probability zero under that hypothesis and so all likelihood ratios with H_1 as second hypothesis are finite.

Thus, we observe again that the weight of evidence $\log(LR)$ is behaves differently than the likelihood ratio itself: while the likelihood ratio does not always on average support the true hypothesis most strongly amongst all possible hypotheses, $\log(LR)$ does.

2.4.6 Likelihood Ratio Versus Weight of Evidence

In any particular case where we have data E, it is of course immaterial whether we calculate the likelihood ratio or its logarithm, but we have noted various properties of the logarithm of the likelihood ratio that seem more natural than the corresponding properties of the likelihood ratio itself, and which suggest that the logarithm of the likelihood ratio might be a better quantification of evidence than the likelihood ratio itself.

In order to further elaborate on this, we start by formulating Bayes' rule in logarithmic form:

$$\log \left(\frac{P(H_1 \mid E)}{P(H_2 \mid E)} \right) = \log(LR(E)) + \log \left(\frac{P(H_1)}{P(H_2)} \right). \tag{2.33}$$

Of course, now we need to *add* $\log(LR(E))$ to our prior log-odds to get our posterior log-odds.

We would like to interpret $\log(LR(E))$ as an amount of information that helps in discriminating between H_1 and H_2. To that end it is helpful to rewrite Bayes' rule as we did in (2.5):

$$\frac{P(H_1 \mid E)}{P(H_1)} = LR(E) \times \frac{P(H_2 \mid E)}{P(H_2)}. \tag{2.34}$$

We can interpret this version as follows: upon learning E, the relative increase in probability of H_1 is $LR(E)$ times as large as the relative increase in probability of H_2. On a logarithmic scale, this reads

$$\log(P(H_1 \mid E)) - \log(P(H_1)) = \log(LR(E)) + \log(P(H_2 \mid E)) - \log(P(H_2)). \tag{2.35}$$

For a random variable X with probability distribution $P(X = x) = p(x)$ the quantity

$$-\sum_x p(x) \log(p(x))$$

is called the *entropy* of that random variable. Entropy can be interpreted in many ways, one of which is as the average amount of information that we obtain upon seeing a realization of X. The quantity $-\log(p(x))$ is interpreted as measuring our "surprise" to see x happen. In that interpretation $\log(LR(E))$ describes the difference between the reduction, induced by learning E, in our surprise if H_1 is true, compared to the corresponding reduction for H_2. Indeed, we do not know whether E makes us more or less surprised to see H_1 or H_2 be true in any absolute sense, but $\log(LR(E))$ tells us to what extent the difference in surprise changes upon learning E, and it makes sense to interpret this as the (new) amount of information that we have at our disposal to distinguish between H_1 and H_2.

Hence

$$E(\log(LR(E) \mid H_i)) = \sum_E P(E \mid H_i) \log(LR(E))$$

is the average amount of information that we obtain if H_i is true.

Expression (2.18) now reads

$$\frac{P(\log(LR) = x \mid H_1)}{P(\log(LR) = x \mid H_2)} = e^x,$$

or

$$\log\left(P(\log(LR) = x \mid H_1)\right) - \log\left(P(\log(LR) = x \mid H_2)\right) = x.$$

This means that the difference in surprise to obtain information of amount x when H_1 is true, compared to when H_2 is true, is equal to x.

With these interpretations, the properties that we have derived for what we have called the weight of evidence justify that terminology. The additivity of $\log(LR)$ for conditionally independent pieces of evidence means that from two identical and conditionally independent pieces of evidence, we expect to obtain twice as much information than from a single one. More generally, the amount of information contained in any two pieces of evidence together, is the same as the amount in the first one, plus the amount in the second one that we had not learned from the first one. Furthermore, properties (2.30) and (2.31) say that on average, if we produce evidence from one of the two hypotheses under consideration, the information in that evidence reduces our surprise in the true hypothesis more than in the false one. Finally, property (2.32) says that, on average, the reduction in surprise is larger for the true hypothesis than for any other one.

These properties suggest that the logarithm of the likelihood ratio is the more natural quantity than the likelihood ratio itself, as a candidate for quantifying evidential value. With some training, it may in fact be easier for many to develop an intuition for the logarithm of the likelihood ratio than for the likelihood ratio itself. Bayes' rule would then be applied in the following way: we may represent the difference in our belief in H_1 as opposed to H_2 as a real number – equal to $\log(P(H_1)) - \log(P(H_2))$ – where the value zero corresponds to no difference, and the larger the value is, the more we believe H_1 rather than H_2. Evidence will induce a change in this, in that we move upwards if E is evidence for H_1 relative to H_2, and downwards if E is relative evidence for H_2. The shift is linear in the amount of information. When we get two equally strong independent pieces of evidence, we shift twice as much as we do for a single one.

In any given case where we obtain evidence E, it is of course immaterial whether we apply (2.34) or (2.33), and traditionally in forensics Bayes' rule is used in its multiplicative form using the likelihood ratio. We will also do so in most of the remainder of this book, but in some places we will return to the logarithm of the likelihood ratio. For example, in Chapter 7 we will further discuss the difference in behavior between the likelihood ratio and its logarithmic counterpart in the specific context of DNA kinship analysis.

2.5 Summary and Conclusions

When we have two competing hypotheses H_1 and H_2, and data E, then we can quantify the evidential value of E with respect to H_1 and H_2 by the likelihood ratio

$$\frac{P(E \mid H_1)}{P(E \mid H_2)}.$$

The likelihood ratio expresses how much more likely the data E is under H_1 compared to H_2. It is a genuinely comparative notion of statistical evidence. We have argued by philosophical arguments on the one hand, and many examples on the other, that only comparative notions of evidence qualify as such. Indeed, if data is better explained by H_1 than by H_2, but even better by H_3 then one cannot say whether or not the data gives support for H_1. It all depends on the alternatives one wants or needs to consider and the plausibility of each of them.

In the end we are not so much interested in the likelihood ratio itself, but rather in the posterior odds

$$\frac{P(H_1 \mid E)}{P(H_2 \mid E)},$$

which can be obtained by multiplying the likelihood ratio with the prior odds $P(H_1)/P(H_2)$.

We have investigated a number of properties of likelihood ratios that a notion of evidence should possess. A likelihood ratio only depends on the probabilities of the actual observed data, and not on data that could have been, but was not observed. Furthermore, a likelihood ratio does not depend on the precise details of the experimental setup: how the data has been obtained, and what the set-up of the experiment was, is no longer important once the data has been gathered.

If H_1 is true, then on average the likelihood ratio is at least 1, a desirable property. If H_2 is true, then the likelihood ratio is (under mild conditions) on average exactly equal to 1. Although this might be considered disappointing, it is at the same time true that when H_2 is true, the probability that the likelihood ratio is larger than k is bounded above by $1/k$. So evidence pointing in the wrong direction is of course possible by the very nature of statistical evidence, but there is some control on how often that will happen.

The logarithm of the likelihood ratio behaves better in the sense that the average logarithm of the likelihood ratio is bigger than 0 when H_1 is true, and smaller than 0 when H_2 is true. The logarithm of the likelihood ratio is often called the weight of the evidence. It has a number of further properties that makes it even more suitable as a quantification of evidence than the likelihood ratio itself. For instance, it is not in general true that the likelihood ratio of H^* versus H_2 will on average support H^*

most strongly when H^* is the true hypothesis. The logarithm of the likelihood ratio does satisfy this elegant property.

If different pieces of evidence are sufficiently independent (the formal requirement is that they are conditionally independent given any of the two hypotheses), then the corresponding likelihood ratios can be multiplied. This should never be routine.

2.6 Bibliographical Notes

The notion of a likelihood ratio is well established in the forensic literature, and its origin goes back to Essen-Möller and Gürtler, who coined the phrase *paternity index*, which is nothing but our likelihood ratio in the case where H_1 states that a certain man is the father of a child, and H_2 states that he is unrelated to the child. The interested reader can consult [82] for a very early discussion of this, and for further references in this direction. See also [74] for an early discussion of the likelihood ratio as a measure of evidence. The book [1] contains a very practical discussion of evidence in forensic science. That book is not so much concerned with probability theory or the general theory behind likelihood ratios, but more with the presentation of ready-to-use formulas for various applications in forensics. The book [127] is aimed at practicing forensic scientists, law students, and legal representatives, and is not intended as an introduction or an in-depth development of the mathematics, or the modeling process. The book by Richard Royall [129] discusses some of the properties of the likelihood ratio that were treated in Section 2.4, see also [146]. The result about repeated experiments in Section 2.4.3 goes back to [168]; see also [126]. Example 2.2.4 is taken from [53]. Proposition 2.4.3 is due to Turing, see [72]. See also [116] for a discussion on likelihood ratios.

3

The Uncertainty of the Likelihood Ratio

After having studied the likelihood ratio in detail, the issue to which we turn our attention now concerns the question of uncertainty around the value of the likelihood ratio. The forensic literature has seen much debate on the topic of uncertainty around the value of a reported likelihood ratio. The question is whether or not the likelihood ratio is to be viewed as a statistical estimate, based on the data, of a certain truly existing quantity, and therefore whether or not it should be accompanied by a confidence interval expressing the uncertainty of that estimate. After all, statistical estimates vary from sample to sample, and statistical estimation therefore typically involves the construction of such a confidence interval which somehow captures the uncertainty in the estimate.

We will argue in this chapter that the likelihood ratio should *not* be accompanied by an interval expressing uncertainty. We will argue that the existing uncertainty has already been taken into account when computing the very likelihood ratio. We illustrate our position with extensive examples, and discuss competing positions in the literature.

We will explain also that it is possible to construct a meaningful interval around a likelihood ratio, not as a classical confidence interval but as an interval that says something about what likelihood ratios we can expect if we were to gather more data. Such intervals can be useful when one needs to decide about whether or not more data should be obtained, but they are irrelevant for the evidential interpretation of the current data.

3.1 The Nature of the Likelihood Ratio

If we want to estimate a physical quantity, like the speed of light or the proportion of a population having a given characteristic, then it is reasonable to assume that the target of our investigation exists and has a certain value. For instance, it simply takes a certain amount of time for light to travel from one place to another, and in a given population, there is a certain proportion of individuals with the investigated characteristic. If we perform (one way or another) measurements or observe certain individuals, we can use these measurements or observations to say something intelligent about the target.

Similarly, when we try to estimate a model parameter, then we would like to know which parameter value fits the data best. The idea, then, is to find a certain statistic, computable from the data, which should be close to the model parameter in the following sense: assuming that the model is correct and that only the (true) value of the parameter remains unknown, the probability that the statistic is far from this true value should be small, and/or when we consider more data, the statistic should in some probabilistic sense converge to the true value.

After obtaining certain measurements, statistical procedures may lead to a point estimate of the quantity of interest, be it a physical quantity or a model parameter as described above. In addition, such a point estimate may, or perhaps even should, be accompanied by a confidence interval, which somehow quantifies the uncertainty of our estimate. These intervals do not tell us what to expect from a new sample, but they contain values of the parameters for which the sample we have observed is not too unlikely. These techniques are completely standard and uncontroversial, but are also the object of many interpretational misconceptions.

The first thing we need to investigate is whether or not a likelihood ratio can be viewed as a model parameter, or perhaps as a physical quantity like the speed of light or the proportion of a population having a certain characteristic. Is there some quantity, physical or within an assumed model, that the likelihood ratio tries to approximate based on the data?

So, what is the nature of a likelihood ratio? To start with, when we compute a likelihood ratio we need to compute two probabilities: the probability of the outcome E assuming that the first hypothesis H_1 is true, and the probability of the outcome E given that a second, competing hypothesis H_2 is true: $LR_{H_1, H_2}(E) = P(E \mid H_1)/P(E \mid H_2)$. A likelihood ratio expresses the weight of the evidence E for H_1 relative to H_2. The two components of a likelihood ratio are both conditional probabilities. Hence, if someone wants to argue that he or she should create a confidence interval around a likelihood ratio then he or she should also be willing to construct such an interval around a reported conditional probability. This, however, is somewhat problematic from a philosophical point of view. What would it mean to make a probabilistic statement about the probability that a certain event takes place? Can one meaningfully speak about the probability that one's probability has a certain value?

Let us consider a simple example. Suppose that a test exists for a disease. Let us say that according to our knowledge, the probability of recovery from this disease is 40%. For anyone with this disease, we therefore say that his or her probability of recovery is 40%. Now, suppose that it is somehow discovered that there are in fact two equally common variants of this disease, a mild one with probability of recovery of 60% and a severe one with probability of recovery of 20%, but that there is for us no way to know which variant a patient has. When we now consider a newly diagnosed patient, would it then make sense to say that the probability of recovery is either 20% or 60%, both with probability 1/2 (since we were told that the variants are equally common)?

The answer is that with our current knowledge that the patient has either the mild or the severe variant, doing this makes no difference: the only probability that we can give for recovery is 40%, whether we write this as $1/2 \times 20\% + 1/2 \times 60\%$ or directly as 40%. The existence of the two variants could be of value in the future, say, if clinical methods could become available to find out which variant a patient has, but in the absence of any way to find out which variant a current patient has, the higher order probabilities do not add anything at all to our current probabilistic assessment. The fact that we have learned that it is in principle possible to distinguish between variants, does not help us for our current assessment of the probability of recovery. The existence of the variants is of no value to us when we do not yet have the information which one we have.

The probability of recovery is not a physically present quantity somewhere. Instead, it reflects, based on the knowledge we have, to what extent we expect recovery to happen. Conversely, given a recovery (or not), it reflects how well we saw that coming. Any probabilistic statement thus reflects our knowledge of the world, rather than the world itself. If our knowledge would be complete, these notions would coincide. In the example we just gave, if we know which of the two variants a patient has, then we can update our probability of recovery to either 20% or 60%. Hence, the probability of recovery that we can assign to a given patient simply depends on the information that we have, and for this, higher order probabilities are not important. To summarize, if our probability is either 20% or 60%, each with probability 1/2, then in fact we should, simply, say that this probability is 40%.

As a second example, suppose that we are given a die, and we are asked to give the probability that upon our first throw, we get a six. If we are told that the die is fair, our answer will be 1/6. This is, in fact, just a reformulation of the property of being fair. But suppose that we are told that the die which we are about to receive, is a special die, namely one with all faces having the same number of eyes. Suppose that we are in addition told that the probability that all faces have n eyes is 1/6, for all $n = 1, \ldots, 6$. Also in this situation, the probability to throw a six is just 1/6. Alternatively one may argue that with probability 5/6 we receive a die with no sixes, while with probability 1/6 we receive a die with *only* sixes. Hence one could perhaps insist that with probability 5/6, the probability to throw a six is 0, and with probability $1/6$, it is 1. However, still this means that we have probability $1/6$ to throw a six. We have not gained anything by "decomposing" our probability of $1/6$ into $5/6 \times 0 + 1/6 \times 1$.

We conclude that, as far as our probabilistic assessments based on our current knowledge is concerned, higher order probabilities do not capture anything that cannot be captured without them. For that purpose they lead to nothing more than an unnecessarily complicated expression. However, we may use these more complicated expressions to reflect that there is possible information to be obtained, whose revelation would alter our probabilistic assessment. In the first example, we may try to obtain knowledge about which variant the patient has, and in the second example, we may try to obtain knowledge about what kind of die we have. But higher order probabilities do not lead to a confidence interval for our current probabilistic assessment, since they add nothing to our *current* probabilistic assessment based on the knowledge we have. Hence a likelihood ratio, being a ratio of two probabilities, should not be accompanied by a confidence interval either.

The interpretation of probability as reflecting our knowledge also means that we can interpret a probability distribution for a model parameter θ as follows. We can think of θ as having a definite yet unknown value, but use a random variable W to express our knowledge and uncertainty about that value. When we are asked what we statistically expect the parameter to be, our answer is the expectation $E(W)$ of W. When we are asked other questions, such as what we statistically expect the square of the parameter to be, we may need other properties of the distribution of W. And when we get new information, the distribution of W will change.

This is also how we regard probabilistic statements in forensic situations. We have argued in Chapter 1 that in the context of forensic science we should interpret probability epistemically and subjectively. With this interpretation of probability, the likelihood ratio tells us how to incorporate evidence E into our belief about the competing hypotheses H_1 and H_2. It tells us how much information is present in the data E that helps in distinguishing between these hypotheses. The more uncertain we are about what data under any of the hypotheses looks like, the less information we can extract.

Probability therefore, in this interpretation, is assigned by an agent, and depends on the relevant knowledge of the agent. The reported likelihood ratios reflect the probabilistic conviction of the expert, and different experts may have different opinions or even different information. Differences between experts who have the same data are not due to randomness in the sampling of those data, but simply to possible difference of opinions, leading to different modeling among the various experts. The fact that different experts may arrive at different likelihood ratios is not a reason to create a confidence interval. In classical estimation of physical quantities, the fact that different values for the estimated parameters are consistent with the sample does indeed lead to the construction of a confidence interval, which is thought to quantify the uncertainty around the estimate in some sense. By construction, the confidence interval contains the true value of the parameter with at least some probability α, in the sense that if we would repeatedly carry out sampling and calculate the confidence intervals, a fraction α of such intervals would contain the true parameter. The fact that more data leave us with less uncertainty is reflected by the confidence intervals usually shrinking as they are computed based on larger samples. Ultimately, we can say that we can approximate the true value of the parameter arbitrarily well if we can conceivably have sample sizes that make the confidence intervals arbitrarily narrow.

But the likelihood ratio of the current data is not a quantity that one could determine, or at least approximate arbitrarily well, if only enough data would be at our disposal. On the contrary, by its very nature, the likelihood ratio is a quantity that depends only on the data that we have seen.

If we would perform more experiments the likelihood ratio would change, but it would be a *different* likelihood ratio depending on *different* data. It would not be a more precise version of the earlier likelihood ratio. Of course, if we would gather more and more data, we would become less uncertain in the sense that the acquisition of knowledge makes probability distributions on parameters converge. One may even imagine a situation in which no uncertainty exists at all anymore, and in which the corresponding likelihood ratio is exactly expressible in terms of model parameters. This will then be the appropriate likelihood ratio in such a situation, but it, simply, expresses something different than a likelihood ratio based on less data.

This position might appear unsatisfactory, because it implies that two pieces of evidence E_1 and E_2 can be equally strong, even if one of them appears to be potentially different than the other one. For example, if a characteristic C_1 that is shared by suspect and offender is known to occur in 10% of the population, we may get a likelihood ratio of 10 in favor of the suspect being the offender. The same likelihood ratio may be obtained for a characteristic C_2 about which little is known, and more information could possibly be gathered. Based on our current knowledge, both pieces of evidence discriminate equally well between the hypotheses.

What might be considered unsatisfactory is that for C_2, there is uncertainty in the sense that we know that given more data, we would arrive at a different evidential value for sharing C_2, whereas for sharing C_1 we know all there is to know. This is certainly true, but it does not affect the interpretations we are currently able to give. However, if we consider to allocate resources in order to get more data, it can certainly be of relevance to consider whether or not more data would lead to a quite different likelihood ratio than the current one. In this chapter we will see that the so-called *posterior likelihood ratio distribution* does exactly that. Therefore, this distribution is relevant as long as we consider getting more data, but it is not for our current assessment.

3.2 A Concrete Example

To illustrate our position, we discuss an important example that has been treated in the literature, see references below. Suppose that at the scene of a crime, a DNA profile Γ has been obtained which we may assume is left by the criminal C. There is a suspect S who has this particular DNA profile, and we write H_1 for the hypothesis that $S = C$ and, therefore, that S left the DNA trace. We write H_2 for the hypothesis that the unknown C is unrelated to S. In a population, the population frequency of this profile will have a certain value θ, as we have explained in Section 1.6. If we know the value θ, then the likelihood ratio would be $1/\theta$.

In practice the precise value of θ is unknown to us and described by a random variable W. To be sure, we do not say that θ itself is a realization of W, but instead that our uncertainty about the true value of θ is described by W, based on our knowledge, e.g., a population sample of profiles and knowledge of the relevant biology and population genetics. We assume for simplicity that W has a density χ_W. We write E_C respectively E_S for the event that C respectively S has characteristic Γ.

How does the expert's uncertainty about θ, expressed via the distribution of W, enter in the computation of the likelihood ratio? To compute the likelihood ratio of H_1 versus H_2 that we obtain in this case we argue as follows. Under H_1 the DNA profile has been seen once (since we assume that $S = C$) and the probability that this happens is

$$\int_0^1 t\chi_W(t)dt = E(W). \tag{3.1}$$

Under H_2 we have seen the DNA profile twice, and the probability of this is given by

$$\int_0^1 t^2\chi_W(t)dt = E(W^2).$$

We conclude that the likelihood ratio is given by

$$LR = \frac{E(W)}{E(W^2)} = \frac{E(W)}{(E(W))^2 + \mathrm{Var}(W)}$$

$$= \frac{1}{E(W) + \mathrm{Var}(W)/E(W)}. \tag{3.2}$$

To properly interpret this formula, we observe that the continuous version of Bayes' theorem gives

$$\chi_{W|E_C}(t) = \frac{P(E_C \mid W = t)\chi_W(t)}{P(E_C)} = \frac{t}{E(W)}\chi_W(t). \tag{3.3}$$

Hence

$$E(W \mid E_C) = \int_0^1 t\chi_{W|E_C}(t)dt = \int_0^1 \frac{1}{E(W)}t^2\chi_W(t)dt = \frac{E(W^2)}{E(W)}$$

$$= E(W) + \text{Var}(W)/E(W).$$

Combining this with (3.2) we conclude that

$$LR = \frac{1}{E(W \mid E_C)}. \tag{3.4}$$

From (3.2) wee see that this likelihood ratio decreases when our uncertainty about θ increases, in the sense of a larger variance. This uncertainty is, therefore, taken into account when computing the likelihood ratio.

It is important to note that the formula for the likelihood ratio is in terms of quantities that relate to the *distribution* of W. The expression is certainly not in terms of the underlying θ directly, which is only reasonable since we do not know the value of θ. The value of the likelihood ratio is, therefore, not a reflection of the true value of θ, but of our *knowledge or uncertainty of that value*.

Example 3.2.1 Let us illustrate this computation with a specific choice for the distribution of W. A choice which is often made is that W has a Beta distribution. The Beta distribution has density given by

$$\chi_W(t) = \frac{\Gamma(a+b)}{\Gamma(a)\Gamma(b)}t^{a-1}(1-t)^{b-1},$$

for all $t \in (0, 1)$, and where $a, b > 0$ are parameters. Here Γ denotes the *Gamma function* defined as

$$\Gamma(z) := \int_0^\infty x^{z-1}e^{-x}dx,$$

for all $z > 0$. This function is a generalization of the factorial function on the natural numbers. It has the property that $\Gamma(1) = 1$ and $\Gamma(z + 1) = z\Gamma(z)$, hence $\Gamma(n) = (n-1)!$ for any integer $n \geq 1$.

If W has such a Beta distribution, then we have

$$E(W) = \frac{a}{a+b} \tag{3.5}$$

and

$$\mathrm{Var}(W) = \frac{ab}{(a+b)^2(a+b+1)},$$

as is well known, and easily computed.

Let us first compute the density $\chi_{W|E_C}$ of the conditional distribution of W given E_C, that is, the conditional distribution of W given that we make the observation that C has the characteristic. First, observe that

$$P(E_C) = \int_0^1 P(E_C \mid W = t)\chi_W(t)dt = \int_0^1 t\chi_W(t)dt = E(W).$$

It then follows from the continuous version of Bayes' rule that

$$\chi_{W|E_C}(t) = \frac{P(E_C \mid W = t)\chi_W(t)}{P(E_C)} = \frac{t}{E(W)}\chi_W(t), \tag{3.6}$$

since after conditioning on $W = t$ we know that C has the characteristic with probability t. Using (3.5), this last expression is equal to

$$\frac{t(a+b)\chi_W(t)}{a},$$

and this is easily seen to correspond to the density of the Beta distribution with parameters $a+1$ and b, using the properties of the Gamma function.

It follows from this and (3.5) that the likelihood ratio in (3.4) is equal to

$$\frac{a+b+1}{a+1}.$$

If C is found not to have the characteristic, then the resulting conditional distribution will be a Beta distribution with parameters a and $b+1$. □

The fact that the likelihood ratio of interest is the reciprocal of an expectation of the distribution of $W \mid E_C$ is, we believe, the source of considerable confusion, and this is best explained using the situation in Example 3.2.1 again. The expectation of this distribution is some function of the underlying parameters a and b. As we have seen above, additional sampling of individuals, together with the information that these do or do not have Γ, will change the distribution by adding 1 to either a or b. Hence, when we think of becoming better informed by increasing a and b, then in the limit all uncertainty about θ will disappear. *If* we would have full knowledge of the frequency θ, then we would obtain a likelihood ratio of $1/\theta$, and indeed this will be the limiting value of our likelihood ratio upon additional sampling with probability 1. This is consistent with our formula $E(W)/E(W^2)$ in (3.2) because in the case of full information, the distribution of W is a point mass at the true θ and (3.2) reduces to $1/\theta$.

But even in the case where we know the frequency, there is a conceptual leap to be made. We will assign the probability that a randomly sampled individual has the characteristic to be numerically equal to the population frequency, but the probability is, as we have argued, an entirely different concept than the frequency. The population frequency exists physically and objectively in the sense that there may a relevant population to consider and that in this population, a number of individuals has the characteristic. The probability that a randomly sampled individual has the characteristic does not exist physically anywhere. If we use the relative frequency of occurrence as probability for a random individual, we must make additional assumptions. For instance, we then have to assume that the sampling is not biased with respect to the characteristic, so that individuals with it are not any more or less likely to be sampled than those without it. In that case, we may numerically equate the required probability with the (relative) frequency. Of course in general we will not know the population frequency. The mental construction to imagine that we do, is therefore of limited value: it will almost never happen and we risk to confuse frequency with probability.

The fact that the limit will be $1/\theta$ does not mean that we are estimating $1/\theta$ when we provide a likelihood ratio. The expert is not asked to give an estimate of $1/\theta$. Instead he is asked to give advice about the evidential value or interpretation of the data, and the expert will do this with a likelihood ratio. If one would be interested in an estimate for $1/\theta$, then this would lead to a more or less classical statistical procedure, with a point estimate and a confidence interval for $1/\theta$ which should be interpreted in a frequentistic way. But the expert is simply not asked to give an estimate of $1/\theta$. The likelihood ratio he is asked to provide, is a function of our *knowledge* about this frequency. It is not θ which is ultimately important, but our knowledge about θ. Hence there is no such thing as a "true but unknown strength of the evidence," a position not shared by Sjerps et al. [137] where we read (page 27):

"We have argued above that it is much more informative for the legal justice system to explore the resulting parametric expression, which represents the *true but unknown strength of the evidence only*, and see what likelihood ratio values we obtain for varying parameter values." (emphasis added)

Furthermore, on page 25 of the same reference, the authors refer to the position of Taroni et al. in [158]. The γ in the quote is the (subjective) probability that an individual drawn at random from the relevant population has the particular DNA profile. The abbreviation TBBA refers to [158]:

"TBBA choose to inform the court about γ. [...] We choose to inform the court about θ."

As we have argued, our position is that we need to assess two probabilities, and that the model parameters are only interesting insofar as they are needed for such assessment.

Of course, the situation in which we know the population frequency θ is a very artificial one, in the sense that it will generally not be possible to even define the precise population of interest, let alone determine for each member whether or not they have the characteristic of interest. In general, there will always be uncertainty about the population frequency and, as we have seen, more uncertainty leads to a lower likelihood ratio in the sense that if two probability densities for the frequency have the same expectation, then the one with the larger variance leads to the lower likelihood ratio. Of course, this sparks our interest in lowering the variance.

Sampling uncertainty is, therefore, not an issue for evidential interpretations: we do not collect a sample to estimate θ, but to be able to obtain values for $E(W)$ and $E(W^2)$ that are supported by more data than what we had prior to the sample. The distribution of W represents our knowledge, and the likelihood ratio is expressed in terms of it. A different sample would have led to a different opinion, but for the purpose of obtaining a distribution for W the obtained sample is the only one we have to deal with. It is indeed the case that a different sample leads to a different evidential value, but this does not change the evidential value of the current sample. It is just as pointless to imagine what another sample would have made us believe as it would be to imagine what we would have been able to conclude had the suspect and the trace shared another characteristic than the actual one.

In the example above the likelihood ratio contains prior information that constitutes subjective choices of the expert, namely the choice of the parameters of the Beta distribution. This is simply the way things are, and as long as the expert is transparent about what choices he or she made, the court can accept his or her witness statement as a subjective probabilistic statement which has incorporated all uncertainty that the expert is aware of.

One cannot start a statistical procedure with absolutely nothing. It is inevitable that probabilities are interpreted as subjective in the sense that they are determined by the probability distributions used by the forensic statistician. In this case, these distributions describe his or her knowledge (or lack thereof) about the frequency of the characteristic. This knowledge is formed by updating the purely personal prior distribution with a population sample. Had the prior distribution been a different one, or if another sample of the same population had been used, then in general a different probability density would have been obtained and also a different likelihood ratio.

Finally, if the likelihood ratio has a particular numerical value κ, say, then this does not mean that the expert claims that the true population frequency of the profile is $1/\kappa$. It does mean, however, that the evidential value obtained is the same as in the case that we know for sure that the population frequency is equal to $1/\kappa$, which is something completely different.

3.3 The Posterior Likelihood Ratio Distribution

We have argued so far that a likelihood ratio completely expresses the weight of the evidence, and there is no rationale to accompany a likelihood ratio with an interval to quantify uncertainty. This is not to say that there is no way to construct an interval around a likelihood ratio that has a well-specified interpretation.

Indeed, we saw that the likelihood ratio has a well-defined distribution when we imagine sampling more data of relevance for the parameters in the model. Since it may be the case that knowing which of H_1 or H_2 is true is relevant for the distribution of these parameters, we may need to distinguish between distributions where H_1 or where H_2 is true.

As we have explained, our position is that the forensic statistician acknowledges that the model parameters θ exist in the sense that there is a true but unknown value θ_0 of them responsible for the generation of the data. These values being unknown, the statistician's knowledge is summarized in a probability distribution.

In the case where θ_0 is known, the likelihood ratio typically can be written as a function $g(\theta_0)$. A possible reasoning that we have discussed, and which is advocated by some, is to consider the likelihood ratio, therefore, as a function of θ. Then, we may obtain an estimate $\hat{\theta}$ of θ, plug it into our function to obtain $\widehat{LR} = g(\hat{\theta})$, and then transfer any uncertainty about the sample statistic $\hat{\theta}$ to an uncertainty applying to $\widehat{LR}$.

In the previous section we have already argued that this procedure is a mistaken one. The likelihood ratio is *not* a function of θ. The likelihood ratio is a function of the distribution of θ, that is, of our *knowledge* about its possible values, and this is something fundamentally different. As such, a confidence interval for θ, obtained by classical statistical procedures, does *not* lead to a corresponding confidence interval for the reported likelihood ratio. All uncertainty about θ is carried over to the likelihood ratio by the change in distribution for θ.

The likelihood ratio being a function of our current knowledge, a natural question to ask is to what extent we would expect our likelihood ratio to *change* if we were able to acquire a larger population sample to inform our probability distribution for W. We can imagine getting such a large sample that for all practical purposes we would be able to say that we know the population frequency in the sense that the remaining variance is much smaller than the expectation of the frequency. We investigate this question in great generality now.

Suppose that the model parameters that occur in the statistical model are summarized by θ and that proponents of H_1 and H_2 each have their own distribution of θ, denoted by $f(\theta \mid H_1)$ and $f(\theta \mid H_2)$ respectively. We can now write

$$LR(E) = \frac{\int P(E \mid \theta, H_1) f(\theta \mid H_1) d\theta}{\int P(E \mid \theta, H_2) f(\theta \mid H_2) d\theta}. \tag{3.7}$$

Assuming that the ratios below do not lead to $0/0$, let

$$LR_\theta(E) = \frac{P(E \mid \theta, H_1)}{P(E \mid \theta, H_2)}$$

be the likelihood ratio we have when the value of θ is known, and let

$$LR(\theta) = \frac{f(\theta \mid H_1)}{f(\theta \mid H_2)}.$$

The reason for the notation $LR(\theta)$ is that we can interpret $f(\theta \mid H_1)/f(\theta \mid H_2)$ as the likelihood ratio that the value θ itself has, in the following sense. If someone would reveal the true value θ_0, then the likelihood of this value under H_1 compared to the likelihood under H_2 would just be $f(\theta_0 \mid H_1)/f(\theta_0 \mid H_2)$. Revealing the true value of θ provides evidence for which hypothesis is correct, and therefore it is consistent to use the notation $LR(\theta)$.

We can rewrite $LR(E)$ as an integral of $LR_\theta(E)$ against an appropriate measure. Indeed, we have (changing the integration variable in the denominator for clarity) that

$$LR(E) = \frac{\int P(E \mid \theta, H_1) f(\theta \mid H_1) d\theta}{\int P(E \mid v, H_2) f(v \mid H_2) dv}$$

$$= \int \frac{P(E \mid \theta, H_1)}{P(E \mid \theta, H_2)} \frac{P(E \mid \theta, H_2) f(\theta \mid H_1)}{\int P(E \mid v, H_2) f(v \mid H_2) dv} d\theta$$

$$= \int LR_\theta(E) LR(\theta) \frac{P(E \mid \theta, H_2) f(\theta \mid H_2)}{\int P(E \mid v, H_2) f(v \mid H_2) dv} d\theta$$

$$= \int LR_\theta(E) LR(\theta) f(\theta \mid E, H_2) d\theta, \tag{3.8}$$

where $f(\theta \mid E, H_2)$ is the distribution for θ supplied by H_2, updated with the occurrence of the evidence E, and where we used the continuous version of Bayes' theorem in the last identity.

Let us pause a moment and reflect on (3.8). First of all, if there is no disagreement concerning the distribution of θ, then $f(\theta \mid H_1)$ and $f(\theta \mid H_2)$ coincide, and the term $LR(\theta)$ disappears. In that case we get

$$LR(E) = \int LR_\theta(E) f(\theta \mid E, H_2) d\theta. \tag{3.9}$$

However, even if $LR(\theta) = 1$, so that the two hypotheses agree on the distribution of θ, they may no longer agree on this distribution given the evidence E, hence in the factor $f(\theta \mid E, H_2)$ we cannot delete the conditioning on H_2. Perhaps this may be seen as problematic by statisticians with a more frequentist inclination. They might argue that θ is fixed but unknown, and that knowledge of E, H_1 or H_2 does not change that fixed but unknown value. At first glance, this seems like a good argument. If θ is fixed, its value is not changed when subsequently a realization of E, H_1, or H_2 occurs. In the context of the example in Section 3.2.1, we may focus on some characteristic with population proportion θ, and then consider that a trace donor C has this characteristic, as well as a suspect S. If θ is fixed then S has this characteristic either with probability 1 or θ, depending on whether $C = S$ or not. However, that is not the situation we are in. We are confronted with two persons C and S that share a characteristic whose population proportion is unknown to us. It is then perfectly reasonable, that if $C \neq S$ the characteristic will, on average, turn out to be more frequent than if $C = S$, simply because chance matches happen more easily for common characteristics than for rare ones. Therefore, it is natural not to assume that $f(\theta \mid E, H_1)$ and $f(\theta \mid E, H_2)$ coincide.

We call the distribution of $LR_\theta(E)$, where θ is supposed to have density $f(\theta \mid E, H_2)$, the *posterior likelihood ratio distribution under* H_2. In the literature, this distribution is simply called the posterior likelihood distribution, but since we will also investigate what happens under H_1 we add the hypothesis under which we work. It follows from (3.9) that the mean of this distribution is equal to $LR(E)$.

What (3.9) expresses, is that assuming H_2 is true, if we sample $LR_\theta(E)$ using the distribution of our current knowledge, then the expectation of the outcome will be precisely $LR(E)$. Sampling according to our current knowledge described by $f(\theta \mid E, H_2)$, can be interpreted as sampling the value of θ that would remain if we were able to reduce, or even eliminate, our uncertainty about θ in the sense that the variance of the distribution describing our uncertainty will be very small. If all uncertainty is removed, then our knowledge about θ will be a point mass at some θ_0 and then the appropriate likelihood ratio is just $LR_{\theta_0}(E)$.

Thus, sampling from the posterior likelihood ratio distribution under H_2 tells us what likelihood ratios we *expect* to obtain if we can eliminate our uncertainty about θ, but we do not expect the likelihood ratio to change in either direction.

If we assume that H_1 is true then things are different. In that case we need to sample θ from the distribution $f(\theta \mid E, H_1)$, and (3.9) does not immediately give us information about what happens in that case. However, we can write

$$\int LR_\theta(E)f(\theta \mid E, H_1)d\theta = \int LR_\theta(E)\frac{f(\theta \mid E, H_1)}{f\theta \mid E, H_2)}f(\theta \mid E, H_2)d\theta.$$

$$= \int LR_\theta(E)\frac{P(E \mid \theta, H_1)f(\theta \mid H_1)}{P(E \mid H_1)}$$

$$\times \frac{P(E \mid H_2)}{P(E \mid \theta, H_2)f(\theta \mid H_2)}f(\theta \mid E, H_2)d\theta$$

$$= \int LR_\theta(E)\frac{P(E \mid \theta, H_1)}{P(E \mid \theta, H_2)}\frac{f(\theta \mid H_1)}{f(\theta \mid H_2)}\frac{P(E \mid H_2)}{P(E \mid H_1)}$$

$$\times f(\theta \mid E, H_2)d\theta$$

$$= \int LR_\theta(E)^2 LR(E)^{-1}f(\theta \mid E, H_2)d\theta$$

$$= LR(E)^{-1}\int LR_\theta(E)^2 f(\theta \mid E, H_2)d\theta$$

$$\geq LR(E)^{-1}LR(E)^2 = LR(E). \tag{3.10}$$

We call the distribution of $LR_\theta(E)$, where θ is supposed to have density $f(\theta \mid E, H_1)$ the *posterior likelihood ratio distribution under* H_1. It has the same interpretation as the posterior likelihood ratio distribution under H_2, the only difference being that we now assume that H_1 is true rather than H_2. It follows from (3.10) that the mean of the posterior likelihood ratio distribution under H_1 is *at least* $LR(E)$. Hence, if H_1 is true, then gathering more information about the model parameters in order to reduce uncertainty about these parameters will on average increase the likelihood ratio.

When we repeatedly sample $LR_\theta(E)$ using either $f(\theta \mid E, H_2)$ or $f(\theta \mid E, H_1)$, we can, by disregarding the, say, 5% most extreme outcomes, construct an interval. This interval tells us something about the values of future likelihood ratios that we would obtain, were we to remove all existing uncertainty about the model parameters θ. A very small interval reflects that obtaining further evidence will have little impact, whereas a large interval reflects that significant changes are possible or even expected. The interval can therefore be useful for such purposes as deciding whether or not we should indeed gather more data. It tells us the potential that gathering further data has: gathering more data will change the likelihood ratio that we have now, and based on our current knowledge we are able not only to evaluate the current data as a likelihood ratio, but also to predict (probabilistically) what future data will look like and how that will have impact on the likelihood ratio. The interval has no interpretation in relation to the *current* likelihood ratio, and in particular cannot be interpreted as expressing its uncertainty.

We have seen that, if H_2 is true, we do not statistically expect the likelihood ratio to change, whereas we do expect it to be larger if H_1 is true. We note that if we reverse the hypotheses, we get

$$\frac{1}{LR(E)} = \int \frac{1}{LR_\theta(E)} f(\theta \mid E, H_1) d\theta.$$

Hence, upon learning more about the model parameters, we expect $1/LR(E)$ to remain the same when H_1 is true, and to become larger when H_2 is true.

We make one final remark. If an expert is, because of lack of knowledge, not willing to suggest a probability distribution for the relevant model parameters, he or she might still be willing to provide upper and lower bounds for them, leading to an interval for the likelihood ratio as well. Again this is not a confidence interval, but a pragmatic way to deal with lack of knowledge. In epistemic language the endpoints of the interval correspond to situations where one would know the model parameters to stay between the upper or lower bound. Such an interval is acceptable if well understood and interpreted. It does not mean that the likelihood ratio comes with a confidence interval, but it can be a pragmatic way to express what we might call the *the sensitivity* of the likelihood ratio, that is, the way the likelihood ratio changes upon varying parameters.

3.4 Examples of Posterior Likelihood Ratio Distributions

In this section we apply the discussion about posterior likelihood ratio distributions of the previous section to three concrete examples.

3.4.1 Continuation of Example 3.2.1

Let us first apply the preceding framework to Example 3.2.1, where we have a shared characteristic between C (the offender) and S (the suspect). The evidence E consists of the pair (E_C, E_S) denoting, respectively, that C and S have the characteristic.

The uncertainty regarding the population frequency of the characteristic is, prior to the observation of E_C or E_S, modeled by $\chi_W(t)$ which we concretize as a Beta distribution with parameters (a, b). We assume that we are here in the situation where there is no difference between the distributions specified by H_1 and H_2, meaning that there is agreement on the relevant population and on the uncertainty about the frequency of the characteristic.

We have seen in (3.4) that

$$LR(E) = \frac{1}{E(W \mid E_C)} = \frac{1}{E(W \mid E_S)}.$$

Since $W \mid E_S$ follows a Beta distribution with parameters $(a + 1, b)$, this means that the likelihood ratio is $(a + b + 1)/(a + 1)$.

Writing the likelihood ratio in the form of (3.9) yields

$$LR(E_S, E_C) = \int \frac{1}{t} \chi_W(t \mid E_S, E_C, H_2) dt,$$

since if θ is known and equal to t, then the likelihood ratio is equal to $1/t$.

The distribution $W \mid E_S, E_C, H_2$ is the Beta distribution with parameters $(a + 2, b)$, since H_2 says that S and C independently have the characteristic. Thus, the likelihood ratio is also the expectation of the inverse of this distribution. It can be easily verified algebraically that indeed the expectation of the inverse of a Beta distribution with parameters $(a + 2, b)$ is equal to $(a + b + 1)/(a + 1)$.

Now we can investigate what would happen if we could eliminate our uncertainty about W by sampling population members and updating our Beta distribution accordingly. If H_1 is true then $W \mid E_C$ summarizes our knowledge. This is also the case when we have found the trace left by C and observed the characteristic, but we do not yet have a suspect S. In both cases, we have one observation. In that case, we expect that upon further sampling the population frequency will turn out to be θ with probability given by the Beta distribution with parameters $(a+1, b)$. For any such value θ_0 we then get likelihood ratio $1/\theta_0$, so the distribution of likelihood ratios we expect to obtain is given by the distribution of $1/(W \mid E_C)$, which in expectation satisfies

$$E\left(\frac{1}{W \mid E_C}\right) \geq \frac{1}{E(W \mid E_C)}, \tag{3.11}$$

by Jensen's inequality. Thus, prior to identifying a suspect, gathering additional information on the characteristic will in expectation increase the evidential value of that characteristic, when observed in a future suspect; and if we have a suspect who is in fact the trace donor, this is also true.

When we have, on the other hand, an innocent suspect, then the situation is different. In that case, if we know that the suspect is not C (or, more precisely, that the suspect has the characteristic independently of C), then our knowledge is summarized by the Beta distribution with parameters $(a + 2, b)$. Sampling from that distribution and calculating $1/\theta_0$ as we did for the first case, now yields a distribution which has mean $LR(E_S, E_C)$. Thus, we learn to what extent the evidential value may change, but we do not statistically expect it to change.

3.4.2 DNA Mixtures

We can also apply the framework in this chapter to DNA mixtures. We will devote Chapter 8 to the analysis of such mixtures, but since they fit naturally in the present discussion, we briefly introduce and discuss them here.

A DNA mixture is a DNA profile (cf. Section 1.6) which cannot be explained by only one contributor. For instance, when blood of a victim and a criminal is mixed in a stain, the profile of this stain can contain the alleles of both contributors at each locus. Historically, attention to mixed DNA profiles has long been confined to profiles where it could be assumed that all alleles of all contributors were observed, and nothing else. Under that (restrictive) assumption, one can calculate the probability that a random person can be excluded as contributor, which is possible for anyone who has at least one allele that has not been observed. The probability of the complement, namely that a random person only has alleles that have been observed, is often denoted $RMNE(M)$ (Random Man Not Excluded), where M denotes the mixture.

To fit this situation in the framework of this paper, consider a suspect S with profile g. This profile g is the parameter that plays the role of θ in the general theory of the previous section. We consider the hypotheses H_1 that S contributed to M versus H_2 that he did not. Let E denote the event that mixture M has been observed, together with the observation that S is not excluded as a donor. Note that E does not reveal the precise profile g of S, only that S is not excluded as a donor to the mixture M. It is easy to see that

$$LR(E) = \frac{1}{RMNE(M)}. \tag{3.12}$$

From (3.9) we see that it is true that (replacing the integral by a sum and the density by a probability, since g can take only finitely many values)

$$\sum_g LR_g(E)P(g \mid E, H_2) = LR(E). \tag{3.13}$$

Furthermore, (3.10) in this case yields

$$\sum_g LR_g(E)P(g \mid E, H_1) \geq LR(E). \tag{3.14}$$

In both expressions we can reduce the sum to all g which are not excluded as a donor of M, since we condition on E and this event implies that the profile of S is not excluded by M.

Since for all g which are not excluded as a donor of M, E is just the event that mixture M occurs, we can for all such g write

$$LR_g(E) = \frac{P(M \mid g, H_1)}{P(M \mid g, H_2)}.$$

Hence, $LR_g(E)$ is the usual likelihood ratio which measures the evidential value of the mixture M for the hypotheses that S contributed to M versus he did not, with knowledge of the profile of S.

We can interpret (3.13) and (3.14) as follows. If initially we only know that the profile of S matches with M, then the appropriate likelihood ratio is $LR(E) = 1/RMNE(M)$. But we can ask what likelihood ratio we expect once we learn the actual profile of S. From (3.13) we see that if S did not contribute to the mixture, then learning the actual profile of S will on average not change the likelihood ratio. On the other hand, if S did contribute, then we see from (3.14) that we expect the likelihood ratio to increase if the profile of S would become known to us. We will rediscover this property in a slightly different way in Section 8.4.3.

It has often been argued in the literature that one of the benefits of the $RMNE$ approach is, apart from its simplicity, the fact that it is on average a conservative assessment of the evidence, in the sense that it underestimates the evidential value. We now see that only in the case of a true contributor, the likelihood ratio is underestimated. In the case of an innocent suspect, the expected likelihood ratio upon learning the profile of S is the same as the current one $LR(E)$.

3.4.3 Height Measurements

Next, we apply our theory to an example given in [80]. Suppose one considers (body) height measurements obtained from camera images, modeled as

$$m_i = h_i + \alpha + \epsilon_i, \tag{3.15}$$

where m_i is the measurement of person i, h_i is the actual height of person i, α is a fixed systematic error and ϵ_i is a random error term, following a $N(0, \sigma^2)$ distribution. The heights h_i of the population are supposed to follow a normal distribution with parameters (μ_l, σ_l^2) which are considered to be known. The model parameters therefore are $(\mu_l, \sigma_l, \alpha, \sigma)$. Only the last two are the object of inference and we denote $\theta = (\alpha, \sigma)$.

A perpetrator has been seen on camera and has been measured as m_p. There is also a suspect with known height h_s. The data do not contain a measurement m_s of the suspect. To compute the likelihood ratio corresponding to the hypothesis that the perpetrator is the suspect, versus the perpetrator being an unknown member of the general population, one must compute the probability of obtaining the measurement m_p under both hypotheses. For the hypothesis where the suspect is the perpetrator, this probability can be computed for fixed model parameters θ, hence also by integration against some density for θ. For the second hypothesis, one needs the probability distribution for the height of a random individual. In order to obtain a data informed probability distribution for θ, a (modest) database B containing (m_i, h_i) for some test individuals is available.

With this setup the likelihood ratio can be written as

$$LR(m_p, h_s) = \frac{P(m_p, h_s \mid H_1, B)}{P(m_p, h_s \mid H_2, B)}.$$

We note that in this setup the model for m_i itself is not disputed and given by (3.15). Thus, $P(\theta \mid H_1, B) = P(\theta \mid H_2, B)$ which we denote by $P(\theta \mid B)$. We can write the likelihood ratio in the form (3.9) as

$$LR(m_p, h_s) = \int LR_\theta(m_p, h_s) P(\theta \mid m_p, h_s, B, H_2) d\theta. \qquad (3.16)$$

First we consider the term $P(\theta \mid m_p, h_s, B, H_2)$. We now need to condition on H_2, even if $P(\theta \mid B, H_2) = P(\theta \mid B)$, because H_2 tells us that m_p and h_s are data on different, independent, individuals. If H_2 is true, then h_s is simply the length of a random population member, and hence is not informative for θ. The measurement m_p is, according to H_2, the length measurement on camera of the perpetrator who is unknown. Therefore m_p is informative for θ, but only very slightly so, since the actual height of the perpetrator is unknown so needs to be considered as a random draw from the height distribution. In theory, θ could be estimated from (3.15) by providing only measurements m_i, but obviously for this model very many such measurements would be needed. Therefore, we omit also m_p from the conditioning. But then

$$P(\theta \mid m_p, h_s, B, H_2) \approx P(\theta \mid B),$$

since in the absence of m_p and h_s the hypothesis is no longer informative for θ, assuming the model for θ is undisputed between H_1 and H_2.

Therefore, we get

$$LR(m_p, h_s) = \int LR_\theta(m_p, h_s) P(\theta \mid B) d\theta,$$

where

$$LR_\theta(m_p, h_s) = \frac{P(m_p, h_s \mid \theta, H_1)}{P(m_p, h_s \mid \theta, H_2)}$$

is the likelihood ratio we get assuming the model parameters in (3.15) are known. We can evaluate this by either developing it as

$$LR_\theta(m_p, h_s) = \frac{P(m_p \mid H_1, h_s, \theta)}{P(m_p \mid \theta)}$$

or as

$$LR_\theta(m_p, h_s) = \frac{P(h_s \mid H_1, m_p, \theta)}{P(h_s)}.$$

The first way to evaluate $LR_\theta(m_p, h_s)$ amounts to comparing draws from $N(\alpha + h_s, \sigma^2)$ with draws from $N(\mu_l, \sigma_l^2) + N(\alpha, \sigma^2)$. In the second case, we compare draws from $N(\alpha - m_p, \sigma^2)$ with draws from $N(\mu_l, \sigma_l^2)$.

In any case, the posterior distribution of the likelihood ratio amounts to sampling from $P(\theta \mid B)$ and evaluating $LR_\theta(m_p, h_s)$. This is exactly what is done in [80], where several distributions are obtained corresponding to different h_s. As we have seen, we can interpret this as the distribution of likelihood ratios that we expect to obtain if we were able to obtain full knowledge of the parameters θ, assuming H_2 is true. That assumption has very limited influence here, but it is not exactly zero. Indeed, if we were to sample under the assumption that H_1 is true, then we sample from $P(\theta \mid m_p, h_s, H_1, B)$. Since, according to H_1, the data m_p and h_s are from the same person, the pair (m_p, h_s) can be added to B as an additional element. Thus, $P(\theta \mid m_p, h_s, B, H_1)$ is slightly (but strictly) better informed about θ than $P(\theta \mid m_p, h_s, B, H_2)$, and therefore we again expect likelihood ratios coming from $P(\theta \mid m_p, h_s, B, H_1)$ to be in expectation larger than $LR(m_p, h_s)$, the expectation of the posterior likelihood ratio distribution.

Now we can interpret a 95% (or any other) interval for the posterior likelihood ratio distribution. This distribution has no impact on the evaluation $LR(m_p, h_s)$ of the evidence that we have at hand when we have B, m_p, and h_s. It does, however, tell us what the likelihood ratios will become when we get to know the precise value of the parameters θ, assuming that the suspect is not the perpetrator. If the suspect were the perpetrator, we get a theoretically different, yet in practice quite the same distribution in this example. The posterior likelihood ratio distribution therefore tells us in which interval, if we were to carry out additional observations to include in B, we are most likely to end up with our likelihood ratio based on the new data.

While this does not change anything for the present evaluation, it may be of use to inform a decision-maker to what extent the likelihood ratio is influenced by the modeling uncertainty. This distribution can be used to make summary statistics answering that question. Hence this answers a question asked in [80]:

"Using the posterior distribution of the likelihood ratio for evidence evaluation can be seen as a hybrid of Bayesian and frequentist methods. It is not fully Bayesian, but it is also not a frequentist analysis. This ambiguity causes interpretation problems. For example, in a fully Bayesian framework, a 95% credible interval of a parameter means that the posterior probability that the parameter lies in that interval is 0.95. A frequentist 95% confidence interval means that given a large number of repeated samples, 95% of the estimated confidence intervals includes the true value of the parameter. What are the properties of the credible intervals for the likelihood ratio that we computed in the current application?"

It is interesting that the approach is considered to be neither Bayesian nor frequentistic. This seems a correct statement. As we have explained in Chapter 1, our position cannot be called "Bayesian" in the classical sense, and it is certainly not frequentistic. We have taken the position of expressing our uncertainty about some underlying parameter in a classical probability distribution, which we update upon further information. The posterior likelihood ratio distribution plays a role in this context, but cannot be properly interpreted in a genuine Bayesian or frequentistic framework.

3.5 Summary and Conclusions

The nature of a likelihood ratio is very different than the nature of a physical parameter or model parameter that needs to be estimated. The likelihood ratio is not a quantity that one could determine, or at least approximate arbitrarily well, if only enough data would be at our disposal. On the contrary, by its very nature, the likelihood ratio is a quantity that depends only on the data that we have seen, and of course on our knowledge that leads us to define the necessary probabilistic models. It is not existing in the physical reality. There is simply no such thing as approximating a likelihood ratio "arbitrarily well" by performing more experiments. If we would perform more experiments the likelihood ratio would change, but it would be a *different* likelihood ratio. It would not be a more precise version of the earlier likelihood ratio.

Sometimes, a likelihood ratio can be expressed as an expression that involves a model parameter θ. This might lead to the idea that the likelihood ratio is a function of this parameter θ. But it is not. Instead, the likelihood ratio is a function of our *knowledge* about this parameter and this is something fundamentally different. The court wants to know what the evidential value of the data is, and this is then expressed by the expert in terms of his or her knowledge about the underlying but unknown θ. So it is not θ which is ultimately important, but our knowledge about θ.

Sampling uncertainty is, therefore, not an issue for evidential interpretations: we do not collect a sample to estimate a parameter θ, but to be able to obtain information about the random variable W representing our knowledge of θ. Of course a different sample would have led to a different opinion, but for the purpose of obtaining a distribution for W the obtained sample is the only one we have to deal with. It is indeed the case that a different sample leads to a different evidential value, but this does not change the evidential value of the current sample. It is just as pointless to imagine what another sample would have made us believe as it would be to imagine what we would have been able to conclude had the suspect and the trace shared another characteristic than this one. The data is what it is, and we simply need to quantify its evidential meaning. It could all have been different than what we actually observed, but alas, it is not.

As a result of all this, a likelihood ratio should not be accompanied by a confidence interval. If we are uncertain about a piece of evidence, then this does not lead to a confidence interval around the likelihood ratio but instead, simply, to a lower likelihood ratio.

There is, however, a way to create a meaningful interval, but this is not a confidence interval. Indeed, when we are given a distribution describing our current knowledge of the likelihood ratio, we can sample from this so-called posterior likelihood ratio distribution and create an interval by discarding, say, the 5% most extreme outcomes. This is not a confidence interval for the likelihood ratio itself, but it says something about future values of the likelihood ratio if we were able to gather more data. If we assume that H_1 is true, then it turns out that we expect the likelihood ratio to increase upon obtaining further information about model paramaters. If H_2 is true, the likelihood ratio remains the same in expectation. This interval can be important for decision problems, but not for the weight of the current evidence. We have illustrated all this with three examples from forensic science.

3.6 Bibliographical Notes

For a philosophical backup of the use and interpretation of epistemic probability as carried out in this chapter, we refer to Richard Swinburne in [156], who has a lot to say about the nature of epistemic probability. The debate about whether or not the likelihood ratio should be accompanied by a confidence interval has received a lot of attention in the literature, see [14, 17, 20, 99, 108, 137, 142, 161]. The example in Section 3.4.3 is taken from [80] and [95]. For an early discussion of posterior likelihood ratio distributions, see [2], which operates a slightly different context. A further discussion can be found in [80], whose author remains somewhat uncertain about the interpretation of the posterior likelihood ratio distribution.

4

Forensic Identification

In 1968, a couple stood trial in a notorious case, known as "People of the State of California vs. Collins." The pair had been arrested because they matched eyewitness descriptions. It was estimated by the prosecution that only one in twelve million couples would match this description. The jury were invited to consider the probability that the accused pair was innocent, and returned a verdict of guilty. Later, the verdict was overthrown, essentially because of the flaws in the statistical reasoning. The case sparked interest in the abstraction of this problem, which became known as the island problem.

In Example 2.2.2 we have discussed the basic version of the island problem. In this chapter we will first elaborate on this basic version, and after that consider various generalizations. In all cases, we will consider a characteristic that a person of interest S has in common with an unknown targeted person C. In the classical version, S is a suspect and C is a criminal, but since the theory applies more generally we prefer to call them person of interest and targeted person, still written as S and C respectively. After having discussed the classical case, we will investigate what happens when the population frequency p of the relevant trait is not completely known to us. A second generalization concerns the fact that populations are in general not homogeneous, and can be partitioned into a number of subpopulations among which the frequency of the relevant trait varies. We also discuss what happens when the trait is measured with the possibility of making a mistake. Finally, the way S is identified also plays a role, as we will see.

The island problems should be seen as idealizations. In practice, the problem can of course typically not be described so neatly. Nevertheless, when we have discussed all the variants and generalizations of the island problem that we announced, we have, at least in theory, covered many of the situations that we will encounter in practice. We will give some examples of such situations in Section 4.5.

We have discussed the likelihood ratio in great detail in Chapter 2. This likelihood ratio measures the strength of the evidence for one hypothesis in relation to another one, and transforms prior odds into posterior odds after seeing the evidence. However, this implies a question which will turn out to be rather important in this chapter, namely which part of the available data should be seen as the evidence, and which part is "just" background information? In other words, exactly which evidence do we want to consider? Indeed, we will see that the value of the likelihood ratio sometimes depends on which of the available information is regarded as background information or as evidence (and of course also on the propositions that one is interested in proving). From a purely mathematical point of view, concentrating on the posterior probabilities, given background information and/or evidence, settles the issue, but from a legal perspective things may not be so obvious.

4.1 The Classical Case

In this section we start with the relatively simple case of a homogeneous population for which we know the probability for each person to have the characteristic of interest. Our starting point is a collection X of $N + 1$ individuals which together form the inhabitants of an island. (We take $N + 1$ instead of N since this is the choice in most of the literature, so this will make comparison with the literature easier.) For a characteristic Γ, for instance a DNA profile, we introduce indicator random variables Γ_x, taking value 1 if $x \in X$ has the characteristic Γ and 0 otherwise.

Before we start, we need to say a few words about the modeling. In this section, we assume that the unknown C and the person of interest S are chosen such that $P(C = S) = \pi$, for some probability π. We think of the labels Γ_x as independent and identically Bernoulli distributed with success probability p.

This description is consistent with various different mathematical models, and we mention two of them here. In the first model, C is randomly chosen such that $P(C = i) = \pi_i$, with $\sum_{i=1}^{N+1} \pi_i = 1$. We then think of S as non-random, so that $P(C = S) = \pi_S$, meaning that the probability π depends on S. Since S is considered fixed this is not problematic.

Alternatively, one can think of a situation in which S is selected in such a way that the probability that $S = C$ is π. This selection is done independent of the labels Γ_x. The probability π can now be seen as somehow quantifying the quality of the selection procedure.

Although these two situation model different procedures, the mathematics below will apply to both. All we need is that C and S are chosen without reference to the labels Γ_x, and such that $P(C = S) = \pi$. In both cases we can think of the labels as being assigned to the members of the population after C and S are chosen.

Suppose now that we obtain the information that $\Gamma_C = 1$. Writing, as before, $E_C = \{\Gamma_C = 1\}$, $G = \{S = C\}$, and $E_S = \{\Gamma_S = 1\}$, we have from Example 2.2.2 that

$$\frac{P(E_C, E_S \mid G)}{P(E_C, E_S \mid G^c)} = \frac{1}{p}. \tag{4.1}$$

Since E_S in itself is not informative for G, we also found

$$\frac{P(E_C \mid G, E_S)}{P(E_C \mid G^c, E_S)} = \frac{1}{p}. \tag{4.2}$$

Therefore,

$$\frac{P(G \mid E_C, E_S)}{P(G^c \mid E_C, E_S)} = \frac{1}{p} \cdot \frac{P(G \mid E_S)}{P(G^c \mid E_S)} = \frac{1}{p} \cdot \frac{P(G)}{P(G^c)} = \frac{\pi}{p(1 - \pi)}, \tag{4.3}$$

and hence the posterior probability $P(G \mid E_C, E_S)$ is given by

$$P(G \mid E_C, E_S) = \frac{\pi}{\pi + (1 - \pi)p}. \tag{4.4}$$

It is interesting to see how (4.4) relates to the total (random) number U of Γ bearers. Before anyone is tested for Γ, U has a binomial distribution with parameters $N + 1$ and p, which we write as a $\mathrm{Bin}(N + 1, p)$-distribution. When it is observed that C has Γ, we condition on $\Gamma_C = 1$ and obtain

$$\begin{aligned} P(U = k + 1 \mid E_C) &= \frac{P(E_C \mid U = k + 1)P(U = k + 1)}{P(E_C)} \\ &= \frac{\frac{k+1}{N+1}\binom{N+1}{k+1}p^{k+1}(1 - p)^{N-k}}{p} \\ &= \binom{N}{k}p^k(1 - p)^{N-k}. \end{aligned}$$

It follows that the probability that $U = k + 1$, given E_C, is equal to the probability that a random variable with a $\mathrm{Bin}(N, p)$-distribution takes the value k, so that conditionally on E_C, U is distributed as $1 + \mathrm{Bin}(N, p)$. Hence we have

$$E(U \mid E_C) = 1 + Np.$$

Comparing this to (4.4) we see that the posterior probability of G is given by

$$P(G \mid E_C, E_S)^{-1} = E(U \mid E_C) + p\left(\frac{1}{\pi} - (N + 1)\right), \tag{4.5}$$

which for the uniform prior case $\pi = 1/(N + 1)$ reduces to

$$P(G \mid E_C, E_S)^{-1} = E(U \mid E_C).$$

Intuitively the last formula makes sense. Indeed, the uniform prior case can be realized by letting C be distributed uniformly on X. In that case we know that C is a Γ-bearer, that any one of the Γ-bearers is equally likely to be C, and that we have found one of them. So we have to compute the expected number of Γ-bearers, given the knowledge that C is one of them.

We also note that we could have conditioned on E_S in the above derivation instead of on E_C; this leads to the same conclusions. Indeed in both cases we use a single observation of Γ.

Resuming, when we also condition on $\Gamma_S = 1$, we first write

$$P(U = k \mid E_S, E_C) = \frac{P(E_S \mid U = k, E_C)P(U = k \mid E_C)}{P(E_S \mid E_C)}. \tag{4.6}$$

The denominator is the probability that S has the trait given that C has it. If $C = S$, an event with probability π, then so does S. If $C \neq S$, then S has the trait with probability p. Hence $P(E_S \mid E_C) = \pi + p(1 - \pi)$.

As for $P(E_S \mid U = k, E_C)$, this quantity is equal to

$$P(E_S \mid G, U = k, E_C)P(G \mid U = k, E_C)$$
$$+ P(E_S \mid G^c, U = k, E_C)P(G^c \mid U = k, E_C),$$

which evaluates to $\pi + \frac{k-1}{N}(1 - \pi)$.

Hence we find that

$$P(U = k \mid E_S, E_C) = \frac{\pi + \frac{k-1}{N}(1 - \pi)}{\pi + (1 - \pi)p} P(U = k \mid E_C)$$

$$= \frac{\frac{(N+1)\pi - 1}{N} + \frac{1-\pi}{N}k}{\pi + (1 - \pi)p} P(U = k \mid E_C).$$

Hence

$$E(U^{-1} \mid E_S, E_C) = \sum_{k=1}^{N+1} \frac{1}{k} P(U = k \mid E_S, E_C) \tag{4.7}$$

$$= \frac{(N + 1)\pi - 1}{N(\pi + p(1 - \pi))} E(U^{-1} \mid E_C) + \frac{1 - \pi}{N(\pi + p(1 - \pi))}. \tag{4.8}$$

It is only when $\pi = 1/(N + 1)$ that this reduces to

$$\frac{1}{1 + Np}. \tag{4.9}$$

This latter result can also be understood in an intuitive way. Indeed, both S and C have Γ, and they are selected independently of one another. Then the probability that they are equal is the inverse of the number of Γ-bearers. This number is unknown, so we have to take expectations, given knowledge of both S and C.

Summarizing, we have found that for the uniform prior case we have

$$P(G \mid E_S, E_C) = (E(U \mid E_C))^{-1} = (E(U \mid E_S))^{-1} = E(U^{-1} \mid E_C, E_S), \quad (4.10)$$

but these rather elegant identities do not carry over to the general case.

4.2 The Effect of a Search

So far, the selection of S did not involve the characteristic Γ. What would happen if we repeatedly select from X – with or without replacement – until a Γ-bearer is found, without keeping any records on the search itself, such as its duration? Will this change the probability that the thus found member of X is C?

Let us denote the thus selected person by S again. Furthermore we assume that the search is carried out in such a way that every time, any member of the population is equally likely to be selected. This assumption implies that S can be seen as a uniform choice among Γ-bearers.

We are interested in the probability that the thus selected person S is C. The search is such that, if the population has k persons with Γ, we are equally likely to find any one of them. Thus the probability that $C = S$ is now

$$\sum_{k=1}^{N+1} \frac{1}{k} P(U = k \mid E_C) = E(U^{-1} \mid E_C). \quad (4.11)$$

Observe that we know the distribution of U given E_C: we have seen that this conditional distribution is just $1 + \mathrm{Bin}(N, p)$. This enables us to explicitly compute $P(S = C \mid E_C)$ as follows:

$$P(S = C \mid E_C) = \sum_{k=1}^{N+1} \frac{1}{k} P(U = k \mid E_C)$$

$$= \sum_{k=1}^{N+1} \frac{1}{k} \binom{N}{k-1} p^{k-1} (1-p)^{N+1-k}$$

$$= \frac{1}{p(N+1)} \sum_{k=1}^{N+1} \binom{N+1}{k} p^k (1-p)^{N+1-k}$$

$$= \frac{1 - (1-p)^{N+1}}{p(N+1)} = \frac{P(U > 0)}{E(U)}. \quad (4.12)$$

Let us take a moment to reflect on what we have computed now. First of all, we have directly computed a posterior probability, without first computing a likelihood ratio. This is only reasonable here, since we only made a statement about the probability that the selected person is C, without specifying who that selected person is, or is going to be.

The posterior probability in (4.12) reflects the quality of the search procedure itself. In other words, it may be seen as a measure of the efficiency of the search, and it is not individually directed to anyone in particular. In situations of this type, the procedure of arriving at posterior odds via prior odds and a likelihood ratio is not the most efficient or natural way. Indeed, in this case it was easier to directly compute the required posterior probability.

This is not to say that a likelihood ratio cannot be computed. Indeed, suppose that we have uniform priors in the sense that all members of the population are a priori equally likely to be C. In that case, the extra knowledge that a given identified person has been selected should lead to the same posterior probability of guilt irrespective of the identity of the person, and this probability must then be the outcome in (4.12).

With this in mind, suppose that the selected person is identified as, say, John Smith. From (4.12) we learn that the posterior odds that John Smith is C, is equal to

$$\frac{P(U > 0)}{E(U) - P(U > 0)}.$$

Plugging in that the prior odds for John Smith to be C are assumed to be $1/N$, we see that the corresponding likelihood ratio of John Smith being C versus not being C (based on the selection of John Smith) must be equal to

$$\frac{N P(U > 0)}{E(U) - P(U > 0)}. \tag{4.13}$$

This can be confirmed with a direct computation, and we think it is instructive to do so. We now take an individual-directed point of view and let E be the event that the selected person is John Smith. Let G be the hypothesis that John Smith is C. We want to compute the likelihood ratio for G versus G^c conditioned on E_C, that is, we want to compute

$$\frac{P(E \mid E_C, G)}{P(E \mid E_C, G^c)}. \tag{4.14}$$

The numerator is easily seen to be equal to the same outcome as in (4.12) since it is obtained with the same computation. Writing $\Gamma_{JS} = 1$ for the event that John Smith has the trait, the denominator in (4.14) is equal to

$$P(E \mid E_C, G^c, \Gamma_{JS} = 1) P(\Gamma_{JS} = 1 \mid E_C, G^c) = p P(E \mid E_C, G^c, \Gamma_{JS} = 1).$$

Conditioned on the event $\{E_C, G^c, \Gamma_{JS} = 1\}$, the distribution of the number U of Γ-bearers can be written as 2 plus a binomial distribution with parameters

$N - 1$ and p. Indeed, we know that John Smith and the criminal both have the trait, and that they are different persons. This explains the 2, and all others simply have the trait with probability p independently of each other. Furthermore, given that $U = k$, and that John Smith has the trait, the probability that he is selected is $1/k$. Hence, similar to the computation above, this leads to the following derivation:

$$P(E \mid E_C, G^c, \Gamma_{JS} = 1) = \sum_{k=2}^{N+1} \frac{1}{k} \binom{N-1}{k-2} p^{k-2}(1-p)^{N+1-k}$$

$$= \frac{1}{p^2 N(N+1)} \sum_{k=2}^{N+1} (k-1) \binom{N+1}{k} p^k (1-p)^{N+1-k}$$

$$= \frac{1}{p^2 N(N+1)} \left(\sum_{k=0}^{N+1} (k-1) \binom{N+1}{k} p^k (1-p)^{N+1-k} \right.$$

$$\left. + (1-p)^{N+1} \right)$$

$$= \frac{1}{p^2 N(N+1)} \left((N+1)p - 1 + (1-p)^{N+1} \right).$$

Keeping in mind that we have to multiply this expression by p, we now take everything together and obtain

$$\frac{P(E \mid E_C, G)}{P(E \mid E_C, G^c)} = \frac{1 - (1-p)^{N+1}}{p(N+1)} \cdot \frac{pN(N+1)}{(N+1)p - 1 + (1-p)^{N+1}}$$

$$= \frac{N(1 - (1-p)^{N+1})}{(N+1)p - 1 + (1-p)^{N+1}}$$

$$= \frac{NP(U > 0)}{E(U) - P(U > 0)},$$

the same answer as in (4.13).

The expression of the likelihood ratio thus found enables us to directly compare the search case with the classical scenario. It is easy to see from either the final expression or the formula preceding it, that when N is large, the likelihood ratio in (4.13) is close to $1/p$, the likelihood ratio corresponding to the classical scenario. Hence the evidential value of a match arising from a search is almost the same as arising from the so-called cold case, in which we have checked only one person who happened to have the trait.

In fact, one expects that in the search case the evidential value is slightly larger, since in the course of the search it may have happened that we have excluded people. This is confirmed by direct computation, as follows.

The likelihood ratio in (4.13) is larger than $1/p$ precisely when

$$\frac{E(U) - P(U > 0)}{P(U > 0)} < Np = E(U) - p.$$

Rewriting this, we see that we need to verify that

$$E(U)(1 - P(U > 0)) < (1 - p)P(U > 0),$$

which is equivalent to

$$(N + 1)p(1 - p)^{N+1} < (1 - p)(1 - (1 - p)^{N+1}),$$

leading to the requirement that $Np(1 - p)^N < 1 - (1 - p)^{N+1}$, or $P(U = 1) < P(U > 0)$, which is clearly true.

4.3 Uncertainty About p

In this section we assume that the Γ-frequency p is not known with certainty. Instead, we describe the frequency with a probability distribution. As explained in Chapter 3 we interpret this not to say that p itself is random, but instead that we have limited knowledge about its value. The basic question we want to answer is how the uncertainty about p affects the likelihood ratio and the posterior probability of G.

We make the same assumptions on the relation between C and S as before, that is, we let $\pi = P(C = S)$. We write $E_S = \{\Gamma_S = 1\}$ and $E_C = \{\Gamma_C = 1\}$ as before.

To model the uncertainty of the Γ-frequency we assume, as we did in Chapter 3, that there is a random variable W, taking values in $[0, 1]$, with probability density χ_W, and such that conditional on $W = r$, the Γ_x are independent Bernoulli variables with $P(\Gamma_x = 1) = r$. We let p denote the expectation of W and σ^2 its variance.

The densities of the random variables W, and W conditioned on E_S, are denoted by χ_W and χ_S respectively. It is not difficult to express χ_S in terms of χ_W. In fact, we already did so in Example 3.2.1 for E_C, but we repeat the argument in our current notation for E_S. Since

$$P(E_S) = \int_0^1 P(E_S \mid W = t)\chi_W(t)dt = \int_0^1 t\chi_W(t)dt = p,$$

the continuous version of Bayes' theorem implies that

$$\chi_S(t) = \frac{P(E_S \mid W = t)\chi_W(t)}{P(E_S)} = \frac{t}{p}\chi_W(t), \tag{4.15}$$

since after conditioning on $W = t$ we are back in the classical situation with p replaced by t.

Next we compute the expectation of W given E_S:

$$E(W \mid E_S) = \int_0^1 t \chi_S(t) dt = \int_0^1 \frac{1}{p} t^2 \chi_W(t) dt = \frac{E(W^2)}{p}. \qquad (4.16)$$

Since $E(W^2) = E(W)^2 + \sigma^2 = p^2 + \sigma^2$, we find

$$E(W \mid E_S) = p + \frac{\sigma^2}{p} =: p'.$$

A few remarks are in order. First of all, $p' \geq p$, which is to be expected, since we have the information that S has the trait. Furthermore, p' does not need the prior probability π on $C = S$. In particular, in a population with uniform prior it does not depend on the population size. This is also to be expected, since learning that a certain member (S) has Γ is not informative about the population size. As we will see later, this changes when we in addition learn E_C, the fact that C has Γ as well. Indeed, in a small population it is more likely that $C = S$. Hence it is more likely in a small population that the fact that C also has Γ is not new information, compared to a larger population. Finally, we note that instead of conditioning on E_S we could have also chosen to condition on E_C to obtain $\chi_C = \chi_S$.

Next we compute the relevant likelihood ratios. As in the classical case, we can interpret E_S as part of the evidence, or as general background information. Starting with the former and writing $G = \{S = C\}$ as before, we compute

$$\frac{P(E_C, E_S \mid G)}{P(E_C, E_S \mid G^c)} = \frac{\int_0^1 P(E_C, E_S \mid W = t, G) \chi_W(t) dt}{\int_0^1 P(E_C, E_S \mid W = t, G^c) \chi_W(t) dt}$$

$$= \frac{\int_0^1 t \chi_W(t) dt}{\int_0^1 t^2 \chi_W(t) dt} = \frac{p}{\sigma^2 + p^2} = \frac{1}{p'}, \qquad (4.17)$$

so the outcome is as in the classical case with p replaced by p'. Note that we obtained this formula already in (3.2).

Of course, E_S is again not informative for G, and indeed an explicit computation confirms this:

$$\frac{P(E_C \mid G, E_S)}{P(E_C \mid G^c, E_S)} = \frac{\int_0^1 P(E_C \mid W = t, G, E_S) \chi_S(t) dt}{\int_0^1 P(E_C \mid W = t, G^c, E_S) \chi_S(t) dt}$$

$$= \frac{\int_0^1 \chi_S(t) dt}{\int_0^1 t \chi_S(t) dt} = \frac{1}{p'}. \qquad (4.18)$$

It follows that we get the answer of the classical case, with p' instead of p, for the posterior probability on G:

$$P(G \mid E_C, E_S) = \frac{\pi}{\pi + (1 - \pi)p'}. \tag{4.19}$$

This means that if we ignore the uncertainty we have about the population frequency of the trait in the population, that is, use p instead of p', then this is unfavorable to the suspect. The uncertainty does not average out in any way. In other words, uncertainty makes the probability of guilt smaller, something which is rather intuitive.

One might naturally wonder why it is p' that replaces p, and not the conditional expectation of W given that both E_S and E_C occur. Of course, the mathematics tells us that this is so, but it is also understandable. Indeed, the likelihood ratio expresses the evidential value of the evidence. It tells us how surprised we should be to find certain evidence. Given that we know that E_S occurs, the likelihood ratio tells us what the evidential value of a potential match with C is. To quantify this we, naturally, should not use the actual match with C itself.

It is, however, still interesting to compute the expectation of W given both E_S and E_C. It is to be expected that this conditional expectation is larger than p'. To verify this, we first compute the density $\chi_{C,S}$ of W conditional on both E_C and E_S. We claim that

$$\chi_{C,S}(t) = \frac{\pi + (1 - \pi)t}{\pi + (1 - \pi)p'} \chi_S(t). \tag{4.20}$$

To see this, note that

$$\chi_{C,S}(t) = \frac{P(E_C \mid W = t, E_S)\chi_S(t)}{P(E_C \mid E_S)} \tag{4.21}$$

$$= \frac{P(E_C \mid W = t, E_S)\chi_S(t)}{\int_0^1 P(E_C \mid W = t, E_S)\chi_S(t)dt}. \tag{4.22}$$

First we compute $P(E_C \mid W = t, E_S)$. When we condition on $W = t$ we are back in the classical situation with p replaced by t. We now further condition on $\Gamma_S = 1$. If $C = S$, an event with probability π, then E_C occurs. If $C \neq S$, an event with probability $1 - \pi$, then the probability that C has Γ is just t. We conclude that

$$P(E_C \mid W = t, E_S) = \pi + (1 - \pi)t,$$

and this gives us the numerator in (4.21). The denominator is equal to

$$\int_0^1 (\pi + (1 - \pi)t)\chi_S(t)dt = \pi + (1 - \pi)p'. \tag{4.23}$$

From this, the claim in (4.20) follows.

Note that $\chi_{C,S}$ depends on π whereas χ_S does not. Now we can compute the conditional expectation of W given both E_C and E_S:

$$p'' := E(W \mid E_C, E_S) = \int_0^1 t \chi_{C,S}(t) dt$$

$$= \frac{1}{\pi + (1-\pi)p'} \int_0^1 t(\pi + (1-\pi)t) \chi_S(t) dt$$

$$= \frac{\pi p' + (1-\pi) \int_0^1 t^2 \chi_S(t) dt}{\pi + (1-\pi)p'}.$$

If we denote by $\sigma^2_{W \mid E_S}$ the variance of χ_S, the above formula can be rewritten as

$$p'' = p' \left(\frac{\pi}{\pi + (1-\pi)p'} + \frac{(1-\pi)(p' + \sigma^2_{W \mid E_S}/p')}{\pi + (1-\pi)p'} \right) \geq p',$$

with equality only if $\sigma^2_{W \mid E_S} = 0$ or $\pi = 1$.

So we have indeed found that

$$E(W) \leq E(W \mid E_S) = E(W \mid E_C) \leq E(W \mid E_C, E_S).$$

Note that using p'' in (4.19) instead of the correct p' would be favorable to the suspect when computing the posterior probability of guilt.

In the case where it is assumed that $\pi = 0$, we obtain $p'' = p' + \sigma^2_{W \mid E_S}/p'$, which gives the largest difference between p'' and p'. This is the same relation as between p and p'. This is understandable since when $\pi = 0$, we know that $S \neq C$, so that we have typed two individuals, one extra compared to when we only condition on E_S or E_C. It is a known forensic practice (referred to as the *size-bias correction*) to calculate match probabilities for DNA profiles from a reference database to which the observed profile is added twice. This amounts to conditioning on both E_S and E_C, assuming that $C \neq S$.

How does the posterior probability of G relate to U, the total number of Γ-bearers? It is easy to see that (4.5) still holds, since the expected number of Γ-bearers, given E_S is given by

$$E(U \mid E_S) = \int_0^1 E(U \mid E_S, W = t) \chi_S(t) dt = \int_0^1 (1 + Nt) \chi_S(t) dt = 1 + Np'.$$

$$(4.24)$$

Likewise, from (4.8) and (4.20) we see that

$$E(U^{-1} \mid E_C, E_S) = \int_0^1 E(U^{-1} \mid E_C, E_S, W = t) \chi_{C,S}(t) dt$$

$$= \frac{(N+1)\pi - 1}{N(\pi + (1-\pi)p')} E(U^{-1} \mid E_S) + \frac{1-\pi}{N(\pi + (1-\pi)p')}.$$

Finally we consider again a search for a Γ-bearer as we did in Section 4.2 in the presence of uncertainty about the trait frequency. We can compute

$$P(S = C \mid E_C) = \sum_{k=1}^{N+1} \frac{1}{k} P(U = k \mid E_C)$$

$$= \int_0^1 \sum_{k=1}^{N+1} \frac{1}{k} P(U = k \mid E_C, W = t) \chi_C(t) dt$$

$$= \int_0^1 \frac{1 - (1-t)^{N+1}}{t(N+1)} \frac{t}{p} \chi_C(t) dt$$

$$= \frac{1}{p(N+1)} \int_0^1 (1 - (1-t)^{N+1}) \chi_C(t) dt = \frac{P(U > 0)}{E(U)},$$

the same expression as in (4.12) in the case in which we know p.

4.4 The Existence of Subpopulations

In this section we consider the situation where the population consists of several subpopulations, each with their own Γ-frequency. We assume that these frequencies are known.

This is a quite general situation. One natural example is to consider DNA profiles, which are not equally rare in all populations. But there are other situations where we may use this framework, for example, if certain tool marks are not equally probable to be left by specific tools, or if fibers that are found can be obtained from different fabrics with different probabilities. In all such and similar cases, the observed characteristic is informative for the question from which subpopulation C originates. If a person of interest S is found who has the required characteristic, an evaluation of E_C and E_S must take into account both the information that the characteristic carries about the subpopulation it may come from, and the fact that S has Γ.

We write the population X as a disjoint union of subpopulations X_i:

$$X = \bigcup_{i=1}^{m} X_i, \tag{4.25}$$

with $X_i \cap X_j = \emptyset$ whenever $i \neq j$. If $x \in X_i$, we say that x is in subpopulation i and write $i = X(x)$.

In the previous cases without subpopulations, we did not know anything about C. With the subpopulations we need to assume that the probability that C is contained in any of them is well defined. Hence we set

$$\beta_i := P(C \in X_i), \tag{4.26}$$

where the β_i's are positive and satisfy $\sum_{i=1}^{m} \beta_i = 1$. The values of the β_i's should be considered as prior information about the identity of C. Note, however, that these prior probabilities are not conditional on $\Gamma_C = 1$. The β_i may depend on S, which we think of as fixed and non-random here.

To model the different probabilities to have Γ over the subpopulations, we let the random variables Γ_x be independent Bernoulli variables with probability of success $p_{X(x)}$; hence they are not identically distributed as their distribution varies for different subpopulations.

The subpopulation to which S belongs is observed, and denoted by $X(S)$. We define $\alpha_S := P(S = C \mid C \in X(S))$, so that the probability π_S that $S = C$ satisfies

$$\pi_S = \alpha_S \beta_S.$$

(In this section we do express the dependence upon S in our notation.) We can retrieve the classical case without subpopulations if we set $\beta_S = 1$, and then α_S coincides with π_S. The posterior probability $P(G \mid E_C, E_S)$ is now well defined. However, for the likelihood ratio there are various choices. Indeed we can compute different likelihood ratios, depending on what we treat as background information or as evidence.

Suppose first that we interpret E_C as background information. Writing p_S for $p_{X(S)}$, we have

$$LR(E_S \mid E_C) := \frac{P(E_S \mid G, E_C)}{P(E_S \mid G^c, E_C)} = \frac{1}{p_S}. \tag{4.27}$$

Indeed, if we know that $S = C$ and that $\Gamma_C = 1$, then we are sure to find the trait, but if $S \neq C$, then the probability that he has the trait is p_S, the probability that applies to the subpopulation that S is from. This likelihood ratio thus compares the competing explanations for S to have Γ.

In order to obtain the likelihood ratio for E_C and E_S simultaneously, we should multiply (4.27) with

$$LR(E_C) := \frac{P(E_C \mid G)}{P(E_C \mid G^c)}.$$

The numerator evaluates to $P(\Gamma_C = 1 \mid C = S) = p_S$, since now we are asking for the probability of S to have Γ. For the denominator, we need

$$P(\Gamma_C = 1 \mid S \neq C) = \sum_{i=1}^{m} P(C \in X_i, \Gamma_C = 1 \mid S \neq C)$$

$$= \sum_{i=1}^{m} p_i P(C \in X_i \mid S \neq C).$$

In order to evaluate this, we write

$$P(C \in X_i \mid S \neq C) = \frac{P(S \neq C \mid C \in X_i)P(C \in X_i)}{P(S \neq C)}$$

$$= \frac{P(S \neq C \mid C \in X_i)\beta_i}{1 - \alpha_S \beta_S}.$$

Now we use that

$$P(S \neq C \mid C \in X_i) = \begin{cases} 1, & X_i \neq X(S), \\ 1 - \alpha_S, & X_i = X(S). \end{cases}$$

Putting these parts together we arrive, after some algebraic manipulations, at

$$LR(E_C) = \frac{p_S(1 - \alpha_S \beta_S)}{\sum_{i=1}^{m} p_i \beta_i - p_S \alpha_S \beta_S} = \frac{1 - \alpha_S \beta_S}{\sum_{i=1}^{m} \frac{p_i}{p_S} \beta_i - \alpha_S \beta_S}. \tag{4.28}$$

Notice that this likelihood ratio is larger than one if $\sum_{i=1}^{m} p_i \beta_i < p_S$, corresponding to Γ being rarer than p_S on average.

Another way to derive (4.28) is to note that

$$P(C \in X(S) \mid E_C) = \frac{p_S \beta_S}{\sum_{i=1}^{m} p_i \beta_i},$$

and hence

$$P(S = C \mid E_C) = P(S = C \mid C \in X(S), E_C)P(C \in X(S) \mid E_C)$$

$$= \frac{\alpha_S p_S \beta_S}{\sum_{i=1}^{m} p_i \beta_i},$$

from which we may verify that $LR(E_C)$ is as stated above.

It may seem strange that E_C, an observation on C, has a likelihood ratio different from one. This is because we consider the subpopulation of the suspect to be already known. Hence the observation of E_C has evidential value because of the varying probabilities p_i.

We now conclude that

$$LR(E_C, E_S) = LR(E_C)LR(E_S \mid E_C) = \frac{1 - \alpha_S \beta_S}{\sum_i p_i \beta_i - p_S \alpha_S \beta_S}, \tag{4.29}$$

which gives us the posterior odds

$$\frac{P(G \mid E_C, E_S)}{P(G^c \mid E_C, E_S)} = \frac{\alpha_S \beta_S}{\sum_i p_i \beta_i - p_S \alpha_S \beta_S}, \tag{4.30}$$

leading to the posterior probability

$$P(G \mid E_C, E_S) = \frac{\alpha_S \beta_S}{\sum_{i=1}^{m} p_i \beta_i - p_S \alpha_S \beta_S + \alpha_S \beta_S}. \tag{4.31}$$

Notice that we can also work the other way around, that is, starting with E_S rather than with E_C, and compute

$$LR(E_C, E_S) = LR(E_S)LR(E_C \mid E_S).$$

In that case, we have

$$LR(E_S) = \frac{P(\Gamma_S = 1 \mid S = C)}{P(\Gamma_S = 1 \mid S \neq C)} = \frac{p_S}{p_S} = 1,$$

and so we must have

$$LR(E_C \mid E_S) = LR(E_C, E_S) = \frac{1 - \alpha_S \beta_S}{\sum_i p_i \beta_i - p_S \alpha_S \beta_S}. \tag{4.32}$$

The observation E_S has no evidential value on its own. This is because S is considered to be known, as is $X(S)$, and therefore knowing that E_S holds, in the absence of E_C, does not tell us anything on $C = S$ or not.

We finally show that we can merge all subpopulations other than the one of S into a single one. To this end, we write $\beta_A := 1 - \beta_S$ and

$$p_A := \beta_A^{-1} \sum_{i:X_i \neq X(S)} p_i \beta_i.$$

Then we can write

$$LR(E_C) = \frac{1 - \alpha_S \beta_S}{\frac{p_A}{p_S} \beta_A + (1 - \alpha_S)\beta_S}, \tag{4.33}$$

$$LR(E_C \mid E_S) = LR(E_C, E_S) = \frac{1 - \alpha_S \beta_S}{p_A \beta_A + (1 - \alpha_S)p_S \beta_S}, \tag{4.34}$$

and

$$\frac{P(G \mid E_C, E_S)}{P(G^c \mid E_C, E_S)} = \frac{\alpha_S \beta_S}{p_A \beta_A + (1 - \alpha_S)p_S \beta_S}. \tag{4.35}$$

These expressions correspond to the general ones above with only two subpopulations. They indeed show that, rather than considering all subpopulations, it suffices to consider the subpopulations other than the one of S as a single one with probability p_A for Γ.

Note that if we want to retrieve the situation without subpopulations then we need to set $\beta_S = 1$. It is easily verified that we then indeed retrieve (4.3), since with $\beta_S = 1$ we have $\alpha_S = \pi_S$.

4.5 Some Examples and Special Cases

The expressions that we found in this chapter are very general. In this section we discuss a few special cases.

4.5.1 Characteristic Rare in Other Populations

If $p_A \ll p_S$, (4.35) is approximately equal to

$$\frac{P(G \mid E_C, E_S)}{P(G^c \mid E_C, E_S)} \approx \frac{1}{p_S} \frac{\alpha_S}{(1 - \alpha_S)}.$$

Indeed, if Γ is much more frequent in $X(S)$ this strongly indicates that $C \in X(S)$ and therefore the posterior odds are well approximated by those that we would obtain if this subpopulation were the only one.

As an example, suppose that bullets found at a crime scene indicated that a gun of a very rare type was fired, since the patterns obtained are such that they are very unlikely to be produced by any other gun type. If such a gun is obtained, the further probative value of that match, given by $1/p_S$, is then limited because most of the guns of this type can be expected to yield such a match and we already know the gun is of the correct type. If α_S is large, then this already raises the odds on this gun being the one that was fired with at the crime scene. It may raise it to such a large degree that it is not really necessary to verify this by firing it and comparing bullet markings. The odds are so large that this is the gun, and that this is almost certainly going to result in a match. In other words, more evidence is possibly obtained then, but it cannot make the total evidence much stronger.

4.5.2 S is the Only Candidate in its Subpopulation

If $\alpha_S = 1$, meaning that S is the only candidate from its subpopulation for C, then the likelihood ratio in (4.34) becomes

$$LR(E_C, E_S) = \frac{1 - \beta_S}{p_A \beta_A} = \frac{1}{p_A},$$

while (4.33) tells us that E_C alone gives evidence

$$LR(E_C) = \frac{p_S}{p_A},$$

and the posterior odds are

$$\frac{P(G \mid E_C, E_S)}{P(G^c \mid E_C, E_S)} = \frac{1}{p_A} \frac{\beta_S}{1 - \beta_S}.$$

That is, we then need to know only whether an alternative candidate for C, who must then come from the alternative population, is likely to have Γ. We can illustrate this with Y-chromosomal DNA profiles, which are DNA profiles obtained from loci on the Y-chromosome. These profiles are inherited from father to son, in principle without modification, and are therefore especially useful to investigate a more distant paternal relationship: if no male relative of S is a candidate for C, then we need to know only how rare the profile is for non-related individuals.

4.5.3 Autosomal DNA Profiles

In [90] it was shown that the Dutch DNA database can be very well described as being composed of essentially three subpopulations, that may be thought of as being characterized by ethnicity. The largest group of 61% has estimated allele frequencies close to European ones and can be thought of as the European cluster, the second as the African cluster of about 27%, and finally there is a group of the remaining 12%. We can investigate how the results in this chapter help evaluating DNA evidence.

Let us denote the three subpopulations above by X_1, X_2, and X_3 respectively, and suppose that a targeted person C has a certain DNA profile whose population frequencies in the three subpopulations are $p_1 = 10^{-14}, p_2 = 10^{-13}$, and $p_3 = 10^{-12}$ respectively. We let the β_i be dictated by the sizes of the subpopulations, that is, $\beta_1 = 0.61, \beta_2 = 0.27$, and $\beta_3 = 0.12$. We then get $P(C \in X_1 \mid E_C) = 0.04$, $P(C \in X_2 \mid E_C) = 0.18$, and $P(C \in X_3 \mid E_C) = 0.78$.

The likelihood ratios $LR(E_S, E_C)$ for suspects of the three subpopulations (for convenience we take $\alpha_S = 0.5$, for all suspects) are $4.63 \cdot 10^{12}$, $6.20 \cdot 10^{12}$, and $1.01 \cdot 10^{13}$, respectively. These are, for the first two subpopulations, smaller than $1/p_S$. It is therefore not the case that it is always advantageous for a suspect to let the likelihood ratio be determined by the population frequency in the subpopulation of the suspect. Rather, and especially for small α_S, the likelihood ratio $LR(E_S, E_C)$ is close to $1/(\sum_{i=1}^{m} p_i \beta_i)$, and this is mostly determined by the largest p_i.

4.5.4 Uniform Priors

The expressions we found do not involve any of the (sub)population sizes. This might seem strange at first sight, since one might be inclined to think that when the size N_S of the subpopulation to which S belongs increases, this should make the posterior probability that $S = C$ smaller. However, what really matters is α_S, not N_S. If one makes the assumption that $\alpha_S = 1/N_S$, then N_S does enter into the equations. Indeed, when we substitute $\alpha_S = 1/N_S$ into the likelihood ratio in (4.37) we find

$$\frac{P(E_C, E_S \mid G)}{P(E_C, E_S \mid G^c)} = \frac{N_S - \beta_S}{N_S \sum_{j=1}^{m} p_j \beta_j - p_S \beta_S}.$$

The posterior odds in (4.30) reduce to

$$\frac{P(G \mid E_C, E_S)}{P(G^c \mid E_C, E_S)} = \frac{\beta_S}{N_S \sum_{j=1}^{m} p_j \beta_j - p_S \beta_S},$$

leading to

$$P(G \mid F_C, F_S) = \frac{1}{(N_S/\beta_S) \sum_{j=1}^{m} p_j \beta_j + 1 - p_S}.$$

It is interesting (and intuitive) that the sizes of the other subpopulations, apart from the subpopulation of S, never play a role.

4.5.5 Hypotheses Using the Evidence

The theory in this section is also relevant for the following situation. We first describe the situation, and then comment on it in light of the findings in this chapter.

Consider a situation in which a crime has been committed, and that the criminal left a DNA profile. Suppose further that there is a suspect with this DNA profile. We consider the hypotheses:

H_1: The suspect is the source of the DNA;
H_2: A person unrelated to the suspect is the source of the DNA found.

The likelihood ratio of H_1 versus H_2 is equal to $1/p$, with p the population frequency of the profile. However, there are other choices possible for the hypotheses. For instance, we could incorporate the fact that we know the profile of the offender in the hypotheses, and take:

H_1: The suspect is the source of the DNA;
H_2: A person unrelated to the suspect with the same DNA profile is the source of the DNA found.

The difference seems harmless. After all, we already know that the donor of the DNA profile must have the profile found at the scene of the crime, so we have only added redundant information. However, the likelihood ratio is now equal to 1, since the evidence is certain under both hypotheses.

Is this paradoxical? No, not really. Recall that

$$\text{posterior odds} = \text{likelihood ratio} \times \text{prior odds}.$$

Since we only added redundant information, the posterior odds must be the same. The fact that the likelihood ratio decreased from $1/p$ to 1 by changing H_2 must therefore be compensated by a corresponding increase of the prior odds. And this is indeed precisely what happens. When we add the requirement that the donor has the given DNA profile, we have to multiply the prior probability of H_2 by a factor p to account for the requirement that the unknown person who is the donor under H_2 must have this particular DNA profile, an event with probability p. This precisely balances the change in the likelihood ratio, therefore leading to the same posterior odds.

We see that the choice of the hypotheses may have a serious effect on the like-lihood ratio obtained, but that this will be compensated for by the prior odds. This will only happen, of course, when the various sets of hypotheses are equivalent after seeing the evidence. Only in that case will the posterior always be the same.

In the framework of this chapter, we can define two populations, the first com-posed of the individuals with the observed DNA profile, and the second composed of persons with another profile. In that case, $p_1 = 1$ and $p_2 = 0$. To evaluate the β_i, we must remember that we have assumed in this chapter that the subpopulation from which S originates is known and is taken into account in all probability assessments. That means in this case that we know that S has the profile of interest. The β_i are formulated knowing that S has this profile, but not conditional on the observation that C has it, hence $\beta_1 = \pi_S + (1 - \pi_S)p$, and $\beta_2 = 1 - \beta_1$. This leads to, using that in this case, $\alpha_1 \beta_1 = \pi_S$,

$$LR(E_C, E_S) = \frac{1 - \alpha_1 \beta_1}{\beta_1 - \alpha_1 \beta_1} = \frac{1}{p},$$

$$LR(E_S \mid E_C) = 1,$$

so that the posterior probability that $C = S$ is

$$\frac{\alpha_1 \beta_1}{p_1 \beta_1 + p_2 \beta_2 - p_1 \alpha_1 \beta_1 + \alpha_1 \beta_1} = \alpha_1.$$

Thus, the posterior probability of $C = S$ is simply the conditional probability α_1 that among all persons with the required DNA profile, the suspect is the one who left the trace. This is of course to be expected under the assumptions made, and is the same result as (4.4). To see this, recall that $\beta_1 = \pi_S + (1 - \pi_S)p$, and that $\alpha_1 \beta_1 = \pi_S$. Writing $\alpha_1 = (\alpha_1 \beta_1)/\beta_1$ leads to (4.4).

We thus see that likelihood ratios can differ enormously, depending on the hypotheses chosen. In this case, conditioning on the profile of C when specifying H_2 has the effect of reducing the likelihood ratio to unity, while bringing the prior odds down. Later we will see another example of such data-driven hypotheses, where there is also an interplay between likelihood ratio and prior odds depending on how the hypotheses are formulated, namely in Chapter 11 where we discuss matches in DNA databases.

4.5.6 Parental Identification

Consider a situation in which the mother M of a child C is known. The father is assumed to be one out of $N + 1$ men which together from the collection of possible fathers X. We assume that we have typed DNA profiles of both mother and child. Now we consider a particular man $S \in X$, type his DNA profile, and ask the question what the probability is that S is the father of C, assuming uniform priors.

Although this is not exactly the same setting as the island problem, we can analyze it with the same ideas. Let us see what happens when the DNA profiles consist of one locus only (the same locus for all individuals involved). Clearly M and C must have at least one allele in common, otherwise M cannot be the mother of C (we ignore mutations). If, say, M has genotype (a, b) and C has genotype (b, c), where a, b and c are all different, then we know that M has passed on b to C, so that the father must have passed on c.

If S has one allele of the correct type (c), then he passes this on with probability $1/2$. An unknown man passes on c with probability p_c, the population frequency of c (see Section 1.6). Hence the likelihood ratio of the hypotheses that S is the father, versus an unrelated man is the father, is $1/(2p_c)$, and the posterior probability that S is the father is $1/(1 + 2Np_c)$, assuming uniform priors. If S has two alleles of the correct type (c), then he passes on c for sure. An unknown man still passes on c with probability p_c, so that the likelihood ratio is $1/p_c$, and the posterior probability that S is the father is $1/(1 + Np_c)$. One should compare these answers to (4.9).

The situation is different when mother and child have the same genotype (a, b), say. In this case it is not known which of the alleles of C is the paternal one. Suppose now first that S has one allele in common with C, say a. If S is the father, then M and S must have passed on b and a, respectively, an event with probability $1/4$. If not S but an unknown man is the father, then the probability that C has (a, b) is $\frac{1}{2}p_a + \frac{1}{2}p_b$, since when the mother passes on a the unknown father must pass on b and vice versa. This leads to a likelihood ratio of $1/(2p_a + p_b)$. If S has both alleles in common with C, that is, $G_S = (a, b)$, then a similar argument leads to a likelihood ratio of $1/(p_a + p_b)$, and these last two answers easily translate into posterior probabilities, as before. We will come back to this setting in Section 13.4.

4.6 Which Likelihood Ratio?

Legal systems generally wish to make a distinction between the strength of the evidence, and the strength of the case. Ideally, the expert witness informs the court about the strength of the evidence (that is, gives a likelihood ratio), and the court combines this information with its prior to draw conclusions about the strength of the case. The prior is not discussed with, or communicated to, the expert. For this to be possible, however, the likelihood ratio should not depend on the prior.

In the case with subpopulations discussed in Section 4.4, there are two likelihood ratios that could be considered as the relevant one to communicate, and we recall them now:

$$LR(E_S \mid E_C) = 1/p_S \qquad (4.36)$$

and

$$LR(E_C \mid E_S) = LR(E_C, E_S) = \frac{1 - \alpha_S \beta_S}{\sum_i p_i \beta_i - p_S \alpha_S \beta_S}. \qquad (4.37)$$

Taking the version of (4.37) with only two subpopulations gives

$$LR(E_C, E_S) = LR(E_C \mid E_S) = \frac{1 - \alpha_S \beta_S}{p_A \beta_A + (1 - \alpha_S) p_S \beta_S}. \qquad (4.38)$$

Notice that this last expression is close to

$$(p_A(1 - \beta_S) + p_S \beta_S)^{-1}$$

when α_S is small, close to $1/p_A$ when α_S is close to 1, and close to $1/p_S$ when β_S is close to 1. In any case, the value $1/\max\{p_A, p_S\}$ is (sometimes very) conservative.

The issue at hand is that we need to decide if the event E_C that C has Γ counts as (legal) evidence against S, or not. If one communicates $LR(E_S \mid E_C)$ as evidential value, then the evidential fact that C has Γ is ignored, and it is not possible to obtain the correct posterior odds without taking $LR(E_C)$ also into account. Therefore, (4.36) is in general simply insufficient to get posterior odds from.

In some cases, (4.36) is the relevant likelihood ratio, if other information is available that narrows down the possible subpopulations that C could be from to only the one from the suspect. Consider, for example, the following hypothetical scenario: at a crime scene, a hair of C is found. Analysis by a forensic hair expert shows that C must belong to subpopulation X_1. Let us denote this information by I. Later, a suspect $S \in X_1$ is found. From the hair a DNA profile is generated, and S's DNA profile matches with it. The court wishes to be informed about the value of that match. Clearly, conditional on I we now have $\beta_S = 1$, so (4.37) coincides with (4.36). Indeed it only makes sense to report p_S, since it is at this point already known from I that S and C are from the same subpopulation.

On the other hand, (4.37) depends on all the prior probabilities β_i, and as such it may not be admissible as legal evidence, since a forensic expert cannot be assumed to be able to assign these probabilities. A possible way out would be for the expert to report all the p_j separately to the court.

4.7 Uncertainty or Measurement Error of the Evidence

People make mistakes. Forensic labs make mistakes. The probability that something goes wrong in the process of determining a DNA profile is likely to be much larger than the population frequency of an observed DNA profile at the scene of the crime. Doesn't this fact jeopardize the significance of match probabilities which can be of the order of one in billions? In other words, does the fact that mistakes are made with probability much larger than one in a billion make such small match probabilities rather meaningless?

Roughly speaking, the answer is no, not really, although it depends a bit what kind of mistake is made. It is of course possible that the DNA of a suspect is assessed incorrectly. Typically such mistakes are rare, and relatively easy to rectify, by taking a new reference sample. We will not go into these errors here. Another possibility, which probably occurs much more frequently and can be more difficult to rectify, is the incorrect assessment of a profile obtained from the evidence from the crime scene. We concentrate on this latter type of mistake. Let us first perform a few elementary computations, and then we comment on the outcomes.

We write $\Gamma_C^{att} = 1$ for the event that we attribute Γ to C, and keep in mind that this may be incorrect. The actual (but not reliably observable) event that C truly has Γ is denoted by $\Gamma_C = 1$. Finally we denote by $\Gamma_S = 1$ the event that the person of interest S has profile Γ and this event is observable.

Suppose that we make the assumption that there is a probability α that a mistake is made in the determination of the profile attributed to C. We write $Z = 1$ if a mistake is made, and $Z = 0$ if not, so we have that $P(Z=1) = \alpha$ and $P(Z=0) = 1-\alpha$. We assume that Z is independent of the event that $C = S$. Thus, we have $P(\Gamma_C^{att} = 1 \mid Z = 1, \Gamma_C = 1) = 0$ and $P(\Gamma_C^{att} = 1 \mid Z = 0, \Gamma_C = 1) = 1$.

The population frequency of Γ is denoted by p. Suppose that we learn that person S has Γ. How incriminating is it for a suspect to have a profile matching one that is possibly erroneous? We will compute the likelihood ratio given by

$$\frac{P(\Gamma_S = 1, \Gamma_C^{att} = 1 \mid C = S)}{P(\Gamma_S = 1, \Gamma_C^{att} = 1 \mid C \neq S)}. \tag{4.39}$$

Our independence assumption implies that the numerator of (4.39) is equal to

$$P(\Gamma_S = 1, \Gamma_C^{att} = 1 \mid Z = 1, S = C)P(Z = 1 \mid S = C)$$

$$+ P(\Gamma_S = 1, \Gamma_C^{att} = 1 \mid Z = 0, S = C)P(Z = 0 \mid S = C)$$

$$= \alpha P(\Gamma_S = 1 \mid Z = 1, S = C)P(\Gamma_C^{att} = 1 \mid Z = 1, S = C, \Gamma_S = 1)$$

$$+ (1 - \alpha)P(\Gamma_S = 1 \mid Z = 0, S = C)P(\Gamma_C^{att} = 1 \mid Z = 0, S = C, \Gamma_S = 1)$$

$$= (1 - \alpha)p.$$

In the denominator, we get by an analogous computation,

$$P(\Gamma_S = 1, \Gamma_C^{att} = 1 \mid S \neq C)$$

$$= \alpha P(\Gamma_S = 1 \mid Z = 1, S \neq C) P(\Gamma_C^{att} = 1 \mid Z = 1, S \neq C, \Gamma_S = 1)$$

$$+ (1 - \alpha) P(\Gamma_S = 1 \mid Z = 0, S \neq C) P(\Gamma_C^{att} = 1 \mid Z = 0, S \neq C, \Gamma_S = 1)$$

$$= \alpha p P(\Gamma_C^{att} = 1 \mid Z = 1, S \neq C, \Gamma_S = 1) + (1 - \alpha) p^2.$$

These considerations lead to

$$\frac{P(\Gamma_S = 1, \Gamma_C^{att} = 1 \mid C = S)}{P(\Gamma_S = 1, \Gamma_C^{att} = 1 \mid C \neq S)} = \frac{1 - \alpha}{p + \alpha(p' - p)}, \tag{4.40}$$

where

$$p' := P(\Gamma_C^{att} = 1 \mid Z = 1, S \neq C, \Gamma_S = 1)$$

is the probability that profile Γ is attributed to C, given that the suspect has Γ, that a mistake has been made and that S is not C. The numerical evaluation of the likelihood ratio (4.40) therefore crucially depends on p', and different scenarios lead to very different numerical answers.

An extreme situation would be that $p' = 1$, meaning that if a mistake is made, it is always the case that the profile of S is attributed to C, for instance via contamination. In this case, the likelihood ratio in (4.40) is equal to $(1 - \alpha)/(\alpha + p(1 - \alpha))$, which is close to $(1 - \alpha)/\alpha$ if p is much smaller than α. Hence, in that case, the likelihood ratio is approximately equal to the odds on there having been made no mistake. The small value of p is completely overthrown by the probability of making a mistake, as intuition requires.

However, in most cases it will not be the case that there is any bias in the direction of a specific profile when making a mistake in the typing. In many cases the profile attributed to C will be similar, but not exactly equal to the actual profile of C and there seems to be no reason to think that p' is of a different order than p. If that is true, then the ensuing likelihood ratio in (4.40) is still of the order $1/p$ which means that the evidential value of the match is not really affected by the possibility of making mistakes.

The rationale behind this is, simply, that although mistakes are relatively frequent compared to DNA profiles, it is not to be expected that a mistake leads to the specific profile of the person of interest. As such, mistakes of the type here considered have less effect on the strength of the evidence than perhaps thought at first sight. In fact, since the likelihood ratio is of the same magnitude, the indication that it gives in favor of $S = C$ is at the same time an indication that no error has been made. Even if α would be ridiculously large, say 10%, this would not meaningfully alter the likelihood ratio associated with a matching profile. The fact that there is a match therefore gives support to the profile of C being correct. With p as small as is typical for DNA profiles, in fact the overwhelming majority of possible DNA profiles are not realized in the population. In almost all cases where a profile has been erroneously determined, there will therefore be no one in the population having that profile.

We conclude that the risks of these mistakes are rather in the other direction. Indeed, since they lead to another profile than C's real profile, they will rather lead to there being a missed match with C than to an adventitious match with an innocent suspect.

4.8 Summary and Conclusions

In this chapter we have discussed a situation in which we learn that an unknown person C has a certain characteristic, like C having a specific DNA profile. For instance, C could be a criminal who has left a DNA profile at the scene of the crime, but we have discussed other applications and examples as well. We assume that the population of interest is well defined. The characteristic is assumed to have population frequency p. A person of interest S also has the characteristic. Our basic question is what we can say about the probability that $S = C$.

For this question to make sense, we have made the assumption that $S = C$ with probability π, and that the choice of C and S does not depend on the characteristic.

Writing E_C and E_S for the events that C, respectively S have the characteristic, and G for the event that $S = C$, the likelihood ratio for G versus G^c is $1/p$ and the posterior probability of G is

$$P(G \mid E_C, E_S) = \frac{\pi}{\pi + (1 - \pi)p}.$$

If we perform a search until someone with the characteristic is found, then the probability that such a search will lead to C is equal to

$$\frac{1 - (1 - p)^{N+1}}{p(N + 1)}.$$

The evidential value of a search result, when having given rise to a specific person, is almost the same as in the classical case, with a likelihood ratio very close to $1/p$.

If we do not know the value of p and our knowledge about p is described by a random variable W with expectation p and variance σ^2, then

$$P(G \mid E_C, E_S) = \frac{\pi}{\pi + (1 - \pi)p'},$$

where $p' = p + \sigma^2/p$. Hence uncertainty about p does not average out but reduces the posterior probability that $S = C$.

When we assume that the population consists of m, say, subpopulations, each with their own probability p_i for the characteristic, the posterior probability for $C = S$ reads as

$$\frac{\alpha_S \beta_S}{\sum_{i=1}^{m} p_i \beta_i - p_S \alpha_S \beta_S + \alpha_S \beta_S},$$

where β_j is the prior probability for C to be in the jth subpopulation, α_S is the probability that $C = S$ given that C belongs to the same subpopulation of S, and p_S is the frequency of the characteristic in that subpopulation.

Although this posterior probability is undisputed, there are several ways to compute likelihood ratios here. If we consider only the fact that S matches as evidence, and the fact that C does as background information, then the likelihood ratio is just $1/p_S$. This, of course, is not enough to obtain posterior odds, since we also need $LR(E_C)$, which depends on the p_i, the a priori probability for a random person in the ith subpopulation to have Γ, and on the β_i, the a priori probability that $C \in X_i$. It is only when the expert may consider that the decision-maker has taken E_C into account, that $LR(E_S \mid E_C)$ is relevant.

If we take into account both E_C and E_S as evidence, the likelihood ratio is given by

$$LR(E_C, E_S) = LR(E_C \mid E_S) = \frac{1 - \alpha_S \beta_S}{\sum_i p_i \beta_i - p_S \alpha_S \beta_S}. \tag{4.41}$$

The fact that these likelihood ratios are not the same is the source of considerable confusion. They are different because they give answer to different questions. Note also that (4.41) contains prior information in the form of the β_i. All this reinforces the point that an isolated likelihood ratio is not meaningful in itself, and that the context and the question of interest need always to be made explicit. Different likelihood ratios give answers to different questions and this must always be kept in mind.

Finally, we argued that potential mistakes in a forensic laboratory are not expected to have a big effect on the evidential value of a match, despite the fact that mistakes are likely to have a greater probability that the random match probability of the involved DNA profile. Essentially this is due to the fact that apart from biased mistakes due to contamination, mistakes will almost never lead to the profile of the suspect. In fact profile probabilities are so small, that it is extremely unlikely that the erroneous profile will exist in the population. The main risk these unbiased mistakes carry is to lead to false exclusions of actual offenders.

4.9 Bibliographical Notes

The formulation and solution of the island problems in this chapter generalize existing texts. The two main references for a rigorous treatment of the island problem are [8] and [146]. Formula (4.12) was published by Yellin in [179] as the solution to this version of the island problem with a search. Sometimes, however, it is incorrectly quoted in the literature (e.g., in [8]) as an incorrect solution to the island problem without search as we have discussed it. The results in Section 4.7 are new, but in [54] another formulation addressing the same problem is discussed.

5

The Bayesian Framework in Legal Cases

In Chapter 2 we have introduced and analyzed the likelihood ratio and the Bayesian framework in great detail, and in Chapter 3 we have investigated the nature of the likelihood ratio. In Chapter 4 we have given derivations of likelihood ratios in idealized conditions. In this chapter we discuss some applications of the theory so far by means of a number of examples and cases. As can be expected, the mathematical theory never fits perfectly, but as we will see, the theory is nevertheless rather useful in many situations. We will encounter serious difficulties in almost all elements of the framework: the choice of the hypotheses, the choice of prior odds, the computation of the likelihood ratio, and last but not least the interpretation of the outcomes by the judiciary. This chapter will also serve as a motivation for further developments in the chapters to come.

5.1 The Link Hammer Case

In 2010 in the Dutch city of Breukelen, a heavily wounded woman was found lying in some bushes. Her skull was severely damaged, and despite an emergency operation, she died the following day. Upon witness statements, a suspect was arrested and charged with murder. In the suspect's house, a link hammer was found and it was subsequently investigated whether or not this link hammer could have been the murder weapon by which the skull of the woman had been beaten. We do not go into the many (interesting) details of the case, but focus on the hypotheses that were brought forward by the Netherlands Forensic Institute (NFI).

To evaluate the evidential value of the evidence, a choice is needed for the alternative murder weapon. A link hammer is a type of hammer within the larger class of claw hammers. We believe, based on the reports, that it was considered that claw hammers could not be ruled out as the murder weapon, but that link hammers were the best candidates.

Table 5.1 *The verbal scale as used by the Netherlands Forensic Institute.*

Number	Verbal
1–2	About equally likely
2–10	Somewhat more likely
10–100	More likely
100–10,000	Much more likely
10,000–1,000,000	Very much more likely
> 1,000,000	Extremely much more likely

In any case, one set of hypotheses considered by the NFI was the following:

H_1: The damage of the skull was caused by beating with the link hammer found in the house of the suspect;

H_2: The damage of the skull was caused by beating with another claw hammer.

The NFI concluded that the damage was "very much more likely" assuming H_1 than when assuming H_2. Although this statement does not immediately give rise to a numerical expression for the likelihood ratio, one could use Table 5.1 (as currently used by the Netherlands Forensic Institute) to get an idea of the intended numerical value.

In addition, the NFI considered the following hypothesis H_3 that restricted the alternative murder weapon to link hammers:

H_3: The damage of the skull was caused by beating with another link hammer.

The NFI concluded that the damage of the skull was (using the same verbal scale) "more likely" assuming H_1 than when assuming H_3. There were no other conclusions in the report of the NFI. The question is what we can conclude from these likelihood ratios.

In fact, this case forms an application of the framework we have developed in Chapter 4 where we evaluated the evidential value, and the posterior odds, after having observed a shared characteristic between suspect and offender. In the notation of Chapter 4, in this case C is the murder weapon and S is the link hammer found in the suspect's house. We let the information E_C be the observed skull damage, and E_S the "match" between the suspect's link hammer and the skull damage. The population of potential murder weapons can be regarded as being composed of several subpopulations: the subpopulation of link hammers, the subpopulation of claw hammers other than link hammers, and the subpopulation of murder weapons other than claw hammers. Let us call these populations population 1, 2, and 3 respectively, and let β_i be the prior probabilities (that is, before observing the skull damage) that the murder was committed by either type of weapon. While it is clearly difficult to attach values to the β_i, it is reasonable to say that β_3 is the largest, since most murders are not committed with hammers.

The likelihood ratio $LR(E_S \mid E_C)$ is then equal to $1/p_S$, see (4.36). In the notation of Chapter 4, p_S is the probability that S has the required characteristic given that S did not leave the trace, valid for the population that S is from. Note that in Chapter 4, we assumed that the suspect has the characteristic with certainty, if he is C. In this case, we are considering specific skull damage and the probability to observe this damage need not be one for the murder weapon. Therefore, we consider E_S to be the event that the suspected link hammer cannot be excluded as being the murder weapon. If we assume furthermore that experts never exclude the actual murder weapon, we can interpret p_S as the probability that a random link hammer cannot be excluded as murder weapon, and so $1/p_S$ is then the likelihood ratio for H_1 versus H_3 as considered by the NFI. From the NFI report we conclude that the quantity $1/p_S$ is now a likelihood ratio falling in the "more likely" verbal scale, that is, it is some number between 10 and 100.

The likelihood ratio for E_C and E_S together, however, is very different. From (4.37) we see that it can be written as

$$LR(E_C, E_S) = \frac{1 - \alpha_S \beta_S}{\sum_i p_i \beta_i - p_S \alpha_S \beta_S}.$$

Now $p_1 = p_S$, which we have already discussed, and p_2 is the probability that a claw hammer (which is not a link hammer) cannot be excluded as murder weapon. We now must take into account that the NFI considered the whole population of claw hammers, including those of link hammers. Therefore the likelihood ratio reported as "very much more likely" is not the likelihood ratio $1/p_2$.

Let us write the reported likelihood ratio as $1/p_C$, then

$$p_C = \frac{p_1 \beta_1 + p_2 \beta_2}{\beta_1 + \beta_2}.$$

Furthermore, other possible types of murder weapon were not considered, on which we base the assumption that this was not necessary since $p_3 \approx 0$. Then the likelihood ratio (4.37) becomes

$$LR(E_C, E_S) = \frac{1 - \alpha_1 \beta_1}{p_1 \beta_1 + p_2 \beta_2 - p_1 \alpha_1 \beta_1} = \frac{1 - \alpha_1 \beta_1}{p_C(\beta_1 + \beta_2) - p_1 \alpha_1 \beta_1},$$

and the posterior probability evaluates to

$$\frac{\alpha_1}{p_1 + p_2 \beta_2 / \beta_1 - p_1 \alpha_1 + \alpha_1} = \frac{\alpha_1}{p_C(1 + \beta_2 / \beta_1) - p_1 \alpha_1 + \alpha_1}.$$

Now we can draw some conclusions. First of all we see that, since $p_3 = 0$, it is irrelevant for the posterior probability on guilt how many murders are committed by other means than making use of a claw hammer. Since these weapons do not play a role here, it does not matter that they might have. What is relevant, however, is how β_2 relates to β_1. We also see that, for the calculation of p_C as we have defined it here following the phrasing of the NFI report, we need the conditional probability of link hammers being the murder weapon given that the murder weapon is a claw hammer. No doubt these probabilities are hard to define. But the above expression in any case allows to judge the impact of these assessments. For example, in the expression for the posterior probability we see that we need a term equal to $p_2\beta_2/\beta_1$. If p_2 is such that this is small compared to p_1 for reasonable choices of β_2/β_1, this term will not have much impact.

To conclude, we see that incorporating the reported likelihood ratios into the assessment of the posterior probability is possible, but requires additional assumptions and we consider it unlikely to be straightforward for non-statisticians.

5.2 Examples of Combination of Evidence

In Section 2.2.1 we have seen that, mathematically, it is clear how to assess various pieces of evidence. But in many concrete cases, no complete mathematical model can be formulated easily, and the combination of evidence then becomes difficult. Since the different pieces of evidence concern the same case, dependencies may easily exist between them. It is therefore important that any claim of conditional independence be argued for carefully. Complete conditional independence might be impossible to claim, and very often the best we can do is convince ourselves that assuming conditional independence is a reasonable thing to do. Hence, although the likelihood ratio approach in principle allows for combination of evidence, in many cases it will be difficult to do so.

We already saw that in many cases forensic experts will not be willing (or able) to report a number for the likelihood ratio of the evidence, but instead will use a verbal formulation. Although they might use a table relating verbal to numerical, it is clear that any such table should be used with care and some skepticism. In many cases, there is simply no suitable mathematical model available which is realistic enough to render numbers very meaningful, and in such a case it will be difficult or impossible to make an explicit meaningful computation. In such a situation, talking about a likelihood ratio, a concept that involves mathematical objects like probabilities, can only be done in some approximate and informal way. This being already an obstacle for an individual piece of evidence, when we combine various pieces of evidence this problems becomes even bigger. Here are some examples.

Example 5.2.1 Suppose that a burglary has taken place in a house, and that we have two pieces of evidence E_1 and E_2. For instance, we have shoe traces that give us information about the shoe size of the culprit, and we have camara images which give us some approximate idea of the length of the culprit. These two traces form two different pieces of evidence, and we can ask ourselves whether or not they are conditionally independent given the hypotheses of interest. Let us call the shoe traces evidence E_1 and the camera image evidence E_2. Suppose that X is a suspect in the case, and that X possesses shoes that seem to match with the traces, and that his length is roughly corresponding to the images. The hypothesis H_1 could be the hypothesis that X committed the burglary, and H_2 the hypothesis that an unknown person did it. We have to compute $P(E_1, E_2 \mid H_1)$, and it seems reasonable to assume that E_1 and E_2 are conditionally independent given H_1. For evaluating the similarity between X's length and the camera images, the shoes that X possesses will not be relevant.

However, under H_2 where X did not commit the burglary, then this may be different. Indeed, it is not far fetched to assume that shoe size and length correlate, so that information about someone's length also contains information about his shoe size. Although this example is somewhat contrived, we see that conditional independence has to be argued for under every hypothesis separately. In this case if E_1 and E_2 are conditionally independent under H_1 but $P(E_2 \mid H_2, E_1) > P(E_2 \mid H_2)$, then by assuming independence under H_2 we will overestimate the evidential weight of the combined evidence. □

Example 5.2.2 In a burglary case, entry into a house was forced by opening the front door with violence. Around the house a crowbar is found with some paint traces on it which match the paint of the front door. Furthermore, upon making test traces with this crowbar it is seen that the traces of break-in on the front seem to match the crowbar's traces made in the test situation. Naturally, we define hypothesis H_1 as the hypothesis that the crowbar was used to break in through the front door, while H_2 is the hypothesis that this is not the case. We have, therefore, two pieces of evidence: E_1 is the event that paint was found on the crowbar which matches the paint of the front door, and E_2 that the traces on the door were found to match the crowbar.

Are these two pieces of evidence conditionally independent given the two hypotheses H_1 and H_2? We can argue against this. If we condition on H_1, the hypothesis that the crowbar was used, then learning that traces were found on the door might give reason to think that the crowbar was used with a lot of force. If in addition to the assumption that the crowbar was used, we also condition on it being used with a lot of force, the probability that paint remains are found on the crowbar should perhaps increase. In the extreme case, we might have that $P(E_1 \mid H_1) \approx P(E_1, E_2 \mid H_1) \approx P(E_2 \mid H_1)$ meaning that if we see either evidence, we are certain to also see the other evidence. Hence there seems to be no reason to think that the two pieces of evidence are conditionally independent given H_1.

Under H_2, we can on the contrary argue for conditional independence. When the crowbar was not used in the burglary, then the traces on the door match the crowbar accidentally, and this match should have no effect on the probability to find paint that matches the front door on the crowbar.

This would mean that $LR(E_1, E_2) \geq LR(E_1)LR(E_2)$, which means that the two pieces of evidence combined are stronger evidence than if they had been independent. In other words, the fact that the first piece of evidence has been observed, makes the second one stronger evidence than if the first piece of evidence had not been obtained. In this case, contrary to the preceding one, assuming independence would thus have a conservative effect on the assessment of the combined evidence.   □

Our final example is a situation in which we combine two pieces of conditionally independent evidence, and in which the defense hypothesis partitions in a natural way into three sub-hypotheses.

Example 5.2.3 Near the scene of a criminal offense an item I is found which is possibly used during the criminal activities. There is also a suspect S. The evidence consists of two pieces. E_1 is evidence which relates S to I, and E_2 is evidence relating I to the crime. To be more concrete, the item could be a crowbar, E_1 could be a fingerprint of S on the crowbar, while E_2 could be traces of the crowbar at the crime scene. We consider the following natural hypotheses:

H_1: S performed the offense-related activity with item I;
H_2: Someone else performed the offense-related activity, and S had nothing to do with it.

As far as H_1 is concerned, we assume that under H_1, S performed the offense-related activity, handling the item during this activity, and that the item was used to perform this activity. Since we distinguish between evidence relating S to I on the one hand, and evidence relating I to the crime on the other, there are several distinct situations that together make up the defense scenario:

H_2^1: S had nothing to do with the offense activity, he did not handle the item during this activity. However, the item was used by the offender to perform the activity;
H_2^2: S had nothing to do with the offense-related activity, but at some point he handled the item. However the item was not used by the offender to perform this activity;
H_2^3: S had nothing to do with the offense-related activity, he never handled the item, and the item was not used by the offender to perform this activity.

Intuitively, it seems reasonable that it is the best strategy for the defense to not contest the strongest link, but dispute the other one. For example, if the evidence linking the suspect to the crowbar is strong, but the evidence that the crowbar was the one used during the crime is weaker, the suspect might not dispute having handled the crowbar, but deny having committed the crime with it. We will see now how the likelihood ratio evaluation makes this clear.

We need to calculate the likelihood ratio of the combined evidence E_1 and E_2, and it seems reasonable to assume that E_1 and E_2 are conditionally independent given each of H_1, H_2^1, H_2^2, and H_2^3. To calculate the likelihood ratio we need the conditional prior probabilities of the H_2^i given H_2, as explained in Section 2.3.1. Let us denote these prior probabilities by π_i, $i = 1, 2, 3$.

Furthermore, under the hypotheses we defined, it is clear that $LR_{H_1, H_2^2}(E_1) = 1$. Indeed, H_1 and H_2^2 agree that the suspect handled the item. Similarly, also LR_{H_1, H_2^1} $(E_2) = 1$. For analogous reasons, $LR_{H_1, H_2^1}(E_1) = LR_{H_1, H_2^3}(E_1)$, since these two alternative hypotheses agree in their statement that the suspect did not handle the item.

Using the various instances of conditional independence we now compute

$$LR_{H_2, H_1}(E_1, E_2) = \frac{P(E_1, E_2 \mid H_2)}{P(E_1, E_2 \mid H_1)} = \frac{\sum_{i=1}^3 \pi_i P(E_1 \mid H_2^i) P(E_2 \mid H_2^i)}{P(E_1 \mid H_1) P(E_2 \mid H_1)}$$

$$= \pi_1 LR_{H_2^1, H_1}(E_1) + \pi_2 LR_{H_2^2, H_1}(E_2)$$

$$+ \pi_3 LR_{H_2^3, H_1}(E_1) LR_{H_2^3, H_1}(E_2).$$

Hence, writing $LR(E_1)$ as shorthand for $LR_{H_1, H_2^1}(E_1) = LR_{H_1, H_2^3}(E_1)$ and analogously for $LR(E_2)$, we find

$$LR_{H_1, H_2}(E_1, E_2) = \frac{LR(E_1) LR(E_2)}{\pi_1 LR(E_2) + \pi_2 LR(E_1) + \pi_3}.$$

We see that indeed the likelihood ratio $LR_{H_1, H_2}(E_1, E_2)$ depends on the prior probabilities π_1, π_2 and π_3. This is to be expected, since the strength of the evidence depends on which of the sub-hypotheses is assumed. We also see that if $LR(E_1) \geq LR(E_2)$, then $LR(E_1, E_2)$ is minimized for $\pi_2 = 1$, as we already pointed out above. $\square$

5.3 The Sally Clark Case

We next discuss a well-known case in which the Bayesian framework was *not* used, and which led to disaster: the Sally Clark case in England.

In December 1996 Sally Clark's firstborn son Christopher was found dead in his bed, aged $2^1/2$ months. He died when Sally was alone in the house with him.

In January 1998 her second child Harry died, aged 2 months, in similar circumstances. Soon afterwards Sally was accused of having murdered her two children by smothering.

Apart from the possibility of a double murder, the possibility of a double Sudden Infant Death Syndrome (SIDS) was considered. The principal prosecution evidence came from a paediatrician, Sir Roy Meadow, who testified that the expected incidence of a child dying from a Sudden Infant Death Syndrome was about 1 in 8,500. He also testified that a second occurrence of SIDS given a first one would be as likely as a first one, resulting in a overall rate of a double SIDS of about 1 in 73 million. This number, apparently, was so overwhelmingly small, that a double SIDS was no longer deemed realistic, and since the only possible alternative that was considered was a double murder, this is what was concluded. Sally Clark was convicted for double murder.

There is a lot to say about this case, and a lot to learn from it as well, and we now discuss the relevant statistical and probabilistic issues.

First we note that the multiplication of the two terms 1 in 8,500 to yield 1 in 73 million, is highly questionable. It is well known that if one child dies of SIDS, this may have an effect on the probability that a second child in the same family dies of SIDS. The independence assumption is not defended and probably not defendable. However, the biggest problems in this case are not about (in)adequate numbers, but instead about the probabilistic logic.

The second thing we note, is that the likelihood ratio approach was not used. As we have seen, a likelihood ratio approach insists on comparing various hypotheses, and forces us to compute the probability of the evidence given both competing hypotheses. In the current case, only one computation was made, under the assumption of innocence. If Sally Clark was not guilty, then the two deaths should have been attributed to a double SIDS, the probability of which was supposed to be extremely small.

That the probability of a double SIDS is small is clear, but we have to ask ourselves whether any competing hypothesis, say the hypothesis of a double murder, could also be very unlikely. After all, we are interested in the question as to how likely it is that Sally Clark murdered both her children. Hence we may consider:

H_1: Sally Clark murdered her two children by smothering;
H_2: The two children died of SIDS.

Below we discuss some alternatives to this pair of hypotheses. What can be said about the probabilities of H_1 and H_2 given the evidence E that two children died? We can invoke Bayes' rule

$$\frac{P(H_1 \mid E)}{P(H_2 \mid E)} = \frac{P(E \mid H_1)}{P(E \mid H_2)} \cdot \frac{P(H_1)}{P(H_2)}.$$

In this particular case, the likelihood ratio is very simple to compute. Indeed under both H_1 and H_2 the two children would have died, so the numerator and denominator of the likelihood ratio are both equal to 1. This means that the evidence E is neutral with respect to H_1 and H_2, something that seems to be in sharp contrast to the conclusions drawn by the expert in the case. The evidence being neutral, the posterior odds of H_1 versus H_2 are equal to the prior odds. However, the prior odds were never discussed in the legal process, since only $P(H_2)$ was considered but not $P(H_1)$. Without making any specific calculation, it should be clear that the prior probability of a double murder is very small indeed. It might be difficult to come up with a reasonable number for this, but the fact that this number never showed up in the legal case already tells us that the conviction of Sally Clark was based on an erroneous use of statistics and probability. A simple application of Bayes' rule would have shown that the 1 in 73 million being very small is, on its own, not relevant for the probability that Sally Clark murdered her children. What really matters is how this probability compares to the prior probability of a double murder.

There are other possible approaches to this case. The two hypotheses used above, H_1 and H_2, were both formulated after seeing the evidence E that two children died. It would also be natural to consider H_1 versus its negation H_1^c. Hypothesis H_1^c does not assume from the outset that the children will die. In fact, as we will now show, this choice is just as fine, and leads to precisely the same conclusion as above. Indeed, the posterior probability of guilt will be the same, and the only thing that will happen is that there will be a shift of "mass" between prior odds and likelihood ratio.

To see this, we first compute the likelihood ratio of H_1 versus H_1^c. In order to clearly see what happens, we write μ for the prior probability of a double smothering, and δ for the prior probability of a double SIDS. Note that δ was estimated to be equal to 1 over 73 million in the legal case against Sally Clark. We already saw that $P(E \mid H_1) = 1$. If we assume that the circumstances of the two dead children were such that the only possible explanations are double smothering or double SIDS, then we compute

$$P(E \mid H_1^c) = P(E \mid H_1^c, H_2)P(H_2 \mid H_1^c) + P(E \mid H_1^c, H_2^c)P(H_2^c \mid H_1^c)$$

$$= P(H_2 \mid H_1^c) = \frac{P(H_2)}{P(H_1^c)}$$

$$= \frac{\delta}{1 - \mu}. \tag{5.1}$$

Hence the likelihood ratio of H_1 versus H_1^c is $(1 - \mu)/\delta$ and the posterior odds are equal to

$$\frac{P(H_1 \mid E)}{P(H_1^c \mid E)} = \frac{1 - \mu}{\delta} \cdot \frac{\mu}{1 - \mu} = \frac{\mu}{\delta}.$$

These posterior odds are exactly the same as the posterior odds of H_1 versus H_2 that we discussed above. This becomes understandable once you realize that, given the evidence E, H_1^c and H_2 are equally likely since we assumed that the evidence (two children found dead in their beds) do not allow for other hypotheses than double smothering and double SIDS.

The likelihood ratio of H_1 versus H_1^c is equal to $(1 - \mu)/\delta$, which may be a huge number. This is, roughly, the number used by Sir Roy Meadow. In contrast, the likelihood ratio of H_1 versus H_2 is equal to 1. The fact that this nevertheless results in the same posterior probability of guilt is due to the fact that the priors are very different, and precisely balances the difference in the likelihood ratio.

It is important now to point out the inadequacy of classical hypothesis testing in the form of p-value procedures for evidential purposes in situations of this type. Suppose we would consider hypothesis H_1 in isolation, and consider H_1^c as our null hypothesis. Suppose further that we would compute the probability of the evidence E given H_1^c as in (5.1). The quantity in (5.1) is a very small number, assuming that the prior probability that Sally Clark would murder her two children must be very small. Following the classical p-value procedure to quantify evidence, this would have led to the rejection of H_1^c. Indeed, the classical argument would be that either something very unusual happened, or H_1^c is false. This is true, but in this case we already know from the outset that something unusual has happened.

The conclusion from a classical p-value procedure would obviously have been completely wrong. This example illustrates the fact that there *must* be something wrong with using a p-value procedure to quantify evidence. What is wrong with it has been mentioned already a few times in this book. It is generally impossible to speak about evidence for a given, isolated, hypothesis. It only makes sense to speak about evidence for a hypothesis compared to another, competing one. Especially in legal cases this is crucial, and the conviction of Sally Clark can be attributed to incompetent experts and a complete misunderstanding of what statistical evidence actually is.

The discussion so far was based on general statistics only. One may naturally wonder whether or not there were any pieces of evidence at the scene of the events that would have been useful. If nothing out of the ordinary was found, then this fact might have been used statistically as well. Indeed, it is probably more likely to find nothing of any interest if the children died of SIDS then when they were murdered. It might be difficult to assign actual numbers to this finding, but it may further point in the direction of innocence.

In the legal case, Sally Clark was convicted for double murder and this was confirmed by the court of appeal. After the second conviction it became apparent that serious statistical mistakes had been made. Finally she was released from imprisonment but she died shortly after.

5.4 The Death of the Linesman

The case of the linesman that we will discuss now caused some uproar in the Netherlands. After an amateur soccer match in 2012, one of the linesmen was attacked by several players and a bystander. Among other things, the linesman was kicked in the head several times. After the attack (which was witnessed by many people), the linesman returned home, apparently without any serious injuries. However, one day later he suddenly died from an arterial bleeding in the neck.

The people who had attacked the linesman were brought to trial. The question, of course, arose as to whether or not the death of the linesman was a result of the attack the day before. The case largely concentrated on medical affairs on which we will not comment. However, also statistics played a role. Indeed, it was brought forward by the defense that general statistics show that a fighting incident without weapons (as was the case here), only leads to death one in every 10,000 times. According to the defense it was, therefore, not to be expected that the death of the linesman had anything to do with the attack.

The figure of one in 10,000 was disputed during the trial. It was argued that an attack which includes hitting against a head cannot be interpreted as a general fight, and that the death rate related to such more specific fights must be much higher. This has to do with the question what the correct reference population is if one wants to interpret probability in a frequentistic way.

This argument that the incorrect reference population was used carries some weight. However, it does not seem to address the biggest misinterpretation in the case. Indeed, we are not interested in the conditional probability of someone dying given that he has been involved in an attack or fight of a certain type. The fact is that someone who was involved in such an attack died, and now we want to know whether this was caused by the attack. This is a completely different question.

We can use the Bayesian framework to see what is going on. As background information I, we take the fact that the linesman was involved in a fight, that he was in his late forties and otherwise healthy. We let H_1 be the hypothesis that the fight was lethal, and H_2 the hypothesis that this was not the case. We denote by E the event that the linesman died not long after the fight.

According to the defense, $P(H_1 \mid I) \approx 1/10,000$. (To be precise, the defense did not explicitly condition on I, but we may safely interpet their claim as we do.) This number was disputed during the trial, so let us say that $P(H_1 \mid I) = \epsilon$, a small number. The prior odds $P(H_1 \mid I)/P(H_2 \mid I)$ are then $\epsilon/(1 - \epsilon)$.

For the likelihood ratio we have $P(E \mid H_1, I) = 1$ and $P(E \mid H_2, I) = \nu$, where we can think of ν as being much smaller than ϵ. Indeed, the probability to die of arterial bleeding, for an otherwise young and healthy man, must be extremely small. Hence the likelihood ratio is equal to $1/\nu$ and the posterior odds satisfy

$$\frac{P(H_1 \mid E, I)}{P(H_2 \mid E, I)} = \frac{1}{\nu} \times \frac{\epsilon}{1 - \epsilon} \approx \frac{\epsilon}{\nu}.$$

Since, as we already mentioned, we have good reasons to assume that ν is much smaller than ϵ, we again conclude that $P(H_1 \mid E, I)$ is large.

The conclusion is that the death of the linesman is likely to be connected to the attack, although a precise number will be difficult to provide. But our argument clearly shows that the claim of the defense is in no way exculpatory for the suspects in this case.

In the legal case, the suspects were found guilty (except for one of them) and sentenced to prison for time periods up to six years.

5.5 The Lucia de Berk Case

We have seen in the Sally Clark case that the occurrence of an event E which has very small probability under a hypotheses H does not imply that H becomes very unlikely. Although it is true that either H is false or an event of small probability has occurred, this fact cannot be used to reject H. For one thing, the event E may also be very rare under any competing hypothesis. Furthermore, there might be reasons to consider H very unlikely a priori. So, small probabilities in themselves should not have any implication in legal affairs like this. We next discuss another case where misinterpreting small probabilities led to disaster.

In The Hague (the Netherlands), on March 24, 2003 the nurse Lucia de Berk was sentenced to life imprisonment for allegedly killing or attempting to kill a number of her patients in two hospitals where she had worked in the recent past: the *Juliana Children Hospital* (JCH) and the *Red Cross Hospital* (RCH).

At the JCH, an unusually high proportion of incidents seemed to occur during the shifts of Lucia de Berk. The precise technical definition of an "incident" is not important here; suffice it to say that an incident refers to the necessity for reanimation, regardless of the outcome of the reanimation. The question arose as to whether Lucia's presence at so many incidents could have been merely coincidental.

After noticing this large number of incidents during her shifts at the JCH, data was also acquired from the other hospital (the RCH) where the suspect had been working in two different wards numbered 41 and 42.

Statistician Henk Elffers, who had looked into the matter at the request of the prosecutor, was asked whether sheer coincidence might be a satisfactory explanation of the data. In broad terms, his conclusion was this. Assuming only that:

1. the probability p that the suspect experiences an incident during a shift is the same as the corresponding probability for any other nurse,
2. the occurrences of incidents are independent for different shifts,

Table 5.2 *The data in de Lucia de Berk case.*

Hospital (and ward number)	JCH	RCH-41	RCH-42
Total number of shifts	1029	336	339
Lucia's number of shifts	142	1	58
Total number of incidents	8	5	14
Number of incidents during Lucia's shifts	8	1	5

then the probability that the suspect has experienced as least as many incidents as she in fact has (in all of the three wards, considered separately), is less than 1 in 342 million. According to Elffers, this probability is so small that standard statistical methodology sanctions rejection of the null-hypothesis of chance, that is, the null-hypothesis of innocence of Lucia de Berk.

Note that Elffers' approach constitutes a *p*-value procedure, which we already saw is very problematic in cases like this. Before we further comment on the case, we explain how Elffers came to his conclusion.

The data on shifts and incidents for the period which was singled out in Elffers' report is given in Table 5.2. The last two columns refer to two different wards of the RCH where Lucia de Berk had been working. When trying to put the situation sketched into a statistical model, one's first choice might be to build a model on the basis of epidemiological data concerning the probability of incidents during various types of shifts; this would allow one to calculate the probability that the suspect would be present accidentally at as many incidents as she in fact witnessed. However, the problem with this approach is that for the most part the requisite data are lacking. And even if the data were available, their use would be a subject of debate between prosecutor and defense.

Because of this, Elffers tried to set up a model that used only the shift data given above. This he achieved by conditioning on part of the data, namely the observed number of incidents.

He first considered the JCH. It is straightforward to compute the conditional probability, given that the number of incidents is eight, that all eight incidents occur during Lucia's shifts. Indeed, in general, if the total number of shifts is n, and Lucia de Berk was responsible for r out of these n shifts, then the conditional probability that she witnessed x incidents, given that a total of k incidents occurred, is

$$\frac{\binom{r}{x}p^x(1-p)^{r-x}\binom{n-r}{k-x}p^{k-x}(1-p)^{n-r-k+x}}{\binom{n}{k}p^k(1-p)^{n-k}} = \frac{\binom{r}{x}\binom{n-r}{k-x}}{\binom{n}{k}}. \qquad (5.2)$$

Note that this quantity does not depend on the unknown parameter p, which is only natural since we conditioned on the total number of incidents. This distribution is known as the hypergeometric distribution, and with this formula one can easily compute the (conditional) probability that the suspect witnessed at least the number of incidents as she actually has, for each ward.

However, according to Elffers, this computation is not completely fair to the suspect. Indeed, the computation is carried out precisely because there were so many incidents during her shifts at the JCH. It would, therefore, be more reasonable (according to Elffers) not to compute the probability that Lucia has witnessed at least as many incidents, but instead the probability that *some* nurse witnessed at least as many incidents. At the JCH, there were 27 nurses taking care of the shifts and therefore, presumably to get an upper bound to this probability, Elffers multiplies his outcome by 27; he calls this the *post hoc correction*. According to Elffers, this correction only needs to be done at the JCH; at the RCH this is no longer necessary since the suspect was already identified as being suspect on the basis of the JCH data.

Elffers arrives at his final number (the aforementioned 1 in 342 million) by multiplying the outcomes for the three wards (with post hoc correction at the JCH, but without this correction at the RCH). That is, he obtains his final p-value by multiplying the three individual p-values.

The similarity with the Sally Clark case is striking, and (part of) our criticism is the same. Exactly as in the Sally Clark case, Elffers uses a p-value procedure to reject the hypothesis of innocence. But we have seen that this procedure is wrong since it may well be the case that the evidence also has very small probability under a competing hypothesis.

There are, however, also some interesting differences between the Sally Clark case and the case of Lucia de Berk. We saw that Elffers ended up at his final figure by multiplication of three p-values, one for each ward. Does this result in a new p-value? In other words, can we interpret his final outcome as a p-value at all? The answer is no. One can in general not multiply p-values to arrive at an overall p-value. This is another problem with the p-value procedure which simply does not arise when you take a likelihood ratio approach.

To see why multiplication of p-values is problematic, a simple thought experiment suffices. Suppose that Lucia de Berk worked in 100 wards (instead of the actual three) and that the hypothesis of innocence is true. Instead of multiplying three p-values we have to multiply a hundred of them. Since each p-value is smaller than 1, this will result in a very small number. Something must be wrong then, since if this were correct, one can always obtain a very small p-values by simply multiplying p-values of independent findings. Clearly, one has to somehow correct for the number of p-values that were considered.

The literature offers a number of possible ways to do this, and we briefly mention one of them. One way to combine (under the null-hypothesis) independent p-values is a method due to Fisher [68]. Denoting the three p-values for the separate tests by p_1, p_2, and p_3, one computes $-2 \sum_i \log p_i$. This statistic is known to have a chi-squared distribution with 6 degrees of freedom under the null hypothesis, and from this fact a global, final p-value can easily be obtained. This p-value will be much larger than the one reported by Elffers.

So we can safely conclude two things. First, a p-value procedure is in general not adequate for evaluating evidence in legal cases, and second, the number produced by Elffers cannot even be interpreted as a p-value.

The post hoc correction suggested by Elffers also deserves special attention. Clearly, this correction is supposed to take care of the fact that it is not completely fair to the suspect that we perform this calculation, because the considered hypothesis that she murdered her patients is clearly data driven. Since Elffers' set up does not allow for prior probabilities, he is forced to treat the data-driven nature of his hypotheses in a different way. Within the likelihood ratio framework, the use of data-driven hypothesis is in principle not problematic, since the fact that the data will support the hypothesis is compensated by a very small prior probability. Not having this mechanism at his disposal, Elffers has to find another, rather ad hoc, method to deal with this, and this results in his post hoc correction.

However, the level at which he applies this correction seems rather arbitrary. Why only look at the ward where the suspect worked? Why not look at all similar wards in the city, in the country? Furthermore, it seems very odd that the number of nurses who worked in this ward should play a role. The probability of guilt of Lucia de Berk should depend on what happened during her own shifts, and not on the number of nurses who worked during the remaining ones.

The question arises whether or not a likelihood ratio approach could have been of any help in this case. We turn to this question now.

5.5.1 A Naive Likelihood Approach

Whether or not the likelihood approach advocated in this book could have been of any help in the case of Lucia de Berk is not an easily answered question. First of all, we note that the specific approach of Elffers does not seem to easily allow for a likelihood approach. Recall that Elffers did not want to use the unknown parameter p, and avoided using this number by conditioning on the number of incidents. But it is only because of the assumption of innocence (that is, incidents occur completely randomly) that the unknown parameter p drops out in the calculations. No straightforward way exists to make a computation under any competing hypothesis because it is not clear how to formulate the hypothesis of guilt in his model. At first sight it seems, therefore, that a likelihood approach is impossible in the framework of Elffers.

This is not to say that likelihood approaches have not been suggested. Econometrician Aart de Vos suggested the following computation. According to de Vos, there were four pieces of evidence that he wished to use in a Bayesian computation. Each of these pieces of evidence were given a likelihood ratio in favor of guilt. That is, de Vos computes a likelihood ratio for the hypotheses H_1 that Lucia de Berk did kill her patients, versus H_2 that she did not. Now follows a list of the pieces of evidence de Vos considered, with (between parentheses) the likelihood ratio that he associates with the appropriate evidence:

1. E_1: The fact that the suspect never confessed ($\frac{1}{2}$);
2. E_2: The fact that two of the patients had certain toxic substances in their blood (50);
3. E_3: The fact that 14 incidents occurred during Lucia's shifts (7,000);
4. E_4: The fact that suspect had written in her diary that "she had given in to her compulsion" (5).

We first briefly comment on the choice of $E_1, \ldots, E_4$. Only E_3 was considered by Elffers. The toxic substance mentioned in E_2 was not discussed before, because this did not play a role in the statistical analysis. The force of this evidence was the source of a big debate in the legal trial. It was taken as important evidence, supporting the claim of Elffers that coincidence was excluded. The note in the diary of Lucia de Berk mentioned in E_4 was another fact that was brought up by the prosecution. Again, it was interpreted as a confirmation that was consistent with the statistical findings.

De Vos even suggested prior odds of 10^{-5}. Assuming (conditional) independence between the various pieces of evidence, he simply multiplied the likelihood ratios to arrive at posterior odds of roughly 8.75. This means that, according to de Vos, the suspect is guilty with probability close to 90%, certainly not enough to warrant conviction.

The numbers obtained by de Vos are in sharp contrast with Elffers' outcomes, but it is not so easy to take his approach seriously. His numbers seem to be completely arbitrary, and impossible to defend. For instance, the circumstances of possible confession vary greatly. Was there pressure, or was the confession done immediately? There are multiple reasons to confess a crime, and multiple different circumstances which cannot be compared to each other so easily. The likelihood ratio mentioned in connection to E_4 seems even more absurd, and seems to have no basis whatsoever. Also the choice of the prior odds seems to be completely arbitrary.

The choice of the relevant pieces of evidence seems to be rather arbitrary as well, and probably different people would have made other decisions. And last but not least, the claimed conditional independence of the pieces of evidence seems clearly wrong. The presence of toxic substance should certainly not be (conditionally) independent of the fact that a certain number of incidents occurred. We must conclude that this approach is not feasible, and if a likelihood approach can be used at all, it is not this one.

5.5.2 Naive Bayes – A Short Detour

The general method of de Vos, that is, identifying a certain collection of pieces of evidence, assuming the appropriate (conditional) independence and multiplying the relevant likelihood ratios, is sometimes referred to in the literature as *naive Bayes*, or sometimes even as *idiot Bayes*. Some people call it *linear Bayes*. But whatever nomenclature is used, there seems to be consensus in the literature that a complex or complicated case should not be approached in this way, for multiple reasons. The dependency structure is typically too complicated, and the necessary numbers are typically not available. Dependency relations between various pieces of evidence can sometimes be made explicit by using *Bayesian networks*. We discuss the usefulness of these networks in some depth in Chapter 6.

The judiciary in the Netherlands sometimes explicitly acknowledges the problem of arbitrariness when using the naive likelihood approach for complex cases, and we now make a short detour from the Lucia de Berk case to illustrate this.

In a recent verdict (to be found under the label ECLI:NL:GHSHE:2018:421), the details of which do not concern us here, the court comments on a report of philosopher Ton Derksen, who had made a Bayesian analysis of the complete case. We read (our translation):

"Furthermore, a selection has been made concerning which aspects are discussed in the report. For instance, in section 2 (according to the technical investigators there had been no theft), it is only discussed that the technical investigators notice that there is no mess in the house; some drawers are open but it is otherwise a neat crime scene.

However, there are also other circumstances that play a role in deciding whether or not there really had been an (attempted) theft. For instance, nothing was stolen. [...] A last aspect concerns that no damage had been discovered to any of the doors or windows, so that it is not clear how possible thieves might have entered the house, and it remains a question how the thieves could have left the place so quickly. The front door was closed and right in front of the back gate, the body of the victim was lying. None of these aspects have been taken into account in the report."

The point made by us in commenting upon de approach of de Vos, and by the court in this quote, is that the selection of pieces of evidence taken into account, is a matter of choice. As such, the numbers arising from a computation along these lines cannot and should not be taken as a statement about the case in its entirety.

A few pages later in the same verdict, the court warns the reader against an overly optimistic use of the likelihood approach (our translation):

"The Bayesian method [...] has received a lot of criticism in the literature. First of all the method assumes that, given the hypotheses, all pieces of evidence are statistically independent of each other. Apart from that it is doubtful whether or not the probabilities [...] are expressible in numbers that we can trust. The use of numbers makes an impression of objectivity. The estimation of prior probabilities [...] can only be done subjectively, and this subjective probability can not be tested in an objective way. Finally it is questionable whether or not degrees of belief obey the axioms of probability theory."

We find this a rather striking summary of some of the problems one encounters when trying to make a Bayesian computation of a full (and often complicated case). The last sentence of the quote might refer to the problems of probabilities that we have discussed in Chapter 1.

We end our small detour by quoting another statement of a Dutch court in relation to the use of likelihood ratios. The quote can be found in verdict numbered ECLI:NL:RBZWB:2016:3060 (our translation):

"The court does not rule out that this method [the court refers to the likelihood approach] if applied correctly, can help in finding the truth, but the final answer to the question whether or not an accusation can be lawfully and convincingly proved, is not a question that can be answered with probability theory. The answer to this question is and remains the responsibility of the judge."

This seems to be a healthy and defendable attitude towards the use of probability in this context. Probability and statistics may certainly help, but will not on their own provide definite and final answers.

5.5.3 Are There Better Statistical Approaches?

We now return to the Lucia de Berk case. We have concluded that the method of Elffers was not suitable, and in addition that his calculation of p-values was downright wrong. The Bayesian approach of Aart de Vos was far from convincing as well. Is there a better way to treat this case from a probabilistic point of view? Can statistics mean anything at all in this case and is there a more convincing way to treat this case with the likelihood ratio approach?

We think that the answer is yes, even when you remain within the realm of Elffers' simple mathematical model. Hence, we take from Elffers' approach that the probability of an incident during a given shift is given by some number p, but now we explicitly want to be able to vary p among nurses and among wards. We would like to choose a *base rate*, that is, a probability of an incident in a particular ward under normal and non-suspicious circumstances. In the first ward at the JCH, this immediately poses a problem, since according to the data, no incident was reported outside shifts taken care of by Lucia de Berk. For this reason we find it hard to believe that data is trustworthy, and we ignore this first ward for the moment and come back to it later.

For the second and third ward we argue as follows. We define the base rate for each ward as the fraction of shifts with an incident outside the shifts of Lucia de Berk. This leads to $4/335$ and $9/281$ for the second and third ward respectively. With these numbers fixed we formulate our hypotheses. The hypothesis of innocence is that Lucia de Berk has the same base rate of incident during her shifts. In addition, for each $x \in [0, 1]$ we define H_x as the hypothesis that the probability of an incident during a shift of Lucia de Berk in RCH-41 is equal to $4/335+331x/335$, and in RCH-42 equal to $9/281+272x/281$. In words, H_x constitutes the hypothesis that there is a probability x that during a shift of Lucia de Berk, an incident takes place that would not have taken place without her. Or, to put it differently, we assume that in RCH-41 there is a base rate of $4/335$ for the probability of an incident. If such a "base-rate incident" does not take place, then there is (under H_x) an additional probability x that Lucia de Berk causes an incident, and similarly in the RCH-42 ward. In this notation, H_0 corresponds to the hypothesis of innocence of Lucia de Berk.

With these hypotheses in place we can compute likelihood ratios corresponding to the simultaneous data in RCH-41 and RCH-42. It is not difficult to compute the likelihood ratio of H_x versus H_0. Indeed, we write

$$p(x) = \frac{4}{335} + \frac{331x}{335}$$

and

$$q(x) = \frac{9}{281} + \frac{272x}{281}$$

for the "success" probabilities in the two wards RCH-41 and RCH-42 respectively. The probability of the observed incidents during the shifts of Lucia de Berk in the two wards together, is

$$f(x) := p(x)\binom{58}{5}q(x)^5(1 - q(x))^{53}.$$

The likelihood ratio $f(x)/f(0)$ of H_x versus H_0 is now easily seen to be maximal for $x = 0.0757$ and in that case is equal to 43.03. The somewhat remarkable fact is, therefore, that in this model, no matter which value of x we take, there is not much evidence for H_x versus H_0. Indeed, in legal cases a likelihood ratio of this magnitude is not convincing evidence at all.

One can also make a different choice for the probability that Lucia de Berk witnesses an incident. For instance, we can let H_x correspond to the hypothesis that this probability is x in either ward. Under this assumption, a computation similar to the one above leads to the conclusion that the likelihood ratio for H_x

versus the innocence hypothesis in which Lucia de Berk simply follows the base rate probabilities, is maximal for $x = 0.102$ and equal to 52.46. So, also under these assumptions the evidence is not very convincing.

The reader may object that we have not used the data from the JCH, and that this part of the data is precisely the most incriminating. As we mentioned before, we find it hard to believe that the data is correct, since incidents will occur also during shifts of other nurses. In fact, this was confirmed in the report of the committee Grimbergen, a special committee that was asked to look into the matter after the court case against Lucia de Berk was already closed. They discovered that the data collection at the JCH was not done properly, and that certain incidents outside the shifts of Lucia de Berk were not reported, and, even worse, certain incidents outside her shifts were actually attributed to her shifts.

So although the ward at the JCH could in principle be treated in the same way as the other two wards, we do not think that this makes any sense given the above considerations. It seems impossible to make any meaningful calculation with the (partly corrupted) data from the first ward. This does not mean that we should ignore this ward completely. From the point of view of the likelihood approach that we discuss in this book, it might be appropriate (at least in principle) to let the data of first ward be summarized into prior odds against Lucia de Berk. Anyone is free to evaluate the (partly corrupted) data of the first ward and to turn these into prior odds. For instance, one might think that the data of the JCH is rather striking (which it seems to be) and as a result assign much higher prior odds against Lucia de Berk than without that data. It remains rather interesting though that the remaining evidence of the other two wards will hardly contribute to evidence against Lucia de Berk, and all in all we conclude that from a statistical point of view there is no strong case against the suspect at all.

In the legal process, Lucia de Berk was convicted for multiple murder twice, both in the original trial and in the court of appeal. After the second conviction, doubt arose and after the report of the aforementioned committee Grimbergen, Lucia de Berk was released from imprisonment, after spending more than seven years in jail.

5.6 The Case of the Information Telephone

The case that we discuss in this section can be found under label ECLI:NL:RBOBR: 2017:6556. The case was about accessory to murder, and concentrated on the question whether or not the suspect had informed the actual murderer about the whereabouts of the victim, by sending text messages from a mobile phone. We will denote this phone as the information phone. Based on the information of this text message, the victim was killed by various gun shots.

We first describe the case, and then discuss the presented statistical analysis, and finally draw some general conclusions.

In this case, various pieces of evidence were available, though none of them provided direct evidence that the suspect had actually sent the text messages to the gunman. The phone from which these messages had been sent had been identified, as well as the phone credit card that was used to activate it. The purchase of that card had been identified as well to have been done at a certain petrol station. The first piece of evidence was that the suspect's car had been recognized by an automatic number plate recognition (ANPR) camera, at a location and time close to the purchase of the card. When the card was purchased, a pack of Marlboro Gold cigarettes was also bought, and this happened to be the brand of cigarettes that the suspect smoked. A phone, from which the text messages were sent to the killer later, was activated moments after the purchase, and this phone seemed to have traveled together with the suspect's phone based on telecom data on the antennas that the phones communicated with, for a considerable amount of time.

A scenario thus was readily available: the suspect had driven her car to the petrol station, bought the card and cigarettes, then had activated the phone and kept it with her, until she sent the messages on the whereabouts of the victim. The phone was shut down after these events.

Let us now discuss the elements of the verdict that are relevant to us. The two main hypotheses were formulated as follows, where for notational convenience later on, we use H_p and H_d instead of H_1 and H_2 respectively:

H_p: The suspect was the user of the information phone;
H_d: Someone else was the user of the information phone.

The three different pieces of evidence were, each separately, taken into account in a likelihood ratio approach. Each of these pieces of evidence was assigned a corresponding likelihood ratio, which were then multiplied with each other. We discuss the pieces of evidence and the corresponding likelihood ratios now first.

The first piece of evidence concerned the suspect's car. In order to define a likelihood ratio for this, the following two sub-hypotheses were introduced:

H_1: The car of the suspect was used to buy the phone card;
H_1^a: Another car was used to buy the phone card.

The evidence (to be denoted by E_1) with respect to these hypotheses consisted of the camera registrations of the car of the suspect. Experts estimated that these camera registrations were 864 times more likely assuming H_1 than when assuming H_1^a. Hence the likelihood ratio of E_1 with respect to H_1 and H_1^a was concluded to be 864.

The verdict offers no insight as to how the number of 864 was calculated. In Chapter 3 we have argued that the likelihood ratio need not be accompanied by an interval reflecting uncertainty, and this is indeed how the likelihood ratio was presented here. However, in order to obtain such a number, we have to integrate over all probability distributions that reflect the expert's uncertainty. In this case, we are dealing with an ad hoc model that has to give a probability for the suspect's car to be registered by the ANPR camera at the moment when it was, and for such a model various choices will undoubtedly have to be made for which defensible alternatives exist that give, slightly or not, different answers. In such a case, we think that these assumptions preferably should also be disclosed, in order to make a proper defense possible. Clearly the hypotheses alone do not allow for a probabilistic assessment, in order to do so one must make various additional assumptions. It is, without computations, clear that the registration of the suspect's car is of some evidential value. A risk in modeling would be that one tunes the model until its result corresponds to one's intuition about the strength of the evidence. In that case, one could have also skipped the model and directly given a number, or order of magnitude, one finds reasonable. This makes it all the more important that the evaluation model is open to being challenged.

In this case, a critical examination was indeed done. The statistical evaluation was reviewed by a statistician who concluded that the model did indeed contain some questionable assumptions, but that in his opinion altering these would not have led to a much different result.

The second piece of evidence concerned the information phone itself. The suspect also had her own phone, and based on location details of both phones (which were obtained from telecom providers), the question arose as to whether the two phones had both been with the suspect, or that they had been traveling independently of each other. To this end, the following sub-hypotheses were considered:

H_2: The phone of the suspect and the information phone were with the same user throughout;
H_2^a: The two phones were with different users.

The Netherlands Forensic Institute (NFI) reported that the evidence E_2 (that is, the location details of both phones) was between 19 and 105 times more likely under H_2 than under H_2^a. Again we have no insight in the precise details of these values, but they were based on statistical considerations of independently moving telephones.

Contrary to for the first piece of evidence, in this case reported an *interval* for the likelihood ratio. In Chapter 3 we discussed intervals around reported likelihood ratios in great detail, and we argued that from a methodological point of view a likelihood ratio does *not* have to be accompanied by such an interval. One reason to do so nevertheless is when the expert has refrained from integrating out all uncertainty. It could, for example, be the case that for some model parameters the expert can identify a lower and upper bound, but does not specify a probability distribution between these bounds. In the latter case, the bounds on the parameters can lead the expert to give bounds on the likelihood ratio, and obtain an interval within which the likelihood ratio lies for any probability distribution of the model parameters that the expert would be willing to consider. The resulting interval provides a lower bound of the strength of the evidence (useful to the prosecution) and an upper bound (useful for the defense).

But as we have also seen in Chapter 3, other types of intervals exist as well and are used by forensic statisticians. If a posterior likelihood ratio distribution is reported, then it must be the case that the expert was able to define all needed probability distributions, but then the likelihood ratio should be given as the number that comes out, and the interval should only be reported as relating to the likelihood ratio that could be obtained if we were to obtain more data on the model parameters. Yet other types of intervals are also in use. In order for anyone to be able to properly interpret the report, it is therefore at the very least necessary to indicate what type of interval is reported. The report in this case did not mention that, so there is no way to know this.

Finally, there was a third piece of evidence, namely that the phone credit card was purchased together with Marlboro Gold cigarettes. It was known that the suspect smoked Marlboro Gold cigarettes. Hence the following sub-hypotheses were formulated:

H_3: The suspect bought the phone credit card;
H_3^a: Someone else bought the phone credit card.

The Netherlands Forensic Institute attributed a likelihood ratio of 8 to the evidence (buying Marlboro Gold cigarettes together with the activity card, denoted E_3) concerning these two hypotheses. Again, we have no way of knowing how this number was obtained.

In order to incorporate these findings into the main hypotheses H_p and H_d, the court now continues by enumerating and summarizing a number of assumptions, namely:

(A1) Suspect was the user of the car on the camera registrations;
(A2) Suspect was the user of her own telephone (not the information phone);
(A3) Suspect smoked Marlboro Gold cigarettes;
(A4) The phone credit card was bought by the user of the information phone;
(A5) Under H_2^a the suspect and the actual user of the information phone traveled independently.

The court then writes that with these additional assumptions, the likelihood ratios obtained for the separate pieces of evidence can be used also as likelihood ratio for the main hypotheses and multiplied with each other. Let us analyze this claim.

First of all, we see that (A4) implies that we need only prove that the suspect bought the card. The court makes this assumption based on the very short period between the purchase of the card and the activation of the phone. However, the court then rules out some possibilities. One alternative could be that the suspect drove to the petrol station in the company of a second person, who bought the card and cigarettes, activated the phone, and then remained with the suspect. Perhaps such a scenario was deemed implausible on good grounds, but no mention of such considerations can be found in the verdict. This assumption explicitly rules out some alternative scenarios, for example, the scenario that the suspect had given her car and phone to a friend, who went to buy the card and cigarettes, activated and used the information phone, and also kept the suspect's phone, while the suspect was at home being a law-abiding citizen unaware of the criminal endeavors of her friend. It is of course inevitable that some scenarios that are not strictly speaking ruled out by the presented evidence are discarded as too unlikely; and it will be impossible to enumerate all of them.

The hypotheses H_1, H_2, H_3 together imply H_p, but in fact, from assumption (A4) H_3 alone already does so. It is therefore implicit in the reasoning that if H_3 holds (the suspect bought the card) that then also H_1 and H_2 hold. For H_1 this makes sense, because the suspect's car was on camera, and by (A1) the suspect was in the car and therefore must have used the car to go and buy the card. For H_2 this follows again from (A4), stating that the buyer of the card is the user of the phone, and therefore if the suspect bought the card she used the phone and it therefore traveled with her own phone by assumption (A2). Therefore under H_p, all three hypotheses H_1, H_2, H_3 hold.

The next question is whether under H_d, all of H_1^a, H_2^a, H_3^a hold. If H_d holds, then the suspect was not the user of the phone. Therefore under (A4), she did not buy it either, so H_3^a holds. If she did not buy the card, then H_1^a holds. If she did not buy the card nor use the phone, the phone must have traveled independently unless it was carried by a second person in the company of the suspect, and we have just seen that this scenario seems to have been tacitly ruled out.

We see that H_p implies H_1, H_2, H_3 and that H_d implies H_1^a, H_2^a, H_3^a. But since H_p and H_d are each other's complement, all hypotheses H_i actually coincide with H_p and all H_i^a with H_d. In other words, if any of the H_i is true then all of them are and H_p as well, and if any of the H_i^a is true then all of them are and H_d as well.

We now write

$$\frac{P(H_1, H_2, H_3 \mid E_1, E_2, E_3)}{P(H_1^a, H_2^a, H_3^a \mid E_1, E_2, E_3)} = \frac{P(E_1, E_2, E_3 \mid H_1, H_2, H_3)}{P(E_1, E_2, E_3 \mid H_1^a, H_2^a, H_3^a)} \times \frac{P(H_1, H_2, H_3)}{P(H_1^a, H_2^a, H_3^a)}$$

$$= \frac{P(E_1 \mid H_1, H_2, H_3)}{P(E_1 \mid H_1^a, H_2^a, H_3^a)} \times \frac{P(E_2 \mid E_1, H_1, H_2, H_3)}{P(E_2 \mid E_1, H_1^a, H_2^a, H_3^a)}$$

$$\times \frac{P(E_3 \mid E_1, E_2, H_1, H_2, H_3)}{P(E_3 \mid E_1, E_2, H_1^a, H_2^a, H_3^a)} \times \frac{P(H_1)}{P(H_1^a)}$$

$$\times \frac{P(H_2, H_3 \mid H_1)}{P(H_2^a, H_3^a \mid H_1^a)}.$$

Looking at the first term in the last expression, if we know that H_1 occurs, then so do H_2, H_3, so we may omit them from the conditioning, similarly in the denominator, and we get the reported likelihood ratio $LR_{H_1, H_1^a}(E_1)$. For the second term, we can again omit H_1, H_3 and their alternatives from the conditioning and we need to know whether the probability of the location data of the phones depends on E_1, the fact that the suspect's car was on the ANPR camera. The telecom data, however, are concerned with the phones only, and so E_1 is not relevant, at least if we assume that the experiments leading to the likelihood ratio for H_2 versus H_2^a were carried out with telephones that started at the same location. For the last likelihood ratio, we need to verify that E_1 and E_2 do not influence the probability of E_3, given either H_p or H_d. Again, we would consider this to be the case.

For the numerator in the last term we argue as follows: once H_1 occurs, then H_2 and H_3 occur as well, and similarly for the denominator. Hence the last term is 1, and

$$\frac{P(H_p \mid E_1, E_2, E_3)}{P(H_d \mid E_1, E_2, E_3)} = \frac{P(E_1 \mid H_1)}{P(E_1 \mid H_1^a)} \times \frac{P(E_2 \mid H_2)}{P(E_2 \mid H_2^a)} \times \frac{P(E_3 \mid H_3)}{P(E_3 \mid H_3^a)} \times \frac{P(H_p)}{P(H_d)}.$$
(5.3)

Thus, in this case we see that the assumptions that were made justify the multiplication of the likelihood ratios, and the claim of the court that

$$LR_{H_p, H_d}(E_1, E_2, E_3) = LR_{H_1, H_1^a}(E_1) \times LR_{H_2, H_2^a}(E_2) \times LR_{H_3, H_3^a}(E_3)$$

is correct.

The next question for the court is how to come up with prior odds. When the hypotheses of interest become more detailed and complicated, it might become more difficult or even impossible to assign prior odds in any meaningful way. How would one assess prior odds on H_p versus H_d above? Because of the assumptions, prior odds on H_1 versus H_1^a are the same as for H_2 versus H_2^a and for H_3 versus H_3^a, and also for H_p versus H_d. In the verdict the court writes that it considers it to be proven that the suspect was the user of the information phone, based on the presented evidence interpreted in a common framework. No assessment of the prior odds is (explicitly) done.

5.7 Two Burglary Cases

In this section we discuss two burglary cases which are rather interesting from a mathematical point of view. The first case because it involves combination of evidence, the second case because it involves an explicit description of prior information.

5.7.1 A Case with Several Weak Pieces of Evidence

During the night of June 22, 2013, a robbery took place. Three men entered a house, used significance violence against the family living there, and disappeared with a certain amount of stolen things. The case (labeled ECLI:NL:GHARL:2015: 5572) is against a man who was suspected to be one of the three intruders.

The suspect had an alibi: he claimed to have spent the night with his girl-friend, something that was confirmed under oath by the girlfriend herself. Nevertheless, there were three pieces of incriminating evidence that were assessed by the court.

The first piece of evidence consisted of DNA material that was found on a weapon which was left behind by the intruders. The source of this DNA material was not disputed, but the suspect claimed that he had used the weapon earlier when shooting for fun at empty cans in the house of one of the other suspects in the case. The court concludes that "the DNA trace in itself does not provide concluding evidence that the trace was left behind during the robbery" (our translation).

The second piece of evidence consisted of a glove that was found in a bedroom in the house of the mother of the suspect. The inside of the glove contained cell material that gave strong evidence in favor of coming from one of the family members in the house that was robbed. But on the glove, there was also some DNA that gave evidence in favor of coming from the suspect versus from an unknown person, and material from at least two other persons as well. The court now claims that the DNA expert in the case concluded that "the hypothesis that the glove contained DNA from the suspect is extremely more likely than the hypothesis that the material came from three random and unknown persons" (our translation). We assume that it was the court, not the report of the expert, that committed the prosecutor's fallacy of mixing up likelihood ratio with posterior odds here.

The court continues with an assessment of the conclusion of the expert. The alternative hypothesis of three unrelated and random persons may not be the appropriate one, according to the court. The bedroom in the house of the suspect's mother was also used by family members of the suspect, for instance by his brother. The verdict does not contain a statement about the likelihood ratio which would correspond to the brother of the suspect being one of the donors of the DNA mixture, something one might have expected perhaps. In any case the court concludes that this piece of evidence cannot be seen as decisive evidence that the suspect was one of the intruders.

The final piece of evidence consisted of a shoe trace which was found some 350 meters away from the scene of the crime. The profile of this shoe trace matched with the profile of one of the shoes that was found in the house of the mother of the suspect. On this shoe, DNA of at least five persons was found, including DNA that gave evidence in favor of being from the suspect relative to being from an unknown person. The suspect claimed that the size of this shoe was not his size, and that the shoe belonged to his brother anyway. The court concludes that the shoe trace was incriminating, but constituted no direct evidence that the suspect was one of the intruders. Therefore, also this piece of evidence cannot serve as evidence that the suspect was one of the intruders.

The court concludes with the statement that there is no compelling evidence that the suspect was one of the intruders, and decides not guilty.

How should we assess the course of affairs in this case? First of all, it is rather strange that the very fact that a glove with cell material that strongly appears to come from one of the family members on it was found at the house of the mother of the suspect, was not identified as a piece of evidence in itself. It would be hard to assign a likelihood ratio to this evidence in relation to the guilt versus not guilt hypotheses, but it is obvious that the presence of the glove is hard to explain if the suspect is not guilty (or his brother for that matter).

However, perhaps the more important issue is the structure of the reasoning of the court. There are three pieces of evidence E_1, E_2, and E_3, namely the DNA on the weapon, the traces on the glove, and the shoe trace, respectively. If these pieces of evidence are judged to be conditionally independent given any of the hypotheses (see Section 2.2.1), then the likelihood ratio corresponding to the three pieces of evidence E_1, E_2, and E_3 together can be obtained by multiplying the individual likelihood ratios. So even when each of the individual likelihood ratios of E_1, E_2, and E_3 are in themselves not convincing, their product can be quite large and rather compelling. Even if each of the pieces of evidence E_1, E_2, and E_3 are not strong evidence on their own (something that can be quite correct here), sub-sequentially concluding that *hence* there is no convincing evidence, is a principle mistake. Many pieces of evidence can accumulate into a very strong piece of evidence when taken together. Of course this incriminating evidence should then also be combined with he exculpatory evidence of the witness statement of the girlfriend of the suspect.

A second issue of interest from our point of view, similar to the previous case, is how the suspect was found in this case. The verdict sheds no light on this matter, so we have to speculate. Perhaps the suspect was found by searching a DNA database with the DNA profile that was found on the weapon. (We discuss DNA databases in detail in Chapter 11.) In that case, the prior probability for the guilty hypothesis H_1 will be small, as is always the case with a data-driven hypothesis. The point is that without knowledge of how the suspect was identified, it is difficult if not impossible to produce posterior odds, and the strength of the full case can in principle not be determined.

This issue, as a side remark, routinely comes up in the legal system of the United States, where jury members are not supposed to know how suspects were identified. Although there are sometimes good reasons for this, we do note that his makes it in principle impossible for jury members to evaluate (subjective) posterior odds. They can decide on the appropriate likelihood ratio (in principle) but not on the full case since they will not be able to produce prior odds. Hence, the mathematics makes it clear that there is a fundamental problem with this specific rule about not being allowed to know about how the suspect was identified.

5.7.2 A Burglary Case in Rotterdam

In 2006 a burglary took place in Rotterdam, and several witnesses described some characteristics of a man running way from the scene of the crime. The burglary took place by smashing a window, and on the curtains behind the window a blood trace was found which was assumed was left behind by the intruder. The DNA profile of this trace was determined but a database comparison did not result in a match and the case remained unsolved.

Three years later, in 2009, a suspect was identified because his DNA (taken from him because he had been convicted for another burglary) matched the DNA of the 2006 burglary. As a result of this match, this person became a suspect in the case. The legal case against this suspect took place in The Hague, and can be found under number LJN:BQ9005.

The DNA profile at the scene of the crime was concluded to have a population frequency of at most one in a billion. However, the suspect declared that he had a fraternal twin brother. So the court asked the Netherlands Forensic Institute (NFI) to compute the probability that a given brother of the suspect had the same DNA profile, based on 15 loci. The NFI declared that this probability was at most one in a million. As such, the possibility that the twin brother of the suspect had the same DNA profile was discarded by the court.

The court now continues with assessing that the evidential value of the DNA match is very high. After that, they state the following (our translation):

"The court also concludes that the suspect, from Moroccan origin, satisfies the description of the witness who had seen the men leaving the place of the burglary. Furthermore, the suspect has been prosecuted before, he worked in the same city as where the burglary took place, and he was declared guilty in a second burglary case. As such, the accusation and the DNA match should not be surprising."

What the court is doing here is assessing prior odds. The DNA match provides very strong evidence, but we have seen that this could possibly be compensated for by very small prior odds. Here, however, the court seems to be aware of this possibility, and explains why certain facts make it not so unreasonable to view suspect as a suspect in this case.

We are not in a position to judge whether or not this course of affairs is legally acceptable. We have presented the case to many legal representatives in the Netherlands and the opinions differ greatly. All we can say is that, from a mathematical point of view, the line of reasoning of the court seems in principle correct.

5.8 Summary and Conclusions

In this chapter we have discussed some well-known, and also some less well-known actual legal cases, and investigated the use of the theory that we have discussed so far in each of these cases. In the case of the link hammer, the discussion was mostly around the choice of the alternative population for the murder weapon: how we can derive posterior odds from likelihood ratios comparing the suspected weapon with different classes of alternatives. We have then gone into the combination of evidence, and gave examples where ignoring conditional dependence may overstate or understate the likelihood ratio. We then discussed two cases, the ones of Sally Clark and the death of the linesman, where a pitfall is to interpret a small probability of the evidence under one hypothesis as a reason to reject that hypothesis. This can both lead to an unjustified conviction (Sally Clark) or unjustified lack of conviction (as could have happened in the linesman case). We also discussed the case of Lucia de Berk, a nurse initially convicted for killing several patients, to be released later. We discussed the evidence, previous analyses of it, and also gave our own evaluation of some of it. In the telephone case, we found an example where the court combined several pieces of evidence, all of which were statistically evaluated, and our main conclusion is that we find this is rather well done. Finally we discussed two burglary cases.

5.9 Bibliographical Notes

The link hammer case was discussed in [89] (in Dutch). The case of Sally Clark was discussed in [53]. The Lucia de Berk case was discussed in detail in [101], and implicitly in [96]. Example 5.2.3 is taken from [56]. Some aspects of the statistical method used in the telephone case in Section 5.6 are discussed in [26]. The other cases that we discussed have, as far as we are aware, not been treated in the literature. A case that has received a lot of attention but has not been treated here is the People v. Simpson case, see for instance [88]. See [135] for a general discussion of the role of statistics in casework.

6

Bayesian Networks

We have seen that analyzing a complicated situation with Bayes' rule is not straight-forward. Many choices have to be made, and dealing with dependencies is a potential source of problems and mistakes. The likelihood ratio framework that we have extensively discussed only allows for a "linear" representation of various pieces of evidence, in the sense that one must evaluate one piece of evidence after another, each time taking care of potential (conditional) dependencies, as in formula (2.13).

When there are many random variables in the model and the situation becomes more complicated, it might become more or less impossible to keep track of all dependencies. For such situations, it has been suggested that using a *Bayesian network* might be more appropriate. A Bayesian network is a qualitative graphical representation of a joint probability distribution of several random variables. In this chapter, we introduce and discuss these Bayesian networks. We will give an interpretation of Bayesian networks suitable for our purposes, and we will investigate the added value of such networks in forensic and legal situations.

6.1 The Basics

In a forensic context we need to deal with various hypotheses, background information and with multiple pieces of evidence. We are primarily interested in (probabilistic) statements about the truth of certain hypotheses, given our background information and given certain pieces of evidence. In our typical notation, we interpret a hypothesis H, background information I or a piece of evidence E as events in an outcome space, and ask for $P(H \mid E, I)$, that is, the probability that H is true, given the available evidence and background information.

A Bayesian network is nothing but a certain graphical representation of a joint distribution of multiple random variables. In order to use a Bayesian network we need to formulate the outcome of an experiment in terms of random variables, and

Figure 6.1 A Bayesian network with two nodes.

there is a simple way to do this. Indeed, we use indicator random variables 1_E for events E, where $1_E = 1$ if E occurs, and $1_E = 0$ otherwise. A node in a Bayesian network corresponding to 1_E will often still be denoted by E, for typographical reasons.

The simplest example of a Bayesian network is the representation corresponding to the joint distribution of two random variables X and Y. We can write

$$P(X = x, Y = y) = P(X = x)P(Y = y \mid X = x),$$

and this factorization can be displayed graphically by a graph with two nodes labeled X and Y respectively, and a directed arrow from X to Y; see Figure 6.1.

We draw an arrow from X to Y since in the factorization the conditional probability of Y given X appears. We say that X is a *parent* of Y and that Y is a *child* of X. Obviously this factorization is not unique, since we can also write $P(X = x, Y = y) = P(Y = y)P(X = x \mid Y = y)$, which is represented by the same nodes but with the direction of the arrow reversed.

The graphical representation in Figure 6.1 only gives a qualitative description of the joint distribution of X and Y. To complete the description we need to assign numerical values to $P(X = x)$ and to $P(Y = y \mid X = x)$ for all possible values of x and y. Since node X has no parent in the graph, we say that $P(X = x)$ is the *prior* probability of $\{X = x\}$.

Obviously, any distribution of a finite number of variables can be represented likewise by a suitable factorization of the joint distribution. For instance, with four variables X, Y, U, and V we can write

$$P(X = x, Y = y, U = u, V = v) = P(X = x)P(Y = y \mid X = x)$$
$$\times\ P(U = u \mid X = x, Y = y)P(V = v \mid X = x, Y = y, U = u).$$

This factorization can also be represented graphically. The term $P(U = u \mid X = x, Y = y)$ yields arrows from both X to U and Y to U, and with this understanding the resulting network is given in Figure 6.2. Both X and Y are now parents of U.

If, for whatever reason, we can factorize the joint distribution of several random variables with fewer factors, then the ensuing Bayesian network will become sparser. For instance, if it so happens that we can write

$$P(X = x, Y = y, U = u, V = v) = P(X = x)P(Y = y) \qquad (6.1)$$
$$\times\ P(U = u \mid X = x)P(V = v \mid X = x, Y = y, U = u),$$

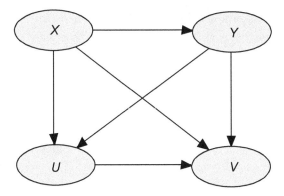

Figure 6.2 A general Bayesian network with four nodes.

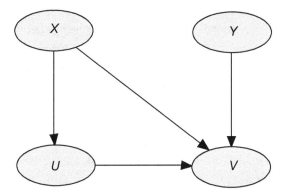

Figure 6.3 The Bayesian network with four nodes corresponding to the representation in (6.1).

then the corresponding network is given in Figure 6.3. X and Y are the *prior* nodes of the network, as they have no parents.

It follows from the construction that a Bayesian network is a directed graph with no cycles, and therefore it is sometimes also called a DAG (directed acyclic graph). In order to complete the description of the network, we need to assign numerical values to the conditional probability distributions of each node conditional on the states of its parents, as well as the distributions of the states of the prior nodes. Then a joint probability distribution on the random variables corresponding to the nodes is defined, thanks to the lack of cycles in the graph.

As we have seen, the Bayesian network is generally not unique for a joint distribution, as already the simple example in Figure 6.1 shows. In large networks, it may not be easy to see whether different networks define the same conditional probability structure. The question arises as to how, when building a network, to choose between the various possible equivalent networks.

Arrows are often interpreted in a causal way: when there is an arrow from X to Y, one may interpret this as X being a cause of the effect Y. We should keep in mind though that from a joint probability distribution itself, one cannot distinguish cause from effect.

When designing a network, it is natural to aim for as few arrows as possible that are needed to describe the joint probability distribution that we have. Suppose that we have our set of random variables selected, and hence we have the collection of nodes. When should there be an arrow between two nodes? We would like not to draw one if we can do without. With our epistemic interpretation of probability, an arrow between X and Y means that (i) knowledge on X is relevant for Y, that is, X and Y are not independent, and (ii) there is no collection of nodes such that knowledge of their states would make knowledge of X irrelevant for the probability distribution of the states Y can be in. The latter requirement means that there is no collection U of nodes such that X and Y are conditionally independent given U.

This leads to an interpretation of one node being a *direct effect* of the other one, where directness only has a meaning within the network, namely that there is no way to gather information on the network nodes that makes the state of the first node irrelevant for the second. This interpretation of direct effect does not have a natural direction stemming from the network: for example, one may equally well argue that a suspect is innocent because there is no DNA match, or that there is no DNA match because the suspect is innocent. Also, the interpretation of direct effect is only valid within the network: in a network at hand, one may have an arrow $X \rightarrow Y$, whereas in a more refined network one might introduce another random variable Z such that we now have $X \rightarrow Z \rightarrow Y$ meaning that X is no longer a direct effect of Y or the other way around; the random variable Z then describes how the effect of X on Y takes place.

Let us now apply all this by considering a simple forensic example where we have a single hypothesis H and one piece of evidence E. In a typical situation we are interested in making probabilistic statements about H given the evidence, but we only know something about the conditional probabilities of the evidence given the truth or falseness of H. Hence, the only *useful* arrow in two-node network with nodes H and E is from H to E as in Figure 6.4. It is not wrong to draw the arrow in the opposite direction, but it will not help us, since we have no way of directly assigning a numerical value to $P(H \mid E)$. Indeed, the whole point of invoking Bayes' rule is to infer something about $P(H \mid E)$ using $P(E \mid H)$, $P(E \mid H^c)$ and $P(H)$ to begin with. Hence the *natural* Bayesian network for this situation is the one in Figure 6.4.

The joint probability distribution of H and E is now determined by the marginal distribution of H together with the conditional distribution of the truth of E given H or H^c. The former is just another name for the prior probability of H and H^c and

Table 6.1 *The probability table of the* Evidence
node in the network in Figure 6.4.

Hypothesis	True	False
True	0.99	0.1
False	0.01	0.9

Figure 6.4 The structure of a Bayesian network with one hypothesis and one evidence node.

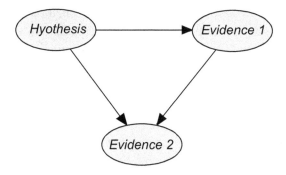

Figure 6.5 The structure of a Bayesian network with one hypothesis and two evidence nodes.

an example of the latter is given in Table 6.1. This table (and all similar tables which follow) should be read as follows. The top row(s) contains the possible values of the appropriate parental node, and the True and False in the first column correspond to the state of the child node. For instance, the value 0.99 in the Table 6.1 is the probability of the occurrence of the evidence given that the hypothesis is true, and likewise for the other entries. From the table we can read off that $LR_{H,H^c}(E)$ is given by $P(E \mid H)/P(E \mid H^c) = 0.99/0.1 = 9.9$.

Next we discuss an example with two pieces of evidence. The structure of the Bayesian network is given in Figure 6.5. In this case we need two tables with conditional probabilities, one for each evidence node. Let us say that that the probability table of the *Evidence 1* node is the same as in Table 6.1 and that the probability table of the *Evidence 2* node is given in Table 6.2. Furthermore, we again set the prior probability for H to be true to 0.1.

Table 6.2 *The probability table of the* Evidence 2
node in the network in Figure 6.5.

Evidence 1	True		False	
Hypothesis	True	False	True	False
True	0.8	0.7	0.1	0.05
False	0.2	0.3	0.9	0.95

We can now perform calculations in this network. For each node one can compute the probability that it is in one of its states. Furthermore, the user can force a specific node into a specific state upon which the software can update the probability distributions of all other nodes, conditioned on the specific state of the specific node. One of the pleasant aspects of Bayesian networks is that various software packages exist which are able to quickly perform computations that would be rather tiresome or downright impossible by hand. The computations in this chapter have been carried out using the Hugin 8.6 © package. Designing efficient computational algorithms for Bayesian networks is a very interesting topic in itself, but we will not delve into that matter in this book.

Within the software, after having designed the network, it is easy to compute the conditional probabilities of any desired event conditioned on any set of outcomes. Since the Bayesian network, together with the probability tables, contains all information about the full joint distribution of the random variables involved, one should in principle be able to compute everything one needs to know about this joint distribution with the software.

Let us again look at Figure 6.5. If we condition on *Evidence 1* to be true, then the software computes the conditional probability for H to be true as 0.5238. Indeed, as we saw, the likelihood ratio is 9.9 and the prior odds were 1/9, so the posterior odds on H are 1.1 and the posterior probability of H is 11/21, which evaluates to 0.5238 with the given precision.

Similarly, if we condition on *Evidence 2* to be true we find that the conditional probability of H is equal to 0.4338. Indeed, $P(E_2 \mid H) = P(E_2 \mid E_1, H)$ $P(E_1 \mid H) + P(E_2 \mid E_1^c, H)P(E_1^c \mid H) = 0.793$ and similarly $P(E_2 \mid H^c) = 0.115$, leading to the likelihood ratio of 793/115 and the computed posterior probability for H.

If both *Evidence 1* and *Evidence 2* are set to be true, then the conditional probability of H is 0.5570. Again the likelihood ratio can be computed to be 792/70, leading to the computed posterior probability.

In a Bayesian network, we can query the nodes. Conditioning on observed evidence therefore give us posterior probabilities, but no likelihood ratios, at least not directly. However, if one wishes, one can easily retrieve the likelihood ratios corresponding to the various pieces of evidence. The easiest way to do so is to let the prior odds on H be even, which implies that the likelihood ratio becomes equal to the posterior odds, so that the likelihood ratio can be obtained from the posterior probability that the network computes for the hypothesis node.

Alternatively we can use the probability tables on the nodes. For this example, from Table 6.1 we read that $LR_{H,H^c}(E_1) = 0.99/0.1 = 9.9$. For $LR_{H,H^c}(E_2)$ we cannot simply refer to Table 6.2. Instead we can condition on H and let the software update the node for E_2, where it will compute $P(E_2 \mid H) = 0.793$ and $P(E_2 \mid H^c) = 0.115$, leading to a likelihood ratio of 6.90. Indeed, since the network, together with the assigned probabilities completely determine the joint distribution, it must be the case that we can retrieve everything we want from the network. It follows, for instance, that in this case, the two pieces of evidence are not conditionally independent, since the likelihood ratio of the combined evidence is not the product of the individual likelihood ratios.

Figure 6.5 can easily be extended to multiple pieces of evidence, say $E_1, \ldots, E_m$. We can condition on any of these pieces of evidence to be true or false, and the Hugin software then easily computes the corresponding likelihood ratios. This network can be used to examine the multiple pieces of evidence one by one, and each time compute a likelihood ratio of the next piece of evidence, given either hypothesis and all previous information, see (2.13).

Does this mean that a Bayesian network can indeed be used in situations with complicated dependencies, a question posed in the introduction of this chapter? We can only use the Bayesian network if we have given all conditional probabilities necessary for the network. Assigning these conditional probabilities already requires knowledge of the interdependencies. As such, what is primarily gained is computational power and the visualization of the joint distribution. A Bayesian network is convenient and useful mostly *because* of the software, and it is perhaps reasonable to say that the Bayesian network is merely serving as a representation of the joint distribution of the variables involved *in order* to take advantage of precisely this software. As such, a Bayesian network is then mainly a computational tool when a joint distribution is already known.

6.2 Conditional Independence

When one designs a Bayesian network as the one in Figure 6.5, with multiple pieces of evidence, then certain conditional independence properties of the various pieces of evidence can be incorporated through the design of the geometry of the network, or through the corresponding conditional probabilities. That is, if we have, say, two pieces of evidence, then we can take a network as in Figure 6.5. If we want to

Table 6.3 *A probability table of the* Evidence 2 *node in the network in Figure 6.5 making the two pieces of evidence conditionally independent given H.*

Evidence 1	True		False	
H	True	False	True	False
True	0.8	0.7	0.8	0.7
False	0.2	0.3	0.2	0.3

make sure that the two pieces of evidence are conditionally independent of each other given H, then we can do one of two things. We can either delete the edge from *Evidence 1* to *Evidence 2*, or we can change the conditional probabilities in Table 6.2 in such a way that the *Evidence 1* node becomes irrelevant for *Evidence 2* given H. For instance, this can be done as in Table 6.3.

If we delete the edge from *Evidence 1* to *Evidence 2*, then the two pieces of evidence are conditionally independent given H for *any* assignment of the remaining (conditional) probabilities. Thus, from the network we will be able to deduce certain conditional independencies that are guaranteed by the structure, but there may be more of them depending on the probability tables. Of course, one would want to delete unnecessary arrows, both because this improves the visual appearance of the network, and because it will be beneficial for the algorithm performing the computations.

It is interesting to investigate how the notion of conditional independence relates to the geometry of Bayesian networks. After all, conditional independence plays an important role in the evaluation of multiple pieces of evidence. We recall that X and Y are conditionally independent given Z if

$$P(X = x \mid Y = y, Z = z) = P(X = x \mid Z = z), \tag{6.2}$$

for all values of x, y, and z. Whether or not X and Y are conditionally independent given Z depends on both the geometry of the network and on the assignment of the (conditional) probabilities. However, there are designs of networks which are such that two collections of nodes are conditional independent given a third collection for *any* assignment of the (conditional) probabilities.

To shed some light on this phenomenon we consider simple networks with only three nodes X, Y, and Z as in Figure 6.6. In the network in Figure 6.6a, X and Y are conditionally independent given Z, irrespective of the numerical values of the (conditional) probabilities involved. This may be obvious from the construction, but it is also easy to check algebraically. Indeed, the Bayesian network in Figure 6.6a corresponds to the factorization

$$P(X = x, Y = y, Z = z) = P(Z = z)P(X = x \mid Z = z)P(Y = y \mid Z = z)$$

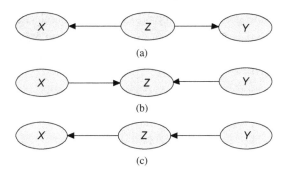

(a)

(b)

(c)

Figure 6.6 Three different Bayesian networks with three nodes. The first and third have the same conditional independence structure, but the second is different.

and hence

$$P(X = x \mid Y = y, Z = z) = \frac{P(X = x, Y = y, Z = z)}{P(Y = y, Z = z)}$$

$$= \frac{P(Z = z)P(X = x \mid Z = z)P(Y = y \mid Z = z)}{P(Z = z)P(Y = y \mid Z = z)}$$

$$= P(X = x \mid Z = z),$$

as required. Similarly, for the network in Figure 6.6c we have

$$P(X = x \mid Y = y, Z = z) = \frac{P(X = x, Y = y, Z = z)}{P(Y = y, Z = z)}$$

$$= \frac{P(Y = y)P(Z = z \mid Y = y)P(X = x \mid Z = z)}{P(Y = y)P(Z = z \mid Y = y)}$$

$$= P(X = x \mid Z = z).$$

Hence, as far as the the relations of conditional independence are concerned, the networks in Figures 6.6a and 6.6c are identical. But they are not identical for our purposes, since which network we wish to use depends on the context and on the available conditional probabilities.

It should be noted that the network in Figure 6.6b is qualitatively different from the viewpoint of conditional independence. Indeed, there are probability assignments under which X and Y are not conditionally independent given Z. For instance, suppose that X and Y are independent and both take values 0 and 1 with probability $1/2$. If $Z = \max\{X, Y\}$ then $P(X = 0 \mid Y = 0, Z = 1) = 0$ but $P(X = 0 \mid Z = 1) > 0$. For another, more forensic-oriented example, let X and Y denote the genotypes of the parents of a child, and Z denotes the genotype of the child. The genotypes of the parents are independent, but given knowledge about their child, this is no longer the case.

When can we in the general case conclude that two collections of nodes S and T are conditionally independent given a third set U? There exists an algorithm that can quickly check for a sufficient condition for this to be true. This algorithm runs as follows:

1. We delete all nodes in the Bayesian network that are not an ancestor of some node in S, T, or U, together with their arrows. (A node is an ancestor of another node, if the second node can be reached in the network by following a directed path starting at the first node.)
2. We add undirected edges between any two nodes that are parents of the same child, if they are not already joined by an arrow.
3. We delete all arrowheads, thus obtaining an undirected graph.
4. Look for a path in this undirected graph from S to T that has empty intersection with U. If there is no such path, then S and T are conditionally independent given U.

The simplest case is where S is a parent node of node T. These nodes are not conditionally independent, whatever we condition on, since the path $S \to T$ does not intersect U for any choice of U.

We do not prove this criterion here, but the complexity of the criterion suggests that conditional independence is not an easy matter, and rather difficult to establish from visual inspection of the network. We should keep this in mind when we discuss the construction of Bayesian networks in complex cases.

Let us apply the algorithm to the networks in Figure 6.6 to query whether X and Y are conditionally independent given Z. Starting with the network in Figure 6.6b, when we follow the steps of the algorithm, we end up with a network with undirected edges $\{X, Z\}$, $\{Z, Y\}$, and $\{X, Y\}$. Since now there is a path from X to Y avoiding Z (namely the direct edge between X and Y) we cannot conclude that X and Y are conditionally independent given Z, and we indeed know that this is not true in general.

When instead we start with the network in Figure 6.6a or 6.6c we end up with a network with only the undirected edges $\{X, Z\}$ and $\{Y, Z\}$. Any path from X to Y must go through Z and therefore the conditional independence property does hold.

What about independence of X and Y? When we take U to be empty, we must remove all nodes that are not an ancestor of either X or Y. The algorithm leads to the undirected graph with edges $\{X, Z\}$ and $\{Z, X\}$ for Figure 6.6a and 6.6c, and leads to isolated nodes X and Y for Figure 6.6b. Thus, only for Figure 6.6b are X and Y independent: in the other two cases there is a path from X to Y, and since any path has empty intersection with the empty set U, we cannot conclude independence.

To make the logic of this even more apparent, suppose that we think of the networks in Figure 6.6 as modeling DNA profiles. The networks may represent, respectively, a parent Z with two children X and Y, a child Z of parents X and Y, and a grandparent Y and grandchildren Z and X. In the first and third situation, the profiles of two children of the same parent are not independent and neither are the profile of a grandparent and grandchild. But, given the profile of the parent, the profiles of both children are independent. The same is true if we know the profile of the child in Figure 6.6c. On the other hand, for Figure 6.6b the parent's profiles are (marginally) independent, but no longer independent when we condition on the profile of their child. In fact, as we shall see in Chapter 7, one cannot distinguish between a grandparent–grandchild and a half-sibling relation using independent pieces of DNA, and the reason for that is essentially that the Bayesian networks in Figure 6.6a and 6.6c encode the same dependency structure.

These examples may provide some intuition as to why the above algorithm does what it promises to do. We remark, however, that the algorithm only provides a sufficient condition for the required conditional independence, and not a necessary one. Indeed, it may be the case, that the assignment of the (conditional) probabilities makes a certain Bayesian network enjoy a certain conditional independence property, whereas another assignment would not. In that case, the algorithm will not allow us to conclude that the required conditional independence property is true, even though it might be in special cases.

6.3 Some Examples of Bayesian Networks

Let us now look at some Bayesian networks that have been used in a forensic or legal context.

6.3.1 Evaluation of a Matching Characteristic

Consider the classical situation of some characteristic X, for instance a DNA profile, found at the scene of a crime and attributed to some source, say the offender, and a suspect who also has this characteristic. If we also want to take into account the possibility that the determinations whether suspect and source actually have the characteristic is imperfect, then the Bayesian network corresponding to this situation is given in Figure 6.7.

In this case the network structure is quite generic. It is not difficult to do the computations by hand. We have, in fact, done this in Section 4.7, to model the situation where the determination of the profile of the trace donor (the "source" in this network) does not always result in the actual profile of the trace donor. Nevertheless, it might be convenient to use this network, as quick computations can be done with the appropriate software. Someone who wants to review the assessment does not have to consider the possibility of errors in the calculation but needs only to inspect the network (including, of course, the conditional probability tables).

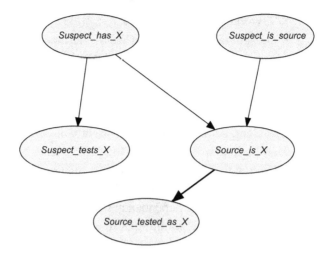

Figure 6.7 A full Bayesian network for a crime stain with a matching suspect.

As such, this network can provide an instance of a situation in which the actual joint distribution of the variables involved is not disputed. The Bayesian network can be used as an efficient calculator but does not offer any new insight.

6.3.2 The Jury Fallacy

In the previous example, the joint probability distribution of the random variables was quite canonical, and the network is used as a calculator. In the next example, however, this is perhaps different.

A jury, in a crime case, has found the defendant not guilty. It is subsequently revealed that the defendant had a previous conviction for a similar crime, something that was not known to the jury. Does this make you, as an outside observer of the case, less confident that the jury was correct in its verdict? Intuition may suggest that this is so: if the defendant has previous convictions, this may lead one to think that there is now a higher chance that he also committed this crime.

However, we can also reason in another way. Even if the defendant was found not guilty, apparently there was reason to charge him. If we further assume that some-one with previous convictions is more easily charged than someone without, then this means that less case-related evidence is needed against someone with previous convictions in order to be charged than for someone without previous convictions. Juries are not told whether there are any previous convictions. Therefore, if one learns about the previous convictions after having heard the not guilty verdict, this means that a good explanation for having been charged is available, and that the probability that there is strong evidence is now less than it was before we knew about the previous convictions. Therefore we actually become more convinced that the defendant is, as was decided by the jury, not guilty.

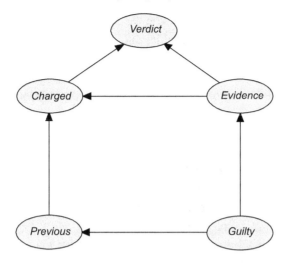

Figure 6.8 The Bayesian network network associated with the jury fallacy.

In order to demonstrate this, the Bayesian network in Figure 6.8 was proposed to study the situation. In this network the nodes *Charged*, *Guilty*, *Evidence*, and *Previous* take values either Yes or No. For the *Previous* node, state yes means that suspect has previously been convicted for a similar offence, while the meaning is clear for the other three nodes. The *Verdict* node takes values *Guilty*, *Not Guilty*, and *N/A*, where the last state refers to the situation in which there was no trial.

In this network, we indeed see the behavior that was announced, at least for certain, not unreasonable, choices of the probability tables: if we condition the verdict node on *Not Guilt*, the probability of the state *Yes* in the Guilty node is raised from its prior to a higher value, because a verdict means that someone was charged, and that happens more often to guilty suspects than to innocent ones. Subsequent conditioning on *Previous* to be Yes, results in a *lower* probability of guilt.

The question now, is whether we have learned this effect (called the jury fallacy) from the network. This is not so clear. It may equally well be the case that the network is designed for the purpose of yielding the intended effect, that was obtained via the qualitative reasoning above, and that the choices of probability tables are such that they provide the effect. Although we do not claim that this happened here, the present discussion highlights that if one produces an ad hoc network, there is a risk of modeling towards the intended effect. The potential exists to keep adapting the network until its results are qualitatively consistent with a conclusion that was already drawn prior to its construction. Unless the network (including its probability tables) is very carefully scrutinized, if possible by independent researchers, we can then not say that we have demonstrated much more than that it is possible to build a network displaying the desired outcomes. In other words, one has found a possible explanation for the effect, but the quality of that explanation is not immediately clear. The designers of this network have designed a joint distribution of five random variables and have visualized this joint distribution into a network. Part of the decision was to isolate precisely these five nodes, and no others. The question is then whether an independent team of researchers would have come up with the same network, based on the description of the situation at the beginning of this section.

The network does allow, once we agree on its structure (the nodes and the states they may have, and the arrows), for an analysis of the influence of the prior probabilities. But it remains unclear what this means. One would have to agree on the states the evidence node can have (does one distinguish between types of evidence, the number of evidential items, their strength?), or the one of the previous convictions (does one count their number, how long ago they were?), and so on. If one can show that the jury fallacy effect persists for many such choices, then perhaps we can draw the conclusion that it is real, without being able to say much on its size. But this was apparently also possible carrying out the heuristic reasoning prior to building the network.

6.3.3 *The Simonshaven Case*

In this section we discuss a murder case in the area of Rotterdam (the Netherlands) which became known as the *Simonshaven case*. We treat this case since an attempt has been made to actually model the full criminal legal case in detail. Of course every case is unique, but we believe that the difficulties encountered in this case are to a large extent generic.

On August 11, 2009, a woman was murdered in the recreational area Simonshaven in Rotterdam when she was there with her husband. The husband was prosecuted and found guilty, and the verdict was confirmed by the Court of Appeal. What makes this case interesting for us is that the defendant did not simply deny the charges but had a rather precise alternative story of events. He claimed that he had not killed his wife, but that she was killed by a man who had suddenly appeared from the bushes and had attacked her without any apparent reason. This story was not taken very seriously at first, but a couple of months after the murder had taken place, it actually happened that a hiding place in the form of a deep pit was found some 150 meters from where the woman was killed, belonging to a man (fictitiously called Perry Sultan in the network) responsible for the violent death of two women, whom he murdered without any apparent reason.

We do not need to spell out all details on the case here, but a number of things should be mentioned in order to be able to read the Bayesian network that we present below. The defendant and his wife were in a process of separation but their relation seemed to have become better lately. There were witness statements about people making love in the car of the defendant, there were witness statements about the car being seen at a petrol station, possibly to get rid of the murder weapon. Furthermore, the area had not been thoroughly searched immediately after the murder, so the number of people around was not really known, but thought to be relevant. The behavior of defendant was also considered to be strange, calling the alarm number 112 only very late and being rather confused when he instead called one of his children. It was also the case that the defendant was hardly wounded by the claimed attack from the man in the bushes, while his wife was killed. Finally, the man that appeared from the bushes a couple of months later possessed a map with certain marks on it, one mark being very close to the location of the murder. This man did not match the description of the man in the bushes as related by defendant, however.

In [67], a Bayesian network to describe this case was designed, and the result is shown in Figure 6.9. We have given enough background of the case so that the reader can understand what the nodes in the network represent. The network has three types of nodes: factual ones whose truth status cannot be observed, evidential ones whose status has been observed and that will be conditioned on, and credibility nodes that have to do with the reliability of the evidence, that is, which determine the effect of the evidence nodes on their parent fact nodes, and then beyond. This Bayesian network is very complicated, even without the assignment of all necessary conditional probabilities. By presenting this Bayesian network the authors implicitly claim that the joint distribution of all variables in the network does have something meaningful to say about the case at hand, and in particular about the question whether or not the defendant committed the murder. We now make a number of remarks about this Bayesian network.

First of all, we see that the motif in Figure 6.10 appears a few times in the network. This motif is included to take care of possible incredibility of certain pieces of evidence. For instance, if the hypothesis is that the defendant's car was at the pump station, and the evidence consists of a witness saying so, then this makes it more likely that the defendant's car was actually at the station if the witness is credible in comparison to the case where he is not. This sounds completely reasonable, but the caveat is the numerical values assigned to, in particular, the credibility node. In the network in Figure 6.9, the assignments for the credibility nodes in Figure 6.9 are summarized in Table 6.4. The numbers in Table 6.4 seem to be hard to defend (why would one takes these values?) and hard to criticize (because then one should argue in favor of different ones, which may be just as difficult). But of course, inferential consequences depend on the reliability of the evidence, and the network makes this apparent by explicitly adding the credibility nodes.

For the defendant's credibility node, the network assumes that the defendant's credibility is the same for the three nodes that are a child of it, even if the statements

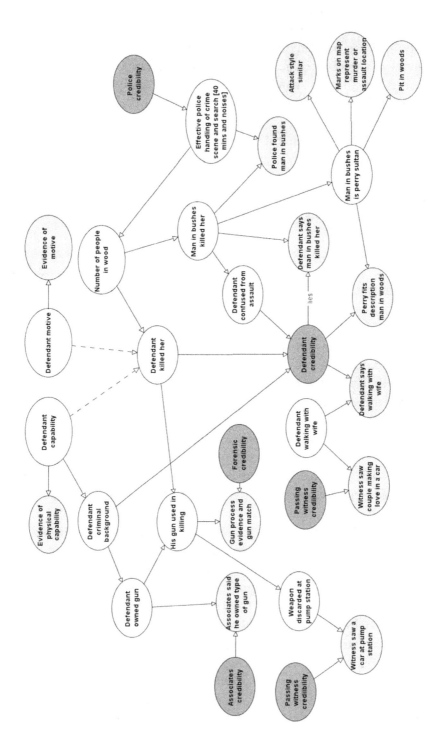

Figure 6.9 A Bayesian network for the Simonshaven case. (Illustration taken from [67] with kind permission.)

Table 6.4 *The assignment of credibilities in Figure 6.9.*
(∗) The figure of 0.53 in the Defendant credibility node
is the result of the priors for this node's parent nodes.

Credibility node	Probability credible
Police	0.9
Forensic	0.9
Defendant	0.53 (∗)
Associates	0.3
Passing witnesses	0.9

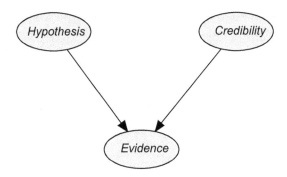

Figure 6.10 The generic credibility motif.

are quite different in nature. Another consequence of this choice is, for example, that if we change the number of people in the woods, then the probability that the defendant's description of the alleged attacker matches Perry Sultan changes, and conversely, that if we condition on this description fitting or not, the probability distribution on the number of people changes. It is not so easy to say whether this is reasonable.

Furthermore, the network contains probability distributions that may not be agreed upon by both parties, such as the conditional probability that the defendant killed his wife, given that he has a motive for doing so. If this is set to zero, then murder is impossible. The question emerges how to assign these probabilities. And one may wonder whether there should not be a direct arrow from motive to walking with wife, since if the defendant had a motive, he might create an opportunity by taking his wife out to an isolated place.

This discussion, while rather ad hoc, shows that using a Bayesian network cannot be done without making very many choices. It is, in other words, not enough to carry out a sensitivity analysis on the conditional probability tables, but one should also do this on the network structure itself. This seems hardly feasible and as a consequence, the posterior probability of 0.74 that the authors computed for the defendant having killed his wife, cannot be viewed as meaning anything outside the network. It is not easy to say to what extent this outcome depends on subjective choices, and to what extent it relies on the application of well-established generic methods. Without that being clear, the outcome cannot be granted a status above the one of an educated guess, at best.

We can compare this case to the telephone case that we have discussed in Section 5.6. Also in that case, various items of circumstantial evidence were evaluated in a unifying framework. However there the ambitions were more modest, being restricted to these evidential items only, and not needing prior probabilities as for the Simonshaven network. Moreover, fewer assumptions were made specifically about the suspect (such as the prior probability of walking with his wife in the Simonshaven case). The assumptions that the court made were clearly stated and in our opinion, the analysis in Section 5.6 is more convincing than the Bayesian network in the current case.

Modeling the whole case within a network is outside the usual province of the forensic expert. They do not normally reconstruct the entire chain of events, and cannot do so without having full access to all details in the case. These details are typically withheld on purpose, to prevent the scientists developing an unintended bias based on information not relevant for the evidence they are asked to evaluate. Therefore one should let a network be developed by others than those evaluating the individual pieces of evidence.

Ultimately it is the court that decides on a certain scenario. Therefore it is also important that it understands the network and its consequences, in all its complexity. In the telephone case, the court appeared to be well aware of the involved statistics. In the Simonshaven case, this Bayesian network was only made after the trial, and it therefore remains unclear whether a court would have accepted it.

6.4 Modeling Competing Arguments with a Bayesian Network

We next draw attention to an interesting phenomenon in the network in Figure 6.9 that has further consequences for the usefulness of modeling full cases with Bayesian networks. In the network two nodes appear which describe mutually exclusive events, namely the nodes *Defendant killed her* and *Man in bushes killed her*. Naturally, the Bayesian network is supposed to model the situation at hand, in which one and only one of these nodes can be True, but from the network in Figure 6.9, this cannot be concluded. It appears at first sight that, for instance, the sum of the probabilities for the two hypotheses to be True, could easily exceed 1, something which should not be allowed with proper modeling. What is going on here?

Moreover, note that the network in Figure 6.9 integrates the different explanations of the murder. More generally, the defense and prosecution may have very different pictures of the probabilistic relations between what has been observed on the one hand, and the guilt or innocence of the defendant on the other hand. They might even have very different opinions about which evidence to take into consideration to begin with. Can two such different scenarios be meaningfully combined into one single network? Since the aim of a Bayesian network is to model a full legal case, this is a very important question, and we further discuss this issue now in detail.

6.4.1 Splitting the Hypothesis Node

It would be most natural to have a network with only a *single* node expressing which hypothesis is true. In the Simonshaven case, this node would take the two values *Man in bushes killed victim* and *Defendant killed victim*. This might indeed be conceived as more natural than the two separate scenarios, since it naturally enforces that one and only one of the two competing hypotheses is true, so that their probabilities add up to 1. Of course, the design of such a network, taking into account all arguments of the various parties, might prove very difficult. Different parties in the case will conceivably insist on different pieces of evidence, and different relations between them, and the fact-finder has to make many choices, and somehow take all suggestions into consideration.

But even if such a network is somehow constructed, two problems may surface. First of all, the network may be so dense that even advanced software will not be able to process it. This can happen when the degree of certain nodes, that is, the number of arrows coming in and going out, is large. Second, the network might become so complicated that it is hard to see what is going on. Since computability and visual transparency are the two major reasons to use Bayesian networks to begin with, these problems must be taken seriously.

One idea now is that one splits the hypotheses node, containing mutually exclusive outcomes one of which must be true, into two nodes each representing one of these scenarios. Such a splitting procedure may indeed contribute to solving both problems identified above. Parental nodes of the original single hypothesis node need not necessarily be a parent of all split nodes. Indeed, if a certain parental node is irrelevant for one of the hypotheses, the link is simply not needed. This will have the effect that the degree of the split nodes might be smaller than the original degree, and hence that processing the model might become feasible. In addition, the network might become easier to read. For instance, the network in Figure 6.9 would be more difficult to read and to understand if the two hypotheses nodes would have been coded into one node.

The splitting of a single node into various other nodes should, if done correctly, leave the marginal probabilities of the hypotheses unchanged. By this we mean that if the original probability of, say, the hypothesis that the defendant killed the victim, was δ, this should still be the case after the splitting in the sense that the node *Defendant killed victim* has probability δ of being True. However, although this must be true if the splitting is carried out properly, the joint distribution of the various hypotheses will in general have changed by the splitting operation. We can check this with a very simple example.

Consider a network with three nodes: A, B, and X, where we think of X as the hypotheses node. Suppose that there are two arrows, one from $A \rightarrow X$ and one from $B \rightarrow X$. Furthermore, suppose that X has two possible states 0 and 1 representing two mutually exclusive scenarios, and that the probabilities $P(X = 0 \mid A = a, B = b)$ and $P(X = 1 \mid A = a, B = b)$ are strictly positive, for any of the values a and b that can be taken by A and B respectively.

Now suppose we split the hypothesis node X into two nodes X_1 and X_2. The new nodes X_1 and X_2 both have A and B as parents, and we set $P(X_1 = \text{True} \mid A = a, B = b) = P(X = 0 \mid A = a, B = b)$ and $P(X_2 = \text{True} \mid A = a, B = b) = P(X = 1 \mid A = a, B = b)$. We now have replaced node X by two nodes X_1 and X_2, in such a way that the probability that X_1 is True is the same as the original probability that $X = 0$, and the probability that X_2 is True is the same as the original probability that $X = 1$. But now note that the probability that X_1 and X_2 are *both* true, is positive. If we would draw a realization of the new network, then it might happen that both X_1 and X_2 are True.

At first sight this seems to be problematic, since we know that only one of the hypotheses can be true. However, we claim that it is *not* problematic, and we now explain why. The purpose of the original network, with only one hypothesis node, was to make a probabilistic assessment of our belief in either of the hypotheses. We were simply interested in the (posterior) probability of any of the relevant hypotheses. In the new network with the split nodes, these probabilities are still available. The marginal probabilities of the hypotheses nodes in the split network are the same as in the original network, and since we are only interested in these marginal probabilities, the split network is just as useful as the original one.

Perhaps it is instructive here to comment on the difference between a distribution and a realization. In forensic probability and statistics we want to make statements about the (subjective) probability of certain hypotheses. That is, we are interested in *distributional* statements. All statements above were distributional. However, one can also draw a realization of the network, by first choosing the states of prior nodes according to their distributions, and use these states to choose the further states of their children nodes, and so on. Finally, this leads to a state of the hypotheses nodes being either True or False. If the distribution allows for it, it may well be the case that in such a realisation, two competing hypotheses are both True. But this is completely irrelevant. No one would consider making a decision on the basis of the thus obtained realization of the network. Instead, a decision-maker will base his decision on the *probability* that a certain hypothesis is true.

So, in the split network both hypotheses can be True, but the crucial fact is that the marginal probabilities of the various hypotheses are the same as in the original model, and these can therefore be used. Therefore, the splitting procedure might be rather useful since it may indeed be the case that the new network is computable. In addition, the new network may be more transparent.

6.4.2 Starting with Different Hypotheses Nodes

Instead of splitting a single hypothesis node into several ones as described above, one can also design a model of a given situation that has two hypotheses nodes from the outset. This is perhaps less intuitive, because then it could easily be the case that the probabilities of the various mutually exclusive hypotheses to be True add up to something strictly larger or strictly smaller than 1, and this, of course, is in fact problematic. This problem did not arise in the splitting procedure that we described above, since the fact that the original network contained only one hypothesis node guaranteed that the sum of the probabilities of the various hypotheses summed up to 1.

But how does one avoid the problem that the sum of the probabilities of the hypotheses to be True is not equal to 1, if these hypotheses are modeled as different nodes? To realize the difficulty of this requirement, note that it must be the case that the posterior probabilities for the various hypotheses must sum up to 1 for *any* choice of the prior probabilities of the network. Clearly, this is in general impossible to achieve.

Let as look at the Bayesian network of Figure 6.9 as an example. In this network, there are two nodes that describe who might have killed the defendant's wife. It is not clear from the network whether the designers of the model started with a single node which they sub-sequently split into two nodes, or that they originally designed the network as having two separate hypotheses nodes. We suspect the latter since the designers used, invisible in the picture, a specific technical device to make sure that one, and only of the two hypotheses nodes has the value True.

How the designers forced this, but which is not shown in the network, is by adding an auxiliary node S that is a common child of both hypotheses nodes, and which has state True if and only if precisely one of the parental nodes is true. By conditioning on this auxiliary node to be True, we force the probability distribution of the network to concentrate on outcomes for which one and only one scenario is true. Here are the details of this construction.

Table 6.5 *The probability table corresponding to S in Figure 6.11.*

A	True		False	
B	True	False	True	False
True	0	1	1	0
False	1	0	0	1

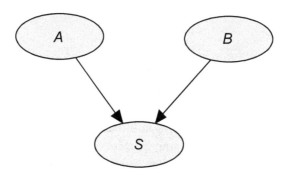

Figure 6.11 A construction to make sure that exactly one of *A* and *B* is true.

Denote the two hypotheses nodes under consideration by *A* and *B* and introduce a common child *S* of *A* and *B* as in Figure 6.11, with corresponding probability table as given in Table 6.5. When we now condition on *S* being True, this conditioning forces that exactly one out of *A* and *B* is true, as required.

Note that this is a statement about realizations, and didn't we just notice that we are not interested in realizations? That is true, but note that this time, ensuring (somehow) that every realization yields exactly one of the hypotheses nodes to be True, guarantees that the sum of the probabilities of the hypotheses is equal to 1. In the above discussion, this was clear from the outset, and therefore this was no issue in the split network. Here, however, it must somehow be forced. We are still not primarily interested in realizations, but if we make sure that in any realization one and only one hypothesis is True, then we can conclude that their probabilities sum up to 1, which is the real issue of interest.

Is this a satisfactory way to proceed? Not really. The conditioning on *S* being True changes the distribution of the network. How the distribution changes depends on the full joint distribution of the network, and of the joint distribution of *A* and *B* in particular. To illustrate this, suppose that *A* and *B* have no common ancestors in the network. To be sure, the procedure of adding *S* to the network does not require this, but if this is the case then an explicit computation is possible. Indeed, if we write $x = P(A = \text{True})$ and $y = P(B = \text{True})$, each conditional on their own ancestors only, then a simple calculation shows that

$$P(A = \text{True} \mid S = \text{True}) = \frac{x(1-y)}{x(1-y) + y(1-x)},$$

which is in general not equal to x. So the addition of S and the conditioning on it to be True gives, in fact, different probabilities for the hypotheses than we had in the separate networks for A and B.

Hence the distribution of the network changes upon adding the auxiliary node S. If a designer believes that his original model describes reality satisfactorily, then there is no guarantee that this is still the case after the conditioning on S being True. Adding a common child S as above to the two hypotheses nodes and conditioning on it being True will force one, and only one, of the hypotheses nodes to be equal to True, but exactly how this can, or should, be interpreted is unclear. Indeed, this "solution" seems to be a rather arbitrary way of defining a joint probability distribution over all variables that play a role and does not seem to correspond to a joint probability distribution of all variables involved that the fact-finder will endorse. It is a purely technical device with unclear consequences.

Here is alternative suggestion that has been advocated in the literature. Instead of one constraint node, this approach uses two constraint nodes, as depicted in Figure 6.12. Suppose now that we again assume that A and B are hypotheses nodes, and suppose that the marginal distributions of A and B in the original network are $P(A = \text{True}) = x$ and $P(B = \text{True}) = y$.

Node X can take the values, a, b, and NA, while node S can take the values True and False. Consider the probability tables of S and X in Tables 6.6 and 6.7, respectively. The idea now is again to condition on S being True. As in the previous case with only one auxiliary node S, this condition will ensure that the state of

Table 6.6 *The probability table for node S in Figure 6.12.*

X	a	b	NA
False	x	y	1
True	$1-x$	$1-y$	0

Table 6.7 *The probability table for node X in Figure 6.12.*

A	False		True	
B	False	True	False	True
a	0	0	1	0
b	0	1	0	0
NA	1	0	0	1

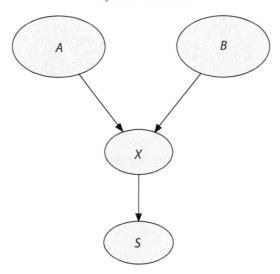

Figure 6.12 A second construction to make sure that exactly one of A and B is true.

the nodes (A, B) concentrate on (True, False) and (False, True). However, this time something interesting happens when the states of A and B can be considered to be independent, for instance, when their ancestors are completely disjoint. In that case the conditioning on S being True results not only in one and only one of A and B to be true, but moreover, that A is true with probability $x/(x + y)$ and B is true with probability $y/(x + y)$. That is, the marginal probabilities of the joint network are proportional to the original probabilities.

If the original probabilities x and y sum up to 1, then the marginal probabilities, therefore, do not change with this procedure. However, as we discussed above, it is essentially impossible to have a network with two hypotheses nodes with the property that their probabilities sum up to 1. The only situation in which this may be achieved is the original situation where we started with one node which we subsequentially split into two nodes. If it so happens that after the splitting the different hypotheses nodes are independent, then the procedure of adding the two auxiliary nodes X and S to the network guarantees that we have designed a network in which one and only one of the hypotheses nodes is True, and in which the marginal probabilities have not changed. However, we have argued above that in that situation, it is not necessary that the new network has the property that one and only one hypothesis is True, since we are only interested in marginal probabilities of the various hypotheses. If, after splitting, these marginal probabilities can be known by successfully running the network, then we simply do not need the auxiliary nodes. If the network can, after splitting, still not be run, then the two auxiliary nodes S and X offer no solution, since the unknown x and y are needed for carrying it out.

Indeed it seems rather difficult to design a network to describe a complicated full legal case. If such a network is to contain and describe all the elements of both parties, the network will be very difficult to execute. Sometimes, splitting the hypothesis node into several other ones as described above may help. For this to be helpful, one does not need auxiliary nodes to ensure that one, and only one of the new, split, nodes is True, since we are only interested in distributional assessments. The auxiliary nodes suggested in the literature either lead to a rather arbitrary model based on a technical device rather than a modeling decision, or they are simply not needed.

All this, perhaps, calls for another approach. In the next section we introduce and discuss a different way to go about the problem of integrating various scenarios into one conceptual framework. This method has been discussed in the literature, and goes under the name *Bayesian network selection*.

6.5 Bayesian Network Selection

It seems reasonable to assume that prosecution and defense independently construct legal arguments, without any guarantee that these involve the same collection of variables. They may take different pieces of evidence into account, they may have vastly different ideas about the relations between various variables, and of course also may have very different ideas about prior probabilities. In short, the two networks designed by either party might have very few things in common.

A possible conceptual way to go about this, is to let both the prosecution and the defense design their own Bayesian network, containing precisely those variables that they wish to include, and without the variables that they do not want to consider. In this section we describe this approach, and we will argue that it is not feasible.

Each of the two parties, prosecution and defence, designs a network that they believe describes the situation best. These two models, including both the graph structure and the probability tables, are denoted m_p and m_d respectively. Both networks are supposed to contain a *Guilt* node, taking the values True or False. The facts, or pieces of evidence, considered in m_p are denoted by f_p and those in m_d by f_d. The collections of facts f_p and f_d need not coincide. Their intersection might even be empty if it so happens that both parties wish to take disjoint pieces of evidence into account. Corresponding to f_p and f_d are the credibility nodes, very similar to the general credibility motif in Figure 6.10, and the values assigned to these credibility nodes are summarized by the parties involved as c_p and c_d respectively. We mention these credibility nodes explicitly, since it may be the case that a factfinder will assign different values to them than the party who designed the network.

Already at this point one can wonder whether this is a realistic starting point to begin with. The defence has no obligation to design a suitable explanation, and could simply state that the defendant is not guilty. But let us see how an approach of this type could be continued.

Typically it should be the case that the two networks will result in very different probabilities for the *Guilt* node. Writing G for the hypothesis that the *Guilt* node is True, the two parties will produce, respectively, $P(G \mid f_p, c_p, m_p)$ and $P(G \mid f_d, c_d, m_d)$, where the former will typically be much higher than the latter. More precisely, the various parties claim that if the fact-finder would follow their arguments, then the fact-finder would end up at the claimed numerical number for his probability that the defendant is guilty.

Consider now a fact-finder who is confronted with the two networks, and who is to formulate a final verdict about guilt or not. Let us denote the union of all considered facts by f, and the credibility values of the fact-finder by c. These credibility values might, and will in general, be different from the credibility assignments of the two parties involved. The fact-finder is now interested in his assessment of the probability of guilt, given all considered facts f and his assessment of the credibilities c. It is clear that this cannot be done without a certain prior belief in both models m_p and m_d, so let us denote the fact-finder's prior probabilities of the two models by $p(m_p)$ and $p(m_d)$, respectively. We assume that these prior probabilities take into account the full network, including both graphical structure, probability tables, and prior probabilities, but not the credibility values which the fact-finder sets for himself. In the sequel, for simplicity we assume that the credibilities of the fact-finder are fixed, and we do not express c in our notation.

We now want to compute

$$P(G \mid f) = \sum_m P(G \mid f, m) P(m \mid f), \tag{6.3}$$

where the sum is over $m = m_p$ and $m = m_d$. Now $P(G \mid f, m)$ can be easily computed: it is a straightforward computation within one of the given models m_p or m_d. Note that in order to compute $P(G \mid f, m)$, one only needs the facts associated with the particular model m.

For $P(m \mid f)$, however, things are different, and we need *all* facts. We now formally write

$$P(m \mid f) = \frac{P(m, f)}{P(f)} = \frac{p(m) P(f \mid m)}{\sum_{m'} p(m') P(f \mid m')}. \tag{6.4}$$

However, note that now there is problem since $p(f \mid m)$ is not defined. Indeed, given that model m is correct, the facts from the competing model are not taken into account, and m gives no information about their probabilities. It is not clear how to deal with this, and there does not seem to be a canonical approach. In [112], where an approach like this is described, the authors choose to define $P(f \mid m_p)$

as the product of $p(f_p \mid m_p)$ and $1/2$ to the power of the number of items in f that is not taken into account in m_p, and similarly for $P(f \mid m_d)$. Hence, not taking into account a fact which is considered by the other party, is penalized by a factor of $1/2$. According to the authors in [112], the ratio behind this choice is that in doing so, one expresses being uninformed about the facts not taken into account by one's own model.

This approach has several problems. First of all, we have seen in Chapter 1 that using the uniform distribution, which is precisely the suggestion here, is not the same as being uninformed. The penalization is, therefore, a rather arbitrary choice, and of course any suggestion will to some extent be arbitrary. Moreover, this method gives rise to a rather perverse incentive to add as many facts as one can, as long as these do not harm your case. Indeed, taking into account more facts will make the penalty for the other party larger. This reinforces the arbitrariness of the proposed method.

But there are more problems. What, precisely, is the relation between the prior probabilities $p(m)$ and the penalizing construction? Suppose, for instance, that the fact-finder finds the model m_d unrealistic because of the many facts that this model ignores. This leads, we assume, to a low prior $p(m_d)$. But the omission of these facts is *again* penalized through the assignment of $p(f \mid m)$, by the very fact that they are missing. Hence, it seems that here is a great risk that certain problems are counted multiple times. Exactly on what the prior probabilities should be based is, then, rather unclear.

We can illustrate the problems with a simple example. Suppose f consists of a DNA match only. The prosecutor's scenario is the scenario as in the classical island problem of Chapter 4. With a uniform prior on a population of size $N + 1$, and a match probability of p, the probability of guilt under the prosecutor's scenario is $1/(1+Np)$, see (4.4). The defence, however, proposes a model with only one node, namely the *Guilt* node, with a (prior) probability of being True of $1/(N+1)$, again taking uniform priors on the population. What happens when we take the approach of the current section?

According to (6.4), using the penalizing suggestion above, we obtain

$$P(m_p \mid f) = \frac{p(m_p)}{p(m_p) + \frac{1}{2}p(m_d)}, \tag{6.5}$$

so that (6.3) gives

$$P(G \mid f) = \frac{1}{1 + Np} \frac{p(m_p)}{p(m_p) + \frac{1}{2}p(m_d)} + \frac{1}{N+1} \frac{\frac{1}{2}p(m_d)}{p(m_p) + \frac{1}{2}p(m_d)}$$

$$= \frac{2p(m_p)/(1 + Np) + p(m_d)/(N + 1)}{2p(m_p) + p(m_d)}.$$

It is easy to see that when Np is very small and N is large, this is about the same as (6.5), and therefore it seems that the evidence has not been used. One may try to argue that the fact-finder will somehow incorporate p in his prior assessment $p(m_p)$ and $p(m_d)$, but then, how? The defence can claim that the fact that they did not use the DNA match has already been penalized by the factor of $1/2$ so that a further penalizing through a low $p(m_d)$ is unfair. Hence in this simple example, the approach behaves very unsatisfactorily and leads to considerable confusion.

Of course, this is a simple example. But a good approach should also work well in a simple example, and since it does not, we must conclude that the Bayesian selection approach that we described in this section, is not a solution to the problem of integrating different scenarios into one single conceptual framework. In addition, all problems about choosing priors and numerical values persist. All problems about designing joint distributions persist, and new problems arise, as we have just showed.

Our view of Bayesian networks has been one of representing, or visualizing joint distributions. Let us, finally, briefly compare this view to another viewpoint brought forward in a forensic context. Dahlman [50] says:

"Critics of the Bayesian method say that it cannot mirror the complexity of the world. In my view, this misses the point of Bayesian thinking. [...] Bayesian Networks are not models of the world. They are models of our reasoning about the world, that help us avoid fallacies and biases."

How to assess this claim? First of all, we agree that no method whatsoever can mirror the complexity of the world. Indeed, this is why they are called models to begin with, so the discussion should indeed not concern this point. Consider the Bayesian network corresponding to the Simonshaven case that we discussed above. This is, indeed, not an *objective* model of the world, but instead a subjective reconstruction that is by its very nature limited by lack of information. But even though it is not objective, it *is* a model. We do not think that an alleged model for our *reasoning* about the world would include numbers. Why would it, if only our reasoning is at stake? The numbers in the above modeling say nothing about the actual reasoning, which is qualitative rather than quantitative in nature. No, these numbers are supposed to relate to our knowledge of the actual world, to say something about the world, so we don't think that the claim of Dahlman stands.

Expressing doubts about an application of a certain method does not, of course, imply that a better one is available. One should not try the impossible, and one should not try to apply a theory beyond its natural scope. A Bayesian approach can be extremely important to aid the reasoning in a case, as we saw for instance in the Sally Clark case discussed in Section 5.3. But actual numbers should only be used when these are both founded and relevant to the case.

6.6 Summary and Conclusions

A Bayesian network is a graphical representation of the joint distribution of a number of random variables. It contains a node for each modeled random variable, and arrows from one variable to another if the first one is always relevant for the second, no matter what knowledge on the other variables might be available. The node from which the arrow departs is called the parent of the child node where the arrow goes to. Given the nodes and the arrows, the joint probability distribution is captured by specifying the probabilities of the states in every child node given the states of its parents, and a probability distribution for the nodes without parents in the network, called prior nodes. Since the network defines the joint probability distribution, it also determines all conditional dependencies and there are algorithms to efficiently verify these.

When designing a Bayesian network, the arrows should be so directed that the corresponding conditional probabilities can be meaningfully given. The construction of a Bayesian network is the result of gut feeling, expert knowledge, experience, and perhaps other, non-mathematical ingredients.

The usefulness of a Bayesian network often lies primarily in the computational possibilities of software. To perform calculations with a given joint distribution, formulating the distribution into a Bayesian network enables powerful software to be used. As such, a Bayesian network is a visual and useful tool, but it gives no real new information that we did not, at least in theory, have before. For example, when modeling DNA transmission in pedigrees the joint distribution is clear, and the Bayesian network is an efficient calculator.

For modeling more complex situations where it is difficult to judge all dependencies, it is sometimes claimed that a Bayesian network is helpful. In principle, a Bayesian network can indeed be used in this situation, but the problem of the interdependencies is of course not taken away when we do so. Indeed, the very construction of the Bayesian network requires these interdependencies to be taken into account.

We have discussed the modeling of a full legal case, the Simonshaven case, by a Bayesian network. Even though the presented Bayesian network contains generic patterns like the credibility motif in Figure 6.10, it does not seem to us that the full network is generic in any way. We should keep in mind that, in the end, the Bayesian network is representing a joint distribution of all random variables involved. It is very unlikely that two independent research groups would eventually come up with the same network geometry and the same collection of random variables. And not only that, a huge number of conditional probabilities is required, many of which must somehow be assigned in one way or another. These choices are highly subjective, and they may have a huge effect on the final probabilistic assessment.

We have also discussed at length the issue of integrating competing stories into one Bayesian network, or at least in one conceptual framework. Integrating competing scenarios into one Bayesian network easily leads to networks which are too large to compile, and which are no longer very transparent. An attempt to solve this problem by splitting a single hypothesis node into several ones can in principle be successful. When the modeling starts with two different hypothesis nodes, each representing a different scenario as, for instance in Figure 6.9, then technical devices to ensure that one and only one of these nodes is True, are not useful. An approach to integrate two potentially very different scenarios into one conceptual framework, called Bayesian model selection, is problematic for many reasons that we have discussed in detail.

We conclude that Bayesian networks have their use in visualizing models, and in allowing for computations with powerful software. Modeling complex cases with a Bayesian network needs so many choices, assumptions and simplifications, that we advice not to do this. The outcomes can hardly be given a meaning relating to the case at hand, and can only be interpreted in the network itself.

6.7 Bibliographical Notes

There are many excellent references for Bayesian networks. For computational issues we refer to [41] and [93]. For a discussion about interpretation the reader can for instance consult [52], [119] [166], and [167]. The book [1] contains a full chapter on Bayesian networks. The Bayesian network in Figure 6.7 is taken from [55]. The network in Figure 6.8 is taken from [65]. For a closely related discussion we refer to [49]. The Bayesian network describing the Simonshaven case in Figure 6.9 is taken from [67]. For a discussion of representing mutually exclusive events by different nodes we refer to [66]. For the issue of integrating various scenarios into one Bayesian network we further refer to [169], [170], and [171]. The model selection problem in the context of Bayesian networks is discussed in [112]. Our approach is somewhat different from theirs.

7

DNA

In this chapter, we focus on forensic DNA profiles, and we bring much of the previously discussed philosophy and theory into practice. In addition, we introduce concepts that are needed in the discussion in later chapters. Section 7.1 is a short introduction to the chemical basis for the typing of DNA profiles for forensic purposes. In Section 7.2 we explain at some length that population frequencies of profiles cannot in general be equated with match probabilities. A population frequency is an existing and measurable property of the population, whereas a match probability expresses the subjective probability for an agent to find a certain profile, given his or her knowledge, information, and personal judgment. The difference is crucial in order to understand what evidence means in the context of DNA. In Sections 7.3 and 7.4 we derive the probability for a randomly chosen population member to have the same profile as a trace donor, the so-called random match probability. We treat this as an instantiation of the island problem with uncertainty about the population frequency of the observed DNA profile, as discussed in Section 4.3. In Section 7.5 we approach profile probabilities and in particular match probabilities from a population-genetic point of view, and we introduce and explain the so-called θ-correction. Section 7.6 is an elementary introduction to likelihood ratios in the DNA context of pairwise kinship, interesting in their own right, and also needed for the discussion on familial searching in Chapter 11.

7.1 Forensic DNA Profiling

In Section 1.6 we gave some background on the biology of DNA. In this section we discuss the process of obtaining DNA profiles suitable for forensic science.

In order to carry out the necessary comparisons, DNA profiles need to be obtained from persons and from traces. For persons typically abundant DNA can be obtained under controlled conditions, which normally leads to unambiguous determination of their DNA profile. Traces, however, need to be recovered. They do not arise under controlled conditions, the amount of DNA that they contain may be small, and the DNA may have been damaged because of, say, exposure to light or water.

In order to better understand the modeling challenges that DNA trace profiles pose, in this section we briefly explain the currently most widely used method by which DNA profiles are generated, namely PCR (polymerase chain reaction) multiplication and detection by capillary electrophoresis. As we explained in Section 1.6, this method records the length of fragments of DNA on so-called STR loci. The resulting categories, called the alleles, can be detected with this technology. The alleles are denoted by numbers, which are determined from their length.

When a sample from a trace is processed by a forensic laboratory, DNA from the cells in the sample is first extracted by chemical reagents. The DNA extract is then stored in the laboratory, and an estimate of the DNA concentration in it can be made. Based on this measurement, a part of the DNA extract can be selected for DNA profiling that contains an amount of DNA optimal for the chosen technique. Often it will be possible to use the extract for several profiling runs, which are then called replicate analyses. The DNA selected for amplification will then be subjected to a series of chemical reactions, the PCR mentioned above. The PCR consists of a number of cycles that are identical in their setup, and which aim to double the amount of detectable STR alleles. In each cycle, DNA sections that contain the alleles of the targeted STR loci are copied, and some are given a fluorescent dye label to be able to detect them by capillary electrophoresis. In principle, the PCR should faithfully copy all alleles in each cycle, but in practice the efficiency is less than 100%. In addition the copying process is not perfect. The most common form of copying error is that an allele is copied as an allele with one repeat unit less than the original allele; such an allele is called a -1 *stutter allele* of its "parent allele." It is also possible to have other errors, such as the loss of two repeat units (a -2 stutter), the insertion of a new repeat unit (a $+1$ stutter), or another modification. Once these imperfect copies have been made they are available for copying in the next PCR cycles.

As a result, the resulting DNA profile is best viewed as an outcome of a stochastic process. The DNA profile is obtained by measuring the amount of alleles of each type after completion of the PCR process by exciting the dyes on the tagged alleles. The amount of fluorescence, expressed in units called *rfu* (relative fluorescence units), is then a measure for the number of tagged alleles. Since there is always some noise, usually only rfu signals exceeding a threshold T, called the *analytical threshold*, are registered as peak heights. The DNA profile from the trace then consists of the peak heights for those alleles where the analytical threshold is reached. That is, the profile can be viewed as a set with elements $\{(a, h_a)\}$, where a can be any of the possible alleles of the loci under consideration, and the heights h_a are at least equal to T.

Because of the various stochastic effects described above, replicate analyses need not always produce the same DNA profile. The heights h_a can be so different that the analytical threshold is sometimes reached and sometimes not. Some alleles that are present in one replicate may therefore be absent in others. In addition, not all alleles that are detected necessarily correspond to an allele that was present in the original sample. There may be alleles in the profile that have arisen as stutter and there may also be so-called *drop-in* alleles that do not originate from the sample at all. The incidence of such alleles can be observed in negative controls. In addition there can be complicating effects like DNA degradation that may affect the profile.

If an allele that is present in one of the contributors of DNA to the sample is undetected, this is called a *dropout*. The probability that an allele drops out depends on the amount of DNA contributed to the sample, the PCR efficiency, and on the analytical threshold. DNA degradation may cause the probability of dropout to be higher for alleles that are on longer fragments in the PCR process. In extreme cases, there may even be no discernible signal from the alleles with large fragment sizes, while the alleles with small fragment sizes are still detected.

Many laboratories subject DNA profiles to an additional, semi-manual cleanup of the profile which aims to remove stutter peaks and other artifacts (the terminology for all registered peaks that are believed not to have come from biological contributors). The final profile to be evaluated therefore need not contain all alleles whose peak height exceeds the analytical threshold, it may be a smaller set. The recognition of alleles as artefactual is not that hard for reference profiles of individuals, but it is clearly difficult for trace profiles where alleles of contributors may coincide with possible artefactual alleles. This manual step is a complication for models that aim to model trace profiles as a result of the PCR process, taking stutter and other artifacts into account.

In this chapter we restrict ourselves to reference profiles of persons and traces that contain DNA of a single individual, all of whose alleles are detected in the resulting DNA profile. This implies that we do not take peak heights into account in this chapter. We will discuss mixed and incomplete traces in Chapter 8, and there peak heights will play a role.

7.2 Population Frequencies Versus Profile Probabilities

The forensic applications of DNA profiling have gradually increased over time. The first application was, naturally, to compare a DNA profile from a trace (coming from an unknown offender C, say) to the DNA profile of a known individual (a suspect S, say). In the case where these profiles are the same, an evaluation of the strength of that evidence is required. We denote by $G_C = g$ the event that C has DNA profile g and by $G_S = g$ the event that S has DNA profile g. To compute the likelihood ratio in favor of $H_1 : S = C$ versus $H_2 : S \neq C$, conditional on $G_C = g$, we note that if $S = C$ and $G_C = g$, then the probability that $G_S = g$ is equal to 1. Hence we obtain

$$LR_{H_1, H_2}(G_S = g) = \frac{1}{P(G_S = g \mid G_C = g, S \neq C)}, \tag{7.1}$$

where we have, as we noted above, assumed that if $S = C$, then we are certain to measure the same profile for both S and C, which in fact means that both the profile of S and C have been unambiguously determined. For a DNA profile of a reference sample this is not a real restriction, but for a trace at a scene of a crime it is.

Note that in (7.1) we have to evaluate the probability of the event $G_S = g$ conditional on $G_C = g$ and $S \neq C$, so we are interested in the probability of a person S having profile g, given that another person C has that profile. Clearly, the fact that DNA is inherited from parent to child makes it impossible to evaluate the required probability without further assumptions on the relatedness between S and C. In a finite population, we can expect some level of *inbreeding*, that is, distant familial relationships between two randomly chosen individuals, and this in turn means that profiles cannot be expected to be independent: we cannot simply say that $P(G_S = g \mid G_C = g, S \neq C) = P(G_S = g)$. However, if the population is large and if S and C are not recently related, then their profiles will be close to independent.

So, as a first approximation, we compute profile probabilities in a very large or even infinite population. In such a population, the probability that the parents of a person are related is zero, and the alleles that a person inherits from the paternal and the maternal side are obtained as two independent random draws from the population of alleles that the parental generation has. This means that, if we know the proportions p_a of type a for all a, then the probability $P_{x,y}$ that a randomly chosen offspring has genotype (x, y) is given by

$$P_{x,y} = (2 - \delta_{x,y}) p_x p_y, \tag{7.2}$$

where $\delta_{x,y} = 1$ if $x = y$ and 0 if $x \neq y$. It follows also that, in the generation of offspring, the allele proportions will not have changed, since for allele a we get proportion

$$P_{a,a} + \frac{1}{2} \sum_{b \neq a} P_{a,b} = p_a^2 + \sum_{b \neq a} p_a p_b$$

$$= p_a \sum_b p_b = p_a.$$

This phenomenon is called *Hardy–Weinberg equilibrium* (HWE).

What we need, however, are not allele or genotype *proportions* but their *probabilities* as assigned to them by, say, a forensic statistician. As we have discussed extensively in Chapter 1, probabilistic statements are epistemic in nature. They are statements reflecting our knowledge of the world, rather than the world directly. Hence, in the absence of full information, it is not the case that match probabilities of DNA profiles are the same as their underlying but unknown population frequency or proportion. We will, therefore, distinguish between population frequencies or proportions on the one hand, and match probabilities on the other. We should assign these match probabilities conditional on what we know. This knowledge includes what we assume to be true about the population and about biology. If the proportions of alleles are known, then we simply define the probability that a randomly selected allele is of type a to be equal to the population proportion of that allele. In that (unrealistic) case, the probabilities of the genotypes naturally satisfy (7.2).

Knowing the allele proportions of the whole population is quite impossible to ever happen. We could have exact knowledge of the allele proportions if we have profiles of all relevant individuals, in which case we would obtain much more information than just the allele proportions, since we also know all relevant profiles themselves. This would remove the need for modeling altogether.

Realistically, we have a sample of alleles at our disposal, and we must base the probabilities for genotypes and profiles on that sample. In that case, the population may well be in HWE but the genotype probabilities that we assign may not. Indeed these probabilities must, as always, reflect what we expect in light of what we know or assume. Quantitatively, if we are not certain what the population proportions of the alleles are, then sampling an allele that turns out to be of type a will increase our probability that the next allele that is sampled is also of type a, and lower the probabilities for the other types.

Interestingly, this is precisely what we would expect as a result of relatedness as well: if we draw two alleles from the population, there is a certain probability that both of them are copies of one and the same ancestral allele, in which case it is certain they are of the same type. This will make our probability that the second allele is of type a, given that the first allele is of type a, larger than our probability that the first allele is of type a. It turns out, perhaps rather surprisingly, that these two different sources of deviation from HWE for the genotype probabilities can be given the exact same probabilistic description. We develop these descriptions below in Sections 7.3 and 7.5, respectively. The mathematics in Sections 7.3 and 7.5 is carried out on a single locus, so before we carry out the analysis, we first discuss how to extend a single-locus analysis to a multiple-loci one.

First we consider two loci that are on different chromosomes. Since the segregation of different chromosomes takes place independently of each other, the inheritance processes on the two loci also evolve independently. We can, simply, view the alleles on the two loci as if they belong to two independently evolving populations. If a parent has genotype (a_1, a_2) on one locus, and (b_1, b_2) on another locus on another chromosome, then the children of that person will inherit each combination (a_i, b_j) with the same probability. We can obtain probabilistic statements about the two loci by simply multiplying probabilities on each single locus, irrespective of the way we arrive at our single-locus statements.

However, if two loci are on the same chromosome, then we need to know more about these loci since then they do not evolve independently. If a chromosome carries allele a on the first locus and allele b on the second locus, we say that the *haplotype* of the chromosome is a/b. For a person with haplotypes a_1/b_1 and a_2/b_2, we can infer from biology that there is a number $0 \le \rho \le 1/2$, such that an offspring of that person inherits any of the two haplotypes a_i/b_i with probability $(1 - \rho)/2$, and any of the two haplotypes a_i/b_j $(j \neq i)$ with probability $\rho/2$. The haplotypes a_1/b_2 and a_2/b_1 are called *recombinant products*, and ρ is called the probability of *recombination*. Throughout, we will assume some idealizations, namely that the recombination probability only depends on the loci under consideration and not on the gender of the person that produces an offspring.

If $\rho = 0$, recombination is impossible and a haplotype, once present in the population, can only be passed on unchanged. If HWE applies it will then also apply to these haplotypes and then we can consider those haplotypes as "alleles" of a "locus" that encompasses both of the considered biological loci.

If $\rho > 0$, then all haplotypes have non-zero probability in every generation except possibly the first one. It is not hard to show that, over time, the proportion of haplotypes a/b will asymptotically converge to the product of the proportions $p_a p_b$. Note that a/b and b/a constitute different haplotypes so that we do not have a factor 2 here. Thus if we assume that the population of interest is sufficiently old and that there are no effects such as selection that make certain combinations (dis)advantageous for reproduction, it is reasonable to assign a probability $p_{a/b} = p_a p_b$ to a haplotype a/b. This is called the assumption of *linkage equilibrium* (LE).

As HWE, LE is a property that a population may or may not have. If a population is known to be in both HWE and LE, and we know the allele proportions in that population, then we should assign the probability of a set of genotypes on several loci as the product over all genotype probabilities. In forensics this is usually known as the *product rule*.

However, whereas HWE and LE are properties of the population, the profile probabilities are based on our *knowledge* of the population, and therefore the product rule will not automatically apply if this knowledge leaves uncertainty about the dependence of alleles between loci. But if we do not call into question the validity

of the biological model that predicts that alleles on different loci are after many generations not informative about each other, then uncertainty about allele proportions
will not affect the validity of the product rule. Put differently, if we want to assign a
probability that randomly selected chromosomes from the population have certain
haplotypes, we can always obtain it as the product of the probabilities per locus.
Again, this is the same as we expect from background relatedness in a very large
population. In that case of background relatedness, if we sample haplotype a/b
from a person, there is a certain probability, say θ, that the next person has allele
a on the first locus because of it being inherited from a common ancestor with the
first person. This probability θ will also apply to the second locus considered on its
own. The question is whether, if the second person shares allele a on the first locus
through a common ancestor, this is predictive for sharing allele b through common
ancestry as well. In principle, this is so. Indeed, if $\rho = 0$ the allele on the first
locus being shared through ancestry means that the allele on the second is as well.
But for recombination probabilities that are not very small in a population that is
large, so that common ancestors are usually quite a number of generations ago, we
can expect this not to be predictive to a relevant extent. Therefore, we will always
restrict ourselves to single loci and apply the product rule for multiple loci.

Of course, in practice a human population may not very well be described as
a large homogeneous population with random mating in which relatedness can
be ignored. Indeed, either we look at a large population where relatedness plays
little role when we sample random alleles from the population, but then we will
typically find substructuring of the population that we need to incorporate, or we
consider a local, more homogeneous population, but that will tend to be smaller
so that coancestry cannot be ignored. The match probabilities to be derived in the
next sections will be applied to both cases. These match probabilities are obtained
per locus and involve a single parameter θ accounting for the variation of allele
frequencies between subpopulations or the level of coancestry in a given random
mating population. While we cannot expect that such a simple model can capture
all population genetic effects, these locus match probabilities can be multiplied
with each other to obtain the match probability of the whole profile if the effect of
substructuring or of coancestry can be expected to play the same role for all loci.
We will assume this to be the case. If necessary, one can use an inflated value for the
parameter θ, the purpose being to avoid the risk to overstate the evidence against a
defendant.

7.3 Uncertainty About Allele Frequencies: The Dirichlet Distribution

In reality, the allele proportions in the relevant population are not precisely known
by a forensic laboratory. Such a laboratory usually has a reference database with

the genotypes of a few hundred up to a few thousand individuals and uses these for assigning allele probabilities.

In this section, we discuss one way to do so. We assume that the studied population is in HWE, and that we do not have full knowledge of the allele proportions. If we know them, we would define allele probabilities as precisely these proportions and then we could use HWE to obtain the genotype probabilities.

Since we have uncertainty about the proportions but nevertheless believe that they exist, we are going to model this uncertainty by setting up a probability distribution reflecting our knowledge on what they could possibly be, as best we can. In the language of Section 4.3, we arrive at a probability distribution for W with density χ_W that describes our uncertainty about the allele frequencies.

As discussed above, if we do not know the allele frequencies in the population, then we cannot simply say that the probability that two randomly selected alleles are both of type a is the square of the probability that a single allele turns out to be of type a. Indeed, the fact that a first allele is of type a makes it more likely that this is a more frequent allele, which in turn increases the probability that the second allele is also type a.

What we need for the calculations is, in general, the probability for a set of alleles that we are about to sample, to be of certain types. If allele frequencies are unknown to us, then sampling more and more alleles from the population will reduce our uncertainty further and further. This means that the probability, given a population sample, that the next allele to be sampled is of type a, depends on the sample, but uncertainty remains. The remaining uncertainty is a remnant of our initial uncertainty that was encapsulated into some prior distribution. This prior distribution describes what we a priori believe the population frequencies to be.

If f_a denotes the density of the distribution describing our knowledge about the frequency of allele a, and we randomly select an allele, then the probability that it is of type a is equal to

$$\int_0^1 x f_a(x)dx,$$

that is, it is equal to the expectation of the frequency of a. Indeed, one obtains this formula by first conditioning on the frequency and then integrate out. Similarly, probabilities of sets of alleles to be of certain types are obtained as expectations of the corresponding products of the random variables. For instance, the probability that two specific alleles are both of type a is equal to

$$\int_0^1 x^2 f_a(x)dx,$$

that is, the second moment of the random variable modeling the population frequency of allele a. Since for any random variable X we have that $E(X^2) \geq (E(X))^2$, the probability to sample two alleles of type a is at least as large as the square of the probability to sample type a in a single draw. This positive correlation is intuitive: if we sample a then this is an indication that a is more frequent then we perhaps thought and hence in the next draw it is more likely to again draw an a.

Indeed, as we argued before, the probability to obtain a certain genotype upon sampling on the one hand, and its population frequency on the other, are two different concepts. The latter is defined in terms of a population (it materially exists but is unknown), whereas the former measures to what extent we expect that a person to be sampled has that genotype (and one could say that it has the precise opposite properties: it does not materially exist but it is known). A genotype is simply the realization of a random variable which is supposed to model the possible combinations of alleles a person can have. If the population would be infinitely large and population frequencies would be known, then this knowledge implies that we define our probabilistic model such that the probability that a randomly selected genotype is g, is the known population frequency of that g. In general, a population frequency cannot be smaller than the reciprocal of the population size, but our probability assessment of seeing a certain genotype in a person to be sampled obviously can.

As anticipated above, we work on a single locus, since we have explained in Section 7.2 how to deal with multiple loci once we know how to work with one. Suppose, then, that in the population, the alleles on the locus under consideration can be of type $a_1, \ldots, a_n$. Let X_i denote the random variable describing our knowledge about the population frequency of the allele of type a_i. The random vector $(X_1, \ldots, X_n)$ takes values in the set $\{(x_1, \ldots, x_n) : 0 \leq x_i \leq 1, \sum_{i=1}^{n} x_i = 1\}$.

The random vector $(X_1, \ldots, X_n)$ is often modeled as having a (joint) Dirichlet distribution, as follows. Since the frequencies of the n alleles sum up to 1, we only need a probability density for the first $n - 1$ alleles; the frequency of the last one is then determined by the requirement that the sum is equal to 1. Hence we only need a joint distribution of $(X_1, \ldots, X_{n-1})$. A choice often made for this is the $(n - 1)$-dimensional Dirichlet distribution with positive parameters $\alpha_1, \ldots, \alpha_n$, defined via the density

$$f_{\alpha_1, \ldots, \alpha_n}(x_1, \ldots, x_{n-1}) := \frac{\Gamma\left(\sum_{i=1}^{n} \alpha_i\right)}{\prod_{i=1}^{n} \Gamma(\alpha_i)} \prod_{i=1}^{n} x_i^{\alpha_i - 1}, \qquad (7.3)$$

where

$$x_n := 1 - \sum_{i=1}^{n-1} x_i, \qquad (7.4)$$

and which is defined on the set

$$U_{n-1} := \left\{ (x_1, \ldots, x_{n-1}) \, : \, x_i \geq 0, \sum_{i=1}^{n-1} x_i \leq 1 \right\}.$$

As in Section 3.2, Γ denotes the Gamma function. The Dirichlet distribution generalizes the Beta distribution which we also came across in Section 3.2.

For notational convenience, we often write $\alpha := (\alpha_1, \ldots, \alpha_n)$ and

$$B(\alpha) := \frac{\prod_{i=1}^{n} \Gamma(\alpha_i)}{\Gamma\left(\sum_{i=1}^{n} \alpha_i\right)},$$

so that we can write

$$f_\alpha(x_1, \ldots, x_{n-1}) = \frac{1}{B(\alpha)} \prod_{i=1}^{n} x_i^{\alpha_i - 1},$$

again noting (7.4). The parameters $\alpha_i > 0$ are prior parameters, and there is no specific natural choice for them. They are intended to summarize our prior knowledge, or lack thereof, of the allele frequencies. In the next subsection, we will say more about the possible choices of these parameters.

Suppose now that we sample one allele from the population. As we saw above, the probability that this will be allele 1 is equal to its expectation $E(X_1)$, which is, writing $\alpha' := (\alpha_1 + 1, \alpha_2, \ldots, \alpha_n)$,

$$E(X_1) = \frac{1}{B(\alpha)} \int \cdots \int_{U_{n-1}} x_1^{\alpha_1} \prod_{i=2}^{n} x_i^{\alpha_i - 1} dx_1 \cdots dx_{n-1}$$

$$= \frac{B(\alpha')}{B(\alpha)} \int \cdots \int_{U_{n-1}} f_{\alpha'}(x_1, \ldots, x_{n-1}) dx_1 \cdots dx_{n-1}$$

$$= \frac{B(\alpha')}{B(\alpha)} = \frac{\alpha_1}{\alpha_1 + \cdots + \alpha_n},$$

making use of the properties of the Gamma function. A similar computation can be done for the other α_i and we conclude that the α_i are proportional to the marginal allele probabilities.

If we sample several alleles, we need to compute expectations of products of the X_j. These have a simple closed form. Indeed, it is not hard to show in the same way as above, that

$$E(X_1^{\beta_1} \cdots X_n^{\beta_n}) = \frac{\Gamma(\sum_{i=1}^{n} \alpha_i)}{\Gamma\left(\sum_{i=1}^{n} (\alpha_i + \beta_i)\right)} \prod_{i=1}^{n} \frac{\Gamma(\alpha_i + \beta_i)}{\Gamma(\alpha_i)}, \qquad (7.5)$$

a formula which is true for general values of the β_i but which we only use for integer values. In particular, taking $\beta_1 = 2$ and $\beta_i = 0$ for $i = 2, \ldots, n$, it follows that

$$E(X_1^2) = \frac{(\alpha_1 + 1)\alpha_1}{\left(1 + \sum_{i=1}^{n} \alpha_i\right) \sum_{i=1}^{n} \alpha_i} \tag{7.6}$$

and

$$E(X_1 X_2) = \frac{\alpha_1 \alpha_2}{\left(1 + \sum_{i=1}^{n} \alpha_i\right) \sum_{i=1}^{n} \alpha_i}. \tag{7.7}$$

In the terminology of the island problem from Section 4.3, the density χ_W representing the probability distribution of the characteristic at hand is the probability density of X_i^2 if the trace is homozygous. If the trace is heterozygous for alleles i and j, then χ_W is the probability density of $2X_i X_j$.

We note from (7.6) and (7.7) that we can think of the α_i as pseudo-counts: the first allele to be sampled has probability $\alpha_i / \sum_{j=1}^{n} \alpha_j$ to be of type i so we can think of an urn containing α_i alleles of type i, for each i. Now suppose that upon sampling such an allele, we put it back together with an extra allele of the same type i, then the probability that the next allele sampled will also be of type i is $(\alpha_i + 1)/\left(\sum_{j=1}^{n} \alpha_j + 1\right)$. Hence, the probability that two alleles are both of type 1 is

$$\frac{(\alpha_1 + 1)\alpha_1}{\left(1 + \sum_{i=1}^{n} \alpha_i\right) \sum_{i=1}^{n} \alpha_i},$$

and the probability of first obtaining type 1 and then type 2 is

$$\frac{\alpha_1 \alpha_2}{\left(1 + \sum_{i=1}^{n} \alpha_i\right) \sum_{i=1}^{n} \alpha_i}.$$

This sampling scheme is known as the Polya urn sampling scheme.

The mathematically convenient way to deal with multiple sampling, along with the flexibility within the family of Dirichlet distributions, are important reasons to model allele probabilities using Dirichlet distributions. Moreover, there exist other (sometimes rather loose) justifications, and we present one of them here.

First of all, one can turn things around, and show that the Dirichlet distribution naturally arises from the Polya urn scheme just described. Suppose we start with an urn containing c_i balls of color i, for $i = 1, \ldots, n$. Now we repeat the following process. We sample a ball uniformly at random from the urn and look at its color. We put the selected ball back in the urn, together with a ball of the same color. If we repeat this process many times, the relative frequencies of the colors in the urn will converge to some random vector, and it can be shown that the probability density on the limiting frequencies is precisely the Dirichlet distribution with parameters c_i.

Next, imagine a population with a large number N of alleles in $N/2$ individuals (we think of one locus). If the population is mating at random and an offspring is produced, two alleles are randomly selected from the population, copied into the new individual, and added to the population. If we allow for self-mating and keep all individuals forever in the population, this process is very similar to the Polya urn sampling scheme. The difference is that we sample two alleles each time, but it nevertheless seems reasonable to assume that in a large population in which we start with N alleles (a number $c_i = Np_i$ of each type to start with) after sufficiently many generations, the allele frequencies of the population assuming no individual ever deceases or becomes incapable of producing offspring are well approximated by an outcome of a Dirichlet distribution with parameters Np_i. This gives at least some justification for using the Dirichlet distribution.

So far we have only defined the prior distribution for the allele frequencies. A first oddity is that the number n representing the number of possible alleles can only be based on a population sample that we have not yet incorporated into the analysis, so the prior is in part obtained from the sample to be incorporated. Moreover there seems to be no obvious choice for the parameters α_i. As we shall see below, forensic laboratories use a particular choice that is also in terms of the sample to be incorporated.

Having discussed the prior distribution of the allele frequencies, we next see what happens when we incorporate a sample of N alleles. Suppose we take a sample of N alleles, and the numbers of alleles of type $a_1, \ldots, a_n$ in the sample are denoted by the random variables $Y_1, \ldots, Y_n$, respectively, where Y_n is redundant and can be written as $Y_n = N - \sum_{i=1}^{n-1} Y_i$. This redundancy means that we may view the Y_i as either $(n-1)$- or n-dimensional. We make the choice that we write the Y_i as n-dimensional.

Using the continuous version of Bayes' rule we have

$$f_\alpha(x_1, \ldots, x_{n-1} \mid Y_1 = y_1, \ldots, Y_n = y_n)$$
$$= \frac{P(Y_1 = y_1, \ldots, Y_n = y_n \mid X_1 = x_1, \ldots, X_{n-1} = x_{n-1}) f_\alpha(x_1, \ldots, x_{n-1})}{P(Y_1 = y_1, \ldots, Y_n = y_n)}.$$

Since

$$P(Y_1 = y_1, \ldots, Y_n = y_n \mid X_1 = x_1, \ldots, X_{n-1} = x_{n-1}) = \frac{N!}{\prod_{i=1}^n y_i!} \prod_{i=1}^n x_i^{y_i}, \quad (7.8)$$

we have, writing $\alpha + y$ for the vector $(\alpha_1 + y_1, \ldots, \alpha_n + y_n)$,

$$f_\alpha(x_1, \ldots, x_{n-1} \mid Y_1 = y_1, \ldots, Y_n = y_n) = \frac{1}{B(\alpha + y)} \prod_{i=1}^n x_i^{\alpha_i + y_i - 1}, \quad (7.9)$$

that is, the conditional distribution of the allele frequencies given the sample is again Dirichlet with parameters $\alpha_i + y_i$. This property is called the *conjugacy* of the multinomial and the Dirichlet distributions.

7.4 Match Probabilities

We have seen that, if we start by modeling allele frequencies by the random vector with Dirichlet distribution $\mathrm{Dir}(\alpha_1, \ldots, \alpha_n)$, and then condition on the obtained population sample with counts $(y_1, \ldots, y_n)$, we get as distribution for the allele frequencies the Dirichlet distribution $\mathrm{Dir}(\alpha_1 + y_1, \ldots, \alpha_n + y_n)$. Forensic laboratories often model the allele frequencies as described by a random vector with a Dirichlet distribution with a different parametrization, namely

$$\mathrm{Dir}\left(\frac{1-\theta}{\theta}p_1, \ldots, \frac{1-\theta}{\theta}p_n\right), \tag{7.10}$$

where $p_i = y_i/N$ is the observed frequency of the allele of type i in the sample, and where $0 \le \theta \le 1$ is a parameter that can be given, as we will see below, a population-genetic interpretation. We can interpret this in our context of uncertainty about the allele frequencies if we can write

$$\alpha_i + y_i = \frac{1-\theta}{\theta}p_i,$$

so let us see whether this is possible.

In order for the Dirichlet distribution to be well defined, we need positive α_i. Since

$$\alpha_i = \frac{1-\theta}{\theta}\frac{y_i}{N} - y_i = y_i\left(\frac{1-(N+1)\theta}{N\theta}\right),$$

we have that $\alpha_i > 0$ if and only if $\theta < 1/(N+1)$. Thus, we can only view the parameters $\frac{1-\theta}{\theta}p_i$ as the posterior parameters of a Dirichlet distribution that was updated with the population database if $\theta < 1/(N+1)$. However, forensic laboratories typically use a larger value for θ, in the range of up to 0.03. The reason for this is that, as mentioned above, precisely the same formulas also arise in a different, population genetic, context. We come back to this in the next section.

Now suppose that trace and suspect have the same genotype. In the notation of Chapter 4, the likelihood ratio $P(E_C, E_S \mid G)/P(E_C, E_S \mid G^c)$ is equal to the inverse of $p' = E(W \mid E_C)$, where W describes the random variable for the characteristic at hand (that is, the relevant genotype) and E_C denotes the information that C has this characteristic.

Whatever the rationale behind (7.10) (modeling uncertain allele frequencies or population genetics), we can now derive the likelihood ratios that we want. Suppose that the genotype is (a_1, a_1). Then the density $\chi_C(t)$ of $W \mid E_C$ is the density of the random variable X_1^2 derived from the Dirichlet distribution with parameters

$$\left(\frac{1-\theta}{\theta} p_1 + 2, \frac{1-\theta}{\theta} p_2, \ldots, \frac{1-\theta}{\theta} p_n \right).$$

Using (7.5), we see that the expectation of this random variable is equal to

$$\frac{\frac{1-\theta}{\theta} p_1 + 3}{\frac{1-\theta}{\theta} + 3} \times \frac{\frac{1-\theta}{\theta} p_1 + 2}{\frac{1-\theta}{\theta} + 2} = \frac{3\theta + (1-\theta)p_1}{1+2\theta} \times \frac{2\theta + (1-\theta)p_1}{1+\theta}. \qquad (7.11)$$

In the case where the characteristic Γ corresponds to being heterozygous with alleles a_1 and a_2, we need the expectation of $2X_1 X_2$, where the X_i follow a Dirichlet distribution with parameters

$$\left(\frac{1-\theta}{\theta} p_1 + 1, \frac{1-\theta}{\theta} p_2 + 1, \frac{1-\theta}{\theta} p_3, \ldots, \frac{1-\theta}{\theta} p_n \right).$$

This expectation is equal to

$$2 \frac{\theta + (1-\theta)p_1}{1+2\theta} \times \frac{\theta + (1-\theta)p_2}{1+\theta}. \qquad (7.12)$$

The two formulas (7.11) and (7.12) are called the *match probabilities* and are used by virtually all forensic laboratories. They represent the conditional probability that a suspect S has the same genotype as the person C who left the trace, given that C has that genotype and that S is not equal to C.

The likelihood ratios are the inverse of these match probabilities. These are then multiplied over all the loci to arrive at the likelihood ratio for the matching genotype on all loci (see the discussion at the end of Section 7.12). A forensic laboratory carries out this procedure for every trace separately. The starting point (7.10) is the same for all traces, but of course the traces themselves are not. This means that the genotype probabilities are case-specifically assigned, since the density χ_C depends on the trace. For example, the assigned probability that an innocent suspect has genotype (a_1, a_1) is, for $\theta > 0$, larger if the trace is (a_1, a_1) than if the trace is different.

In the derivation in Section 7.3, we modeled the genotypes as conditionally independent given the allele frequencies. That means that we assume that there is no relatedness between S and C. Interestingly, if we start with a finite population where there must be some relatedness, we can derive the very same match probabilities, and this we will do in the next section.

7.5 Population Genetics and the θ-Correction

We have seen that one can arrive at the match probabilities in (7.11) and (7.12) by considering uncertainty about allele frequencies, with the Dirichlet distribution (7.10) as our starting point. This can only be achieved for $\theta < 1/(N + 1)$. Otherwise, if θ is larger, we overestimate the remaining uncertainty that we have about the allele frequencies: whatever our initial parameters α_i were, the sample of N alleles that we subsequently incorporate cannot leave as much uncertainty as we have when we use $\theta > 1/(N + 1)$ in (7.10).

Somewhat surprisingly perhaps, there is a completely different way to arrive at the match probabilities in (7.11) and (7.12), which does not assume the Dirichlet distribution from the outset and which is interpretable for larger θ. In this section we will show how these match probabilities are naturally obtained if we work in a non-homogeneous population with subpopulations where mutations and immigration take place, and where θ is explicitly interpreted as the probability that two alleles in a (random) subpopulation have a common ancestor, that is, are *identical by descent* (IBD). In this interpretation there is no restriction on the numerical value of θ.

Consider, then, a randomly mating subpopulation, partly isolated from a larger population. We denote by N the subpopulation size, that is, the number of alleles under consideration. Upon tracing back the history of an allele, several things may happen. The allele may have appeared in the population by *immigration* from a different subpopulation, or the allele came into the population by means of a *mutation* of another allele. When we consider two arbitrary alleles in the population we can also consider the possibility that when we trace back their respective lineages, these lineages *coalesce* before an immigration or mutation event occurs with either of them, that is, the two alleles are two copies of the same ancestral allele.

We are interested in the probability of such a coalescence. Obviously, one can only make sense out of such a probability when making certain idealistic assumptions. We assume that when going back in time, coalescence of two lineages happens after an exponentially distributed waiting time with parameter $1/N$. We say that coalescence occurs at *rate* $1/N$. The waiting times (when going backwards in time) for pairs of alleles are independent of each other. At the same time, the waiting time for the event that either an immigration or a mutation event occurs in a single lineage is assumed to have an exponential distribution with parameter $\mu/(2N)$, and we assume that this waiting time does not depend on any coalescence event, and that they are also independent for different lineages.

It follows from elementary properties of the exponential distribution that the total rate of mutation or immigration in the two lineages of two alleles together is simply the sum of the two rates, and thus equal to μ/N. When we trace back the two lineages, it also follows from elementary properties of the exponential distribution that the probability that coalescence of two lineages takes place before any mutation or immigration event occurs with either of them is equal to

$$\theta := \frac{1/N}{1/N + \mu/N} = \frac{1}{1 + \mu}. \tag{7.13}$$

We interpret this number as the probability for any two alleles to be IBD.

We can, with this definition of θ, compute the probability that a number of alleles drawn from the subpopulation have certain types. To illustrate this, let p_a be the probability that in a population in equilibrium, any given allele is of type a, so p_a is the population frequency of a. If we now take two alleles, then the probability that they are both of type a can be expressed in terms of θ as

$$\theta p_a + (1 - \theta)p_a^2. \tag{7.14}$$

Indeed, these two alleles are IBD with probability θ and if this is the case, then we only need their common ancestor to be of type a, an event with probability p_a. If they are not IBD, an event with probability $1 - \theta$, then the types of the two alleles are independent of each other, and each of them is a with probability p_a.

Similarly, the probability that the two drawn alleles contain one allele of type a and one allele of type b is equal to $2(1 - \theta)p_a p_b$. To see this, note that the alleles can only be of different type if they are not IBD, an event with probability $1 - \theta$. In that case, their types are independent, and the formula follows.

7.5.1 The General Allele Sampling Formula in the IBD Interpretation

We next derive the general formula for the probability that a random sample from the subpopulation consists of specified numbers of alleles of each type. For simplicity we restrict ourselves to the situation in which there are only two different alleles in the population, but the argument immediately generalizes to the case with an arbitrary number of possible alleles.

To be precise, we will show that, if we have already sampled r alleles of type a and s alleles of type b, the probability that the next allele that we sample is of type a is equal to

$$\frac{r\theta + (1 - \theta)p_a}{1 + (r + s - 1)\theta}. \tag{7.15}$$

From this recursion set-up, any desired probability statement about numbers of alleles in random draws can be easily computed.

Notice that part of the claim is that only the number r of alleles of type a that has already been sampled is relevant, and not the order in which they appeared. It follows that the probability to obtain a sequence of alleles with the positions of the alleles of each type specified, only depends on the total number of alleles of each type in that sequence. So if we write $P(a^r b^s)$ for the probability to obtain the specific sequence that first contains r alleles of type a and then s alleles of type b, then the probability $P(r,s)$ to obtain r alleles of type a in a sample of $r + s$ alleles is given by

$$P(r,s) = P(a^r b^s) \binom{r+s}{r}.$$

The binomial coefficient simply counts how many sequences exist with r alleles of type a and s alleles of type b.

We will prove (7.15) by induction on $r + s$. Readers not particularly interested in the rather involved combinatorics can safely skip the rest of this subsection and recall the result.

When $r + s = 0$, (7.15) reduces to p_a and the formula is correct. The case $r + s = 1$ has been dealt with above: in that case, if one allele of type a has been sampled (that is, $r = 1, s = 0$), the probability that the next sampled allele is of type a is $\theta + (1 - \theta)p_a$, and if the first sampled allele was not of type a (that is, $r = 0, s = 1$) then the probability that the second allele is type a is $(1 - \theta)p_a$, in accordance with (7.15).

Now suppose that we randomly sample $r + s + 1$ alleles from the population, and that we are interested in the probability $P(r + 1, s)$ of the event that we obtain $r + 1$ alleles of type a and s alleles of type b. The claim (7.15) is equivalent to stating that

$$P(r+1,s) = P(a^r b^s) \frac{r\theta + (1 - \theta)p_a}{1 + (r + s - 1)\theta} \binom{r+s+1}{s}. \tag{7.16}$$

With $r + s + 1$ alleles we have $(r + s + 1)(r + s)/2$ pairs among them, so the total rate of coalescence is $(r + s + 1)(r + s)/(2N)$. The total rate of the mutation/immigration processes is $(r + s + 1)\mu/(2N)$. By the properties of the exponential distribution, which describes the waiting time for a coalescence or mutation/immigration event when we go backwards in time, these rates imply that the probability that we encounter a coalescence before any allele disappears into a mutation or immigration event is

$$\frac{r+s}{r+s+\mu} = \frac{(r+s)\theta}{1 + (r + s - 1)\theta},$$

where we have used (7.13). With the remaining probability, namely

$$\frac{1 - \theta}{1 + (r + s - 1)\theta},$$

upon tracing back the alleles, we will lose one as a result of a mutation/immigration event before any pair has coalesced together into a single ancestral allele.

Suppose now first that a coalescence happens before a mutation/immigration event. In that case there are two ways in which our sample of $r + s + 1$ alleles can have $r + 1$ alleles of type a. Either, there were r alleles of type a before the coalescence which involves type a alleles, or there were $r + 1$ alleles of type a before the coalescence which involves type b alleles. Since in a sequence of $r + s$ alleles any allele is equally likely to be the coalescing one, we see that conditional on a coalescence being the first event when we trace the $r + s + 1$ alleles back in the past, the probability that we get $r + 1$ alleles of type a and s of type b is

$$P(r,s)\frac{r}{r+s} + P(r+1,s-1)\frac{s-1}{r+s}$$

$$= P(a^r b^s)\binom{r+s-1}{r-1} + P(a^{r+1}b^{s-1})\binom{r+s-1}{r+1}.$$

Next, by considering how $P(a^r b^s)$ and $P(a^{r+1}b^{s-1})$ can both be obtained from a situation with r alleles of type a and $s - 1$ alleles of type b by sampling an allele of type b or a respectively, we have, using the induction hypothesis, that

$$P(a^{r+1}b^{s-1}) = P(a^r b^s)\frac{r\theta + (1-\theta)p_a}{(s-1)\theta + (1-\theta)p_b}. \tag{7.17}$$

This allows us to take out a factor $P(a^r b^s)$, corresponding to conditioning on the event of having selected r alleles of type a and s alleles of type b.

Now consider the second possibility, namely that a mutation/immigration event was the first event that was encountered when going backwards in time. In that case, this mutated allele is either allele a or allele b and by a similar argument as above, the probability that the $r + s + 1$ alleles contain $r + 1$ alleles of type a is easily seen to be

$$p_a\binom{r+s}{r}P(a^r b^s) + p_b\binom{r+s}{s-1}P(a^{r+1}b^{s-1}).$$

Thus, taking all these terms together we conclude that $(1+(r+s-1)\theta)P(r+1,s)$ is equal to $P(a^r b^s)$ multiplied with

$$(r+s)\theta\left[\binom{r+s+1}{r-1} + \frac{r\theta + (1-\theta)p_a}{(s-1)\theta + (1-\theta)p_b}\binom{r+s-1}{r+1}\right]$$

$$+ (1-\theta)\left[p_a\binom{r+s}{r} + p_b\binom{r+s}{s-1}\frac{r\theta + (1-\theta)p_a}{(s-1)\theta + (1-\theta)p_b}\right].$$

Thus, $((s - 1)\theta + (1 - \theta)p_b)(1 + (r + s - 1)\theta)P(r + 1, s)$ is equal to $P(a^r b^s)$ multiplied with

$$(r + s)\theta \left[\binom{r + s - 1}{r - 1}((s - 1)\theta + (1 - \theta)p_b) + (r\theta + (1 - \theta)p_a)\binom{r + s - 1}{r + 1} \right]$$

$$+ (1 - \theta)\left[p_a \binom{r + s}{r}((s - 1)\theta + (1 - \theta)p_b) + p_b \binom{r + s}{s - 1}(r\theta + (1 - \theta)p_a) \right],$$

which we can rewrite as

$$((s - 1)\theta + (1 - \theta)p_b)\left[(r + s)\theta\binom{r + s - 1}{r - 1} + (1 - \theta)p_a\binom{r + s}{r}\right]$$

$$+ (r\theta + (1 - \theta)p_a)\left[(r + s)\theta\binom{r + s - 1}{r + 1} + (1 - \theta)p_b\binom{r + s}{s - 1}\right].$$

Since

$$(r + s)\binom{r + s - 1}{r - 1} = r\binom{r + s}{r}$$

and

$$(r + s)\binom{r + s - 1}{r + 1} = (s - 1)\binom{r + s}{r},$$

this reduces to

$$((s - 1)\theta + (1 - \theta)p_b)\binom{r + s}{r}(r\theta + (1 - \theta)p_a)$$

$$+ (r\theta + (1 - \theta)p_a)\binom{r + s}{r + 1}((s - 1)\theta + (1 - \theta)p_b)$$

which equals

$$((s - 1)\theta + (1 - \theta)p_b)(r\theta + (1 - \theta)p_a)\left[\binom{r + s}{r} + \binom{r + s}{r + 1}\right]$$

$$= ((s - 1)\theta + (1 - \theta)p_b)(r\theta + (1 - \theta)p_a)\binom{r + s + 1}{r + 1},$$

and the desired result follows.

7.5.2 The θ-Correction in Forensic Practice

The sampling formula (7.15) is equivalent to (7.10). Indeed, if we model allele frequencies (X_a, X_b) as a random vector distributed as $\mathrm{Dir}\left(\frac{1-\theta}{\theta} p_a, \frac{1-\theta}{\theta} p_b\right)$, then if we have sampled $r + s$ alleles where r were of type a, the distribution of the allele frequencies conditional on this sample is $\mathrm{Dir}\left(\frac{1-\theta}{\theta} p_a + r, \frac{1-\theta}{\theta} p_b + s\right)$. Then the probability that the next allele to be sampled is of type a is easily seen to be the same as (7.15). This means that from the population genetic model in the previous section, we also get the match probabilities (7.11) and (7.12).

To see how this sampling formula relates to forensic practice, let us discuss the assumptions needed for it. When we trace back alleles, they coalesce or are introduced by the mutation/immigration process, meaning that ultimately all alleles are introduced by the latter mechanism. The allele probabilities p_a are the probabilities that this mechanism introduces new alleles in the population of type a. If we assume that the global population is in equilibrium and has reached stable allele frequencies, we may use the allele counts in a reference sample of that global population to be unbiased estimators of p_a. This is also true for data on any subpopulation, but since the global population is larger we obtain a better estimate from that, larger, population.

So let us assume that we have a sample from the global population. For any subpopulation of it, it holds that if we sample a random allele, the probability that it is of type a is p_a. If we keep sampling alleles from the same subpopulation that we sampled the first allele from, we get the sampling formula (7.15). Thus, what (7.15) gives us, is the average probability, over all subpopulations, for such a sample to have a specific outcome.

We think of the subpopulations to have evolved all in the same way, i.e., with the same rates on coalescence and mutation/immigration events. In particular, this means that the probability, in any subpopulation, that a randomly selected allele is type a is p_a. In view of the above description, the probability that an allele is type a is also interpretable as a realization of X_a when we make a random draw from a Dirichlet distribution with parameters $(1 - \theta) p_i/\theta$.

This in turn means that we can estimate θ if we do have data on allele frequencies from various subpopulations. Indeed, the variance of the random variable X_a modeling the allele frequency of allele a is given by

$$\mathrm{Var}(X_a) = E(X_a^2) - E(X_a)^2 = \theta p_a(1 - p_a),$$

so that

$$\theta = \mathrm{Var}(X_a)/(p_a(1 - p_a)).$$

All subpopulations can, as explained above, be viewed as giving realizations of X_a. Therefore, if we have data on $p_a^{(i)}$, the allele frequencies of allele a in subpopulation i, then we can estimate θ with the above formula by estimating $\text{Var}(X_a)$ with the sample variance in the $p_a^{(i)}$ and p_a by the average of the $p_a^{(i)}$.

We see now that θ is interpretable in several ways. We introduced it as the probability that two randomly selected alleles in a given subpopulation are identical by descent. If we additionally assume that all subpopulations have undergone the same random process in their genetic history, then the variance in the allele frequencies between the subpopulations is a measure for the level of coancestry in each subpopulation.

To illustrate this, imagine for example that the subpopulations are small so that θ is large. Then all of the subpopulations will rapidly undergo genetic drift, and will lose genetic variation, but there is no preference for which of the alleles will become more frequent. We can therefore expect a large variation in allele frequencies between the different subpopulations. On the other hand, in very large populations with random mating, common ancestors are so many generations ago that there is hardly any coalescence before a migration/mutation event, so θ is very small. In such populations, allele frequencies hardly change, so that in all subpopulations the allele frequency of a is very close to the average p_a.

Of course, the assumption that all subpopulations can be seen as identical independent realizations of the same evolutionary process is a strong one, and in reality different subpopulations may for example have different sizes and different levels of coancestry. This makes the estimator above unsuitable, but the idea remains that we can establish a connection between the IBD sharing within subpopulations and the variation in allele frequencies between them. The match probabilities thus are average match probabilities across all subpopulations, where we condition on all alleles being drawn from the same subpopulation, but not which subpopulation that is. Indeed, if we have data on the relevant subpopulation that we want to make a statement about, we should use those.

The habit of using (7.11) and (7.12) goes under the name *θ-correction*. This correction is supposed to account for the fact that we have data on a global population, but we want to assume that S and C are from the same (unknown) subpopulation (this may or may not be warranted by our actual knowledge of the situation), since this is beneficial for the defendant S if innocent.

In practice, however, the population sample used by the forensic laboratory to estimate p_a need not be representative of the offender population, it may be a convenience sample from the local population not containing individuals from all populations that are represented in the offender population. In that case, the framework for the sampling formula does not apply: we want to make statements on match probabilities outside those in the reference sample, but what we get from the sampling formula (7.15) are the match probabilities in subpopulations within the population the reference sample is from. Estimates of the value of θ for the latter are then not sufficient. However, augmenting θ beyond that estimate results in practice in larger match probabilities and therefore lower likelihood ratios.

The θ-correction should, then, be mostly viewed as a pragmatic way to arrive at a conservative value for the likelihood ratio obtained against a suspect. By using a generous value of θ, one can ensure that a likelihood ratio calculated with allele frequencies obtained from one population, does not exceed the likelihood ratio obtained in a second population from which the profile truly originates. Empirical studies have shown that a value as high as 0.03 is needed to achieve this. By doing so, one abandons both the interpretation of θ as a measure of uncertainty about the allele frequencies in the population the sample is from, as well as the interpretation as expected match probability in a subpopulation. One then simply inserts a value that in practice lowers the likelihood ratio to such an extent that it is a conservative value no matter which population one would have preferred to work with had data about it been available.

7.6 Kinship

Since DNA is inherited from parent to child, the DNA profiles of relatives have a different joint probability distribution than those of unrelated individuals. This can be exploited to arrive at a likelihood ratio investigating possible ways for how the individuals could be related. In this section we will consider one of the simplest forms of such likelihood ratios, namely those that compare the possibility that two individuals are related according to some given pedigree, as opposed to being unrelated, where the only genetic data available are those of the two individuals under consideration. Throughout, we assume that we consider loci in linkage equilibrium and we ignore the possibility of mutations.

7.6.1 The Inbreeding Coefficient of an Individual

We start with two important notions, namely *relatedness*, and being *inbred*. Individuals X and Y are said to be related if they have at least one ancestor in common. Real populations are obviously finite, and this means that many people are related, either closely or dating back many generations. Thus, if two persons are related, there exists a connected pedigree $\mathcal{P}$ that contains both these persons, with at least one common ancestor. There is a non-zero probability that such a common ancestor has passed on the same allele via the pedigree to both individuals, implying that if we select random alleles, one from X and one from Y, there is a non-zero probability that these alleles can be traced back to the same allele, so that they are identical by descent.

If the parents of a person are related, we say that this person is *inbred*. For an inbred person, if we consider his or her two alleles on a given locus, the probability that these are IBD is not zero. Indeed, since the parents are related, the alleles of the parents could be IBD and these can be passed on to their children. With these definitions, however, (virtually) all individuals in a finite population will be related to each other, and they will be inbred as well. Therefore we will only consider two individuals to be related if their common ancestor is present in a pedigree that we provide. Hence relatedness that goes back too far is simply not counted if it falls outside the scope of the pedigree under consideration.

Suppose now that there is a pedigree connecting the individuals X and Y. We may then wonder how this pedigree affects their genetic similarity. One measure of this is the probability that a randomly selected allele from X is IBD (within the pedigree) to a randomly selected allele from Y (at the same locus of course). This probability is called the *coancestry coefficient* or *kinship coefficient* and denoted by $\theta_{X,Y}$. Furthermore, for any individual X we denote by F_X the probability that the two alleles that X has on a given locus are IBD.

For a child I of X and Y, we have

$$F_I = \theta_{X,Y}, \tag{7.18}$$

since the two alleles of I (on a given locus) can be seen as random choices of the alleles of the parents X and Y. The probability that these are IBD is, therefore, the same as $\theta_{X,Y}$.

For an individual X we have $\theta_{X,X} = (1 + F_X)/2$. Indeed, if we sample two random alleles from X, then with probability $1/2$ we sample the same alleles, and then they are IBD. If we sample different alleles, then they are IBD with probability F_X.

Suppose next that X is a parent of Y and that the parents of Y are unrelated. If the alleles of X are IBD, then two randomly chosen alleles from X and Y are certainly IBD if for Y we choose the allele that is inherited from X. This happens with probability $F_X/2$. If the alleles of X are not IBD, then the only way for the two alleles to be IBD is that the chosen allele at X is passed on to Y, and that this allele is chosen for Y. The probability of this is $(1 - F_X)/4$ so that $\theta_{X,Y} = F_X/2 + (1 - F_X)/4 = (1 + F_X)/4$.

If X and Y are siblings with unrelated parents A and B, we claim that $\theta_{X,Y} = (2 + F_A + F_B)/8$. To see this, observe that if we choose alleles at X and Y which come from different parents, then they cannot be IBD since we assume that the parents are unrelated. If both chosen alleles come from parent A, then they are IBD with probability $\theta_{A,A} = (1+F_A)/2$, as explained above. The total probability of this possibility is, therefore, equal to $1/4 \times (1/2 + F_A/2)$. The computation in the case where both chosen alleles come from B is similar, leading to the claimed formula.

In a pedigree, we always include either both or none of the parents of each individual. Let the *founders* of the pedigree be those persons whose parents are not included in it. The founders are assumed to be unrelated to each other, meaning that no allele of a founder is IBD to an allele of another founder. It is natural to assume this, since the pedigree contains all the relations one wants to consider. Thus, if one wants the founders to be related, they should not have been founders but one should extend the pedigree beyond them instead.

We do allow for the founders to be inbred: the alleles of any founder are allowed some non-zero probability of being IBD. Thus, even if (as we just motivated) it is a natural choice to let the founders be unrelated to each other, we do still allow for each founder to be the result of a complicated pedigree including inbreeding.

The next question is whether or not there is a natural choice for the founders. In principle any pedigree can be extended by including the parents of some founder(s); if no additional relatedness is introduced, this will not alter the relatedness between the individuals of interest. If the individuals of interest are X and Y and we consider a pedigree without inbreeding, then they will have most recent common ancestors, which are those common ancestors that have no descendants who are also common ancestors of X and Y. Since there is no inbreeding, there will be a unique path from each such most recent common ancestor to X and one unique path to Y. Any IBD allele sharing between X and Y must come from one of the most recent common ancestors. Therefore we will restrict the pedigree to let these be founders and allow for all founders to have a positive inbreeding coefficient.

7.6.2 *Computing the Coancestry Coefficient for Non-inbred Individuals*

Consider two non-inbred individuals X and Y who are related to each other in a pedigree as we just described, that is, such that their common ancestors are also their most recent common ancestors. For each common ancestor A, there is a unique path in the pedigree from A to X and also a unique path from A to Y. Let there be $n_1 \geq 0$ allele transmissions from A to X and $n_2 \geq 0$ from A to Y.

If we select a random allele in X, the probability that this allele is IBD with an allele in A is equal to $(1/2)^{n_1}$. Hence, if we take a random allele a in X and b in Y, the probability that both of them are equal to an allele in A is $(1/2)^{n_1+n_2}$. The probability that these two alleles in A are furthermore IBD to each other is $\theta_{A,A} = (1 + F_A)/2$ as we saw above.

Thus, the probability that if we select a random allele in X and a random allele in Y, these alleles will be a pair of IBD alleles that is coming from ancestor A is equal to $(1/2)^{n_1+n_2+1}(1 + F_A)$. Note that $n_A = n_1 + n_2 + 1$ is the number of individuals in the path $X \to A \to Y$ in the pedigree.

Of course, X and Y may have several common ancestors. For example, siblings have both parents as common ancestors. However, when we consider a random allele a of X and a random allele b of Y, they can only be IBD if they are copies of an allele of one and the same common ancestor since we assume that the ancestors are unrelated. Thus, summing over all the common ancestors of X and Y now leads to the formula

$$\theta_{X,Y} = \sum_A \left(\frac{1}{2}\right)^{n_A} (1 + F_A).$$

7.6.3 Likelihood Ratios for Pairwise Relatedness

Now we turn to likelihood ratios that investigate pairwise relatedness between two individuals X and Y. We are interested whether the genotypes g_X of X and g_Y of Y give support for the hypothesis that X and Y are related according to some pedigree $\mathcal{P}$. For simplicity we will suppose that $\mathcal{P}$ is such that there is no inbreeding within this pedigree $\mathcal{P}$. We will, however, allow inbreeding and background relatedness in the population. This is done by using (7.15) for the joint probability distribution of the alleles of the founders, i.e., by assuming that any two alleles drawn at random from the population are IBD with probability θ. Recall that we obtained this interpretation of θ by defining the probabilities to select sets of alleles as moments of the distribution of $(X_1, \ldots, X_n)$, which are random variables distributed as a Dirichlet distribution with parameters $\frac{1-\theta}{\theta} p_i$ for $1 \leq i \leq n$, where $p_i = y_i/N$ denotes the relative frequency of the observed alleles of type i in a sample of size N.

We have defined $\theta_{X,Y}$ as a measure for the genetic proximity of X and Y. For likelihood ratio calculations this is not sufficient, since we need to calculate the genotype probabilities of X and Y, and then $\theta_{X,Y}$ is obviously not enough information. For example, when the founders are non-inbred then $\theta_{X,Y}$ is equal to 1/4 both for a parent–child relationship as well as for a sibling relationship. This expresses the fact that we expect the same amount of allele sharing for these two relationships, but it is also clear that the likelihoods of a pair of genotypes is not the same for both relationships: parents and children must share one IBD allele, whereas siblings may have 0, 1, or 2 such IBD pairs.

Since we model genotypes of founders as outcomes of random variables, the genotypes of X and Y are also outcomes of random variables that we denote G_X and G_Y. Given a pedigree $\mathcal{P}$, let $H_{\mathcal{P}}$ denote the hypothesis that X and Y are related as prescribed by $\mathcal{P}$, and let H_0 denote the hypothesis that X and Y are unrelated. The likelihood ratio we need to look at is then

$$LR_{H_{\mathcal{P}}, H_0}(g_X, g_Y) = \frac{P(G_X = g_X, G_Y = g_Y \mid H_{\mathcal{P}})}{P(G_X = g_X, G_Y = g_Y \mid H_0)}. \tag{7.19}$$

If we assume that $P(G_Y = g_y \mid H_P) = P(G_Y = g_y)$ and similarly for X and/or H_0, then the expression in (7.19) reduces to either

$$\frac{P(G_X = g_X \mid G_Y = g_Y, H_P)}{P(G_X = g_X \mid G_Y = g_Y, H_0)} \qquad (7.20)$$

or

$$\frac{P(G_Y = g_Y \mid G_X = g_X, H_P)}{P(G_Y = g_Y \mid G_X = g_X, H_0)}. \qquad (7.21)$$

We therefore need to be able to calculate conditional genotype probabilities of X, given the genotype of Y and the pedigree connecting them.

We start by calculating these likelihood ratios on a single locus, assuming Mendelian inheritance such that there are no mutations possible. When we consider IBD relations between the alleles of X and those of Y then we note that the absence of inbreeding ensures that neither the alleles of X nor those of Y can be IBD with each other via $\mathcal{P}$ (in the case where X or Y is a founder we will assume that they are not inbred). However, there can be pairs of IBD alleles within $\mathcal{P}$ between the alleles in g_X and those in g_Y; there may be either zero, one or two such pairs. Zero pairs means that the genotypical relation between X and Y is that of unrelated individuals; one pair is genetically the same as being parent–child, and two pairs corresponds genetically to being monozygotic twins. The precise genetic relation between X and Y is a linear combination of the three mentioned relations, with weights which are determined by the pedigree $\mathcal{P}$. This motivates the following development.

Let X and Y be connected by a pedigree $\mathcal{P}$ without inbreeding. We define $\kappa_i(X, Y)$ as the probability that X and Y have exactly i pairs of IBD alleles inherited via pedigree $\mathcal{P}$. The κ_i are called the *IBD coefficients*. Note that $\theta_{X,Y}$ is easily expressed in terms of the $\kappa_i(X, Y)$: for non-inbred individuals related by pedigree $\mathcal{P}$ we have

$$\theta_{X,Y} = \frac{1}{4}\kappa_1(X, Y) + \frac{1}{2}\kappa_2(X, Y). \qquad (7.22)$$

Indeed, if there is one pair of IBD alleles, then the probability to select two IBD alleles is $1/4$, and if there are two such pairs, then this probability is $1/2$. If we know the $\kappa_i(X, Y)$, then we can compute the conditional probabilities (7.20) and (7.21) by conditioning on the number of IBD pairs. Indeed, denoting by I the number of IBD pairs between the genotypes of X and Y, we have

$$P(G_Y = g_Y \mid G_X = g_X, H_P) = \sum_{i=0}^{2} \kappa_i(X, Y) P(G_Y = g_Y \mid G_X = g_X, I = i).$$

$$(7.23)$$

We write $PI(g_X, g_Y)$, referred to as the *parental index* (also called paternity index when it is more specifically investigated whether a certain man can be the father of a certain child), for the likelihood ratio for the hypotheses that X and Y are parent–child (versus unrelated) and $MZ(g_X, g_Y)$ for the likelihood ratio for the hypotheses that X and Y are monozygotic twins (versus unrelated). With this notation, (7.23) can be written as

$$LR_{H_P, H_0}(g_X, g_Y) = \kappa_0(X, Y) + \kappa_1(X, Y)PI(g_X, g_Y) + \kappa_2(X, Y)MZ(g_X, g_Y). \tag{7.24}$$

Next we claim that $LR_{H_P, H_0}(g_X, g_Y)$, which of course depends upon the allele frequencies of the alleles occurring in the genotypes, only depends on the frequencies of those alleles that occur in both g_X and g_Y. This is easy to see for the case where X and Y have genotypes without alleles in common: if they share no alleles then $LR_{H_P, H_0}(g_X, g_Y) = \kappa_0(X, Y)$, which is a constant independent of the allele frequencies. If they share two alleles, there is nothing to show, so we need only further look at the case where they share one allele.

If $g_X = (a_1, a_2)$ and $g_Y = (a_1, a_3)$, the likelihood ratio will only depend on the frequency of a_1. Intuitively this is easy to understand: under both scenarios, a sequence of alleles needs to be drawn from the population. The probability to draw a particular sequence of alleles does not depend on the order in which the alleles appear, only on the total number of each type. The alleles that are not shared need to be drawn from the population for both hypotheses, and we may for convenience assume that these are the first ones to be drawn. The likelihoods will therefore only differ because different numbers of the alleles that are shared are drawn from the population under both hypotheses. The probability to draw these alleles does not involve other allele frequencies than those of the selected alleles, cf. (7.15).

We confirm this with an explicit computation. The relevant conditional probabilities are listed in Table 7.1. In Table 7.2 we repeat Table 7.1 with $\theta = 0$. Note that when one takes the ratio of the two probabilities on the same line, the frequencies of the alleles that are not shared cancel, and only shared alleles turn out to matter.

For unlinked loci, the segregation of alleles between the loci is independent and hence (since we assume linkage equilibrium) likelihood ratios are obtained by multiplying the likelihood ratios obtained per locus. While this has the advantage of facilitating computations, it means that it is impossible to distinguish between pedigrees with the same $\kappa_i(X, Y)$.

For linked loci, however, pedigrees with the same IBD probabilities marginally per locus may have different joint distributions of IBD probabilities. We will now explain this phenomenon, recalling the concept of recombination that we described in Section 7.2.

Table 7.1 *Conditional genotype probabilities for unrelated individuals and parent–child pairs for genotypes with alleles in common.*

g_X	g_Y	$P(G_Y = g_Y \mid G_X = g_X, I = 0)$	$P(G_Y = g_Y \mid G_X = g_X, I = 1)$
(a_1,a_1)	(a_1,a_1)	$\frac{2\theta+(1-\theta)p_1}{1+\theta}\frac{3\theta+(1-\theta)p_1}{1+2\theta}$	$\frac{2\theta+(1-\theta)p_1}{1+\theta}$
(a_1,a_1)	(a_1,a_2)	$2\frac{(1-\theta)p_2}{1+\theta}\frac{2\theta+(1-\theta)p_1}{1+2\theta}$	$\frac{(1-\theta)p_2}{1+\theta}$
(a_1,a_2)	(a_1,a_2)	$2\frac{\theta+(1-\theta)p_1}{1+\theta}\frac{\theta+(1-\theta)p_2}{1+2\theta}$	$\frac{1}{2}\left(\frac{\theta+(1-\theta)p_1}{1+\theta}+\frac{\theta+(1-\theta)p_2}{1+\theta}\right)$
(a_1,a_2)	(a_1,a_3)	$2\frac{(1-\theta)p_3}{1+\theta}\frac{\theta+(1-\theta)p_1}{1+2\theta}$	$\frac{1}{2}\frac{(1-\theta)p_3}{1+\theta}$

Table 7.2 *Table 7.1 with $\theta = 0$.*

g_X	g_Y	$P(G_Y = g_Y \mid G_X = g_X, I = 0)$	$P(G_Y = g_Y \mid G_X = g_X, I = 1)$
(a_1,a_1)	(a_1,a_1)	p_1^2	p_1
(a_1,a_1)	(a_1,a_2)	$2p_1p_2$	p_2
(a_1,a_2)	(a_1,a_2)	$2p_1p_2$	$\frac{1}{2}(p_1 + p_2)$
(a_1,a_2)	(a_1,a_3)	$2p_1p_3$	$\frac{1}{2}p_3$

We let, for individuals X, Y in a given pedigree $\mathcal{P}$, $\kappa_{i,j}(X,Y)$ be the probability that X and Y have i pairs of IBD alleles on the first and j pairs on the second locus. The coefficient $\kappa_{i,j}(X,Y)$ is a function of the recombination probability ρ. The following example shows that it is possible that due to recombination, the joint IBD coefficients of X and Y in two pedigrees are different, while the marginal ones are identical.

Example 7.6.1 The IBD coefficients for half-siblings are $\kappa_0 = \kappa_1 = 1/2$ and $\kappa_2 = 0$. For the relation between grandparent and grandchild, we have the same numbers. Hence, these two relations are genetically indistinguishable on a single locus.

However, recombination changes this, as we can see from the following computation. Two half-siblings have no IBD alleles if and only they receive different alleles from their common parent. This is possible when the common parent passes on alleles without recombination twice (in which case the probability of there being no IBD alleles between X and Y is $1/2$), or with recombination twice (with the same result), but not if there is recombination towards one offspring and not towards the other one. Thus, $\kappa_{0,0}(X,Y) = (1-\rho)^2/2 + \rho^2/2 = 1/2 - \rho + \rho^2$. But this gives us the other $\kappa_{i,j}(X,Y)$ as well: for instance $\kappa_{0,1}(X,Y) + \kappa_{0,0}(X,Y) = \kappa_0$ since the two possibilities on the left-hand side together give the probability that there are no IBD alleles on the first locus. Therefore $\kappa_{0,1}(X,Y) = \rho - \rho^2$ and we similarly obtain $\kappa_{1,0}(X,Y) = \kappa_{0,1}(X,Y)$ and $\kappa_{1,1}(X,Y) = \kappa_{0,0}(X,Y)$.

For grandparent–grandchild it is not difficult to see that $\kappa_{0,0} = \kappa_{1,1} = (1-\rho)/2$ and $\kappa_{0,1} = \kappa_{1,0} = \rho/2$. Indeed, any child of the grandparent has one chromosome with alleles which come from the grandparent under consideration. The probability that none of these will be in the grandchild's genotype is (see Section 7.2) $(1-\rho)/2$, which is therefore precisely equal to $\kappa_{0,0}$. The other coefficients follow from similar arguments. $\square$

We have, similar to (7.24), that

$$LR_{H_P, H_0}(g_X, g_Y) = \sum_{i,j=0}^{2} \kappa_{i,j}(X,Y) LR^{i,j}(g_X, g_Y), \qquad (7.25)$$

where $LR^{i,j}$ is the likelihood ratio in favor of having a relationship with i pairs of IBD alleles on the first and j on the second.

Finally, if we consider more than two linked loci, and I_j denotes the number of IBD alleles on locus j, we need to compute all

$$\kappa_{i_1,\ldots,i_n}(X,Y) = P(I_1 = i_1, \ldots, I_n = i_n \mid H_P), \qquad (7.26)$$

that is, the probability that there are i_j pairs of IBD alleles on locus j. To compute this, we can use that if we consider the loci in their ordering on the chromosome, I_j is conditionally independent of all $I_i, i < j-1$ given I_{j-1} (assuming recombination events across the chromosome are independent). Thus,

$$P(I_j = i_j \mid I_1 = i_1, \ldots, I_{j-1} = i_{j-1}, H_P) = P(I_j = i_j \mid I_{j-1} = i_{j-1}, H_P).$$

Indeed, if we know how many IBD alleles we have on the locus preceding locus j, then the pedigree and the recombination probability determines how many pairs we will get at locus j.

Beyond pairwise relationships, in kinship analysis one encounters pedigrees in which multiple persons have known DNA profiles. For example, in a missing persons case a few relatives of the missing person may have been genotyped. While the computations become more laborious in such cases, the underlying model remains the same. The profiles of the persons in the pedigree will, in combination with the genotype probabilities of the untyped founders and the pedigree, yield a probability distribution for the genotypes of the persons in the pedigree whose DNA profile is unknown. In particular, one obtains a probability distribution for the genotype of the missing person. The likelihood ratio for an unidentified person with genotype g to be that missing person, as opposed to being unrelated to that missing person, is then the ratio between the probability that the missing person has that genotype given the pedigree and the information of genotypes of those individuals for which the genotypes are known, and the probability that an unrelated person has that profile.

Several algorithms and software solutions exist that enable the computation of the likelihood of genetic data on pedigrees, including the possibility to take linkage and mutations into account.

7.6.4 Expectation of the Likelihood Ratio for Pairwise Kinship

In this section we consider the expectation of the likelihood ratio for pairwise kinship, assuming that allele frequencies are known. We will show the rather remarkable fact that, given the number L of possible alleles on a locus, the average (expected) likelihood ratio for pairwise kinship does not depend on the allele frequencies on the locus, but only on L. Sometimes, L is referred to as the length of the *allelic ladder* at the locus.

We first introduce some notation and terminology that allow us to carry out the necessary computations, and then we will compute the expected value of the likelihood ratio. Recall that for pairwise kinship, genotype likelihoods depend on the IBD coefficients $\kappa_i(X, Y)$. Indeed, once we know these coefficients, we can compute the likelihood ratio as a weighted average as explained in the previous section.

Suppose that the likelihood ratio compares the hypothesis H_κ that the two individuals are related by a pedigree with $\kappa = (\kappa_0, \kappa_1, \kappa_2)$ to the hypothesis that they are unrelated. Furthermore, we do not assume that the true relation between the individuals is necessarily the same as the one tested for in the likelihood ratio: the true relationship is a pedigree with IBD coefficients $\kappa' = (\kappa'_0, \kappa'_1, \kappa'_2)$.

If we consider genotypes (g_X, g_Y) from persons with IBD coefficients $\kappa_i(X, Y)$, then we write the probability to obtain them as

$$P(g_X, g_Y \mid H_\kappa) = \sum_{i=0}^{2} \kappa_i(X, Y) P(g_X, g_Y \mid H_i), \tag{7.27}$$

where H_i is the hypothesis that $\kappa_i(X, Y) = 1$. We also let LR_i for $i \in \{0, 1, 2\}$ be the likelihood ratio of H_i versus H_0, and LR_κ be the likelihood ratio that compares the hypotheses of being related according to κ, versus being unrelated. Then, since obviously $LR_0 = 1$, we have

$$LR_\kappa(g_X, g_Y) = \kappa_0(X, Y) + \kappa_1(X, Y) LR_1(g_X, g_Y) + \kappa_2(X, Y) LR_2(g_X, g_Y), \tag{7.28}$$

which is simply another way of writing (7.24).

Recall that we test for the relation defined by κ while the true relationship is κ'. Since the genotypes (g_X, g_Y) are outcomes of a random variable selecting individuals related with IBD coefficients κ', we can write $LR_\kappa \mid H_{\kappa'}$ for the random variable that gives the likelihood ratio in favor of H_κ versus H_0 on genotypes randomly selected with IBD coefficients κ'. From (7.27) and (7.28) it now follows that we can compute the expectation of this random variable as

$$E(LR_\kappa \mid H_{\kappa'}) = \sum_{i,j=0}^{2} \kappa_i \kappa'_j E(LR_i \mid H_j), \qquad (7.29)$$

which we can also write as a matrix product

$$E(LR_\kappa \mid H_{\kappa'}) = \kappa \cdot E(LR_i \mid H_j) \cdot (\kappa')^t.$$

Now it is easy to see that when $i = 0$ or $j = 0$, we have $E(LR_i \mid H_j) = 1$, so it remains to compute only four expectations. We will do so explicitly for the parent–child case, that is, for $i = j = 1$.

Assume first that the child has genotype $G_C = (a, a)$. In that case, the possible genotypes of its father, alongside with their probabilities (given $G_C = (a, a)$) and the corresponding likelihood ratios are listed in Table 7.3.

From this table, we see that

$$E(LR_1 \mid G_C = (a, a), H_1) = p_a \frac{1}{p_a} + (1 - p_a) \frac{1}{2 p_a} = \frac{1 + p_a}{2 p_a}.$$

Next, suppose that the child has genotype (a, b) where we assume that $a \neq b$. Then we obtain Table 7.4.

From this table it is not difficult to check that

$$E(LR_1 \mid G_C = (a, b), H_1) = \frac{1}{2} + \frac{p_a + p_b}{8 p_a p_b}.$$

Summing over all possible genotypes of the child, we arrive at the expected likelihood ratio in the case where we evaluate a true father–child pair with unspecified genotypes:

Table 7.3 *Likelihood ratios in favor of paternity if* $G_C = (a, a)$.

g	$P(G_F = g \mid G_C = (a,a), H_1)$	LR_1
(a, a)	p_a	$1/p_a$
$(a, b), b \neq a$	p_b	$1/(2 p_a)$

Table 7.4 *Likelihood ratios in favor of paternity if $G_C = (a,b)$.*

g	$P(G_F = g \mid G_C = (a,b), H_1)$	LR_1
(a,b)	$(p_a + p_b)/2$	$(p_a + p_b)/(4 p_a p_b)$
$(a,x), x \notin \{a,b\}$	$p_x/2$	$1/(4 p_a)$
$(b,x), x \notin \{a,b\}$	$p_x/2$	$1/(4 p_b)$
(a,a)	$p_a/2$	$1/(2 p_a)$
(b,b)	$p_b/2$	$1/(2 p_b)$

$$
E(LR_1 \mid H_1) = \sum_a p_a^2 \frac{1 + p_a}{2 p_a} + \sum_{a,b:a<b} 2 p_a p_b \frac{p_a + p_b + 4 p_a p_b}{8 p_a p_b}
$$

$$
= \sum_a p_a \frac{1 + p_a}{2} + \sum_{a,b:a<b} \frac{p_a + p_b + 4 p_a p_b}{4}
$$

$$
= \sum_a \frac{p_a}{2} + \sum_a \frac{p_a^2}{2} + \sum_{a,b:a<b} p_a p_b + \sum_{a,b:a<b} \frac{p_a + p_b}{4}.
$$

The first term equals $1/2$. The second and third term together also give $1/2$, since they together enumerate all genotypes on the locus under consideration, and count half their probability.

Finally, to evaluate the last term, we observe that in the double sum

$$
\sum_a \sum_{b:b>a} (p_a + p_b)
$$

each of the possible p_i appears precisely $L - 1$ times. Hence the last term is equal to $(L - 1)/4$. We conclude that

$$
E(LR_1 \mid H_1) = \frac{1}{2} + \frac{1}{2} + \frac{L - 1}{4} = \frac{L + 3}{4},
$$

which only depends on L and not on the allele frequencies. Thus, for likelihood ratios that evaluate the hypothesis of being parent–child versus unrelated to each other, the expected value of this likelihood ratio for true parent–child pairs is equal to

$$
\prod_i \frac{L_i + 3}{4}, \tag{7.30}
$$

where L_i is the length of the allelic ladder of locus i and we take the product over all genotyped loci, assuming independence.

Similar computations lead to the full matrix

$$E(LR_i \mid H_j)_{i,\,j=0,1,2} = \begin{pmatrix} 1 & 1 & 1 \\ 1 & (L+3)/4 & (L+1)/2 \\ 1 & (L+1)/2 & L(L+1)/2 \end{pmatrix} \qquad (7.31)$$

and plugging these expressions into (7.29) we obtain

$$E(LR_\kappa \mid H_{\kappa'}) = \kappa_0 + (1 - \kappa_0)\kappa_0' + \kappa_1\kappa_1'\frac{L+3}{4} + (\kappa_1'\kappa_2 + \kappa_1\kappa_2')\frac{L+1}{2}$$
$$+ \kappa_2\kappa_2'\frac{L(L+1)}{2}. \qquad (7.32)$$

Note that this expression is symmetric in κ and κ'.

If $\kappa = \kappa'$, (7.32) reduces to

$$E(LR_\kappa \mid H_\kappa) = \kappa_0(2 - \kappa_0) + \kappa_1^2\frac{L+3}{4} + 2\kappa_1\kappa_2\frac{L+1}{2} + \kappa_2^2\frac{L(L+1)}{2}, \qquad (7.33)$$

which is readily seen to be equal to

$$E(LR_\kappa \mid H_\kappa) = \alpha L^2 + \beta L + (1 - \alpha - \beta), \text{ where} \qquad (7.34)$$

$$\alpha = \frac{\kappa_2^2}{2} \text{ and } \beta = \frac{\kappa_1^2 + 4\kappa_1\kappa_2 + 2\kappa_2^2}{4}.$$

Finally, we note that if $L > 1$, we obtain

$$E(LR_2 \mid H_1) > E(LR_1 \mid H_1).$$

We see that among all LR_κ, the highest average LR_κ is not for the LR_κ that postulates the actual relationship. This gives us the example announced in Section 2.4.5.

7.6.5 Linked Loci

We next investigate various loci which may or may not be linked. Consider a pair of possibly linked loci 1 and 2 with L_1 and L_2 possible alleles respectively, and with recombination probability p.

Let $H_{j_1,\,j_2}$ be the hypothesis that there are j_1 pairs of IBD alleles on the first locus and j_2 on the second. Similarly let $H_j^{(i)}$ be the hypothesis that on locus i there are j pairs of IBD alleles. Using the assumption of linkage equilibrium we can write

$$P((g_1^{(1)}, g_1^{(2)}), (g_2^{(1)}, g_2^{(2)}) \mid H_{j_1, j_2}) = P(g_1^{(1)}, g_2^{(1)}) \mid H_{j_1}^{(1)}) P(g_1^{(2)}, g_2^{(2)}) \mid H_{j_2}^{(2)}),$$

where $g_i = (g_i^{(1)}, g_i^{(2)})$ is the genotype of person i on the two loci.

The likelihood ratio factorizes and we have

$$LR_{i_1, i_2}(g_1, g_2) := LR_{H_{i_1, i_2}, H_{0,0}}(g_1, g_2)$$

$$= LR_{i_1}^{(1)}(g_1^{(1)}, g_2^{(1)}) LR_{i_2}^{(2)}(g_1^{(2)}, g_2^{(2)}),$$

where $LR_i^{(j)}$ denotes LR_i on locus j. Therefore

$$E(LR_{i_1, i_2} \mid H_{j_1, j_2}) = E(LR_{i_1}^{(1)} \mid H_{j_1}^{(1)}) E(LR_{i_2}^{(2)} \mid H_{j_2}^{(2)}), \qquad (7.35)$$

where the expectations on the right-hand side are given in (7.32). This formula expresses the likelihood ratio of H_{i_1, i_2} versus $H_{0,0}$ when in fact the true relation is according to H_{j_1, j_2}.

In general, $E(LR_{\mathcal{P}} \mid H_{\mathcal{P}'})$ can be written as

$$\sum_{j_1, j_2, i_1, i_2=0}^{2} \kappa_{i_1, i_2}(X, Y) \kappa'_{j_1, j_2}(X, Y) E(LR_{i_1}^{(1)} \mid H_{j_1}^{(1)}) E(LR_{i_2}^{(2)} \mid H_{j_2}^{(2)}), \qquad (7.36)$$

where the $\kappa_{i_1, i_2}(X, Y)$ and $\kappa'_{j_1, j_2}(X, Y)$ are derived from the pedigrees $\mathcal{P}$, respectively $\mathcal{P}'$.

The above formula readily extends to more than two loci. Indeed, considering n loci, let $\rho = (\rho_1, \ldots, \rho_{n-1})$, where ρ_i is the recombination probability between loci i and $i+1$, and let $\kappa_{i_1, \ldots, i_n}(X, Y)$ be the probability of having i_j IBD alleles at locus j, for all $j = 1, \ldots, n$. Obviously this probability depends on the precise pedigree. Then we can write (in the obvious extension of our notation),

$$E(LR_{\mathcal{P}} \mid H_{\mathcal{P}'}) = \sum \kappa_{i_1, \ldots, i_n}(X, Y) \kappa'_{j_1, \ldots, j_n}(X, Y) E(LR_{i_1, \ldots, i_n} \mid H_{j_1, \ldots, j_n})$$

$$= \sum \kappa_{i_1, \ldots, i_n}(X, Y) \kappa'_{j_1, \ldots, j_n}(X, Y) \prod_{k=1}^{n} E(LR_{i_k}^{(k)} \mid H_{j_k}^{(k)}). \qquad (7.37)$$

Thus, for any number of loci, the expected value of the likelihood ratio $LR_{\mathcal{P}}$, realized on members of a possibly different pedigree $\mathcal{P}'$ does not depend on the allele frequencies but only on the lengths of the allelic ladders of the loci and the recombination probabilities.

It also follows that if IBD coefficients are the same on single loci, as is the case for instance for half-siblings, grandparent–grandchild and uncle–nephew, then the expected likelihood ratios involving these relationships are the same for fully linked loci, as well as for independent loci. When ρ is strictly between 0 and 1/2 this is no longer the case anymore. In particular, for a number of n (fully) linked loci, we get, with L_i the number of alleles that exist for locus i,

$$E(LR_{\mathcal{P}} \mid H_{\mathcal{P}}) = \kappa_0(2 - \kappa_0) + \kappa_1^2 \prod_{k=1}^{n} \frac{L_k + 3}{4} + 2\kappa_1\kappa_2 \prod_{k=1}^{n} \frac{L_k + 1}{2}$$

$$+ \kappa_2^2 \prod_{k=1}^{n} \frac{L_k(L_k + 1)}{2}. \tag{7.38}$$

While this can be a very large value, if there are no alleles shared on all loci then the likelihood ratio is κ_0. It is only with probability $1 - \kappa_0$ that the individuals will share IBD alleles on all loci. If alleles are sufficiently rare, this will result in a likelihood ratio in favor of $H_{\mathcal{P}}$, so then the probability that $P(LR_{\mathcal{P}} \geq 1 \mid H_{\mathcal{P}}) \geq 1 - \kappa_0$. If the tested individuals do not share alleles identical by descent, they may share alleles by chance. But if all loci are linked, one locus without shared alleles allows to conclude that there are no identical by descent alleles at all. As more loci are considered it becomes less likely that the individuals will share alleles on all considered loci by chance. Therefore for many loci $P(LR_{\mathcal{P}} \geq 1 \mid H_{\mathcal{P}})$ will be only slightly larger than $1 - \kappa_0$. This implies that when using a series of linked markers if κ_0 is large, we either get (with small probability) very strong evidence in favor of $H_{\mathcal{P}}$, or (with large probability) very weak evidence against it, i.e., the LR distribution is very skewed.

7.6.6 Likelihood Ratio and Weight of Evidence

We have seen that $E(LR_\kappa \mid H_{\kappa'})$ does not depend on the allele frequencies. This means that if we reduce the allele frequency p_a of an allele until it vanishes completely, the expected value has a discontinuity at $p_a = 0$. From a practical point of view this means that we cannot determine the expected value of the likelihood ratio for a certain population, since unless we have genotyped the whole population, we cannot know with certainty all the alleles on the loci under consideration.

Since $P(LR_\kappa > 0 \mid H_\kappa) = 1$, $E(\log(LR_\kappa \mid H_\kappa))$ is well defined. Contrary to $E(LR_\kappa \mid H_\kappa)$, it does depend on all allele frequencies. In Section 2.4.5 the $\log(LR)$ was called the weight of the evidence, measuring the amount of information in the evidence.

As an example, consider the situation in which $\kappa = (0, 0, 1)$, that is, we look at genetic identity. We have claimed that $E(LR_2 \mid H_2)$ is equal to $L(L + 1)/2$ (cf. (7.34)), which is the number of genotypes on a locus with L alleles. This is rather easy to see, since by conditioning on the genotype g of the first person, we obtain

$$E(LR_2 \mid H_2) = \sum_a p_a^2 E(LR_2 \mid g = (a,a), H_2)$$

$$+ \sum_{a,b:a<b} 2 p_a p_b E(LR_2 \mid g = (a,b), H_2)$$

$$= \sum_a p_a^2 \cdot 1/p_a^2 + \sum_{a,b:a<b} 2 p_a p_b \cdot 1/(2 p_a p_b)$$

$$= L + \frac{L^2 - L}{2} = \frac{L(L+1)}{2}.$$

On the other hand,

$$E(\log(LR_2 \mid H_2))$$

$$= \sum_a p_a^2 \cdot \log(1/p_a^2) + \sum_{a,b:a<b} 2 p_a p_b \cdot \log(1/(2 p_a p_b))$$

$$= -2 \sum_a p_a^2 \log(p_a) - 2 \log 2 \sum_{a<b} p_a p_b - 2 \sum_{a<b} p_a p_b \log(p_a)$$

$$- 2 \sum_{a<b} p_a p_b \log(p_b)$$

$$= -2 \sum_a p_a^2 \log(p_a) - \log 2 \left(1 - \sum_a p_a^2\right) - 2 \sum_{a\neq b} p_a p_b \log(p_a)$$

$$= -2 \sum_a p_a^2 \log(p_a) - \log 2 \left(1 - \sum_a p_a^2\right) - 2 \sum_a p_a(1 - p_a) \log(p_a)$$

$$= -\log 2 \left(1 - \sum_a p_a^2\right) - 2 \sum_a p_a \log(p_a).$$

Hence the expected weight of evidence involves the term $1 - \sum_a p_a^2$, which is the *expected heterozygosity* on the locus. It also involves the *entropy* $-\sum_a p_a \log(p_a)$ of the allele frequency distribution.

A similar computation for the parent–child likelihood ratio gives

$$E(\log(LR_1 \mid H_1)) = -2 \log 2 \left(1 - \sum_a p_a^2\right) + \sum_a p_a(p_a^2 - p_a - 1) \log(p_a)$$

$$+ \sum_{a<b} p_a p_b(p_a + p_b) \log(p_a + p_b).$$

We see that this expression again involves the expected heterozygosity, and terms that seem to be related to the entropy.

In any of these expressions we see that $E(\log(LR_i \mid H_i))$ is continuous in the allele frequencies, whereas $E(LR_i \mid H_i)$ is not. An allele that becomes rarer still contributes the same to the expected likelihood ratio, but less to the expected log of the likelihood ratio. This means that, contrary to $E(LR_i \mid H_i)$, we can estimate $E(\log(LR_i \mid H_i))$ from a sample of population alleles: the presence of rare alleles does not influence it very much. So although equivalent in any particular case, the likelihood ratio and the logarithm of the likelihood ratio behave differently in terms of expectation. This analysis reinforces our conclusion in Section 2.4.5 that the logarithm of the likelihood ratio is the better behaved quantity.

7.7 Summary and Conclusions

First we have described the basics of DNA profiles, which consist of the alleles at a certain number of loci. Next we carefully set out the difference between the population frequency of a profile on the one hand, and its random match probability on the other. The former is a population statistic that we typically do not know, while the latter is a subjective probability that a randomly chosen person has the profile. This last probability depends on our current knowledge.

We have explained the notions of Hardy–Weinberg equilibrium and linkage equilibrium, and have argued that we can work with these notions per locus for the random match probability, despite the possible linkage between various loci.

The uncertainty about allele frequencies is often described with a Dirichlet distribution, and we explained how, starting with such a distribution, additional sampling of profiles leads to a new Dirichlet distribution with adjusted parameters. Forensic laboratories often work with a choice of parameters which involves a number $0 \leq \theta \leq 1$, and which leads to the famous sampling formulas

$$\frac{3\theta + (1-\theta)p_1}{1+2\theta} \frac{2\theta + (1-\theta)p_1}{1+\theta} \tag{7.39}$$

and

$$2\frac{\theta + (1-\theta)p_1}{1+2\theta} \frac{\theta + (1-\theta)p_2}{1+\theta}, \tag{7.40}$$

which represent the conditional probabilities that a suspect S has the same genotype as the person C who left the trace, given that C has that genotype and that S is not equal to C in the homozygous case (7.39), respectively the heterozygous case (7.40).

We have subsequently shown that the same formulas result from a completely different, population-genetic, approach with background relatedness, mutation, and migration. In this interpretation, there is no further restriction on the values of θ. Using these formulas is known as applying the θ-correction.

In the second part of this chapter, we have explained in detail how to make computations for likelihood ratios in a kinship context. The basic formula is

$$LR_{H_{\mathcal{P}}, H_0}(g_X, g_Y) = \kappa_0(X, Y) + \kappa_1(X, Y)PI(g_X, g_Y) + \kappa_2(X, Y)MZ(g_X, g_Y),$$
(7.41)

which expresses the likelihood ratio for kinship via pedigree $\mathcal{P}$ versus unrelatedness in terms of the IBD (identical by descent) coefficients κ_i: $\kappa_i(X, Y)$ is the probability that two individuals X, Y have i IBD alleles via the pedigree $\mathcal{P}$ under investigation. In this formula, PI is the parental index, that is, the likelihood ratio corresponding to the hypotheses parent/child versus being unrelated. This familial relationship guarantees one IBD allele. Similarly, MZ stands for the likelihood ratio of being monozygotic twins versus being unrelated. Being monozygotic twins implies having two IBD alleles. Hence, the actual likelihood ratio is a weighted combination of these likelihood ratios, with the weights determined by the pedigree of relatedness.

This likelihood ratio only depends on the frequencies of alleles occurring in both g_X and g_Y. Expectations of such kinship likelihood ratios tend to have the somewhat surprising property that they only depend on the alleles involved via the number of possible alleles at a given locus, and not on the population frequency of these alleles.

7.8 Bibliographical Notes

The book [5] by David Balding is suitable further reading for the evaluation of DNA evidence, as is the collection of essays in [30]. For HWE and LE we refer to [63], in which also a discussion of the use of the Dirichlet distribution as in this chapter can be found, and much more. The θ-correction goes back to Balding and Nichols in [12] and [13]. For estimation of population substructure, we refer to [176]. Much of the discussion on kinship calculations can be found in [144] and [145].

8

Statistical Modeling and DNA Mixture Evaluation

It happens very often that a trace turns out to contain DNA material from multiple individuals. Calculations of likelihood ratios for such traces is generally perceived as much more difficult than for single source traces. In this chapter we discuss various concrete ways to go about such mixture evidential interpretation. In order to do so, we first need to investigate what kind of statistical modeling we actually need, and what level of detail is adequate for our purposes. Much of our discussion, especially in the beginning, is on an almost abstract level. This is necessary so as to develop a suitable philosophical and practical position in this large and ever extending field. We will discuss in detail what mixture evaluation really amounts to, and what can be expected from the likelihood ratios that we obtain upon using various different models and approaches.

8.1 Mixture Likelihood Ratios

We have explained in Section 7.1 that a trace profile consists of a set of detected alleles, together with their peak heights. If we want to fully process the evidence, we therefore must define a model that gives a probabilistic description of such peak heights. The history of mixture interpretation is simply a history of defining models that reduce the data less and less, moving from evaluating matches/non-matches, to the set of detected alleles, and finally to full trace profiles.

Let us denote the (data to be evaluated in the) trace profile by M, and let S be the person of interest with DNA profile g. There may be other profiles available from persons that play an undisputed role, for instance of a victim whose contribution is considered to be certain, and we denote by I the collection of all such profiles, excluding g.

We wish to calculate the likelihood ratio in favor of S having contributed to M. The data pertaining to the case that are relevant for this are, of course, the trace profile M and the profile g of S. That is, we wish to compute the likelihood ratio for these data under the two hypotheses:

$$LR(M, g \mid I) = \frac{P(M, g \mid H_1, I)}{P(M, g \mid H_2, I)} = \frac{P(M \mid H_1, g, I)}{P(M \mid H_2, g, I)} \frac{P(g \mid H_1, I)}{P(g \mid H_2, I)}, \tag{8.1}$$

where H_1 states that S contributed to M and H_2 states that S did not. We assume that H_1 and H_2 only differ in their description of who contributed with respect to the alleged contribution of S. That is, the relationship between S and the persons whose profiles are in I is the same for H_1 and H_2. This implies that the identity

$$P(g \mid H_1, I) = P(g \mid H_2, I) \tag{8.2}$$

holds for the probability of S to have profile g. This identity is violated if the hypotheses make different statements as to how the profile of S depends on those in I. For example, H_1 may state that S contributed and is unrelated to all persons in I and H_2 may state that S did not contribute and also state some form of relatedness, for instance that S is a child of one of the persons in I.

In the case where (8.2) holds, the last term in (8.1) is equal to 1, and we obtain

$$LR(M, g \mid I) = \frac{P(M \mid H_1, g, I)}{P(M \mid H_2, g, I)}. \tag{8.3}$$

8.1.1 Mixture Models, Abstractly

Abstractly, we introduce parameters θ in the model, with a probability density f describing our knowledge about them. We can make computations by integrating over θ (where in the notation we omit the space over which we integrate), for instance:

$$P(M) = \int P(M \mid \theta) f(\theta) d\theta = \int P_\theta(M) f(\theta) d\theta.$$

We can evaluate $LR(M, g \mid I)$ by integrating out the parameters θ. If we make the assumptions that $f(\theta \mid H_1, I) > 0$ if and only if $f(\theta \mid H_2, I) > 0$, that is, the support of f is the same under both hypotheses, then we can write (as we did in Chapter 3):

$$LR(M, g \mid I)$$

$$= \frac{\int P_\theta(M, g \mid H_1, I) f(\theta \mid H_1, I) d\theta}{\int P_\psi(M, g \mid H_2, I) f(\nu \mid H_2, I) d\nu}$$

$$= \int \frac{P_\theta(M, g \mid H_1, I)}{P_\theta(M, g \mid H_2, I)} \frac{P_\theta(M, g \mid H_2, I) f(\theta \mid H_2, I)}{\int P_\nu(M, g \mid H_2, I) f(\nu \mid H_2, I) d\nu} \frac{f(\theta \mid H_1, I)}{f(\theta \mid H_2, I)} d\theta$$

$$= \int LR(M, g \mid I, \theta) f(\theta \mid M, g, H_2, I) LR(\theta \mid I) d\theta, \tag{8.4}$$

where

$$LR(M,g \mid I, \theta) := \frac{P_\theta(M,g \mid H_1, I)}{P_\theta(M,g \mid H_2, I)}$$

is the likelihood ratio assuming parameter values θ under both hypotheses, and where

$$f(\theta \mid M, g, H_2, I) := \frac{P_\theta(M,g \mid H_2, I) f(\theta \mid H_2, I)}{\int P_v(M,g \mid H_2, I) f(v \mid H_2, I) dv}$$

is the density $f(\theta \mid H_2, I)$ further updated with M and g using the (possibly continuous version of) Bayes theorem, and finally where

$$LR(\theta \mid I) := \frac{f(\theta \mid H_1, I)}{f(\theta \mid H_2, I)}$$

can be interpreted as the likelihood ratio that the value θ *itself* gives in favor of H_1 versus H_2.

Thus, what the calculation of $LR(M, g \mid I)$ amounts to can be understood in the following way, assuming that there is no value of θ that can rule out any of the hypotheses. First we derive the updated probability distribution of θ assuming H_2 holds and conditioning on all data, i.e., the trace M, the profiles in I, and the profile g of S. Then we weight the likelihood ratio corresponding to all possible θ, using weights that are determined by both the probability that θ is indeed the true value as given by $f(\theta \mid M, g, H_2, I)$, and by the evidential value of θ itself.

We must, therefore, wonder under which conditions there is evidential value in θ, that is, whether the different hypotheses entail different probability distributions. The hypotheses investigate the possible contribution of S. Traditionally they are often called H_p and H_d since they are imagined to be supplied by the prosecution, respectively the defense. This is perhaps reasonable when DNA evidence is gathered in addition to already existing evidence at a moment where there is already a suspect with a defense, and that both parties advocate a certain scenario. But the gathering of traces is often done in the investigative phase, and at that point they need not have a specific suspect in mind. In the investigative phase there typically are no specific scenarios brought forward, in any case not in such detail as to have consequences for mixture evaluation parameters. There may be a person of interest, but not yet a formal prosecution or defense. There are no parties advocating a specific scenario, there is merely the question who may have contributed to the trace. It will therefore usually not be the case that we would change our odds on the hypotheses in case we had a revelation of (some of) the parameters.

Therefore we assume, unless there turn out to be case-specific circumstances that dictate otherwise, that we have $f(\theta \mid H_1, I) = f(\theta \mid H_2, I)$. If that is the case, then (8.4) simplifies to

$$LR(M, g \mid I) = \int LR(M, g \mid I, \theta) f(\theta \mid M, g, H_2, I) d\theta. \qquad (8.5)$$

We note that $f(\theta \mid H_1, I) = f(0 \mid H_2, I)$ does not imply that $f(\theta \mid H_1, M, g, I) = f(\theta \mid H_2, M, g, I)$. Indeed, under H_1 the profile g is the profile of a contributor, which can be informative for θ in a different way than if g is the profile of a non-contributor.

In fact, to a good approximation we can simplify (8.5) a little bit more. First we observe that in the generic situation where we consider that H_1 states that S is a contributor and H_2 that S is unrelated to all contributors, the only difference between H_1 and H_2 is that H_1 fixes one profile of the contributors to be g whereas H_2 does not. Under H_2 we do not say that there is no contributor with profile g, we only do not say that there is one. Persons from the general population may also have profile g.

We can now wonder to what extent the conditioning on g in $f(\theta \mid M, g, H_2, I)$ plays a role. The profile g is, under H_2, the profile of a non-contributor. For most parameters it has no influence on them. If we allow for dependence between profiles of persons from the general population (as we discussed in Section 7.5), then the observation of a profile of a non-contributor has some impact on the probabilities for subsequent individuals to have certain alleles. This may introduce some impact on θ but it will not be large. Mixture interpretation would clearly be infeasible if the observation of profiles of persons having nothing to do with the case were of serious influence. Therefore, to a good approximation we will have $f(\theta \mid M, g, I, H_2) = f(\theta \mid M, H_2, I)$.

Returning to (8.5), the question is of course, which parameters θ consists of. The model that needs to give a probability to M must, at the very least, be able to assign probabilities for alleles to be detected in the trace profile. These are, of course, to be (at least possibly) explained by the presence of DNA of persons in the sample, and therefore we need to take into θ the profiles of the possible contributors, and hence also a specification (probabilistic or fixed) of the number of such contributors.

The question of interest usually is whether or not person of interest S contributed to the mixture with profile M. The question *how many* persons contributed in total is another question that is usually not explicitly asked for. Judging the number of contributors has, at least historically, been regarded as an important element of the analysis, because the evidential value may depend on it, and also because it may be of criminalistic relevance, shedding light on what happened in the case that the sample is from.

Therefore, θ includes, in all models we consider, the set of profiles of all contributors. For those that are unknown to us (since they are not specified by I), we need to have prior information about their distribution. This is supplied by choosing allele frequencies, and possibly there is relevant information in I as well, e.g., I may stipulate that S is the brother of a contributor, or that there are related contributors. In any case, the number n of such contributors automatically emerges as a parameter that we need. This parameter stands out, since it is reasonable to view it as having an unknown but truly existing value, contrary to more abstract parameters that are needed in the statistical model. Later, we will nuance this distinction.

If π describes our probability distribution for the number of contributors, then we may write

$$P(M \mid H, g, I) = \sum_{n \geq 0} \pi(n \mid H, g, I) P(M \mid H, g, I, n).$$

If we assume that $\pi(n \mid H_1, I) = \pi(n \mid H_2, I)$, then we get from (8.5) that

$$LR(M, g \mid I) = \sum_n LR^{(n)}(M, g \mid I) \pi(n \mid M, g, H_2, I), \qquad (8.6)$$

where $LR^{(n)}$ stands for the likelihood ratio assuming n modeled contributors.

We will discuss below in Section 8.5 why for large enough n the likelihood ratio $LR^{(n)}$ tends to stabilize, but also advocate that there is another way to overcome the problem of having to assign a number of contributors. If we can define an ordering on the contributors, for example by decreasing contribution, then we can target the first k, or any specific one, with the likelihood ratio calculation. It is then not necessary to know the number of contributors one would take if contribution in general were tested.

Next, we take the profiles of the contributors out of θ for explicit, separate integration. We still call the remaining parameters θ, slightly abusing notation. From (8.6) we see that we need to be able to carry out likelihood ratio calculations assuming a fixed value n for the number of contributors. We then need to calculate, for the appropriate hypothesis H,

$$P(M \mid H, g, I, n) = \int_\theta \sum_{g_1, \ldots, g_n} P_\theta(M \mid g_1, \ldots, g_n, H, g, I, n)$$
$$\times P(g_1, \ldots, g_n \mid H, g, I, n, \theta) f(\theta \mid H, g, I, n) d\theta. \qquad (8.7)$$

If we consider n to be chosen, then we will omit it from the notation and write

$$P(M \mid H, g, I) = \int_\theta \sum_{g_1, \ldots, g_n} P_\theta(M \mid g_1, \ldots, g_n, H, g, I)$$
$$\times P(g_1, \ldots, g_n \mid H, g, I, \theta) f(\theta \mid H, g, I) d\theta. \qquad (8.8)$$

In (8.8), the term $P_\theta(M \mid g_1, \ldots, g_n, H, g, I)$ is the probability that we would see M if the contributors have profiles $g_1, \ldots, g_n$, conditional on H, g, I and if the model parameters are θ. Clearly, here the conditioning on H, g, I is irrelevant and can be omitted: if we know the profiles of the contributors and the values of θ, then H, g, I carry no additional information for the profile.

The term $P(g_1, \ldots, g_n \mid H, g, I, \theta)$ tells us how likely the g_i are as contributor profiles, based on H, g, I and the model parameters θ, but not based on the trace. None of the events conditioned on, except θ (which describes the way mixtures profiles are generated) can in general be omitted. Indeed, H specifies how g and I come into the trace as contributors. For example, conditioning on H_1, according to which S contributes, there must be (at least) one of the g_i equal to g, namely the g_i that represents the profile of S.

Finally, we will assume that we can also write $f(\theta \mid H, g, I) = f(\theta)$, which amounts to assuming that without having observed the profile M, we do not change our opinion on what the parameter values could be.

Taking these considerations into account, we can write (8.8) as

$$P(M \mid H, g, I) = \int_\theta \sum_{g_1, \ldots, g_n} P_\theta(M \mid g_1, \ldots, g_n) P(g_1, \ldots, g_n \mid H, g, I) f(\theta) d\theta.$$

(8.9)

We call $P_\theta(M \mid g_1, \ldots, g_n)$ the *statistical model*, since it reflects our assessment of how trace profiles are generated if the parameters θ are known. We call $f(\theta)$ the *probabilistic model*: it reflects our assumptions as to which parameters are deemed possible and should be used as weights by the statistical model. In other words, f describes our prior probability distribution for the parameters. Finally, the probabilities $P(g_1, \ldots, g_n \mid H, g, I)$ reflect our *population genetic model* for the unknown contributors conditioned on the assumptions on contribution as specified by H and I. If S is assumed to have contributed, we need to specify which index i is the one of the profile g of S. Therefore we introduce $H_{1,i}$ by letting it put S in position i, that is, it lets g_i be g in $P(g_1, \ldots, g_n \mid H_{1,i}, g, I)$. In the sum over the g_i, all g_i run over all possible profiles.

For some models, $P(M \mid H_{1,i}, g, I)$ may be the same for all i. Then the likelihood ratio $LR(M, g)$ is not specifically targeting any of the contributors. Other models aim to distinguish between the contributors on the basis of their relative contribution, and we next explain how that can be done in (8.9).

In order to differentiate between the contributors we need contributor-specific parameters in the statistical model. For example, we may have a separate dropout probability d_i per contributor (for a *discrete* model in which we only take alleles into account and not their peak heights), or a parameter r_i that measures the relative contribution of contributor i (for a *continuous* model in which peak heights are taken into account). Suppose now that we let $f(\theta)$ be non-zero only for increasing probabilities of dropout $d_1 < d_2 < \cdots < d_n$ or for decreasing relative contributions

$r_1 > r_2 > \cdots > r_n$. Then the $P(M \mid H_{1,i}, g, I)$ are different, so we arrive at contributor-specific likelihoods. For example, the mixture likelihood $P(M \mid H_{1,1})$ corresponds to letting S be the most contributing person, and $P(M \mid H_{1,n}, I)$ corresponds to letting S be the least contributing person to M. Therefore, we now have hypotheses refining H_1 into $H_{1,i}$ that state that S is the ith contributor, and we define $LR_i(M \mid g, I)$ as the likelihood ratio for $H_{1,i}$ versus H_2.

For such cases, we have contributor-specific likelihood ratios $LR_i(M, g \mid I)$. These are related to the likelihood ratio $LR(M, g \mid I)$ through the conditional probabilities $\pi_i = P(H_{1,i} \mid H_1)$ stating which contributor S can be. Taking $\pi_i = 1/n$ we obtain

$$LR(M, g \mid I) = \frac{1}{n} \sum_{i=1}^{n} LR_i(M, g \mid I), \qquad (8.10)$$

which is simply the average of the contributor-specific likelihood ratios.

8.1.2 Explicit Examples

So far the discussion has been completely general, and the next step is to make (8.9) more explicit. First we discuss a discrete method in which case M is reduced to its detected alleles, and $\theta = (d_1, \ldots, d_n, c)$, where d_i is the dropout probability for the contributor with profile g_i and c is a parameter for drop-in. In this model it is assumed that the number of alleles that drop in per locus is Poisson distributed with fixed parameter c, and that the alleles that do drop in come (independently from each other) from the known distribution of allele probabilities. Under these assumptions an allele a is detected with probability

$$P_\theta(a \in M \mid g_1, \ldots, g_n) = 1 - e^{-cp_a} \prod_{i=1}^{n} d_i^{n_{i,a}}, \qquad (8.11)$$

where $n_{i,a} \in \{0, 1, 2\}$ is the number of alleles a in g_i. The probability that M is the observed set of alleles is obtained from (8.11) by multiplication, assuming conditional independence of detection of alleles given the g_i, the d_i, and c. We take $f(d_1, \ldots, d_n)$ to be uniform on $[0, 1]^n$ and for c we use (here) some fixed value so that $\theta = (d_1, \ldots, d_n)$. This is a model that cannot distinguish between different contributors, so $LR(M, g \mid I)$ is the likelihood ratio in favor of being a contributor, not in favor of being any specific one.

Equation (8.9) in this case reduces to (writing x_i for d_i for obvious typographical reasons)

$$P(M \mid H, g, I) = \int_0^1 \cdots \int_0^1 P_\theta(M \mid g_1, \ldots, g_n) P(g_1, \ldots, g_n \mid H, g, I) dx_1 \ldots dx_n. \qquad (8.12)$$

Still, if the dropout probabilities d_i that best explain the trace M are different from each other, this is taken into account in the likelihood ratio. Indeed, by (8.5) the likelihood ratio $LR(M, g \mid I)$ is determined mostly by the probabilities of dropout that best explain the trace profile under H_2. This probability density is invariant under permutations, but may be supported mostly on vectors $(d_1, \ldots, d_n)$ whose entries are different from each other.

As a second example, we globally describe the continuous model used by Euro-ForMix. Now M is the set $\{(a, h_a) : h_a \geq T\}$, where a is an allele, h_a its peak height measured in rfu, and T is the analytical threshold. Peak heights are assumed to follow Gamma distributions. The parameters θ are (related to) the expected peak height, their variance, the relative proportions of contribution r_i for contributor i and the degradation rate. On each locus, the expected peak height for contributor i is considered to be proportional to r_i. Furthermore, a separate peak height distribution for drop-in alleles is needed. If stutter is modeled, still more assumptions are needed.

Then, maximum likelihood estimates (MLE) are obtained for the parameters for the peak height expectation and variance, the proportions r_i and the degradation rate. This is done conditional on H_i, I, g, and M such that we obtain $\hat{\theta}_1$ and $\hat{\theta}_2$. These values are plugged into (8.8), but note that we cannot write this as (8.9) because of the dependence of the parameters of the hypotheses and on the data M, g, I. The model computes $P(M \mid H_1, g, I, \hat{\theta}_1)/P(M \mid H_2, g, I, \hat{\theta}_2)$. This resembles the contributor-specific likelihood ratios $LR_i(M, g \mid I)$, the likelihood ratio in favor of S being the i-contributor. Now i depends on the ML estimate of the relative proportion that S is responsible for, assuming H_1.

8.1.3 The Interpretation of the Likelihood Ratio

We now return to the general expression (8.5). As we have seen, for the parameters θ we need a probability distribution $f(\theta)$ describing our knowledge about θ. As usual, our position is that we assume that there is an actual value θ_0 for the parameters such that our data were generated by the statistical model for θ_0, but that we do not know that value. Our knowledge about it is expressed in $f(\theta)$.

We may then ask the question what the relation is between $LR(M, g \mid I)$ and $LR_{\theta_0}(M, g \mid I)$. The latter is the likelihood ratio which we would obtain if we had full knowledge about all relevant parameters; see also Chapter 3. If the prior distributions reflect whatever information we have about θ, then $LR(M, g \mid I)$ captures the evidential value based on our current knowledge. In practice, however, there may be various, at first glance all plausible, distributions available and we may tend to choose one that facilitates the computations. Then $f(\theta)$ becomes a *convenience prior*, used because of its appeal in terms of simplicity.

Therefore $LR(M, g \mid I)$ obtained with the convenience prior $f(\theta)$ is not exactly what we would have obtained if we had been able and had taken the trouble to really use all relevant knowledge.

Let us consider two examples to illustrate this, one with a convenience prior and one with a naturally informed choice of prior distribution. First we consider the probabilities of dropout $(d_1, \ldots, d_n)$ for the discrete model (8.11). In this case, we take a uniform prior probability on $[0, 1]^n$ as $f(d_1, \ldots, d_n)$. For these probabilities, no prior seems sensibly available; even if we knew them for past traces, there is no reason to consider the dropout probabilities of past traces to be predictive for the current ones. One can to some extent investigate how influential the ad hoc uniform prior distribution actually is. One can for instance verify by simulation whether the likelihood ratio $LR(M, g \mid I)$, using the ad hoc uniform density, is approximately equal to the likelihood ratio that we get for the true parameters $(d_1, \ldots, d_n)$.

If, on the other hand, we consider the profiles of the unknown contributors as parameters, then we are also in the situation that we believe that these profiles exist but are unknown. This time, however, there is a natural prior density, namely that given by the allele frequencies and population genetic model. Again, we may wonder whether the likelihood ratio that we obtain by integrating out all the profiles of the unknown contributors is close to the likelihood ratio that we would get if we knew all the profiles of the contributors. Suppose that we compute $LR_i(M, g)$ in favor of S being the ith contributor. Knowing the profiles, this is simply a match/no match evaluation so we get either 0 (if the profile of the contributor i is not g), or $1/p(g)$ (if it is), where $p(g)$ is the probability that a randomly chosen individual has that profile.

The examples show that the comparison between $LR(M, g \mid I)$ and LR_{θ_0} $(M, g \mid I)$ is fundamentally different depending on whether θ_0 represents the profiles of the contributors or the dropout probabilities. If $f(\theta)$ encodes our knowledge, then for the assessment of $LR(M, g)$ nothing more needs to be done than taking this into account in the modeling. But if $f(\theta)$ is a convenience prior, we need to assess if and how much we deviate from the likelihood ratio we would obtain with knowledge of the parameters.

8.1.4 Probabilistic Genotyping

A second way to evaluate the likelihood ratio (8.1) is as

$$
LR(M, g \mid I) = \frac{P(g \mid M, H_1, I)}{P(g \mid M, H_2, I)} \frac{P(M \mid H_1, I)}{P(M \mid H_2, I)}
$$
$$
= \frac{P(g \mid M, H_1, I)}{P(g \mid M, H_2, I)},
$$

using that throughout we consider models and hypotheses which satisfy $P(M \mid H_1, I) = P(M \mid H_2, I)$. Note that since we do not condition on g here, this means that in the absence of the profile of the person of interest, we do not expect different profiles for the trace per hypotheses. This is violated, for example, if H_1 states that S is a contributor and that all other contributors are unrelated to each other and to S, whereas H_2 states that S is a not a contributor and all unknown contributors are full siblings. We do not take such situations into account here.

Suppose now that the hypotheses postulate no relatedness between S and the profiled persons in I. If we regard profiles of unrelated individuals as independent, then $P(g \mid M, H_2, I)$ is just the probability $p(g)$ that a randomly chosen population member has profile g, and we obtain

$$LR(M, g \mid I) = \frac{P(g \mid M, H_1, I)}{p(g)}. \tag{8.13}$$

The relation $P(g \mid M, H_2, I) = p(g)$ is not exactly true when we introduce dependence between the profiles of persons, such as when the standard subpopulation correction (see Section 7.5) is applied. However, in any case, (8.13) remains approximately true and we will think of it as if it is. The terminology *probabilistic genotyping* refers to the fact that, as (8.13) shows, one may regard likelihood ratio calculations as determining a probabilistic assessment $P(g \mid M, H_1, I)$ of the profiles of the contributor(s) described by H_1.

The preceding arguments can be easily used to show that on the level of individual contributors we have

$$LR_i(M, g \mid I) = \frac{P(g \mid M, H_{1,i}, I)}{p(g)}, \tag{8.14}$$

that is, $LR_i(M, g \mid I)$ is large if we predict profile g to be that of contributor i with a probability that is much larger than the population probability $p(g)$.

If we write (8.14) as

$$P(g \mid M, H_{1,i}, I) = LR_i(M, g \mid I) p(g), \tag{8.15}$$

and call the probability distributions $P(g \mid M, H_{1,i}, I)$ for $1 \leq i \leq n$ the *deconvolution* of the profile M, we see that likelihood ratio calculations provide such deconvolution.

Since S can only be one of the mixture contributors, we expect that if S is contributor j, then (see 8.10)

$$LR(M, g \mid I) \approx LR_j(M, g \mid I)/n, \tag{8.16}$$

since then $LR_j(M, g \mid I)$ will be expected to be much larger than all the other $LR_k(M, g \mid I)$.

8.1.5 The Impact of the Quality of the Model

At first sight, the ambition of a mixture evaluation model is to distinguish between contributors and non-contributors as well as possible, such that contributors obtain likelihood ratios in favor of being a contributor, and non-contributors against. However, some thought reveals that this is not quite right. Instead, we need to say in which of either directions the evidence points and how strongly, and this is really something different.

There are many choices to be made, but once a probabilistic model is in place and the terms $P_\theta(M \mid g_1, \ldots, g_n)$ in (8.9) can be calculated, the likelihood ratios obtained will have all the usual properties described in Chapter 2. We need to realize though, that while we think of H_1 and H_2 as statements only on the level of specifying the contributors of the trace, what we implicitly also do is assume that the mixture is generated as described by (8.9). Sampling from H_2 then means sampling individuals from the general population, while keeping $f(\theta)$ and the model $P_\theta(M \mid g_1, \ldots, g_n)$ fixed. The population of random individuals is usually well described by the population genetic model. Sampling from H_1, however, does not mean that we sample from the actual profile contributors, but that we sample from the probability distribution induced by the deconvolution in (8.15). This is a distribution for profiles of contributors conditional not only on the trace M but also on the model. There may be very many profiles that give support in favor of H_1. Whether or not this set contains the profiles of the actual trace contributors is what primarily determines the quality of the model. The rates $P(LR(M, g) \geq t \mid H_1)$ that exist within the model do not reflect the quality of the model: they reflect the power of the model assuming that it is an accurate description of how M was generated. Judging that accuracy amounts to model validation.

For example, regardless of the model, one always has that

$$P(LR(M, g \mid I) \geq t \mid H_2) \leq 1/t. \tag{8.17}$$

Indeed, for all likelihood ratios $LR_\theta(M, g \mid I)$ evaluated assuming parameter values θ, this follows from Proposition 2.4.2. Since the probabilistic model $f(\theta)$ is independent of S, this inequality also applies to $LR(M, g \mid I)$. For any model drawing random profiles (as described by H_2) and subjecting them to a likelihood ratio calculation cannot yield many strong false positives because of this property. Fear that a misspecification of the model may lead to many strong false positives is therefore misplaced.

To illustrate this, we discuss two examples. An extreme example is that we, regardless of what M is, randomly select some number n of profiles $g_1, \ldots, g_n$ and consider them to be the profiles of the contributors. If S has one of these profiles, say g_1, we get $LR(M, g \mid I) = 1/n \times 1/p_{g_1}$, and $LR(M, g \mid I) = 0$ otherwise.

Within such a model, the g_i are the contributor's profiles; clearly it is impossible to see whether this is accurate without extra information. With this model non-contributors will with virtual certainty all be excluded. On the other hand, no actual contributor is likely to ever be identified. Such a procedure is therefore useless, not because of elevated false positive risks but because it fails to identify the actual contributors.

A less artificial example is to model a mixture profile which in reality has three contributors, as being a two-person mixture. Both the two- and three-person models are well-defined probabilistic models and therefore (8.17) applies to them. Again, it is impossible to get strong support in favor of being a contributor while not being one, because of the bounds of (8.17). For the H_1-contributors as modeled by either the two-person or three-person evaluation, however, the difference will be larger. Any profile that could belong to a contributor assuming that there are two contributors, can also be a profile of a contributor assuming that there are three, but not the other way around. It may happen that an actual trace contributor is then excluded as being one of two contributors, but obtains support in favor of being one of three contributors. Modeling the mixture as having too few contributors therefore entails the risk of failing to identify actual trace contributors, without leading to false positive rates violating (8.17). Conversely, modeling the trace as having too many contributors makes the set of profiles supporting H_1 larger, but of course not so large as to violate (8.17).

It is only when our description of random persons is not accurate that (8.17) may appear to be violated. While it holds within the model, it needs not hold within the population that we are actually working in. For example, if we use allele probabilities of a certain population, and then calculate likelihood ratios for persons issued from another one, then our description of H_2 follows another probability distribution than the profiles of the persons that we actually test. In that case, the bounds provided by (8.17) do not apply to the tested population.

8.2 The Concept of a Contributor

The number of contributors is typically not part of the original question that was asked, namely to determine whether there is evidence that the person of interest contributed DNA to a sample. But since in any model, according to (8.9), a trace profile of the sample is viewed as a superposition of (possibly partial) profiles, with in addition the possibility of non-allelic peaks having another origin, we must assume some number n of contributors (or a probability distribution for it) to be able to calculate (8.9).

It is therefore inevitable to introduce some number n of contributors. In the model, this number n has a clear meaning. But what do we really mean when we talk about the (number of) contributors to a DNA mixture? We can think of three possible, but different, interpretations: sample contributors, profile contributors, and modeled contributors.

The *sample contributors* are the persons whose DNA in reality is present in the sample with some minimum amount to be defined (say, one cell). This number may be known in laboratory experiments, but usually otherwise it is not. However, since we do not subject the sample to calculations, but the DNA profile obtained from it, we believe this number is not of ultimate interest. Indeed it may be that sample contributors have not been detected in the profile. It then would not make much sense to still include these persons as contributors in calculations on a profile from which they are absent.

Looking at the profile itself, by a *profile contributor*, we mean those sample contributors whose DNA has actually been detected in the resulting DNA profile. Or, a bit more precisely, we could define them as the sample contributors the removal of which would have led to a different profile. By definition there are at most as many profile contributors as sample contributors, possibly strictly fewer. The difference in numbers will depend on the profiling technology (the sensitivity, the profile analysis procedure, the analytical threshold, etc.), and of course on the amounts of DNA of the sample contributors to the sample. For any given trace profile, imagine that we increase the analytical thresholds. As we do so, the profile will contain fewer and fewer alleles and hence we lose profile contributors, until there aren't any left. The number of sample contributors is obviously unchanged, and hence we see that inferences about all sample contributors, based on the profile, are not always possible.

The number of profile contributors has a subtlety. If we believe it exists as a single number valid for all loci, we must define it on the basis of the full profile. But if some loci are more sensitive than other loci, it may be that on these loci alleles are obtained from sample contributors who remain undetected on other loci. Similarly, degradation may cause some loci not to register any alleles. These loci, when considered on their own, show zero profile contributors. Yet, when other loci show alleles and the profile is then classified as (say) having three contributors, then one has to classify the whole profile as a three-person profile. This makes it impossible to definitively establish the number of profile contributors, since that number could always be subject to upward change depending on the results of additional DNA typing. At best, one can therefore only establish a lower bound for the number of profile contributors. Even this is difficult, because a profile contributor may have contributed very little. In our opinion this is a drawback.

Finally, there is the number of *modeled contributors*. This is the number n in (8.9). A modeled contributor is foremost a concept within the probabilistic model for the likelihood calculations, but what this concept represents (i.e., what it is really modeling) varies over the different approaches.

The earliest approaches made no attempt to distinguish between contributors. The first, most basic models (sometimes called the binary or combinatorial method) only dealt with traces where all contributors were supposed to be fully detected in the profile, and no additional alleles were supposed to be present in the trace. The detected alleles, not the peak heights, were subjected to calculations. A contributor in this model is a strong concept: since all of the contributors are modeled as fully detected, the mixture likelihood strongly depends on their number, hence so does the likelihood ratio. On the bright side, with this assumption the mixture likelihood depends so strongly on the number of modeled contributors that maximum likelihood estimation of that number works fairly well (cf. [76]).

A first generalization was the family of discrete models as implemented in LRmix(Studio) (cf. [77]), where dropout is allowed for, but all unknown contributors are modeled as having the same probability of dropout (assumed contributors with known DNA profile may each be given their own probability of dropout). The set of all detected alleles is therefore regarded as a superposition of partial DNA profiles of persons, where the unknown contributors are expected to be equally partially detected. As for the previous model without dropout, this induces a large dependence of the mixture likelihood on the number of contributors: if the detected alleles are a superposition of (for the unknown contributors) equally partial profiles, it is of importance how many unknown contributors there are. It is then only reasonable that the likelihood ratio can depend strongly on the chosen n. A contributor is a weaker concept than it was for the binary models, but still quite a strong one since the mixture likelihood (8.9) is determined by terms where all profiles corresponding to unknown contributors have the same probability to have their alleles detected in the trace.

This is different for models that distinguish between the contributors based on their possibly different contribution. A modeled contributor is now a much weaker concept: it is someone that we *may*, but *need not*, see alleles of in the profile when computing (8.9). A contributor may be now be (almost) making no contribution, without this being so for others as well. The dependence of the likelihood ratio on n will then be different. Increasing the number of model contributors no longer means that the same alleles must be fairly divided over a larger number of persons; the superfluous model contributors may be estimated to have made no (meaningful) contribution to the trace profile.

This means that we can expect that if the number n of modeled contributors is less than the number of profile contributors, not all profile contributors can be recovered. It may however still be perfectly possible that an underestimate does not affect the likelihood ratio for the most prominent contributors. Contrary to the modeled contributor notions of the earlier models, it is now conceptually unproblematic (but it is computationally unwise) to work with more modeled contributors than profile contributors, or even with a number exceeding the number of sample contributors. This is so since if the model makes a likelihood-driven estimate of parameters (this is the $f(\theta \mid M, g, H_2, I)$ in (8.5)) including the individual contributions or probabilities of dropout, then superfluous contributors can be expected to have their contribution estimated to be close to zero. Nothing is learned about a contributor if we see no alleles of that person. This means that for the superfluous contributors we will have $LR_i(M, g \mid I) = 1$ for all g, cf (7.5). Since the likelihood ratio is, as in (8.10), the average of the likelihood ratios targeting the separate modeled contributors, we can predict what happens if we augment the number of modeled contributors. For a person of interest who is not a profile contributor, we will usually have $LR_i(M, g \mid I) \ll 1$ if modeled contributor i is well resolved. This means that $LR(M, g \mid I) \ll 1$ if n is at most equal to what is minimally needed as the number of profile contributors. Adding superfluous contributors k who have $LR_k(M, g \mid I) = 1$ will bring the $LR(M, g \mid I)$ towards m/n, where m is the number of such superfluous contributors and n the total number of modeled contributors. As a result, strong exclusions are no longer possible. But this is only logical: if we take into account the possibility that there are more contributors than needed to explain the trace, we cannot rule out that our person of interest made such a small contribution that it went (practically) undetected.

Finally we note that since related individuals tend to share more alleles than unrelated individuals, one must make a choice for the (lack) of relatedness between the contributors whenever their number is to be estimated. In practice contributors are always supposed to be unrelated. This may lead to an underestimate of the number of contributors. For example, consider three brothers producing a trace together. The number of profile contributors may then be three. But three brothers together have at most four distinct alleles on every locus, which will lead to an allele count based estimate of there being two contributors. In fact, three brothers together amount to 1.75 unrelated contributors, since for both of their parents the probability that there is one of their alleles that has not been passed on to any of the three siblings is 0.25. Thus, each parent (if heterozygous) will in expectation give rise to $1 \cdot \frac{1}{4} + 2 \cdot \frac{3}{4} = 1.75$ distinct alleles in the three siblings together. In general, if we assume related contributors, we will obtain a probability distribution for how many alleles occur in the profiles, together with a probability distribution of their multiplicity due to identical by descent (IBD) sharing of alleles. The number of distinct alleles that we expect on a locus will generally not be an integer.

In view of all this we view contributors primarily as model concepts, needed to draw pairs of alleles out of the reference population that can, but need not be, detected. This is why we prefer to speak of a trace *modeled with n* contributors, rather than of a trace *having n* contributors. Even if we know that the laboratory used n contributor samples to generate the profile, this does not mean that we should use that number in likelihood calculations. Using less than n modeled contributors often implies some sample contributors cannot be found. Using more is, for a good model, harmless. It makes strong exclusions impossible, but this is reasonable: if we take into account the possibility of non-detected contributors, anyone could be one of these.

8.3 Analogies Between Mixtures and Kinship Evaluations

Abstractly, kinship analysis and mixture analysis are the same problem. In mixture analysis we use the trace profile to make inferences about the profile of a contributor of interest; in kinship analysis we use the profiles of biological relatives of a person S to make inferences about the profile of person of interest S. In both cases, we use a model (the mixture evaluation model, respectively the pedigree inheritance model) to make these inferences based on observations (the trace profile, respectively the relatives) that carry information on what we want to describe (the profiles of the contributors, respectively the person targeted by the kinship computations).

For example, the role of the single source trace in mixture analysis is played by the monozygotic twin in the kinship case: in both cases we directly observe the profile we want to derive. A poor mixture profile is comparable to having distant relatives of S only: in both cases we have little information. Because of this analogy we think that some aspects of DNA mixture evaluation can be better understood when we compare them with the analogous ones in kinship analysis. For this reason we work out some of these analogies in this section.

We first comment on the uncertainty about genotypes, modeling requirements, and the distribution of the likelihood ratio in the kinship context. After that we formulate the equivalent properties for mixture analysis.

8.3.1 Uncertainty About Genotypes

Suppose that two parents have reported a child of theirs as missing, and that no DNA profile of that child is available, whereas the profiles of the parents are known. These parents may produce, ignoring mutations, on every locus considered in isolation up to four different children. Indeed each parent has two alleles one of which may be passed on to the child (with equal probability). This may result in fewer than four possible genotypes, but for the sake of exposition we consider that they may produce on all considered loci four different genotypes for their children.

When considering k loci, there are then 4^k possibilities for the profile of a child, meaning that as the number of loci increases, so does our inability to predict the profile of a child: there are 4^k possibilities, each having probability 4^{-k}. With $k = 20$, this means that the number of possible profiles for a child is $4^{20} \approx 10^{12}$, that is, a thousand billion. At most a handful (the number of children the couple actually has) of these occur in their actual children. However, all of these profiles may occur in an unrelated person, and if we would classify everyone with such a profile as a child these will be false positives.

And yet, if we do so and classify any person as child who has one of the 10^{12} profiles, we will make a mistake with vanishingly small probability. The reason is that, the loci being much more polymorphic than just containing the alleles of the parents, this set of 10^{12} profiles is an extremely small subset of the set of all possible profiles, and hence, the probability to see such a profile (anyone in particular, or even one in the whole set) in an unrelated individual is extremely small.

As a ball park figure, if there are 14 equally frequent alleles on every locus, there are about 100 genotypes possible on each locus, so about 10^{40} on all 20 loci, and the probability to select from that set one of the 10^{12} genotypes a child may have is around 10^{-28}. In other words, seeing a particular profile that could be of a child is an event that is unexpected both if it is actually from a child (it had probability 10^{-12} to occur then), but it is much more unexpected for a random individual in the population (where the average profile probability is about 10^{-40}). The mere fact that our probabilistic model gives profiles small probability to occur under one hypothesis (being from a child) is in itself of absolutely no concern. If the alternative has an even much harder time explaining the profile, that means we have good discrimination power, resulting in large likelihood ratios.

8.3.2 Modeling Requirements

A second example from kinship analysis shows how modeling shortcomings primarily affect the ability to recognize actual relationships, rather than leading to false positives.

Suppose we carry out paternity testing (with or without the mother available, let's say without). In principle, this is simple: letting AF be the alleged father and C the child, we set up hypotheses H_1 where AF is C's father, and H_2 where AF is unrelated to C. Several choices need to be made that affect the likelihoods. Here we focus on the choice whether or not to apply a mutation model for inheritance. If we do without, then we assume that every child must on every locus share an allele with its father. If we do apply a mutation model, we allow for the possibility that an allele, when passed on from father to child, mutates into another variant than the father was in the process of passing on. The probability for a mutation to occur is, in reality, small but non-zero for the forensic STR loci, so in a large majority of cases where there is paternity, we do not need to consider mutations to make paternity possible if there are not very many loci typed.

If we decide to use a mutation model, a subtlety arises. In that case, the allele frequencies will in general change over time. If, on some locus, the allele frequencies are p_i in some generation, then the probability that an allele that is passed on by a father to the next generation is allele i, is $q_i = \sum_i p_i \mu_{i,j}$, where $\mu_{i,j}$ is the probability that allele i is transmitted by a male as allele j. Typically, we will have $q_i \neq p_i$. In that case H_2 needs to specify in which generation the child is, if AF is not its father. That is because the probability to see the genotype (a_i, a_j) is $2p_i p_j$ in the first generation, but $2q_i q_j$ in the next one. For the alleles of the mother, we need to make similar choices, defining a mutation model for females. Setting up a mutation model involves many choices, such as which mutations are possible? Is the mutation model allowed to create new alleles? The data on mutations are too scarce to measure all possible $\mu_{i,j}$, so some kind of model is needed.

All this detail is needed, since in order to do calculations we simply must make choices. The point of this exposition is not to advocate a particular choice, but to show that they are needed, and that another choice leads to (perhaps only very slightly) different likelihoods and likelihood ratios.

Any reasonable model will reflect that mutations are rare, that is, has the property that $1 - \mu_{i,i}$ is very small. If we now have AF and C who have an identical allele on every locus, it is essentially immaterial whether we use a mutation model or not. This will hardly affect the likelihoods since (i) mutations are (modeled as) rare events and (ii) that event is not needed for the explanation of the profiles. However, when we do encounter a parent–child pair where a mutation has occurred and has given rise to a lack of shared alleles, then the likelihood ratio will be zero when we do not use a mutation model, no matter how strong the support is on the loci where alleles are shared. Thus, not applying a mutation model reduces our ability to recognize true fathers as such.

If we do apply a mutation model, we are using a model closer to reality and recognize more fathers as such. Note though that when we compute likelihoods with a mutation model we will no longer classify an allele as having come from the father: for example, if an alleged father has genotype $(16, 17)$ and the child has $(17, 17)$, then the likelihood contains a component corresponding to the 16 having been passed on and a component corresponding to the 17 having been passed on. We see that classification is neither required, nor possible. But our task is not to learn which allele came from the father, it is to compute likelihoods and judge the strength of the evidence for paternity.

What about recognizing non-fathers as such? Without a mutation model, most non-fathers will be categorically excluded, and the ones that by coincidence share an allele with the child on all loci get a likelihood ratio in favor of paternity. When we use a mutation model, say one where all $\mu_{i,j} > 0$, then there are no likelihood ratios equal to zero anymore. The distribution of likelihood ratios for unrelated individuals will change, giving a slightly smaller likelihood ratio to those that share an allele on the child on all loci compared to when we do not model mutations, but having a positive likelihood ratio for everyone. Regardless of whether we use a mutation model or not, the average likelihood ratio stays the same: we will have $E(LR \mid H_2) = 1$. For this expectation we have to keep in mind that H_2 does not only represent unrelatedness but also a probability distribution for unrelated individuals, and for these we may need the allele frequencies p_i or others (e.g., the q_i mentioned above), depending on which generation is modeled to have allele frequencies p_i.

In this discussion, we have considered paternity investigation, where the choice of a using a mutation model can be very important. If we would instead compute a likelihood ratio for two persons in favor of being siblings, then we can safely completely ignore the possibility of mutations in our modeling. Indeed siblings need not share any parental alleles: the probability that they do not share any alleles identical by descent is one in four (marginally on each locus). This probability is so large compared to the probability of a mutation, that introducing a realistic mutation model would not change the likelihood to an extent that is relevant for the further inferential process.

8.3.3 (In)dependence of Loci and (A)symmetry of Likelihood Ratio Distributions

Suppose two persons are genetically tested in order to investigate their relatedness, either as, say, first cousins or as unrelated individuals. If on a certain locus, these persons do not share any alleles, then the likelihood ratio in favor of being first cousins versus being unrelated is $3/4$. This is because first cousins can only have the observed genotypes if they share no IBD alleles, an event with probability $3/4$, and if indeed they share no alleles identical by descent they are effectively unrelated on that locus. In the notation of Section 7.6, we have $\kappa_0 = 3/4$ and $\kappa_1 = 1/4$.

If we consider $k > 1$ loci simultaneously, then we can multiply the likelihood ratios per locus provided the loci segregate independently to offspring. By that we mean that if a person X has genotype $(g_{i,1}, g_{i,2})$ on locus i, the probability for all offspring of X, independently of each other, to receive alleles g_{i,a_i} (for $1 \leq i \leq k$) is $(1/2)^k$ for all choices of a_i. If not, then we need to consider the joint segregation probabilities of these loci. Considering two loci, it may for example be the case that alleles $g_{1,1}$ and $g_{2,2}$ are passed on with probability more than $1/4$, because the alleles $g_{1,1}$ and $g_{2,2}$ are on the same chromosome. Since we cannot observe whether or not this is the case, for a first offspring the probabilities for any combination $(g_{1,i}, g_{2,j})$ are $1/4$, provided that on the basis of the genotypes $(g_{1,1}, g_{1,2})$ and $(g_{2,1}, g_{2,2})$ it is equally likely that $g_{1,1}$ is on the same chromosome with $g_{2,1}$ or with $g_{2,2}$.

This, in turn, is the case if the genotypes on both loci are independent, in which case we say the loci are in linkage equilibrium. Since random mating populations of arbitrarily large size asymptotically reach linkage equilibrium, in the absence of other forces such as selection effects, it is reasonable to assume that the forensic loci satisfy this. Thus, the fact that the segregation is not independent has no effect if we consider a single offspring, but once we have observed one, it will change the probabilities for the next one.

The opposite extreme of independent segregation is that the loci are fully linked. Then, the alleles of these loci that are on a chromosome of X either are all passed on, or none of them are. This happens, for example, for loci on the Y-chromosome, but also the other chromosomes can contain sets of loci that behave in this way. Suppose this is the case for k autosomal loci under consideration. If we compare the hypotheses of being first cousins versus being unrelated, based on the genetic data of the two concerned individuals on these loci, then two outcomes are possible. The first is that there is at least one locus where the individuals do not have an allele in common. In that case, we know that they have no identical by descent alleles at all, and hence the likelihood ratio is $3/4$ on these k loci considered together; see also formula (7.25).

The second case is that they do share an allele on all considered loci. Then, the likelihood ratio can be arbitrarily large. Thus, whereas this set of loci can provide strong evidence in favor of one hypothesis (of being first cousins), it cannot at all provide strong evidence in favor of the other hypothesis (of being unrelated). In fact, for 75% of the actual cousins, there is no IBD sharing and then it will be unlikely that they share an allele on all loci by chance if we consider many polymorphic loci. Hence for almost 75% of first cousins, the likelihood ratio in favor of being first cousins is $3/4$. We see that for first cousins in most cases the likelihood ratio does not give support to the true hypothesis. This is not in any way an error: it is a consequence of the genetic behavior of these loci. The fact that the majority of cousin pairs does not get a likelihood ratio pointing towards their relationship, is simply due to there being 75% probability that first cousins pairs are only genealogically, but not genetically related on these loci.

We see, as we also did in Section 2.4.4, that there is no reason why likelihood ratio distributions should be symmetric: it may be possible to obtain strong support for one hypothesis but not for the other one.

8.3.4 Mixture Equivalents of the Kinship Properties

In the preceding paragraphs we have considered kinship modeling. We can now draw analogies with mixture modeling. We start with the missing child considered in Section 8.3.1. As we saw in (8.15), mixture analysis can be viewed as assessing the probability that a contributor has a certain DNA profile. In some cases we may be able to unambiguously derive the profile of the targeted contributor. In many cases, we are not. Conceptually that is as unproblematic for DNA mixtures as it is for kinship. If our model would select a billion genotypes as possibly being from that profile contributor, we would even have done a better job than in the kinship example in Section 8.3.1. The situation where there is just one possibility for the profile contributor and we have a match/no match situation is a special case, but does not fundamentally differ from the general case with remaining uncertainty. Not fully resolving the profiles of the contributors is compatible with having fully and correctly processed all relevant information.

The fact that many profiles give support in favor of being from a profile contributor is not necessarily due to a lack of understanding or modeling precision. In the paternity example in Section 8.3.1, we simply cannot do better: nature is such that children's genotypes have probability $1/4$ each on every locus. Similarly, for mixtures, sometimes we cannot precisely predict the profiles of the contributors. That simply means that we get lower likelihood ratios compared to if we could have done that. It does not mean that the likelihood ratio we obtain when uncertainty remains is to be regarded differently than a likelihood ratio of the same value, where no uncertainty remains (for instance, on fewer loci corresponding to a direct unambiguous match).

Next, we consider the paternity testing in Section 8.3.2. From that example we see that a simple model will suffice, provided that the omitted model aspect is not needed for the explanation of the data and is sufficiently unlikely a priori. In the paternity case, if no mutations are needed to explain the genetic data, it is unproblematic to use an inheritance model without mutations. We also saw that for the more difficult cases (for instance actual fathers with a mutation) incorrect conclusions may be obtained. These conclusions are incorrect, because the model does not recognize a mechanism that exists in reality. These affect the persons who are actually father, and only to a much smaller extent the persons who in reality are not.

We now draw the following analogy with mixtures. For some peaks there may be various explanations, they may be allelic, they may be stutter, they may be a drop-in, or something else; there usually isn't even any reason to suppose they are exclusively of one such type. For peaks that are large enough, the probability that they are entirely non-allelic is negligible. While these peaks may be not entirely allelic, they would also have been detected if their non-allelic part had not been there.

For a person of interest that is compared with such peaks, it will be not so important to have an accurate model for the non-allelic part of the peaks (stutter, drop-in). These alleles that can be with (near) certainty be ascribed to profile contributors are comparable to the alleles that can be with (near) certainty be ascribed to the father in the kinship example in Section 8.3.2.

On the other hand, if a person of interest has alleles that, in the trace, correspond to peaks that may also be explained as stutter or another non-allelic mechanism, we need to model those peaks much better. Again, this will mostly impact our ability to find those profile contributors, and be less important for the non-contributors. As for the mutation example, we will not need to classify these peaks as being of some type. What we need to do is compute the likelihood of seeing these peaks with a probability model that reflects the actual mechanism to a satisfactory extent. Just as there are very many mutation models and many more could be easily invented, models for stutter, drop-in etc. abound as well.

Next, we consider the (in)dependence of loci in Section 8.3.3. As we have seen, in the kinship case the independence of loci for likelihood ratio calculations depends on the loci being linked or not. For a pair of linked loci, if we consider two children of two parents, the alleles transmitted to the first child will give information on which alleles are on the same chromosome in the parents. Therefore, this would alter the probabilities for the second child's genotypes. In this case, we do not know from the genotypes what the phasing of the alleles in the parents is, that is, which alleles they have on which chromosome. If we knew that, then the profiles of several children would be independent again. In other words, we can introduce model parameters indicating which allele is on which chromosome, whose values we have not observed. Therefore we use a probability distribution for it, which amounts to assigning probability $1/2$ to each possibility if we assume linkage equilibrium. This distribution is then averaged over in the likelihood calculations, which technically speaking amounts to integrating over the unobserved parameters.

For mixtures, we have a similar phenomenon. The considered loci may well be independent, in the sense that they are in linkage equilibrium so that the probability for a person to have a certain profile factorizes over the loci. Now we are not concerned with inheritance, but we have the parameters θ in the statistical model whose values are unobserved. It is usually also the case that, given values for all parameters θ of the statistical model, the probability $P(M \mid g_1, \ldots, g_n, \theta)$ factorizes over the loci as well. As in the linkage case, that does not mean that $LR(M, g \mid I)$ can be obtained by multiplication over the loci, as if we could have worked with each locus separately. By considering (8.5) we see that even if all $LR(M, g \mid I, \theta)$ factorize over the loci, the fact that $f(\theta \mid M, I)$ is a density based on the entire trace M on all loci, means that the final expression $LR(M, g \mid I)$ generally does not factorize.

We can also understand this intuitively. If we use, for example, a discrete model with probabilities of dropout d_i for contributor i, then for any choice of d_i the likelihood ratios can be computed locus by locus and obtained by multiplication. But this is different if we do not know the probabilities of dropout. In that case we would model our uncertainty about them by specifying the density $f(d_1, \ldots, d_n)$ (with n modeled contributors). If, for example, the first locus shows no alleles, then this leads to a new distribution with more support for larger values for the d_i. This means that what we expect to see on a subsequent locus is affected by what we have seen so far, and therefore we cannot reduce the computations to single loci. In particular, adding a locus with no registered alleles to the mixture profile will change the likelihood ratios, even if for all choices of $d_1, \ldots, d_n$ the likelihood ratio on that locus considered in isolation is equal to one.

For mixture models we may, as for kinship calculations, arrive at likelihood ratio distributions that are very different and asymmetric. It may well be that the likelihood ratios for actual contributors can be very large, although not all of them are, whereas for non-contributors only a weak likelihood ratio favoring non-contribution is obtained. Whether or not this happens depends on the employed model. If we employ a model that allows for a distinction between the contributors then, if there are n modeled contributors, we have (cf. (8.10))

$$LR(M, g \mid I) = \frac{1}{n} \sum_{i=1}^{n} LR_i(M, g \mid I),$$

where $LR_i(M, g \mid I)$ is the likelihood ratio in favor S being the ith contributor (in some ordering within the model, for instance by decreasing contribution), versus being unrelated to all contributors. If n is larger than needed, there are superfluous modeled contributors and their $LR_i(M, g \mid I)$ will be around one, since for these contributors the posterior density $f(\theta \mid M, H_d, g, I)$ is mostly supported around values corresponding to them having a small, or even no, contribution. That means that, whereas for an actual contributor strong evidence can be obtained, because then a $LR_i(M, g \mid I)$ can be up to $1/p(g)$ in which case $LR(M, g \mid I) \approx 1/(np(g))$, we always have $LR(M, g \mid I) \gtrsim m/n$ for non-contributors where m is the number of superfluous contributors whose contribution is near zero.

In the kinship case, we would have the same behavior if a pedigree contained n missing persons: we would compare a person S to all these missing persons in the pedigree, and compute $\frac{1}{n} \sum_{i=1}^{n} LR_i(D, g)$, where D is the analogue of M and represents the relevant pedigree and all known DNA profiles. Now $LR_i(D, g)$ is the likelihood ratio in favor of being the ith missing person in the pedigree, versus not being related to the pedigree at all. If the pedigree contained a missing person for whom no very informative relatives were available, we would also get that the $LR_i(D, g)$ for this person would be around one.

In the example with first cousins in Section 8.3.3, we saw that persons who are actual genealogical first cousins, may provide evidence in favor of being unrelated. This is because on the considered loci, they are genetically unrelated and we have, from the profiles, inferred that there is no IBD sharing. Similarly, imagine we have a laboratory generated mixed profile made with some sample contributors. Some of these may have contributed so little that their DNA is not reflected in the profile, so that they are effectively not a contributor. We can then expect that for them, we will not find evidence in favor of being a contributor, because effectively they are not one, similar to how cousins can be effectively unrelated.

8.4 Models for Mixture Likelihoods

In this section we discuss some concrete models for the evaluation of likelihoods ratios. These methods differ in what they process as evidence, that is, what data they take into M, and how they statistically model the evidence they process.

8.4.1 No Model: Ignore Mixtures

The simplest is to ignore mixture profiles altogether and not carry out any calculations on them. Although clearly not the optimal strategy, choosing to systematically ignore relevant information may be the only sensible choice in case it is not clear how to process that information at all. It is not an uncommon practice to disregard relevant data: in many cases the evidence that is subjected to likelihood ratio calculations does not consist of all obtained data but of a selection or summary of it.

One should be wary, however, of the potential to introduce a bias towards one of the hypotheses that one would like to make statements about, since in order not to introduce any bias, the decision to ignore all information should be independent of which hypothesis is true. This means that the decision whether or not to process information present in a DNA profile from a trace should be purely trace-dependent and not based upon a comparison of the trace and the suspect's profile. Bias towards H_1 would, for example, be introduced in case we report that there is a match if there is one, but report that no conclusions can be drawn in case there is none. That would entail that for innocent suspects (whose profiles will usually not match) a statement of having obtained no information is made, but for guilty suspects (whose profiles match) a statement about evidential value is made. A bias against innocent suspects then arises.

8.4.2 Inclusion/Exclusion Probabilities

The first mixtures that were subjected to calculations were those where it was possible to reasonably assume that all alleles of all contributors were detected in the trace profile, and no other artefactual alleles.

As in Chapter 3 we denote by $RMNE(M)$ (an abbreviation of "Random Man Not Excluded") the probability that a person, selected randomly from the population, cannot be excluded as a profile contributor to such a mixture profile that is supposed to have n contributors. This is the case if the alleles of that person appear in the profile on all loci, and the profile has less than $2n$ alleles on the loci where that person is homozygous (because otherwise, the other $n - 1$ contributors would have to explain $2n - 1$ alleles, which is impossible). This approach of inclusion probabilities is firmly rooted in the match/no match paradigm. Indeed it is nothing but an extension of random match probabilities for single source profiles to mixtures. As for single source profiles, the inclusion probability depends only on the trace.

For single source profiles, if the random match probability is p, then the likelihood ratio for a suspect with a matching profile to be the source of the profile (versus being a random individual) is $1/p$. This is also true for the inclusion probability: if a suspect is not excluded, we can set up hypotheses that state that the suspect is a mixture contributor, versus is a random person unrelated to any of the mixture contributors, and then the likelihood ratio that belongs to not being excluded is $1/RMNE(M)$. Indeed, if we merely take as processed evidence that someone is not excluded, we get this result since actual contributors have this property with certainty, and unrelated non-contributors with probability $RMNE(M)$.

If dropout is thought to have possibly occurred, things become more difficult. In principle it is, given drop-out probabilities, straightforward to compute the probability $P(E_k \mid H_2)$ that for a random individual exactly k of their alleles are not present in the mixture profile on all loci together. However, this is no longer sufficient for a likelihood ratio computation. If we observe E_k stating that a suspect has k alleles that are not observed in the mixture profile, we need the probability for this to happen both for a mixture contributor and for a random individual to be able to arrive at $LR(E_k) = P(E_k \mid H_1)/P(E_k \mid H_2)$. Therefore the computation of $P(E_k \mid H_2)$ alone does not determine the evidence carried by E_k. The likelihood ratio will be at most $1/P(E_k \mid H_2)$, but possibly much smaller; it could also be in favor of the suspect being a non-contributor.

8.4.3 Likelihood Ratios Based on Matching Profiles

A simple refinement of the inclusion/exclusion approach for mixtures where all alleles of all contributors are detected and nothing else, is to take into account which alleles have been observed. In the likelihood computations one lets M be the set of detected alleles, and $P(M \mid g_1, \ldots, g_n)$ is equal to 1 if and only if M is, on every considered locus, exactly equal to the set of alleles of the g_i on that locus; otherwise it is equal to 0. The resulting $LR(M, g)$ is non-zero precisely when S with profile g is not excluded as contributor.

By using Proposition 2.17, we compute

$$P(LR > 0 \mid H_2) = \sum_{k:k>0} P(LR = k \mid H_2) = \sum_{k:k>0} \frac{1}{k} P(LR = k \mid H_1)$$

$$= E(LR^{-1} \mid H_1),$$

where the last step follows since $P(LR = 0 \mid H_1) = 0$. From Jensen's inequality we now conclude that

$$E(LR \mid H_1) \geq \frac{1}{P(LR > 0 \mid H_2)} = \frac{1}{RMNE(M)}. \tag{8.18}$$

Since $1/RMNE(M)$ is the likelihood ratio when only the match itself is taken as evidence, we see that for actual contributors of the mixture, the evidence in favor of their contribution is on average stronger if the likelihood ratio is calculated taking their profile into account, compared to when only the match itself is considered as evidence.

For non-contributors, we use that for $x \geq 0$ we have, according to an argument similar to the one leading to Proposition 2.22, that

$$E(LR \mid LR > x, H_2) = \frac{P(LR > x \mid H_1)}{P(LR > x \mid H_2)}.$$

When applied with $x = 0$, this reduces to

$$E(LR \mid LR > 0, H_2) = \frac{1}{RMNE(M)}.$$

Thus, for non-contributors we see that if they by chance cannot be excluded as contributors, on average we obtain the same likelihood ratio for them in favor of being a contributor that we already had, upon finding out which alleles they have. Perhaps the evidence will usually decline since matches by chance tend to be with the most common alleles, but it must also sometimes increase.

We remark that in Section 3.4.2 we drew the same conclusions, via a slightly different route, namely by using the posterior likelihood ratio distributions.

8.4.4 Discrete Versus Continuous Models

To be able to calculate likelihood ratios for mixtures where dropout may have occurred, a model for the probability to observe the mixture profile is needed, where we take into account that not all alleles of all contributors need to be observed with certainty. A first approach is to only model the presence or absence of alleles in the mixture profile, without taking the peak heights into account.

We have seen an example of such a model in Section 8.1.2, more specifically in (8.11) and (8.12). Suppose we model the mixture as having n contributors, and let d_i be the probability of dropout for contributor i. We can think of d_i as the probability for any allele of contributor i not to make a contribution to the mixture profile, homozygous alleles being treated as two independent alleles. Furthermore, drop-in of alleles can be modeled as a process independent of the observation of the alleles of the contributors. If we model the number of alleles dropping in at each locus as a Poisson process with parameter c, then we define the probability to observe allele a in the trace profile by (8.11).

This equation is the only formula needed, since we model all alleles to be detected or to drop out independently of each other, given the profiles of the contributors, the d_i and c. The probability to detect a set A of alleles is then the product of (8.11) for the alleles in A, multiplied by the complement of (8.11) for the alleles not in A.

It remains then to handle the fact that in general, neither the probabilities of dropout nor the profiles of all contributors are known. We integrate both of these away to obtain (8.12). In particular, we use a uniform density on $[0, 1]^n$ for the probabilities of dropout. We do not do so because we claim that our knowledge is that all probabilities $(d_1, \ldots, d_n)$ are equally likely. Rather, we do this so that, whatever the true probabilities of dropout are, they influence the likelihood ratio in the same way in (8.5).

If one wishes to take all generated data into account, it is necessary to have a model that predicts peak heights. These heights, measured in rfu, correspond to the number of post-PCR amplicons, and that number is informative for the number of pre-PCR copies. Therefore, any continuous model will need to include model parameters both for the relative contribution that the contributors have with respect to each other, and for the absolute contribution of all contributors together.

Many models have been suggested and certainly more would be possible. A first important aspect is the distribution from which peak heights are drawn, once other parameters are conditioned on (for instance, the profiles of the contributors, the mixture proportions). Some models use Gamma distributions (for instance, the model developed in [43], reprogrammed as EuroForMix in [24], the software LiRa [123], LikeLTD [150], and also [98]), others use a log-normal distribution (for instance, STRMix [160]), other choices are made for TrueAllele [121], and in [154], and no doubt more would be reasonably possible.

In addition to modeling peak heights of alleles, decisions need to be made as to (1) whether and how to model stutter (e.g., not at all, -1 stutters, -2, $+1$, -2 stutters, etc.), (2) the peak height distribution of them (e.g., conditional on the length of the parental allele, or on the longest uninterrupted sequence, conditional on the locus), (3) how to model drop-in alleles (e.g., their peak height distributions, their probabilities, whether or not they are taken into the subpopulation correction or not), (4) locus specific sensitivity and degradation, and more. It is easy to envisage dozens or even hundreds of models that are all slightly different from each other. In addition it has been noted [39, 40] that especially for small amounts of input DNA, peak height distributions need not be unimodal and hence are not well described by any of the above mentioned distributions.

One may wonder how one should or could make a choice from all these existing models. Even more important perhaps is the question which of these models describes reality best. In what follows in this chapter, we will argue that the specific peak height distribution is less important than perhaps thought at first sight, and we now illustrate the idea behind this claim with a first elementary example.

Consider a single source trace, and suppose we have a locus with alleles $(12, 16)$ with peak heights $(1000, 1100)$. If we have a person of interest with genotype $(12, 16)$ then the model needs to predict by what probability one would get peak heights exactly equal to $(1000, 1100)$. For an unknown individual, all possible genotypes need to be considered, but the contribution to the profile likelihood coming from genotypes other than $(12, 16)$ will be negligible, and the likelihood is almost equal to the probability of seeing $(12, 16)$ in the person of interest if it is not a contributor, multiplied by the probability to obtain peak heights $(1000, 1100)$ for such a person. In the likelihood ratio this probability cancels out and we get the inverse of the random match probability for genotype $(12, 16)$. Thus, the whole peak height model drops out of the equation and the likelihood ratio is model-independent. The model becomes important only when the alleles have non-negligible probability to be not from the contributor, but instead are a result of stutter or drop-in. This means that basically any peak height distribution (that has a larger expected peak height for contributors with a larger amount of template in the sample) will lead to the same result, namely a likelihood ratio almost equal to the inverse of the random match probability.

For a mixture the conclusion need not be different. Suppose we consider a locus with detected alleles $(15, 16, 17, 18)$ with peak heights $(2500, 1000, 1100, 2600)$. Some peaks may have a stutter component but they are too large to be purely stutter. The only possibility really playing a role is the one corresponding to the corresponding genotypes being $(15, 18)$ and $(16, 17)$. The probability to see *exactly* the observed heights is not relevant because it is needed for both hypotheses for the same genotypes. The only crucial assumption is that contributors tend to have higher peaks if their contribution is larger. Different models will predict the profiles with different probabilities, but the ratio between these probabilities under both hypotheses, that is, the likelihood ratio, is the same for such profiles.

These toy examples illustrate that the importance of the details of the peak height model depends on how well the trace profile allows to distinguish between the contributors. For contributors that can be well distinguished, based on the peak heights and the basic assumption that more DNA corresponds to higher peaks, the precise peak height model is not so important and the evidential value is quite model independent. Therefore, continuous models can be expected to give the same results on straightforward comparisons where a person of interest is tested as being the unique major contributor. On the other hand, it also means that models that return that likelihood ratio, need not have a probability model that makes any sense at all beyond predicting higher peaks for contributors which left more DNA. We cannot infer that if a model performs well for some simple category of traces, it also works well on more challenging categories where more modeling aspects are needed.

8.5 The Top-down Approach

The methods so far use the approach of (8.9), that is, they model the whole trace, with or without the peak heights. When this modeling is done we are able to calculate likelihood ratios taking the whole trace into account. If we cannot distinguish between contributors, then we get a likelihood ratio $LR(M, g \mid I)$ in favor of being any contributor. If we can distinguish between the contributors, then we get contributor-specific likelihood ratios $LR_i(M, g \mid I)$. But, as we have seen with examples, since peak heights scale with DNA contribution, it may be possible to target contributors directly by looking at alleles that could possibly be theirs. This is the idea behind the following method, where we define sub-profiles of the trace which are aimed at containing the alleles of the k most prominent contributors, for some suitable k. The method that we are about to introduce and discuss is of a hybrid form, with both continuous and discrete aspects.

Suppose that the model orders the contributors from larger to smaller contribution, and that the model provides a probabilistic description of the possible genotypes of each contributor. The more the probabilistic description for contributor i resembles a point distribution, the more $LR_i(M, g \mid I)$ approaches $1/p(g)$ and the better "resolved" we say the contributor is.

If we work under the assumption of n contributors for the trace profile, then from point of view (8.9) we see that we need to take all profiles $g_1, \ldots, g_n$ into account. From point of view (8.15) these computations amount to predicting the genotypes of all contributors. For large n this becomes computationally prohibitive at some point.

On the other hand, if we have a mixture with different mixture proportions for all contributors and we order them according to decreasing contribution, then we expect to be, for most mixtures, able to resolve contributor 1 better than contributor 2, etc., because a higher contribution leads to larger peaks, more detection of alleles, and less uncertainty as to whether the resulting peaks are allelic or not. This also means that we heuristically expect that generally

$$E(LR_1(M, g \mid I) \mid H_{p,1}) \geq \cdots \geq E(LR_n(M, g \mid I) \mid H_{p,n}).$$

It may very well be the case that the last contributors can be only so poorly resolved that no useful likelihood ratio is to be expected. In that case, we would need to model the trace with a very precise model, and even then we would perhaps not be able to gather evidence strong enough to be useful. Moreover the likelihood ratios for the last contributors have the potential to depend much more heavily on the specifics of the chosen model than for the well-resolved contributors. Above, we argued that for well-resolved contributors the precise model is of minor importance.

If we are interested only in the most prominent contributor, it would be enough to compute $LR_1(M, g \mid I)$. In view of (8.16) we would be done if that yields strong evidence. We would have obtained evidence in favor of being the most prominent contributor, and hence by (8.10) and (8.16), also evidence in favor of being any contributor. The difference is a factor n depending on how we formulate the hypotheses (to get evidence in favor of being this particular contributor, or just any contributor). If we would have computed $LR_1(M, g \mid I)$ and we would not have found evidence, we could then consider the second contributor and compare it with S. In other words, we can approach our problem of determining whether there is evidence in favor of S having contributed, by computing the series

$$LR^{(1)}(M, g \mid I) = LR_1(M, g \mid I),$$
$$LR^{(2)}(M, g \mid I) = (LR_1(M, g \mid I) + LR_2(M, g \mid I))/2,$$
$$LR^{(3)}(M, g \mid I) = (LR_1(M, g \mid I) + LR_2(M, g \mid I) + LR_3(M, g \mid I))/3,$$
$$\cdots = \cdots,$$

which ends with $LR^{(n)}(M, g \mid I) = LR(M, g \mid I)$ as the nth computation, at least if the full trace is considered to have n contributors. This series can be terminated if we find some $LR^{(j)}(M, g \mid I) \gg 1$ sufficiently large for our purposes, or if the computations become too complex. These computations amount to answering the following series of questions:

1. Is there evidence that the person of interest is the most prominent contributor? If yes, we are done. If not,
2. Is there evidence that the person of interest is among the two most prominent contributors? If yes, we are done. If not,
3. Is there evidence that the person of interest is among the three most prominent contributors? If yes, we are done. If not,
4. ...

If we could do this, we can avoid the modeling of contributors that we are at that point not interested in. Finding evidence for belonging to a certain top-k is sufficient, regardless of how many contributors we would need beyond the first k. The method we will discuss is inspired by this way of approaching the contributors in the order of contribution.

The top-down approach is quite natural and reminiscent to human judgment. If there is a clear major component to the mixture, its contributor(s) are easily recognizable, without having to know much about the underlying minor contributors, not even how many there are. In DNA casework, sometimes profiles with many contributors are encountered, but with only a few major contributors. It is then not uncommon to derive (manually) a profile which is thought to correspond to the alleles from those most prominent contributors, and subject only that profile to calculations. The top-down approach is an objectified and unbiased automated version of this manual approach.

The minor contributors are generally harder to distinguish, and finding evidence in favor of their contribution requires much more subtle modeling than for the major components. The top-down method does not aim to find these. Instead it aims to give a method to find the prominent contributors requiring the least effort. We will show in Section 8.5.2 that this is in practice very possible, even if there are many profile contributors.

8.5.1 The Top-down Likelihood Ratio

We can now explain the top-down approach to mixture evaluation. We want to use the principle that contributors with a larger relative contribution are responsible for larger peaks. Therefore we define M_α, locus by locus, and replicate by replicate, as the sub-profile of M that contains the smallest set of peaks such that the sum of the peak heights in M_α is at least a fraction α of the total sum of peak heights. We define this sub-profile by carrying out this procedure on all loci separately, and if applicable, on every replicate analysis of the trace. In this way, on every locus M_α targets alleles of the most prominent contributors that together have contributed at least a fraction α of the total peak height. On every locus, M_α can be iteratively constructed, by taking in peaks starting with the largest one, and stopping when a fraction α or more of the total sum of peak heights has been taken into M_α. We only take alleles into M_α, not their peak heights, since we will use the discrete model (8.12) on the M_α.

For example, suppose a trace has alleles $(10, 11, 12, 13, 14, 15, 15.3, 16, 17)$ with peak heights $(112, 733, 2265, 301, 527, 729, 486, 534, 1430)$ rfu. Then the sum of the peak heights is 7117 rfu, and we now describe M_α for $\alpha = 0.1, 0.2, \ldots, 0.9, 1$. First $M_{0.1} = \{12\}$ since allele 12 alone has 2265 rfu, which is more than the targeted $\alpha = 0.1$. For the same reasons, $M_{0.2} = M_{0.3} = \{12\}$, whereas $M_{0.4} = M_{0.5} = \{12, 17\}$, $M_{0.6} = \{11, 12, 17\}$, $M_{0.7} = \{11, 12, 15, 17\}$, $M_{0.8} = \{11, 12, 14, 15, 17\}$, $M_{0.9} = \{11, 12, 14, 15, 15.3, 16, 17\}$, and finally M_1 is the whole trace.

Of course the sub-profiles M_α need not contain all alleles of all profile contributors to M_α and they may also contain some alleles that do not belong to the contributors we targeted. If several contributors share the same allele, its (in reality stacked) peak height may be so large that it is taken into M_α. Since in M_α we only register absence or presence of alleles, this is only undesirable when none of the targeted contributors have that allele. We do not claim (or aim for) a perfect derivation of a sub-profile containing precisely the alleles of the most prominent contributors, but our procedure is such that we do target them since we collect the largest peaks, which reasonably come from the most contributing persons. We note that the same holds for the full trace profile $M = M_1$. In that profile we need not have all alleles of all contributors (there may be dropout) and we may have alleles detected not belonging to them (drop-ins or artifacts).

We compute likelihood ratios on all the M_α using dropout probabilities and drop-in, just as we would do for the trace $M = M_1$. For notational convenience we write

$$LR_\alpha := LR(M_\alpha, g \mid I),$$

which we can compute using the discrete model specified in (8.12), where the number of modeled contributors n_α used for M_α is taken to be the minimal required number $n_\alpha = \lceil m_\alpha / 2 \rceil$, with m_α the maximum number of peaks observed on the loci of M_α. So, we use the peak heights only for the definition of the sub-profiles, and carry out calculations using only the alleles in these.

It remains to define a final result, denoted $LR_{\text{top-down}}(M, g \mid I)$, from the LR_α. We define

$$LR_{\text{top-down}}(M, g \mid I) = \max_\alpha LR_\alpha, \tag{8.19}$$

that is, we take the *largest* likelihood ratio obtained on any of the sub-profiles M_α. The choice of taking the largest may seem counterintuitive, and in the next subsections we elaborate in detail on this choice.

8.5.2 Examples of the Top-down Approach

We now proceed with two examples where we compute the $LR_\alpha(M, g)$, one for a mixture with four replicates and another example for one with a single analysis. In these examples, we do not condition on anything and therefore we omit I in out notation.

As will be presented in more detail below, we have subjected laboratory generated profiles to this method. For the two next examples, we use two laboratory generated mixtures described in [23], consisting of mixtures analyzed on the NGM loci, with either two or three contributors in various mixture proportions, some with replicate analyses.

In Figure 8.1 we plot $\log(LR_\alpha(M, g))$, for the profiles g of the sample contributors, where M is the trace with code name 0.24 in [23] (two contributors in a targeted 5:1 proportion, four replicate analyses), as a function of α, for $\alpha \in \{0.05, 0.1, 0.15, \ldots, 0.95, 1\}$. We have omitted the $LR_\alpha < 1$ in this graph for more convenient scaling of the $\log(LR_\alpha)$-axis, and plotted them as $LR_\alpha = 1$ instead. In addition we plot the likelihood ratios obtained with EuroForMix, using the MLE approach, taken from [23]. These likelihood ratios are computed on the whole trace. For visual comparison purposes we plot them as a horizontal line.

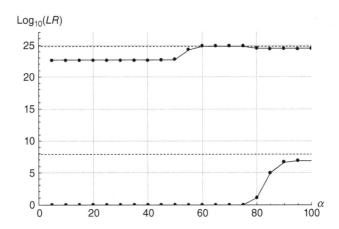

Figure 8.1 Likelihood ratios LR_α as a function of α (labeled in percentages; top graph with dots: major contributor; lower graph with dots: minor contributor), compared with the likelihood ratio obtained by EuroForMix (MLE) (values plotted as dotted lines for better comparison).

From Figure 8.1 we see that the likelihood ratios obtained with the continuous model are best approximated by the largest LR_α for both the contributors. For the major contributor, the likelihood ratio is maximal for $\alpha = 0.7$, and for the minor contributor at $\alpha = 1$, i.e., when the whole trace is modeled. For the major contributor, the maximal likelihood ratio once obtained, remains (approximately) stable when α increases. This can be explained by properties of the discrete model. The likelihood ratio it computes by integration over the probabilities of dropout is dominated by the likelihood ratios for probabilities of dropout that best explain the evaluated profiles (cf. (8.5)). The four replicates are best explained by one contributor without and one with dropout. The different reproducibilities of the alleles then give information about which alleles come from the same contributor. The largest contribution to the likelihood (8.9) is obtained when alleles with similar reproducibility are from the same contributor. Therefore, when alleles from the minor contributor become taken into M_α, they do not influence the likelihood ratio for the major contributor much.

For a continuous model, the largest contribution to the mixture likelihood is similarly obtained: it is largest when the genotypes fit the peak heights. If the profile of a prominent contributor can be well resolved, a continuous model therefore can be thought of as automatically conditioning on the profile of the major contributor.

If only a single analysis has been done, then in the absence of replicates the dropout model cannot use reproducibility. Thus, when α grows and M_α contains more alleles, the newly added alleles cannot be recognized by the discrete model as coming from new contributors. Therefore the LR_α will decrease after a maximum has been reached on the M_α, since alleles taken into a larger M_α cannot be distinguished as coming from another contributor and the number of modeled contributors grows. For the continuous model, the likelihood ratio for a contributor is much less affected by the presence of less prominently present contributors, since it can still use the peak heights also on a single analysis as it does when there are replicates. This dependence on the likelihood ratio for a mixture with a single analysis is exemplified in Figure 8.2 where we display the LR_α obtained by the three contributors to mixture 12.5. This is a mixture with $(500, 50, 50)$ pg of DNA for the contributors.

In Figure 8.2, we see that the likelihood ratio for the major contributor is practically the same with the top-down method as with the continuous model, and that for the minor contributors, the likelihood ratio with the top-down method is conservative with respect to that of the continuous model. However, the likelihood ratio for the major contributor is easily retrieved: this likelihood ratio is found at $\alpha = 0.55$ and remains constant up to $\alpha = 0.7$. Until then, the M_α are actually modeled with a single contributor.

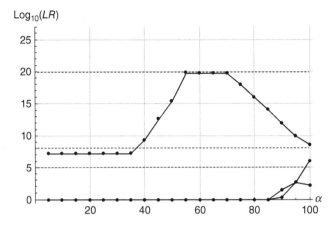

Figure 8.2 Likelihood ratios LR_α (for all three contributors) as a function of α (labeled in percentages, graphs with dots) compared with the likelihood ratio obtained by EuroForMix (MLE) (values plotted as dotted lines for better comparison).

For our final example, we ran the top-down approach on a set of mixtures with known composition, analyzed on the 23 autosomal loci of the PPF6C multiplex. In total, 120 traces were generated, each in principle with three replicates. These traces and computations on them with EuroForMix are reported upon in [16]. These 120 traces were divided into 30 traces with two, three, four or five persons, in various mixing proportions. We treated each replicate separately, thus having 354 traces (6 profiles did not pass a laboratory quality control step), and we computed the top-down likelihood ratio with each of the 30 individuals that together were the contributors of all traces. These traces contained, for the five-person mixtures the following amounts of input DNA: (300, 150, 150, 150, 150), (300, 30, 30, 30, 30), (150, 150, 60, 60, 60), (150, 30, 60, 30, 30), or (600, 30, 60, 30, 30) pg of DNA. These series are denoted as series A, B, C, D, or E, respectively. For the traces with $k < 5$ contributors, the first k of each of these combinations were used. For example the four-person traces of the D-series had (150, 30, 60, 30) pg of input DNA for the four contributors. There is thus variation in the relative proportions, in the absolute amounts, and in whether or not a single prominent contributor stands out.

We restricted the top-down likelihood ratio to sub-profiles with at most three modeled contributors, thus stopping if more than three were needed. If a sub-profile M_α was not subjected to computations because more than three contributors would be modeled, all likelihood ratios with this sub-profile were set equal to 1. Therefore, according to (8.19), if g is such that all LR_α with at most three contributors turned out to be less than one, we get $LR_{\text{top-down}}(M, g) = 1$ if there are sub-profiles with more than three contributors.

As calculations using EuroForMix were time consuming, likelihood ratio calculations were performed on a subset of possible comparisons as described in [16]. No computations were done with EuroForMix on five-person traces. The calculated likelihood ratios for sample contributors were usually not with the most prominent ones. We present the comparison of the available results, as well as a summary of the results for all contributors and for the non-contributors.

A drawback of the mixture proportions of the mixtures we consider here is that there are many contributors with precisely the same input DNA amount. If we sort the contributors according to contribution we say that the first k form an identifiable top-k if all contributors beyond the kth have contributed strictly less than the kth. For example, in a mixture with proportions $(300, 300, 150, 150)$ the top-1 is not identifiable, the top-2 is, the top-3 is not, and the top-4 is. None of the mixtures in this study with more than three contributors have an identifiable top-3. Therefore we restricted attention to the identifiable top-1 and top-2.

First of all we compare the results of the top-down method with those of the classical discrete method. The latter results corresponds to the evaluation of the full profile. By construction, the top-down method gives an likelihood ratio that is at least equal to the likelihood ratio of the discrete method, and is larger if there is a strict sub-profile giving a larger likelihood ratio than the full profile. We have separated the likelihood ratios realized by actual contributors and by non-contributors. In Figure 8.3 we display a comparison of the likelihood ratios for the contributors. From this figure we see that there are several effects at work. First, there is the category of traces that have not been evaluated by the discrete method since the number of contributors is too large, meaning that more than three modeled contributors are needed. These corresponds to the dots on the vertical axis. It is clear that many of these traces harbor evidence that already can be extracted at the expense of modeling at most three contributors.

A second category is formed by the points for which the resulting likelihood ratio is the same: these are comparisons where the person of interest's likelihood ratio is maximal when the full trace is modeled. We see that almost all of the smallest likelihood ratios are of this type, which is to be expected since these will be the comparisons with the most minor contributors. The third category consists of those points where the top-down likelihood ratio is larger than the discrete likelihood ratio. These points correspond to contributors that give a large likelihood ratio on the sub-profiles. We see that the difference in likelihood ratio can be very substantial, and that we can extract these large likelihood ratios using only the profile data to define the sub-profiles. The computational effort to retrieve these larger likelihood ratios is for most points considerably less than the one for the smaller likelihood ratio obtained with the classical discrete method on the whole profile.

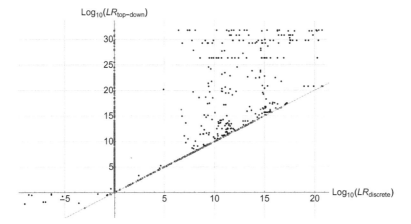

Figure 8.3 Likelihood ratios for contributors (1235 comparisons) with the classical discrete method and with the top-down method; dashed line corresponding to equality.

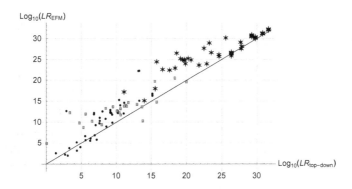

Figure 8.4 Comparison of likelihood ratios for identifiable top-1 up to top-3 in three- and four-person mixtures. Stars correspond to the contributors in the identifiable top-1, gray squares to those in the identifiable top-2 (but not top-1), and black dots to the contributors in the identifiable top-3 (and not in the top-2 or top-1: there are such contributors for the three-person mixtures only).

The results for the identifiable top-1, top-2, or top-3 contributors for all three- and four-person mixtures where a computation with EuroForMix has been carried out are in Figure 8.4. For the four-person mixtures there is never an identifiable top-3. We see that the top-down method retrieves the targeted contributors with a likelihood ratio that is conservative with respect to those of EuroForMix. For most cases, the obtained evidence is very strong with both methods. There is one comparison that yields $LR = 1$ for the top-down method (the 60-pg-contributor in a four-person E-series mixture, with input (600, 30, 60, 30) pg).

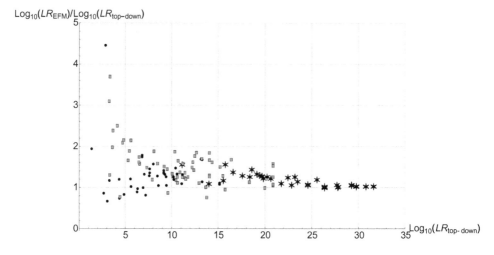

$\mathrm{Log}_{10}(LR_{\mathrm{EFM}})/\mathrm{Log}_{10}(LR_{\mathrm{top-down}})$

Figure 8.5 Comparison of all likelihood ratios obtained by EuroForMix, with those obtained by top-down method, on the two-, three-, and four-person mixtures. Stars correspond to the contributors in the identifiable top-1, gray squares to those in the identifiable top-2 (but not top-1), and black dots to the contributors in the identifiable top-3 (and not in the top-2 or top-1: there are such contributors for the three-person mixtures only).

In order to see the convergence between the results of the top-down method and the continuous method, we give a presentation of the results for all contributors in the two-, three-, and four-person mixtures that are targets of the way we applied the top-down method here, i.e., who are in an identifiable top-k with $k \leq 3$. This time, we compare the likelihood ratio obtained by the top-down method with the likelihood ratio obtained by the continuous method, by considering the ratio of the weight of evidence of the continuous model with that of the top-down method.

For the four-person mixtures, there being no identifiable top-3 in any of them, only contributors in the identifiable top-1 and top-2 could be included in Figure 8.5. These mixtures do not have an identifiable top-3, so for contributors beyond the identifiable top-1 and top-2 we cannot expect the top-down likelihood ratio to have reached its maximum when targeting the top-3.

In Figure 8.5 we clearly see the trend for the likelihood ratios of both methods to differ relatively less from each other, as the weight of evidence becomes larger. We note, however, that we do not intend the results of EuroForMix to serve as a golden standard. Also for different continuous models we expect that it will be the case that the ratio between their obtained weights of evidence is larger for smaller weight of evidence, since these will depend more heavily on the more subtle choices in the model, such as the way stutter is modeled.

Finally we look at the likelihood ratios for the non-contributors as obtained with the top-down method. As expected, a large proportion of these were precisely

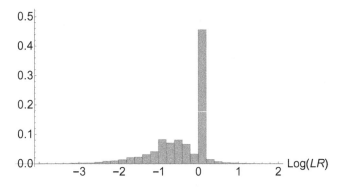

Figure 8.6 Likelihood ratios for the non-contributors of the PPF6C profiles.

equal to 1. A histogram of the obtained likelihood ratios on logarithmic scale is presented in Figure 8.6. The largest likelihood ratio observed for a non-contributor was equal to 82.

These examples confirm that the top-down approach is sufficient to reproduce the likelihood ratios obtained with a continuous model for the most prominent contributor, at least if the difference in contribution with the remaining contributors is large enough. For less prominent contributors, it is a conservative approach. Indeed, apart from the first one, we do not target the contributors directly. The M_α form an increasing series of sub-profiles, each expected to contain most of the trace alleles coming from the first k contributors, and also some of the alleles of subsequents ones, mostly from contributor $k + 1$. The sequence of subsequent $LR_\alpha(M, g)$ therefore resembles a sequence containing the various $LR_1(M, g)$, $(LR_1(M, g) + LR_2(M, g))/2$, $(LR_1(M, g) + LR_2(M, g) + LR_3(M, g))/3$, etc., interpolating between these. A continuous model can directly compute the $LR_i(M, g)$ in favor of being contributor i, and therefore we expect the top-down likelihood ratio to be increasingly conservative as we go deeper into the mixture.

8.5.3 Heuristics and Further Discussion of the Top-down Approach

The top-down approach, with its simple definition, has several advantages over more refined modeling. Using the conceptually simple model (8.12) on the sub-profiles implies that we do not need to make distributional assumptions on the peak heights. The algorithm to query contributors serially, in a top-down fashion, also guarantees computational simplicity. When the whole trace profile is modeled, then the computation time is determined by the number of modeled contributors. With the top-down approach this is different. For an algorithm implementing the top-down approach, various choices must be made. In principle, since there are only finitely many alleles in a trace M, there are also finitely many different LR_α, hence all of these can be determined. In practice, one may choose to discretize the interval [0,1] in a trace-independent way, and in this chapter we have always carried out calculations on α in multiples of 0.05. This means that as many as 20 sub-profiles are created so that at most 20 computations must be done. Further, the number of sub-profiles to be analyzed depends on the criterion for stopping: one can decide to stop when a likelihood ratio threshold is reached, when a certain α is reached, or when more than a certain number of contributors needs to be modeled. The runtime for the likelihood ratios on sub-profiles using n contributors are, by construction, the same as for any trace that is modeled with n contributors. Therefore, when the top-k is searched, several computations, each involving $1 \leq n \leq k$ contributors, must be done.

Thus, the top-down approach allows to carry out computations until either we have found strong evidence for contribution to a top-k, or until the whole trace is analyzed, or until the computation becomes too complex. The criterion for being too complex can be decided beforehand: one can decide, for example, to aim only for the three most prominent contributors regardless of the total number.

In contrast to other methods, the total number of contributors is not a parameter of the top-down method. The previous examples indicated that taking the largest LR_α as top-down likelihood ratio, as we defined it in (8.19), gives us a good approximation of the likelihood ratio obtainable with a continuous model. As we saw, for a continuous model we would expect the likelihood ratio not to decline after it has reached the maximum LR_α if we were to work with sub-profiles with such a method.

Next we further discuss heuristically why we believe that working with sub-profiles, and hence discarding information on the trace beyond that contained in the sub-profile maximizing LR_α, can be expected to have the properties that we want.

First we emphasize that not only sub-profiles are incomplete. Often the whole trace $M = M_1$ can also be thought of as a sub-profile of an (unobserved) larger profile that we would obtain with other sensitivity settings. It would be a concern if likelihood ratios obtained on M would usually decrease if we would have that larger profile. The reason that such a decline in evidence should not occur is broadly speaking the following. At $\alpha = 0$ we start with the empty profile M_0. Then, as α increases, we obtain the alleles of the contributors where their order of appearance is roughly according to decreasing contribution. For every contributor there will be a smallest α such that this contributor's alleles in M are all in M_α. Letting α increase further, we will add more alleles to the subsequent sub-profiles. That does not affect the likelihood ratio for the already present contributors, if the newly added peaks are sufficiently smaller so as to be best explained as coming from other contributors. We therefore believe that, if we would use a continuous model that reflects the reality of mixture profile generation adequately, LR_α will rise to some maximal value and then remain constant, if we use the peak heights in the mixture likelihood calculations for the M_α.

The top-down method does not use a continuous but a discrete model for the actual computations on the sub-profiles M_α. This means that on any M_α, the peak heights are no longer taken into account; they only play a role in the definition of the M_α. Contrary to what we expect to happen for a continuous model, the LR_α can therefore be expected to decrease when M_α takes in more and more alleles especially when no replicates are available. This is indeed what we saw in Figure 8.2.

A concern with (8.19) may be that for a non-contributor we seem to maximize the opportunity to obtain a likelihood ratio in favor of contribution. We think, however, that false positives are not to be expected to be more of a concern than for other models. Indeed, since we argued that the LR_α, viewed as a function of α, interpolate between the various $LR^{(k)}(M, g)$, the false positive rates will be, we expect, similar to those of a serial query for being either contributor 1, and if not then for being contributor 1 or 2, etc. This again should roughly correspond to the combined false positive rates of several queries for the contributors directly with the $LR_k(M, g)$.

It is possible to give crude bounds. We know from Proposition 2.4.2 that $P(LR \geq t \mid H_2) \leq 1/t$. This bound applies to all the LR_α on the sub-profiles. Suppose we approximate (8.19) by discretizing $[0, 1]$ using a number k of sub-profiles M_α, say for $\alpha \in \{1/k, 2/k, \ldots, (k-1)/k, 1\}$. If all the M_α would be independent the bound $1/t$ will become approximately k/t for large t, if t is the top-down likelihood ratio, i.e., the maximal likelihood ratio on all sub-profiles. Therefore it is impossible to have a large probability for strong false positives, with k/t being a very crude upper bound for the probability that a non-contributor has a top-down likelihood ratio exceeding $t \gg 1$, if we take k sub-profiles M_α. However, the M_α, being an increasing series of sub-profiles, are far from independent. Any person fitting well into a particular M_α will also fit in the larger ones, but not conversely. This will reduce the false positive probabilities far below this crude bound. In Section 8.5.2 we saw that the likelihood ratios for non-contributors on the described set of mixtures were almost all at most equal to one, and never large. This is in agreement with the preceding arguments.

Continuous models need to have probability distributions for the heights of all types of peaks, including stutter peaks, drop-in peaks, and other artefactual peaks. Also factors like degradation and inhibition that may cause peak heights to differ across the loci need to be taken into account. Different sensitivity across the loci, leading some loci to show alleles of more sample contributors than other loci, requires careful locus specific peak height modeling. It is less relevant for the top-down method, because rescaling all peak heights by the same factor does not affect the M_α. Indeed, this is why we have not defined the sub-profiles in terms of absolute peak heights by moving the analytical threshold, but in terms of the heights relative to the total on each locus separately. This was chosen to better deal with different sensitivities and degradation across loci. Of course, different approaches to defining the subsets analogous to our M_α could still be envisaged, for example, one might take a locus specific approach and take in peaks above a locus-dependent peak height threshold. Alternatively, one could first normalize the peak heights to sum up to one, and then lower the analytical threshold. If a continuous interpretation method were applied to the sub-profiles, such choices might be more suitable for those models. Perhaps such an approach would even outperform the one presented here. We have not trialled other methods and therefore cannot carry out a comparison. The choice for M_α described here turned out to give results that were in our opinion satisfactory enough, and the rationale behind it is easy to understand.

The number of profile contributors is not the most important factor for determining the complexity of a mixture. Rather, this complexity is determined by the mixture *proportions* and the total amount of DNA in the sample. More even mixture proportions and smaller amounts reduce the possibility to target the affected contributors individually, and hence sequentially. Those contributors who have a contribution similar to that of others, are more difficult to find evidence for. This hinders the top-down approach, but lack of information in peak heights also hinders a continuous model. Evenness of mixture proportions is a complexity measure which is inherent to the problem, and not specific for a chosen model.

8.6 Maximum Likelihood Versus Integration

Some mixture evaluation methods do not compute the integrals (8.8) but instead compute

$$LR_{ML}(M, g \mid I) := \frac{P(M \mid H_1, g, \hat{\theta}_1, I)}{P(M \mid H_2, g, \hat{\theta}_2, I)}, \qquad (8.20)$$

where $\hat{\theta}_i$ maximizes $P(M \mid H_i, g, \theta, I)$ over all θ, and where ML stands for "maximum likelihood." The quantities $\hat{\theta}_1$ and $\hat{\theta}_2$ are called *ML estimates*. The quantity in (8.20) is, methodologically speaking, very different from $LR(M, g \mid I)$. Despite our notation, the quotient in (8.20) is not a likelihood ratio, but instead it represents how much better the best explanation for the data under H_1 is than the best explanation under H_2.

How does this number relate to $LR(M, g \mid I)$? First of all we have, by definition of the $\hat{\theta}_i$, that

$$LR_{\hat{\theta}_2}(M, g \mid I) = \frac{P(M \mid H_1, g, \hat{\theta}_2, I)}{P(M \mid H_2, g, \hat{\theta}_2, I)} \leq \frac{P(M \mid H_1, g, \hat{\theta}_1, I)}{P(M \mid H_2, g, \hat{\theta}_2, I)}$$

$$\leq \frac{P(M \mid H_1, g, \hat{\theta}_1, I)}{P(M \mid H_2, g, \hat{\theta}_1, I)} = LR_{\hat{\theta}_1}(M, g \mid I), \qquad (8.21)$$

so that $LR_{ML}(M, g \mid I)$ is always between the two likelihood ratios corresponding to the separate likelihood ratios at the maximum likelihood values $\hat{\theta}_2$ and $\hat{\theta}_1$.

Heuristically the ML estimates of θ can be expected to give a better estimate of the true value θ_0 as more data are specified. The difference between H_1 and H_2 is that H_1 fixes a profile of a contributor which under H_2 is free to be any profile. If H_1 is true, so that the person of interest S is indeed a contributor, then we can expect that $\hat{\theta}_1$ is a more accurate estimate of θ_0 than $\hat{\theta}_2$. The likelihood ratio $LR_{ML}(M, g \mid I)$ can in that case therefore be expected to be conservative with respect to the best estimate $LR_{\hat{\theta}_1}$.

On the other hand, if the person of interest did not contribute to the trace, then the ML estimate from H_1 is conditional on information that is incorrect and therefore we can expect that $\hat{\theta}_2$ is the better estimate. But with respect to that estimate, $LR_{ML}(M, g \mid I)$ is anti-conservative, being larger. Therefore, we can expect that, while $LR_{ML}(E)$ does not overstate the evidence for actual contributors and will be closer to the likelihood ratio at the true parameters θ_0 for those, it will be anti-conservative to do so for non-contributors. This behavior is a drawback of the ML method. Methodologically, the ML procedure tries to learn about θ from the presence of the person of interest, whereas the aim should be to do the opposite: indeed we should try to learn about the presence of the person of interest from our knowledge of θ.

It therefore needs to be verified whether in practice, the model and the optimized parameters are such that the degree of anti-conservatism is limited for non-contributors. In any case, if the likelihood ratios at $\hat{\theta}_1$ and $\hat{\theta}_2$ are close to each other then by (8.21), the effect of the separate maximization is small. We need to be more worried when the likelihood ratios obtained from these estimates are very different then if they agree fairly well. These being generally not accessible in software, the only remaining proxy is to verify whether the estimates $\hat{\theta}_1$ and $\hat{\theta}_2$ correspond.

In some cases the computational effort required may be a reason to prefer maximum likelihood over integration. In practice the existing approaches are hybrid, applying ML to some parameters and integration to others. An obvious question then is which parameters are subjected to ML estimation and which are not. One natural choice is to use ML for those parameters where no prior $f(\theta)$ is readily available, for instance for case-dependent aspects such as mixture proportions, but to use integration for the parameters that have a natural prior, such as the profiles of the unknown contributors.

8.6.1 The Profiles of the Unknown Contributors as Model Parameters

In this section we work out the difference between maximization and integration for a specific choice of model parameters, namely the profiles of the unknown contributors.

First of all, applying maximum likelihood estimation to all parameters, including the profiles of the contributors, we arrive at

$$LR_{ML}(M \mid g, I) = \frac{\max_{\theta \in \Theta_1} P_\theta(M \mid g, I)}{\max_{\theta \in \Theta_2} P_\theta(M \mid g, I)},$$

where $\Theta_1 \subset \Theta_2$, the difference being that in Θ_1 the profile of the targeted contributor is equal to the profile g of the person of interest S.

This is, in fact, a classical frequentist likelihood ratio test where the parameters are optimized over two domains, one being included in the other. If we do so, we get $LR_{ML}(M \mid I, g) \leq 1$ by construction. The maximal value $LR_{ML}(M \mid I, g) = 1$ is obtained if the ML estimate in H_2 gives the same likelihood as the one in H_1, which will happen if the most likely profiles of the contributors also yield g as profile for the contributor that we query. The smaller $LR_{ML}(M \mid I, g)$ becomes, the better one can explain the data M without contribution of S. Thus, the ML estimator has no likelihood ratio interpretation and now has become a frequentist instrument for hypothesis testing.

Next, we explicitly integrate over the profiles of the unknown contributors, as in (8.5). We will see that this gives us another derivation of the link between probabilistic genotyping and likelihood ratios in (8.15).

Assume that the mixture has n contributors, whose profiles we interpret as model parameters, as we discussed before. We would like to apply (8.5), but in order to do so we need to discuss for which sets of hypotheses this is allowed in the sense that we have $f(\theta \mid H_1, I) = f(\theta \mid H_2, I)$, as we discussed before in Section 8.1. In most situations encountered in practice these distributions will be the same, for example if S is modeled as unrelated to any of the contributors, or as the brother of one of them. It will, however, not always be the case, for example if H_2 says all contributors are siblings, or that S is a parent of each of the mixture contributors, then the joint distribution of the g_i will be different under H_2 than under H_1. Bearing this in mind, we will now assume that $f(\theta \mid H_1, I) = f(\theta \mid H_2, I)$ so that we can use (8.5).

The two ingredients in this formula are the likelihood ratio for a fixed value of the parameters, and the updated density $f(g_1, \ldots, g_n \mid M, g, H_2, I)$. As for the likelihood ratio, fixing the parameters now means fixing the profiles of the contributors and we need to compute

$$LR(M, g \mid g_1, \ldots, g_n, I) = \frac{P(M, g \mid g_1, \ldots, g_n, H_1, I)}{P(M, g \mid g_1, \ldots, g_n, H_2, I)}, \qquad (8.22)$$

where both probabilities are for the trace profile to be M and the profile of S to be g, given the profiles g_i of the contributors, the hypothesis and I.

Evaluating the probabilities in (8.22), we see that the probability to see M does not depend on H anymore if we know all the g_i. As for the profile g of S, under each hypothesis its probability no longer depends on M once we know the profiles of the contributors either.

In the case where we choose H_1 the hypothesis that S is the first contributor, we have that (8.22) can be written as

$$LR_1(M, g \mid I) = \frac{\delta_{g, g_1}}{P(g \mid g_1, \ldots, g_n, H_2, I)}.$$

The updated probability distribution for the profiles required in (8.5) is

$$P(g_1, \ldots, g_n \mid M, g, H_2, I),$$

and hence (8.5) reduces to

$$LR_1(M, g \mid I) = \sum_{g_1, \ldots, g_n} \frac{\delta_{g, g_1} P(g_1, \ldots, g_n \mid M, g, H_2, I)}{P(g \mid g_1, \ldots, g_n, H_2, I)}.$$

In the case where H_2 prescribes unrelatedness between S and any of the contributors, and we furthermore have a population in which we model the profiles of unrelated individuals as independent, the denominator is just $p(g)$, the probability for a random population member to have profile g.

Using this assumption, the likelihood ratio further simplifies into

$$LR_1(M, g \mid I) = \frac{1}{p(g)} \sum_{g_1, \ldots, g_n} \delta_{g, g_1} P(g_1, \ldots, g_n \mid M, g, H_2, I)$$

$$= \frac{1}{p(g)} P(g \mid M, g, H_2, I) \tag{8.23}$$

$$= \frac{P(g \mid M, H_2, I)}{p(g)}, \tag{8.24}$$

where in the last line we have again used the assumption that profiles of unrelated individuals are independent. In the last expression, the probability in the numerator is that of the first contributor to have profile g, based on the trace profile, hypothesis H_2 stating that S did not contribute, and I.

Thus we arrive at an equivalent formulation of (8.15), saying that likelihood ratio calculations are equivalent to probabilistic genotyping. Notice however that the different expressions for the same probabilities reflect that we argued differently. We now see that we can interpret probabilistic genotyping as a rewriting of the likelihood ratio, if we treat the profiles of the contributors as model parameters and integrate them out according to the general scheme of (8.4). Indeed, if we do so, we must consider which profiles are best supported by M, and then directly match these with the person of interest's profile.

8.7 Summary and Conclusions

For a DNA mixture M and a person of interest having genotype g, the basic formula for the likelihood ratio of this person having contributed to the mixture versus being unrelated to all mixture contributors, is given by

$$LR(M,g \mid I) = \int LR(M,g \mid I,\theta) f(\theta \mid M,g,H_2,I)d\theta, \qquad (8.25)$$

where θ represents model parameters, I represents profiles of undisputed contributors to the mixture, and the density $f(\theta \mid M,g,H_2,I)$ describes our conditional knowledge about θ. In other words, the likelihood ratio is a weighted average of likelihood ratios assuming θ is known. The expression in (8.25) applies to any θ with undisputed prior density, that is, when $f(\theta \mid H_1,I) = f(\theta \mid H_2,I)$. If we assume that there is such an undisputed distribution for the number N of contributors, then we get

$$LR(M,g \mid I) = \sum_n LR^{(n)}(M,g \mid I)P(N = n \mid M,g,H_2,I), \qquad (8.26)$$

where $LR^{(n)}$ stands for the likelihood ratio assuming n modeled contributors.

The mixture model itself can be discrete, that is, only incorporating the typed alleles with or without drop-in and dropout, or continuous, in which case also the peak heights are taken into account. For discrete models, the number of possibilities is limited, but modeling peak heights can be done in very many ways, and it is not always clear whether or not certain modeling assumptions are realistic or only a mathematical convenience. It so happens that in many likelihood ratio computations, the precise modeling of the peak heights drops out of the calculation and is therefore of less importance.

Whenever one wants to perform computations on a mixture, one needs to say something about the number of contributors, either as a fixed number of as an unknown with a certain distribution. This is in principle problematic, since neither a number nor a reasonable distribution may be available. We have argued at length though that this number may be of less importance than generally assumed. The reason for this is that the main contributors of a mixture can very well be resolved without knowledge of the number of contributors. In the top-down method, the full profile including the peak heights, are taken as a starting point, after which a discrete calculation is performed on the most prominent alleles. This hybrid approach between discrete and continuous models is typically sufficient for the main contributors, and conservative for the minor ones. The point of the top-down approach is that it is in general not needed to be very precise about the exact modeling of the mixture at all, since contributors will be resolved anyway, with or without taking details of the modeling into account. Indeed, such details will not have a significant effect on conclusions concerning the main contributors.

We also discussed the concept of a contributor, distinguishing between sample contributors, whose DNA is in fact in the mixture, profile contributors whose contribution has been detected, and modeled contributors which is the number used in the model and computations.

One can also take a maximum likelihood approach to mixture evaluations. Indeed, one may compute

$$LR_{ML}(M, g \mid I) := \frac{P(M \mid H_1, g, \hat{\theta}_1, I)}{P(M \mid H_2, g, \hat{\theta}_2, I)}, \tag{8.27}$$

where $\hat{\theta}_i$ maximizes $P(M \mid H_i, g, \theta, I)$ over all θ. Methodologically, this procedure tries to learn about θ from the presence of the person of interest, whereas the aim should be to do the opposite: we should try to learn about the presence of the person of interest from our knowledge of θ.

Finally we have argued that there are many similarities between mixture and kinship evaluations. In some sense, they amount to the same problem. In both cases we use a model to make inferences from observations that carry partial information on what we want to describe. Hence, understanding kinship helps understanding mixtures and vice versa.

8.8 Bibliographical Notes

We already gave many references in the text. For more information about the actual generation of DNA profiles we refer to [32] and [39] . Formula (8.26) appears in [143]. For the discrete method, see [139]. For the continuous model of Euro-ForMix, see [24] and [42]. For MLE in the context of early mixture models, see [76]. See [22] and [139] for the effect of adding modeled contributors. The contributor concept has been discussed in [31]. What they call the target, respectively correct, respectively assigned, number of contributors corresponds closely to our notions of sample, profile, and modeled contributors. The authors of [31] state that, as the first two numbers will not be known in casework, one can only make a reasonable choice for the assigned number in the calculations. This is in agreement with our discussion. The extent to which continuous methods obtain, on average, stronger evidence in favor of the correct hypothesis, has been investigated in, e.g., [23], [140], and [150]. The material in Section 8.5 comes from [141].

9

p-Values of Likelihood Ratios

As we have extensively explained, the likelihood ratio is the appropriate quantity to quantify the evidential value of data, where this evidential value is always taken to be relative to two competing hypotheses. Data constitute evidence in favor of one hypothesis with respect to another one if the data is more likely under the first than under the second hypothesis.

One naturally wonders why classical statistical procedures seem to fail in our context (and in fact in many other situations as well). In this chapter we will explain this in great detail. Roughly speaking, we will argue (as anticipated before in Section 1.7 and Chapter 2) that *p*-values, simply, cannot in general be used for evidential purposes. This is a general claim, but for the context of this book of crucial importance, since it is precisely evidential purposes that we are concerned with.

9.1 *p*-Values of Likelihood Ratios

In the classical frequentistic setting, one often formulates only one hypothesis, the null hypothesis. Typically this is the hypothesis that one would like to reject. For example, the null hypothesis may state that a new drug is no better than an old one, or that a certain gene has no effect on a certain disease. Researchers then set out to gather data, because they believe that the null hypothesis is false, meaning the new drug is superior, or a certain gene does have an effect on a certain disease.

In a frequentistic procedure with *p*-values, one proceeds by defining a *rejection region*. The null hypothesis is rejected precisely when an appropriate test statistic falls into this rejection region. In this setting, one usually accepts a previously determined probability α of a false rejection of the null hypothesis, which can be controlled by the specific choice of the rejection region. Indeed, the probability of an outcome in the rejection region assuming that the null hypothesis is true must be bounded above by α. This means that when many such tests are carried out, a proportion α of the instances where the null hypothesis was actually true will result in a false rejection of it.

It is, on the other hand, not possible to say which of the decisions to reject or not that have been taken were correct: α controls the probability to reject the null hypothesis if it is true, which is obviously not the same as the probability that the null hypothesis is true, if it is rejected.

There is a certain amount of asymmetry around this classical frequentistic procedure. This asymmetry is caused by the fact that the significance level α is often interpreted as a measure of the evidence against the null hypothesis. This is the reason that α needs to be controlled, whereas the probability of a false negative is only *optimized* under the constraint of a maximal α. A small α is in this approach thought to be essential, whereas a small probability of false negatives is only desirable.

It may seem reasonable to use this framework in the legal setting and take the hypothesis of innocence as null hypothesis. That would correspond to the presumption of innocence, which is accepted as a starting point and only abandoned when there is sufficient evidence against it. However, reasonable as this may sound, we have already seen that this approach is very problematic in a legal or forensic context. Indeed, in Section 5.3 and Section 5.5 we saw that this procedure led to the rejection of the null hypotheses of innocence, whereas it turned out that there was no statistical reason for guilt at all. These instances reinforced the importance of alternative hypotheses. The question should not be "Is the data reason so unlikely under the null hypothesis that we abandon it?," but instead "Are there other hypotheses that explain the data better than the null hypothesis, and how plausible are they?" In this chapter we will illustrate with a number of further examples and principles how the inadequacy of p-values as a measure of evidence comes about.

It has been suggested to use a particular kind of p-value, namely *the p-value of the likelihood ratio* for evidential purposes. Suppose we compute a likelihood ratio having value x for H_1 versus H_2. The p-value of an obtained likelihood ratio can take several forms. If we let H_2 play the role of null hypothesis, then we can consider

$$P(LR_{H_1, H_2}(E) \geq x \mid H_2)$$

as p-value. If H_2 is the hypothesis corresponding to innocence, this measures how unlikely it is for an innocent suspect to have evidence of at least the observed strength pointing towards H_1. Naturally, its application would be to abandon the hypothesis of innocence if the evidence is strong enough.

Similarly, we can also call

$$P(LR_{H_1, H_2}(E) \leq x \mid H_1)$$

a *p*-value. If H_1 is the hypothesis of guilt, this represents the probability that the obtained evidence E gives a likelihood ratio of at most the observed value. Its application is now to abandon the hypothesis of guilt, if the evidence in favor of it is not strong enough. We note that in these definitions it is E that is regarded as random, but we have not been very specific about exactly how we should regard it as random. This will indeed turn out to be one of the various problems with *p*-values, see Section 9.3 below.

Several arguments have been put forward that justify the use of *p*-values in the context of likelihood ratios, one of them being that *p*-values would be an alternative way to present the strength of the evidence that is easier to explain in court than likelihood ratios.

In this chapter, we will present several arguments and examples from which we can conclude that *p*-values of likelihood ratios can certainly *not* be used for this purpose. *p*-Values simply do not convey the strength of the evidence. The likelihood ratio measures the strength of the evidence, while a *p*-value measures how rare it is to find evidence that is equally strong or stronger, which is something fundamentally different.

We will show that *p*-values, in some circumstances, show behavior that is very problematic if we want to give them an evidential interpretation. First of all, a *p*-value depends on the probability distribution (under the hypothesis under consideration) on the collection of possible outcomes that were not observed. We will argue that this is problematic, in general but also with forensic genetic examples.

We will also see that a *p*-value is not always unambiguous. There can be several canonical ways to formulate H_1 and H_2 that give the same likelihood ratio and the same posterior odds, but different *p*-values. Hence a *p*-value need not even be unambiguously defined, which seems highly problematic in view of a possible evidential interpretation. Also, we will see that *p*-values sometimes seem to support the wrong hypothesis.

In the following three sections we will treat these problems with evidential interpretations of *p*-values of likelihood ratios one by one. Following, in Section 9.5 we reflect on all this, and discuss error rates and the prosecutor's fallacy in connection with *p*-values. In Section 9.6 we will discuss some consequences of all this for forensic practice. After that, we discuss additional problems of *p*-values in general, not necessarily restricted to likelihood ratios or forensic science.

9.2 *p*-Values May Change if the Distribution of Unobserved Possibilities Changes

Suppose that we have two persons, and that we wish to determine whether they are full siblings or unrelated. Suppose person one has genotype (a_1, a_2) on a certain

DNA-locus, and person two has genotype (a_1, a_3) on the same locus. We assume that allele frequencies of the relevant population are known and denote by p_i the population frequency of allele a_i.

In Chapter 7 we have explained how one can compute the likelihood ratio for the hypothesis H_1 that these persons are siblings, versus the hypothesis H_2 that they are unrelated. If we condition on the genotype (a_1, a_2) of the first person, then the probability that a sibling has genotype (a_1, a_3) is given by $(p_3 + 2p_1p_3)/4$. Since the probability that an unrelated person has this genotype is $2p_1p_3$, this results in a likelihood ratio given by $1/4 + 1/(8p_1)$. If, say, $p_1 = 1/7$ then this last expression reduces to $9/8$.

Note that this likelihood ratio only depends on the population frequency of the allele a_1 that the two persons have in common, since all other frequencies cancel in the computation. This, in fact, is something that we expect in this context. The argument for this was given in Section 7.6.3 and we recall it here. If we have the genotypes of two individuals, and we wish to quantify how much evidence we have that they are related in a specific way versus being unrelated, then only the shared alleles can possibly be informative about this. The shared alleles could, under the assumption of relatedness, be identical by descent, and it is precisely the probability that this happens under the assumption of relatedness which differentiates between the two hypotheses of interest. In other words, a test for relatedness is a test for identical by descent probabilities. Alleles that are different cannot be identical by descent. It is not relevant what the population frequency is of the alleles that are not identical by descent. They are observed to have arisen in the genotypes of the individuals by independent random sampling from the population alleles, and whether this is a likely or unlikely event is not relevant since it is not discriminating.

In this example so far, we have seen that only shared alleles matter for the question of relatedness between two individual. Although the alleles a_2 and a_3 were in fact observed, their probabilities do not matter, since these are not discriminating between the two alternatives. In general, we submit that if we want to draw evidential conclusions about an hypothesis H, based on certain data, then the probability that the distribution under H assigns to *unobserved data* should never play a role. We already mentioned this in Section 2.3.1, and we recall the argument here.

Suppose that we consider two hypotheses H_1 and H_2, and that the observed data has the same probability under both hypotheses. Furthermore, suppose that the distribution of unobserved values differ under the two hypotheses, either by assigning different probabilities to shared outcomes, or by simply having different possible outcomes, or both. An observer, confronted with the actual data, now has no way whatsoever to distinguish between the two hypotheses. He has no way of telling whether the data comes from H_1 or from H_2, since the observed outcomes have precisely the same distribution under either of them. It follows that for any reasonable quantification of evidential value which involves H_1 should give the same outcome were H_1 to be replaced by H_2. Indeed, the only way that data could have been discriminating between them, would be the observation of data that has not been observed. We conclude that only the distribution of the observed data should matter for any reasonable notion of evidential value.

Likelihood ratios adhere to this condition, but p-values do not. We further illustrate this with a continuation of the genetic example above.

Let us further assume (for the sake of the argument) that the same genotypes as above are observed on 14 other loci (with the same allele frequencies), then this results in a likelihood ratio equal to $(9/8)^{15} \approx 6$, since we may assume that likelihood ratios may be multiplied due to conditional independence. We now have DNA profiles (consisting of genotypes on 15 autosomal loci) that are about six times as likely to arise if the involved individuals are actually siblings than if they are unrelated, and this number should be used to arrive at posterior odds on these hypotheses.

For the reasons explained above, on each locus we do not need allele frequencies other than the one of the shared allele. But now suppose that we wish to compute the p-value of the obtained likelihood ratio, by computing the probability that two randomly chosen persons unrelated to each other would produce a likelihood ratio of at least 6 on the 15 loci under consideration. In other words, we want to compute how unlikely it is to obtain a likelihood ratio of *at least* 6 if in fact the persons are unrelated. The suggestion is that if this is small, it provides evidence for relatedness (although we already know that this suggestion is not correct).

If we want to compute this, then we do need the allele frequencies of all alleles, since unrelated individuals randomly select two alleles from the full population. Thus, this p-value depends on the frequencies of all possible alleles, not only of the shared or even observed ones.

We can now investigate, by performing a simulation experiment, how large the p-value (the probability to obtain a likelihood ratio of at least 6 under the assumption of unrelatedness) is, under various circumstances concerning the possible other, not observed alleles. We distinguish between three different situations, in each of which $p_1 = 1/7$. Remember that in our example, on each locus the genotypes are (a_1, a_2) and (a_1, a_3).

1. If, on each locus, there are four possible alleles $a_1, \ldots, a_4$, with population frequencies $1/7, 1/7, 1/7$ and $4/7$ respectively, then the p-value $P(LR \geq 6 \mid H_2) = 0.02$.
2. If, on each locus, there are seven possible alleles $a_1, \ldots, a_7$, each with population frequency $1/7$, then the p-value $P(LR \geq 6 \mid H_2) = 0.004$.
3. If, on each locus, there are 103 possible alleles $a_1, \ldots, a_{103}$, with population frequencies $1/7, 1/7, 1/7, 4/700, \ldots, 4/700)$, then the p-value is $P(LR \geq 6 \mid H_2) = 0.00007$.

Thus, the p-value changes as the loci become more polymorphic even though the frequencies of the alleles that we have observed do not change. This fact makes it very problematic to use p-values for evidential interpretation purposes. Indeed, our original observation of alleles that we started out with, leading to a likelihood ratio of about 6, could have been done in any of the three circumstances discussed here. In any of these three cases, the evidence would have been identical – recall that the likelihood ratio in this case only depends on the shared alleles, in this case only on a_1. However, the corresponding p-values would have been very different.

The fact that the p-value changes when other allele frequencies change is in itself understandable. Indeed, the set of pairs of unrelated individuals for which the null hypothesis of unrelatedness would be falsely rejected depends on the possible outcomes of the likelihood ratio for such pairs. If there are many alleles, then the unrelated individuals are easier to discern and fewer will obtain a likelihood ratio of 6 or more, hence the smaller p-value.

This in itself should be convincing enough not to use p-values for evidential purposes. However, we can make things even more absurd by realizing that in the above context, we may initially be in situation 1 (with four possible alleles) but later learn that we were actually in situation 2 (with seven possible alleles). For example, suppose that we initially used a technology that discriminates on each locus between four different alleles a_1, a_2, a_3, a_4 with frequencies $1/7, 1/7, 1/7$, and $4/7$ respectively. We then compute the p-value, equal to 0.02, and do not reject unrelatedness at the 1% significance level. A subsequent technology may reveal that on each locus the allele a_4 actually has four sub-variants $a_{4,1}, a_{4,2}, a_{4,3}$, and $a_{4,4}$, all measured as allele a_4 with the previous technology but notably distinct with the new technology. The new technology does not reveal any new variants for alleles a_1, a_2, and a_3 so that we have now the seven alleles as described in situation 2 above. Then our new p-value becomes 0.004 so that now, we should reject unrelatedness at the 1% significance level.

How should we interpret this from an evidential point of view? Does it mean that, if the new technology has been introduced after the profiles have been obtained with the old technology and the p-value of 0.02 has been computed, the p-value computation should be done again and the conclusion revised? It seems absurd to re-evaluate evidence that has not changed with the introduction of a new technology, yet it is what has to be done if we want to use p-values for evidential purposes. The old p-value does not suffice any more, since the data that we could possibly observe has changed.

Therefore, all p-values obtained with the old technology are incorrect as soon as the new technology is introduced. This implies that p-values are temporary. But when the old technology is in place and a new one is not in sight, a p-value is calculated and it is impossible to know that it will later turn out to have to be corrected.

As a last thought experiment one could even imagine a researcher reviewing the case on the basis of the allele designations, but unaware of which technology had been used. Although that is irrelevant for the obtained data, which are independent of the technology in this particular case, such a reviewer would be unable to compute the appropriate *p*-value.

Note that the likelihood ratio does not suffer from such problems. If evidence obtained with an old technology is re-examined and no new information is obtained, then the likelihood ratio does not change. It can only change if the new technology reveals more about the evidence than we already knew, and this is precisely what a measure of evidence should do. If we learn more about the actual evidence, then the evidential value should (be able to) change as well.

9.3 *p*-Values are Ambiguous

As a second problem for an evidential interpretation of *p*-values, we claim that the *p*-value is ambiguous in the sense that there may be several *p*-values associated with the same likelihood ratio for the same hypotheses. The reason is (again) that the *p*-value is concerned with evidence that we could have obtained but did not. Hence we need to precisely describe what we consider as randomly obtained evidence and what we consider as fixed evidence. After all, the *p*-value results as the frequency of certain outcomes when we repeatedly sample under one of the hypotheses. But it may very well happen that there are multiple ways to perform this sampling, and in each of the different ways to do this, a different *p*-value may surface. A simple example illustrates our point.

Consider two persons with observed genotypes g_1 and g_2 and the likelihood ratio that compares the hypotheses of them being related in some specified way (H_1) versus unrelatedness (H_2). We can write the corresponding likelihood ratio in three different ways. Indeed we have

$$
\begin{aligned}
LR_{H_1, H_2}(g_1, g_2) &= \frac{P(g_1, g_2 \mid H_1)}{P(g_1, g_2 \mid H_2)} \\
&= \frac{P(g_2 \mid g_1, H_1)}{P(g_2 \mid g_1, H_2)} \frac{P(g_1 \mid H_1)}{P(g_1 \mid H_2)} = \frac{P(g_2 \mid g_1, H_1)}{P(g_2 \mid g_1, H_2)} \\
&= \frac{P(g_1 \mid g_2, H_1)}{P(g_1 \mid g_2, H_2)} \frac{P(g_2 \mid H_1)}{P(g_2 \mid H_2)} = \frac{P(g_1 \mid g_2, H_1)}{P(g_1 \mid g_2, H_2)},
\end{aligned}
$$

since, of course, the marginal probability of a person's profile is always equated to the population frequency.

Suppose now that this likelihood ratio is equal to *x*. The three ways of writing the likelihood ratio correspond to three ways of interpreting the evidence. In the first expression, we treat both g_1 and g_2 as random and then we should compute

Table 9.1 *The genotypes of two persons at the 10 SGMplus loci.*

Locus	Person P_1		Person P_2	
D3S1358	13	16	16	18
VWA	19	21	19	19
D16S539	11	13	11	13
D2S1338	16	22	22	24
D8S1179	10	12	10	12
D21S11	24.2	29.2	28	30
D18S51	18	19	13	15
D19S433	15	15	14	15.2
TH01	9	10	6	7
FGA	20.2	23	20	23

the corresponding p-value $P(LR(E) \geq x \mid H_2)$ as the probability that the likelihood ratio is at least x for two randomly chosen unrelated individuals. That is, sampling under the hypothesis of unrelatedness boils down to randomly choosing two unrelated individuals, and compute their likelihood ratio.

In the second expression, we condition on the genotype g_1 and we only view g_2 as random. With that interpretation the p-value is the probability that, for an unrelated person, the likelihood ratio in favor of being a relative of someone with genotype g_1 is at least equal to x, and there is no reason whatsoever why this p-value should be the same as the first one. The third p-value is obtained in a similar way with the roles of g_1 and g_2 interchanged. Again there is no reason why this third p-value is the same as any of the previous two. These three p-values are probabilities of three different events and therefore there is no reason for them to coincide, as the next example illustrates.

We consider in Table 9.1 the DNA profiles of two individuals P_1 and P_2, typed on 10 autosomal loci (those in the SGMPlus kit). One of the individuals has more rare alleles than the other one. It turns out that $SI(P_1, P_2) = 1.4$, where, as mentioned before, SI stands for "sibling index," another name for the likelihood ratio in the case where we test sibling relationship versus being unrelated. In this case, the sibling index constitutes almost neutral evidence.

If we formulate as null hypotheses the hypotheses of unrelatedness, we can follow three different procedures which all use the obtained $SI(P_1, P_2) = 1.4$ as reference value. Suppose we test at a 0.01 significance level. In the first case, we fix the profile of person P_1 and consider the sibling index that unrelated individuals have with person P_1. In that case, we approximate the distribution of the likelihood ratios by taking a random sample of 100,000 unrelated individuals and compute the sibling index with person P_1 with each of them. We find 274 cases where this sibling index is larger than $SI(P_1, P_2)$, and thus we have a p-value of 0.00274 and we reject the null hypothesis of unrelatedness: for unrelated individuals, the probability that they have a sibling index with person P_1 that is at least as large as what we have observed is below 0.01.

On the other hand, if we carry out the same procedure but now calculate the sibling index with person P_2, we find a p-value of 0.026, which is not small enough to reject unrelatedness. Thus we are in the peculiar situation that if we consider P_1 fixed we reject the hypothesis that person P_2 is unrelated to person P_1, but if we consider P_2 fixed we do not reject the hypothesis that person P_1 is unrelated to person P_2.

Finally, we can also compute a p-value where we keep none of the individuals fixed and take as distribution that of the sibling index between two unrelated individuals. This gives us a p-value of 0.028, again not small enough to reject unrelatedness.

We conclude that although the likelihood ratio is the same for all these approaches in the sense that the three expressions above coincide, the associated p-values are not. There is no canonical way to choose among the three given possibilities, and hence there is no canonical way to express any evidential value in terms of p-values.

The fact that the three likelihood ratios are all equal to each other reinforces the idea that the likelihood ratio indeed precisely captures the evidential value of the observations. The value of the evidence should not depend on which choice we make. Likelihood ratios comply to this constraint whereas p-values do not.

9.4 p-Values May Appear to Support the Wrong Hypothesis

The considerations above should be convincing enough to disqualify the use of p-values for any evidential purpose. But there is more. Strangely enough, the use of p-values in connection with the likelihood ratio may lead to supporting the hypothesis which is explicitly not supported by the data. In order to make our point we start with an example with coin flips.

Suppose we have a coin which we know is biased in either the heads or the tail direction. We know that either heads has probability $1/4$ to come up, or tail has probability $1/4$, but we do not know which of the two possibilities is true. Let us denote by H_1 the hypothesis that heads has probability $3/4$, and by H_2 the probability that heads has probability $1/4$. We now flip the coin 30 times, and suppose we obtain 12 heads. Since the two competing hypotheses are symmetric and 12 is below $30/2 = 15$, it is no surprise that this outcome provides rather strong evidence in favor of H_2 compared to H_1. Indeed a small computation shows that the corresponding likelihood ratio in favor of H_1 is equal to $1/729$, so the outcome is 729 times more likely when assuming H_2 is true than when assuming H_1 is true.

However, this is not to say that the outcome of 12 or more heads is in any way likely under H_2. Indeed, one easily verifies that under H_2 the probability of seeing 12 or more heads is slightly below 0.05. Hence if we were to perform a p-value procedure to test H_2 in isolation, then we would reject H_2 at significance level 0.05 despite the fact that the data actually provides quite a lot of evidence in favor of it, when compared to the only possible alternative. The point is that an outcome of 12 heads is very unlikely under *both* hypotheses, a phenomenon that we saw earlier in a forensic context in Sections 5.3 and 5.5. It is not so relevant that the outcome has small probability under H_2 because its probability under the alternative is even much smaller. As such, a p-value procedure might reject the wrong hypothesis.

We note that, of course, the hypothesis H_1 would also be rejected on the basis of p-values. The example illustrates, however, that p-values may lead to the rejection of a hypothesis for which there is actually support by the likelihood ratio.

After this introductory example we turn to a forensic example with DNA evidence. Consider the DNA mixture depicted in Table 9.2, also discussed in [78] and in [91]. We evaluate the following two competing hypotheses:

H_1: victim (V), suspect (S) and an unknown person are contributors;

H_2: victim (V) and two unknown persons are contributors.

We compute the likelihood ratio using the discrete model of Section 8.1.2, with a drop-in probability of 0.05 and a dropout probability of 0.1 for all contributors, using allelic frequencies from a Norwegian database for SGMplus. (See Chapter 8 for a discussion about computations with mixtures.) The likelihood ratio equals approximately 0.4, so the evidence is about 2.5 times more likely if the victim and two unknown persons contribute to the mixture than if the victim, the suspect and one unknown person contribute to the mixture. Hence, there is no evidence that the suspect contributed to the mixture (at least, assuming these two hypotheses are the relevant ones, which we do for the sake of argument).

However, if we compute the p-value of the likelihood ratio we obtain

$$P(LR \geq 0.4 \mid H_2) \approx 0.0008, \tag{9.1}$$

where we consider likelihood ratios one would obtain by replacing the suspect with a randomly chosen person. Hence, approximately one out of every 1,250 random persons would attain a likelihood ratio as least as large as the current suspect. One might erroneously interpret this as strong evidence that the suspect is a contributor to the mixture. But the fact that it is quite rare to find such strong evidence for a

Table 9.2 *A mixture profile at the 10 SGMplus loci. The likelihood ratio for victim, suspect and one unknown person being contributors versus the victim and two unknown persons equals 0.4, which means that the evidence is not incriminating for the suspect. The p-value, however, equals approximately 0.0008, which might be erroneously interpreted as evidence that the suspect is a contributor.*

Locus	Mixture				Victim (V)		Suspect (S)	
D3S1358	14	16	17		14	16	15	17
VWA	16	17	18		17	19	18	19
D16S539	11	12	13	15	11	15	13	13
D2S1338	17	19	20		17	24	17	20
D8S1179	9	10	13	14	10	14	13	13
D21S11	29	31	32		29	31	30	30
D18S51	12	16			16	16	12	20
D19S433	12	14	15.2	16	14	15.2	12	15
TH01	6	9.3			6	9.3	6	9.3
FGA	19	24	26		24	26	19	20

random suspect does not make the evidence stronger. In fact, the evidence is slightly more probable if the suspect is not a contributor than if the suspect is, which means that there is some support for H_2, despite the very small p-value.

9.5 Error Rates and the Prosecutor's Fallacy

In the example in the previous section, the p-value of 0.0008 corresponded to a likelihood ratio of 0.4. Again, this means that for only 0.08% of the non-contributors, we would find evidence pointing towards their contribution at least as strongly as what we have found for the current suspect. In other words, if we carry out a database search and accept a false positive rate of 0.08%, then we should set a likelihood ratio threshold equal to 0.4. In that case, we would use the p-value in line with its definition: it predicts how many non-contributors are found if we use that threshold.

One reason to advocate p-value statistics is that they can be interpreted as error rates. For example, in [120], where the p-value is called a (generalized) random match probability, it is formulated in the context of DNA mixtures as "While the likelihood ratio summarizes evidence, the random match probability estimates error. Both statistical measures assist a trier of fact in understanding DNA evidence." In this section we will further argue that the error rate as measured by the p-value does not assist the trier of fact at all.

By definition, the p-value is only concerned with a single hypothesis H, say. Indeed typically one would take the hypothesis to be the one where the suspect is not the source of the DNA-evidence. In a frequentistic framework, one would say that H is the null hypothesis and that we reject it if the evidence against it is sufficiently strong. Rejection does not necessarily mean that one actually believes that H is not true, it may simply mean that one takes some action to further investigate which hypothesis is true, for example, by doing additional DNA testing on a set of loci that has not been typed yet. Not rejecting then means that one does not take that action, and does not further investigate which hypothesis is true, which again does not mean that one has a specific belief about them, but only that the evidence against H is not sufficiently strong to warrant further scrutiny.

With this understanding, if we allow for many repetitions of H (that is, imagine a large series of situations where H is the true hypothesis), then the relative frequency by which we incorrectly reject H is under control. The p-value therefore makes a prediction: if the p-value equals p and we were to sample from H a large number (say, N) times, then we expect to encounter Np cases where we would decide against (or to further investigate) H.

The point is that this prediction is not useful any more once a decision has been taken. It does not allow us to say anything about the probability that a given decision is correct. For instance, when we search a database with N individuals for the donors of a DNA mixture, and none of the donors is actually in the database, then the p-value predicts that we will retrieve Np persons from the database, but all of these will be false positives regardless of how small the p-value is.

A second problem, specific to the interpretation of DNA mixtures, is that the hypothesis H is not simply that the person of interest did not contribute to the DNA mixture, but usually says that the person of interest is not related to any of the mixture donors. Therefore, rejecting H does not at all imply the acceptance of H', which says that the person of interest contributes. The rejection of H means a decision in favor of there being a contributor to the mixture who is not unrelated to the person of interest (and in particular, may be the person of interest him- or herself). Indeed in many cases, especially siblings of the mixture contributors may give a likelihood ratio that is relatively large for non-contributors (resulting in a small p-value $P(LR_{H',H} \geq x \mid H)$ but which is also relatively small for contributors (resulting in a small $P(LR_{H',H} \leq x \mid H')$. Indeed, if neither hypothesis H' or H is true, then conceivably one may encounter a likelihood ratio that has a value which is unusual for both hypotheses.

Finally, we say a few words about the fact that likelihood ratios are often misunderstood, and the suggestion that p-values would be less prone to wrong interpretations. For likelihood ratios, the interpretation of a likelihood ratio as the posterior odds is called the *prosecutor's fallacy* (although in practice not exclusively committed by prosecutors). For example, if the likelihood ratio in favor of having contributed to a sample is one million, this is often understood as there being a one in a million chance that the suspect did not contribute. However, only if the prior odds had been equal to 1, then the posterior odds would have been equal to the likelihood ratio. Only in that case, the conclusion that the odds are a million to one in favor of the first versus the second hypothesis is correct.

For *p*-values it is easy, but in some sense even "more wrong," to understand them in the same fallacious way, and to interpret them as a probability statements as to whether the suspect contributed. For example, in our example above with a *p*-value of 0.0008 one might think that the computed *p*-value means there is a probability of 0.0008 that the suspect did not contribute to the mixture. This time, however, there are no prior odds that would make this reasoning correct. There is no one-to-one correspondence between *p*-values and likelihood ratios, since the same likelihood ratio may come from different likelihood ratio distributions.

Therefore, someone who only knows the *p*-value but does not know the model by which it was computed, cannot reconstruct the likelihood ratio it is associated with. It follows that from the *p*-value alone no inference can be made.

Finally, since from Proposition 2.4.2 we have for all $x > 0$ that

$$P(LR_{H_1, H_2} \geq x \mid H_2) \leq \frac{1}{x},$$

the *p*-value is *always* less than the reciprocal of the relevant likelihood ratio. The interpretation of the *p*-value as strength of evidence therefore leads to even more serious mistakes than the prosecutor's fallacy does.

9.6 Consequences for Casework

Many pertaining questions in daily forensic and legal work have to do with the relevance of the distribution of the likelihood ratio. In this section we discuss three such questions, and show how the insights of the current chapter help us answering these.

9.6.1 Unusually Strong or Weak Evidence

For a half-sibling test where the two individuals under consideration are in fact half-siblings, we usually get a lower likelihood ratio than for a full sibling test when they are in fact siblings. Recall that if we test for being (half)-siblings versus being unrelated, we call the likelihood ratio the (half)-sibling index, abbreviated $(H)SI$. For example, in Figure 9.1 we plot histograms of a random sample of sibling indices (for siblings) and half-sibling indices (for half-siblings) computed on the 23 autosomal loci of the Powerplex Fusion 6C multiplex using Dutch allele frequencies from [177]. In each case we have drawn a random sample of size 100,000. In these figures, we see for example that a likelihood ratio of 10^6 is a

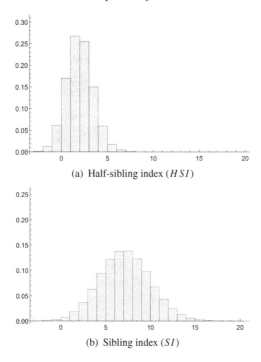

(a) Half-sibling index (HSI)

(b) Sibling index (SI)

Figure 9.1 Histogram of $\log_{10}(LR)$ where (a) $LR = HSI$ or (b) $LR = SI$ on 23 loci, for true siblings and true half-siblings, respectively.

common value for siblings, but unusually high for half-siblings. On the other hand a likelihood ratio of 10 is a common value for half-siblings, but small for siblings.

The question is, does this mean that a likelihood ratio means something different for a half-sibling test than for a full sibling test? For example, a likelihood ratio of at least 10^6 is much more exceptional for half-sibling tests than for full sibling test. Do we need to take this fact into account, as intuition perhaps suggests? In general, when evaluating a likelihood ratio, should we take into account whether or not this likelihood ratio is obtained in a test where this is a relatively high or low value?

To answer this question, let H_{hs}, H_s, H_u denote the hypotheses that the considered pair are half-siblings, siblings, or unrelated, respectively. One way to reformulate the first part of the question is to state that

$$P(HSI \geq 10^6 \mid H_{hs}) \ll P(SI \geq 10^6 \mid H_s). \tag{9.2}$$

In this case, we empirically find $P(HSI \geq 10^6 \mid H_{hs}) = 0.005$ whereas $P(SI \geq 10^6 \mid H_s) = 0.655$. The question is whether or not the fact that the evidence in the half-sibling case is unusually high, whereas it is not for the sibling case, somehow carries additional weight in the half-sibling case that it does not have in the sibling case.

Similarly, if we obtain a likelihood ratio of 10 in a case where we compute the SI, and also in another case where we compute the HSI, we might be tempted to have more confidence in the first pair being half-siblings than the second pair being siblings, since the obtained result is a very normal one in the half-sibling case, but is not in the sibling case.

From Bayes' rule we see that, if the likelihood ratios for two sets of hypotheses are the same, the odds on both pairs of investigated hypotheses change by the same factor. The inequality in (9.2) merely states that the corresponding p-values are very different. This has no effect whatsoever on the evidential value that we obtain with respect to the hypotheses under investigation.

However, if we consider that there may be more possibilities for the ground truth than just the two hypotheses we have the likelihood ratio for, the fact that the obtained likelihood ratio is unusual under both hypotheses may alert us that none of these hypotheses might be true. For example, if in the case where we investigated the possibility of being half-siblings versus unrelated, we also do not strictly exclude that the investigated individuals are full siblings, then we may be triggered to also investigate that possibility. If full siblings are subjected to a HSI computation, then the obtained likelihood ratio of a million is not unusual at all, as we see from Figure 9.2.

In this case, an obtained $HSI = 10^6$ is unusually large for half-siblings ($P(HSI \geq x \mid H_{hs})$ very small), but of course it is even more unexpectedly large for unrelated individuals (since $P(HSI \geq 10^6 \mid H_u) \leq 10^{-6}$). This may prompt us to formulate other hypotheses to investigate. We may, for example, obtain $HSI = 10^6$ and $SI = 10^9$. This means that the odds on being siblings versus half-siblings increase by a factor of 1,000. If we had prior probabilities mainly concentrated on half-siblings or unrelated, for instance $P(H_u) = P(H_{hs}) = 0.4995$ and $P(H_s) = 0.001$, then we arrive at posterior probabilities on these hypotheses equal to, respectively, $3 \cdot 10^{-7}, 0.33$, and 0.67. Thus, although the possibility of the individuals being siblings could be a priori considered as a very unlikely, dormant hypothesis, it is the most likely one given the genetic data and the prior probabilities. In this case the fact that the calculated likelihood ratio for being half-siblings is unusually high was used to prompt the investigation of that dormant hypothesis. If this hypothesis had been involved in the computations from the beginning, then of course there would have been no additional information in the distribution of the likelihood ratio for half-siblings.

Similarly, if we find $SI = 10$, then we see that this value is unusually large for unrelated individuals, and unusually small for siblings. However, such a result is not unusual if the tested pair are actually half-siblings (cf. Figure 9.2) and this may prompt us to consider the possibility to compute HSI as well. From the SI and HSI we can then arrive at posterior odds on these three hypotheses.

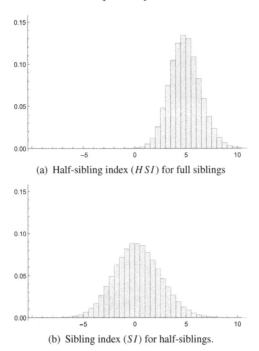

(a) Half-sibling index (HSI) for full siblings

(b) Sibling index (SI) for half-siblings.

Figure 9.2 Histogram of $\log_{10}(LR)$ where (a) $LR = HSI$ or (b) $LR = SI$ on 23 loci, for true siblings and true half-siblings, respectively.

9.6.2 Rates of Misleading Evidence

Likelihood ratios, or rather data, can be misleading in the sense that they can provide evidence for a false hypothesis. When we compute the likelihood ratio for H_1 versus H_2, then we can compute how often a large likelihood ratio of at least a given value will be obtained when in fact H_2 is true. The question is, does the frequency of such misleading evidence matter in any way?

This situation is more subtle than the one in Section 9.6.1, so let us introduce a numerical example in order to make things more concrete. Suppose that we have two cases with hypotheses H_1, H_2 respectively H_1', H_2', each producing a likelihood ratio of 1,000. Furthermore suppose that the p-values, when sampling under H_2 and H_2' respectively, of the likelihood ratios are different, namely equal to 10^{-4} in one case and 10^{-5} in the other. This means that a likelihood ratio of at least 1,000 is seen under H_2 one in 10,000 times, and a likelihood ratio of at least 1,000 is seen under H_2' one in 100,000 times. Should this difference influence the inference we make in each case?

Again, the answer is no: the prior odds have to be multiplied by 1,000 in each case. Given the likelihood ratio, the consequences for the odds are determined solely by that likelihood ratio. But of course, when we do not yet have the likelihood ratio, what we expect to obtain differs for H_1, H_2 on the one hand and for H_1', H_2' on the other. If we define a decision rule that chooses the first hypothesis whenever the likelihood ratio is at least 1,000, then we will erroneously reject H_2 once every 10,000 cases but we will erroneously reject H_2' once every 100,000 cases. This can be useful information if such numbers of cases are going to be carried out, for example. We will get back to the topic of decision rules in Chapter 10.

As an example of such a situation, we consider a search for siblings in a heterogeneous database where some of the profiles in the database consist of the 10 loci of the SGMPlus kit, and the others of the 15 loci of the NGM kit. For each threshold $x \geq 0$ we can compute $P(SI \geq x \mid H_s)$ and $P(SI \geq x \mid H_u)$ where H_s and H_u denote the hypotheses that the tested individuals are siblings or unrelated, respectively. These probabilities can be conveniently visualized in a so-called *ROC-curve*, where we plot

$$(\log_{10}(FPR(x)), TPR(x)) = (\log_{10}(P(SI \geq x \mid H_u)), P(LR \geq x \mid H_s)),$$

where FPR stands for "false positive rate," TPR stands for "true positive rate," and ROC stands for "receiver operating characteristic." Upon changing the parameter x, the TPR and FPR change, and the ROC-curve describes their relation. Since there is no place for the symbol x on the axis, one sometimes writes its values near the plotted coordinates.

These curves are plotted in Figure 9.3. The probabilities $FPR(x)$ and $TPR(x)$ have both been computed from a random sample of size 100,000 obtained on actual siblings, where for the probabilities $FPR(x)$ we have used importance sampling, that is, we applied Proposition 2.4.2.

From Figure 9.3 we observe that for a likelihood ratio value of 1,000 (look for the "3" on the curves) we have approximately the same false positive probabilities of one in 10,000 using either system, but different true positive probabilities. Thus, if we apply a likelihood ratio threshold of 1,000 in both parts of the database, we expect to find about one in 10,000 unrelated individuals in both parts. If a true sibling is present, the probability to find it is about 50% in the SGMPlus part, and around 75% in the NGM part. Again, these considerations are useful prior to carrying out the actual search, and can be used to judge whether the number of false positives that are to be expected is reasonable compared to the probability of actually finding a true sibling.

9.6.3 No Additional Evidence Found

Suppose we have obtained a likelihood ratio of 1,000 in favor of two individuals being siblings versus unrelated, based on DNA profiles typed on 10 loci. Suppose we do additional testing on 10 more loci and obtain a likelihood ratio

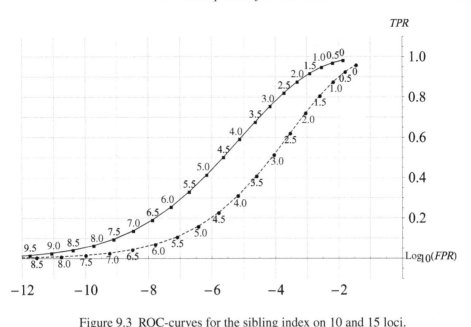

Figure 9.3 ROC-curves for the sibling index on 10 and 15 loci.

of 1 on these extra 10 loci, so that we still have a likelihood ratio of 1,000 on all loci together. The question is, does this outcome of the additional test make it more likely that the tested pair is not a sibling pair?

In this case, we start with genetic information pointing towards relatedness, but when we obtain additional genetic information then no further evidence either way is obtained. If, for example, we would have found this pair of individuals in a database search for siblings retrieving all individuals that have a likelihood ratio of at least 1,000, then we might be inclined to think that this new genetic information points in the direction of the pair being unrelated after all. By construction of the search we have made sure that the likelihood ratio on the first set of loci is sufficiently large and we know that most of the retrieved individuals will turn out to be unrelated. Furthermore, since the expectation of the likelihood ratio under unrelatedness is, according to (2.23), equal to 1, we might think that the new information that we have is in line with unrelatedness.

However, a likelihood ratio equal to one does not change the odds on the hypotheses. A likelihood ratio equal to one occurs with the same probability for pairs of siblings and for pairs of unrelated individuals, see Proposition 2.4.1. For the choice between the pair being siblings or unrelated, the probability by which that happens is not important.

However, as we discussed above as well, it may be that a likelihood ratio of 1 is a very unusual value, in the sense that it is unusually high for unrelated individuals, and unusually low for siblings. This corresponds to a p-value statement that

$P(LR \geq 1 \mid H_2)$ and $P(LR \leq 1 \mid H_1)$ are both small, where H_1 is the hypothesis of relatedness (being siblings) and H_2 the hypothesis of unrelatedness. Thus, either something highly unusual has happened, or neither hypothesis is correct. It may, for example, be the case that the considered individuals are an uncle–nephew pair that happened to have a large likelihood ratio for being siblings versus unrelated on the loci that were initially considered. If this is a possibility and we formulate it as a third hypothesis, then it may well be that the odds on being siblings versus another relationship (e.g., uncle–nephew) decrease, while those on being siblings versus unrelated stay the same.

Such a situation could for example arise when we carry out a search for siblings in a database. Suppose we retrieve all individuals from the database with a sibling index equal to at least 1,000. If there is in reality no sibling but an uncle, nephew, or half-sibling in the database, we may find this person with the sibling search. For example, from (the data underlying) Figure 9.2b we see that there is a probability of about 12% that the sibling index will exceed 1,000 for individuals truly related as half-siblings (or genetically equivalent on independent loci, such as uncle–nephew). By construction, the search only returns candidates whose sibling index is at least 1,000. If we then investigate a new independent set of loci, it is not at all unusual to find a sibling index close to 1, as we can see from Figure 9.2b again. In fact, on 10 autosomal loci (data not shown) the probability that an actual half-sibling yields a sibling index between 1/10 and 10 is about 50%: half-siblings having a form of relatedness that is intermediate between unrelatedness and a sibling relationship, often have genotypes that can be explained approximately equally well by unrelatedness and by being siblings.

To summarize, if the likelihood ratio is equal to one on the new loci, we have not learned anything that can help us to discriminate between the pair being siblings or unrelated. The odds on these hypotheses relative to each other are unchanged. But if the new evidence is very unlikely under both hypotheses, then it may be a trigger to consider additional hypotheses that possibly provide a better explanation.

9.7 More Problems with Evidential Interpretations of *p*-Values

In the preceding sections we have concentrated on *p*-values of likelihood ratios, and we have shown that *p*-values of likelihood ratios cannot be interpreted evidentially. The likelihood ratio expresses the value of the evidence, and associated *p*-values do not contribute to this in any way.

In this section we provide some additional reasons why evidential interpretations of *p*-values in general lead to absurdities. Although the significance level α is often interpreted as a quantification of the evidential values, this interpretation is incorrect. The only correct interpretation of α is the predictive probability of making the mistake of rejecting the hypothesis of interest incorrectly when data will be gathered. The examples and issues in this section are not necessarily of a forensic nature, but we think they are important enough to be discussed in any book on applied probability and statistics.

9.7.1 Multiple Peeks at Data

Suppose a researcher sets out to disprove a certain hypothesis H. For ease of exposition, we consider the example in which the researcher wants to disprove that the success probability of a certain experiment is equal to $1/2$. Initially the researcher decides to do 20 experiments. Now suppose that these 20 experiments resulted in 14 successes. Fixing $\alpha = 0.05$, the researcher asks how likely it is that the number of successes after 20 experiments deviates by at least 4 from the expected 10 successes under H. That is, he asks how likely it is to have at most 6 or at least 14 successes. (In special circumstances the researcher might only be interested in values larger than 10. In such a *one-sided* case he would only ask for the probability of at least 14 successes. This would not change anything conceptually in the forthcoming discussion.)

A small computation with the binomial distribution reveals that the probability of having at most 6 or at least 14 successes when performing 20 experiments is about 0.115, too big to reject H. The researcher realizes, though, that had he observed 15 successes instead of 14, then he would had been able to reject H. Indeed, the probability to see 15 successes or more is about 0.0206 which is small enough to warrant rejection of H in this paradigm. Hence the researcher concludes that rejection at this point is not possible, but only barely not. He decides to perform 20 more experiments, in the hope that this will be sufficient for the rejection of H.

Suppose now that the researcher is lucky and that the second series of 20 experiments results in 19 successes. His overall score is now 33 successes in 40 experiments. The probability under hypothesis H to have at least 33 successes out of 40 is about 0.0000211 and this is clearly small enough to reject the hypothesis H with significance level 0.05.

Is the researcher justified in rejecting H in this situation? The answer is no, he is not. In fact, even if the researcher would have performed 1,000,000 additional experiments, every single one of which would have been successful, even then he would not have been in a position to reject H at significance level 0.05. Obviously this sounds rather absurd, since that many successes should certainly be evidence that H is not correct. In fact it is, but this cannot be quantified with the p-value approach of the researcher, which reinforces the inadequacy of p-values for evidential purposes once more. The evidence can, for that matter, be quantified perfectly well with likelihood ratios. We will explain all of this now.

Why is it that the researcher cannot conclude that H can be rejected at the 0.05 level of significance? In a significance test of this form, one needs to specify a rejection region R. If the data falls into R, the hypothesis H is rejected, otherwise it is not. In the current example, the rejection region of the researcher consisted of the union of two parts. Indeed, he would have rejected H if the deviation from the mean would have been at least 5 after 20 experiments, but also if the deviation from the mean would have been at least 7 after 40 experiments (the probability of having 27 successes or more after 40 experiments is about 0.019). But the first part of this rejection region already has probability of almost 0.05 under H, so the total rejection probability is simply too large. In fact, ignoring the fact that because of the discrete character of the problem, a type-I error probability will be somewhat smaller than α, the point is that the first part of the rejection region already "uses up" the total type-I error probability the researcher is willing to allow for. Any additional possibility to reject H will make the probability of making such a type-I mistake larger than the allowed α.

Had the researcher looked *only* after 40 experiments, then he would have been correct, at least in his interpretation of the error probability under hypothesis H. Common sense, however, dictates that now the additional experiments have been done and the data has been collected, it would be very strange if these additional experiments cannot somehow be used in an evidential procedure against H.

The phenomenon that we just described is a strong argument against using p-values for evidential procedures. Moreover, in concrete experiments it is impossible to check whether or not the researcher had not been able to resist the temptation to peek and – upon finding that the evidence is not yet significant – to continue until it is. A procedure of this type is very prone to scientific fraud.

How does peeking at the data (and possibly continuing the experiments after that) fit in the framework of likelihood ratios? The answer is simple and clear: there is no problem whatsoever, and the whole problem sketched above does not come up in a likelihood ratio framework. The only difference, of course, is that a likelihood ratio approach can only be done comparatively, so we need to introduce an alternative hypothesis. This in itself is reasonable enough, as we have discussed extensively in this book. If the experiment is about finding out whether or not a coin is fair (or a much more sophisticated version of a question of this type), then we already know the answer and we do not need to perform an experiment: there is, simply, no fair coin in the world. There is no mechanism to generate a perfect sequence of Bernoulli $1/2$ trials. So certainly hypothesis H is wrong. But that is not the point. The point is whether or not there is an alternative hypothesis that would explain the data (much) better than H. The alternative depends on the circumstances.

As an illustration, suppose that the researcher above wants to compare $H: p = 1/2$ to $H': p = 3/4$. The researcher then performs his first series of 20 experiments,

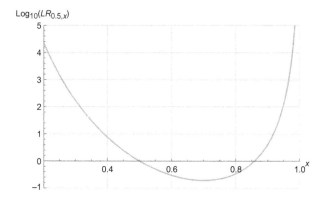

Log$_{10}$(LR$_{0.5,x}$)

Figure 9.4 The logarithm of the likelihood ratio in favor of success probability 0.5 versus success probability x, based on 14 out of 20 successes, as a function of x.

and observes 14 successes. The probability of this under H is 0.037 and the probability under H' is 0.168. Hence the corresponding likelihood ratio is equal to 0.219 and the data therefore supports H' over H by a factor of 4.6. If the alternative is $H'' : p = 1/3$ then the corresponding likelihood ratio of H versus H'' would be about 52 in favor of H. Whether or not the data supports H depends on the alternative.

To illustrate this further, we note that we need not fix the alternative to $p = 1/2$ in advance in the sense that we can compute the likelihood ratio versus all alternatives. In Figure 9.4, we plot $\log_{10}(LR_{0.5,x})$ where $LR_{0.5,x}$ is the likelihood ratio in favor of success probability 0.5 versus success probability x.

From Figure 9.4 we see, for example, that the evidence in favor or against a success probability of 0.5 versus success probability x is rather weak, say at most 10, for all x between 0.39 and 0.92. In particular, the support for the maximum likelihood value, $x = 0.7$, versus the hypothesis of interest that $x = 0.5$, is not very strong, about 5.2.

The interesting point is now that there is no reason whatsoever not to perform additional experiments. If the researcher wishes (for good, bad, or even unethical reasons) to perform 20 additional experiments, he is statistically allowed to do so. After observing, say, 33 successes in 40 experiments, he can again compute the likelihood ratio of H versus H'. A small computation shows that this likelihood ratio is now equal to 0.000199, so much stronger supporting H' over H than the likelihood ratio after 20 experiments. The data is what it is, and given two hypotheses, a likelihood ratio can be computed. There is no point in saying that H in isolation is rejected (or not) after a certain number of experiments with any evidential implication, and certainly the associated significance level α does

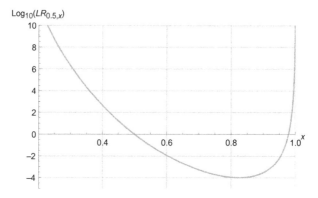

Figure 9.5 The logarithm of the likelihood ratio in favor of success probability 0.5 versus success probability x, based on 33 out of 40 successes, as a function of x.

not quantify the evidence. The evidence is quantified by a likelihood ratio in the presence of an alternative hypothesis.

In Figure 9.5 we see that these numbers provide much stronger evidence than the data based on 20 experiments. In particular the support of the maximum likelihood value, $x = 33/40$, versus $x = 0.5$ is now approximately 10,000. We can also see, for example, that the support for a success probability of $33/40$ versus being equal to x, is at least 10 for all x outside the interval $(0.67, 0.93)$ and is at least 100 for all x outside the interval $(0.60, 0.95)$.

Suppose now, finally, that the researcher wants to perform a certain experiment which has an unknown success probability p. His goal is to reject the hypothesis $H: p = 1/2$. He is in principle willing to perform 20 experiments, but after 10 experiments wants to have a look at the data, and wants to allow for the possibility to stop at that point. He works with significance level 0.05 and suggests the following rejection region: reject H if either (i) after 10 experiments the number of successes is at least 9 or at most 1, or (ii) after 20 experiments the total number of successes is at least 16 or at most 4. Elementary computations with the binomial distributions show that the probability to reject H if it is in fact true, is less that 0.05, so this is a correct procedure. However, the problems with an evidential interpretation do not disappear. Indeed, suppose that the researcher finds 3 successes after 10 experiments, and a total of 5 successes after 20 experiments. In that case he would not reject H. But another researcher who has the exact same results but who has not peeked at the data after 10 experiments, would in fact reject H, since the rejection region after 20 experiments, with significance level 0.05 is $\{0, 1, \dots, 5\} \cup \{15, \dots, 20\}$. So although he researchers find the same results, one of them rejects H but the other does not.

One could argue that this is perhaps not a real problem. After all, the procedures that led to the two different conclusions is different, so deviating conclusions might, perhaps, be reasonable and expected. Certainly there are situations in which this would be true. If two researchers receive different information about the data, then different conclusions are to be expected. But in this case, the researchers have the exact same information. If it is the case that an evidential quantification differs between different procedures where, eventually, the same information is obtained, then we think that such an evidential quantification is unacceptable. Likelihood ratios do not suffer from this problem. If two researchers agree on the model, and receive the same information, then they will produce the same likelihood ratio. Thus, likelihood ratios lead to a canonical way of quantifying evidence, whereas *p*-values do not.

9.7.2 Manipulating p-Values?

Suppose the same researcher as above again sets out to reject H, the hypothesis that the success probability of the experiment is equal to $1/2$. He decides again to take $\alpha = 0.05$. He has learned something from the critique in the precious section, and this time performs 40 experiments in one swap, without looking after 20 experiments. He observes 29 successes. Being a responsible researcher he opts for a two-sided test, and computes the probability of deviating at least 9 from the mean under the null hypothesis H. This probability turns out to be rather small, namely 0.0003. He realizes that this probability is so small that it warrants rejection of H at a much lower significance level than the one he started out with. Indeed, even the two-sided version warrants rejection of H under $\alpha = 0.01$ so this is what he reports.

Is this correct? Surely not. One must choose α before performing the experiment, and one cannot change α afterwards. The reason is that α is measuring the probability of falsely rejecting the hypothesis H of interest. It is a property of the statistical *procedure*. An α of 0.05 means that if the researcher were to repeat the experiment many times, he would falsely reject H in at most 5% of the cases. The value of α is a value that is associated to the test at large, and certainly not to an individual outcome. Hence changing the value of α after a certain observation simply makes no sense. It takes away the only meaningful thing α can express, namely the probability of falsely rejecting H.

However, reporting the actually obtained *p*-value has an interpretation that is correct, as follows. Let X be a statistic and assume that we reject the null hypothesis if X is too large. If we write F for the distribution function of X under the null hypothesis, then when $X = x$ is observed, the *p*-value is $1 - F(x)$ (we assume for simplicity that F is continuous and strictly increasing). Now note that $F(X)$ is a random variable which has, under the null hypothesis, a uniform distribution on $(0, 1)$, since

$$P(F(X) \le y) = P(X \le F^{-1}(y)) = F(F^{-1}(y)) = y$$

for all $y \in (0, 1)$. Hence a researcher can correctly claim that upon reporting p-values of concrete experiments, in all cases that the null hypothesis is correct, the reported value is uniformly distributed over the unit interval. As a result, the frequency of reporting a p-value of at most $\delta > 0$, say, is δ among those cases in which the null hypothesis is actually true. This is a statement about the whole ensemble of tests performed by one or more researchers. This is not to say that the statement has a sound evidential interpretation for any given individual test. We know it does not, and p-values should not be mentioned in this connection. But reporting p-values without previously having chosen a significance level α has an interpretation that is correct in the sense described above.

9.7.3 Multiple Hypotheses

One of the authors of this book (RM) relates the following story. A personal friend working on a PhD thesis in psychology at some point in time went to see her supervisor. The research was not going so well, and she had not made a lot of progress on her original research question. Somehow, the data that she had collected did not seem to point in a specific direction, and this seemed to jeopardize her complete research project. The answer of her supervisor was, roughly, the following: "Indeed that is not so good, but well, don't worry, as no doubt *something* will be significant."

This rather shocking answer of the supervisor refers to the phenomenon that if one tries enough hypotheses, sooner or later one of these hypothesis can be rejected at any specified significance level α. Indeed, with $\alpha = 0.05$, the probability to incorrectly reject the hypothesis of interest if this hypothesis is actually true, is 0.05 (assuming such a rejection region exists, for the sake of argument). So on average, one out of every 20 trials in which the hypothesis is correct, will lead to the rejection of it.

So suppose that we are interested in the hypothesis that one's favorite color has an effect on the success probability when flipping a coin, the only thing needed to do is to come up with (1) sufficiently many different colors, and (2) for each color a person declaring that color to be his or her favorite one. Now we simply let everyone perform a certain number of coin flips, and we may find that indeed, in one out of 20 times the null hypothesis of $p = 1/2$ is rejected at the $\alpha = 0.05$

significance level. If this happens to happen with the person favoring the color green, then we have statistically proven that preference for green implies being skillful at flipping coins.

Of course, the example is anecdotal. But it is in principle not different from the suggestion of the supervisor mentioned above. This phenomenon is often called *publication bias*, and potentially undermines the credibility of many a statistical conclusion in the scientific literature. The point is that the number of hypotheses you test interferes with the significance level and therefore also with the decision to reject or not. A standard approach is to apply the Bonferroni correction, which is to divide the significance level α by the number of tests carried out. This supposes, of course, knowledge of n. If several laboratories carry out experiments unaware of each other, they will each divide α by their own number, instead of by the total number of experiments.

To illustrate the problems with multiple tests further, suppose we have 20 colors, and for each color there is a person flipping a coin 10 times. Then the hypothesis H that $p = 1/2$ for the person liking green will be rejected if the number of successes is 0, 1, 9, or 10. Suppose, however, that we are interested in the hypothesis H' that $p = 1/2$ for all of the 20 colors. Then the region defined by the requirement that at least one person must have 0, 1, 9, or 10 successes has a much too large probability, namely about $1/3$. Instead, we can define a rejection region as those outcomes for which at least one person sees *only* heads or *only* tails. The probability of this set, assuming H' is true, is about 0.04, so the significance level is attained. Now suppose that the person liking green sees 9 heads, and all the others see a number of heads in the range from 1 to 9. In that case, H would be rejected, but H' would not. For someone only interested in green this sounds rather strange; the bare fact that other colors were investigated as well make him change his decision, whereas the number of heads obtained by himself does not change.

As usual, the problem simply does not arise when working with likelihood ratios instead. Of course, working with likelihood ratios means that sometimes evidence is obtained in favor of the incorrect hypothesis, see Proposition 2.4.2. This phenomenon – evidence in favor of an incorrect hypothesis – cannot be avoided, by the nature of probability and statistics. But it is very different to accept that evidence sometimes points in the wrong direction than to purposely seek for hypotheses which happen to be supported by the data. In addition, the likelihood ratio must always be seen in conjunction with prior probabilities for the various hypotheses. We take it that when we compare, say, $p = 1/2$ to $p = 2/3$ for people favoring the color green, not many people will be willing to assign more than an extremely small prior probability to the possibility that $p = 2/3$. So even if the data happens to point towards $p = 2/3$, this does not automatically imply that we assign a large posterior probability to that possibility. If one finds evidence for $p = 2/3$, this does not mean one believes it. Common sense still plays a role when working with likelihood ratios, via the choice of the prior probabilities. In the p-value framework it is much more difficult to see how common sense can be used as a safeguard to absurd conclusions, since prior probabilities do not play a role in that framework.

9.7.4 The Illogic of p-Value Procedures

Finally, we briefly comment on some strange issues associated with the choice between one- or two-sided p-value procedures. We have extensively argued that p-values do not quantify evidence. They quantify something quite different instead, namely the probability for the data to be more extreme (in a certain sense) than what has actually been observed. There is one more, rather curious fact about p-value procedures which also jeopardizes their evidential interpretation.

Suppose again that we are interested in the unknown success probability p of a binomial distribution. Suppose the hypothesis of interest is $H: p = 1/2$, and that we perform the experiment 100 times. When we take $\alpha = 0.05$ then we should reject H if the number of successes is either at least 61 or at most 39, as is easily checked by direct computation. Note that we reject H if the number of successes is either too large or too small to be explainable by $p = 1/2$.

However, if our hypothesis of interest is one-sided, say $H': p \leq 1/2$, then we should only reject H' if the number of successes is too high. This one-sided version of the test leads to the rejection region (still with $\alpha = 0.05$) of $\{59, 60, \ldots, 100\}$. Now suppose that the number of successes is 60. This is enough to reject $p \leq 1/2$. Rejecting $p \leq 1/2$ implies that $p = 1/2$ is rejected as well, but the curious fact is that the outcome of 60 successes is not enough to reject the hypothesis H that $p = 1/2$. We reject $p \leq 1/2$ but we do not reject the much stronger hypothesis that $p = 1/2$. This is a rather illogic state of affairs, of course.

With likelihood ratios this issue simply does not come up, since we always consider two competing simple hypotheses. The issue of one-sided versus two-sided therefore, simply does not arise.

9.8 Summary and Conclusions

We have argued extensively that p-values should not be used for evidential purposes. In particular, the p-value of a likelihood ratio does not add anything to the evidential value or interpretation of this likelihood ratio. We have given several arguments for this position. First of all, the p-value depends on the probability assigned to unobserved outcomes, while we insist that a measure of evidential value should only depend on the distribution on what has been actually observed. When unobserved possibilities change, for instance because of technological advancement, then the p-value can also change, even if the observed data does not.

Second, p-values are ambiguous in the sense that it is not always the case that there is only one canonical pair of hypotheses. If we want, for instance, to make an assessment about whether or not two persons are siblings, then one has several options. One can fix the DNA profile of one of them as background information, and treat the DNA of the other person as evidence, or vice versa. These two options lead to the same evidential value, but not to the same p-values. Treating both profiles as evidence leads to yet another p-value but, again, to the same evidential value.

Finally, it is very possible, as we have shown by a number of examples, that when we compare two hypotheses H_1 and H_2, the likelihood ratio in favor of H_1 is smaller than 1, while the corresponding p-value is also very small. The small p-value might erroneously be interpreted as evidence in favor of H_1, while in fact the data supports H_2 over H_1 since the likelihood ratio is smaller than 1.

We have also discussed several consequences of using p-values for evidential purposes in general. We concluded that using p-values for this purpose leads to further absurdities.

This is not to say that p-values are useless. By their very nature, p-values of a likelihood ratio say something about the distribution of this likelihood ratio. They give answers to questions of the following kind: "How often should we expect a likelihood ratio of at least a certain (observed) value in a situation as specified by, say, the defense hypothesis." The answers to such questions are not relevant for the evaluation of the evidence in a particular case. However, if it so happens that the findings are extremely unlikely under both hypotheses considered, then this may be an indication that there is a third hypothesis which explains the data better than the two hypotheses under consideration.

One can also use p-values in the process of deciding whether or not to further investigate certain possibilities. If the likelihood ratio distribution indicates that obtaining certain type of data will very likely lead to obtaining evidence of a certain strength, then this may lead to the decision of not gathering that data. The p-value, therefore, can be used to make meaningful and useful statements about the process of finding evidence, or about the choice of the hypotheses but as soon as we have decided which hypotheses we wish to consider, and have obtained the data, the p-value is silent about the evidential value in that particular instance.

9.9 Bibliographical Notes

The use of p-values goes back all the way to Fisher [68]. For very forceful arguments against using p-values for evidential purposes in general, see [129], from which some examples in this chapter originate. Discussions about the problems of presenting likelihood ratios in court can be found in [30], [159], and [175]. p-Values in an evidential role are defended in, e.g., [70], [107], and [120]. Some computations of p-values for likelihood ratios can be found in [58]. Much of the material of this chapter is taken from [91]. References [73] and [81] contain further critique on using p-values.

10

From Evidence to Decision

As we have extensively discussed, likelihood ratios express the degree of support that evaluated data give for one hypothesis over another one. That statement does not tell us which hypothesis is true, it only tells us which one is the better explanation of the data and also how much better it is. Of course, the reason to gather and evaluate the evidence in the first place is usually because we want to make some decision, or take some action, that we would ideally take using knowledge of which hypothesis is true. Since we cannot observe directly which hypothesis is true, we gather evidence that is informative for that. We will consider that knowledge of H_1 to be true would prompt us to carry out action A_1, and knowledge that H_2 is true would prompt us to carry out action A_2. An action could be, for instance, a conviction or acquittal, it could also be the decision to gather more data, or the decision to abandon the investigation altogether. What is important here is only that the follow up is a binary choice: all cases of H_1 lead to A_1 and all cases of H_2 lead to A_2. If we are uncertain about which hypothesis is true then we run the risk of deciding for A_1 while H_2 is in fact true, or the other way around, and it may be that we want to avoid one such scenario even more than the other one.

In this chapter we give some attention to how one could take such a decision. First, in Section 10.1, we will discuss decisions that are based on the evidence alone. We then enter the realm of frequentist statistics and error probabilities that tell us how often a decision will be correct or incorrect if either of the hypotheses is true. Not having prior probabilities implies not having posterior probabilities and therefore not knowing how likely a given decision is to be correct. Of course, one would like the error rates to be as small as possible. The classical theory, developed by Neyman, Pearson, and others, in short says that a decision based on the evidence is best based on the likelihood ratio. We will formulate and prove the exact optimality statement. We give several examples of their applications in Section 10.2.

Next, in Section 10.3 we discuss the situation where we do have prior probabilities, and only want to carry out A_i if the probability of H_i is sufficiently large. Then, it may be that neither A_1 nor A_2 is decided for, but a third decision is taken, A_0, which could represent gathering additional evidence, or abandoning the investigation. A possible way to formalize this approach is by using cost functions. We then associate a cost to making a wrong decision, say cost c_1 if we do A_1 if H_2 is true, c_2 if we do A_2 if H_1 is true, and A_0 comes at a cost c_0. If we know the prior odds on the hypotheses, then we can work out a strategy whose expected cost will be minimal, which as we shall see boils down to doing A_2 if the likelihood ratio is sufficiently small, A_1 if it is sufficiently large, and A_0 in all remaining cases. If A_0 corresponds to the acquisition of more data, we can also investigate how likely it is that these data will allow for a decision A_1 or A_2 when we have obtained them.

Forensic evidence is of course to be used in a court case where a judge or jury needs to reach a decision. What constitutes statistical evidence need not always be legally acceptable evidence. Moreover the admissibility or role of prior probabilities in legal court cases is not directly clear. For instance, giving a probabilistic translation that does justice to the presumption of innocence does not seem easy, to say the least. We discuss these issues briefly in Section 10.4, with the primary aim not being to be comprehensive, but rather to raise awareness of their existence.

10.1 Neyman–Pearson Theory

In this chapter we suppose that there are two relevant hypotheses H_1 and H_2, one of which is true, and we are interested in which one that is. If we knew that H_1 were true, then we would take action A_1, and if we knew that H_2 were true, then we would take action A_2. We suppose here that we have evidence E at our disposition, and nothing else, and that we need to choose either A_1 or A_2. That is, in this section we either do not have or disregard prior probabilities on the hypotheses when it comes to deciding for A_1 or A_2.

We could interpret A_1 as "accepting H_1" and A_2 as "rejecting H_1," but this interpretation is not necessary. For example, A_1 and A_2 could also be very different actions, such as to gather further data or not.

Neyman–Pearson theory basically claims that if we need to take a decision based on the data E alone, the best way to do so is based on the likelihood ratio $LR_{H_1, H_2}(E)$, deciding in favor of H_1 if and only if there is sufficient evidence in favor of it, that is, when $LR_{H_1, H_2}(E) \geq t$ for some t. Any such decision criterion optimizes error rates in a certain way that we discuss now.

In general, we consider a test procedure that we intend to apply to evidence we are yet to obtain. Hence, for all data we can potentially obtain, we define the decision we would take if we were to obtain it. That is, we define a region R such that if the evidence falls in R then we choose A_2, and if not we choose A_1. Traditionally, in the context of the accepting and rejecting paradigm that we mentioned above, R is called a *rejection region*: if the evidence falls into it, we take action A_2 which in this context consists of rejecting H_1. Our framework is somewhat more general, but we will adopt the name "rejection region" for R, keeping in mind though that A_2 does not necessarily consists of rejecting anything

Since we regard the evidence as random, with its probability distribution depending on the hypothesis which is true, we can speak of the probability that we call for A_2 when in fact H_1 is true. In the absence of a probability on the hypotheses, we cannot speak of the probability that H_1 is true if A_2 is called for.

The probability that we choose A_2 if H_1 is true is denoted α. In the accept/reject interpretation, this is the probability that we erroneously reject H_1, and the error that we then commit is called a *type-I error*. The probability that we choose A_1 when H_2 is true is called β, and this error is called a *type-II error*. It is customary to call α the *significance level* and $1 - \beta$ the *power* of the test.

The following famous result says that if the rejection region of the test corresponds to a likelihood ratio threshold, that is, if we choose for A_1 precisely when the evidence for H_1 relative to H_2 is sufficiently strong, then there can be no more powerful test at its significance level.

Proposition 10.1.1 (Neyman–Pearson lemma) *Suppose that on the basis of evidence E we choose between actions A_1 and A_2 by means of a likelihood ratio threshold t, that is, we choose for A_1 if $LR = LR_{H_1, H_2}(E) \geq t$ and for A_2 if $LR = LR_{H_1, H_2}(E) < t$. Let $P(LR < t \mid H_1) = \alpha$ and let $P(LR \geq t \mid H_2) = \beta$. If another test procedure T has significance level $\alpha_T \leq \alpha$, then it must have power $1 - \beta_T \leq 1 - \beta$.*

Proof. Let $R_t = \{E : LR_{H_1, H_2}(E) < t\}$ be the rejection region for the likelihood ratio test with threshold t: if the likelihood ratio is less than t, then we choose for A_2 and otherwise we choose for A_1. Now suppose that we have another test T, which also leads to a choice for A_1 or A_2 based on the obtained evidence.

Let R be the rejection region for this test T, and suppose that

$$\alpha_T = P(E \in R \mid H_1) \leq P(E \in R_t \mid H_1) = \alpha.$$

By considering how R and R_t overlap, we have

$$\alpha_T = P(E \in R \mid H_1) = P(E \in R \cap R_t \mid H_1) + P(E \in R \cap R_t^c \mid H_1)$$

and

$$\alpha = P(E \in R_t \mid H_1) = P(E \in R \cap R_t \mid H_1) + P(E \in R_t \cap R^c \mid H_1),$$

and hence $\alpha_T \leq \alpha$ is equivalent to

$$P(E \in R \cap R_t^c \mid H_1) \leq P(E \in R_t \cap R^c \mid H_1). \qquad (10.1)$$

Similarly, we have

$$1 - \beta_T = P(E \in R \mid H_2) = P(E \in R \cap R_t \mid H_2) + P(E \in R \cap R_t^c \mid H_2)$$

and

$$1 - \beta = P(E \in R_t \mid H_2) = P(E \in R_t \cap R \mid H_2) + P(E \in R_t \cap R^c \mid H_2),$$

so we need to show that

$$P(E \in R \cap R_t^c \mid H_2) \leq P(E \in R_t \cap R^c \mid H_2).$$

Since by construction, every outcome in R_t (respectively R_t^c) is at most (respectively at least) t times more likely under H_1 than under H_2 we have, using (10.1) that

$$P(E \in R_t \cap R^c \mid H_2) \geq \frac{1}{t} P(E \in R_t \cap R^c \mid H_1)$$

$$\geq \frac{1}{t} P(E \in R \cap R_t^c \mid H_1)$$

$$\geq P(E \in R \cap R_t^c \mid H_2),$$

which is what we needed to show.   □

From the proof of the Neyman–Pearson lemma we see that for the optimality of a likelihood ratio test, it does not matter whether we set $R_t = \{E : LR(E) < t\}$ (with strict inequality) or $R_t = \{E : LR(E) \leq t\}$ (with non-strict inequality). Therefore, we are free to include the evidence with $LR(E) = t$ into the rejection region or not; this will alter α and β since the rejection region changes, but it will not change the optimality condition. In view of this, we can also *randomize* the decision when E is such that $LR(E) = t$. Doing so, we can achieve any α (or, alternatively, β) that we aim for, which in turn implies that we need consider *only* such rejection regions. If we have any other test with some rejection region that gives significance level α, we can achieve the same α with some likelihood ratio threshold (possibly involving randomization for evidence yielding a likelihood ratio equal to the threshold), and this region can only improve on β.

We also note that a rejection region may coincide with such a likelihood ratio rejection region, even if not formulated in such a way. A simple example where this happens is in the context of DNA matches with unambiguous single source traces. If we decide that the suspect has left the trace if his profile matches with that of the trace, we get the same decisions as when we decide so if the likelihood ratio is larger than zero.

In the statement of the Neyman–Pearson lemma, one fixes the probability α of a type-I error, and then shows that a likelihood ratio test with that α has the largest power possible. However, one may also opt for treating α and β on the same footing by minimizing the sum $\alpha + \beta$ instead. Since everything is symmetric now, it is no surprise that the sum $\alpha + \beta$ is minimal for a likelihood ratio threshold of 1 and we can see this as follows. When we take a likelihood ratio threshold of t we can write

$$\alpha = \sum_{E:P(E|H_1)\leq t P(E|H_2)} P(E \mid H_1)$$

and

$$1 - \beta = \sum_{E:P(E|H_1)\leq t P(E|H_2)} P(E \mid H_2).$$

Hence we obtain that

$$\alpha + \beta = 1 + \alpha - (1 - \beta) = 1 + \sum_{E:P(E|H_1)\leq t P(E|H_2)} \left(P(E \mid H_1) - P(E \mid H_2) \right).$$

When $t = 1$, the summation includes all terms which are negative, and no terms which are positive. Increasing t means including E for which the summand is positive, and decreasing t means leaving out E for which the summand is negative. Both options imply that the sum increases, and hence the sum is minimal when $t = 1$. On the threshold $t = 1$ itself, it is immaterial for the sum $\alpha + \beta$ what we decide.

If we use a likelihood ratio threshold equal to t, then by Proposition 2.4.2 the probability that we choose A_1 if H_2 is true, is at most $1/t$. In other words, $\beta \leq 1/t$, and the power of the test is at least $1 - 1/t$. Of course this is only an informative statement for $t > 1$ and it may be the case that a small α, that is, a small probability to choose A_2 if H_1 is true, means that we have to choose a threshold $t < 1$ in which case we may not have any power at all.

10.1.1 Example: Kinship Likelihood Ratios on a Single Locus

The Neyman–Pearson lemma says that if a rejection region is defined either directly as, or such that it coincides with, all possible data E such that $LR(E) \leq t$ for some t, then we cannot simultaneously improve on both of the resulting error rates.

Significance tests typically use rejection regions that consist of all data that are least likely under the null hypothesis, disregarding the alternative altogether.

Table 10.1 *Probabilities and likelihood ratios*
if $p_a = 0.2, p_b = 0.1, p_c = 0.7$.

g	$P(g \mid H_1)$	$P(g \mid H_2)$	$LR(g)$
(a,a)	0.36	0.04	9
(a,b)	0.06	0.04	1.5
(a,c)	0.42	0.28	1.5
(b,b)	0.0025	0.01	0.25
(b,c)	0.035	0.14	0.25
(c,c)	0.1225	0.49	0.25

We will now give an example that illustrates that with such an approach, we may end up with suboptimal rejection regions.

Consider a person P_1 who is homozygous (a,a) on a locus with three possible alleles a, b, and c, with allele frequencies $p_a = 0.2, p_b = 0.1$ and $p_c = 0.7$ respectively. We consider the genotype of P_1 as fixed, and we want to set up a test to identify siblings of P_1, assuming that a person to be tested is either a sibling of P_1 or unrelated. In that case the genotype probabilities for siblings, for unrelated individuals and the likelihood ratio distribution is summarized in Table 10.1, where H_1 is the hypothesis of being siblings, and H_2 the hypothesis of being unrelated.

The computations that lead to Table 10.1 have been explained in Chapter 7, but for the convenience of the reader we explain the number 0.36 in the first line. A sibling of P_1 can have genotype (a,a) in three ways: (1) he may receive the same alleles as P_1 from their parents, an event with probability $1/4$; (2) he may receive one allele a that was passed on to P_1, while the other was not passed on to P_1 but happens to be a as well, this is an event with probability $p_a/2$, or (3) he receives the two parental alleles that were not passed on to P_1, which both happen to be a, an event with probability $p_a^2/4$. Summing up, and using that $p_a = 0.2$ gives 0.36.

From Table 10.1 we see that the three most likely genotypes for a sibling are $(a,c), (a,a)$, and (c,c). If we define the rejection region as the complement of the three most likely genotypes, then one would reject sibling-ship if the observed data (the genotype of the tested person) are among the least likely outcomes if the tested hypothesis (siblings) is true. However, one sees from the table that this rejection region does not correspond to a rejection region defined by a likelihood ratio threshold. Hence we may be able to improve on this test if we use a likelihood ratio threshold rejection region. This indeed turns out to be the case, as we see in Table 10.2 summarizing various tests and their error rates.

If we reject the hypothesis of being siblings if the genotype is one of the three least likely genotypes of siblings, then we have a type-I error rate of $\alpha = 0.0975$

Table 10.2 *Rejection regions R and error rates for various tests based on Table 10.1.*

R	α	β	Threshold
$\emptyset$	0	1	$t < 0.25$
$\{(b,b),(b,c),(c,c)\}$	0.16	0.36	$0.25 \leq t < 1.5$
$\{(a,b),(a,c),(b,b),(b,c),(c,c)\}$	0.64	0.04	$1.5 \leq t < 9$
All	1	0	$t \geq 9$
$\{(a,b),(b,b),(b,c)\}$	0.0975	0.81	None
Not (a,c)	0.58	0.28	None
Not (a,a) or (a,c)	0.22	0.32	Randomized on $t = 1.5$
Not (a,a) or (a,b)	0.58	0.08	Randomized on $t = 1.5$
If $(b,b),(b,c),(c,c)$ then reject 50%	0.08	0.68	Randomized on $t = 0.25$

and a type-II error rate of 0.81 as we read off from the fifth row in the table. The type-II error rate is large due to the fact that the genotype (c,c) is very common: it is among the three most likely genotypes for siblings, but this is only because allele c is so common in the general population.

We can simultaneously achieve lower error rates of both types. For example, as the last line in Table 10.2 indicates, we can decide to reject the hypothesis of being siblings in a randomized way by rejecting with probability $1/2$ if the genotype is $(b,b),(b,c)$, or (c,c). In that case we find $\alpha = 0.08$ and $\beta = 0.68$, which is an improvement of both error rates compared to the strategy corresponding to row five.

Thus, rejecting a hypothesis if one of its least likely outcomes occurs (at the chosen significance level) may sound at first glance like a reasonable procedure, but we then ignore that any outcome must be explained one way or another and this may lead to suboptimal error rates.

10.1.2 Composite Hypotheses and Nuisance Parameters

The Neyman–Pearson lemma has its roots in frequentist statistics, where no probability is attached to events that have already occurred without the outcome being known. Since this is quite a different point of view than the one we have elaborated upon in Chapter 1, we digress here to discuss the differences between the concept and the applicability of the likelihood ratio in the frequentist framework on the one hand, and in our subjective epistemic framework on the other.

In the frequentist framework, the concept of probability refers to how likely the various outcomes of future experiments are, where probability is interpreted as relative frequency. By conceivably carrying out an experiment many times in the future, the probability of a specific possible outcome is the same as the expected relative frequency of that outcome. Then it is possible to make a probabilistic prediction about data that will be generated by a hypothesis, provided the hypothesis is *simple*, by which we mean that the probability distribution of E exists as frequentist probabilities. If both H_1 and H_2 are simple, the likelihood ratio $LR_{H_1, H_2}(E)$ exists in the frequentist framework, and it is for such hypotheses that the Neyman–Pearson lemma makes sense in the frequentist framework. In that case, its evaluation corresponds to the one we have developed. For example, consider a likelihood ratio for paternity versus unrelatedness in a population with known allele frequencies. Then the frequentist's evaluation of the required profile probabilities depend on genetic inheritance and allele frequencies, and the frequentist likelihood ratio coincides with ours. We also note though that, for the distribution of E and hence of the likelihood ratio under each hypothesis, we also need to take into account the way the experiment is set up. For example, in Section 9.7.1 we discussed the example of a researcher who tosses a coin 10 times, and then decides on the basis of the outcomes whether or not to toss it 10 more times. In order to compute the distribution of likelihood ratios, we need to take that into account, but of course the likelihood ratio of an obtained outcome of the experiment only depends on what was obtained and not on how the experiment was set up, cf. Section 2.3.2.

Hypotheses that are not simple are called *composite*. In the frequentist framework, the likelihood ratio for composite hypotheses H_1 and/or H_2 is defined differently. For example, suppose H_2 is composite. One then needs to decompose H_2 into simple ones $H_2 = \cup_i H_2^{(i)}$, often making use of some parametrization. Then, since $P(E \mid H_2)$ does not exist in the frequentist framework, one takes the maximum of all $P(E \mid H_2^{(i)})$ instead. In the resulting ratio, we compare the best explanation a simple sub-hypothesis of H_1 provides, with the best explanation any simple sub-hypothesis of H_2 provides. The Neyman–Pearson lemma then does not apply anymore. Note that is somewhat reminiscent to the discussion in Section 8.6.

By contrast, with our subjective epistemic interpretation, the probability of an event reflects our conviction that it is true, on the basis of our knowledge. In particular it is immaterial whether the event has already occurred or not. Therefore, $P(E \mid H)$ always exists for us, regardless of whether the hypothesis would be called simple or composite from a frequentist point of view, and to obtain it we need to summarize the knowledge H provides into a probability distribution for E. This may be easy or difficult in practice, but to us, there is no intrinsic difference between simple and composite hypotheses.

From the proof of the Neyman–Pearson lemma we see that it does not rely on the hypotheses being simple, but only on the existence of the probability distributions induced by it. Therefore it applies to any pair of hypotheses in our subjective epistemic framework. If our model involves a parameter θ we write, as in Chapter 3,

$$P(E \mid H_1) = \int P(E \mid H_1, \theta) f(\theta \mid H_1) d\theta,$$

where the density $f(\theta \mid H_1)$ denotes the distribution of θ under H_1. With a similar decomposition for H_2, we get

$$LR_{H_1, H_2}(E) = \frac{\int P(E \mid \theta, H_1) f(\theta \mid H_1) d\theta}{\int P(E \mid \theta, H_2) f(\theta \mid H_2) d\theta},$$

cf. (3.7).

In general, we may view the realization of our evidence E as the result of a process where we first sample parameters θ from a probability distribution $f(\theta \mid H_1)$ (for H_1) or from $f(\theta \mid H_2)$ (for H_2), and then sample E from the evidence distribution $P(E \mid \theta, H_i)$, conditional on θ, for $i = 1$ or $i = 2$. We call θ a *nuisance parameter* if it is not mentioned in the hypotheses as they were formulated to the forensic laboratory. For nuisance variables we will assume that they satisfy $f(\theta \mid H_1) = f(\theta \mid H_2)$ for all θ, that is, their distribution is independent of the hypotheses, and they have no evidential value on their own.

For example, if the question asked is whether there is evidence that a person of interest contributed to a mixture profile, we regard the number of contributors as a nuisance variable. If the question is whether a trace has two or more than two contributors, then clearly it is not.

For nuisance variables, since they have no evidential value on their own, revelation of their value would not alter the odds on the hypotheses. Therefore, if we choose a threshold for $LR_{H_1, H_2}(E)$ to define a rejection region, we can simply apply the same threshold to all $LR_{H_1, H_2}(E \mid \theta)$.

If a parameter is not a nuisance parameter so that in general $f(\theta \mid H_1) \neq f(\theta \mid H_2)$, then things are different: the threshold on $LR_{H_1, H_2}(E)$ will entail different thresholds on the $LR_{H_1, H_2}(E \mid \theta)$. We will illustrate this with examples in Section 10.2.

10.1.3 The Evidential Value of a Decision

The Neyman–Pearson lemma tells us that error rates are optimal when rejection regions are defined by likelihood ratio thresholds. A threshold t corresponds to the probability $\alpha = P(LR < t \mid H_1)$, the probability of a type-I error where we take action A_2 while H_1 is true, and to the type-II error probability $\beta = P(LR \geq t \mid H_2)$ of taking action A_1 while H_2 is true.

If we know not only which action was taken, A_1 or A_2, but also which likelihood ratio was obtained, then this carries more information than the decision. But if we do not know that, and only observe which decision was taken, then we can say that the likelihood ratio in favor of H_1 corresponding to the decision A_1 having been made, is equal to

$$LR_{H_1, H_2}(A_1) = \frac{1 - \alpha}{\beta}. \tag{10.2}$$

This likelihood ratio uses the decision that was taken as evidence, rather than the processed data that led to that decision. To do so, one does not need to use the fact that the rejection region is formulated in terms of a likelihood ratio threshold.

If a likelihood ratio threshold equal to t was used, then we can write

$$LR_{H_1, H_2}(LR \geq t) = \frac{P(LR \geq t \mid H_1)}{P(LR \geq t \mid H_2)}$$

$$= \frac{1}{E(LR^{-1} \mid H_1, LR \geq t)}$$

$$= E(LR \mid H_2, LR \geq t)$$

$$\geq t$$

by using Proposition 2.4.2. In particular we see that setting the threshold equal to the obtained likelihood ratio post factum, leads to an overstatement of the obtained evidence.

In some cases it may not be clear whether a likelihood ratio threshold was used. For example, if forensic practitioners make a decision as to whether two samples are of the same source or not, we are provided with decisions A_1 or A_2, but not with the likelihood ratio threshold that was used, nor with the likelihood ratios that they obtained; in fact, they may not have used such an approach at all. In that case, we can think of this process as a black box giving a binary answer. The empirically obtained error rates are all that we know about the black box. From these error rates one cannot infer the probability of interest, namely the probability that if action A_1 is chosen, H_1 is true. In such case we can only use the error rates to evaluate the likelihood ratio corresponding to the decision, as $(1 - \alpha)/\beta$ in favor of H_1 if A_1 was chosen, and $(1 - \beta)/\alpha$ in favor of H_2 if A_2 was chosen.

In order to obtain strong evidence that H_1 is true, given that A_1 came out of the black box, it is mostly important that β is small, and this makes sense. This is the error where A_1 is called for, when H_2 is true, and for the evidential strength of A_1, it is important that this is small. Decreasing α from small, to 10 times smaller, will have little impact on the evidential value of A_1. On the other hand, decreasing β tenfold increases the evidential value by a factor of 10. The value of α determines how often A_1 is declared when H_1 is true, but has less impact on the value of that decision, once taken. This also shows how important it is not to confuse α, the probability to take action A_2 if H_1 is true, with the probability that H_1 is true when action A_2 is taken.

10.1.4 Is a Decision Correct?

In this section, we assume that $H_2 = H_1^c$ so that the truth is described by either H_1 or H_2. If the likelihood ratio $LR_{H_1, H_2}(E)$ were equal to zero, then we would know that H_2 must be correct, while a likelihood ratio of infinity implies that H_1 is the truth. If likelihood ratios are neither zero nor infinite and hence do not reveal the truth, it is possible that we will make a decision that we would not have made if we had known the truth. One could call a decision an error if it is not the decision one would have taken knowing the truth of the hypotheses. One might also argue that this decision is not erroneous, only unfortunate, since we took this decision on the grounds that we agreed upon when setting up the procedure. In any case, the likelihood ratio tells us which hypothesis best explains the data. There is nothing erroneous about the likelihood ratio itself, it merely expresses a property that the evidence really has. If we agree that we decide for A_1 when $LR(E) \geq t$, we accept the risk to find such evidence when H_2 is true. Nevertheless, it is common to call the probabilities to take action A_1 if H_2 is true and vice versa, error rates. In the language of Chapter 2 we would rather speak of misleading evidence, however, not errors.

The error rates predict the proportion of desirable decisions amongst the cases where each hypothesis is true, but if we want to make a statement about the probability that a decision that has been taken is the desirable one, we need more than the error rates, namely priors.

Suppose we believe the same prior probabilities π_1 and π_2 to apply to a long series of independent cases. If we could observe whether H_1 or H_2 was realized, we would be able to estimate π_1 and π_2 from the proportion of cases where H_1 or H_2 is realized. If we do not observe H_1 or H_2 directly, but only get to know whether decision A_1 or A_2 was taken, then we may still be able to estimate π_1 and π_2 provided that the decisions are informative about H_1 and H_2, which is the case when $\alpha + \beta \neq 1$, as follows from (10.2). Now, $\alpha = P(LR < t \mid H_1)$ and $\beta = P(LR \geq t \mid H_2)$, so $\alpha + \beta = 1$ if and only if $P(LR < t \mid H_1) = P(LR < t \mid H_2)$. This is only possible for t at least as large as the maximal possible likelihood ratio ($\alpha = 1, \beta = 0$, always choosing A_2), or less than the smallest possible obtainable likelihood ratio ($\alpha = 0, \beta = 1$, always choosing A_1). In all other cases, deciding on the basis of a likelihood ratio yields $\alpha + \beta < 1$, and then the fact that a decision has been taken is of some evidential value.

So, suppose that we base our decision for A_1 or A_2 on a likelihood ratio threshold t with known error rates α, β. If we record the decisions that we have taken in a series of tests, and these tests were, independently of each other, having a probability π_1 for H_1 to be true and π_2 for H_2 to be true, then we can compute the expected number of decision for A_1 and A_2. The proportion of cases where A_1 is chosen is then expected to be $\pi_1(1 - \alpha) + \pi_2 \beta$ and, of course, the proportion of cases where

A_2 is chosen is expected to be $\pi_1\alpha + \pi_2(1-\beta)$. The proportion of cases where we take the undesired decision is $\pi_1\alpha + \pi_2\beta$, and this number, of course, lies between α and β. From this, it follows that (provided $\alpha + \beta \neq 1$) if p_{A_1} is the proportion of decisions where A_1 was chosen, and similarly for p_{A_2}, that

$$\pi_1 = \frac{\beta - p_{A_1}}{\alpha + \beta - 1}, \quad \pi_2 = \frac{\alpha - p_{A_2}}{\alpha + \beta - 1}, \tag{10.3}$$

that is, we can retrieve π_1 and π_2. From the error rates and the decisions taken we can estimate the proportions of cases where each hypothesis was true. Note that if $\alpha = \beta = 0$ then we simply get $\pi_i = p_{A_i}$, as we should since no mistakes are made then.

One can make a statement about the probability that a decision, once taken, is correct. The likelihood ratio in favor of H_1, given that we have decided action A_1, is

$$\frac{1 - \alpha}{\beta} \tag{10.4}$$

and hence

$$P(H_1 \mid A_1) = \frac{(1-\alpha)\pi_1}{(1-\alpha)\pi_1 + \beta\pi_2}. \tag{10.5}$$

If we know π_1 and π_2, we can then work out posterior probabilities. If we plug in the solutions from (10.3), we get

$$P(H_1 \mid A_1) = \frac{(1-\alpha)(\beta - p_{A_1})}{p_{A_1}(\alpha + \beta - 1)}, \qquad P(H_2 \mid A_2) = \frac{(1-\beta)(\alpha - p_{A_2})}{p_{A_2}(\alpha + \beta - 1)}. \tag{10.6}$$

Let us discuss the applicability of (10.6). The probability $P(H_1 \mid A_1)$ depends, for a particular case, on the sequence of cases that this case comes from. Here, we retrieve π_1 and π_2 from the α, β and the fractions p_{A_1}, p_{A_2} of decisions either way. The probabilities α and β are properties of the test, and apply to all cases where this test is used. However, p_{A_1} and p_{A_2} have nothing to do with the specific case at hand: they are based on the whole set of tests. It is only when this set is considered to be relevant, in the sense of being of predictive value for the test we are doing now, that we can set up priors. These priors then have a frequentist interpretation. This interpretation has as a consequence that we are more inclined to believe that, say, a parent–child relation is true in a laboratory where many such investigated relations are in fact true, then we are if we do the same test with the same test result in a laboratory where many investigated relations do not exist. This is so because π_1 is larger in the first institute than in the second one.

10.2 Applications

We have seen that deciding on the basis of the likelihood ratio is, in the absence of priors, the best one can do based on the evidence. One can predict how likely mistakes of either type are, and from those the evidential value of the taken decision A_1 or A_2 can be determined. Given prior probabilities, this gives posterior probabilities that a decision was correct, but of course these posterior probabilities are not based on the evidence itself, but only on the test properties and the taken decision (that is, whether the likelihood ratio exceeded the employed threshold).

Imagine, for example, that paternity cases would be decided upon in this way. Given the distribution of the likelihood ratios for parent–child pairs and for unrelated pairs, one can determine a threshold such that, say, one in 10,000 unrelated pairs would be admitted as parent–child pairs. The probability that a parent–child pair is admitted as such is then also determined. For the sake of argument, suppose this is 0.999. If we apply this threshold, we will be able to decide in each case, but we will not know any more which decision is correct. The number of decisions taken in the long run, together with the error rates, will allow us to say which proportion of the cases were parent–child and unrelated pairs, and therefore we can also say which proportions of decisions were correct and incorrect. But these statements apply to the series of decisions, and do not allow us to distinguish between two cases in which the same decision was reached, because all we know about the genetics is the decision that was taken on the basis of it.

Therefore it is only when one is not particularly interested in which decision is incorrect, but merely in how many incorrect decisions are to be expected, that we believe this procedure can be applied in a forensic context. Such situations do occur, for example in the context of database searches.

If a database is searched in order to find items of interest, hidden in a potentially very large number of items that are not of interest, it may be feasible to further inspect a limited number of candidate items in the database, but not all of them. In the DNA context, an example is the search for a relative of an unknown offender in a DNA database. This is called *familial search* and we will discuss this in detail in Chapter 12. A similar example is a search in a missing persons database that contains genetic data of relatives of missing persons.

A first application is simply the observation that one cannot gain any improvement in the error rates by letting other statistics than the likelihood ratio come in. When familial searching was introduced in the UK, sibling searches were conducted as a two-step process. First, the individuals in the database sharing sufficiently many alleles were selected, and then the likelihood ratio in favor of being siblings was computed (cf. [97]). A decision for further investigation was then taken on the basis of the likelihood ratio exceeding a threshold. This means that the rejection region is formulated as follows: a person is further investigated if the likelihood ratio exceeds threshold t and the number of shared alleles is sufficiently large. While this procedure may be computationally helpful in reducing the number of likelihood ratios to be calculated, it does not satisfy the Neyman–Pearson condition and hence there is no guarantee of optimality.

The Neyman–Pearson lemma may also be applied to tell us how to deal with inhomogeneous databases, that is, databases that contain more information for some items than for others. For example, a DNA database with profiles of suspects and offenders need not have the same loci typed for everyone in the database: for some persons there may be more genetic information than for others. Similarly, a DNA database containing relatives of missing persons can contain more informative relatives for one missing person than for another one. For instance, for some missing persons one may have both parents, while for others only a sibling may be available. For the identification of missing persons with more informative relatives, we can expect a larger likelihood ratio than for one with less informative relatives. Should we take that into account when searching the database? Should we compensate for the fact that the search yields less strong evidence for some missing persons, by lowering the likelihood ratio threshold for those? It is clear that if we use the same threshold for the whole database, some missing persons have a higher probability to be identified than others. So if we want to have the same probability of identification, no matter of what type the relatives are, we have to use different thresholds for each type.

In [110] this problem was discussed in the familial searching context for the database of California. This database, at the time of writing, contained individuals for whom 15 loci are typed, and others for whom 13 out of these 15 are typed. The authors attempted to correct for the missing information in the less informative part, by plugging in values for the two missing loci that are expected given relatedness, which they call enhancing the profiles. The authors note that with a threshold applied to all profiles (the enhanced 13-locus profiles and the 15-locus profiles) "it was seen that inclusions of enhanced 13-locus relatives improved but coincided with decreased inclusions of relatives with full 15-locus profiles. This was the unavoidable consequence of also increasing the likelihood ratios of unrelated offenders with 13-locus profiles."

This observation is, in fact, predicted by the Neyman–Pearson lemma. With the construction as we described it, one uses a single threshold on the database, but not on the likelihood ratio of the data it contains. The 13-locus profiles are all augmented with the same values for the last two loci, which amounts to multiplying the likelihood ratio on the 13-locus profiles with a fixed number t_0. The threshold t

that is subsequently applied therefore really is a pair of likelihood ratio thresholds: on the 13-locus profiles it is t/t_0 and on the 15-locus profiles it is t.

From the Neyman–Pearson lemma it follows that as long as the the inhomogeneity of the database is independent of the hypotheses of interest, the number of loci typed is irrelevant, and we should treat all profiles on the same footing only considering the likelihood ratio they yield. We explain now how this conclusion follows.

We consider a search in a database, where most (perhaps all) of the database members are unrelated to the profile g_C of person C we search with. The (possibly) remaining individuals are related to C, and we consider that if they are related, the relatedness is as stated by the first hypothesis of the likelihood ratio we calculate. In reality of course there may be relatives of several types (parents, siblings, uncles, cousins, etc.) in the database, but if we find such individuals in addition to those we search for, the search is also successful. Therefore we do not overestimate our success rates by ignoring that there may be other relatives than we search for.

Hence, we view the database as a series of items, where each database item is either a profile of an appropriate relative, or from an unrelated person, independently of each other. In reality, again, this is not precisely the case, as there is a limit on how many items can come from the first hypothesis. This is a slight deviation from the Neyman–Pearson setting, which means that it may be possible to obtain results slightly outside of its stated optimality, and we will go into that matter in Chapter 12. For now, we consider the database items to be independent realizations of profiles, either of relatives or of unrelated individuals.

To model the heterogeneity we decompose the database into $\mathcal{D} = \cup_i \mathcal{D}_i$, a disjoint union, such that for the persons in part $\mathcal{D}_i$ their profile in the database consists of their genotypes on the loci in the set $\mathcal{L}_i$. Suppose now that we know the profile g_C of person C we wish to identify. If this profile is obtained on the set of loci $\mathcal{L}_C$, then likelihood ratio calculations for relatedness between a person in $\mathcal{D}_i$ and C need only be done on the loci in $\mathcal{L}_i \cap \mathcal{L}_C$ since the other loci are not informative about the relationship in question.

According to the Neyman–Pearson lemma, if we search $\mathcal{D}_i$ with a likelihood ratio threshold t_i, then the error rates α_i, β_i on $\mathcal{D}_i$ are optimal on that part: on each part alone, a larger power cannot be obtained with the same (or smaller) significance level.

On the whole database $\mathcal{D}$, the evidence obtained consists for each person of two parts: the set of loci this person's profile is determined on, and the actual profile on that set.

Suppose we observe for a databased person the data $(\mathcal{L}, g)$, denoting that we have a profile g on the set $\mathcal{L}$ of loci. Using somewhat informal notation, we write the likelihood ratio of these data as

$$LR(\mathcal{L}, g \mid g_C) = \frac{P(\mathcal{L}, g \mid H_1, g_C)}{P(\mathcal{L}, g \mid H_2, g_C)} = \frac{P(\mathcal{L} \mid H_1, g_C)}{P(\mathcal{L} \mid H_2, g_C)} \times \frac{P(g \mid \mathcal{L}, H_1, g_C)}{P(g \mid \mathcal{L}, H_2, g_C)}. \quad (10.7)$$

If we now make the assumption that the set $\mathcal{L}$ of loci that are typed does in no way depend on H_1 or H_2 being true, then the first factor on the right-hand side is equal to 1, and only the last term

$$LR(g \mid g_C) = \frac{P(g \mid \mathcal{L}, H_1, g_C)}{P(g \mid \mathcal{L}, H_2, g_C)} = \frac{P(g \mid H_1, g_C)}{P(g \mid H_2, g_C)} \quad (10.8)$$

remains.

The Neyman–Pearson lemma tells us that optimal error rates are obtained if we base our decision on a threshold of the likelihood ratio of the pair $(\mathcal{L}, g)$, but since $\mathcal{L}$ is not informative for the hypotheses, it follows that we need only compute $LR(g \mid g_C)$. If this likelihood ratio exceeds a certain threshold, then we choose for one action, and if it does not, we choose for the other. Hence we should treat all profiles in the database on the same footing, and we should act in precisely the same way, independently of the set of loci the likelihood ratio is obtained on. In reaching this conclusion, it is of course crucial that the set of typed loci does not depend on whether H_1 or H_2 is true. We expect that this assumption is reasonable: it amounts to assuming that knowing the loci $\mathcal{L}$ a database member is typed on, without knowing the profile itself, is not informative for the question whether or not this person is a relative. Although there might be a little information in the set $\mathcal{L}$, indicating a period in time when this profile was obtained, in turn indicating the possible age of the databased person, in turn influencing the a priori probabilities of relatedness given an estimate of the age of C, it seems safe to say that this an effect we might almost always simply ignore.

Any likelihood ratio threshold now corresponds to a certain α and β, which are weighted averages of the corresponding quantities in each of the $\mathcal{D}_i$. Indeed in the obvious notation we have

$$\alpha(t) := P(LR(g \mid g_C) \le t \mid H_1)$$

$$= \sum_i P(LR(g \mid g_C) \le t \mid H_1, \mathcal{L}_i) P(\mathcal{L}_i \mid H_1)$$

$$= \sum_i \alpha_i(t) \pi_i,$$

where $\pi_i = |\mathcal{D}_i|/|\mathcal{D}|$ is the fraction of the profiles in $\mathcal{D}$ with loci $\mathcal{L}_i$, assuming (again) that $P(\mathcal{L}_i \mid H_1) = \pi_i$, and similarly for H_2, and where we write $\alpha_i(t) := P(LR(g \mid g_C) \leq t \mid H_1, \mathcal{L}_i)$ for the significance level on $\mathcal{D}_i$ corresponding to the threshold t.

Now suppose we use different thresholds t_i on the different $\mathcal{D}_i$. This will give certain error rates $\alpha = \sum \alpha_i(t_i)\pi_i$ and $\beta = \sum \beta_i(t_i)\pi_i$. The Neyman–Pearson lemma now says that if we would have taken a single likelihood ratio threshold t that gives the same $\alpha(t) = \alpha$, we have $\beta(t) \leq \beta$. Thus, with a threshold t applied to all profiles, we get optimal ratios of how many unrelated individuals are selected per related individual. Searching with a lower threshold in a less informative part is necessary if we want to secure a higher probability of finding relatives it contains, but we will also find more unrelated individuals, and (provided relatives are equally likely to occur in each part) doing so leads to, on average, more work per identification.

Thus, a threshold t_i leads to optimal searches on the parts of $\mathcal{D}_i$ in isolation, but not on $\mathcal{D}$ as a whole. What, now, about a sequence of searches aiming to identify person $C_1, C_2, \ldots$? So far, we have worked conditional on g_C, that is, considering the profile g_C as fixed. The conclusion is that for a given case, any likelihood ratio threshold yields optimal error rates on the database. If we have several profiles $g_{C_1}, g_{C_2}, \ldots$, we are likewise interested in a strategy that allows for as many identifications of persons C_i at the expense of also investigating as few unrelated individuals as possible. Now, we can make a similar argument: if we apply threshold t_{C_i} for the identification of C_i, then we get α_{C_i} and β_{C_i} that tell us how likely relatives and unrelated individuals are to exceed threshold t_{C_i}. If we assume that all C_i are equally likely to have relatives in $\mathcal{D}$, then, by reasoning analogously to what we did for the inhomogeneous database above, we see that optimal error rates are obtained if we take all t_{C_i} equal to the same t. We conclude that a case-independent likelihood ratio threshold gives optimal error rates, provided the heterogeneity on its own carries no information for identification, and that all unknown persons we wish to identify are a priori equally likely to have relatives in $\mathcal{D}$.

The crucial assumption to arrive at a uniform threshold that evaluates the genetic evidence on a heterogeneous database, is that the part of the database that the profile belongs to is in itself no indication for which hypothesis is true. One can imagine situations in which this condition is violated, and then we need to take that into account. We illustrate this with an example.

Suppose that an unidentified person with profile g_C is found in country A, and that one tries to identify this person by searching the missing persons database of country A, as well as the one from neighboring country B. A missing persons database is very inhomogeneous in the sense that for each missing person different genetic information is available. For instance, for missing person 1 we have the DNA profile of two brothers, whereas for missing person 2 we have a profile of his or her parents.

Obviously many other types of genetic information are possible. Analogously to the previous example, we now consider the genetic information g_C of the unidentified victim C as given and fixed, and we can interpret the union of the databases in countries A and B as one big inhomogeneous database. For the ith missing person MP_i in that large database we have a triplet of information (C_i, ped_i, g_{ped_i}): the label C_i of the country (A or B), the pedigree structure, and the genetic data in the pedigree.

For instance, we observe that for a certain missing person (1) the person is from country A, (2) we have genetic information from a parent of the person, and (3) we have the specific genetic information of that parent.

The analogue of (10.7) now is

$$LR(x, ped, g_{ped} \mid g_C) = \frac{P(x, ped, g_{ped} \mid H_1, g_C)}{P(x, ped, g_{ped} \mid H_2, g_C)}$$

$$= \frac{P(x \mid H_1, g_C)}{P(x \mid H_2, g_C)} \frac{P(ped \mid H_1, x, g_C)}{P(ped \mid H_2, x, g_C)} \tag{10.9}$$

$$\times \frac{P(g_{ped} \mid H_1, x, ped, g_C)}{P(g_{ped} \mid H_2, x, ped, g_C)}. \tag{10.10}$$

We (assume that we) can remove the label x in the two conditional probabilities in the last factor, which is the likelihood ratio of the genetic data. The first factor $P(x \mid H_1, g)/P(x \mid H_2, g) = P(x \mid H_1)/P(x \mid H_2)$ in (10.9) need not be equal to 1 now. If the unidentified person is found in country A then under H_1 we would give a larger probability to have country label A than under H_2. The second factor in (10.9) needs an assignment of how likely it is that we have pedigree ped and country label x under H_1 and H_2, so we need to ask ourselves the question whether we think that, if our unidentified person is a certain missing person from country x, it is more likely that this missing person will have relatives in pedigree $\mathcal{P}$ taken into the missing persons database than if our unidentified person is not related to this missing person. Again, this likelihood ratio need not be equal to 1. For example, if we know that the unidentified person is a highly aged person, then it may be unlikely that this person's parents are in the missing persons database, compared to when the unidentified person is known to be a child.

Let us now, for the sake of argument, assume that this factor is equal to 1, so that $LR(x, ped, g_{ped} \mid g_C)$ is equal to the genetic likelihood ratio, multiplied with the likelihood ratio that label x provides. If the fraction of profiles with label A in the overall database is π_A we set $P(A \mid H_2) = \pi_A$. Let us further assume that $P(A \mid H_1) = 0.9$ reflecting that we think the probability that the unidentified person is from country A is 0.9. If $\pi_A = 0.6$ this means that $LR(A \mid g_C) = 0.9/0.6 = 1.5$ and $LR(B \mid g_C) = 0.1/0.4 = 0.25$.

We then find from (10.9) that

$$LR(A, ped, g_{ped} \mid g_C) = 1.5 \frac{P(g_{ped} \mid H_1, ped, g_C)}{P(g_{ped} \mid H_2, ped, g_C)}$$

and similarly,

$$LR(B, ped, g_{ped} \mid g_C) = 0.25 \frac{P(g_{ped} \mid H_1, ped, g_C)}{P(g_{ped} \mid H_2, ped, g_C)}.$$

For optimal error rates, we use likelihood ratio threshold t on the whole database. It follows from the above expressions that the genetic information of the profiles with label B should be treated differently from that with label A. To be specific, if the thresholds for genetic information when A is observed is denoted t_A and t_B is defined similarly, we learn from the last two expressions that $t_B = 6t_A$. Since the unidentified person was found in country A, and we therefore assign higher probability to identify this person as a missing person in country A than in country B, we need stronger genetic evidence for missing persons from country B to take action than for missing persons from country A.

10.3 Bayesian Decision Theory

So far we have discussed how decisions on the hypotheses can be taken on the basis of the likelihood ratio, and how decisions taken by a black box procedure can be given an evidential value.

With prior probabilities $P(H_1)$ and $P(H_2)$ at our disposal, we can use Bayes' rule to obtain posterior odds and we are then, for these odds, not concerned with error rates. These error rates come into play again if we want to define a decision making procedure, and in this section we consider a procedure that takes the consequences of a wrong decision into account. The consequences of one error (say, declaring non-paternity when there in fact is) may be considered less bad, or worse, than those of the other type (declaring paternity when this is not the case). This may depend on the context of the case: in an immigration context where persons claim to be related, what is at stake for the tested individuals is different than in a paternity case for a pregnancy following a rape.

In many cases it may be possible to choose for a third option, namely gathering more data and delaying the decision until the additional data have also been evaluated. In a paternity case this step would be the typing of additional DNA loci, for example.

Delaying a decision comes with a price as well, and it is only to be considered reasonable if its cost is smaller than that of a wrong decision of either type. Therefore let us fix the cost of delaying the decision to be 1, and let $1 + c_i$ be the cost incurred when H_i is true but the wrong decision is taken. We assume that $c_i > 0$, reflecting that delaying a decision is less costly than an error of either type. We also assume that taking the correct decision has no costs.

Given the posterior probabilities $P(H_i \mid E)$, taking decision A_1 has expected cost $P(H_2 \mid E)(1 + c_2)$: it is only when H_2 is true that there is a cost. Similarly taking decision A_2 has expected cost $P(H_1 \mid E)(1 + c_1)$, and of course delaying the decision has a cost of 1.

Let us now see when we would choose for A_1. We would choose for A_1 if the expected cost of taking that decision is smaller than the expected costs of both A_2 and delaying a decision. In other words, we need to have $P(H_2 \mid E)(1 + c_2) \leq P(H_1 \mid E)(1 + c_1)$ and also $P(H_2 \mid E)(1 + c_2) \leq 1$. The first condition is equivalent to

$$\frac{P(H_1 \mid E)}{P(H_2 \mid E)} \geq \frac{1 + c_2}{1 + c_1},$$

and the second to the posterior odds being at least c_2. Thus we choose A_1 if the posterior odds are at least $\max\{(1 + c_2)/(1 + c_1), c_2\}$. Similarly we choose A_2 if the posterior odds are at most $\min\{(1 + c_2)/(1 + c_1), 1/c_1\}$.

In the remaining cases, we choose A_0 which denotes the delayed decision. Now, it is easy to see that $\max\{(1 + c_2)/(1 + c_1), c_2\}$ is equal to c_2 if $c_1 c_2 \geq 1$ and to $(1 + c_2)/(1 + c_1)$ otherwise. Similarly, $\min\{(1 + c_2)/(1 + c_1), 1/c_1\}$ is equal to $1/c_1$ if $c_1 c_2 \geq 1$ and otherwise it is $(1 + c_2)/(1 + c_1)$. If $c_1 c_2 = 1$, then all three numbers $(1 + c_2)/(1 + c_1)$, c_2, and $1/c_1$ coincide.

Thus, if $c_1 c_2 \leq 1$ we will never decide for A_0: the costs c_1 and c_2 are both too small. But if $c_1 c_2 > 1$, meaning that at least one error is considered to be serious, then there is a region where we decide A_0, namely if the posterior odds are between $1/c_1$ and c_2. This seems to be a reasonable outcome. Indeed, if the posterior odds are large enough, we choose A_1, where "large enough" is with respect to the cost c_2 of taking decision A_1 if H_2 is actually true. Entirely similarly, we choose A_2 if the likelihood ratio in favor of H_2 is large enough, where "large enough" now is measured with respect to the error of the other type. If the posterior odds are not large enough in either direction, we delay our decision until we have gathered and evaluated more data, and come to an inconclusive result for now.

The impact of new data can also be assessed with this machinery if we know what to expect from these data. More precisely, suppose that we denote the present evidence by E and that we set out to gather new evidence E^*. Let us, as usual, denote the likelihood ratio of the new data E^* by $LR(E^* \mid E)$, expressing the fact that we already have seen data E before observing E^*.

Let

$$\alpha(t) := P(LR(E^* \mid E) < t \mid H_1)$$

and

$$\beta(t) := P(LR(E^* \mid E) > t \mid H_2)$$

represent the probability distributions of the likelihood ratio for the new evidence E^*, given the present evidence E under H_1 and H_2 respectively. What is now the expected cost after acquiring E^*? Our present assessment is that H_i is true with probability $P(H_i \mid E)$. If H_1 is true, then we will have costs after having acquired E^* in two cases. If the new posterior odds $P(H_1 \mid E, E^*)/P(H_2 \mid E, E^*) < 1/c_1$ we will choose A_2 and incur cost $1 + c_1$, and if they are between $1/c_1$ and c_2 we will again make decision A_0, delaying again a decision, and incur a cost of 1. Putting this together, we claim that the expected cost of a decision if H_1 is true, is equal to the sum of

$$P\left(LR(E^* \mid E) < c_2 \frac{P(H_2 \mid E)}{P(H_1 \mid E)} \mid H_1\right)$$

and

$$c_1 P\left(LR(E^* \mid E) < \frac{1}{c_1} \frac{P(H_2 \mid E)}{P(H_1 \mid E)} \mid H_1\right).$$

Indeed, since the posterior odds are obtained by multiplying the likelihood ratio with the prior odds, the posterior odds being smaller than a number c is equivalent to the likelihood ratio being smaller than c divided by the prior odds. This expression reduces to

$$\alpha\left(c_2 \frac{P(H_2 \mid E)}{P(H_1 \mid E)}\right) + c_1 \alpha\left(\frac{1}{c_1} \frac{P(H_2 \mid E)}{P(H_1 \mid E)}\right).$$

For H_2 we can make a similar computation. Taking these together, we conclude that the expected cost of a decision, after acquiring E^*, is equal to

$$
\begin{aligned}
&P(H_1 \mid E) \left(\alpha\left(c_2 \frac{P(H_2 \mid E)}{P(H_1 \mid E)}\right) + c_1 \alpha\left(\frac{1}{c_1} \frac{P(H_2 \mid E)}{P(H_1 \mid E)}\right)\right) \\
&+ P(H_2 \mid E) \left(c_2 \beta\left(c_2 \frac{P(H_2 \mid E)}{P(H_1 \mid E)}\right) + \beta\left(\frac{1}{c_1} \frac{P(H_2 \mid E)}{P(H_1 \mid E)}\right)\right).
\end{aligned}
\tag{10.11}
$$

The expected cost is a function of the current posterior odds $P(H_1 \mid E)/P(H_2 \mid E)$, the costs c_i, and the likelihood ratio distributions of the data that is to be gathered, as expressed by the distribution functions $\alpha(\cdot)$ and $\beta(\cdot)$.

In the case where several possibilities for E^* are considered, we can use (10.11) to choose the type of additional evidence to gather that corresponds to the lowest cost in expectation. For example, when investigating kinship where linkage affects the likelihoods, we may choose linked or unlinked loci. Linked loci can provide stronger evidence in favor of relatedness than an equal set of loci that are independent, but weaker evidence in favor of unrelatedness. If H_1 is considered likely to be true, we may choose linked DNA loci to confirm this, but if H_2 is considered more likely based on E, we would rather choose independent loci.

This approach is an elegant and powerful one, but it also requires more, namely the specification of the costs c_i. These represent the gravity of making a wrong decision, and it seems difficult to attach a number to those consequences.

One could choose to work without priors and aim simply for the report of a likelihood ratio that is sufficiently strong in one direction or another. A laboratory, however, is sometimes expected by law to report a posterior probability (for instance, in paternity cases, see below), which effectively means that the laboratory has no other choice than to use prior probabilities. Traditionally, in paternity cases equal prior probabilities are assigned to the hypotheses of paternity and unrelatedness so that the likelihood ratio coincides with the posterior odds. Suppose that posterior odds of 10,000 are required, then c_2 can be defined as 10,000. For the lower bound c_1 that determines when we find the evidence strong enough to conclude non-paternity, no natural bound arises from the legal obligations. One could argue that a uniform prior on paternity also implies that one is equally easily led to a decision in both directions, and then we would set $c_1 = 10,000$ as well.

In that case (10.11) simplifies to, using $c_1 = c_2 = c$ and a uniform prior probability,

$$\frac{LR(E)}{LR(E)+1}\left(\alpha\left(\frac{c}{LR(E)}\right) + c\alpha\left(\frac{1}{cLR(E)}\right)\right)$$
$$+ \frac{1}{LR(E)+1}\left(c\beta\left(\frac{c}{LR(E)}\right) + \beta\left(\frac{1}{cLR(E)}\right)\right),$$

where we use that uniform priors $P(H_i) = 1/2$ imply that

$$P(H_1 \mid E) = LR(E)/(LR(E)+1).$$

This expression now only involves the likelihood ratio distributions for E^*, the already obtained likelihood ratio $LR(E)$ and the bounds c to be achieved.

10.4 Evidence and Decision in a Legal Context

In this chapter, we have so far discussed decision making from a statistical point of view, either working with priors (obtaining posterior probabilities pertaining to the case at hand) or without (obtaining error rates but losing control over the posterior probabilities). Let us now consider to what extent these considerations are compatible with similar ones in legal reasoning.

First we can compare the notions of error. From a legal point of view, a legal decision may be perceived as wrong if its conclusions turn out to not be what happened in reality. If a person who is convicted later turns out to be innocent, the initial conviction is often considered to be a miscarriage of justice.

Statistically, we would consider the initial conviction to be potentially erroneous when the evidence was not fairly judged, e.g., if a likelihood ratio was computed with a statistical model that is biased and not carrying out a proper probabilistic assessment. All cases where the decision would reasonably have been different with a proper evaluation would then count as cases with errors. But if the evidence was, at the time, properly evaluated and put into context, then there may be unfortunate cases where there is enough evidence to convict an innocent person or not enough to convict a guilty one. Of course one should strive to minimize the occurrence of these events and put a system in place where a fair re-evaluation is possible if it is suspected later that an innocent person has been convicted. But even if this has happened, it does not necessarily mean that errors have been made.

The application of likelihood ratios and Bayes' rule in a legal context is not straightforward, for many reasons. One such reason was already mentioned in Section 1.5. When the law dictates that a conviction should only be based on evidence in the case, then this seems to leave no room for prior probabilities, which by their very definition, *precede* the evidence. But if we are to make a probabilistic assessment, the likelihood ratio only says how our probabilities change relative to each other, and we need prior probabilities as well to arrive at posteriors. A formulation of priors should not violate the presumption of innocence, and it is the object of debate how to do so. On the other hand, if a decision has to be taken on the basis of evidence itself, this is possible but then one cannot say much about posterior probabilities any more, as we have explained above.

It seems intuitive that the minimum evidence needed for a conviction should be stronger in a case where the consequences of an erroneous conviction are more severe, e.g., that one should avoid more strongly to convict someone to several years of imprisonment for a murder that he or she did not commit, compared to, say giving a fine for shoplifting. One can wonder how this criterion can be translated to specific requirements for the evidence. On the one hand, we can translate the requirement to having another bound that is needed for the posterior probability of the guilt scenario in order to convict. On the other hand, we can translate it into a case-dependent bound on the p-value telling how often evidence of minimally the strength in the case at hand is expected to happen for innocent suspects. The first approach translates into a bound on the likelihood ratio, which then needs to be higher in order to convict for cases where there is more at stake for the defendant, if the prior odds in those cases are the same. The second approach translates into different bounds for how often one accepts the conviction of an innocent suspect in cases such as the one at hand, requiring this probability to be smaller for more severe cases. While this seems like a sensible approach at first sight, one may then encounter situations where the p-value is small and yet the evidence favor the innocence hypothesis, as we saw in Chapter 9. Therefore, we concluded that the likelihood ratio itself should be the basis of a decision, whether or not prior probabilities are used.

In Section 5.7.2 we have discussed a case in which the court summarized some indirect background information and evidence into something that we recognized as prior odds, upon which the direct evidence in the form of DNA evidence was computed with a likelihood ratio. Whether or not this procedure is legally acceptable we are not to judge, but we have noted that not all legal scholars and practitioners have the same opinion on the matter. From a statistical point of view, the procedure seems to make sense.

There are legal situations in which the law explicitly requires a posterior probability. For example this is so in the Netherlands, where applicants of family reunification may be asked to provide DNA evidence if there is no documentation available confirming the relationships. The law then asks the investigating institute to report a posterior probability which forces it to use a prior. Routinely, priors giving equal probability to the claimed relationship and no relationship are used. Such priors can hardly be viewed as a summary of our epistemic uncertainty. As a result, effectively decisions are taken on the basis of a likelihood ratio threshold, even if by appearance they seem to be based on posterior probabilities.

A related and challenging question is how we should value and incorporate so-called *naked statistics* in our evidential assessment. By naked statistics we mean contextual frequency statistics that do not directly relate to a case at hand. We have already seen an example of this type, namely in (10.2), where the likelihood ratio was expressed in terms of error rates.

Are naked statistics allowed when one assesses the strength of the evidence in a specific court case? Let us give an example. It has been noticed that when a married woman is killed in the Netherlands, in about 52% of the cases the husband turned out to be the killer (see [115], in Dutch). This is a general, naked statistic. Clearly it is relevant for investigating authorities: if a married woman is murdered, they are well advised to investigate her husband. But can, or should, we use this statistic as the prior probability for a man to be the murderer of his wife in court, if she is murdered and he is accused?

This seems problematic, because the naked statistic is not directly related the case at hand. It is a frequentistic number obtained from other cases that have a certain similarity, but it is unclear if and how it should be used in an evidential way as if it pertains to this case. It has been argued (e.g., see [173]) that a conviction based on naked statistics is unacceptable, since it conflicts with the autonomy and individuality of the suspect. Precisely his autonomy, the capability to act differently from others, is completely ignored when we concentrate on naked statistics. The husband of the murdered woman will claim that it is utterly irrelevant for the present case at hand, that other husbands have murdered their wives. The only thing that matters is *his* behavior.

This is a strong argument, but it has been contested, for instance in [130]. Few people will deny that a witness statement (like the one in the burglary case in Section 5.7.2) is case-specific. Nevertheless, when we ask ourselves how we should value a witness statement, then one might suggest to take naked statistics into account about the general reliability of witnesses. It might be reasonably well known how often, generally speaking, witnesses are reliable, and this might be taken into account when evaluating the evidential value of a witness statement. This, then, seems to suggest that also a case-specific piece of evidence cannot always be properly interpreted or used without using naked statistics, and it, ultimately, begs the question whether or not naked statistics can be avoided.

This is an interesting argument, and we do not claim that we have the full answer to concerns of this type. But we notice two things which we think are relevant in thinking about these issues. First of all, in the case of the naked statistics around the killed wives, ignoring this statistic would remove *all* evidential value about the husband being the murderer. If we are not allowed to use this statistic, then the fact that most murdered wives are killed by their husbands, is utterly unimportant for any specific case at hand. If, on the other hand, we remove the reference to the naked statistics around the witness statement, then the witness statement itself remains. The fact that the witness statement remains, even if we do not know how to quantitatively assess it, means that this piece of evidence is of a different nature than the statistics about husbands killing their wives.

Second, what is at stake in a specific trial, is not the evaluation of an "average" witness. It is a *specific* witness, and the judge has to assess the reliability of this particular witness. It is clear, we think, that simply plugging in a general statistic about the reliability of witnesses is not reasonable, and that instead, any judgment on the reliability of the witness should involve arguments pertaining to this specific witness as well. If we use general reliability figures we essentially treat the witness as random. But we also know that witness reliability can be variable, so if our final judgment would rely on the witness statement, then we need to further motivate our reasons to find this particular witness credible or not. The argument that witness statements can only be assessed using naked statistics seems difficult to defend.

In general, if there is missing knowledge in a court case, then it does not seem satisfactory to substitute general knowledge for this especially if it is of importance for the decision we reach.

We already mentioned in Section 1.5 that probability theory is not optimally equipped to deal with missing information. In certain circumstances so-called belief functions are more suitable. We discuss these in Chapter 13.

10.5 Summary and Conclusions

In this chapter we have discussed the theory around taking decisions based on likelihood ratios. We first discussed the classical theory of Neyman–Pearson, to the effect that if the rejection region of a test corresponds to a likelihood ratio threshold, then there can be no other test procedure with the same or smaller significance level that has more power. We noted the fact that the decision itself has evidential value, without knowing on what data the decision was based. Without priors, we cannot make any statement about the probability that a taken decision was correct, but in the presence of prior probabilities for the relevant hypotheses, we can.

We have applied the theory to a number of forensic examples. We showed that in a inhomogeneous database, with different loci typed for different members, we should base a decision on the genetic information only, and not on the number of loci typed. This perhaps somewhat surprising result is only true if the number of loci typed does not depend on whether H_1 or H_2 is true. We also discussed a forensic situation where this latter assumption is violated, namely one where we consider a database of missing persons in two countries. In that situation, one can still use the Neyman–Pearson result for the overall likelihood ratio, but in this case this will lead to different strategies for the two countries. We also gave an example in which the rejection region of a significance test consists of all outcomes that are least likely under the null hypothesis, but where this seemingly reasonable choice leads to suboptimal decision procedures.

Next we discussed and applied Bayesian decision theory where decisions involve certain costs, and where the actual decision is based on minimizing such costs. Although elegant and powerful, this approach requires specification of costs and this may certainly not always be feasible or realistic in legal cases.

Finally we have reflected on the way statistics and legal science fundamentally differ, and how this affects their interaction. From a legal point of view, a legal decision is wrong if its conclusions as to what happened do not correspond to what really happened. Statistically a decision is wrong if the evidential value is over- or understated, which in itself has nothing to do with what really happened.

10.6 Bibliographical Notes

We already gave a number of references in the text. The theory of Neyman–Pearson is standard and classical and can be found in any introductory textbook on mathematical statistics. Richard Royall [129] discusses the evidential value of a decision. In Section 10.3 we have largely followed the exposition in [162]. The error rates of decision rules based on both the number of shared alleles and the likelihood ratio for various kinship likelihood ratios have been investigated in [69]. In [7], it was shown that the error rates can be improved upon by rejection regions defined by the likelihood ratio alone, in agreement with the Neyman–Pearson lemma. Suitable references for the problem of "naked statistics" are the classics [35], [113], and [173]. For discussion on the admissibility of statistical evidence and the discrepancy between legal and statistical evidence, we refer to [117] and [149]. A very interesting discussion focused on establishing prior probabilities needed for the posterior probabilities for DNA database matches to be with the trace donors can be found in [4]. Discussion about the question whether high posterior probability of guilt warrants conviction can be found in [15] and [149]. For the distinction between frequentist and Bayesian statistics, see for instance [45].

11

The Interpretation of DNA Database Matches

So far we have mainly discussed the evaluation of evidence in the light of hypotheses, without discussing where that evidence came from or why the hypotheses were defined as they were. In this chapter we discuss a particular and important kind of evidence, namely evidence generated by database searches. If a database search is conducted, this is often (but not always) done without having specific prior interest in any individual whose data are stored in a database. In that case, an individual becomes interesting only after the search, for example if a person turns out to provide a match with a crime scene DNA sample. The hypotheses that are then subsequently considered, namely whether or not that person is the source of the trace, become of interest after the search result, and by construction this leads to a likelihood ratio in favor of that hypothesis.

In the forensic literature there has been a fierce discussion as to what the evidential value of such a database match is. Is the evidence stronger compared to a situation in which only one person is typed and found to match?

In this chapter we provide a full mathematical and interpretative treatment of unique database matches. We deviate here from our habit of postponing bibliographical notes to the end of the chapter. The reason for this is that the discussion about the so-called database controversy cannot be satisfactorily described without including the historical course of events. To see what is at stake, we now first describe this database controversy.

11.1 The Database Controversy

The debate about database matches reached its peak around the beginning of this century [6, 10, 51, 102, 103, 124, 125, 151]. The controversy circled around the question whether or not a unique match of a trace profile in a DNA database constitutes weaker or stronger evidence compared to a scenario in which only one suspect is typed and found to match. When we compare a database search to such a scenario, there are two opposite effects. On the one hand the database search could give rise to coincidental matches, but on the other hand the search result also excludes a number of potential candidates to be the donor of the crime trace. So on the one hand, it could be felt that some correction ought to be put in place to account for the fact that many comparisons are done, but on the other hand, it can also be argued that the database result gives more evidence against the matching individual than if he or she had been the only person that was compared. The fact that other persons can no longer be the source of the trace is also to some extent evidence against the matching suspect.

Initially, a report of the National Research Council [124] advised to circumvent this perceived problem by simply not taking the match into account as evidence in court, and to only use it to be able to define the matching individual to be a suspect. Additional DNA testing would then supply evidence that can be subjected to a probabilistic assessment yielding a statistic (random match probability or like-lihood ratio) to be used in court.

Clearly, this is not an optimal solution. For one thing, it could very well be the case that the same single match would also have been obtained if fewer loci had been used in the search. Therefore, exactly which loci can be used as evidence depends on the database search settings, even if all data are precisely the same. From a practical point of view, in some cases it means that no DNA evidence can be used, for example if there is no trace material left to analyze for further DNA typing.

Several publications subsequently appeared concerning the issue of database matches. In [37] the use of likelihood ratios was advocated because of their opti-mality in (frequentist) decision making, but a so-called "Bonferroni correction" was proposed for the match probability. If we assume for the moment that each profile in the database matches with the trace profile with probability p, the correction was proposed to be $1 - (1 - p)^n$. It represents the probability of having at least one match by chance in a database of size n, and is about np for $np \ll 1$.

Other authors, using likelihood ratios as well, but subsequently applying Bayes' rule to obtain probabilistic assessments on hypotheses concerned with the guilt or innocence of the suspect, claimed that a database search yields stronger DNA evidence against the suspect than a single comparison would. For example, [9] argues against the frequentist hypothesis testing framework for the evaluation of DNA evidence in general. For database searches it notes that "In a wide range of settings, the DNA evidence is slightly stronger when it is obtained after a search," explaining that the intuition behind that result is the fact that the search excludes other individuals as trace donors. In [10] this point of view is further elaborated.

In 1996, a second report of the National Research Council in the United States [125] appeared, which aligned with the frequentist intuition. The report stated that

"If the only reason that the person becomes a suspect is that his DNA profile turned up in a database, the calculations must be modified," where the calculation that was referred to is the calculation of the random match probability (that is, the inverse of the likelihood ratio). It was recommended (Recommendation 5.1) to multiply the random match probability with the number n of persons in the database "to describe the impact of the DNA evidence under the hypothesis that the source of the evidence sample is someone in the database." Even though the hypothesis that someone in the database left the trace is explicitly mentioned, it is not immediately clear from the phrasing of the report whether the number $1/(np)$ was intended to play a role in a Bayesian analysis, or rather was intended as a frequentist instrument to correct for the number of hypotheses tested, such as the Bonferroni correction. The report also mentioned that this correction was proposed as suitable for databases that contain only a small fraction of the whole population and that, if this were not the case, a more complicated analysis would be required, without going into the details of what such an analysis should then be like.

This recommendation was criticized by many, because it goes against the Bayesian analysis that had previously been provided. To strengthen those arguments, absurd conclusions were derived assuming the evidence weakens in larger databases. One of the arguments put forward indeed was that if the database grows to the full population, clearly a unique match must identify the trace donor with certainty, whilst the evidential value as per NRC-II (ignoring that the report had explicitly stated the correction to be applicable only for relatively small databases) has the opposite effect because of the division by n.

In 1999, the NRC-II recommendation gained some statistical support when Stockmarr [151] provided a rationale for the evidential value of $1/(np)$. He showed that this is the likelihood ratio of a unique match when considering the hypotheses that the donor of the trace profile is in the database versus its negation.

Now that both $1/p$ and $1/(np)$ can appear as likelihood ratio, a controversy was born: which one should be used? It was rapidly argued by various authors [51, 102] that the choice of the hypotheses, and hence of the ensuing likelihood ratio, was *mathematically* unimportant in the sense that they lead to the same posterior odds. This last fact is understandable, since after finding a unique match, the hypothesis that the matching person is the trace donor is equivalent with the hypothesis that the donor is in the database. However, even if the choice of hypotheses is mathematically unimportant, it is another issue which likelihood ratio a forensic laboratory should *report*. Various authors have argued that only hypotheses involving the identified suspect are admissible. For example, in [51] it is argued that "Stockmarr makes a fundamental logical error when he suggests that the court can replace these hypotheses by H_p and H_d (hypotheses on the database containing the trace donor) and still use the resulting likelihood ratio as if it were directly relevant to the case against Smith (the identified suspect)." Similar arguments were used in [62] and [174] and more recently in [18].

In many jurisdictions, a forensic laboratory has the task to assess the strength of the evidence, and to communicate this to the investigating authorities or to fact finders such as judges or juries. It is our impression that a likelihood ratio of $1/p$ is usually chosen, although the German Stain Commission issued a recommendation in favor of reporting a likelihood ratio of $1/(np)$ in [131].

Meanwhile, the forensic databases have grown considerably, and millions of comparisons are routinely made with crime stain profiles. The difference between $1/p$ and $1/(np)$ can therefore, depending on p, be of significant importance. It is well known that likelihood ratios are often erroneously interpreted as odds on the hypotheses, a mistake that we have seen and is known as the prosecutor's fallacy. The implications of such a fallacy also depend on whether $1/p$ or $1/(np)$ is presented as the likelihood ratio.

It is therefore perhaps not a surprise that the debate is still ongoing. In fact not only the debate is still ongoing, but also more generally there is discussion as to which are the relevant probabilities that influence the evidential value or the prior/posterior odds on the hypotheses. One's intuition could lean more toward $1/p$ as most natural value for the evidential value or more towards $1/(np)$. Both values can be perceived as being natural.

In the literature most (if not all) explicit calculations have been made assuming some ad hoc model for the population and typically uniform prior distributions for the trace donor in the population and for the database as a subset from the population. The uniform prior has some appeal in the sense that it facilitates computations, but it often is not realistic, and care must be taken not to extend conclusions for the uniform prior case as conclusions for the general case.

We will explain in this chapter that in this particular situation the general case is actually the simplest one, and treating it in full generality makes it clear where the aforementioned problems appear and also how they can be approached. We will first derive a surprisingly simple formula for the posterior odds upon a unique match which is valid in *all* circumstances, irrespective of the question whether or not the suspect became suspect as a result of the match, or whether there was already interest in him or her. Although in most papers on this subject uniform prior odds are assumed, we deviate from this habit for the reasons given above. With our general formula, it becomes clear exactly which quantities are important for the calculation of posterior odds and likelihood ratios, and which are not.

In this chapter we will shed light on the controversy, by showing that proper modeling, understanding, and interpretation makes the controversy disappear. Both suggested likelihood ratios can be used, depending on the circumstances and on the question that was originally asked. In the ensuing sections we first develop the mathematical modeling of database searches, and in Section 11.7 we will explicitly address the criticism that the use of $1/(np)$ and $1/p$ as likelihood ratio has received. We will argue that none of these arguments are convincing.

11.2 Mathematical Modeling and the Basic Formula

We will consider the most general situation, because this will allow us to derive all further results as special cases, and because we believe it already sheds a lot of light on the problem. Consider a population $\mathcal{P}$ of individuals, and a DNA database $\mathcal{D} = \{d_1, \ldots, d_n\}$ of n DNA profiles of members of $\mathcal{P}$. We allow for the possibility of an inhomogeneous database, in the sense that there may be different loci typed for the different d_i. The reason for this inhomogeneity is that historically the DNA typing technology has advanced to give genetic information on more and more loci. Therefore, older profiles typed with previous technology may have data on fewer loci. Moreover, sometimes not all loci are successfully typed, so that for some profiles data on a few loci are missing.

Furthermore, there is a DNA profile g_C of a person $C \in \mathcal{P}$. The individual C is unknown to us, but we assume that we have prior probabilities $P(C = i)$, for all $i \in \mathcal{P}$. Typically g_C is retrieved from a crime scene, and C represents the unknown donor.

We will consider the case in which some d_i is the only profile in $\mathcal{D}$ that is indistinguishable from g_C. We say that in that case d_i is the only *match*, or rather, that d_i is the only *non-exclusion*. In particular we are interested in the evidential value of such a unique match in view of the hypotheses that the donor of d_i is the same as C or not. Two profiles match if they are the same on all *common* loci. In order to evaluate this evidential value, we need the probability of the match to happen by chance, by which we mean the probability that a randomly chosen person matches with g_C on all common loci of d_i and g_C. The fact that $\mathcal{D}$ is not homogeneous implies that these match probabilities of the profiles d_i are not all the same. We are aware of the fact that this might be counterintuitive, so we first briefly elaborate on this.

If a certain profile in $\mathcal{D}$ involves, say, 12 loci, then this profile matches if it agrees with g_C on these 12 loci (assuming that these loci are typed for g_C as well). If another profile consists of these 12 loci, plus two extra, then in order for this profile to match it must *in addition* also agree on the extra two loci. Hence, the probability that a randomly chosen individual, unrelated to C, matches with g_C on all loci that are typed for both g_C and d_i, is in general not the same for all i. This probability is called the *random match probability* (RMP) of profile d_i. When we increase the number of typed loci, the random match probability decreases.

We denote the RMP of d_i by p_i. At this point we have introduced the d_i, the p_i and the crime trace g_C. Which of these quantities are known to us, and which are not? This is an important question since the answer to it will direct our mathematical modeling of the situation. The answer to this question is different for different agents in the process. In principle, we can model the profiles $d_1, \ldots, d_n$ and the trace profile g_C all as being random, but various agents in the process may have knowledge about certain quantities, and hence they will condition on the outcomes. The administrator of the database, for instance, may have full knowledge of the profiles in it, so he or she might condition on the actual profiles in the database and work from there.

From the position of the investigating authorities, the situation is reversed. For them, the crime trace g_C is known, but the database profiles are not. Here we come across, once more, the epistemic and subjective character of probability in forensic science. Agents in different positions will have their own probabilistic assessments, based on the information or knowledge they have. In what follows, we place ourselves in the position of the investigating authorities, which is the most natural position for us. This means that we treat the profiles in the database as random, and that we will condition on the trace profile g_C.

In what follows, we describe the mathematical model, using the convention that upper case letters refer to random variables, whereas the corresponding lower case letters refer to realizations. We let G_C be a random profile, representing the profile found at the crime scene, assuming it is left by the criminal C. For each of the persons $i = 1, \ldots, n$, we let D_i be the random profiles in the database. In order to not complicate matters unnecessarily, we consider the collection of loci typed for D_i to be non-random.

For each $i = 1, \ldots, n$ we can write

$$G_C = (F_i, H_i),$$

where F_i denotes the profile of G_C restricted to the loci that are typed both for G_C and for D_i, and where H_i denotes the profile on the remaining loci.

Similarly we can write

$$D_i = (K_i, L_i),$$

where K_i is the profile of D_i restricted to the loci that are shared with G_C, and L_i the profile on the remaining loci. Note that F_i, H_i, K_i, and L_i are also random.

The investigating authorities now learn that $G_C = g_C$ and ask the database administrator whether or not the profile g_C has a match in $\mathcal{D}$. We are interested in the situation in which it is reported that there is a unique match with D_i. If that is the case, the investigating authorities know that the following event E_i occurs:

$$E_i := \{K_i = F_i \text{ and } K_j \neq F_j \text{ for all } j \neq i, G_C = g_C\}.$$

How does the occurrence of E_i affect the probability that $C = i$, assuming that we have prior probabilities $P(C = x)$ at our disposal, for all $x \in \mathcal{P}$?

One might perhaps think that in order to answer this question, we need a lot of additional modeling. After all, we do not know anything about the nature of the comparisons with d_j for $j \neq i$, that is, we have no knowledge about the random match probabilities of the members of $\mathcal{D}\backslash\{i\}$.

However, it suffices to have a prior probability $P(C = i)$, to know the random match probability p_i of individual i, and to have assessed the probability $P(C \in \mathcal{D})$ that the database contains C. Indeed, we claim that in that case, the posterior odds of $C = i$ versus $C \neq i$ are given by

$$\frac{P(C = i \mid E_i)}{P(C \neq i \mid E_i)} = \frac{1}{p_i} \frac{P(C = i)}{P(C \notin \mathcal{D})}. \tag{11.1}$$

To prove this, note that the left-hand side of (11.1) is equal to

$$\frac{P(C = i \mid E_i)}{P(C \notin \mathcal{D} \mid E_i)}, \tag{11.2}$$

since conditioned on E_i, the events $C \neq i$ and $C \notin \mathcal{D}$ are equivalent. It is, therefore, enough to show that the likelihood ratio of the evidence E_i for the hypotheses $C = i$ versus $C \notin \mathcal{D}$) is equal to $1/p_i$. Thus we compute

$$\frac{P(E_i \mid C = i)}{P(E_i \mid C \notin \mathcal{D})} = \frac{P(K_i = F_i \text{ and } K_j \neq F_j \text{ for all } j \neq i, G_C = g_C \mid C = i)}{P(K_i = F_i \text{ and } K_j \neq F_j \text{ for all } j \neq i, G_C = g_C \mid C \notin \mathcal{D})}$$

$$= \frac{P(K_j \neq F_j \text{ for all } j \neq i, G_C = g_C \mid C = i)}{P(K_j \neq F_j \text{ for all } j \neq i, G_C = g_C \mid C \notin \mathcal{D})}$$

$$\times \frac{P(K_i = F_i \mid K_j \neq F_j \text{ for all } j \neq i, G_C = g_C, C = i)}{P(K_i = F_i \mid K_j \neq F_j \text{ for all } j \neq i, G_C = g_C, C \notin \mathcal{D})}$$

$$= \frac{1}{P(K_i = F_i \mid K_j \neq F_j \text{ for all } j \neq i, G_C = g_C, C \notin \mathcal{D})}.$$

When the realization g_C is known, we can also know the outcomes of F_i and H_i, since we assumed that the loci typed for the database profiles are not random. Hence we can write $g_C = (f_i, h_i)$, and the last expression can be written as

$$\frac{1}{P(K_i = f_i \mid K_j \neq F_j \text{ for all } j \neq i, G_C = (f_i, h_i), C \notin \mathcal{D})}. \tag{11.3}$$

So far, we have not made any assumption about independence. If we assume that all profiles are independent of each other, then the last expression reduces to $1/P(K_i = f_i | G_C = (f_i, h_i), C \neq i)$ that is, the probability that the profiles D_i and G_C agree on the overlapping loci, conditioned on $G_C = g_C = (f_i, h_i)$ and on $C \neq i$. This proves (11.1), using Bayes' rule.

However, we note that according to (11.3), formally p_i must be calculated conditional on the event that the profile $G_C = g_C$ has been observed already, and on the information about the K_j for $j \neq i$. It would be rather tedious to incorporate the latter information, and in any case the effect would be essentially vanishing. Conditioning on $G_C = g_C$, however, should be taken into account. This is usually achieved with the standard θ-correction which we discussed in Section 7.5. The denominator of (11.3) is approximately equal to the RMP

$$P(K_i = f_i \mid G_C = (f_i, h_i), C \neq i),$$

and this expression then replaces p_i in (11.1). Similar remarks apply to similar formulas below, but we will not mention this anymore.

It is customary to denote the matching individual by S, standing for *suspect*, since providing a match with g_C of course usually leads to suspicion of being C. Once the unique match is there and the index i of the matching person is revealed, S is defined, and we can speak about the (prior) probability $P(S = C)$ that the uniquely matching person is C. Denoting by E_S the event that there is a unique match with the so found S, we can rewrite (11.1) as

$$\frac{P(C = S \mid E_S)}{P(C \neq S \mid E_S)} = \frac{1}{p_S} \frac{P(C = S)}{P(C \notin \mathcal{D})}, \tag{11.4}$$

and this is the form which we typically use.

Upon a unique match with an identified person S and knowing g_C, the quantities $P(C = S)$, $P(C \notin \mathcal{D})$, and p_S can be defined, and the right-hand side of (11.4) can be computed. The first two probabilities are prior probabilities of C being either S or not belonging to $\mathcal{D}$, and with the prior of C in hand these can be computed. The quantity p_S is just the random match probability of the found S, as explained above.

Before we continue, we take a moment to reflect on the three probabilities that determine the posterior odds on $C = S$. First of all, we need the random match probability p_S of S. This makes perfect sense: if the probability that S would be indistinguishable from C if S and C were different persons becomes smaller, the probability that $C = S$ becomes larger, all other circumstances being equal. We also observe that the *only* random match probability of relevance is the one with S. How likely it was beforehand that other members of $\mathcal{D}$ would be excluded is not important anymore, once S is the only non-excluded individual. We only need to know that all others are excluded, nothing else. Our notation, allowing for varying random match probabilities, makes this explicit, and the fact is easy to miss if we would assume that all random match probabilities would be the same.

Second, we need the prior probability that $C \in \mathcal{D}$, and this also makes sense. Indeed, the better the database is suited for our purpose, the larger the probability that if we find a single match, it is with the right person, all other circumstances being equal. Finally, we need the prior probability that $C = S$, and this is understandable as well: the stronger the case against S without the database result, the stronger the case will be with the database result, again of course assuming all other circumstances are equal.

We next draw attention to the fact that (11.4) is a completely general expression, applying whenever there is just a single person in the database who cannot be excluded as trace donor. In particular it is valid for database searches without having a prior specific suspicion against any database member, or for a search where there is already interest in the matching individual beforehand, or for a probable cause case where there is no one tested except S, which simply means that $\mathcal{D} = \{S\}$. The estimation or assignment of the relevant three probabilities on the right-hand side in (11.4) depends on the further context and will be different for each of the three scenarios that we just mentioned.

We stress the fact that some quantities that could perhaps be thought to be relevant for the posterior odds on $C = S$ do not explicitly enter into (11.4), such as the size of the (general or offender population) or the size of the database. These quantities will therefore only be interesting for us if we employ a model in which they are needed to estimate any of the probabilities in the right-hand side of (11.4), and in any case they are only of indirect relevance. Once the probabilities in (11.4) are known, the posterior odds are known as well, so in a different (offender) population with the same p_S, $P(C = S)$, and $P(C \in \mathcal{D})$, they would be the same even if $\mathcal{D}$ itself were different.

The posterior odds in (11.4) are not in the form of a likelihood ratio times prior odds for a hypothesis versus its negation, but in several ways we can rewrite it as such a product. First of all we may write

$$\frac{P(C = S \mid E_S)}{P(C \neq S \mid E_S)} = \frac{1}{p_S} \frac{P(C = S)}{P(C \notin \mathcal{D})} \frac{P(C \neq S)}{P(C \neq S)} = \frac{1}{p_S} \frac{1}{P(C \notin \mathcal{D} \mid C \neq S)} \frac{P(C = S)}{P(C \neq S)}.$$
(11.5)

Hence the likelihood ratio corresponding to $C = S$ versus $C \neq S$ is given by

$$\frac{1}{p_S} \frac{1}{P(C \notin \mathcal{D} \mid C \neq S)},$$
(11.6)

which is *at least* equal to $1/p_S$.

On the other hand, when we condition on E_S, the hypotheses $C \in \mathcal{D}$ and $S = C$ are equivalent. Hence $P(C \in \mathcal{D} \mid E_S) = P(C = S \mid E_S)$ and we therefore also have

$$\frac{P(C \in \mathcal{D} \mid E_S)}{P(C \notin \mathcal{D} \mid E_S)} = \frac{1}{p_S} \frac{P(C = S)}{P(C \notin \mathcal{D})} \frac{P(C \in \mathcal{D})}{P(C \in \mathcal{D})} = \frac{1}{p_S} P(C = S \mid C \in \mathcal{D}) \frac{P(C \in \mathcal{D})}{P(C \notin \mathcal{D})}.$$
(11.7)

Hence the likelihood ratio of $C \in \mathcal{D}$ versus $C \notin \mathcal{D}$ is equal to

$$\frac{1}{p_S} P(C = S \mid C \in \mathcal{D}) \tag{11.8}$$

and this quantity is *at most* $1/p_S$.

In both formulations, we see that the likelihood ratio reduces to just $1/p_S$ in the case where $\mathcal{D} = \{S\}$, which corresponds to the classical probable cause situation in which only the profile of a suspect S is compared with that of C. The hypotheses $C = S$ and $C \in \mathcal{D}$ are then equivalent. In the case of a uniform prior of C on $\mathcal{D}$, (11.8) reduces to $1/(np_S)$, that is, we retrieve Stockmarr's (cf. [151]) expression.

11.3 Evaluation of the Probabilities in Particular Cases

We have seen that (11.4) is our basic expression, valid in all circumstances where only a single individual S in a set $\mathcal{D}$ turns out not to be excluded as candidate for being C. For the formal derivation of this result, it was irrelevant how large the database is, whether or not there was a suspicion against S, why the search was conducted, or in which order evidence was gathered. None of these additional aspects are needed to derive (11.4) and therefore they will not change (11.4) algebraically. But in order to assess the required probabilities, of course different situations can lead to different *numerical* evaluations of these relevant probabilities, and therefore also to different posterior odds.

To illustrate this, we next treat some special cases in more detail. For database searches, we distinguish between various different scenarios. In the first one we assume the search is carried out without any other relevant information about C other than the obtained profile, that is, there is no additional evidence against any database member. We call this a *cold case search*. After the search we are informed that there is a match with a profile in the database, typically with the identity (i.e., the index i) of the donor of the matching profile.

A second type of search, which we call a *targeted search*, arises if a suspect S has been identified and that suspect happens to already be in the database, say $S = i$. We then carry out the search to confirm this suspicion. In that case, a single match with another person would have surprised us much more than if we indeed obtain E_i, a single match with the already identified suspect.

The classical *probable cause* situation is the one where the identified suspect S is the only person whose profile is compared to that of C. Mathematically, this corresponds to a targeted database search in a database consisting only of S.

11.3.1 Cold Case Search

First, we assume that we have carried out a cold case search, meaning that we have done the database search because the identity of C is unknown and we believe that

C might be one of the members of $\mathcal{D}$. In this case, defining a prior $P(C = S)$ from scratch seems hard and therefore (11.5) is hard to evaluate directly. However, if we take the route (11.7) then within $\mathcal{D}$ things are easier: without any further information about the individuals in the database, the only option is to choose $P(C = S \mid C \in \mathcal{D}) = 1/n$. Therefore (11.7) becomes

$$\frac{P(C = S \mid E_S)}{P(C \neq S \mid E_S)} = \frac{P(C \in \mathcal{D} \mid E_S)}{P(C \notin \mathcal{D} \mid E_S)} = \frac{1}{np_S} \frac{P(C \in \mathcal{D})}{P(C \notin \mathcal{D})}. \tag{11.9}$$

It remains to provide a numerical assessment of $P(C \in \mathcal{D})$. One way to do so is to let $P(C \in \mathcal{D})$ be equal to the proportion of traces that have been previously searched with, and have given rise to a match in the database. In doing so, one implicitly assumes that all previous matches were with the true donor of the trace, and that the traces that were searched with in the past form a sufficiently representative sample to be useful for an estimate of $P(C \in \mathcal{D})$. This assumption is not entirely unproblematic. If we take the type of crime into account, the estimate for $P(C \in \mathcal{D})$ may change depending on whether the case is, for example, a burglary case, a homicide, or a sexual assault case. Furthermore, one may argue that the trace donor C need not be the actual offender. This, however, is also possible for previous searches; the probability $P(C \in \mathcal{D})$ therefore applies to C as trace donor and not to C as offender.

Bearing these cautions in mind, it is not uncommon for databases to be sufficiently large as to have odds $P(C \in \mathcal{D})/P(C \notin \mathcal{D})$ that are within one order of magnitude of being even. If that is the case, the posterior odds are of the same order of magnitude as the likelihood ratio, and we can then say that the odds on the match being with the trace donor are within one order of magnitude of $1/(np_S)$. If, for example, $P(C \in \mathcal{D}) = P(C \notin \mathcal{D}) = 0.5$, $n = 10^6$, and $p_S = 10^{-9}$, the odds are 1000:1 that the match is with the actual trace donor. Of course, when the specifics of the crime and of the uncovered suspect are brought into consideration, these odds will need to be further updated. If, for example, it turns out the match is with a person yet to be born when the crime was committed, they will be reduced to zero. But this cannot happen very often, since there will be a thousand true matches for every coincidental one for these values of n and p_S.

In the case where the match is indeed with the trace donor, and the trace donor is the actual offender, further evidence can potentially be uncovered which will raise the odds from 1000:1 to a larger number. When further non-genetic evidence I is found and taken into account, the result (11.4) still applies, but all probabilities need to be conditioned on I. This has no effect on the match probability p_S but now $P(C = S \mid I) > P(C = S)$. For $\mathcal{D}$, since additional evidence against one of its members S has been found, the probability that $\mathcal{D}$ contains C cannot decrease and hence we have $P(C \notin \mathcal{D} \mid I) \leq P(C \notin \mathcal{D})$. Putting this together we see that the posterior odds on $C = S$ increase, reflecting the strengthening of the case against S due to the new evidence I.

11.3.2 Targeted Search

The preceding discussion naturally brings us to the targeted search case. In this case, evidence against S is found before the database search is done. Since there is no temporal order for probabilities, we must arrive at the same posterior odds regardless of whether S is identified via the database cold case search and further evidence is subsequently found, or when this happens in the reverse order. If we take into account the additional evidence before we process the evidence E_S, we will no longer have $P(C = S \mid C \in \mathcal{D}) = 1/n$, but a much larger value, approaching $P(C = S \mid C \in \mathcal{D}) \approx 1$ as more and more evidence against S is uncovered. In that case, S was – before the database search – pretty much the only plausible candidate for C, which in turn means that $P(C = S) \approx P(C \in \mathcal{D})$, making the hypotheses $C = S$ and $C \in \mathcal{D}$ much closer to being equivalent than in the cold case.

In terms of (11.5) and (11.7), both terms $P(C = S \mid C \in \mathcal{D})$ and $P(C \notin \mathcal{D} \mid C \neq S)$ are close to 1, so that the likelihood ratio is close to $1/p_S$, regardless of whether we start out with hypotheses about S (in which case the likelihood ratio is larger than $1/p_S$) or about $\mathcal{D}$ (in which case it is smaller). The exclusions that the database search has provided are, in other words, essentially irrelevant since we already believed that S was by far the most plausible candidate for being C before carrying out the search. Learning that the other database members, who we already believed not to be C, are indeed not C, then has only very little impact.

11.3.3 Probable Cause

Now we arrive naturally at the probable cause case, which we can think of in various ways. We can set $\mathcal{D} = \{S\}$ so that no other comparisons have been done other than between S and C, who turned out to have matching profiles. Alternatively, we can think of a database in which all individuals apart from S were already excluded prior to the search, that is, $P(C = S \mid C \in \mathcal{D}) = P(C \notin \mathcal{D} \mid C \neq S) = 1$. The latter formulation is nothing but an extreme case of the targeted search case which we discussed above. Regardless of how we think about it, the hypotheses $C = S$ and $C \in \mathcal{D}$ are then equivalent prior to learning E_S, so that (11.5) and (11.7) coincide. The likelihood ratio in favor of $C = S$ (or in favor of $C \in \mathcal{D}$, which is now the same hypothesis) is then equal to $1/p_S$.

11.3.4 Casework

Of course, a case is not going to be confined to one of these three categories once and for all, but at any given point in time we will have information that makes us regard the case as most similar to one of the three types above. For example, a cold case search may be initially carried out, after which evidence against S is found. When that evidence is taken into account, we are in the same situation as for a targeted search. Conversely, a suspect may be identified via other means than the database, and be the only one that is compared to the trace profile. If, subsequently, a database search is carried out and no further matches are found, this is also equivalent to a targeted search. If, on the other hand, the evidence leading to the identification of S as suspect turns out to be erroneous and is dismissed, we could also come close to a situation best described as a cold case search, because there is no evidence any more distinguishing S from the other database members other than the matching profile.

11.3.5 The Multi-stain Problem

As a somewhat recreational yet also quite instructive final example, we now turn things around and consider a person C compared with a set $\mathcal{D}$ of traces (all with different profiles), instead of a trace from C with a set of persons $\mathcal{D}$. We may then wonder what the probability is that, if C matches one of the traces, C indeed left that trace.

This is, in fact, exactly the same problem as the database problem. We need to assume that the person C we compare the traces with, can have left at most one of them, and that exactly one of these traces, denoted S, gives a match with our person C. The hypothesis $C = S$ then states that C left the particular trace S, whereas $C \in \mathcal{D}$ means that C left one of the traces in $\mathcal{D}$. We then get that the probability that C left the trace S depends on the same three probabilities as before. First, there is p_S, the random match probability (which is now the random match probability of the trace: it is the probability that if a trace was left by a random person and compared on the same loci with C as S, it would on those loci have the same profile as we observed in S). Second, we need $P(C = S)$: the probability that C would have left this particular trace, and finally, we need $P(C \in \mathcal{D})$: the probability that C would have left any of the traces we are comparing with.

Again the assessment of these probabilities will depend on the situation. We will again need quantities such as $P(C = S \mid C \in \mathcal{D})$, which now means the probability that if C left any of the traces, it was the one the match is with; or $P(C \notin \mathcal{D} \mid C \neq S)$ which now means the probability that C did not leave any of the traces, if he did not leave this one.

Contrary to the database search, it may now be reasonable that $P(C \in \mathcal{D})$ does not grow with the size of $\mathcal{D}$. For example, if $\mathcal{D}$ represents the set of traces recovered at a particular crime scene, then the probability $P(C \notin \mathcal{D})$ that C has nothing to do with it, would be largely independent of the size of $\mathcal{D}$. The odds on $P(C = S)$ may actually decrease if a larger number of traces is recovered and compared with C. If the prior for S on $\mathcal{D}$ is uniform, meaning that *if* C left one of the traces, it was any of them with the same probability, then the likelihood ratio is $1/(np)$. In that case, both the evidence and the case against C are stronger if a single match with one trace has been found than if a single match with one of many traces has been found. This is reasonable, since if the probability of C being involved does not depend on the number of traces recovered and compared, then we would prefer to link C to one out of a few instead of many traces. All additional traces do is create more opportunity for chance matches.

In other situations where C is suspected to have played a certain role and indeed matches with the trace corresponding to that role (for instance, a car is searched for traces, C is suspected to have driven it and a trace with his profile is recovered from the steering wheel and not from other places like the back seat), one would expect that things are different: then we get high odds on $C = S$ also if many traces are compared. This is because now $P(C = S \mid C \in \mathcal{D})$ is large: if C left a trace, we expect it to be this one.

11.4 Which Likelihood Ratio?

So far, we have seen that the evaluation of the posterior odds on $C = S$ is, at least mathematically, straightforward via (11.4). As expression (11.4) also makes clear, the relevant hypotheses following the search result are that $C = S$ or that $C \notin \mathcal{D}$. Writing these posterior odds as a likelihood ratio times prior odds on a hypothesis versus its negation is possible in two ways, but both are a little artificial. Either, we obtain the likelihood ratio for the hypotheses $C \in \mathcal{D}$ versus $C \notin \mathcal{D}$, which reflect the initial questions (at least, in a cold case search) but not the question that has come up following the search, namely whether $C = S$ or $C \neq S$.

Alternatively, we work with $C = S$ versus $C \neq S$ throughout, which does not reflect that prior to the search we were (in the cold case search) not especially interested in S and which gives by construction strong evidence in the form of a large likelihood ratio. Mathematically, there is no harm in either approach but we do not think they express the situation any better than (11.4) does.

One way out is to abandon the likelihood ratio approach and to directly focus on the matter of interest via (11.4). However, forensic laboratories are often asked (see, e.g., [60]) to provide an assessment of the evidence in terms of a likelihood ratio, which makes it inevitable to choose one. As is clear from (11.6) and (11.8), two candidates emerge here: the suspect centered likelihood ratio $1/(p_S P(C \notin \mathcal{D} \mid S \neq C)) \geq 1/p_S$, or the database centered likelihood ratio $P(S = C \mid C \in \mathcal{D})/p_S \leq 1/p_S$. How large the difference between these is depends on the situation, hence we will discuss the cold case search and targeted search once more. (The latter includes the probable cause case as a special case, as remarked above.)

11.4.1 Cold Case Search

In this case, suppose that we do not know anything about C, and assume uniform prior odds for C within $\mathcal{D}$. Then the discrepancy between the likelihood ratios is large: it is either at least $1/p_S$, or equal to $1/(np_S)$. Which one should we prefer? Obviously, from a mathematical point of view there is no problem: both lead to the same posterior odds, each within their own context. So, another question emerges: what is the most natural context here?

Initially, the question addressed was whether $C \in \mathcal{D}$. A forensic laboratory may receive a generic question to produce a DNA profile from a crime stain sample and compare the resulting profile with the database $\mathcal{D}$. Up to that point, no one in the database stands out. But when the match result E_S is obtained, attention shifts to S and the ultimate issue for a court is whether $C = S$ or not. Hence the context changes along the way. There is, therefore, no obvious choice from the contextual point of view either. Either $1/(np_S)$ is reported reflecting the original question that has been asked, or $1/p_S$ is reported reflecting the fact that the case now revolves about S.

Is there then, perhaps, a *practical* reason to choose for either likelihood ratio? We believe that this may indeed be the case, and that $1/(np_S)$ then has a practical advantage. We next explain why. First of all, we remark that probabilistic assessments are difficult to convey to judges and juries and that intuition may lead to wrong conclusions. A common pitfall is to understand likelihood ratios as posterior odds, a mistake commonly referred to as the prosecutor's fallacy. Those who do not make such mistakes will be able to both interpret the likelihood ratio $1/p_S$ (for initial hypotheses whether $S = C$ or not) or $1/(np_S)$ (for initial hypotheses whether $C \in \mathcal{D}$ or not) and make the correct inference for the posterior odds. However, since the posterior odds in the cold case search case based on the information known at the time of issuing the report are much closer to $1/(np_S)$ than to $1/p_S$, the harm done by a prosecutor's fallacy is much less if $1/(np_S)$ is reported in such a case than if $1/p_S$ is reported. Such a report could for example be as follows:

"A request has been received to generate a DNA profile from item X, and use that profile to search for its trace donor in the database $\mathcal{D}$. From item X a DNA profile has been generated and compared with the DNA profiles of the database $\mathcal{D}$. The findings are that a single match with database member S has been found and that the probability for S to produce a match, if not the trace donor, is p_S (e.g., $p_S = 10^{-9}$). At the time of the search the database contained n profiles (e.g., $n = 1{,}000{,}000$). Furthermore the laboratory is not aware of any non-DNA information pertaining to specific database members as to the possibility that they are more plausible candidates for being the trace donor than others. From this it is concluded that the obtained database search result is $1/(np_S)$ $(1{,}000)$ times more likely if the database contains the trace donor than if the database does not contain the trace donor. Furthermore S is now the only person in $\mathcal{D}$ who can be the trace donor. Averaged over all cases, the database contains about a proportion α (e.g., 40%) of the trace donors that are searched in it. This figure would lead to odds of $(1/(np_S)) \times (\alpha/(1-\alpha))$ to one (667:1) in favor of S being the trace donor. Further information pertaining to the case and to S can be used to revise the odds on S being the trace donor to a larger or smaller number."

The advantage of this approach is that it describes an evaluation of all involved probabilities, and that a prosecutor's fallacy is less likely to occur. A practical disadvantage is that the number n changes rapidly over time, so that each report contains different numbers of n and perhaps α. Another concern is that in order to know whether $1/(np_S)$ as a likelihood ratio applies, one has to know whether a uniform prior is applicable to the database or not. It seems to us that in most cases, using a uniform prior where there is more information available, will be in the interest of the matching individual, since for the n and p_S used in practice, most of the matches are with the true trace donors, so more information is usually information pointing towards the matching suspect S.

A final concern is that laboratories may only be expected or permitted to give likelihood ratios. In that case, one could adapt the above report so as to leave out the estimate of the odds on $C \in \mathcal{D}$.

11.4.2 Targeted Search

In this case a search has been done where S was already, prior to the search, a plausible candidate for being the trace donor C. We assume that the forensic laboratory has been requested to generate a DNA profile from item X and compare it with the DNA profiles in database $\mathcal{D}$, and in particular to the DNA profile of S. In that case $P(C = S \mid C \in \mathcal{D}) \neq 1/n$, and $1/(np_S)$ is not the likelihood ratio for $C \in \mathcal{D}$. Both the purpose of the search and of the ensuing further investigation are to investigate whether $C = S$ and then it is natural to report also the corresponding likelihood ratio for these hypotheses, which is $1/p_S \times 1/P(C \notin \mathcal{D} \mid S \neq C) \geq 1/p_S$. Thus, a report could be phrased along the following lines:

"A request has been received to generate a DNA profile from item X, and use that profile to search for its trace donor in the database $\mathcal{D}$ with particular attention to individual S. From item X a DNA profile has been generated and compared with the DNA profiles of the persons in $\mathcal{D}$. The findings are that a single match with database member S has been found and that the probability for S to produce a match, if not the trace donor, is p_S. This provides evidence that S is indeed the trace donor. Based on the information described up to now, the match with S increases the odds on S being the trace donor by at least a factor $1/p_S$, compared to what they were prior to the search result. Further information pertaining to the case and S will allow to revise these odds to a larger or smaller number."

Of course it is also possible that a request is done to carry out a targeted search, leading to a match with a different individual S' than the expected one S. In that case, we are back into a cold case search case.

11.5 Only a Unique Match is Known

So far we assumed that upon a unique match, we are not only informed about this unique match, but also about the identity of the donor and the matching profile. Suppose now that we only get to know that there is a unique match with *some* person S, without any further information such as p_S or the identity of the matching person. Writing E for this information, can we still say anything meaningful about the (or a) posterior probability that the matching person is C given E?

A little reflection shows that we need more information. It is intuitively clear that in the absence of any individual information about the matching profile, we will need the random match probabilities of *all* database profiles. So let us assume now that all p_i's are known to us.

We claim that

$$P(C = S \mid E) = \frac{\sum_{i=1}^{n} \frac{P(C=i)}{1-p_i}}{\sum_{j=1}^{n} \frac{P(C=j)}{1-p_j} + P(C \notin \mathcal{D}) \sum_{j=1}^{n} \frac{p_j}{1-p_j}}, \qquad (11.10)$$

with corresponding odds

$$\frac{P(C = S \mid E)}{P(C \neq S \mid E)} = \frac{\sum_{i=1}^{n} \frac{P(C=i)}{1-p_i}}{P(C \in \mathcal{D}) \sum_{j=1}^{n} \frac{p_j}{1-p_j}} \frac{P(C \in \mathcal{D})}{P(C \notin \mathcal{D})}, \qquad (11.11)$$

and we prove this next.

From (11.1) and (11.2) we conclude that

$$P(C = i \mid E_i) = \frac{P(C = i)}{P(C = i) + p_i P(C \notin \mathcal{D})}. \qquad (11.12)$$

Next we write

$$P(C = S \mid E) = \sum_{i=1}^{n} P(C = i \mid E_i) P(E_i \mid E).$$

Writing

$$\Pi_i := \prod_{j \neq i}(1 - p_j),$$

we have

$$P(F_i) = P(C = i)\Pi_i + P(C \notin \mathcal{D})p_i\Pi_i.$$

Hence

$$P(E_i \mid E) = \frac{P(E_i)}{P(E)} = \frac{P(E_i)}{\sum_{j=1}^{n} P(E_j)}$$

$$= \frac{P(C = i)\Pi_i + P(C \notin \mathcal{D})p_i\Pi_i}{\sum_{j=1}^{n}\left(P(C = j)\Pi_j + P(C \notin \mathcal{D})p_j\Pi_j\right)}$$

$$= \frac{\frac{P(C=i)}{1-p_i} + P(C \notin \mathcal{D})\frac{p_i}{1-p_i}}{\sum_{j=1}^{n}\left(\frac{P(C=j)}{1-p_j} + P(C \notin \mathcal{D})\frac{p_j}{1-p_j}\right)},$$

assuming that the $p_i < 1$ for all i. Therefore, using (11.12) we find

$$P(C = S \mid E) = \sum_{i=1}^{n}\left(\frac{P(C = i)}{P(C = i) + p_i P(C \notin \mathcal{D})}\right.$$

$$\left. \times \frac{\frac{P(C=i)}{1-p_i} + P(C \notin \mathcal{D})\frac{p_i}{1-p_i}}{\sum_{j=1}^{n}\left(\frac{P(C=j)}{1-p_j} + P(C \notin \mathcal{D})\frac{p_j}{1-p_j}\right)}\right)$$

$$= \frac{\sum_{i=1}^{n}\frac{P(C=i)}{1-p_i}}{\sum_{j=1}^{n}\frac{P(C=j)}{1-p_j} + P(C \notin \mathcal{D})\sum_{j=1}^{n}\frac{p_j}{1-p_j}},$$

proving (11.10) and (11.11).

In the case where all the p_i's are the same and equal to p, the likelihood ratio that appears in (11.11) reduces to

$$\frac{\sum_{i=1}^{n}\frac{P(C=i|C\in\mathcal{D})}{1-p_i}}{\sum_{j=1}^{n}\frac{p_j}{1-p_j}} = \frac{\sum_{i=1}^{n}\frac{P(C=i|C\in\mathcal{D})}{1-p}}{\sum_{j=1}^{n}\frac{p}{1-p}} = \frac{1}{np}. \tag{11.13}$$

Hence, this is another situation in which $1/(np)$ is the correct likelihood ratio.

11.6 An Intermediate Situation

In some cases, for instance in searches between different jurisdictions, the database that has been searched returns the matching profile but no further personal details about the person whose profile that is. The queried database only confirms that it holds a unique non-excluded individual and gives the databased profile of that person. What can we say in this situation about the probability that the uniquely matching individual is C?

Let us still denote the matching person by S, but note that S is unknown. Since S is only defined upon finding a unique match, we do not use the unconditional probability $P(C = S)$. We can, however, speak about the probability that $C = S$ given that there is a unique match. The random match probability p_S is still available, and for notational reasons we write $p = p_S$ in this section.

To start the analysis, we denote by $\mathcal{D}_p$ the subset of members of $\mathcal{D}$ with the same RMP p as S, and by $\mathcal{D}_p^c$ its complement. The size of $\mathcal{D}_p$ is denoted by n_p. We write E for the event that there is a unique match in $\mathcal{D}_p$, and F for the event that there is no match in $\mathcal{D}_p^c$. Assuming that $P(C \in \mathcal{D}_p)/P(C \in \mathcal{D}) = n_p/n$, that is, the RMP p is not informative about C, we claim that

$$\frac{P(C = S \mid E, F)}{P(C \neq S \mid E, F)} = \frac{1}{np} \frac{P(C \in \mathcal{D})}{P(C \notin \mathcal{D})}. \tag{11.14}$$

To prove this, we write

$$\begin{aligned}\frac{P(C = S \mid E, F)}{P(C \neq S \mid E, F)} &= \frac{P(F \mid C = S, E)}{P(F \mid C \neq S, E)} \times \frac{P(C = S \mid E)}{P(C \neq S \mid E)} \\ &= \frac{P(F \mid C = S, E)}{P(F \mid C \neq S, E)} \frac{1}{n_p p} \frac{P(C \in \mathcal{D}_p)}{P(C \notin \mathcal{D}_p)},\end{aligned} \tag{11.15}$$

where we have used formula (11.13).

The numerator of the first fraction is the probability that there is no match in $\mathcal{D}_p^c$, given that C is not a member of $\mathcal{D}_p^c$. Denoting this probability by π, we have that the denominator is equal to $\pi P(C \notin \mathcal{D}_p^c \mid C \notin \mathcal{D}_p)$, which is equal to $\pi P(C \notin \mathcal{D} \mid C \notin \mathcal{D}_p)$. Hence (11.15) is equal to

$$\frac{1}{P(C \notin \mathcal{D} \mid C \notin \mathcal{D}_p)} \frac{1}{n_p p} \frac{P(C \in \mathcal{D}_p)}{P(C \notin \mathcal{D}_p)} = \frac{1}{np} \frac{P(C \in \mathcal{D})}{P(C \notin \mathcal{D})},$$

proving (11.14).

Next, let $\mathcal{D}'$ be *any* subset of $\mathcal{D}$, and denote by $E_{\mathcal{D}'}$ the event that there is a unique match S in $\mathcal{D}$ for some $S \in \mathcal{D}'$. What can we say about the odds that $C = S$ given this information?

The event $E_{\mathcal{D}'}$ can be decomposed as follows: (1) the event that in $\mathcal{D}'$ there is a unique match, and (2) the event that there are no matches outside $\mathcal{D}'$. The odds of the first event follow from (11.14), where we take $\mathcal{D}'$ instead of $\mathcal{D}$ and the cardinality n' of $\mathcal{D}'$ instead of n. Conditional on the first event, the odds for the second event are computed in the same way as above, and they are equal to $1/P(C \notin \mathcal{D} \mid C \notin \mathcal{D}')$. Hence the posterior odds of $S = C$ versus $S \neq C$ are given by

$$\frac{P(C = S \mid E_{\mathcal{D}'})}{P(C \neq S \mid E_{\mathcal{D}'})} = \frac{1}{P(C \notin \mathcal{D} \mid C \notin \mathcal{D}')} \frac{1}{n' p_S} \frac{P(C \in \mathcal{D}')}{P(C \notin \mathcal{D}')}$$

$$= \frac{1}{n' p_S} \frac{P(C \in \mathcal{D}')}{P(C \notin \mathcal{D})}. \tag{11.16}$$

11.7 A Further Analysis of the Controversies

The interpretation of database searches yielding a single match has seen fierce debates [10, 21, 102, 103, 151, 178], where especially the likelihood ratio $1/(np)$ has often been ridiculed. In this section we take a closer look at the various arguments that have been proposed in this debate in favor of or against the use of one of the likelihood ratios, or in favor of or against the use of the various hypotheses of interest. Authors sometimes provide direct arguments why a specific choice should be used, but more often it is the case that arguments are provided against other choices. We will consider the arguments one by one. In every instance that a general rejection of one type of likelihood ratio or hypothesis is suggested, we will argue that this is unjustified.

We distinguish between a strong *case* on the one hand and strong *evidence* on the other. A case always refers to posterior odds or probabilities, while evidence always refers to a likelihood ratio. We should keep in mind though that typically various different likelihood ratios are possible, so that we should be careful whenever we speak about evidence. In this section we assume that all members of the database have RMP equal to p. This is mainly for simplicity, since it will make it easier to explain why the various arguments against either likelihood ratio are incorrect. Also, we will see that the discussion of the controversies leads to certain facts about unique database matches that we find interesting enough to discuss, and which have not appeared in print before, as far as we are aware.

11.7.1 Against $1/(np)$: A Large Database Should Give Strong Evidence

One of the first arguments against the use of the likelihood ratio $1/(np)$ was that it would imply that the larger the database is, the weaker the evidence against the suspect, and that this must be absurd. In the extreme case where the whole population would be in $\mathcal{D}$, the evidence would be the weakest possible (still according to adversaries of the $1/(np)$ likelihood ratio) while it clearly provides the strongest evidence possible; see, for instance [57].

How should we evaluate this argument? First of all, this argument can only be put forward when the $1/(np)$ likelihood ratio applies. As we have seen, this is so in a cold case search case when the prior for C on $\mathcal{D}$ is uniform, and in the case where we do not know the identity of S. Here we consider the latter case, and we use the prior and posterior odds as expressed in (11.14) and (11.16). Below, in the discussion of the so-called cunning defense lawyer argument, we will also discuss what happens when S is identified and C is uniform on $\mathcal{D}$.

Suppose now that the whole population is in the database. In that case $P(C \in \mathcal{D}) = 1$ and $P(C \notin \mathcal{D}) = 0$ which means that the prior odds for these hypotheses are infinite. It then follows that the posterior odds are infinite as well. Rather than giving rise to absurdities, this leads to a posterior probability on $C = S$ equal to 1, as it should. Indeed, if S is the only match and the full population is in $\mathcal{D}$, then the posterior probability that $C = S$ must be 1.

How can we reconcile this with the fact that the likelihood ratio is very small in this case, namely equal to $1/(np)$? We can better see what happens when we assume that *nearly* everyone is in $\mathcal{D}$ so that $P(C \notin \mathcal{D})$ is small but not zero. In that case, the prior odds on $C \in \mathcal{D}$ are very large, but the likelihood ratio $1/(np)$ may even be smaller than one. Note that np is the expected number of matches in the database, assuming that $C \notin \mathcal{D}$ and that the random match probability p applies to all database members. If the number of matches found (being one) is smaller than the expected number np of such matches, then indeed this result provides evidence *against* $C \in \mathcal{D}$; this is only reasonable. Hence the posterior probability on $C \in \mathcal{D}$ decreases, but since it is now totally concentrated on the uniquely matching individual S, the posterior odds on the match being with the trace donor are very high. Of course, np could in principle also be very large but in a situation with a unique match this will not happen often, since it would correspond to a trace occurring much less frequently in $\mathcal{D}$ than predicted by p.

We conclude that there is no contradiction in the proper use of the likelihood ratio $1/(np)$, even when the database is very large.

11.7.2 Against $1/(np)$: Growing Database

A second argument put forward against the $1/(np)$ likelihood ratio, or the use of hypotheses $C \in \mathcal{D}$, involves hypothetically growing databases. It is clear that if a match with S is found in the database, and there are no further matches found at a later point in time when the database has grown, the additional exclusion of new individuals can only increase the posterior odds that S is the trace donor. It may seem that this provides an argument against using $1/(np)$. In order to purely assess the effect of the growth of the database, we disregard the identity of S. Consider a subset $\mathcal{D}' \subset \mathcal{D}$. For example, $\mathcal{D}'$ may be the database at some point in time, and

$\mathcal{D}$ the database at a later moment when new persons have been added. Suppose we first find a unique match in $\mathcal{D}'$ and, after that, we find no further matches in $\mathcal{D}$. Alternatively, we first find the match with S in $\mathcal{D}$, and then find out that $S \in \mathcal{D}'$. At the end of this procedure, we have a unique match in $\mathcal{D}$, but now we also know that this unique match is in fact in $\mathcal{D}'$. This knowledge changes the situation compared to the earlier analysis with $\mathcal{D}'$ and $\mathcal{D}$, as we can verify using (11.14), which is the expression for the posterior odds in precisely this situation. Indeed, we learn from (11.14) that

$$\frac{P(C = S \mid E_{\mathcal{D}'})}{P(C \neq S \mid E_{\mathcal{D}'})} = \frac{1}{n'p} \frac{P(C \in \mathcal{D}')}{P(C \notin \mathcal{D})}$$

$$\geq \frac{1}{n'p} \frac{P(C \in \mathcal{D}')}{P(C \notin \mathcal{D}')},$$

since $P(C \in \mathcal{D}) \geq P(C \in \mathcal{D}')$. Thus, in complete generality, the additional exclusions in $\mathcal{D} \backslash \mathcal{D}'$ provide further evidence for $C = S$, as is to be expected.

So far, we have considered that we first learn that S provides a single match in $\mathcal{D}'$, and then the database grows into $\mathcal{D}$ and no additional matches are found. Next, we consider a different situation: we assume that we know that S provides a unique match in the larger database $\mathcal{D}$, and then we learn that $S \in \mathcal{D}'$ for some subset $\mathcal{D}' \subset \mathcal{D}$. How does that change the odds on $C = S$?

Learning that $S \in \mathcal{D}'$ changes the posterior odds on $C = S$ from (11.14) into (11.16). The ratio between the new odds, when we have learned that $S \in \mathcal{D}'$, and the odds when we only knew that $S \in \mathcal{D}$, is, by using (11.14) and (11.16),

$$\frac{P(C \in \mathcal{D}')/n'}{P(C \in \mathcal{D})/n}. \tag{11.17}$$

If $\mathcal{D}'$ is a subset of $\mathcal{D}$ such that the average prior $P(C \in \mathcal{D}')/n'$ is larger than the corresponding average prior for $\mathcal{D}$, then the knowledge that $S \in \mathcal{D}'$ increases the probability that $C = S$, and the opposite is of course also possible.

In the case where the prior for C is uniform on the population, we have that $P(C \in \mathcal{D})$ is equal to the proportion of the population that is in the database, in which case we get unity in (11.17), expressing that it neither strengthens nor weakens the case against S if we learn that $S \in \mathcal{D}'$, whatever $\mathcal{D}'$ is.

11.7.3 Matches in a Larger Database are not Necessarily More Likely to be With the Trace Donor

It might be perceived that a larger database is better in the sense that a higher proportion of the unique matches is with the actual trace donors. This, however, is not true in general. We can already see this from (11.16). Indeed, consider two databases $\mathcal{D}'$ and $\mathcal{D}$ of sizes $n' < n$ respectively. Let us write $f_\mathcal{D}$ for $P(C \in \mathcal{D})/P(C \notin \mathcal{D})$ and define $f_{\mathcal{D}'}$ similarly. Then the ratio between the posterior odds for a unique match in $\mathcal{D}'$ to be with the actual trace donor, and those for a unique match in $\mathcal{D}$ to be with the actual trace donor, is

$$\frac{f_{\mathcal{D}'}/n'}{f_\mathcal{D}/n}. \tag{11.18}$$

The above expression holds for any two databases, it is not necessary to assume that one is a subset of the other. Let us now assume that $\mathcal{D}' \subset \mathcal{D}$ to see how the odds on the match being with the trace donor may change from matches in $\mathcal{D}'$ to matches in $\mathcal{D}$.

We see that in that case, if the odds on $C \in \mathcal{D}$ compared to those on $C \in D'$ grow more than the sizes of the databases, then in $\mathcal{D}$ a larger proportion of the matches is with the actual trace donors. If the prior for C on $\mathcal{D}$ is uniform, this is the case since then $f_{\mathcal{D}'} = n'/(N - n')$ and $f_\mathcal{D} = n/(N - n)$ so (11.18) evaluates to $(N - n)/(N - n')$, which is smaller than one if $n' < n$.

Thus, if we assume uniform prior probabilities for C then a unique match in a larger database is always more likely to be with C than a unique match in a smaller database.

In general, however, it is possible that (11.18) is larger than one, which means that the posterior odds on a unique match to be with the trace donor are smaller in the larger database than those for matches in a subset of it.

As an example, let us assume that $P(C \in \mathcal{D}) = \sqrt{n/N}$, where N is the size of the population and n the size of $\mathcal{D}$. Then a small fraction of the population in the database corresponds to a relatively large $P(C \in \mathcal{D})$. For instance, if $n/N = 0.01$ we have $P(C \in \mathcal{D}) = 0.1$. This is not an unnatural property at all, since the proportion of traces that yield a match may be much larger than the fraction of the population in the database.

We write $x = n/N$, so that $P(C \in \mathcal{D}) = x^{1/2}$. From (11.16) we have that the posterior odds on a match in $\mathcal{D}$, for size $x = n/N$, being with the trace donor are given by

$$\frac{1}{Np} \frac{x^{-1/2}}{1 - x^{1/2}}. \tag{11.19}$$

It is easy to see now that these posterior odds are minimal for $x = 1/4$: they *decrease* between $x = 0$ and $x = 1/4$, and then increase towards infinity as $x \to 1$. As n increases, so does $P(C \in \mathcal{D})$, as well as the possibility for adventitious matches. Both of these effects influence the posterior odds in the case of a single match. For a uniformly sampled database, the increase of $P(C \in \mathcal{D})$ always outweighs the increased opportunity for adventitious matches, but we now see that this need not be so in general.

Thus, it is not generally true that a larger database is better in the sense that in a larger database, there may be a smaller proportion of the unique matches with the trace donor than in a smaller database. Formula (11.18) tells us that it may be the case that the posterior odds on the match being with the trace donor are smaller, larger or the same in an expanded database $\mathcal{D}$ than in a smaller $\mathcal{D}'$. If we learn that we have a match in $\mathcal{D}$, the odds on it being with the trace donor can be smaller, larger or identical to those that we get if we learn that we have a match in $\mathcal{D}'$ without knowing about $\mathcal{D} \backslash \mathcal{D}'$.

11.7.4 Against $1/(np)$: Cunning Defense Lawyer

A further argument that has been put forward against the $1/(np)$ rule is at first sight quite convincing [10]. Imagine that a match with a suspect has been obtained, outside the database. Then the suspect would be well advised by a cunning defense lawyer to insist a database search be carried out. Indeed, if no additional matches are found, the failure to find additional matches will substantially weaken the evidence against his or her client, since the likelihood ratio is now $1/(np)$ instead of $1/p$. On the other hand, if additional matches are found, then this is even better news for the suspect.

Convincing as this may sound, this argument against the $1/(np)$ rule is not correct. Clearly it is impossible that the *case* against the suspect weakens irrespective of the outcome of a database search, and indeed this is not what follows from our (or, for that matter, from any sound) analysis, be it based on the suspect-driven hypothesis $S = C$ or on $C \in \mathcal{D}$. We next explain this in detail.

First of all, we note that the $1/(np)$ rule is only valid under specific circumstances. With an identified S, we can only apply it when the prior of C is uniform on $\mathcal{D}$, see the discussion following (11.7) and (11.8). But in the situation described above, with a suspect already identified before carrying out a database search, uniform priors are not realistic. Every further tested person would have to have the same prior probability to be C as the suspect S, something which is clearly impossible to realize given the fact that S had been suspect before the search has been carried out. In other words, this argument against the use of the $1/(np)$ rule is as a practical argument flawed from the very start, since the assumptions are not fulfilled.

It is interesting and illuminating, though, to see what our analysis has to say about the cunning defense lawyer argument if we make the (unrealistic) assumption that the $1/(np)$ likelihood ratio applies. We already mentioned above that further exclusions cannot make the case against an already identified suspect weaker. This can indeed also be shown in the current situation, this time using either (11.5) or (11.7). In (11.5), we do not use the $1/(np)$ rule, but it is illuminating to see what is going on there. The likelihood ratio in (11.5) is $1/p \times 1/P(C \notin \mathcal{D} \mid S \neq C)$. If first S alone is compared with the trace we have, at that point, that $\mathcal{D} = \{S\}$ so that the likelihood ratio is $1/p$. If we then compare the profile of C with a database $\mathcal{D}'$ and let $\mathcal{D} = \mathcal{D}' \cup \{S\}$, the odds are further updated with a factor $1/P(C \notin \mathcal{D} \mid S \neq C)$, which is always in favor of $S = C$ (possibly neutral in the case $P(C \in \mathcal{D}') = 0$, a situation unlikely to be encountered but not outside the scope of (11.5)). Thus, it is certainly not true that the case against S becomes weaker as a result of not finding any further matches.

We can also argue this from (11.7), where the likelihood ratio is $1/(np)$, assuming (as we have to in order to apply the $1/(np)$ rule) a uniform prior for C on $\mathcal{D}$. This runs as follows. Again we first have the situation that S is the only investigated person, so that $\mathcal{D} = \{S\}$ in (11.7). The posterior odds are then equal to

$$\frac{1}{p}\frac{\alpha}{1-\alpha},\tag{11.20}$$

where $\alpha := P(C = S)$ is the prior for S.

Next we investigate $n - 1$ further individuals, none of which matches. Note that in order to comply to the requirement that all investigated persons have the same prior α as S, we must have that $n\alpha \leq 1$. Now we can apply (11.7) again, this time with $\mathcal{D}$ defined as the full set of n tested persons. The posterior odds in (11.7) are now equal to

$$\frac{1}{np}\frac{n\alpha}{1-n\alpha} = \frac{1}{p}\frac{\alpha}{1-n\alpha}.\tag{11.21}$$

Since clearly (11.21) is at least as large as (11.20), we again conclude that the case against S cannot have weakened upon finding a number of further exclusions. Note that when $n\alpha = 1$, the posterior odds are infinite, hence the posterior probability that $S = C$ is 1. This is perfectly reasonable since in that case the database contains all persons with positive prior, and they are all excluded, except S. Hence S must be C.

We conclude that there is no way in which the cunning defense lawyer argument can be made correct. Either the argument does not apply because the assumptions are not fulfilled, or, when they are, the conclusion of the argument is incorrect. The cunning defense lawyer argument is, after all, not as cunning as it seemed.

11.7.5 Against $1/p$: Data-Driven Hypotheses

Not only the likelihood ratio of $1/(np)$ has been challenged, also the $1/p$ likelihood ratio has received serious criticism. Probably the main argument against using (11.5) and the corresponding likelihood ratio of (at least) $1/p$ is that the hypothesis $S = C$ is *data driven* in the sense that it is only formulated *after* observing the match with S [151]. Without this match, there would perhaps be no reason whatsoever to consider this hypothesis and this seems unfair towards the suspect S. From this point of view the division by n in the $1/(np)$ rule is supposed to compensate for the data-driven nature of the hypothesis. Is this criticism justified?

Although there is some truth in the idea that a data-driven hypothesis must be compensated for, it is not the division by n that takes care of this, but instead the prior odds of $S = C$ versus $S \neq C$. When we compare (11.5) to (11.7), the prior in the former is smaller than in the latter, and this, simply, compensates for the fact that $S = C$ is a data-driven hypothesis. When using a data-driven hypothesis, the likelihood ratio tends to be large, but this is compensated by small prior odds. We conclude that there is in principle no problem in using such data-driven hypotheses, as long as the interplay between likelihood ratio and priors is understood; see also [103] for more details on this phenomenon. Hence this argument against the $1/p$ rule is unsound.

11.7.6 Relevance of (Offender) Population Size

In [178] it is argued that the size of the active criminal population plays a role in the computation of posterior odds. In their setup, $P(S = C \mid C \in \mathcal{D}) = 1/n$, so that the posterior odds in (11.7) reduce to

$$\frac{1}{np} \frac{P(C \in \mathcal{D})}{P(C \notin \mathcal{D})}. \tag{11.22}$$

These posterior odds involve only one more ingredient apart from n and p, namely the prior probability $P(C \in \mathcal{D})$ for the database to contain the offender. The paper [178] attaches importance to the size of the active criminal population, but that is a quantity absent from (11.22). Hence, we would be interested in the size of the criminal population (whatever this may be) *only if* this size were essential for the estimation of $P(C \in \mathcal{D})$.

But the authors in [178] estimate the size N of this active criminal population by assuming that $\mathcal{D}$ is a random sample from it, and then estimate the size N of that population from the estimate $P(C \in \mathcal{D})$. They use a mark-and-recapture framework to estimate the size of the active criminal population N as $N = n/P(C \in \mathcal{D})$, and then plug this into the formula for the posterior odds.

However, this analysis is redundant because all that is needed to arrive at the posterior odds is an estimate of $P(C \in \mathcal{D})$, which is the very starting point of their procedure to estimate the size of the offender population. In terms of a criminal population, $P(C \in \mathcal{D})$ may be thought of as the coverage of the population by the database. How the coverage relates to the size of that population is another issue, immaterial for the present problem.

11.7.7 Inadmissibility of Hypotheses About $C \in \mathcal{D}$

Several authors (e.g., [10], [18]) have claimed that, even though the posterior odds (11.5) and (11.7) both provide the same answer, the only relevant hypothesis is whether $S = C$ or not, since the trial is concerned with S and not with $\mathcal{D}$ as a whole. We fail to see, however, how providing the likelihood ratio for $C \in \mathcal{D}$ versus $C \notin \mathcal{D}$, which allows equally well to arrive at a correct evaluation of the posterior probabilities the court is interested in, should be banned from being reported.

A court is indeed not concerned with the collective guilt or innocence of all database members, but in the case of a single match, this collective guilt reduces only to S, so these viewpoints coincide. Moreover, in the case where the identity of S is not (yet) known, the most natural way to proceed is by using the hypotheses $C \in \mathcal{D}$ versus $C \notin \mathcal{D}$. The prior probability $P(C = S)$ is not available in case S is not known, and the analogue of (11.14) or variants thereof should be used.

In the case of a targeted search where there is already an existing suspicion, the $1/(np)$ likelihood ratio does not apply anymore to the hypotheses $C \in \mathcal{D}$ versus $C \notin \mathcal{D}$. In that case, both frameworks can still be used, and the difference between them is then far less pronounced, both leading to a likelihood ratio not differing much from $1/p_S$.

Even if dismissed by some statisticians, in the legal community, the relevance of the hypothesis $C \in \mathcal{D}$ and the matter of how to assign a probability to it, has not gone unnoticed. In [4], page 1451, we read:

"[..] to apply Bayes' rule, the probability that the database contains the source of the forensic DNA, assessed prior to any consideration of whether an individual in the database actually matches, becomes a crucial input in determining the (posterior) likelihood that a particular matching defendant is the source of the forensic DNA."

We have argued that this is a completely reasonable position, and we conclude that there is no reason to deem the hypotheses $C \in \mathcal{D}$ versus $C \notin \mathcal{D}$ inadmissible.

11.7.8 A Frequentist Interpretation

The original motivation to believe that the value of the evidence decreases when n comparisons are done came from a frequentist framework, making a correction for multiple testing. The original $1/(np)$-rule was motivated from this point of view. However, we have seen in our expression for the posterior odds (11.4) that it is only p_S that we need, which is the probability for the matching individual to match by chance if innocent. Hence there is no need to think of p as being relevant for comparisons to all database members. Even if sometimes it would be appropriate to think of p as constant for some applications in real databases, we believe it could be detrimental for understanding the problem to act as if p is always constant. If that assumption is needed to reach a conclusion, it cannot be a conclusion pertaining to the general case. The same is of course true for conclusions only valid assuming a specific prior probability for C or $\mathcal{D}$.

With this in mind we mention the paper [152], which aims to reconcile the frequentist and Bayesian points of view. Using uniform priors for C and for $\mathcal{D}$ on a population of size N, and assuming p to be constant on the database, the authors derive expressions for two different "p-values." The first one is obtained by deriving the probability to find a single but coincidental match in the database. The second one is obtained by conditioning on there being a single match, computing the conditional probability that this match is not with the trace donor. The authors observe that the latter p-value is actually nothing but the posterior probability on $C \neq S$, and they conclude that with the conditional frequentist approach the Bayesian and frequentist answers coincide. They write that "quantification of the evidence based on frequentist (p-values) and Bayesian (posterior probabilities) points of view coincide" in that case. They go on to remark that "Simultaneously we show that the unconditional case corresponds (approximately) to the np rule and we argue that this lack of conditioning is an argument against using the np rule."

We disagree with all of these comments. We first remark that the agreement they reach between frequentist and Bayesian quantities is by construction, since they simply *define* the p-value as the Bayesian posterior probability. Second, p-values do not represent a quantification of evidence against a hypothesis, and the strength of the evidence in the Bayesian framework is not represented by the posterior probabilities on the hypotheses but by the likelihood ratio.

The first p-value they derive is $P(E_S, C \notin \mathcal{D})$, the probability that the trace donor is not in $\mathcal{D}$ and that nonetheless there is a single match. This can be written as $P(E_S \mid C \notin \mathcal{D})P(C \notin \mathcal{D})$. To take account of the fact that a match has been observed, the second p-value they propose is $P(C \notin \mathcal{D} \mid E_S)$. None of these have much to do with likelihood ratios. When the authors remark that the unconditional approach gives a result approximately equal to np, they refer to $P(E_S \mid C \notin \mathcal{D})P(C \notin \mathcal{D})$. If p is constant on the population then the first term of this expression can be reasonably approximated by np if $np \ll 1$. But $np \ll 1$ does not in any way imply that $P(C \notin \mathcal{D}) \approx 1$, which would be needed to arrive at the conclusion that the unconditional p-value is approximately np. It is the case in their framework where they assume $n \ll N$ and that $P(C \in \mathcal{D}) = n/N$, but this is not an assumption one needs to make. The authors seem to conclude that, because a Bayesian quantity (the $1/(np)$ likelihood ratio) is, under special circumstances, somewhat similar to a result obtained with a suboptimal frequentist approach, that gives an argument against that likelihood ratio. But our comments above indicate that this argument is not convincing.

11.8 Analogies with Example 2.2.1

We next return to the card example that we treated in Example 2.2.1. The reason for this is that already in that early example, we considered a data-driven hypothesis in the same vein as in the database problem, and there are parallels between that situation and the database search discussed in this chapter.

We recall the situation. Consider a deck of 52 card, where each card has a number between 1 and 52 (inclusive). The hypothesis H_n states that the deck is a normal deck of cards, where each number between 1 and 52 is used once. The hypothesis H_u states that all cards in the deck have the same (unspecified) number. Writing H_i, $i = 1, \ldots, 52$ for the hypothesis that all cards have number i, we can write $H_u = \bigcup_{i=1}^{52} H_i$.

Suppose that we shuffle the deck, draw one card, and the result is the number 12. Denoting this event by E we can easily see that $LR_{H_n, H_{12}}(E) = 1/52$. The observation of the number 12, therefore, is evidence for H_{12} relative to H_n. This may seem unfair to some, since whatever card is chosen, there will be this amount of evidence that the deck is uniform with the chosen number. It seems then to be the case that the simple act of drawing of any card always provides evidence against a normal deck of cards.

However, we concluded that this is not quite true. The hypothesis H_{12} is an example of a so-called *data-driven* hypothesis, that is, a hypothesis that one formulates only after obtaining the evidence. Obviously, when we tailor a hypothesis around the data, the data will appear to support this very hypothesis and the strength of the evidence will be high.

Instead, we can also compute $LR_{H_n, H_u}(E)$, the likelihood ratio of two hypotheses which are not data driven. If we make the additional assumption that $P(H_i \mid H_u) = 1/52$ for all i, then we showed that $LR_{H_n, H_u}(E) = 1$, so the evidence of obtaining a 12 gives no information whatsoever about the deck being normal or uniform, as expected.

The DNA database search controversy is in many ways analogous to the trick deck example. Indeed, consider the case of a database with a million profiles in it, and a single match is found, assuming a RMP of $p = 10^{-6}$ for all database members. Let us for simplicity assume that we have a uniform distribution for the offender on the database, that is, if the database contains the offender then each person in the database has an a priori probability of one in a million to be the

Table 11.1 *Analogy between tricked deck and database search.*

Card example	DNA database
H_u: the deck is uniform (tricked)	$C \in \mathcal{D}$: the database contains the offender
H_n: the deck is normal	$C \notin \mathcal{D}$: the database does not contain the offender
E_{12}: the drawn card is 12	E_S: a single match with S
H_{12}: the deck contains only 12's	$C = S$: the offender is S
$LR_{H_{12}, H_n}(E) = 52$: evidence that the deck is uniform 12 versus normal	$LR_{C=S, C\notin\mathcal{D}}(E_S) = 1/p$: evidence that the offender is S, versus the offender is not in the database
$P(H_u \mid E_{12}) = P(H_u)$: no evidence for tricked deck	$P(C \in \mathcal{D} \mid E_S) = P(C \in \mathcal{D})$: no evidence that $C \in \mathcal{D}$
$P(H_{12} \mid E_{12}, H_u) = 1$: if uniform then with 12's	$P(C = S \mid E_S, C \in \mathcal{D}) = 1$: if $C \in \mathcal{D}$ then $S = C$
$P(H_{12} \mid H_u) = 1/52$	$P(C = S \mid C \in \mathcal{D}) = 10^{-6}$

offender. Now suppose that there is a single match in the database, with S. Then the analogy is drawn up in Table 11.1.

We conclude that the database search situation and the trick deck example share many of the same features. In both cases, it is possible to set up hypotheses in such a way that there is by construction support for them, because they are based on the data that we have at hand. Either we set up the hypothesis that the person who matches in the database is the trace donor, or we set up the hypothesis that the deck contains only cards with the number 12 because that is what we have happened to see. In both cases, this gives a likelihood ratio favoring our data-driven hypotheses over its alternative, which is to be expected since our first hypothesis is tailored to the data. If we proceed our analysis by considering prior and posterior odds, then we see that we are perfectly entitled to do so. However, the obtained likelihood ratio can easily mislead those who are not trained to involve the odds on the hypotheses explicitly in their reasoning. The likelihood ratio in favor of our data-driven hypothesis need not imply that its alternative (the trace donor not being in the database, or the deck not being tricked) has become less likely, and this is easily overlooked.

11.9 Summary and Conclusions

We have first derived a general expression for the posterior odds for the situation of a unique match in a database search, namely

$$\frac{P(C = S \mid E_S)}{P(C \neq S \mid E_S)} = \frac{1}{p_S} \frac{P(C = S)}{P(C \notin \mathcal{D})}. \tag{11.23}$$

This expression is valid for database searches without having a prior specific suspicion against any database member, or for a search where there is already interest in S beforehand, or for a probable cause case where there is no one tested except S, which simply means that $\mathcal{D} = \{S\}$. We do *not* make a uniform prior assumption, since this assumption (1) is often not realistic, and (2) obscures the picture of which quantities play a role and which do not.

We see that only three ingredients affect the posterior directly, namely:

1. The random match probability p_S of the suspect S.
2. The prior probability $P(S = C)$ that the suspects is the criminal (or rather the donor of the trace) C.
3. The probability $P(C \notin \mathcal{D})$ that the database does not contain the criminal C.

All other quantities, such as the database size, database coverage, population size, offender population size, only affect the poster odds indirectly, if at all.

The estimation or assignment of these depends on the further context, and will be different for the three scenarios that we just mentioned. They may be numerically different in different situations, but it is important to conclude that there is no principle difference between a cold case database search, a targeted search, or a probable cause case. They are all covered by our analysis.

We have seen that (11.23) can be written as a product of a likelihood ratio and prior odds in two ways. The hypotheses $C = S$ versus $C \neq S$ lead to a likelihood ratio of at least $1/p_S$, and for $C \in \mathcal{D}$ versus $C \notin \mathcal{D}$ it leads to a likelihood ratio which is *at most* $1/p_S$ and which is under the assumption of uniform priors equal to $1/(np_S)$.

As far as the choice of the set of hypotheses is concerned (and along with that choice, the choice of the relevant likelihood ratio), we have argued that the best choice does not exist, and that the actual choice one makes should depend on the original question asked and further context. The $1/(np_S)$ likelihood ratio (if we assume uniform priors) following from the pair of hypotheses $C \in \mathcal{D}$ versus $C \notin \mathcal{D}$ is far less dangerous than using $1/p_S$, in the sense that a possible wrong interpretation as posterior odds will be not so harmful since the prior odds for these hypotheses are typically of order 1.

We have also shown that the existing arguments against the $1/(np_S)$ rule are unsound. We have furthermore shown that it may very well be the case that single matches from an enlarged database have a smaller probability to be matches with the actual trace donor, falsifying the idea that matches in a larger databases always lead to stronger cases against the identified suspect than smaller databases.

Our conclusions show that it is helpful to express the odds and likelihood ratios in their most general form, and by doing so, all fallacies and controversies disappear. The evaluation of the required probabilities depends on the model that is thought to best reflect the circumstances of the case, and depending on those, the most natural way to express the likelihood ratio may lean towards $1/p_S$ or towards $1/(np_S)$.

11.10 Bibliographical Notes

We have given most of the relevant references in the text already, for reasons explained at the beginning of this chapter. Much of this chapter can be found in [104], except that the derivation of formula (11.16) in [104] was not complete. Formula (11.1) is a more general version of a formula that appears in [51]. For an in-depth discussion on cold cases we refer to [4]. For the multi-stain problem in Section 11.3.5, the $n = 2$ case was developed by [102], although the authors did not explicitly make clear that it is in fact not another problem, but the same database problem in disguise. See also [164] for a discussion of this problem. See [136] for a discussion of the balance between likelihood ratio and priors.

12

Familial Searching

The database searches of the previous chapter were concerned with matches. We searched the database for a profile indistinguishable from the trace profile, and we extensively studied the situation in which a unique such match results. However, a comparison with a database need not result in a match. Having no match though, does not necessarily imply that the database cannot be otherwise useful. Since DNA is inherited, we might to some extent be able to find out whether or not the database contains a (close) *relative* of the donor of the trace profile. In other words, we can imagine that we are looking for some "special" person possibly present in a database, for instance a sibling, parent, or child of the trace donor. The act of searching a DNA database in order to find relatives of an unknown person is called *familial searching*.

The UK was the first country to apply this technique. Various other countries have since also introduced it. The Netherlands adopted a law in 2012 which allows the use of familial searching under some conditions.

We note also that although familial searches are mostly used to identify unknown (typically male) offenders, the technique is also useful for other purposes, such as the identification of unknown victims or to search for the parents of abandoned babies. In the case of a rape leading to conception the profile of mother and child may be used to search for the perpetrator.

Within the context of DNA, we could also be looking for a contributor to a DNA mixture, either any contributor or a specifically targeted one such as the most contributing individual (see Chapter 8). Outside the DNA context, we may imagine we compare a glass particle obtained from a suspect with a database of glass fragments to determine its source, or a recovered MDMA tablet with a database of other tables to investigate whether the recovered tablet has the same origin as a known one. What such searches have in common with familial searching is that for many database items, categorically exclusionary statements are not possible, i.e., that many likelihood ratios between the reference item and the database items are non-zero.

In this chapter we restrict ourselves to familial searching in the DNA context. Since DNA databases mostly contain autosomal DNA profiles, most comparisons are based on autosomal loci. However, autosomal DNA is quickly diluted: at every generation, half of it is not passed on to offspring and therefore autosomal DNA kinship analysis on relatively few loci, as they are available in DNA databases, is only worthwhile for close relationships such as parent–child and sibling relationships.

Hence familial searches based on autosomal DNA profiles are usually done aimed at parents, children and siblings. They are performed by computation of the appropriate likelihood ratios between the unknown individual and the database members, called parental (or paternity) index (PI) and sibling index (SI) respectively, which we introduced in Chapter 7. If we assume that the database contains at most one special item, we will see below in Proposition 12.1.1 how from these likelihood ratios one can make a probabilistic assessment of which item, if any, may be that special item.

A second possibility is the comparison of the Y-chromosomal DNA profile of the case profile with Y-chromosomal DNA profiles in the database (see Section 4.5.2 for a short discussion of Y-chromosomes). This may uncover paternal relatives that are more distantly related, but it is in general not possible to be precise as to how many generations are between two people who share the same Y-chromosomal profile. Typing additional Y-chromosomal loci may be helpful in this situation. Finally, familial searches have also been carried out based on a single, very rare autosomal allele, by investigating those persons in the database who also have that allele.

For ease of comparison between different strategies, we assume throughout that the database contains at most one relative of the type we are looking for, in addition to unrelated individuals. This is, of course, a somewhat restrictive assumption. However, when we are looking for, say, the most important donor of a DNA mixture, then there is naturally only one such person possible, and then the assumption is not restrictive at all. In Section 8.3 we noted that mixture evaluation and kinship problems have in common that in both cases, we have a probability distribution describing the profiles of the person we look for (a relative of a trace donor for familial searching, or a mixture contributor). If more relatives are present, this can of course only increase the probability of a search uncovering at least one relative.

The chapter is structured as follows. In Section 12.1 we present a probabilistic analysis yielding posterior probabilities, assuming that we have prior probabilities for each database member to be related to the targeted individual. In Section 12.2 we discuss various strategies that may be used after we have compared the trace profile to all the profiles in the database. After that, in Section 12.3, we investigate the performance of the strategies from Section 12.2. This we do, somewhat uncharacteristically for this book, by simulation since there seems to be no way to do this in a more analytical way. In Section 12.4 we discuss the relation between the performance of search strategies and the Neyman–Pearson lemma.

12.1 Probabilistic Assessments for Familial Searching

When we discussed database matches in the previous chapter, we put ourselves in the epistemic position that we did not know the actual profiles present in the database. They were considered to be random for us.

We concluded that for the probabilistic inference about the question whether or not the uniquely matching person was the donor of the trace profile, we only needed prior probabilities about the identity of the donor, together with the random match probability p_i for the matching person. The fact that all other persons did not match meant that all these other persons had a likelihood ratio of zero, excluding them as donor. So, one can say that in the database search, knowledge of all pairwise likelihood ratios between trace profile and database members, together with appropriate prior information was all we needed.

The first thing we will show now, is that this is also the case in the more general context of familial searching. This time, however, there will in general be many likelihood ratios that are non-zero. For instance, when we look for a sibling relationship, *all* persons in the database will have a positive likelihood ratio since two siblings need not share any autosomal allele at all.

Let $\mathcal{D}$ denote a database of size n containing autosomal profiles $g_1, \ldots, g_n$. We denote the special item by R, and write $R = i$ for the event that i is the special item. When the special item is not in $\mathcal{D}$ we write $R \notin \mathcal{D}$. We let $\pi_i = P(R = i)$, for $i = 1, \ldots, n$, and define

$$\pi_{\mathcal{D}} := \sum_{i=1}^{n} \pi_i = P(R \in \mathcal{D})$$

to be the prior probability that the special item is in the database. Finally, we let

$$\pi_0 := 1 - \pi_{\mathcal{D}}$$

be the prior probability that it is not. The person C whose relative we seek has profile g_C, and we call g_C the *case profile*. We assume that the prior probabilities do not depend on g_C. We also assume that the DNA profiles of the persons in the database are conditionally independent given R and g_C. This is true in an infinite population with random mating and known allele probabilities. In the language of Chapter 7, it is not exactly true if we consider non-zero identical by descent probabilities between the alleles of any two individuals in the population. In that case, we have (see Section 7.5) $\theta > 0$ so that the DNA profiles of individuals selected randomly from the population are not independent.

We are interested in the probabilities

$$P(R = i \mid g_1, \ldots, g_n, g_C), \tag{12.1}$$

that is, the probability that item i is the special item, given all the profiles in the database and the case profile.

We write r_i for the likelihood ratio that we get for item i in favor of being special, as opposed to being generic (which in the DNA context means that the person is unrelated to the donor of the case profile). Of course, we take the likelihood ratio that corresponds to the type of relatedness that we are interested in: if we look for siblings, then r_i is the sibling index, etc. Let us denote the vector of obtained likelihood ratios by $LR_{\mathcal{D}} = (r_1, \ldots, r_n)$. In the following result we immediately state the appropriate posterior probabilities, without first computing likelihood ratios. Following, however, we will discuss the likelihood ratios that correspond to it, in order to be able to compare with the previous chapter.

Proposition 12.1.1 *Given the database information $g_1, \ldots, g_n$ and the case profile g_C, the probability that the special item is item i is equal to*

$$P(R = i \mid g_1, \ldots, g_n, g_C) = \frac{\pi_i r_i}{\sum_{k=0}^{n} \pi_k r_k},$$

where we define $r_0 := 1$.

Proof. We write $\mathbf{g} = (g_1, \ldots, g_n)$ for the vector of the profiles in the database. We are interested in

$$P(R = i \mid \mathbf{g}, g_C) = \frac{P(\mathbf{g} \mid R = i, g_C) P(R = i)}{P(\mathbf{g} \mid g_C)}, \tag{12.2}$$

where we have used the assumption that $P(R = i \mid g_C) = P(R = i)$.

The denominator in (12.2) can be expanded as

$$P(\mathbf{g} \mid g_C) = \sum_{k=1}^{n} P(\mathbf{g} \mid R = k, g_C) P(R = k) + P(\mathbf{g} \mid R \notin D, g_C) P(R \notin \mathcal{D}).$$

Therefore,

$$\frac{1}{P(R = i \mid \mathbf{g}, g_C)} = \sum_{k=1}^{n} \frac{P(\mathbf{g} \mid R = k, g_C) P(R = k)}{P(\mathbf{g} \mid R = i, g_C) P(R = i)}$$

$$+ \frac{P(\mathbf{g} \mid R \notin \mathcal{D}, g_C) P(R \notin \mathcal{D})}{P(\mathbf{g} \mid R = i, g_C) P(R = i)},$$

which by conditional independence reduces to

$$\sum_{k=1}^{n} \frac{P(g_i \mid R = k, g_C)P(g_k \mid R = k, g_C)P(R = k)}{P(g_i \mid R = i, g_C)P(g_k \mid R = i, g_C)P(R = i)}$$

$$+ \frac{P(g_i \mid R \notin \mathcal{D}, g_C)P(R \notin \mathcal{D})}{P(g_i \mid R = i, g_C)P(R = i)}.$$

The first fraction in the sum is the ratio of the probabilities of seeing g_i given that $R = k$ respectively $R = i$. In the first case i is generic, and in the second case i is the special item. Hence this fraction is the reciprocal of r_i. Similarly, the second fraction is equal to r_k, while the final fraction in the sum is π_k/π_i. The rightmost fraction is just $\pi_0/(r_i \pi_i)$ so we obtain

$$\frac{1}{P(R = i \mid \mathbf{g}, g_C)} = \sum_{k=1}^{n} \frac{r_k}{r_i} \frac{\pi_k}{\pi_i} + \frac{1}{r_i} \frac{\pi_0}{\pi_i} = \frac{\sum_{k=0}^{n} \pi_k r_k}{\pi_i r_i},$$

which is what we needed to show. $\square$

It follows that the only information from the database that we need to compute the posterior probabilities on $R = i$ are the prior probabilities, together with the likelihood ratios $r_1, \ldots, r_n$, and we have

$$P(R = i \mid \mathbf{g}, g_C) = P(R = i \mid LR_{\mathcal{D}} = (r_1, \ldots, r_n)). \tag{12.3}$$

In order to compute the probability that the special element is item i we only need all the likelihood ratios that we have obtained, and we do not need the actual genetic data itself. We have drawn similar conclusions before, for instance in Chapter 2. It reinforces (again) the idea that all evidential information of the data is summarized by the appropriate likelihood ratios. If we would have had different profiles in the database with the same likelihood ratios $(r_1, \ldots, r_n)$, then the posterior probabilities would have been the same. Hence, once we have calculated the likelihood ratios $r_1, \ldots, r_n$ we do not have to take the underlying evidence $(\mathbf{g}, g_C)$ into account any more.

For the database as a whole, the probability that it contains the special item is now equal to the sum of all posterior probabilities (recall that $r_0 = 1$):

$$P(R \in \mathcal{D} \mid \mathbf{g}, g_C) = \sum_{i=1}^{n} P(R = i \mid \mathbf{g}, g_C)$$

$$= \frac{\sum_{i=1}^{n} \pi_i r_i}{\sum_{k=0}^{n} \pi_k r_k}.$$

Equivalently, we may write

$$\frac{P(R \in \mathcal{D} \mid \mathbf{g}, g_C)}{P(R \notin \mathcal{D} \mid \mathbf{g}, g_C)} = \frac{1}{\pi_0} \sum_{i=1}^{n} \pi_i r_i$$

$$= \frac{1}{\pi_{\mathcal{D}}} \sum_{i=1}^{n} \pi_i r_i \times \frac{P(R \in \mathcal{D})}{P(R \notin \mathcal{D})}. \qquad (12.4)$$

Although, having computed the posterior probabilities, we may not be so interested in the likelihood ratio anymore, we do point out that it follows from (12.4) that the likelihood ratio of $R \in \mathcal{D}$ versus $R \notin \mathcal{D}$ is equal to

$$\frac{P(\mathbf{g}, g_C \mid R \in \mathcal{D})}{P(\mathbf{g}, g_C \mid R \notin \mathcal{D})} = \frac{1}{\pi_{\mathcal{D}}} \sum_{i=1}^{n} \pi_i r_i = \sum_{i=1}^{n} P(R = i \mid R \in \mathcal{D}) r_i. \qquad (12.5)$$

We see now that we have a generalization of the database-centered likelihood ratio from Section 11.2. In that case we were looking at exact matches. The r_S of the uniquely matching person S is in that case equal to $1/p_S$, with p_S the random match probability of S. All other r_i are equal to 0. Hence in that case, (12.5) reduces to $P(R = S \mid R \in \mathcal{D})/p_S$, which is precisely what we found in (11.8). We remark that the analysis in this section is applicable in the situation of the previous chapter, since the assumption of at most one special person is naturally satisfied in the case of identification.

The likelihood ratio (12.5) is a weighted average of the likelihood ratios obtained with the database, where the weights correspond to the conditional probabilities that R is person i, given that R is in the database. In the case where we assume that the prior probabilities are uniformly distributed within $\mathcal{D}$, this expression reduces to $\sum_{i=1}^{n} r_i/n$, the arithmetic mean of all the likelihood ratios obtained with the database members.

For a subset $\mathcal{D}' \subset \mathcal{D}$, we similarly have that the likelihood ratio in favor of R being a member of $\mathcal{D}'$, versus not being in the database $\mathcal{D}$ at all, is

$$\frac{P(\mathbf{g}, g_C \mid R \in \mathcal{D}')}{P(\mathbf{g}, g_C \mid R \notin \mathcal{D})} = \frac{\sum_{i \in \mathcal{D}'} \pi_i r_i}{\sum_{k \in \mathcal{D}'} \pi_k} = \sum_{i \in \mathcal{D}'} P(R = i \mid R \in \mathcal{D}') r_i, \qquad (12.6)$$

which is a generalization of (11.14). The posterior probability for $R \in \mathcal{D}'$, assuming $R \in \mathcal{D}$, is

$$P(R \in \mathcal{D}' \mid \mathbf{g}, g_C, R \in \mathcal{D}) = \frac{\sum_{i \in \mathcal{D}'} \pi_i r_i}{\sum_{k \in \mathcal{D}} \pi_k r_k}. \qquad (12.7)$$

In the case of a uniform prior, the π_i cancel out. In that case, the conditional posterior probability that R is in $\mathcal{D}'$, given that R is in the database $\mathcal{D}$, is equal to the fraction of the total sum of likelihood ratios in $\mathcal{D}$ that is achieved by the elements of $\mathcal{D}'$.

12.2 Search Strategies

While Proposition 12.1.1 tells us what the probability for each item is to be the special item, at least when prior probabilities are available, it does not immediately tells us what to *do*. We therefore see that some kind of *search strategy* is required: based on the likelihood ratios $r_1, \ldots, r_n$, and possibly the prior probabilities $\pi_1, \ldots, \pi_n$, one would like to select a number of individuals, and investigate these further.

By a search strategy, we mean the selection of a subset $\mathcal{D}' \subset \mathcal{D}$ such that the follow up for $\mathcal{D}'$ and the remaining items differ. We imagine that the items in $\mathcal{D}'$ are considered for further investigation, whereas those outside $\mathcal{D}'$ are not. In the context of familial searching this further investigation could consist of additional DNA analyses to confirm or invalidate the possibility of relatedness, or it could consist of tactical investigation by the investigating authorities. Ideally, the set $\mathcal{D}'$ is such that it is not prohibitively large but at the same time has a high probability to contain the special item (if present). Obviously, the choice $\mathcal{D}' = \mathcal{D}$ is typically not feasible in practice, as this would amount to having to further investigate all database members. The same holds in many cases for the set $\mathcal{D}' = \{i : r_i > 0\}$ of all strictly non-excluded items: for siblings we would still have $\mathcal{D}' = \mathcal{D}$ but even for a parent–child search, depending on the size of the database and the number of comparable loci, this can also be a very large set.

The results of Section 12.1 allow us to conclude that a possible strategy to make a selection should only be based on the collection of likelihood ratios $r_1, \ldots, r_n$, possibly together with prior probabilities $\pi_1, \ldots, \pi_n$.

But what is a good strategy? How do we measure the "goodness" of a strategy? There are, at least, two conflicting quantities. First of all, there is the *success rate* of a strategy, that is, how often are we able to retrieve the special element, if present. But this rate is not the only issue at stake. The *workload*, that is, how many generic elements are also retrieved as by-catch, is also important. In other words, when discussing the quality of a strategy we are interested in error rates. Note, however, as discussed extensively throughout this book, that once we have computed the likelihood ratios, these error rates become irrelevant since we are then dealing with a particular case and particular data. It does not matter any more then, by which probability we would have found these data.

If we base our selection on sibling or parental indices, then the error rates associated with a search strategy are determined by the distributions of these very indices. Knowledge of the distributions of these likelihood ratios can then be used to predict how often certain actions will be taken, and what the results will be, hence to assess the quality of a possible strategy. We can then decide whether or not the strategy is promising enough to be carried out at all, or use it to make a selection of cases for which it is worthwhile to carry it out.

We now consider various ways to define a selection $\mathcal{D}'$. The selection $\mathcal{D}'$ will be based on the $r_1, \ldots, r_n$ and possibly on the $\pi_1, \ldots, \pi_n$. It defines $\mathcal{D}'$ as a random subset of $\mathcal{D}$ if we regard all $g_1, \ldots, g_n$, hence all likelihood ratios $r_1, \ldots, r_n$ as the outcome of random variables. We can therefore speak of probabilities involving $\mathcal{D}'$, and statements such as, for instance, $P(\mathcal{D}' = A \mid R \notin \mathcal{D})$ make sense, for any subset A of $\mathcal{D}$. We introduce six different strategies. We will discuss their properties below, and simulate their performance in Section 12.3.

Perhaps the simplest strategy is what we call the *top-k* strategy. This strategy consists simply of choosing $\mathcal{D}'$ to be the collection of the k items with the largest likelihood ratios, for some previously given k.

Instead of choosing the largest likelihood ratios one can also decide to choose those items that give a sufficiently strong indication to be special. In other words, this boils down to setting

$$\mathcal{D}' := \{i : r_i \geq t\}$$

for some appropriate number t which we call the *threshold*. If we choose t once and for all, applying it to all case profiles, this strategy goes under the name *LR-threshold* strategy.

We can also combine the top-k and the LR-threshold strategy, yielding the so-called *threshold top-k* strategy, as follows. Renumber the items in $\mathcal{D}$ such that $r_1 \geq \cdots \geq r_n$ and let

$$\mathcal{D}' := \{i : 1 \leq i \leq k, r_i \geq t\},$$

that is, we take $\mathcal{D}'$ to be the set of largest likelihood ratios that exceed threshold t, but we do not take in more than k elements.

The three strategies so far only use the likelihood ratios $r_1, \ldots, r_n$ and no further information or assumptions. In particular, they do not use the distribution of the likelihood ratios for relatives or unrelated individuals. But there is a straightforward way to use that distribution explicitly, as follows. First we choose $\alpha \in (0, 1)$, and then we let

$$\mathcal{D}' := \{i : r_i \geq t_{C,\alpha}\},$$

where $t_{C,\alpha}$ is the largest value of t such that the probability that a relative of the case profile donor C has likelihood ratio t at least t is at least α. This strategy is tailored around the actual case profile, and is therefore called the *profile-centered* strategy. Contrary to the LR-threshold strategy, we can now for every C choose a new threshold $t_{C,\alpha}$ such that we ensure that relatives of C are found with probability at least α.

None of the four strategies above used prior information, they only used likelihood ratios. For the *conditional* strategy this is different. Again we first choose $\alpha \in (0,1)$. Based on (12.7), we include sufficiently many items in $\mathcal{D}'$ as to have a probability α to include the special item, if present. In other words, $\mathcal{D}'$ is defined as the smallest subset of $\mathcal{D}$ such that

$$P(R \in \mathcal{D}' \mid LR_{\mathcal{D}} = (r_1, \ldots, r_n), R \in \mathcal{D}) \geq \alpha.$$

Finally, we mention the *posterior threshold* strategy, which also uses prior information. It consists of selecting all items with a sufficiently high posterior probability, that is,

$$\mathcal{D}' := \{i : \pi_i r_i \geq t\}$$

for some appropriate threshold t.

The listed strategies are very different in nature. To name but a few differences: the last two use prior probabilities, while the others do not. The profile-centered and conditional strategy need an auxiliary α, the others do not need that. The LR-threshold strategy includes a given i in $\mathcal{D}'$ on the basis of the value of r_i only, while for the top-k threshold, the other likelihood ratios do play a role. Below, in Section 12.2.1 we somewhat elaborate on these differences.

All of these strategies may select different subsets $\mathcal{D}'$, and of course a next question is then which strategy is most suitable for use in practice. We thus need some evaluation comparing the strategies to see which one is better, where the definition of "better" may change in various circumstances. In this connection, we remark that the Neyman–Pearson lemma (Proposition 10.1.1) seems to suggest that the LR-threshold strategy is the best one. Indeed, this lemma says that, if some LR-threshold is used to decide whether or not to put item i into $\mathcal{D}'$ then there is no alternative strategy possible that improves on both error rates we thus obtain. However, this may not always be correct: if we assume that the database contains zero or one special item, then the various comparisons are no longer completely independent, and the Neyman–Pearson lemma no longer applies. We discuss this in detail in Section 12.4.

12.2.1 Strategy Properties

First, we will make more precise what we want to compare when looking at the various strategies. We have a database $\mathcal{D}$ of size n. We already mentioned that we would like to make the success rate as high as possible. To this end, we define the *probability of detection* of a strategy in a database $\mathcal{D}$ of size n as the probability that R is in the subset $\mathcal{D}'$ selected according to the strategy, if $\mathcal{D}$ would consist of one realization of R and $n-1$ realizations of generic elements. In this definition, we think of the case profile as being random as well. If one so wishes, one can also define a case-specific probability of detection, for a given case profile g_C.

For some strategies, the probability of detection depends on n, while for others it does not. For instance, the probability of detection for the top k strategy depends on n, since adding additional profiles to the database affects the probability that there are k items with a larger likelihood ratio than the special item. On the other hand, for the LR-threshold strategy, the number n is clearly irrelevant as far as the probability of detection is concerned, since an item is chosen into $\mathcal{D}'$ based on its own likelihood ratio only.

We already mentioned the workload. Formally, we define the workload of a strategy in a database of size n as the expected size of $\mathcal{D}'$, if $\mathcal{D}$ would consist of n generic elements. Again, we think of the case profile as random here, and again, one may consider a case-dependent workload. As the probability of detection, the workload may or may not depend on n, depending on the strategy. For the top-k strategy it obviously does not, while for the LR-threshold strategy it certainly does.

The probability of detection and the workload are generalizations of the classical notions of true and false positive rates, which we retrieve for $n = 1$. Indeed in that case, the probability of detection is the probability that a relative is classified as such, whereas the workload is the probability that an unrelated individual is classified as being related.

For a likelihood ratio threshold t, we can also define true and false positive rates. Writing LR_R for the likelihood ratio of the special item, we let

$$TPR(t) := P(LR_R \geq t),$$

where TPR stands for *true positive rate*: the probability that for a randomly chosen case profile g_C, a random relative of the appropriate type exceeds likelihood ratio threshold t. That is, $TPR(t)$ is the probability that a random pair of related individuals has a likelihood ratio at least equal to t. If we fix g_C, then

$$TPR(t \mid g_C) := P(LR_R \geq t \mid g_C)$$

is the probability that a random relative of someone with profile g_C exceeds likelihood ratio threshold t.

Similarly, writing LR_G for the likelihood ratio of a generic person, we let the *false positive rate* (FPR) be

$$FPR(t) := P(LR_G \geq t),$$

which amounts to the probability that the likelihood ratio is at least t computed on two randomly chosen unrelated individuals. Finally, we let

$$FPR(t \mid g_C) := P(LR_G \geq t \mid g_C)$$

be the probability that a generic person exceeds the likelihood ratio threshold t in favor of being related to a person with profile g_C. Let us now briefly discuss the probability of detection and the workload for each of the six strategies that we introduced above.

Top-k. With this strategy the workload is fixed at precisely k, which may be advantageous for planning purposes. The probability of detection is in principle computable using order statistics, and depends on n.

LR-threshold. For the LR-threshold strategy with threshold t, the probability of detection is $TPR(t)$ and the workload is $n \times FPR(t)$. Indeed, this strategy includes an item in $\mathcal{D}'$ purely on the basis of its own likelihood ratio. The true relative is selected with a probability determined by a different distribution function than a generic element.

The workload can be calculated from the likelihood ratio distribution for generic items, or estimated with importance sampling using Proposition 2.4.2. According to this proposition, the workload is bounded above by n/t. One can similarly compute the case-specific workloads.

In a database with n generic items, the top-k strategy yields the same results as an LR-threshold strategy with a false positive rate of k/n. Indeed, with that false positive rate, the LR-threshold strategy will select around $n \times (k/n) = k$ items, and these will then be the items with the highest likelihood ratios.

Threshold top-k. This strategy has a workload of at most k, since we restrict the top-k method to those likelihood ratios that are large enough. The probability of detection depends on the database size, and can in principle be computed using order statistics.

Profile-centered. For the profile-centered strategy, the probability of detection, if we search for a relative of a person with profile g_C, is equal to $TPR(t_{C,\alpha} \mid g_C)$, and the workload is $n \times FPR(t_{C,\alpha} \mid g_C)$. This method has, by construction, a probability of detection of (at least) α, for every individual g_C. The workload can be computed similarly as for the LR-threshold method with the appropriate value of the threshold.

Conditional. According to this strategy, we renumber the database items such that $\pi_1 r_1 \geq \cdots \geq \pi_n r_n$ and then let $\mathcal{D}' := \{1, \ldots, k\}$ for the minimal k such that $\sum_{i=1}^{k} \pi_i r_i \geq \alpha \sum_{i=1}^{n} \pi_i r_i$. By construction, this strategy guarantees a probability of detection of at least α, where the prior probabilities are taken into account.

For the workload we assume that $R \notin \mathcal{D}$. The expected sum of the likelihood ratios is, in view of (2.23), equal to n. In principle one can, for a given type of relatedness, compute the workload. In the case where only small likelihood ratios are obtained, many persons may be needed in $\mathcal{D}'$.

Posterior threshold. This strategy selects item i in $\mathcal{D}'$ if $\pi_i r_i \geq t$. Therefore in the case of a uniform prior, the method is in fact a LR-threshold strategy corresponding to threshold nt.

12.3 Strategy Performance

The various strategies are of very different nature, and are not so easy to compare, especially when non-uniform priors are taken into account. When it comes down to compare the various strategies, it seems reasonable to compare the strategies in the case of a uniform prior. In this section we will shed some light on the behavior of some of the strategies, by setting up various simulations.

12.3.1 The Top-k Strategy

We take the top-k strategy as a benchmark, and we will compare its behavior with other strategies. We start with some observations about this top-k strategy itself. For now we fix the relationship that we seek (siblings), the database size (100,000), and the set of loci that we type (SGMPlus, consisting of 10 autosomal loci).

In a top-k strategy, the workload is fixed and non-random. It is in principle not difficult to empirically find the probability of detection for a top-k strategy. For example, we could simulate a large number of databases, each containing one relative of a randomly drawn case profile and count how many of the relatives are found in the top-k likelihood ratios in each of the databases.

This procedure produces one unique number for the probability of detection, corresponding to a top-k search in database of this size, the type of relatedness, allele frequencies and employed genetic inheritance model. However, not all case profiles are equally suitable for finding relatives. Therefore we instead investigate the probability of detection for different case profiles, obtaining the unconditional probability of detection as the average.

For a case profile g_C, assuming we investigate the probability of detection in a database of size n, we first sample $n - 1$ likelihood ratios $r_i = LR(g_C, d_i)$ for unrelated individuals d_i. In practice the r_i are all distinct, so we re-order them such that $r_1 > \cdots > r_{n-1}$. Then, using the distribution of the likelihood ratio for relatives of g_C, we take as probability of detection in the top-k the probability that a relative of g_C has a likelihood ratio larger than r_k. Indeed, in that case, the true relative would have been detected in the top-k in the simulated database if we had augmented it with that relative.

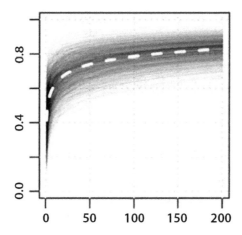

Figure 12.1 Probability to find a sibling in the top-k, as a function of k. The dashed line indicates the average over all 1,000 simulated profiles. The database size n is equal to 100,000.

We carried out this procedure for siblings of 1,000 case profiles, independently drawn. In Figure 12.1 (reprinted from [92]) we have summarized the results. On the horizontal axis we let k run from 1 to 200. For each of the 1,000 case profiles, we have checked whether it is in the top k, for $k = 1, \ldots, 200$, resulting in 1,000 "curves." The dashed line is the average curve over all 1,000 profiles, and serves as an estimate for the probability of detection of the top-k strategy in general.

We observe rather volatile behavior, in the sense that the individual probability of detection varies greatly among the various case profiles. We also observe that enlarging k beyond, say $k = 100$ has only limited effect on the probability of detection.

In [92] a simulation study was carried out, where some of the above mentioned strategies were involved, namely the top-168, the LR-threshold, the profile-centered, and the conditional strategy. The somewhat odd choice of the number 168 has to do with the fact that for practical reasons, this strategy is often applied [110]. We discuss some of the findings of [92] here.

Given the probability of detection of the top-168 strategy, the other strategies were carried out with parameters such that they had the same probability of detection, where, in the case of the conditional strategy, uniform priors were used. To be precise, writing α_{168} for the achieved probability of detection in the top-168 strategy, for the LR-threshold strategy, t was chosen such that $P(SI \geq t \mid \text{sibs}) = \alpha_{168}$, where SI denotes the usual sibling index. For the profile-centered strategy, the threshold t_C needed for the probability of detection to be α_{168} conditional on g_C is then different for different case profiles. For the conditional strategy, we use (12.7) with uniform priors.

Table 12.1 *Workloads, together with the standard deviation of the size of the selected set, obtained in a simulation experiment in which the parameters are chosen such that the probability of detection is equal among the four strategies.*

Strategy	Workload	Standard deviation
Top-168	168	0
LR-threshold	162.22	33.59
Profile-centered	200.80	161.13
Conditional	240.34	192.52

The results of this simulation is summarized in Table 12.1, reprinted from [92]. Again, the results are based on simulations of 1,000 databases of size $n = 100,000$ each, using the SGMPlus multiplex with Dutch allele frequencies.

We see from the table that the smallest workload was achieved with the LR-threshold method, which had a workload of about 162. The price we have to pay for that, compared to the top-168 strategy, is that the standard deviation is positive, and hence the workload can be larger than the fixed workload of 168 in the top-168 strategy.

The LR-threshold strategy clearly outperforms both the profile-centered and the conditional strategy, in terms of both average workload and standard deviation. Especially the large standard deviation of the conditional strategy stands out. The conditional strategy selects likelihood ratios until a fraction of the sum of all likelihood ratios has been sampled. If there are no profiles with exceptionally high likelihood ratios, then one needs many items in order to have the required fraction of the sum of all likelihood ratios.

Next we will compare the top-k strategy with the LR-threshold and threshold top-k strategies in some more detail.

12.3.2 Comparison of the LR-threshold and Threshold Top-k Strategies With the Top-k Strategy

We have compared the top-k strategies (for $1 \leq k \leq 1,000$) with LR-threshold strategies with threshold t for $1 \leq t \leq 10^7$; see Figure 12.2. The database size was again taken to be 100,000 (SGMPlus loci) and we performed 100,000 simulations. Figure 12.2 requires some explanation which we now provide.

The probability of detection on the vertical axis is obtained by simply counting how often the relative is contained in the top-k, or having a likelihood ratio at least equal to t (for the two strategies respectively). On the horizontal axis, we mark the average fraction of $\mathcal{D}$ that was selected in the databases of size 100,000 *containing*

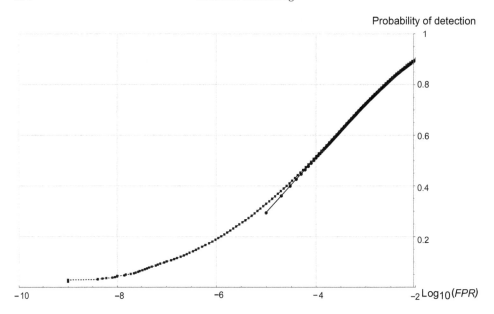

Figure 12.2 ROC-curves of LR-threshold strategies (dotted) and top-k strategies based on 100,000 sibling searches. See the text for more explanation.

only unrelated persons. We call this the false positive rate (FPR), but note that it applies only to unrelated individuals in a database that consists entirely of unrelated individuals. In other words, the false positive rate is simply the workload divided by n. With our database size of 100,000, the FPR of the top-k strategy is obviously k/n and cannot be smaller than 10^{-5}, so this is the reason that the lower curve stops there. However, for the LR-threshold strategies, this is not the case. Although in the figure, one cannot immediately see what the values of k and t are that correspond to the plotted points, the LR-threshold with the same probability of detection as the top-1 strategy is, roughly, at $t = 10^4$.

Despite the fact that the values of k and t cannot be read off from the ROC-curve, the plot allows for convenient comparison between the two strategies. We see that the curve corresponding to the LR-threshold strategies is above the curve for the top-k strategies. This implies two things: (1) for a given FPR, the LR-threshold strategy has a higher probability of detection, and (2) for a fixed probability of detection, the LR-threshold strategy has a lower FPR. In other words, the LR-threshold strategy is superior to the top-k strategy.

On the other hand, it is clear from Figure 12.2 that the LR-threshold strategy is only slightly better than the top-k strategy. For small k the difference is largest: with $k = 1$ we found in the top-1 strategy a probability of detection of 0.295, at a false positive rate of 10^{-5}. For threshold $t = 10^{3.85}$ we found a probability of

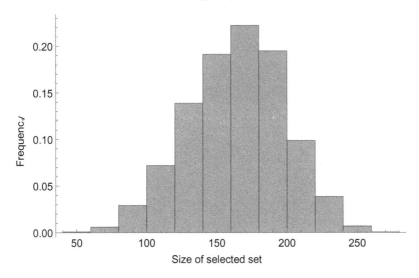

Figure 12.3 Histogram for the size of the selected set in the LR-threshold strategy, for threshold t such that the probability of detection is the same as for the top-168 strategy.

detection of 0.329, at almost the same false positive rate. For larger k, the difference is smaller, with the LR-threshold strategy only very slightly outperforming the top-k strategies.

Looking again at the special case of the top-168 search, we found that the top-168 strategy yields a probability of detection of 0.769. The LR-threshold that yielded the same probability of detection was, at least in in this simulation, $t = 10^{1.7126}$. With this threshold, in total 16,347,860 unrelated individuals were selected in the databases of unrelated individuals, which is an improvement over the top-168 search for which precisely 16,800,000 unrelated individuals were selected.

The variance in size of the selected set is quite large, however, and we plot a histogram of the sizes in Figure 12.3. Thus, while the LR-threshold strategies outperform the top-k strategies, they have the practical disadvantage of yielding a quite variable number of individuals for further inspection.

Next we compare the threshold top-k strategy with the LR-threshold strategy. We make the same comparisons as for the top-k versus LR-threshold strategies, and we display the case with $k = 1$ in Figure 12.4. The curves arise from varying the threshold t.

The threshold top-1 strategy cannot take in more than one item, and for small enough thresholds coincides with the top-1 strategy. Therefore, its graph reaches an endpoint (at $FPR = 10^{-5}$), whereas the LR-threshold graph is not fully displayed

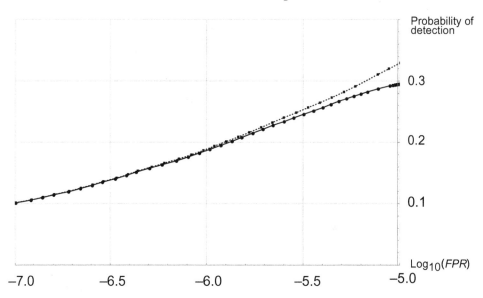

Figure 12.4 ROC-curves of threshold top-1 strategy (black curve) and LR-threshold strategies (dotted curve) based on 100,000 sibling searches, with running parameter the threshold t.

in Figure 12.4 and continues to the right, taking larger subsets and achieving a higher probability of detection.

We see from Figure 12.4 that, as before, the LR-threshold strategy outperforms the compared strategy. For very large t, virtually no unrelated individuals reach threshold t, and then the threshold top-1 strategy almost coincides with the LR-threshold strategy. For small thresholds, the truncation plays less of a role and ultimately with $t = 0$ we reach the top-1 strategy, which is outperformed by the LR-threshold strategy.

As k increases, the two strategies coincide already for smaller t. In Figure 12.5 we plot the same graphs as in Figure 12.4 but now for the truncated top-100 strategy. We see that now the strategies have almost the same performance. This time the graph for the truncated top-100 ends, of course, at $FPR = 10^{-3}$ since for low thresholds we take in 100 out of 100,000 individuals.

Neither the (threshold) top-1 nor the top-100 strategy can reach the probability of detection achieved by the top-168 strategy, so in order to make a last comparison with the top-168 strategy, we must increase k. With the top-168 strategy, in the 100,000 searches we simulated, we found 76,913 relatives. The LR-threshold strategy extracted the same number of relatives for $t = 1.17126$, yielding 16,347,860

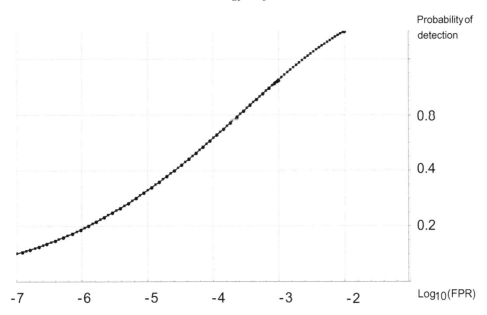

Figure 12.5 ROC-curves of the threshold top-100 strategy and the LR-threshold strategies based on 100,000 sibling searches, with running parameter the threshold t.

unrelated individuals. However, the LR-threshold strategy sometimes produces large subsets, the largest one containing 270 individuals in our simulation.

A result very similar to the LR-threshold strategy can be obtained with the threshold top-200 strategy. We found that taking $t = 1.7029$ yielded 76,913 relatives and a total of 16,453,251 selected individuals, only slightly more than with the above mentioned LR-threshold strategy. However, by construction, the subset size is under control since it cannot exceed 200. We plot a histogram of the subset sizes in Figure 12.6.

Thus, it is possible to control the maximal amount of work needed using a threshold top-k strategy, whilst not losing any meaningful amount of search performance.

We can heuristically understand these outcomes. Indeed, for the threshold top-k, the truncation has a different effect depending on the threshold employed and depending on k. For large enough thresholds t, there will typically not be k individuals exceeding threshold t so that the threshold top-k and the LR-threshold strategy will select the same subsets. For decreasing thresholds, the truncation will at some point mean that not all likelihood ratios exceeding t are included and the strategy is now almost the same as the top-k strategy. Therefore, the threshold

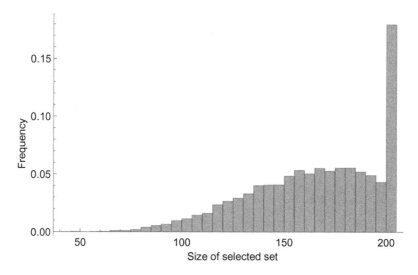

Figure 12.6 Histogram of the size of the selected set for the top-200 threshold strategy, with parameters such that the probability of detection is the same as for the top-168 strategy.

top-k interpolates between the LR-threshold strategy and the top-k strategy, meaning in practice that it can have the advantage of the LR-threshold strategy (an optimal combination of probability of detection and workload) and the advantage of the top-k as well (a bound on the size of the selected subset).

12.4 Search Strategies and the Neyman–Pearson Lemma

The Neyman–Pearson lemma says that if, for a given profile of a person, we need to decide on relatedness with C, deciding on the basis of a LR-threshold is optimal, in the sense that one cannot improve upon $TPR(t \mid g_C)$ and $FPR(t \mid g_C)$ that correspond to a LR-threshold t. If we have n such profiles, each of which is independently related to the case profile g_C with probability π, then we expect to find $n \times \pi \times TPR(t \mid g_C)$ relatives, and $n \times (1 - \pi) \times FPR(t \mid g_C)$ unrelated individuals. Hence, if we view the database as a sequence of profiles, each independent of the other ones with a probability π to be related, then we cannot find a strategy that retrieves more related individuals and fewer unrelated ones.

In reality, a database can perhaps almost, but not precisely viewed as such. If we know that a certain individual is related, this decreases the probability that others are related, simply because we do not expect that there are many related individuals. In the extreme case where there is at most one relative in the database, having found it means that we are sure all other database members are unrelated. In practice, to view the database profiles as independent realizations of profiles of related or unrelated individuals, where the probability of relatedness is less than $1/n$, leads to a description where the probability to have more than one relative is included is very small. This explains why the LR-threshold strategy turns out to be optimal among all considered strategies, even if we are not precisely in the setting of the Neyman–Pearson lemma.

Here, we should be somewhat careful with the word "optimal." We can optimize either over *all* cases, or we can optimize for a given particular case profile. The Neyman–Pearson lemma ensures that if we aim to optimize our strategy over all cases together, using a fixed LR-threshold is optimal in the long run over all cases.

In every case considered individually, however, any LR-threshold gives an optimal strategy in the Neyman–Pearson sense for that particular case, still assuming that items are considered independently for uptake into $\mathcal{D}'$. Therefore the profile-centered strategy is optimal for the case at hand for any $t_{C,\alpha}$, but in the long run, fixing α and thereby varying $t_{C,\alpha}$ is not optimal. Essentially, it leads to very large sets $\mathcal{D}'$ for the least informative case profiles. This is reflected by the large variance in the workload observed in Table 12.1.

Using a fixed *case-independent* threshold does mean, however, that the probability of detection and workload are not entirely under control in a particular case. They can be derived from the likelihood ratio distributions obtained with the specific case profile. For the workload we have, in view of Proposition 2.4.2 in expectation at most n/t items in $\mathcal{D}'$ regardless of the composition of $\mathcal{D}$ into parts with different loci typed.

A stronger deviation of the Neyman–Pearson set-up, where we decide on individual items unaffected by data for previous items, is achieved if we assume that the database does contain precisely one relative. We then add knowledge that we do not make use of when applying the Neyman–Pearson lemma. In order to see whether better results than with the LR-threshold strategy can be obtained, we have carried out simulations on such databases, again being interested in how often the relatives are detected, as well as in the total amount of work to be done, reflected by the size of the selected subsets.

The result of our simulations is summarized in Figure 12.7. We see that in this case, the threshold top-1 strategy indeed outperforms the LR-threshold strategy for some parameter choices: it is possible to find the relative equally well with the threshold top-1 strategy as with the LR-threshold strategy, at the cost of (slightly) fewer selected individuals. The difference is not large, and for practical purposes probably not at all important. But this illustrates the point that the LR-threshold decision strategy can be improved upon, in a situation that is not precisely in the realm of the Neyman–Pearson lemma.

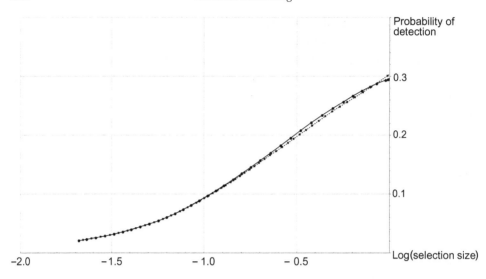

Figure 12.7 ROC-curves of threshold top-1 strategy (black curve) and LR-threshold strategies (dotted curve) based on 100,000 sibling searches, with running parameter the threshold t, when we search in a database with one special item.

12.5 Summary and Conclusions

In this chapter we have investigated the situation in which we are looking for a special element, possibly present in a database. The most prominent example is that of a familial search, in which we aim at finding a certain relative of the donor of a case profile. For each element i in the database, we can compute the likelihood ratio r_i associated to the hypotheses of being special versus being generic. In general, there may be (very) many indices i for which $r_i > 0$. In the case where only one special element is present, we first computed the probability that item i is the special one. This probability depends on the prior probabilities, and on the likelihood ratios which we just mentioned. The main result says that this probability is proportional to $\pi_i r_i$, where π_i is the prior probability that item i is the special one.

After that we discussed six different search strategies, whose aim is to make a selection of not too many items, which contains the special issue with high probability. These two objectives clearly contradict each other to some extent, so compromising is necessary. For each of the six strategies, we discussed the workload (that is, the expected size of the set of selected items of the strategy in a database of size n with only generic elements) and the probability of detection (probability of containing the true special element, given that the database contains precisely one special element and $n - 1$ generic items).

The most important strategies are based on either selecting the k objects with the highest likelihood ratio (the top-k strategy), or on selecting all items whose likelihood ratio is sufficiently high (the LR-threshold strategy). A combination of these two strategies is the threshold top-k strategy, which selects all items with high enough likelihood ratio but restricts the total number to at most k.

We investigated the performance of the various strategies by simulations. The LR-threshold strategy outperforms the top-k strategy in the sense that it achieves the same probability of detection at the cost of a smaller subset of selected items. The disadvantage of the LR-threshold strategy compared to the top-k strategy is that the size of the selected set, although on average smaller, may be large in certain situations.

The threshold top-k strategy is found to also have advantages. In our simulations, it turned out to be possible to choose its parameters (the threshold and k) such that it has practically the same probability of detection and workload as a LR-threshold strategy, but by construction we never retrieve more than k items.

12.6 Bibliographical Notes

For a discussion of searching strategies we refer to [92] and [148]. Further statistical considerations can be found in [11, 34, 44, 46, 87, 97, 110, 128, 138, 147]. A publication for the larger public is [106]. Ethical considerations can be found in, for example, [79] and [153]. Figure 12.1 is reprinted from [92]. For more information and background about ROC-curves, we refer to [163].

13

Belief Functions and their Applications

In Section 1.5 we argued that classical probabilities may not always capture the nature of epistemic uncertainty in a satisfactory way. In particular, we concluded that the requirement that $P(A) + P(A^c) = 1$ for all events A is perhaps too restrictive. More generally, it may very well be the case that we have some knowledge about the occurrence of $A \cup B$, but no further individual knowledge about the occurrence of A or B. In such a case we have no reason to believe in the truth of either A or B individually, but we do have reason to believe in the truth of $A \cup B$.

In this chapter, we explore a way to overcome some of these problems by generalizing the concept of probability. We will introduce, study, and apply the concept of a *belief function*, originally introduced by Shafer in 1976 [132]. Belief functions generalize probability distributions: every probability distribution is also a belief function. Belief functions are flexible enough as to be able to model complete ignorance, and they are not necessarily additive. The calculus of belief functions, however, is not straightforward, and different ways to define conditional beliefs exist in the literature. We will develop the notion of conditional belief in the text from scratch, and apply the theory to a number of forensic problems. There are, in addition, also ways to philosophically back up the use of belief function for epistemic uncertainty, and we will – briefly – explain some of these as well.

13.1 The Basics of Belief Functions

A probability distribution on the (finite) outcome space Ω is determined by the probabilities it assigns to each outcome. Saying that a probability distribution P describes the knowledge of an agent about a given situation, means that the agent assigns probability $P(\{\omega\})$ to every $\omega \in \Omega$.

It is, however, possible that an agent does not have enough information to assign a probability to each and every possible outcome. For instance, he may somehow receive the information that the criminal is one out of a set of two given persons. If this is really all the agent knows, then there seems to be no reason to assume that the two remaining possibilities are equally likely. Indeed, we already concluded in Chapter 1 that ignorance cannot be expressed by a probability distribution.

So, how can an agent express his information, if this is not possible with an ordinary probability distribution? There are many situations in which this can be done by a probability distribution on *subsets* instead of on individual outcomes, and we now first illustrate this idea with a simple example.

Consider an experiment in which a number between 1 and 10 is drawn (inclusive), and consider various agents who are faced with the problem of expressing their knowledge about this experiment. The various agents do not have the same information though. The first agent receives the information that the number is simply drawn uniformly at random between 1 and 10 inclusive. This agent will be happy to assign probability $1/10$ to each of the singletons 1 up to 10. In other words, this agent describes his information in terms of an ordinary probability distribution.

The second agent, however, only receives partial information about the experiment. He is only told that the probability of an even number is $1/2$, and that the probability of an odd number is $1/2$ as well. This agent would like to assign probability $1/2$ to each of the *sets* $\{1, 3, 5, 7, 9\}$ and $\{2, 4, 6, 8, 10\}$, since this is precisely what he knows. What happens within each of these sets is not known by the agent, and therefore he makes no probabilistic assessment about that at all.

The third agent receives no information at all about the experiment, other than that the outcome is a number between 1 and 10. If that really is all he knows, then this information or knowledge may be summarized by saying that the probability of the set $\{1, 2, \ldots, 10\}$ is 1.

Hence, the idea is that an agent can sometimes only express his knowledge via a probability distribution on subsets, not necessarily on individual outcomes. The starting point of the discussion in this chapter, therefore, is a probability distribution m on the *subsets* of Ω. We denote the space of subsets of Ω by 2^{Ω}, a notation which is motivated by the fact that there are exactly $2^{|\Omega|}$ subsets of Ω, where $|\Omega|$ denotes the number of elements in Ω.

Definition 13.1.1 A function $m : 2^{\Omega} \to [0, 1]$ is called a *basic belief assignment* if $m(\emptyset) = 0$ and

$$\sum_{C \subset \Omega} m(C) = 1. \tag{13.1}$$

The second agent above has the information that the collection of odd numbers and the collection of even numbers both have probability $1/2$ to contain the outcome, and this translates into $m(\{1,3,5,7,9\}) = m(\{2,4,6,8,10\}) = 1/2$, and all other subsets having m-probability 0. This agent has no way to further assess the probability that, say, the number 8 is drawn. Indeed, for all the agent knows, it could be the case that whenever an even number is drawn, the outcome is 6. He has, simply, no information that can exclude that possibility. The basic belief function of the third agent is a very simple one: it assigns m-probability 1 to the set $\{1,2,\ldots,10\}$ and m-probability 0 to all other subsets of $\{1,2,\ldots,10\}$.

We define the belief in a set $A \subset \Omega$ as the sum of all m-probabilities of sets that entail A, that is, are contained in A.

Definition 13.1.2 The function $\mathrm{Bel}: 2^{\Omega} \to [0,1]$ given by

$$\mathrm{Bel}(A) := \sum_{C \subset A} m(C) \qquad (13.2)$$

is called the *belief function* corresponding to the basic belief assignment m, and $\mathrm{Bel}(A)$ is called the *belief* in A.

It is easy to check that Bel is a probability distribution if and only if m concentrates on singletons in the set Ω.

Returning to the example above in which a number between 1 and 10 is drawn, we see that the belief function of the first agent is just the uniform probability distribution on $\Omega = \{1,2,\ldots,10\}$.

The basic belief assignment of the second agent, however, is given by $m(\{1,3,5,7,9\}) = m(\{2,4,6,8,10\}) = 1/2$, and $m(A) = 0$ for all other subsets of the outcome space. Since the second agent has no full information, his basic belief assignment is not concentrated on singletons, and as a result his belief function is not a probability distribution. Indeed we have, for instance, $\mathrm{Bel}(\{1,3,5\}) = \mathrm{Bel}(\{7,9\}) = 0$, but $\mathrm{Bel}(\{1,3,5,7,9\}) = 1/2$ so Bel is not additive. The belief in, say, the set $\{1,2,3,4,5,7,9\}$ is equal to $1/2$, since it contains the collection of odd outcomes. The basic belief assignment m describes the information that the agent has about the experiment, and the belief in a set A is then precisely the m-probability that the outcome is contained in A.

The third agent has basic belief assignment given by $m(\Omega) = 1$ and $m(A) = 0$ for all strict subsets A of Ω. This m puts all probability mass on the set Ω itself. The corresponding belief function, representing complete ignorance, assigns belief 0 to every strict subset of Ω.

We have introduced the probability distribution m as arising from lack of information. The ensuing belief function Bel is sometimes also interpreted as a quantification of *provability*: $\mathrm{Bel}(A)$ is then seen as the degree to which the event is deemed to be provable, since it measures the probability of the collection of all subsets which entail A.

A notion related to the belief in A is that of the *plausibility* of A, which is nothing but the sum of all basic belief assignments of sets that have non-empty intersection with A.

Definition 13.1.3 The *plausibility* of an event A is defined as

$$\text{Pl}(A) :- \sum_{C \cap A \neq \emptyset} m(C) - 1 \quad \text{Bel}(A^c). \tag{13.3}$$

We say that the plausibility of A is the m-probability that the outcome of the experiment is *consistent*, or *compatible*, with A.

As an example, we consider an experiment in which a number between 1 and 3 is chosen. Suppose an agent does not receive full information about the probability distribution of this experiment. Instead, he is told that in one out of three cases a 1 is chosen, and similarly for 2. In addition, he is told that in only one out of six cases a 3 was chosen. Finally, he is told that in the remaining one out of six cases, the outcome is a 1 or a 3.

To describe this with a belief function, we take $\Omega = \{1, 2, 3\}$, and the basic belief assignment m given by $m(\{1\}) = m(\{2\}) = 1/3$, $m(\{3\}) = 1/6$, and $m(\{1,3\}) = 1/6$. The corresponding beliefs and plausibilities are then as in the following table:

A	$\emptyset$	$\{1\}$	$\{2\}$	$\{3\}$	$\{1,2\}$	$\{1,3\}$	$\{2,3\}$	$\{1,2,3\}$
Bel(A)	0	1/3	1/3	1/6	2/3	2/3	1/2	1
Pl(A)	0	1/2	1/3	1/3	5/6	2/3	2/3	1

Conversely, we can retrieve m from the first row of the table (and since the rows determine each other, also from the second row) algorithmically as follows.

First, for all singletons i we have $m(\{i\}) = \text{Bel}(\{i\})$. Next we consider sets of size 2. The belief in $\{1,2\}$ is $2/3$, and this is already taken care of already by the sum of the basic belief assignments of the two singletons $\{1\}$ and $\{2\}$, so $m(\{1,2\}) = 0$. The belief in $\{1,3\}$, however, is $2/3$ while the sum of the basic belief assignments of $\{1\}$ and $\{3\}$ is only $1/2$. The missing mass of $1/6$ is therefore assigned to $m(\{1,3\})$. In this case we are done, since the total mass of the already assigned basic belief assignments is 1 now, but in general we continue this way until this is the case. In fact, there is [132] a concise formula expressing m in terms of Bel, namely

$$m(A) = \sum_{B \subset A} (-1)^{|A \setminus B|} \text{Bel}(B), \tag{13.4}$$

but we do not prove this here.

There is a characterization of belief functions in terms of inclusion-exclusion formulas. Such formulas are well known in probability theory: any probability distribution P satisfies

$$P(A \cup B) = P(A) + P(B) - P(A \cap B),$$

for all events A and B. From this, the higher order formulas follow by induction, giving

$$P\left(\bigcup_{i=1}^{n} A_i\right) = \sum_{\substack{I \subset \{1,\dots,n\} \\ I \neq \emptyset}} (-1)^{|I|+1} P\left(\bigcap_{i \in I} A_i\right), \tag{13.5}$$

for all integers n. It turns out that a function Bel: $\Omega \to [0,1]$ is a belief function if and only if it satisfies these inclusion-exclusion formulas with *inequality* instead of equality.

Theorem 13.1.4 Bel: $2^\Omega \to [0,1]$ *is a belief function if and only if:*

(B1) $\text{Bel}(\emptyset) = 0$ *and* $\text{Bel}(\Omega) = 1$;

(B2) For all $A_1, A_2, \dots, A_n \subset \Omega$, *we have*

$$\text{Bel}\left(\bigcup_{i=1}^{n} A_i\right) \geq \sum_{\substack{I \subset \{1,\dots,n\} \\ I \neq \emptyset}} (-1)^{|I|+1} \text{Bel}\left(\bigcap_{i \in I} A_i\right). \tag{13.6}$$

Proof. Suppose first that Bel is a belief function given by (13.2). Then (B1) follows immediately. To prove (B2), fix subsets $A_1, \dots, A_n$, and set, for each $B \subset \Omega$,

$$I(B) := \{i \ : \ B \subset A_i, 1 \leq i \leq n\}.$$

We now write

$$\sum_{\substack{I \subset \{1,\dots,n\} \\ I \neq \emptyset}} (-1)^{|I|+1} \text{Bel}\left(\bigcap_{i \in I} A_i\right) = \sum_{\substack{I \subset \{1,\dots,n\} \\ I \neq \emptyset}} (-1)^{|I|+1} \sum_{B \subset \cap_{i \in I} A_i} m(B)$$

$$= \sum_{\substack{B \subset \Omega \\ I(B) \neq \emptyset}} m(B) \sum_{\substack{I \subset I(B) \\ I \neq \emptyset}} (-1)^{|I|+1}$$

$$= \sum_{\substack{B \subset \Omega \\ I(B) \neq \emptyset}} m(B) \left(1 - \sum_{I \subset I(B)} (-1)^{|I|}\right).$$

It is well known and easy to verify that for any finite, non-empty set A we have that $\sum_{B \subset A} (-1)^{|B|} = 0$, hence the last expression is equal to

$$\sum_{\substack{B \subset \Omega \\ I(B) \neq \emptyset}} m(B) = \sum_{\substack{B \subset \Omega \\ B \subset A_i \text{ for some } i}} m(B),$$

and this quantity is clearly bounded above by $\text{Bel}(A_1 \cup \dots \cup A_n)$.

For the converse, assume that Bel satisfies (B1) and (B2). Now *define m* as in (13.4). By standard Möbius inversion, Bel can be expressed in terms of *m* as in (13.2). In order to show that Bel is a belief function, we need to show that *m* is a basic belief assignment. The only non-obvious thing to prove is that $m(A) \geq 0$ for all $A \neq \emptyset$. To prove this, take $A = \{x_1, \ldots, x_n\}$ and let $A_i := A \setminus \{x_i\}$, for $i = 1, \ldots, n$. Any strict subset B of A can be expressed as an intersection of some of the A_i, so we find

$$m(A) = \sum_{B \subset A} (-1)^{|A \setminus B|} \text{Bel}(B)$$

$$= \text{Bel}(A) + \sum_{\substack{I \subset \{1, \ldots, n\} \\ I \neq \emptyset}} (-1)^{|I|} \text{Bel}\left(\bigcap_{i \in I} A_i\right)$$

$$= \text{Bel}(A) - \sum_{\substack{I \subset \{1, \ldots, n\} \\ I \neq \emptyset}} (-1)^{|I|+1} \text{Bel}\left(\bigcap_{i \in I} A_i\right),$$

and this is non-negative by (B2). ☐

One may at this point already loosely argue that the inequalities in (13.6) are indeed suitable for describing degrees of belief, as follows. Taking $n = 2$ in (13.6) for simplicity gives $\text{Bel}(A \cup B) \geq \text{Bel}(A) + \text{Bel}(B) - \text{Bel}(A \cap B)$. A loose interpretation now is as follows. If we have supporting evidence for either A or B, then of course we have also supporting evidence for $A \cup B$. However, supporting evidence for both A and B is then counted twice and must be subtracted on the right-hand side. Now notice that it is possible that there is supporting evidence for $A \cup B$, but not for A or B individually (something we already remarked above) leading to the inequality in the formula.

We have introduced a basic belief assignment as a probability distribution on the subsets of an outcome space Ω. The basic belief assignment is supposed to capture the information an agent has about an experiment. There is a very natural way to associate a belief function with a collection of probability distributions, as follows.

One can think of $m(A)$ as the probability mass that is confined to A but which can be distributed over the elements of A in any desired way. If, for all $A \subset \Omega$, we distribute the mass $m(A)$ over the elements in A in some way, we end up with a probability distribution. For instance, with the basic belief assignment above leading to the table above, we had $m(\{1\}) = m(\{2\}) = 1/3$, $m(\{3\}) = 1/6$, and $m(\{1,3\}) = 1/6$. The m-probability mass $1/6$ assigned to $\{1,3\}$ can be distributed over the singletons $\{1\}$ and $\{3\}$ in many ways. For instance, they can both receive $1/12$. In that case, the total mass assigned to $\{1\}$ is $1/3 + 1/12 = 5/12$, the total mass assigned to $\{2\}$ is $1/3$, and the total mass assigned to $\{3\}$ is $1/6 + 1/12 = 1/4$.

The collection of all probability distributions obtainable this way is called the collection of probability distributions which are *consistent* with the belief function. One interpretation of this collection is the following. If the agent, with the given belief function, were able to obtain more information, to the extent that he could express his belief with a probability distribution, then the consistent probability distributions would be precisely the possible candidates for such a probability distribution. In other words, we can think of the consistent probability distributions as all candidate probability distributions which could possibly describe the experiment given full information.

Let us denote the collection of consistent probability distributions by $\mathcal{P}$. We now claim that

$$\text{Bel}(A) = \min\{P(A) : P \in \mathcal{P}\}, \qquad (13.7)$$

that is, Bel is the *lower envelope* of $\mathcal{P}$. Indeed, when we distribute the mass as described above, then the minimum amount of mass that will end up in a set A, is precisely the sum of $m(B)$ for all $B \subset A$, since this mass simply cannot escape from A. All other mass could end up outside A, so that the minimum mass ending up in A is precisely $\text{Bel}(A)$.

In the sense of (13.7), belief functions are conservative, which is consistent with the idea that we do not want to make stronger probabilistic statements than warranted by the information we have. We observe, though, that it is *not* true that the lower envelope of any collection $\mathcal{P}$ of probability distributions is necessarily a belief function. To give a counterexample, consider the outcome space $\Omega = \{1, 2, 3\}$ and the collection of all probability distributions $\mathcal{P}$ on Ω with the property that each element has probability at most $1/2$, that is,

$$\mathcal{P} := \{P : P(\{i\}) \le 1/2, i = 1, 2, 3\}.$$

Suppose now that the lower envelope of $\mathcal{P}$ is a belief function Bel with corresponding basic belief assignment m. Since for each i, $\mathcal{P}$ contains a distribution P with $P(\{i\}) = 0$, we must have that $m(\{i\}) = 0$ and hence $\text{Bel}(\{i\}) = 0$, for $i = 1, 2, 3$. On the other hand, $\mathcal{P}$ contains a distribution P with $P(\{1\}) = 1/2$, but this is the maximal value. Hence $P(\{2, 3\}) \ge 1/2$, where equality is possible. It follows that $m(\{2, 3\}) = 1/2$ and similarly for $m(\{1, 3\})$ and $m(\{1, 2\})$. But this is a contradiction since the total sum of the basic belief assignments cannot exceed 1.

We end this section with a first forensic example of a belief function. We explain how the classical island problem from Section 4.1 can be formulated in terms of a belief function in such a way that we impose no prior information about the identity of C other than that C has the characteristic of interest.

Example 13.1.5 (The Island Problem) In this example, we model a version of the classical island problem from Section 4.1 with a belief function. To do this, let $X = \{1, \ldots, N + 1\}$ be the population of the island. At the scene of the crime a DNA profile Γ is found which we know has frequency $p \in (0, 1]$ in the population. We assume it a certainty that this profile was left by C. Furthermore, there is a selected person S who will be checked for having Γ or not.

In this example, we first identify the relevant items about which we have or seek information. First of all there is C, then we have S, and finally we have the indicators Γ_i telling us whether or not person i has the profile Γ. We may now take as our outcome space simply the product space corresponding to all relevant items. That is, we set $\Omega = X \times X \times \{0, 1\}^{N+1}$ and let $C \colon \Omega \to X, S \colon \Omega \to X$ and $\Gamma_i \colon \Omega \to \{0, 1\}$ correspond to, respectively, the first, second, and $(i + 2)$th coordinate, and where $\Gamma_i = 1$ indicates that the ith individual on the island has characteristic Γ.

The next issue is to determine what information we have. We have no information about the identity of C other than that he has Γ. We have information about the identity of S though, and let us for simplicity now assume that we know that $S = s$. Furthermore, we know that each individual has the profile with probability p, independently of everybody else. This means that all we know about the situation is described by the following basic belief assignment on Ω. We set

$$m(C \in \{i \in X \;:\; y_i = 1\}, S = s, \Gamma_1 = y_1, \ldots, \Gamma_{N+1} = y_{N+1})$$
$$= \frac{p^k(1 - p)^{N+1-k}}{1 - (1 - p)^{N+1}} \tag{13.8}$$

if $\sum_{i=1}^{N+1} y_i = k > 0$, and $m(A) = 0$ for all other subsets A of Ω. It is easy to see that this m indeed is a probability distribution on the subsets of Ω, since it essentially describes the assignments of the labels conditioned on the event that not all labels are 0. Indeed, the normalizing factor $1 - (1 - p)^{N+1}$ in (13.8) comes from the fact that we know that at least one person on the island has the characteristic, namely C.

It follows from (13.8) that

$$\mathrm{Bel}(C = i) = \frac{p(1 - p)^N}{1 - (1 - p)^{N+1}}$$

for all $i = 1, \ldots, N + 1$, while at the same time $\mathrm{Bel}(C \in X) = 1$. Indeed, we can only be sure that $C = i$ when i has the characteristic and all others do not. □

We will continue this example below in Section 13.3, where we are going to compute the conditional belief that $C = s$ given that s has Γ. In order to be able to do that, we first have to develop the notion of conditional belief, a task to which we now turn.

13.2 Conditional Belief

For forensic purposes, conditional probability is a crucial concept. After all, we would like to know how new information updates our prior probability for certain events, and the single most important concept of this book, the likelihood ratio, is the quotient of two such conditional probabilities. So it needs no further argument to say that we need a notion of conditional belief as well. For instance, in Example 13.1.5 we want to condition on the event that S has the characteristic in question, and see how this finding affects our belief in the event that $S = C$.

In the classical context, one can think of conditional probabilities from the viewpoint of relative frequencies, or from the viewpoint of mass distribution. In the first interpretation, the conditional probability of A given H is the frequency of A occurring in the subsequence determined by the occurrence of H. That is, if we write x_i for the outcome of the ith experiment, then the conditional probability of A given H must be equal to the limit of $n \to \infty$ of

$$\frac{\sum_{i=1}^{n} 1_{A \cap H}(x_i)}{\sum_{i=1}^{n} 1_{H}(x_i)}. \tag{13.9}$$

In the second interpretation the conditional probability of A given H is obtained by leaving out all mass outside H, renormalize, and then simply look at the resulting mass in $A \cap H$. Both approaches lead to the well-known formula $P(A \mid H) = P(A \cap H)/P(H)$.

Neither of these two interpretations is immediately applicable to belief functions. Indeed, the problem is that we (or rather, the agent) do not receive complete information about the experiment. Only in the special case in which $\mathrm{Bel}(H) = \mathrm{Pl}(H)$, all sets C with $m(C) > 0$ are contained in either H or H^c. In that case, for any $A \subset \Omega$, the conditional belief in A given H should simply be that part of the mass in m that implies that A occurs, normalized by the belief in H. In other words, the conditional belief should in that case equal

$$\mathrm{Bel}(A \mid H) = \frac{\mathrm{Bel}(A \cap H)}{\mathrm{Bel}(H)}, \tag{13.10}$$

at least when $\mathrm{Bel}(H) > 0$.

If, however, $\mathrm{Bel}(H) < \mathrm{Pl}(H)$, with strict inequality, then there is at least one set with positive basic belief assignment which intersects both H and H^c. We have, then, no way of knowing how often H occurs, and things are not so clear. However, what we can do is look at the collection $\mathcal{P}$ of all probability distributions P which are consistent (see Section 13.1 for a discussion of the notion of consistent probability distributions) with the basic belief assignment, and compute $P(A \cap H)/P(H)$ for each such P. We claim that when we minimize this expression over all $P \in \mathcal{P}$, we obtain

$$\frac{\mathrm{Bel}(A \cap H)}{\mathrm{Bel}(A \cap H) + \mathrm{Pl}(A^c \cap H)}. \tag{13.11}$$

The reader who is prepared to believe this can skip the remainder of this paragraph, but for those who want to understand where this expression comes from, we offer an explanation. Let B be a set with $m(B) > 0$. We have to distribute the mass $m(B)$ over the elements of B. If $B \subset A \cap H$, then it does not matter how we do that, since $A \cap H$ and H both will receive everything. If $B \cap (A^c \cap H) \neq \emptyset$, then in order to minimize $P(A \cap H)/P(H)$ we should move all the mass to elements in $A^c \cap H$, since in that case the numerator receives nothing and the denominator receives the maximal amount. In all remaining cases we simply move all mass outside H, so that this mass does not contribute at all. The reason to do this, is that the alternative would be to move the mass to $A \cap H$ but this would add the same amount to both numerator and denominator, thereby increasing the ratio. From this it follows that (13.11) is the minimum of $P(A \cap H)/P(H)$ over all $P \in \mathcal{P}$. Note that if $\mathrm{Bel}(H) = \mathrm{Pl}(H)$, then (13.11) reduces to (13.10).

Given that the expression in (13.11) minimizes $P(A \mid H)$ over all consistent probability distributions P, we know that we will never overestimate our conditional belief in A when we use this formula. This is in line with the conservative character of belief functions, in which we do not want to make stronger statements than warranted by our information. These reflections then naturally lead to the following definition of conditional belief.

Definition 13.2.1 Assume that $\mathrm{Pl}(H) > 0$. We define the conditional belief in A given H by

$$\mathrm{Bel}(A \mid H) := \frac{\mathrm{Bel}(A \cap H)}{\mathrm{Bel}(A \cap H) + \mathrm{Pl}(A^c \cap H)}, \tag{13.12}$$

whenever this expression is well defined.

Note that since $\mathrm{Pl}(A) = 1 - \mathrm{Bel}(A^c)$, we can rewrite (13.12) completely in terms of Bel:

$$\mathrm{Bel}(A \mid H) = \frac{\mathrm{Bel}(A \cap H)}{\mathrm{Bel}(A \cap H) + 1 - \mathrm{Bel}(A \cup H^c)}, \tag{13.13}$$

which is sometimes easier to compute than (13.12).

Furthermore, observe that in the case where $\mathrm{Bel}(H) = \mathrm{Pl}(H)$, this definition coincides with (13.10), as it should. Note also that if Bel is a probability distribution, we find

$$\mathrm{Bel}(A \mid H) = \frac{\mathrm{Bel}(A \cap H)}{\mathrm{Bel}(H)} = \frac{\mathrm{Pl}(A \cap H)}{\mathrm{Pl}(H)}, \tag{13.14}$$

which means that this notion of conditioning generalizes the classical notion.

In classical probability theory, $P(\cdot \mid H)$ is again a probability distribution, at least when $P(H) > 0$. This is important, since it allows for subsequent conditioning on a series of events. In the current context of conditional belief functions, this turns out to also be the case: one can prove that $\text{Bel}(\cdot \mid H)$ is again a belief function. The proof of this fact, however, is surprisingly involved and falls outside the scope of this book.

We next give some examples of computations with conditional belief functions.

Example 13.2.2 Consider $N + 1$ individuals, labeled $1, 2, \ldots, N + 1$ forming the space $X = \{1, 2, \ldots, N + 1\}$, an empty vase, and a fair coin. First a coin is flipped. If heads comes up, person number 1 puts a black ball in the vase while all other persons put a white ball in the vase. If tails comes up, then everybody puts a black ball in the vase.

Next, a ball is drawn from the vase, and we are told that the drawn ball is black. The question now is whether or not, given this information, the drawn ball is the ball put in the vase by person number 1 (without knowing the result of the coin flip). As we will see below, our answer to this question will depend on the (lack of) information we have about *how* the black ball was drawn. In particular, we cannot assume from the outset that the ball was chosen uniformly at random, and we should keep in mind that the draw of the ball may depend on the coin flip or on other things.

We work in the space

$$\Omega = \{0, 1\} \times \{B, W\}^{N+1} \times X.$$

The first coordinate refers to the outcome of the coin flip, the next $N+1$ coordinates refer to the color of the balls put in the vase by persons $1, 2, \ldots, N + 1$ (in that order), and the last coordinate refers to the origin of the drawn ball. We denote the coordinates by $A, \Gamma_1, \ldots, \Gamma_{N+1}$, and F respectively.

Case 1. Ball drawn uniformly at random. Suppose that we are informed that the ball drawn from the vase is chosen randomly, with each ball being equally likely. We are now in a classical situation which can be satisfactorily described with probabilities. To allow comparison with the upcoming cases, however, we prefer to give the basic belief assignment m^{cl} corresponding to this case. This basic belief assignment is given by

$$m^{cl}(0, B, B, B, \ldots, B, i) = \frac{1}{2}\frac{1}{N+1}, \tag{13.15}$$

and

$$m^{cl}(1, B, W, W, \ldots, W, i) = \frac{1}{2}\frac{1}{N+1}, \tag{13.16}$$

for all $i = 1, \ldots, N + 1$. Since m^{cl} concentrates on singletons, the corresponding belief function Bel^{cl} is a probability distribution.

Write $H = \{\Gamma_F = B\}$, the event that the drawn ball is black, and $E = \{F = 1\}$, the event that the drawn ball came from person 1. We are now interested in $\mathrm{Bel}^{cl}(E \mid H)$ (which is the same as the classical probability of E given H since Bel^{cl} is a probability distribution). We compute

$$\mathrm{Bel}^{cl}(E \mid H) = \frac{\mathrm{Bel}^{cl}(E \cap H)}{\mathrm{Bel}^{cl}(E \cap H) + \mathrm{Pl}^{cl}(E^c \cap H)}$$

$$= \frac{\frac{1}{N+1}}{\frac{1}{N+1} + \frac{1}{2}\frac{N}{N+1}} = \frac{2}{N+2}.$$

Case 2. No information about the drawn ball. In the classical case, we assumed that the ball from the vase was randomly drawn. Without this information, the basic belief assignment m we start out with should have the following form:

$$m(A = 0, \Gamma_1 = B, \ldots, \Gamma_{N+1} = B) = 1/2, \tag{13.17}$$

and

$$m(A = 1, \Gamma_1 = B, \Gamma_2 = W, \Gamma_3 = W, \ldots, \Gamma_{N+1} = W) = 1/2. \tag{13.18}$$

Indeed, in this case we have no information whatsoever about the way the ball is drawn from the vase. It is easy to see that none of the sets in (13.17) and (13.18) is contained in $E \cap H$, and therefore we find that $\mathrm{Bel}(E \mid H) = 0$.

Discussion. We have distinguished between two cases, obtaining two different answers: $\frac{2}{N+2}$ and 0. These are different answers which correspond to different situations, and we next argue that each of these answers is reasonable given the information we have.

In the first, classical, case we simply draw a uniform ball, and ask what the probability is that the ball came from 1 given that it is black. It is not a surprise that the answer tends to 0 when N gets larger. Indeed, most instances where the drawn ball is black will come from a situation in which $A = 0$, in which case the probability that the ball came from 1 is only $1/(N + 1)$.

The situation in the second case is very different. In the classical case, we have much more information about the way the procedure is carried out. In the second case we do not know how the balls are drawn, and cannot exclude the possibility that the procedure is such that we only get to know that a black ball has been drawn, when in fact the drawn ball is not coming from person 1. There is no way to discover this on the basis of our information, and hence it is completely reasonable to have zero conditional belief in E.   □

13.3 The Island Problems with Belief Functions

In this section, we continue Example 13.1.5, and for the benefit of the reader we
repeat the context. A crime has been committed on an island with $N+1$ inhabitants,
so that we can be sure that one of them is the culprit. Now some characteristic of the
criminal, e.g., a DNA profile, is found at the scene of the crime and we may assume
that this profile originates from the culprit. Then we somehow select an individual
S from the island, who has the same characteristic as the criminal. The question
is what we can say about the probability or belief in the event that S is in fact
the criminal. This is not an answerable question yet, as it depends on the way S
was found.

Belief functions allow us to assign a zero prior belief in the guilt of any of the
individuals of the island, while at the same time assigning belief one to the full
population. This seems better suited to the legal context than the classical setting,
since it overcomes having to assign a non-zero prior probability to an individual. As
we shall see, the outcomes are different than in the classical outcome: if we assume
total prior ignorance, then the belief that S is the culprit is in our setting different
from the classical probability under a uniform prior. We turn to the examples now.

13.3.1 The Classical Case

In the notation of Example 13.1.5 we suggested the following basic belief assignment, which assumes that we know the identity of S being s:

$$m(C \in \{i \in X \ : \ y_i = 1\}, S = s, \Gamma_1 = y_1, \ldots, \Gamma_{N+1} = y_{N+1})$$

$$= \frac{p^k(1-p)^{N+1-k}}{1-(1-p)^{N+1}}, \tag{13.19}$$

if $\sum_{i=1}^{N+1} y_i = k > 0$.

We want to condition on $H_s := \{\Gamma_s = 1\}$ and compute $\mathrm{Bel}(C = s \mid H_s)$. It seems
reasonable to call this conditional belief the *posterior* belief in $C = s$. To this end,
observe that $\mathrm{Bel}(H_s)$ and $\mathrm{Pl}(H_s)$ are both given by the sum of all basic belief of
events with $y_s = 1$, that is,

$$\mathrm{Bel}(H_s) = \mathrm{Pl}(H_s)$$

$$= \sum_{y_s=1} m(C \in \{i \in X \ : \ y_i = 1\}, S = s, \Gamma_1 = y_1, \ldots, \Gamma_{N+1} = y_{N+1})$$

$$= \frac{1}{1-(1-p)^{N+1}} \sum_{j=0}^{N} \binom{N}{j} p^{j+1}(1-p)^{N-j}$$

$$= \frac{p}{1-(1-p)^{N+1}}. \tag{13.20}$$

Although we performed a formal computation here, it is useful to remark that we also could have obtained the answer without any computation. Indeed, we recall that the belief in an event A is the sum of all basic belief assignments of sets that entail A. Since the basic belief assignment m is a probability distribution on the subsets of Ω, we can still see m as describing a classical probabilistic experiment with a known distribution, but rather than having a probability of elements of Ω, we have probabilities of subsets. So, if we draw a subset according to m, the belief in A is just the probability that the drawn subset implies A. In the last computation, the drawn subset implies that H_s occurs, precisely when the drawn subset happens to have $\Gamma_s = 1$. The m-probability to draw such a subset is just $p/(1 - (1 - p)^{N+1})$, since we need only look at Γ_s to decide whether or not this is the case.

Since $\text{Bel}(H_s) = \text{Pl}(H_s)$, conditioning boils down to

$$\text{Bel}(C = s \mid H_s) = \frac{\text{Bel}(\{C = s\} \cap H_s)}{\text{Bel}(H_s)}$$

$$= \frac{1 - (1 - p)^{N+1}}{p} \text{Bel}(C = s, \Gamma_s = 1). \tag{13.21}$$

A set in (13.19) contributes to $\text{Bel}(C = s, \Gamma_s = 1)$ precisely when $\Gamma_s = 1$ and all other individuals do not have the characteristic. This gives a total contribution of $p(1 - p)^N/(1 - (1 - p)^{N+1})$. Hence we find

$$\text{Bel}(C = s \mid H_s) = (1 - p)^N. \tag{13.22}$$

This formula has a simple interpretation: the belief that s is the criminal is just the probability that all other members of the population are excluded since they have another profile. It will turn out that all computations with belief functions lead to formulas that can be analogously interpreted.

It is interesting to compare this answer to the classical one, in which uniform priors are taken. In the classical case, the posterior probability that $C = S$ is equal to

$$\frac{1}{1 + Np}, \tag{13.23}$$

see (3.3). Since

$$\frac{1}{1 + Np} > (1 - p)^N, \tag{13.24}$$

the belief that $C = S$ is always smaller than the posterior probability that $C = S$ in the classical case, something we can perhaps intuitively understand by recalling that we did not use any assumptions about the criminal other than that the criminal has the characteristic. To give some indication of the difference between the two answers, if $p \sim N^{-1}$ (for $N \to \infty$), then (13.23) $\sim \frac{1}{2}$, while (13.22) $\sim e^{-1}$.

Since belief functions generalize probability distributions, we should be able to re-derive (13.23) using our approach, and we now show that this is indeed the case. If we take a uniform prior for the criminal, but full knowledge that $S = s$, then the basic belief assignment, denoted by m^{cl}, is as follows. We set

$$m^{cl}(C = t, S = s, \Gamma_1 = y_1, \ldots, \Gamma_{N+1} = y_{N+1}) = \frac{1}{N+1} p^k (1-p)^{N-k} \quad (13.25)$$

if $y_t = 1$ and $\sum_{i=1}^{N+1} y_i = k+1$. Note that we do not have the normalizing factor $1 - (1-p)^{N+1}$ here, since all probability mass is now contained in an event which implies $y_t = 1$. The factor $1/(N+1)$ comes from the uniform prior on C. Note that the corresponding belief function is a probability distribution, since only singletons have positive basic belief.

Next we condition on the same event $H_s = \{\Gamma_s = 1\}$ as before. We compute

$$\mathrm{Bel}^{cl}(H_s \cap \{C = s\}) = \frac{1}{N+1}. \quad (13.26)$$

Indeed, if $C = s$, an event with m^{cl}-probability $1/(N+1)$, then it is automatically the case that H_s occurs. Furthermore,

$$\mathrm{Pl}^{cl}(H_s \cap \{C \neq s\}) = \frac{Np}{N+1}. \quad (13.27)$$

Indeed, the probability that $C \neq s$ is $N/(N+1)$ and in that case, we need a further term p for the probability that S has the characteristic. Hence

$$\mathrm{Bel}^{cl}(C = s \mid H_s) = \frac{\mathrm{Bel}^{cl}(H_s \cap \{C = s\})}{\mathrm{Bel}^{cl}(H_s \cap \{C = s\}) + \mathrm{Pl}^{cl}(H_s \cap \{C \neq s\})} = \frac{1}{1 + Np}, \quad (13.28)$$

as required.

This example further illustrates that we lose nothing by working with belief functions, and that belief functions only add flexibility. If a certain classical prior is reasonable then we can take that prior and work with it. If there are reasons to have a non-classical prior, for instance complete ignorance within a given population, then belief functions are flexible enough to deal with this.

13.3.2 The Search Case

In the search variant, we check the inhabitants one by one in a random order, until an individual with the relevant characteristic is found. However, we only take into account the result of the search, and not any information about the search itself.

This time we have information about the way S is found, and this information can be incorporated into our basic belief assignment. Indeed, the procedure boils down to selecting S as a uniform choice among all individuals having the characteristic. Hence we set

$$m(C \in \{i \in X : y_i = 1\}, S = x, \Gamma_1 = y_1, \ldots, \Gamma_{N+1} = y_{N+1})$$
$$= \frac{1}{k} \frac{p^k (1-p)^{N+1-k}}{1 - (1-p)^{N+1}} \tag{13.29}$$

if $y_x = 1$ and $\sum_i y_i = k > 0$. Note that there are two differences compared to the classical case: we have to assume that $y_x = 1$, and we have to divide by k.

Next we incorporate the information that we found a suspect with the characteristic by conditioning on $H_s = \{S = s\}$. Note that the conditioning does not contain information about the length of the search or the identity of searched individuals. We only know that s was the first one to be found with the characteristic. We again have $\mathrm{Bel}(H_s) = \mathrm{Pl}(H_s)$ with

$$\mathrm{Bel}(H_s) = \mathrm{Pl}(H_s)$$
$$= \sum_{y_s=1} m(C \in \{i \in X : y_i = 1\}, S = s, \Gamma_1 = y_1, \ldots, \Gamma_{N+1} = y_{N+1})$$
$$= \frac{1}{1 - (1-p)^{N+1}} \sum_{j=0}^{N} \binom{N}{j} \frac{1}{j+1} p^{j+1} (1-p)^{N-j}$$
$$= \frac{1}{N+1} \frac{1}{1 - (1-p)^{N+1}} \sum_{j=0}^{N} \binom{N+1}{j+1} p^{j+1} (1-p)^{N-j}$$
$$= \frac{1}{N+1}, \tag{13.30}$$

since the final summation is the probability that a binomially distributed random variable with parameters $N+1$ and p does not take the value 0, and this is just $1 - (1-p)^{N+1}$.

To compute the conditional belief in $\{C = s\}$ conditioned on H_s, we claim that

$$\mathrm{Bel}(H_s \cap \{C = s\}) = \mathrm{Bel}(C = S = s) = \frac{p(1-p)^N}{1 - (1-p)^{N+1}}. \tag{13.31}$$

Indeed, we can only be sure that $C = S = s$ if s is the only individual with the characteristic, hence $k = 1$. We conclude that

$$\mathrm{Bel}(C = s \mid H_s) = (N+1)\mathrm{Bel}(H_s \cap \{C = s\})$$
$$= \frac{(N+1)p(1-p)^N}{1 - (1-p)^{N+1}}, \tag{13.32}$$

which is different compared to the classical case.

There is a very natural interpretation of the expression in (13.32). In the numerator, we have the probability that a random variable with a binomial distribution with parameters $N + 1$ and p is equal to 1. The denominator is the probability that this random variable is positive, so that (13.32) is the conditional probability for such a random variable to be 1 given that it is positive. This makes sense, since we can only know for sure that $C = s$ when s is the only one with the characteristic. Notice that (13.32) equals zero if $p = 1$ and if $p < 1$ we can rewrite (13.32) as

$$\frac{N+1}{\sum_{k=0}^{N}(1-p)^{-k}}. \tag{13.33}$$

In the classical case, starting with a uniform probability distribution, the posterior probability that $C = s$ is equal to

$$\frac{1-(1-p)^{N+1}}{(N+1)p} = \frac{1}{N+1}\sum_{j=0}^{N}(1-p)^{j}, \tag{13.34}$$

see (4.12). Note that (13.34) is the arithmetic mean of $1, 1 - p, (1 - p)^{2}, \ldots,$ $(1 - p)^{N}$, while (13.33) is the harmonic mean of the same sequence. Hence the answer using our approach is – as it was in the cold case – smaller than the classical answer.

We finally demonstrate that we can also re-derive this classical result with belief functions. In the classical case, we set the basic belief assignment to be

$$m^{cl}(C = t, S = x, \Gamma_1 = y_1, \ldots, \Gamma_{N+1} = y_{N=1}) = \frac{1}{N+1}\frac{1}{k+1}p^k(1-p)^{N-k} \tag{13.35}$$

if $y_t = y_x = 1$ and $\sum_{i=1}^{N+1} y_i = k + 1$.

Note that the corresponding belief function is a probability distribution, since only singletons have positive basic belief assignments. We condition on $H_s = \{S = s\}$, and in the same way as before we find

$$\mathrm{Bel}^{cl}(H_s) = \mathrm{Pl}^{cl}(H_s) = \frac{1}{N+1}. \tag{13.36}$$

We then compute the belief

$$\text{Bel}^{cl}(H_s \cap \{C = s\}) = \frac{1}{N+1} \sum_{k=0}^{N} \binom{N}{k} \frac{1}{k+1} p^k (1-p)^{N-k}$$

$$= \frac{1}{(N+1)^2} \frac{1}{p} \sum_{k=0}^{N} \binom{N+1}{k+1} p^{k+1} (1-p)^{N-k} \qquad (13.37)$$

$$= \frac{1}{(N+1)^2} \frac{1}{p} (1 - (1-p)^{N+1}),$$

to conclude that

$$\text{Bel}^{cl}(C = s \mid H_s) = \frac{\text{Bel}^{cl}(H_s \cap \{C = s\})}{\text{Bel}^{cl}(H_s)} = \frac{1 - (1-p)^{N+1}}{(N+1)p}, \qquad (13.38)$$

as required.

13.4 Parental Identification

Our next example concerns the situation in which we have DNA profiles of mother and child, but we do not know who the father is. This is precisely the situation discussed in Section 4.5.6. We assume that there is a set $X = \{1, \ldots, N+1\}$ of potential fathers. We would like to make belief statements about the possible paternity of a given individual in X, based on the DNA profile of this individual. We first consider inference based on only one specific locus of the DNA, and we ignore mutations.

13.4.1 Paternal Allele Known

We first assume that mother and child are not both heterozygous with the same alleles, so that we know the paternal allele of the child. We denote this paternal allele by a.

Every potential father i in X has two alleles at the locus under consideration. We write $\Gamma_i = 0$ if none of them is a, and $\Gamma_i = 2$ if they are both a. If precisely one of the two alleles is a, then we do not know which allele is passed on to a child of this father. In our mathematical model, we take care of this by writing $\Gamma_i = 1^+$ if this allele is passed on by the potential father and $\Gamma_i = 1^-$ if this allele is *not* passed on by the potential father. Note that the 1^+ and the 1^- labels are not observable. Given that a potential father has one allele a, we let each of the labels 1^+ and 1^- have probability $1/2$.

In order to set up our prior belief function, we set

$$\Omega = X \times X \times \{0, 1^-, 1^+, 2\}^{N+1},$$

and let $F: \Omega \to X, S: \Omega \to X$ and $\Gamma_i: \Omega \to \{0, 1^-, 1^+, 2\}$ be the projections on respectively the first, second, and $(2+i)$th coordinates. F represents the actual father, and S the selected individual, which is the putative father. We denote by p_a the population frequency of allele a, and for simplicity we assume that the population is in Hardy–Weinberg equilibrium (see Section 7.2).

As in the island problem, we assume that we know that $S = s$. One could, if so desired, also incorporate prior knowledge about the choice of S, but we stick to this case. We set the prior basic belief assignment to be

$$m\left(F \in \{i \in X : y_i \in \{1^+, 2\}\}, S = s, \Gamma_1 = y_1, \dots, \Gamma_{N+1} = y_{N+1}\right)$$

$$= \frac{(1 - p_a)^{2k_0} (p_a(1 - p_a))^{k_1^+ + k_1^-} p_a^{2k_2}}{1 - (1 - p_a)^{N+1}}, \tag{13.39}$$

where $k_0 = \sum_{i=1}^{N+1} 1(y_i = 0)$, $k_1^+ = \sum_{i=1}^{N+1} 1(y_i = 1^+)$, $k_1^- = \sum_{i=1}^{N+1} 1(y_i = 1^-)$, $k_2 = \sum_{i=1}^{N+1} 1(y_i = 2)$, and $k_1^+ + k_2 > 0$. (Our notation is that $1(A) = 1$ if A is true, and 0 otherwise.) We explain this formula now.

As before, this basic belief assignment is a summary of what we know, and is formulated in terms of items that can be well described by classical probabilities. The normalizing factor $1 - (1 - p_a)^{N+1}$ comes from the fact that we know that at least one individual i (namely the actual father) passes on a, since a is the paternal allele observed in the genotype of the child. Every allele that is passed on has label a with probability p_a, hence the denominator. The factor $(p_a(1 - p_a))^{k_1^+ + k_1^-}$ comes from the probability $2p_a(1 - p_a)$ that a person has one allele of type a, multiplied by $1/2$, the probability that it is passed on (in the case of 1^+) or not (in the case of 1^-). The term $(1 - p_a)^{2k_0}$ is obtained from the probability $(1 - p_a)^2$ that a person has no alleles of type a, and similarly for $p_a^{2k_2}$. With these last terms we do not have to worry about passing on the correct allele or not, since this is never, respectively always the case.

Now we have to distinguish between two scenarios: the chosen person has one or two alleles of type a. We first look at the case in which he has two such alleles. So, we want to condition on

$$H_2 := \{\Gamma_s = 2\}. \tag{13.40}$$

We write $E(y_1, \dots, y_{N+1})$ for the event in (13.39), and we compute

$$\text{Bel}(H_2) = \text{Pl}(H_2)$$

$$= \sum_{y_s=2} m(E(y_1, \dots, y_{N+1})) \tag{13.41}$$

$$= \frac{p_a^2}{1 - (1 - p_a)^{N+1}},$$

and

$$\text{Bel}(\{F = s\} \cap H_2) = \sum_{y_s=2, \forall i \neq s \ y_i \in \{0, 1^-\}} m(E(y_1, \ldots, y_{N+1}))$$

$$= \frac{p_a^2 (1 - p_a)^N}{1 - (1 - p_a)^{N+1}}. \tag{13.42}$$

From this, it follows that

$$\text{Bel}(F = s \mid H_2) = (1 - p_a)^N. \tag{13.43}$$

The interpretation of this result is the same as the interpretation of (13.22). Indeed, we can only be sure that $F = s$ if all other potential fathers do not pass on a. Since we do not know the genotypes of the other individuals in X, all we can say is that any of them would pass on a with probability p_a.

Next we consider the case in which the putative father has one allele of type a. We do not know if the putative father passes on this allele, hence we condition on

$$H_1 := \{\Gamma_s \in \{1^-, 1^+\}\}. \tag{13.44}$$

We compute

$$\text{Bel}(H_1) = \text{Pl}(H_1)$$
$$= \sum_{y_s=1^-} m(E(y_1, \ldots, y_{N+1})) \tag{13.45}$$
$$+ \sum_{y_s=1^+} m(E(y_1, \ldots, y_{N+1})).$$

In the first sum, s itself does not pass on a, so we must make sure that someone else does. In the second sum, s itself passes on a so we do not have to worry about that. These considerations lead to

$$\text{Bel}(H_1) = \text{Pl}(H_1)$$
$$= \frac{p_a(1 - p_a)(1 - (1 - p_a)^N)}{(1 - (1 - p_a)^{N+1})}$$
$$+ \frac{p_a(1 - p_a)}{(1 - (1 - p_a)^{N+1})} \tag{13.46}$$
$$= \frac{2p_a(1 - p_a)(1 - \frac{1}{2}(1 - p_a)^N)}{(1 - (1 - p_a)^{N+1})},$$

and

$$\text{Bel}(H_1 \cap \{F = s\}) \sum_{y_s=1^+, \forall i \neq s \ y_i \in \{0, 1^-\}} m(E(y_1, \ldots, y_{N+1}))$$

$$= \frac{p_a(1 - p_a)(1 - p_a)^N}{1 - (1 - p_a)^{N+1}}. \tag{13.47}$$

From this, it follows that

$$\mathrm{Bcl}(F = s \mid II_1) = \frac{\frac{1}{2}(1 - p_a)^N}{1 - \frac{1}{2}(1 - p_a)^N}. \tag{13.48}$$

Again, this formula has an illuminating interpretation. In the denominator we have the probability, given that we know that s has one allele a, that at least one person passes on a. In the numerator, we have the probability $1/2$ that s passes on a multiplied by the probability that all the others do not pass on a. Hence the expression in (13.48) is the conditional probability that s is the only one who passes on a, given that at least one person does so.

Furthermore, it is not difficult to check that (13.48) is smaller than (13.43). This makes intuitive sense indeed: our belief that someone with two alleles a is the father should be higher than for a person who has only one such allele. Note that in (13.43) we do not need to condition on someone passing on a since s already does that.

In Section 4.5.6 we obtained the classical answers, assuming uniform priors. If the person of interest has genotype (a, a), then the posterior probability that he is the father is $1/(1 + Np_a)$. In the case where he has only one allele a, then the posterior probability that he is the father is $1/(1 + 2Np_a)$.

We can reconstruct these classical answers with the machinery of belief functions, as follows. We claim that the proper basic belief assignment is given by

$$m^{cl}(F = t, S = s, \Gamma_1 = y_1, \ldots, \Gamma_{N+1} = y_{N+1})$$

$$= \frac{1}{N + 1} \frac{(1 - p_a)^{2k_0}(p_a(1 - p_a))^{k_1^+ + k_1^-} p_a^{2k_2}}{p_a}, \tag{13.49}$$

whenever $k_0 = \sum_{i=1}^{N+1} 1(y_i = 0)$, $k_1^+ = \sum_{i=1}^{N+1} 1(y_i = 1^+)$, $k_1^- = \sum_{i=1}^{N+1} 1$ $(y_i = 1^-)$, $k_2 = \sum_{i=1}^{N+1} 1(y_i = 2)$, and $y_t \in \{1^+, 2\}$. The factor $1/(N + 1)$ comes from the uniform prior on F. The p_a in the denominator comes from the fact that we condition on F passing on the correct allele, and the remaining terms are as before. We write $J(t, y_1, \ldots, y_{N+1})$ for the event in (13.49), and compute

$$\mathrm{Bel}^{cl}(H_2 \cap \{F = s\}) = \sum_{y_s = 2} m(J(s, y_1, \ldots, y_{N+1}))$$

$$= \frac{p_a}{N + 1}.$$

To see the last equality, observe that we simply add the probabilities in the numerator of (13.49) of those outcomes that have $y_s = 2$. This gives p_a^2, which should then be divided by p_a.

Furthermore, we have

$$Pl^{cl}(H_2 \cap \{F \neq s\}) = \sum_{t \neq s, y_s = 2} m(J(t, y_1, \ldots, y_{N+1}))$$

$$= \frac{Np_a^2}{N+1}.$$

To see this, observe that in order to be compatible with $H_1 \cap \{F \neq s\}$, we need that s has two alleles a, and that the real father F passes on a. This gives a total probability of p_a^3 which upon dividing by p_a gives the factor p_a^2. The factor $N/(N+1)$ comes from the requirement that we need consistency with $F \neq s$.

Thus, from the definition of conditional belief we then find

$$\mathrm{Bel}^{cl}(F = s \mid H_2) = \frac{1}{1 + Np_a}, \tag{13.50}$$

as required.

Finally we consider the classical case in which s has only one allele of type a. This gives

$$\mathrm{Bel}^{cl}(H_1 \cap \{F = s\}) = \sum_{y_s = 1^+} m(J(s, y_1, \ldots, y_{N+1}))$$

$$= \frac{(1 - p_a)}{N+1},$$

for similar reasons as above. Furthermore, we have

$$Pl^{cl}(H_1 \cap \{F \neq s\}) = \sum_{t \neq s, x = s, y_s \in \{1^+, 2\}} m(J(t, y_1, \ldots, y_{N+1}))$$

$$= \frac{2Np_a(1 - p_a)}{N+1}.$$

Thus we obtain

$$\mathrm{Bel}^{cl}(F = s \mid H_1) = \frac{1}{1 + 2Np_a}, \tag{13.51}$$

again as required.

13.4.2 Paternal Allele Not Known

In the case where mother and child have the same heterozygous genotype (a, b), it is not clear what the paternal allele of the child is. In this subsection we discuss this case, but we will not provide all the computations. We have seen that answers arising from the theory of belief functions can be suitably interpreted, and the consistency of these interpretations allows us to predict the answer in new cases.

There are five possibilities for the genotype of the putative father, namely (a,a), (a,b), (b,b), (b,c), and (a,c), for some allele c different from both a and b.

The product space on which we work needs an extra factor $\{a,b\}$ to denote which allele is passed on by the mother. In addition, it is convenient now to take the genotype of all members of X into account, together with the allele they pass on. When we write that an individual in X has (a^*,b), we mean that he has genotype (a,b) and passes on a. That is, the characteristics are in the set

$$Y := \{(a,a), (a^*,b), (a,b^*), (b,b), (a,c^*), (a^*,c), (b,c^*), (b^*,c), (c,c)\},$$

where c denotes any allele different from a and b. Note that homozygous genotypes need no $*$ since the label of the passed on allele will always be the same.

We now consider

$$\Omega = X \times X \times \{a,b\} \times Y^{N+1},$$

where the coordinates represent, respectively, the true father F, the selected person S, the allele Σ passed on by the mother, and the characteristics Γ_i of the members of X. We again assume that $S = s$.

For $\Sigma = \sigma, \Gamma_1 = y_1, \ldots, \Gamma_{N+1} = y_{n+1}$, we let $J(\sigma, y_1, \ldots, y_{N+1})$ be the collection of members of X that could be the father if the mother passes on σ. For all $\sigma, y_1, \ldots, y_{N+1}$ for which $J(\sigma, y_1, \ldots, y_{N+1}) \neq \emptyset$, the basic belief assignment

$$m(F \in J(\sigma, y_1, \ldots, y_{N+1}), S = s, \Sigma = \sigma, \Gamma_1 = y_1, \ldots, \Gamma_{N+1} = y_{n+1})$$

is proportional to

$$\frac{1}{2} p_a^{2k_{a,a}} p_b^{2k_{b,b}} p_c^{2k_{c,c}} \prod_{i \neq j} (p_i p_j)^{k_{i^*,j}+k_{i,j^*}},$$

where the $k_{\alpha,\beta}$ count the number of indices i for which $y_i = (\alpha, \beta)$.

With this basic belief assignment and the corresponding belief function, we can make computations very similar to the ones in Section 13.4.1. We do not give the full computational detail, but only the results, together with a suitable interpretation.

Writing $H_{(a,a)}$ for the event that $S = s$ has genotype (a,a), we find

$$\text{Bel}(F = s \mid H_{(a,a)}) = \frac{\frac{1}{2}(1 - p_a)^N}{1 - \frac{1}{2}(1 - p_b)^N}. \tag{13.52}$$

We can explain this result as follows. We have to condition on the event that some-one passes on a and someone passes on b, an event with probability $1 - \frac{1}{2}(1 - p_b)^N$. Indeed, the condition only fails if the mother passes on a and no member of X passes on b. We can only be sure that s is the father if the mother passes on b and no one else does passes on a, an event with probability $\frac{1}{2}(1 - p_a)^N$. This gives (13.52).

Next we consider the case in which s has genotype (a, b). We again have to condition on the event that someone passes on a and someone passes on b, an event with probability $1 - \frac{1}{4}(1 - p_a)^N - \frac{1}{4}(1 - p_b)^N$. We can only be sure that s is the father if either (i) the mother passes on a, s passes on b, and no one outside s passes on b, or (ii) the mother passes on b, s passes on a, and no one outside s passes on a. The probability of this event is $\frac{1}{4}(1 - p_b)^N + \frac{1}{4}(1 - p_a)^N$. Hence, writing $H_{(a,b)}$ for the event that $S = s$ has genotype (a, b), we find

$$\mathrm{Bel}(F = s \mid H_{(a,b)}) = \frac{\frac{1}{4}(1 - p_a)^N + \frac{1}{4}(1 - p_b)^N}{1 - \frac{1}{4}(1 - p_a)^N - \frac{1}{4}(1 - p_b)^N}. \tag{13.53}$$

Finally, we consider the case in which s has genotype (a, c). The event that a and b are not both passed on by anyone, has probability $\frac{1}{2}(1 - p_b)^N + \frac{1}{4}(1 - p_a)^N$, where the first term comes from the mother passing on a, and the second term comes from the mother passing on b, s passing on c, and no one else passing on a. We can only be sure that s is the father if the mother passes on b, s passes on a, and no one else passes on a, an event with probability $\frac{1}{4}(1 - p_a)^N$. This leads, writing $H_{(a,c)}$ for the event that $S = s$ has genotype (a, c), to

$$\mathrm{Bel}(F = s \mid H_{(a,c)}) = \frac{\frac{1}{4}(1 - p_a)^N}{1 - \frac{1}{2}(1 - p_b)^N - \frac{1}{4}(1 - p_a)^N}. \tag{13.54}$$

We can also obtain the classical answers, assuming uniform priors, with this machinery, in very much the same way as above, and we do not give the details here.

13.4.3 Multiple Loci

In the previous subsections we have seen how to compute beliefs for paternity based on one locus. In reality, we would like to base our belief on multiple loci. To do this, all we have to do is properly combine formulas (13.43), (13.48), (13.52), (13.53), and (13.54). The denominators in each of these formulas represent the probability of the event on which we need to condition, namely that the neces-sary alleles are indeed passed on by someone. (In (13.43), the denominator is equal to 1, since we know that s passes on the correct allele.) In the multiple loci situation, we simply need to condition on *all* these events, for each locus, and since we assume independence between the loci, we simply have to multiply all these probabilities.

In the numerators of the formulas above, we have the probability of the event that implies that s must be the father. When we work with multiple loci, it is enough to conclude that s must be the father when this must be so on one locus. In fact, since we only have genetic information about s, and not about any other member of X, the only way to conclude that s must be the father is when this follows from one (or more) loci. Hence, to compute the numerator associated with observing multiple loci, we compute $1 - \prod_{i \in I}(1 - \epsilon_i)$, where ϵ_i is the numerator corresponding to the ith locus.

In short, if the expression for our belief that s is the father based on locus i is ϵ_i/δ_i, understood in the sense above, then the belief that s is the father based on a collection I of loci, is equal to

$$\frac{1 - \prod_{i \in I}(1 - \epsilon_i)}{\prod_{i \in I} \delta_i}.$$

13.5 Finding Persons with Special Features

In this section we consider the following general situation. We have a collection X of $N + 1$ individuals which we denote by $X = \{0, \ldots, N\}$. The collection X is, with the exception of one individual, part of a population in which the probability to have DNA profile γ is equal to $p_G(\gamma)$. We assume that there is one exceptional individual in X, denoted by X_0, whose probability distribution for the profile is not p_G but p_B. As an example, one can think of the situation in which we are looking for a sibling of a given person whose DNA profile is known. When we assume that the collection X of $N + 1$ individuals contains precisely one sibling of the given person, then this sibling has a different probability distribution governing his or her DNA profile than all the others. The situation in Section 13.4 is a special case, in which the special person was the actual father. It is also similar to the situation as discussed in Section 12.1.

Suppose, then, that we observe the DNA profiles of all members of X and that we want to make a probabilistic assessment about the identity of X_0. If one is willing to accept prior probabilities $\pi_i := P(X_0 = i)$ for the probability that i is the exceptional person, then we can perform an elementary classical computation using Bayes' rule. This runs as follows.

Suppose that we have observed that i has profile α_i, for all $i = 0, \ldots, N$. We denote the vector of observed profiles by $\alpha := (\alpha_0, \ldots, \alpha_N)$. We compute

$$P(X_0 = i \mid \alpha) = \frac{\pi_i P(\alpha \mid X_0 = i)}{\sum_{j=0}^{N} \pi_j P(\alpha \mid X_0 = j)}$$

$$= \frac{\pi_i \delta_i}{\sum_{j=0}^{N} \pi_j \delta_j}, \tag{13.55}$$

where

$$\delta_i := p_B(\alpha_i) \prod_{j \neq i} p_G(\alpha_j). \tag{13.56}$$

Instead of observing all profiles of the members of X, it is also possible that we need to make an assessment on the basis of one observed profile only. Assume that we only observe that individual i has profile α_i. We then compute, using the same priors as above,

$$P(X_0 = i \mid \alpha_i) = \frac{P(\alpha_i \mid X_0 = i)\pi_i}{\sum_{j=0}^{N} P(\alpha_i \mid X_0 = j)\pi_j}$$

$$= \frac{\pi_i p_B(\alpha_i)}{\pi_i p_B(\alpha_i) + (1 - \pi_i)p_G(\alpha_i)}, \tag{13.57}$$

as is all standard of course.

These computations are undisputed if proper prior probabilities can be formulated. However, if no meaningful prior probabilities can be defined, such a computation cannot be performed. Often, uniform prior probabilities are suggested to model complete ignorance, but we have seen in Section 1.5 that this may be somewhat problematic. We will now show how we can use the theory of belief functions to make a probabilistic assessment without using prior information.

In order to use belief functions, we need to define an outcome space and a basic belief assignment which properly describe the situation. In the current situation, with one exceptional individual about whose identity we have no information whatsoever, this is not completely straightforward. The outcome space which simply lists the profiles of $0, \ldots, N$ is not useful, since we do not know who the exceptional person is. We do not want to impose any prior knowledge, and hence there is no way to assign a prior probability to, say, the event that $X_0 = 0$.

To overcome this problem, we argue as follows. There is an individual X_0 (unknown to us) who is special. All the other persons are generic, and we can think of them as being labeled $X_1, \ldots, X_N$ by someone, but in such a way that we have no information whatsoever about their identities. In other words, we put ourselves in the epistemic position that we know a labeling exists, but without us having any information about it other than that $\{X_0, X_1, \ldots, X_N\} = X$, and that X_0 is the exceptional person.

Let us denote by Γ the set of possible profiles. Our outcome space can now be taken to be

$$\Omega = X^{N+1} \times \Gamma^{N+1}, \tag{13.58}$$

where the first $N + 1$ coordinates refer (in that order) to the labeling $X_0, \ldots, X_N$ of the elements in X. A typical element of Ω is written as

$$\omega = (x_0, \ldots, x_N, \gamma_0, \ldots, \gamma_N), \tag{13.59}$$

where γ_i is the profile that belongs to x_i, for $i = 0, \ldots, N$. We refer to the coordinates of ω by capitals. For instance, the set of outcomes ω for which $x_0 = x$ and $\gamma_0 = \gamma$ is denoted by $\{\omega : X_0 = x, \Gamma_0 = \gamma\}$ or just by $\{X_0 = x, \Gamma_0 = \gamma\}$.

The knowledge that we have is captured by the following basic belief assignment:

$$m(\{X_0, \ldots, X_N\} = X, \Gamma_0 = \gamma_0, \ldots, \Gamma_N = \gamma_N) = p_B(\gamma_0) \prod_{i=1}^{N} p_G(\gamma_i). \tag{13.60}$$

Indeed, this basic belief assignment precisely expresses that X_0 is the exceptional person with a non-generic distribution for the profiles, but it does not reveal any information about the identity of X_0.

It is convenient (and it is also often reasonable) to assume that the profiles that can be observed can be ordered according to some previously determined rule. Now suppose that we observe the traits $\alpha_0 < \alpha_1 < \cdots < \alpha_N$ and denote this event by H_α. (We assume for simplicity that the α_i are all different.) Note that in this notation, α_i does not correspond to i. For notational convenience we write S_i for the individual corresponding to α_i.

Without any prior information about the identity of X_0, the belief that $X_0 = i$ is 0 for all i, as follows from (13.60). This is only natural, since we simply have no information whatsoever about the actual identity of X_0. There are, however, nontrivial events with nontrivial beliefs. Indeed, the belief that the donor of, say, α_k is the special person, is in fact nontrivial, as we now show.

We compute $\mathrm{Bel}(S_k = X_0 \mid H_\alpha)$, which corresponds to the conditional belief (given H_α) that the person S_k who carries α_k is the exceptional one X_0. For this, we need to compute $\mathrm{Bel}(\{S_k = X_0\} \cap H_\alpha)$ and $\mathrm{Bel}(\{S_k = X_0\} \cup H_\alpha^c)$. When inspecting the basic belief assignment in (13.60) we see that for H_α to occur we need the set $\{\gamma_0, \ldots, \gamma_N\}$ to be equal to the set $\{\alpha_0, \ldots, \alpha_N\}$. If, in addition, $\{S_0 = X_0\}$ is required, then we also need $\gamma_0 = \alpha_k$. The remaining N items can be ordered in any of $N!$ ways, each with the same basic belief assignment. This leads to

$$\text{Bel}(\{S_k = X_0\} \cap H_\alpha) = N! p_B(\alpha_k) \prod_{i \neq k} p_G(\alpha_i).$$

For the term $\text{Bel}(\{S_k = X_0\} \cup H_\alpha^c)$ we argue as follows. Since each set with positive basic belief assignment is contained in either H_α or H_α^c, we have that

$$\text{Bel}(\{S_k = X_0\} \cup H_\alpha^c) = \text{Bel}(H_\alpha^c) + \text{Bel}(H_\alpha \cap \{S_k = X_0\})$$
$$= 1 - \text{Bel}(H_\alpha) + \text{Bel}(H_\alpha \cap \{S_k = X_0\})$$
$$= 1 - \text{Bel}(H_\alpha) + N! p_B(\alpha_k) \prod_{i \neq i} p_G(\alpha_i).$$

Using (13.13), this gives

$$\text{Bel}(S_k = X_0 \mid H_\alpha) = \frac{\text{Bel}(\{S_k = X_0\} \cap H_\alpha)}{\text{Bel}(\{S_k = X_0\} \cap H_\alpha) + 1 - \text{Bel}(\{S_k = X_0\} \cup H_\alpha^c)}$$
$$= \frac{N! p_B(\alpha_k) \prod_{j \neq k} p_G(\alpha_j)}{\text{Bel}(H_\alpha)}.$$

Since it is not difficult to see that

$$\text{Bel}(H_\alpha) = \sum_{i=0}^{N} p_B(\alpha_i) N! \prod_{j \neq i} p_G(\alpha_j),$$

we finally find that

$$\text{Bel}(S_k = X_0 \mid H_\alpha) = \frac{p_B(\alpha_k) \prod_{j \neq k} p_G(\alpha_j)}{\sum_{i=0}^{N} p_B(\alpha_i) \prod_{j \neq i} p_G(\alpha_j)}$$
$$= \frac{\delta_k}{\sum_{i=0}^{N} \delta_i}. \tag{13.61}$$

We now observe the interesting fact that (13.61) is the same as the answer in (13.55) in the case of a uniform prior, that is, if $\pi_i = 1/(N+1)$ for all $i = 0, \ldots, N$. But note that although the two answers are the same, they were obtained by answering different questions. In (13.55) we compute the posterior probability that a previously identified person is the exceptional one, whereas in (13.61) we compute the belief that the donor S_k of α_k is X_0. A priori, that is, before knowing the profiles $\alpha_0, \ldots, \alpha_N$, any member of X could turn out to be S_k. After learning $\alpha_1, \ldots, \alpha_N$, all members of X are assigned a belief by (13.61) that they are the exceptional person, and the answer is the same as the classical answer with uniform priors.

The ensuing belief function is in fact a probability distribution. Using belief functions in a meaningful way in this case forces us to start with a different question than in the classical case. However, in the end, we have in this special case the same information as when we would have worked with classical probabilities with a uniform prior.

13.6 The Legal Practice with Belief Functions

How could the theory of belief functions as developed in this chapter possibly work in a legal context? After all, the concept of a likelihood ratio does not exist in the context of belief functions, and this raises the question how forensic experts and the judiciary work together when using belief functions.

To shed some light on this matter, let us review the classical procedure. The odds form of Bayes' rule states that

$$\frac{P(H_1 \mid E)}{P(H_2 \mid E)} = \frac{P(E \mid H_1)}{P(E \mid H_2)} \cdot \frac{P(H_1)}{P(H_2)}. \tag{13.62}$$

As we have discussed extensively, formula (13.62) describes how the prior odds $P(H_1)/P(H_2)$ are transformed into the posterior odds $P(H_1 \mid E)/P(H_2 \mid E)$, by multiplying the prior odds with the likelihood ratio $P(E \mid H_1)/P(E \mid H_2)$.

In theory, the likelihood ratio is in the provenance of the forensic expert. This expert can, in certain circumstances at least assign a probability to the evidence under various hypothesis, and thereby compute the likelihood ratio. The expert does not express how likely these hypotheses themselves are, that is, the expert says nothing about the prior probabilities $P(H_1)$ and $P(H_2)$. Hence, the expert does not make a statement about the posterior probabilities $P(H_1 \mid E)$ and $P(H_2 \mid E)$.

However, even in the classical process, this idealistic picture is not always realistic. In many situations that we have encountered, the likelihood ratio did depend on prior information, for instance in (3.2) where the likelihood ratio depended on the distribution W which expressed prior uncertainty about a certain parameter θ. Hence the clear distinction between the contribution of the judiciary and the expert that we described above, and which is advocated in many texts, is not always realized. The strength of the evidence as expressed through a likelihood ratio may depend on prior information that lies with the fact finder.

The main reason to be interested in the likelihood ratio is, as we have insisted many times in this book, that a likelihood ratio expresses the evidential value of one hypothesis with respect to another one. We were interested in what statistical evidence *is*, and how this can be quantified. We have concluded that evidence is relative and should be expressed by a likelihood ratio.

But what one really needs in the end are the posterior probabilities $P(H_1 \mid E)$ and $P(H_2 \mid E)$, so we need the *joint distribution* of all variables involved. In any case, it is only through the joint effort of expert and legal representative that the joint distribution can be computed. We need information from the expert, and we need a probabilistic assessment of the judiciary. In other words, the complete joint distribution of H_1, H_2, and E can only be determined as a joint effort of both expert and legal representative. They both contribute to the joint distribution, albeit in different ways, and as such they both contribute to the posterior odds as well. The representation (13.62) is, from this point of view, just one way to express certain aspects of the joint distribution of H_1, H_2 and E – a representation that has the pleasant interpretation just described, but which is no more than just that: a specific way of obtaining posterior odds or probabilities.

The theory as developed in this chapter suggests a slightly different procedure to end up with a statement about the way the hypotheses and the evidence relate to each other, when working with belief functions. The prior probabilities from the classical approach are replaced by a suitable basic belief assignment, which contains ingredients to be delivered by either the legal representative or the forensic expert. For instance, in the basic belief assignment (13.8) in the classical island problem, the algebraic form of the basic belief assignment represents the information of the legal representative, but the actual value of p must come from the DNA expert. Note that we do not have to worry about choosing prior probabilities. Indeed, these are replaced by the design of the basic belief assignment.

In our setting, if the legal representative confirms that there is no prior information, one takes an uninformative prior as far as the criminal C is concerned, and the expert can simply report, say (13.22), which in that situation contains all the available information in the case. If we have no prior information, then no unfounded or subjective choice for a prior needs to be made, apart from the choice of the relevant population. If there is prior information, then one can set up the corresponding prior basic belief assignment, and compute the conditional belief, conditioned on the evidence, according to the theory explained above.

We have seen in the examples in the island problem that the numbers obtained are typically less impressive than in the classical case. This is not surprising: starting out with an uninformative prior instead of a uniform prior gives us *less* information to start out with. Is this a weakness of the theory of belief functions as we have set out in this thesis? We do not think so. It is, in our opinion, better to have a less impressive number which is well founded and not so easy to challenge, than to have a more impressive number which may depend on unfounded arguments or assumptions, and which might be easier to dismiss.

Finally, we remark that in the literature, attempts have been made to come up with alternatives for the posterior odds in case we work with belief functions.

To be precise, we are aware of three such suggestions. Let Bel be a belief function and H be an hypothesis of interest. Define

$$BR_1 := \frac{\text{Bel}(H_1)}{\text{Bel}(H_2)}, \tag{13.63}$$

$$BR_2 := \frac{\text{Pl}(H_1)}{\text{Pl}(H_2)}, \tag{13.64}$$

and

$$BR_3 := \frac{\text{Bel}(H_1) + \Theta}{\text{Bel}(H_2) + \Theta}, \tag{13.65}$$

where $\Theta = \frac{1}{2}(1 - \text{Bel}(H_1) - \text{Bel}(H_2))$, that is, the mass that does not contribute to either the belief in H_1 or H_2 is evenly spread over numerator and denominator.

Are such *belief ratios* useful in the theory of belief functions? We do not think so, and to explain our position here, let us go back to the classical situation once more. Unlike the likelihood ratio, which as a measure for the strength of the evidence is naturally and necessarily a relative notion, the prior and posterior odds in the classical situation are only a *convenience*. It is convenient to write Bayes' rule in the odds form (13.62), because the likelihood ratio, the relative strength of the evidence, appears in it. The prior and posterior odds in *themselves* are not important. The individual probabilities $P(H_1 \mid E)$ and $P(H_2 \mid E)$ are important, but not their ratio. When $H_2 = H_1^c$, then the posterior odds allow for the computation of posterior probabilities, but in general this is not possible. Hence, in the classical case, posterior odds are convenient, since they can be placed into a nice formula which contains the likelihood ratio and the prior odds, but in the end, a juror or judge is only interested in the posterior probability of the hypotheses of interest.

Now note that the belief ratios in (13.63), (13.64), and (13.65) are not informative about the individual beliefs, *not even when* $H_2 = H_1^c$. In fact, the attempts in (13.64) and (13.65) involve other ingredients than beliefs only, and for that reason do not seem very appropriate from the outset. In the classical theory, odds are informative about probabilities when the hypotheses are each other's negation, as we remarked above, so that at least in these cases, odds could be used instead of probabilities. But in any of the belief odds discussed above, this is not the case. Small belief in *both* H_1 and H_1^c is compatible with high odds, very much in the same way as high classical posterior odds of H_1 versus H_2 do not imply that the posterior probability of H_1 is high, in the case where H_2 is not the negation of H_1. To give a simple numerical example, if $\text{Bel}(H_1) = 0.1$ and $\text{Bel}(H_1^c) = 0.0001$, then the odds in (13.63) are 1,000 but both beliefs are small. So in general we cannot conclude much from high belief ratios.

This seems to rule out any proper use of belief ratios in criminal law. When H_1 represents the guilt of a certain suspect, say, and H_1^c his innocence, then it would be very inappropriate to use the odds in (13.63) in any argument for conviction. The odds can be very high while the actual belief in H_1 is very small, and clearly a small belief in H_1 does not warrant any decision in its favor. Belief ratios simply do not measure any relevant quantity in criminal law: they measure a ratio of beliefs from which the individual beliefs cannot be reconstructed. It seems, therefore, inappropriate to take these ratios into account for a decision.

However, in civil law, a verdict is not necessarily a choice between two competing hypotheses, and it is interesting to contemplate that a decision can possibly be made on the basis of the beliefs of the various hypotheses of interest. We still think that even in that situation, uncommitted support should never play a role, and the only candidate would be the ratio in (13.63). Whether or not one would be willing to base a verdict in civil law on the ratio in (13.63) depends on one's notion of fairness. If no more information can be gathered, and the belief functions have been agreed upon, then it does not seem impossible to defend the point of view that a decision should be taken proportional to the current ratio, which represent all there is to know.

13.7 A Philosophical Back-up of Belief Functions

In this section we explain how the use of belief functions to model epistemic uncertainty can be philosophically justified. We have chosen for a characterization of belief functions in the same spirit as Theorem 1.4.4 for probability distributions. One can interpret this theorem as a characterization of probability distributions in behavioral terms: the total price an agent is willing to pay for a collection of bets $A_1, \ldots, A_N$ exceeds the corresponding total price for the collection $B_1, \ldots, B_M$ if and only if for any outcome of the experiment, the number of the A_i that occur is at least as large as the number of the B_j that occur.

There is a similar characterization for belief functions, and we develop this now. The first step is to rewrite Theorem 1.4.4 in terms of so-called *truth valuations*. A function $\mathcal{T}: 2^\Omega \rightarrow \{0, 1\}$ is a truth valuation provided that:

(i) $\mathcal{T}(A) = 0$ if and only if $\mathcal{T}(A^c) = 1$;
(ii) If $\mathcal{T}(A) = 1$ and $A \subset B$, then $\mathcal{T}(B) = 1$;
(iii) If $\mathcal{T}(A) = 1$ and $\mathcal{T}(B) = 1$, then $\mathcal{T}(A \cap B) = 1$;
(iv) $\mathcal{T}(\Omega) = 1$.

A truth valuation can be thought of as a statement about the truth of events and their interrelations. Indeed, (i) means that if A is true, A^c is not, and vice versa. In (ii) it is stated that if A is true, and $A \subset B$, then B must also be true. Condition (iii) formulates that if A and B are both true, then so is their intersection. Condition (iv), finally, says that something must be true.

We first claim that every truth valuation $\mathcal{T}$ is of the form $\mathcal{T}(A) = 1_A(\omega)$ for some $\omega \in \Omega$. To see this, it follows from (i) and (iv) that $\mathcal{T}(\emptyset) = 0$, and then from (iii) that sets A and B with $\mathcal{T}(A) = \mathcal{T}(B) = 1$ cannot be disjoint. Hence there is a minimal set C such that $\mathcal{T}(C) = 1$, in the sense that all sets D with $\mathcal{T}(D) = 1$ contain C: indeed, simply take C to be the intersection of all sets whose truth valuation is 1. If C is not a singleton, then it contains at least two elements, and by minimality of C it then follows that for all $x \in C$ we have $\mathcal{T}(\{x\}) = 0$. Therefore, for all $x \in C$ we have $\mathcal{T}(\{x\}^c) = 1$, by (i). Hence, from (iii) it follows that

$$\mathcal{T}\left(\bigcap_{x \in C} \{x\}^c\right) = 1,$$

but this intersection is just C^c which we know must have $\mathcal{T}(C^c) = 0$, by (i). Hence C must be a singleton, and by (ii) we now find that $\mathcal{T}(A) = 1$ if and only if A contains the singleton C.

With this characterization of truth valuations in place, we can reformulate Theorem 1.4.4 as follows.

Theorem 13.7.1 *A function $P: 2^\Omega \to [0,1]$ is a probability distribution if and only if:*

(P1) $P(\Omega) = 1$.
(P2∗) For all $A_1, A_2, \ldots, A_N \subset \Omega$ and $B_1, B_2, \ldots, B_M \subset \Omega$ such that for all truth valuations $\mathcal{T}$ we have

$$\sum_{i=1}^{N} \mathcal{T}(A_i) \geq \sum_{j=1}^{M} \mathcal{T}(B_j), \tag{13.66}$$

it is the case that

$$\sum_{i=1}^{N} P(A_i) \geq \sum_{j=1}^{M} P(B_j). \tag{13.67}$$

The four defining properties of truth valuations are quite natural. When we want to develop a theory about *beliefs* rather than about truths, then each of these properties should still be true, with the exception of the first one. Indeed, as we have argued above, it should be possible to have no belief in both A and A^c. However, if one believes A to be true, then one should assign zero belief to A^c. This observation motivates us to introduce the notion of a *belief valuation*, in which we weaken the first requirement in the definition of a truth valuation.

A function $\mathcal{B}\colon \Omega \to \{0, 1\}$ is called a *belief valuation* provided that:

(i) $\mathcal{B}(A) = 1$ implies that $\mathcal{B}(A^c) = 0$;
(ii) if $\mathcal{B}(A) = 1$ and $A \subset B$, then $\mathcal{B}(B) = 1$;
(iii) if $\mathcal{B}(A) = 1$ and $\mathcal{B}(B) = 1$, then $\mathcal{B}(A \cap B) = 1$;
(iv) $\mathcal{B}(\Omega) = 1$.

Note that properties (i)–(iv) can also be understood from the interpretation of a belief function as provability.

We first claim that for any belief valuation $\mathcal{B}$ there is a set C so that $\mathcal{B}(A) = 1$ if and only if $C \subset A$. The proof of this is very similar to the corresponding result for truth valuations that we gave above. Indeed, it follows from (i) and (iv) that $\mathcal{B}(\emptyset) = 0$, and then from (iii) that sets A and B with $\mathcal{B}(A) = \mathcal{B}(B) = 1$ cannot be disjoint. Hence there is a minimal set C such that $\mathcal{B}(C) = 1$, in the sense that all sets D with $\mathcal{B}(D) = 1$ contain C. This time we cannot conclude that C is a singleton. Indeed the step from $\mathcal{T}(\{x\}) = 0$ to $\mathcal{T}(\{x\}^c) = 0$ has no analogue now. However, again (ii) implies the desired conclusion. We call $\mathcal{B}$ the belief valuation *associated* with C.

With this characterization of belief evaluations in place, we can prove the following result, which characterizes belief functions in the same way as Theorem 13.7.1 characterizes probability distributions.

Theorem 13.7.2 *A function* $\mathrm{Bel}\colon 2^{\Omega} \to [0, 1]$ *is a belief function if and only if:*

(Q1) $\mathrm{Bel}(\Omega) = 1.$
(Q2) For all $A_1, A_2, \ldots, A_N \subset \Omega$ *and* $B_1, B_2, \ldots, B_M \subset \Omega$ *such that for all belief evaluations* $\mathcal{B}$ *we have*

$$\sum_{i=1}^{N} \mathcal{B}(A_i) \geq \sum_{j=1}^{M} \mathcal{B}(B_j), \tag{13.68}$$

it is the case that

$$\sum_{i=1}^{N} \mathrm{Bel}(A_i) \geq \sum_{j=1}^{M} \mathrm{Bel}(B_j). \tag{13.69}$$

Proof. First assume that Bel satisfies (Q1) and (Q2). We will use the characterization of belief functions in Theorem 13.1.4 to show that Bel is a belief function. For two sets A and B, we write $1(A \subset B) = 1$ if $A \subset B$ and $1(A \subset B) = 0$ otherwise.

Let $C_1, \ldots, C_n \subset \Omega$ be arbitrary, and fix $S \subset \Omega$. Consider the belief valuation $\mathcal{B}$ associated with S so that $\mathcal{B}(A) = 1(S \subset A)$. We will apply (Q2) with

$$A_1 = \bigcap_{i=1}^{n} C_i,$$

all other sets A_i of the form

$$\bigcap_{\substack{I \subset \{1,\dots,n\} \\ I \neq \emptyset, |I| \text{ even}}} C_i,$$

and the B_j of the form

$$\bigcap_{\substack{I \subset \{1,\dots,n\} \\ I \neq \emptyset, |I| \text{ odd}}} C_i.$$

We claim that

$$1\left(S \subset \bigcup_{i=1}^{n} C_i\right) + \sum_{\substack{I \subset \{1,\dots,n\} \\ I \neq \emptyset, |I| \text{ even}}} 1\left(S \subset \bigcap_{i \in I} C_i\right) \geq \sum_{\substack{I \subset \{1,\dots,n\} \\ I \neq \emptyset, |I| \text{ odd}}} 1\left(S \subset \bigcap_{i \in I} C_i\right).$$

$$(13.70)$$

To see this, we distinguish between three cases. If S is not contained in $\bigcup_{i=1}^{n} C_i$, then all terms are 0. If $S \subset \bigcup_{i=1}^{n} C_i$ but $\sum_{i=1}^{n} 1(S \subset C_i) = 0$, then the left-hand side is 1 while the right-hand side is 0. Finally, if $\sum_{i=1}^{n} 1(S \subset C_i) = k > 0$, then it is not difficult to see that the left-hand side is equal to

$$\sum_{\substack{j \in \{0,\dots,k\} \\ j \text{ even}}} \binom{k}{j}$$

and the right-hand side is equal to

$$\sum_{\substack{j \in \{0,\dots,k\} \\ j \text{ odd}}} \binom{k}{j}.$$

The last two sums are equal, as is well known, and this proves (13.70).

Since any belief valuation $\mathcal{B}$ is of the form $\mathcal{B}(E) = 1(S \subset E)$ for some S, we have from (Q2) that

$$\text{Bel}\left(\bigcup_{i=1}^{n} C_i\right) + \sum_{\substack{I \subset \{1,\dots,n\} \\ I \neq \emptyset, |I| \text{ even}}} \text{Bel}\left(\bigcap_{i \in I} C_i\right) \geq \sum_{\substack{I \subset \{1,\dots,n\} \\ I \neq \emptyset, |I| \text{ odd}}} \text{Bel}\left(\bigcap_{i \in I} C_i\right). \quad (13.71)$$

Since $C_1, \ldots, C_n$ were arbitrary, Bel satisfies the inclusion-exclusion inequalities in (13.6), and we conclude from Theorem 13.1.4 that Bel is a belief function.

Conversely, suppose that Bel is a belief function. Then (Q1) is immediate and we have to show (Q2). Let $m : 2^\Omega \to [0, 1]$ be the corresponding basic belief assignment of Bel. Let $A_1, A_2, \ldots, A_N \subset \Omega$ and $B_1, B_2, \ldots, B_M \subset \Omega$ be such that (13.68) holds for all belief evaluations. In particular, it holds for the belief evaluations $\mathcal{B}_S(A) := 1(S \subset A)$, for any $S \subset \Omega$. Hence

$$\sum_{i=1}^{N} \mathrm{Bel}(A_i) = \sum_{S \subset \Omega} m(S) \sum_{i=1}^{N} 1(S \subset A_i)$$

$$\geq \sum_{S \subset \Omega} m(S) \sum_{j=1}^{M} 1(S \subset B_j) \tag{13.72}$$

$$= \sum_{j=1}^{M} \mathrm{Bel}(B_j),$$

so (Q2) holds. □

We finally briefly indicate that the relation between belief and plausibility in (13.3) is what you expect when interpreting the belief in A as the price an agent is willing to pay for a bet that pays out 1 if A occurs, and the plausibility of A as the selling price of such a bet.

To this end we introduce a *risk function* R, which indicates, for an event A and two real numbers α and β, whether or not an agent is willing to accept a bet with a net result of α if A turns out to be true and a net result of β if A turns out to be false. We interpret $R(A, \alpha, \beta) = 1$ as an affirmative response and $R(A, \alpha, \beta) = 0$ as a negative response. More formally, a risk function is defined as follows.

Definition 13.7.3 A function $R : 2^\Omega \times [-1, 1] \times [-1, 1] \to \{0, 1\}$ is a *risk function* if the following holds for all events A:

(R1) $R(A, \alpha, \beta) = R(A^c, \beta, \alpha)$;

(R2) $R(A, \alpha, 0) = \begin{cases} 1 & \text{if } \alpha \geq 0, \\ 0 & \text{if } \alpha < 0; \end{cases}$

(R3) $R(A, \alpha', \beta') \geq R(A, \alpha, \beta)$ if $\alpha' \geq \alpha$ and $\beta' \geq \beta$.

These conditions do not necessarily capture everything any reasonable agent should adhere to. However, the conditions formulate the very basics. Condition (R1) is obvious. Condition (R2) says that agents should be willing to risk guaranteed non-negative net results and are never willing to risk guaranteed negative net results. Condition (R3) says that if an agent is willing to take a risk, he should be willing to take a risk (on the same event) in which both results are better.

Now note that $R(A, 1 - \alpha, -\alpha) = 1$ indicates that an agent is willing to *buy* the bet on A for a price of α. Similarly, $R(A, \alpha - 1, \alpha) = 1$ indicates that he is willing to *sell* the bet for a price of α. We are interested in the maximal price for which he is willing to buy, and the minimal prices for which he is willing to sell.

Definition 13.7.4 Let R be a risk function. The *buy function* $\text{Buy}_R : 2^\Omega \to [0, 1]$ is given by

$$\text{Buy}_R(A) := \sup\{\alpha \; : \; R(A, 1 - \alpha, -\alpha) = 1\}. \tag{13.73}$$

The *sell function* $\text{Sell}_R : 2^\Omega \to [0, 1]$ is given by

$$\text{Sell}_R(A) := \inf\{\alpha \; : \; R(A, \alpha - 1, \alpha) = 1\}. \tag{13.74}$$

The relation between buy and sell functions is as follows:

$$
\begin{aligned}
\text{Sell}_R(A) &= \inf\{\alpha \; : \; R(A, \alpha - 1, \alpha) = 1\} \\
&= \inf\{\alpha \; : \; R(A^c, \alpha, \alpha - 1) = 1\} \\
&= \inf\{1 - \alpha \; : \; R(A^c, 1 - \alpha, -\alpha) = 1\} \\
&= 1 - \sup\{\alpha \; : \; R(A^c, 1 - \alpha, -\alpha) = 1\} \\
&= 1 - \text{Buy}_R(A^c).
\end{aligned}
\tag{13.75}
$$

This shows how buy and sell functions are dual in the sense that Sell_R is completely determined by Buy_R and vice versa. It also shows that for any belief function, Bel and Pl satisfy this natural general relation between buying and selling prices, and this may add to one's confidence in an epistemic interpretation of belief functions.

13.8 Summary and Conclusions

A belief function is a generalization of a probability distribution. A belief function Bel is not necessarily additive, and so for instance $\text{Bel}(A) + \text{Bel}(A^c)$ need not be equal to 1. It is, therefore, possible to withhold belief, and to assign a certain belief to ignorance. In the classical framework this is not possible. To construct a belief function, we start with a probability distribution m on the *subsets* of the outcome space so that $\sum_C m(C) = 1$, and define $\mathrm{Bel}(A) = \sum_{C \subset A} m(C)$. The m describes the information that we have. For instance, if a number between 1 and 10 (inclusive) is drawn and all we know is that even and odd numbers are equally likely, then we have $m(\{2,4,6,8,10\}) = m(\{1,3,5,7,9\}) = 1/2$, keeping the option open that, say, a 6 is drawn with probability $1/2$, a 3 with probability $1/4$, and a 9 also with probability $1/4$.

This construction is much more flexible than probability distributions. In particular, we can express complete ignorance in terms of belief functions, something which is not possible in classical probability theory.

We have defined the notion of conditional belief, and with this calculus in hand, we have applied belief functions to a number of forensic problems. To get an idea about the difference between classical answers and belief answers, consider the classical island problem. The classical answer of the posterior probability of guilt if we take uniform priors, is $1/(1 + Np)$, where p is the probability of the trait and $N + 1$ is the population size. The answer in terms of belief functions, when we use no more prior information than that the culprit is in the population, is $(1 - p)^N$.

Further forensic problems that we have investigated using belief functions are parental identification and finding items with special features. We have also described a number of examples outside forensics, to further illustrate the theory. The construction of belief functions makes detailed modeling possible, and the information one has can sometimes be better described with such belief functions than with classical probabilities.

Finally, we have given a philosophical backup of belief functions in terms of epistemic uncertainty in the same spirit as our philosophical underpinning of the Kolmogorov axioms for epistemic uncertainty in Section 1.4, and we concluded that belief functions are suitable candidates for describing epistemic uncertainty.

13.9 Bibliographical Notes

Belief functions were introduced by Shafer in [132], in which all basic results discussed in Section 13.1 can be found. See also [133] and [134]. One can consult the recent books by Fabio Cuzzolin [47, 48] for a lot of information about the use of belief functions in a decision-making context. Other approaches to model and describe epistemic uncertainty can be found in [35] and [172]. Formula (13.4) is a special case of the famous Möbius inversion theorem from combinatorics, e.g., see [75]. Formula (13.12) was obtained by Fagin and Halpern in [64] and by Dubois and Prade [59], and with a different approach also by [86]. In [64] it was shown that $\mathrm{Bel}(\cdot \mid H)$ is again a belief function if $\mathrm{Bel}(H) > 0$.

The forensic examples of the use of belief functions are mostly taken from [83] and [85], with the exception of the examples in Section 13.4, which are essentially taken from [28], noting though that in that reference a different concept of conditional belief is used. The philosophical backup of belief functions in Section 13.7 is taken from [84], building upon work in [172]. The ratios in Section 13.6 are suggested and discussed in [111]; see also the commentary in [100].

14

Recommendation Reports

We have seen in this book that the discipline of forensic statistics and probability can be difficult, and that mistakes are easily made. Given what is at stake it is no surprise, therefore, that over the years various recommendation reports have appeared to assist the forensic scientist and the judiciary in their task. At the end of this book we spend a chapter on some of these recommendation reports, in order to assess to which extent these recommendations align with our conclusions in this book. Of course, we will confine ourselves to those recommendations or remarks in the reports that have to do with the subject of this book: the use of probability and statistics in the context of forensic science and law. We comment on six such documents:

1. *ENFSI Guideline for Evaluative Reporting in Forensic Science* [60].
2. The PCAST report to the president *Forensic Science in Criminal Courts: Ensuring Scientific Validity of Feature-Comparison Methods* [118].
3. *Twelve Guiding Principles and Recommendations* ensuing from a meeting of forensic scientists in Cambridge 2017 [165].
4. DNA commission of the International Society for Forensic Genetics: Assessing the value of forensic biological evidence – Guidelines highlighting the importance of propositions [71].
5. *SWGDAM Interpretation Guidelines for Autosomal STR Typing by Forensic DNA Testing Laboratories* [155].
6. The article "A guideline for validation of likelihood ratio methods used for forensic evidence evaluation" [105].

14.1 *ENFSI Guideline for Evaluative Reporting in Forensic Science*

The ENFSI guidelines were initiated by the European Network of Forensic Science Institutes. The aim of the project was to "standardize and improve evaluative reporting in ENFSI laboratories." The project was undertaken by a "core group of scientists from member institutes." Many of the recommendations in the document concern the use of probability and statistics, and the likelihood ratio in particular. In what follows we will not discuss the guidelines and recommendations one by one, but make a selection on the basis of relevance for us. Our quotes are from the approved version 3.0 of the report (2015).

The report is unambiguous about the use of the likelihood ratio, and about the fact that classical statistical methods should not be used for evidential purposes. On page 6 we read:

"Evaluation [...] is based on the assignment of a likelihood ratio. Reporting practice should conform to these logical principles. This framework for evaluative reporting applies to all forensic science disciplines. The likelihood ratio measures the strength of support the findings provide to discriminate between propositions of interest. It is scientifically accepted, providing a logically defensible way to deal with inferential reasoning. Other methods (e.g., chemometrical methods) have a place in forensic science, to help answer other questions at different points of the forensic process (e.g., validation of analytical methods, classification/discrimination of substances for investigative or technical reporting). Equally, other methods (e.g., Student's t-test) may contribute to evaluative reports, but they should be used only to characterize the findings and not to assess their strength. Forensic findings as such need to be distinguished from their evaluation in the context of the case. For the latter evaluative part only a likelihood ratio based approach is considered."

This is an important principle. It emphasizes that only a likelihood ratio can measure the strength of the evidence, and that other statistical methods can *not* do that. This principle is in line with the findings in this book, as made explicit in Chapters 1, 2, and 9.

The principle implicitly assumes that one can only meaningfully speak about evidential value in a comparative way. This is made explicit on page 10 of the report, where we read:

"The findings should be evaluated given at least one pair of propositions: usually one based upon one party's account of the events and one based upon an alternative (opposing party's) account of the events. If no alternative can be formulated, the value of the findings cannot be assessed. In that case, forensic practitioners should state clearly that they are not reporting upon the value of the findings."

A similar statement can be found on page 13:

"The report should stress that in the absence of an alternative proposition, it is impossible to evaluate the findings."

The report also discusses the way the forensic expert should formulate his or her findings. On page 10 we read:

"The conclusion shall be expressed either by a value of the likelihood ratio and/or using a verbal scale related to the value of the likelihood ratio. The verbal equivalents shall express a degree of support for one of the propositions relative to the alternative. The choice of the reported verbal equivalent is based on the likelihood ratio and not the reverse. The report shall contain an indication of the order of magnitude of the likelihood ratio."

Hence, this guideline is concerned with the interplay between numerical outcomes and verbal qualifications as in our Table 5.1. We have some concerns about using a table like this in the way suggested by the report. First of all, we do not see what one really gains with a verbal scale, where the scales correspond to fixed intervals of the likelihood ratio. If verbal scales correspond to numbers it seems hard to find an argument not to present these numbers. In addition the defined intervals need not fit well. As we argued in Chapter 3, a forensic statistician in principle obtains a single number as likelihood ratio. In order to do this, he or she must specify probability distributions reflecting all uncertainty about model parameters. If the expert does not do this, but instead does something cruder, such as specifying intervals for the parameters, then the result will be an interval for the likelihood ratio. In some cases this interval may be more narrow than in others and there need not be an interval of the verbal scale that contains the obtained interval, or conversely there may be one that is much wider than the interval the forensic scientist had in mind. In both cases the pre-defined intervals for verbal scales do not correspond well to the obtained interval, and hence choosing one (or several) interval(s) on the verbal scale amounts to a loss of information.

A second drawback is that qualifications such as "much more likely" or "extremely much more likely" are arbitrary and in themselves meaningless. We fear that they are easily understood as referring to the strength of the case (the posterior odds) and not to the strength of the evidence.

Finally, perhaps a forensic scientist may feel more comfortable to report a verbal scale than its numerical equivalent, because of his or her uncertainty about the model choice and parameter choices. However, if this is so, we think the only reasonable conclusion we can draw is that the forensic scientist should also not report the verbal scale. Therefore, we do not think using verbal scales solves any problems; rather, they introduce a superfluous source of confusion and misinterpretations.

The report also addresses the question whether a likelihood ratio of, say, 1,000 means the same in different circumstances. We have discussed this issue at length in Chapter 9, and argued that the specific context has no effect on the interpretation of the numerical outcome. This is confirmed in the report on page 18, where it is insisted that the verbal scales should be the same for all disciplines. Indeed, without fixed and discipline-independent numerical definitions of the verbal scales it may be tempting for a discipline to characterize evidence which, for their discipline, is the strongest possible, as strongest possible on the verbal scale. In other words, the risk is that each discipline uses its own connection between the same verbal translation and a range of likelihood ratios. The report makes it clear that this should be avoided:

"Although the choice of terms, number of steps and intervals may vary between laboratories, the scale and its principles will apply across all forensic disciplines covered within a laboratory (or group of laboratories). The purpose is to assist the court in relation to the strength of the findings. Therefore, it is incorrect to use different scales for different types of evidence (e.g., DNA and glass)."

We have discussed the uncertainty of the likelihood ratio at great length in Chapter 3, and in Section 3.3 defined the sensitivity of the likelihood ratio as the way the likelihood ratio changes upon changing the parameters. On this topic, we read on page 9:

"Based on the findings of the examination and their probabilities assigned during pre-assessment, a likelihood ratio is assigned. The assigned probabilities (at the pre-assessment stage) may be refined in the light of the findings e.g., a rare glass or fibre type. Justification for changes will be documented. According to their uncertainty, forensic practitioners should consider exploring the sensitivity of the likelihood ratio to different probabilities by examining the effect of assigning different probabilities,"

and on page 16:

"Forensic practitioners often experience difficulty in assigning and justifying probabilities when the assignments are based on expert knowledge. However, likelihood ratios can be informed by subjective probabilities using expert knowledge. These probability assignments shall still be expressed by a number between 0 and 1 rather than by an undefined qualifier (such as frequent, rare, etc.). Such personal probability assignment is not arbitrary or speculative, but is based on a body of knowledge that should be available for auditing and disclosure. The forensic practitioner should not mislead the recipient of expert information as to the basis of the personal assignment, and the extent to which the assignment is supported by scientific research. Forensic practitioners should consider exploring the sensitivity of the likelihood ratio to different probabilities by examining the effect of assigning different probabilities according to their personal uncertainties."

These recommendations appear to be in line with our own philosophy and conclusions in Chapter 3, although the extent to which depends on the exact interpretation of the report's phrasing. In Chapter 3 we have considered the concepts of uncertainty, lack of knowledge, and sensitivity. By uncertainty we mean that we do not know the precise value of some quantity of interest (for instance, a model parameter), but that we do believe that it does actually have a value and that the information that we have allows for a probabilistic assessment of it. In that case, we arrive at a likelihood ratio that incorporates that uncertainty, and there is then no reason (on the contrary) to evaluate the likelihood ratio at specific values of the parameters for which we have probability distributions.

By lack of knowledge we mean that we cannot specify the required probability distributions, and then we agree with the report that one should calculate the likelihood ratio for different choices of parameters that are all considered to be possible. The resulting dependence of the likelihood ratio is what we called its sensitivity. Therefore, we agree with the report that sensitivity analyses are to be carried out in the case of lack of knowledge (which can also include model uncertainty). Such sensitivity analysis need not be carried out in the case where the expert has formulated probabilistic descriptions expressing his or her knowledge to the extent that the likelihood ratio can be calculated by integration.

In this connection, it is interesting to see what the report has to say about situations in which only limited data are available. On page 11 we read:

"When there are insufficient data, the likelihood ratio approach provides the practitioner with a framework for structured and logical reasoning based on his experience, as long as he can explain the grounds for his opinion together with his degree of understanding of the particular trace type,"

and on page 15:

"Note that if a likelihood ratio cannot be assigned by the forensic practitioner (due to a lack of knowledge for example), then no appropriate evaluative assessment of the findings can be made."

Basically, the report says that the likelihood ratio framework should always be used regardless of available data, and that if it does not allow to give a result, then no evaluation is possible. This is, in fact, tantamount to what was said previously, namely that the likelihood ratio framework is the only acceptable one.

We agree that the practitioner must always evaluate the data at hand to the best of their ability, and if the data is sparse or very incomplete, then this should lead to a weaker likelihood ratio. We remark that the report gives no guidance as to when data should be considered sufficient or not, hence also not when a likelihood ratio can or cannot be assigned. However, we think this is understandable as it seems difficult to formulate a general rule for this, so that the decision to assign a likelihood ratio or not when data are sparse remains ad hoc and to be motivated per case individually.

If there is complete lack of knowledge to the extent that even a sensitivity analysis is impossible (if not even parameter bounds can be given, for example because it is not clear what a model for evaluation should be), then we agree that there is nothing to report.

Finally, the ENFSI report contains a philosophical statement about the use of probabilities. On page 23 we read:

"Your subjective probability is the measure for your belief in the occurrence of an event. A number between 0 and 1 represents this measure. The laws of probability apply to these probabilities just as they apply to calculated probabilities.

A measure of belief might be obtained by doing thought experiments, and possibly further informed by ad hoc small-scale physical experiments. Expert knowledge elicitation is a more technical approach to obtain subjective probabilities."

If a forensic practitioner is able to define probability distributions for, say, a parameter, then indeed the laws of classical probability apply. But as we have argued in Chapter 1, the required step of defining these distributions is not a trivial one. If we allow for not defining them, then probabilistic assessments are nevertheless still possible, although these lie outside classical applications of probability theory. One such alternative, the theory of belief functions, has been studied in some detail in Chapter 13.

14.2 The PCAST Report to the President

The 2016 report by the US President's Council of Advisors on Science and Technology (PCAST) [118] has made a number of recommendations for the future development of forensic science. The report is concerned with the whole field of forensic science, including those fields where computations are generally not made (for instance, bite mark comparisons), and where conclusions are based on expert opinions that are sometimes not very transparent. We should keep that in mind when reading quotes from the report.

The PCAST report has received serious criticism. For example, in [61] we read in the abstract that "we find that the PCAST report recommendations are founded on serious misunderstandings" and that there are "many sources of confusion in the PCAST report." We agree with this, and in this section we provide our own brief analysis that explains this position.

The PCAST report does not contain a clear introduction with an overview of how the report views the objectives and methodology in forensic science. We can therefore only make our own inferences on how the authors regard these issues from their commentary on more specific topics.

The first thing to be noticed is that the PCAST report often commits the prosecutor's fallacy of mixing up posterior odds with likelihood ratios. For instance on page 114 we read:

"Footwear analysis is a process that typically involves comparing a known object, such as a shoe, to a complete or partial impression found at a crime scene, to assess whether the object is likely to be the source of the impression."

This is, of course, mistaken. The quote suggests that the goal of forensic research is to come up with a certain probability, verbal or numerical, that two objects have the same source. In other words, the PCAST report seems to have identification as objective. We have argued that, on the contrary, identification is not the objective, but finding evidence is, and evidence is quantified by the likelihood ratio.

This mistake just quoted appears in various places in the report. For instance, on page 65 we read:

"To establish foundational validity for a forensic-comparison method, the following elements are required: (a) a reproducible and consistent procedure for [...] determining, based on the similarity between the features in two sets of features, whether the samples should be declared to be likely to come from the same source."

Again we see the PCAST report seems to have as objective something that is generally impossible, namely a probabilistic statement on the probability that a crime scene sample comes from a certain known source (for instance, a suspect).

The next problem is that the PCAST report seems to believe that in order to make same source declarations, one should first determine whether or not the features obtained from two samples match. Let us consider the following quote (page 5):

"By objective feature-comparison methods, we mean methods consisting of procedures that are each defined with enough standardized and quantifiable detail that they can be performed by either an automated system or human examiners exercising little or no judgment. By subjective methods, we mean methods including key procedures that involve significant human judgment – for example, about which features to select within a pattern or how to determine whether the features are sufficiently similar to be called a probable match."

This quote contains several elements: there are statements about objectivity versus subjectivity and about probable matches. We discuss these one by one. First of all, it seems that the PCAST report confuses repeatability with objectivity. Of course, once certain standards have been set, and, say, a piece of software is ready to use, this piece of software can be used repeatedly. But it is certainly not purely objective, since at some point *someone* must have decided about what (not to) include in the analysis, what model to use, etc. We do not view this as a problem per se. In fact, we have argued at length that the only meaningful interpretation of probability in forensic and legal affairs is epistemic and subjective in nature.

Before we come to the phrase "probable match" at the end of the quote, first we further pursue the position on subjectivity of the PCAST report. On page 66 we read:

"For subjective methods, foundational validity can be established *only* through black-box studies that measure how often many examiners reach accurate conclusions across many feature-comparison problems involving samples representative of the intended use. In the absence of such studies, a subjective feature-comparison method cannot be considered scientifically valid."

At this point the report is concerned about situations in which an expert gives his or her opinion, without giving insight about the way this conclusion is reached. We fully share that concern, and agree that conclusions should be as transparent as possible, and that one should aim to document all steps that were made in the process towards the obtained conclusion. At the same time we also acknowledge that sometimes no real arguments can be given by the expert, other than claiming that the statement results from experience and knowledge. We agree with the report that such statements should be interpreted with caution, but we would go further than that: if an expert declares samples to have the same source, then we know this statement is in general incorrect. That is, the statement may factually happen to be correct, but it is not always possible for an expert to be able to arrive at that conclusion.

Nevertheless, if such a statement is made, it does have evidential value. Once we know how often the expert declares same source for comparisons that are truly from the same source, and analogously for different sources, we can infer the evidential value of these declarations. As we have shown in Chapter 10, we can attach evidential value to such decisions coming from a black box situation as described above. Given error rates α and β, where α is the probability of rejecting H when H is in fact true, and β is the probability not to reject H when H is not true, we can use as our evidence the very decision taken by the expert.

This is in fact a correct procedure in the current situation, since indeed all we know is the decision itself, without any information as to how the decision was reached – that is precisely what a black box means. We do not have the data, but only the decision at our disposition. Therefore the evidence that we must evaluate here is the statement of the expert, not the underlying samples. This leads to a likelihood ratio of either $\alpha/(1 - \beta)$ or $(1 - \alpha)/\beta$, depending on the decision of the expert. These numbers constitute the evidential value of the decisions, and provide the way of dealing with such black box scenarios.

The PCAST report is in this quote – clearly – also referring to the two types of mistakes that the expert can make: declaring that two traits come from the same source where in fact this is not the case, and vice versa. The quote strongly suggests, without being explicit, that knowing the error rates would allow us to determine with which probability a match/no match decision is correct in the sense of corresponding to the same or a different source. As we just explained, that is incorrect.

Let us now return to the phrase "probable match" that we came across in the earlier quote. It seems that the PCAST report refers to the situation where the trace profile (or perhaps also the reference profile although this would happen less often) cannot be derived with certainty, for example if a DNA profile is obtained that may be incomplete, for instance when there is allelic dropout. Again, the PCAST report seems to believe that the goal is to decide whether or not there is a match, and that a probable match would lead to a same source attribution with a lower probability than an undisputable match.

That the PCAST report indeed still resides in the match/no match paradigm is clearly visible in a phrase on page 48 which sheds some light on the full philosophical position of the PCAST report, and of the confusion it gives rise to.

"To meet the scientific criteria of foundational validity, two key elements are required:

(1) a reproducible and consistent procedure for (a) identifying features within evidence samples; (b) comparing the features in two samples; and (c) determining, based on the similarity between the features in two samples, whether the samples should be declared to be a proposed identification ('matching rule').

(2) empirical measurements, from multiple independent studies, of (a) the method's false positive rate – that is, the probability it declares a proposed identification between samples that actually come from *different* sources and (b) the method's sensitivity – that is, probability that it declares a proposed identification between samples that actually come from the *same* source."

In the quote, (1) unambiguously refers to a notion of matching. This is even reinforced further down on the same page, where we read:

"To declare a proposed identification, they should calculate whether the features in an evidentiary sample and the features in a sample from a suspected source lie within a pre-specified measurement tolerance."

According to the PCAST report, therefore, determining whether there is a match is key, while we know that it is not at all the case. Given the evidential value as expressed by the likelihood ratio, we do not need to know whether this evidence is of the "match" type or not. Obviously, a match in the sense of the report would correspond to a large evidential value for that type of evidence, but that does not mean that one should determine whether there is a match or not. Given the evidential value, it does not matter whether the data consist of a "match" or not.

To make this point as clearly as possible, let us consider the specific field of the interpretation of DNA profiles. Initially, the required amount of DNA for profiling was so large that typically single source profiles were obtained and it was relatively easy to verify whether two profiles are the same or not. In the case of a no-match, it could be excluded that the profiles were of the same person, and in the case of a match, the likelihood ratio in favor of the samples having the same origin is simply the inverse of the match probability. Thus, for such profiles having a match and having evidence in favor of contribution is equivalent. But that does not imply that, in general, in order to know whether there is evidence, we need to know whether there is a match. In Chapters 7 and 8 we have extensively considered likelihood ratios investigating kinship and for contribution to mixed DNA profiles. What we need in those cases is a model predicting the observations. The match concept is not needed to formulate such a model.

In the above quote we see a lot of misunderstandings becoming apparent. At the end of (1) we see explicitly how the report sees matching rules as the objective, and in (2) we see the importance the report attaches to error rates. How they should be used is not mentioned.

To sum up our findings, we conclude that the PCAST report seems to have identification as objective (a first misconception), to propose matching rules as the key to finding these identifications (another misconception), and to see the error rates of these matching rules as giving the probability that a proposed identification is correct (a third misconception). Although the report also contains valuable recommendations, we therefore strongly disagree with the entire framework within which these are made.

14.3 *Twelve Guiding Principles and Recommendations*

A group of participants of the program "Probability and Statistics in Forensic Science" held at the Isaac Newton Institute for Mathematical Sciences, Cambridge (July–December 2016) have produced a document entitled *Twelve Guiding Principles and Recommendations for Dealing with Quantitative Evidence in Criminal Law*, with the subtitle "For the use of statisticians, forensic scientists and legal professionals" [165]. The authors of this book participated in the program, but not in the writing of the document.

In this section, we comment on a number of the recommendations from this report as far as they are immediately related to the content of this book. Each time we quote the principle together with the associated recommendations (bulleted), and then we comment on it, before moving on to the next principle. The numbering of the principles corresponds to the numbering in the original document.

Principle 1. Probability is intrinsic to understanding the impact of evidence. Evidence which indicates facts that are certain is rare. There is virtually always some degree of uncertainty and, since probability is the mathematical science of uncertainty, it is the right framework to handle it.

- Law schools and forensic courses should teach sufficient basic statistical and probabilistic thinking to recognize and avoid common fallacies such as the prosecutor's fallacy.
- Statisticians (including the class of experts who should be more accurately referred to as Forensic Mathematicians) should learn the legal rules for admissibility of evidence and duties of expert witnesses.
- Statisticians need to take responsibility for challenging the claims that probability is inconsistent with legal reasoning.

This principle firmly states that probability theory is *the* mathematical framework to deal with uncertainty. We agree with this, although the probability theory that may be needed may be more than just classical probability, which we think the authors refer to. Therefore, although we agree with the first two recommendations, we have some reservations about the third one. In our view, (classical) probability, rather than being inconsistent with legal reasoning, may be too restrictive to apply to all legal reasoning, since it cannot always model ignorance satisfactorily. To name but one example that we have discussed, how the presumption of innocence is to be modeled with a probability distribution is debatable, but it can easily be modeled with a belief function, see Chapter 13.

Principle 4. All evidence is subject to potential errors that should be articulated and, if possible, quantified. When a lay witness (such as an eyewitness) makes an assertion (such as defendant "was at crime scene"), it is accepted that the actual truth of the assertion depends on the accuracy of the witness. The same is almost invariably the case when an expert witness, such as a forensic scientist, makes an assertion like "two samples match." Errors can and do occur at every level of evidence evaluation: sampling, measurement, interpretation of results, and presentation of findings.

- Forensic scientists should articulate, and attempt to quantify, possible sources of error, such as contamination rates and false positive rates where relevant, once such rates are reliably established.
- Statisticians should attempt to include all sources of uncertainty about their parameters and models. Where this is not feasible, the possible errors should be explained in accompanying text.
- Legal professionals should understand and expect this information, and probe for possible sources of uncertainty when it is not presented by the experts.

These recommendations can hardly be challenged, but the way they are formulated does not really guide the expert as to *how* this should be done. Also, the recommendations do not clearly indicate what one should do with the obtained error rates or sources of uncertainty. The recommendations do not, for example, take a position in the question of whether or not one should quantify uncertainty with an interval around the likelihood ratio. We refer to Chapter 3 for a discussion of that topic.

Principle 6. Most cases consist of multiple interdependent items of evidence which need to be combined correctly. Evidence synthesis is the process of assessing the combined weight of all relevant pieces of evidence. When there is a need to quantify the overall impact of multiple pieces of evidence involving various related hypotheses (such as source level, activity level and offense level hypotheses), simplistic solutions that inappropriately assume independence are inadequate. Graphical representations of evidence can be very helpful to model dependencies.

- All those involved in evidence analysis at all stages of a criminal investigation should be aware of the need to model dependencies, and of the existence of methods, such as graphical methods, that support this.
- Interactive software exists to perform computations on probabilistic graphical models (Bayes nets), enabling users to explore the impacts of different assumptions. While it may be difficult to introduce such methods directly in court, they are helpful for evidence synthesis at any of the phases of an investigation preceding the trial.

We have expressed our concerns about the use of Bayesian networks in Chapter 6. It is extremely difficult to deal with dependencies, especially when modeling a complete legal case. A graphical representation can be made for a given joint distribution, but then its use reduces to being a computational tool. We think that a statement such as "Graphical representations of evidence can be very helpful to model dependencies" are overly optimistic, as we concluded in Chapter 6. When drawing a network from scratch by defining arrows that are thought to reflect direct (causal) effects, it may also be the case that a dependency structure is created rather than that it is decided.

Principle 7. The word "match" is often taken to mean "of the same origin," whereas in fact it means that the measured characteristics of two items are the same to within an agreed tolerance.

- It is not necessary, and often not desirable, to reduce the results of forensic analyses to a statement that two items "match." Instead, the degree of similarity should be assessed. If possible, the degree of similarity should be expressed statistically, as should its implications for the hypotheses.

Of course we agree with statement, which is in agreement with our own conclusions in this book. It is interesting to compare this principle with the confusion around this issue in the PCAST report which we discussed in the previous section. Again we note though, that the recommendation does not give directions as to how the degree of similarity should be expressed statistically, in particular likelihood ratios are not mentioned.

Principle 10. Well-founded subjective assumptions can play an important role in forensic analysis. For a procedure to be scientific these assumptions should be made explicit. Subjective assumptions are an unavoidable component of any criminal investigation. This is not merely the province of judges or juries.

- In reports and testimony, forensic experts need to explicitly articulate all key subjective assumptions being made, as well as their justifications, and their implications for the evaluation of the probability of hypotheses.
- Statisticians ditto.
- Legal professionals should probe for assumptions that have not been made explicit.

This principle acknowledges the importance of subjectivity in the evaluation of evidence. We agree with the intention behind it. We do think, however, that it may not be feasible for a forensic expert to explicitly articulate all key subjective assumptions. It is difficult to think of an assumption that does not have any subjective component, so this list might be rather long. For a DNA report on a DNA mixture profile, listing all population genetic assumptions, and all assumptions made by, e.g., an evaluation model, would yield a very long list, especially if all these assumptions were also accompanied by a justification and assessment of their implications, as suggested by this principle.

We would therefore amend and relax this principle, and instead call for review of the methods. For methods that are intended to be used in large case volumes, such as methods for DNA evaluations, this could be done via scientific publications. For models of a more ad hoc nature, developed for a certain particular case, we think it is important that the method be reviewed by, if possible, an independent expert.

Principle 11. Bayesian analysis is a standard method for updating probabilities after multiple items of evidence are observed, and is therefore highly suited for evidence synthesis. Anybody who must make a judgment about a hypothesis such as "guilt" (including pre-trial investigators, judges, juries) informally starts with some prior belief about the hypothesis and updates it as evidence is re-vealed. Sometimes there may even be objective data on which to base a prior probability. Bayesian inference is a valid method for calculating the updated probability.

- Forensic scientists can provide likelihoods without having to consider prior probabilities if they are asked only to evaluate the probative value of the evidence.

- When using Bayesian reasoning, statisticians should justify prior assumptions wherever possible, for example, using external data; otherwise, they should use a range of values for priors, and a sensitivity analysis to test the robustness of the outcome with respect to these values.
- Basic statistical and probabilistic thinking taught in Law schools should cover Bayes' Theorem.

Again, this principle is one we adhere to as well, but we do have some critical remarks. When comparing two simple hypotheses, it is indeed the case that one does not need to know their prior probabilities in order to evaluate the likelihood ratio. But in more complex situations where there are compound hypotheses, the priors on the sub-hypotheses of the compound hypotheses enter the likelihood ratio. We have seen many instances of this, for instance in the database situation of Chapter 11.

Furthermore, the principle does not touch upon the problem of the formulation of the relevant hypotheses for which likelihoods are to be calculated.

Finally, we think that it is perhaps optimistic to assume that, as the principle states, anybody who must make a judgment about a hypothesis informally starts with some prior belief and updates it. Indeed, the classical statistical procedures such as significance testing do not take that approach. We think it is conceivable that sometimes judges or juries will reason along similar lines, rejecting the "null" hypothesis of innocence when there is sufficient evidence that is unlikely under that hypothesis.

14.4 DNA Commission of the International Society for Forensic Genetics

The 2018 report [71] is primarily concerned with the importance of choosing suitable propositions, or hypotheses as we have typically called them. They offer both "recommendations" and "considerations," which are generally worthwhile reading. We comment on some of these in this section.

The authors of the report attach significant value to what they call a "dual role" of the forensic DNA scientist. On page 190 we read that the DNA scientists:

"have a dual role: they are asked to provide investigation leads and to provide the value of a comparison in the context of a case. It is crucial to distinguish between these two roles, in particular with reference to the propositions used."

This dual role is elaborated upon in their Consideration 1, which reads as follows (POI is an abbreviation of 'person of interest'):

Consideration 1. The scientist works in an investigative mode if there is no person of interest in the case. If a suspect is identified, then generally the scientist switches to evaluative mode with respect to this suspect and needs to assign the value of their results in the context of the case. If there is new information (in particular from the POI), the scientist will need to re-evaluate the results. It is thus important that reports contain a caveat relating to this aspect.

Although we of course agree that the forensic scientist can play a role either when there is or when there is not a person of interest, we do not see that a categorical difference. In fact, *any* likelihood ratio is a summary of the evidential value with the information that is available at that time. If new information becomes available, the likelihood ratio will change into another likelihood ratio that gives the evidential value with the new information incorporated. This applies to either of the two modes distinguished by the authors of [71], and therefore as far as the interpretation of the likelihood ratio is concerned, the distinction is unnecessary.

However, there may be some additional value in discriminating between the two modes because either mode requires their own type of hypotheses. This seems a reasonable position. As an example of an investigative mode, [71] mentions a database search, and suggests the following hypotheses, writing $X_1, \ldots, X_n$ for the individuals in the database:

H_1: The DNA is from candidate X_i;
H_2: The DNA is from some unknown individual.

Indeed a database search without any particular suspect in mind is something one would classify as investigative. However, if the question is whether or not the database contains the donor of the DNA profile, the more appropriate hypotheses would be:

H_1: The DNA is from someone in the database;
H_2: The DNA is from someone outside the database,

as we have argued at length in Chapter 11. This latter pair of hypotheses is not considered in the report, but in our opinion it reflects the actual question in the investigative mode. Indeed, the request to search the database is done, not because of the specific individuals in it, but only because it exists and has been useful in the past. Thus while we do not totally agree with the way this database example has been worked out in the report, we do agree that it may be wise to let the formulation of the hypotheses reflect the questions that are investigated, and these are different in investigative compared to evaluative mode.

The report also comments on the nature of a likelihood ratio in its Consideration 2:

> *Consideration 2.* [...] There are no true likelihood ratios, just like there are no true models. Depending on our assumptions, our knowledge and the results we want to assess, different models will be adopted, hence different values for the likelihood ratio will be obtained. It is therefore important to outline in our statements what factors impact evaluation (propositions, information, assumptions, data, and choice of model).

We agree with this consideration inasfar that no true likelihood ratio exists (see the discussion in Chapter 3), but at the same we also think that in a given situation, some models are certainly more appropriate than others. Even if we do not believe that the authors intended to say so, the consideration could be taken to suggest that since there are no true models, any model goes, and that is certainly not the case. The consideration does not mention, for example, anything about validation of the possible models.

The report elaborates on the choices of the hypotheses, and it has a number of useful and interesting remarks about this. It stresses, for instance, that *observations* should not be interwoven with hypotheses. So an hypothesis like "The matching DNA comes from candidate *S*" is (in the report) not appropriate, since it uses the observation of a match. This connects to our discussion on data-driven hypotheses in the context of DNA database searches. We saw there that there is no fundamental objection to such hypotheses, but that one should be especially cautious not to interpret the resulting likelihood ratio as the posterior odds. Indeed for such hypotheses the likelihood ratio is typically large by construction, but the hypothesis that is supported may be a priori very unlikely to be true.

The report states that ideally, hypotheses "should be set *before* knowing the result of the comparison between the contested DNA and a possible contributor" (page 193), but then it seems to run into problems when a database match leads to a suspect. A new hypothesis that this matching person is the donor of the DNA is set up *after* knowing the result of a comparison. We do not think that this is very problematic, as we just explained, since an ensuing high likelihood ratio will be compensated for by small prior odds; see Chapter 11 for a discussion of this.

The report also contains a discussion of the problems that can arise when several (say, two) persons are both seen as potential contributors to a mixed DNA profile. In the report, they are called Mr. Smith and Mr. Doe, and it is observed that a large likelihood ratio can be obtained for the hypotheses that they both contributed, versus that they both did not, even if in reality only one of them contributed. Non-contributor tests are seen as a possible solution. Such a test amounts to replacing one of the suspects by randomly chosen persons from an appropriate population, and to calculate likelihood ratios as above, to see how often a larger likelihood ratio is obtained than the one for the two suspects in the case at hand. This boils down, in fact, to computing a *p*-value. In Chapter 9 we have argued at length that such a *p*-value has no evidential interpretation, but could be useful to draw attention to alternative hypotheses. According to the report,

"Consequently, it is entirely possible that a large likelihood ratio can be achieved when one (Mr Smith) is the ground truth donor and the other (Mr Doe) is not. It is therefore desirable to explore whether this is the case *and there are two methods to do this*: individual likelihood ratio calculations (for evaluative and investigative purposes) and non-contributor tests (that are particularly appropriate in investigative mode, when there are no suspects in order to decide whether one should search the mixture in a national database)." (emphasis added)

In Recommendation 3 we read the following:

Recommendation 3. Propositions should be formulated in order to help answer the issue at hand and be based on the case information (not on the results of the comparison). They should be formulated without knowledge of the results of the comparison made between the trace and the person whose DNA presence is contested (e.g., the suspect's). When the issue regards the possible presence of DNA from several persons of interest, effort should be made to evaluate the profiles separately, and not as a whole. This is especially important if the information available from one part of the profile (e.g., major) is different from the other (minor, partial). For evaluation, this can be achieved by considering the result of the comparison between the given person and the trace and calculating individual likelihood ratios for each person. The report should be fully transparent on what propositions have been considered and on what basis. For investigative purpose, it might be useful to explore whether the results support the proposition that the two persons together are (or not) the source of the DNA. In such a case, one can assign one likelihood ratio. A non-contributor test can be helpful, *also* for investigative purposes. (emphasis added)

Here, we tend to disagree with the report. In the case where several (say, two) suspects each separately give support in favor of being a contributor, we do believe that it is important to also include in the report whether there is evidence that both of them contributed. This may, but need not be the case, and it is important for ensuing decision making. However, non-contributor tests are not needed. For example, if for a mixed profile $LR(S_1)$ (the likelihood ratio in favor of S_1 having contributed) is large and so is $LR(S_2)$, then there is evidence for both of them that they contributed. That does not mean that there is evidence that they both contributed. To investigate this, one should calculate and report $LR(S_2 \mid S_1)$ (the likelihood ratio in favor of S_1

having contributed, assuming that S_1 has) or $LR(S_1 \mid S_2)$ as well. Indeed, we have $LR(S_1, S_2) = LR(S_1 \mid S_2) \times LR(S_2) = LR(S_2 \mid S_1) \times LR(S_1)$. If $LR(S_1 \mid S_2)$ is close to one, then $LR(S_1, S_2)$ does not differ much from $LR(S_2)$. Another way to deal with such a situation is to consider four hypotheses, corresponding to letting each of S_1, S_2 be a contributor or not, and evaluate the likelihoods of all four hypotheses to see which one(s) are best supported. This is nothing but an extension of the likelihood ratio framework to more than two hypotheses.

In the phrasing of the report, we consider this to be done in evaluative mode as well, and not only in investigative mode. We do not see the helpfulness of a non-contributor test here: since the profiles of the possible contributors are known, there is no need to consider arbitrary non-contributors.

Finally, we mention their Recommendation 4, which deals with the number of contributors in DNA mixture analysis.

> *Recommendation 4.* The scientist should assign a value (or several) to the number of contributors to the trace. This will be based on case information, the observation of the DNA profiles of the trace and of the persons whose DNA presence is not contested (e.g., a victim in an intimate swab). The reasoning to support this decision should be indicated.

We have argued in Chapter 8 that this principle is not always appropriate. In the top-down method described in Chapter 8, we have concluded that one can compute likelihood ratios for a suspect being among the, say, three most important contributors, without needing the actual total number of contributors. It is certainly true that for a specific computation, one should use information about persons whose DNA is not contested, but it is certainly not always necessary to assign a value to the total number of contributors to a trace. This number may be of interest from a criminalistic point of view, but for the calculation of the evidence in favor of contribution it is not always needed.

14.5 The SWGDAM Interpretation Guidelines

The Scientific Working Group on DNA Analysis Methods, better known by its acronym of SWGDAM, is a group of scientists representing federal, state, and local forensic DNA laboratories in the United States and Canada. Its subcommittees discuss topics of interest to the forensic DNA community and develop documents to provide direction and guidance for the community. The guidelines we discuss here were presented to the SWGDAM membership and approved on January 12, 2017. They provides guidelines for the interpretation of DNA typing results.

For us, the section concerning likelihood ratios is, of course, the most important part of the guidelines on which we concentrate in this short commentary. Our general impression is that the report contains useful discussions and guidelines, but that in places its statements are only approximately correct. Let us give some examples.

On page 57, the discussion on likelihood ratios starts with some general principles. In the language of the report, the inclusionary hypothesis is an hypothesis which implies that a given suspect contributed to a mixture, while an exclusionary one is an hypothesis in which this is not the case. The likelihood ratio is introduced, and then the report says:

"4B.1. The likelihood ratio for a given locus is the numerator probability divided by the denominator probability.

4B.2. The likelihood ratio for the profile is produced by multiplying the likelihood ratio values from each locus. The resultant value is the ratio of the probabilities of the evidence profile if the inclusionary hypothesis is true as opposed to if the exclusionary hypothesis is true.

4B.2.1. A final likelihood ratio value greater than 1 indicates support for the inclusionary hypothesis.

4B.2.2. A final likelihood ratio value less than 1 indicates support for the exclusionary hypothesis.

4B.3. When the evidence profile is determined to be single source, and the reference and evidence profiles are identical at all loci, the likelihood ratio is reduced to 1 / the Random Match Probability (RMP).

4B.4. The likelihood ratio for mixtures is conditioned on an assumed number of contributors, and may use peak height information (restricted approach) or not (unrestricted approach) when including genotype combinations for proposed contributors into the likelihood ratio."

We discuss these statements one by one. The point 4B.1 is certainly correct, but 4B.2 is not necessarily true. Even if we assume that the genotypes of unrelated individuals are independent over the considered loci, it does not have to follow that the likelihoods, for mixed DNA profiles, factorize over the loci. Note that we get conditional independence of the locus likelihoods for fixed model parameters (for instance, probabilities of dropout). If we do not know these parameters, then the likelihoods are obtained via integration over the probability distributions for them, and as a result, the likelihoods of the loci are no longer independent. In order to understand this more intuitively, suppose that we work with a discrete model assuming that there are contributor-specific probabilities of dropout. If we consider these to be known, the observations on one locus are not predictive for those on the next one. But if the probabilities of dropout are not known, they are. Observing four alleles in a two-person trace on a locus increases our belief in small dropout probabilities, and hence increases the probability to observe alleles on the next locus. It therefore alters the locus likelihood of the next locus. Thus, in general, the likelihood ratio is not the product of the likelihood ratios on each locus. Depending on the employed model, this may or may not be the case.

Moving on to 4B.2.1 and 4B.2.2, we find them not so carefully formulated. We have seen in Chapter 2 that it is possible that a likelihood ratio is larger than 1, while the actual probability of the first hypothesis goes down. It would, therefore, be more appropriate to say that a likelihood ratio larger than 1 indicates support for the inclusionary hypothesis *relative to* the exclusionary one. The next item 4B.3 is correct, but only provided the evidence profile is not only single source, but also a complete profile with certainty. Otherwise, we need to take the possibility of dropout into account. As for 4B.4, we also want to bring in some nuance. Surely one can model the trace and then one needs to assign a number of contributors. But we have also seen in Section 8.5 that likelihood ratio computations are possible without assuming a value for the total number of contributors, by considering hypotheses of the form "suspect is one of the k major contributors."

The report then proceeds by discussing a large number of mixture examples with an advice as to how to compute the likelihood ratio in each case. It differentiates between a "restricted approach" in which peak heights are not taken into account (we called this a discrete model), and an "unrestricted approach" in which they are (we called this a continuous model). We now first give an example of a recommendation which is mostly correct, and after that argue that in some other places, the report is incorrect. The numbering again refers to the numbering in the report.

Example 4B.4.3. In this example, the report considers a mixture that on a particular locus only has allele 8 with height 2,000 rfu. We read:

"Based upon the examination of the entire DNA profile, the mixture is determined to have originated from only two contributors at a close ratio of contributors with no reasonable assumption of dropout. Furthermore, the evidence is intimate to the victim.

The victim is genotype (8,8) at this locus. The POI is also genotype (8,8) at this locus. The likelihood ratio might be for the propositions that the mixture is comprised of the victim and the POI, as opposed to the victim and an unknown individual. The numerator of both the unrestricted and restricted likelihood ratio would assume the presence of both the victim and the POI. The probability of observing this electropherogram would be 1 if this hypothesis is true. The numerator equals 1.

The denominator of both the unrestricted and restricted likelihood ratio assume the presence of the victim, but assume the second contributor to be unknown. Since dropout is considered unreasonable, the only genotype that is reasonable for the second contributor is (8,8). The restricted likelihood ratio has no further information available than the unrestricted likelihood ratio with which to eliminate unreasonable genotypes. As such the denominator for both the unrestricted and restricted likelihood ratio would be $p_8^2 + p_8(1 - p_8)\theta$."

Here θ is the θ-correction as discussed in Chapter 7: it is just formula (7.14) written in a slightly different form.

This example is correctly worked out in that indeed both a discrete and continuous model give the same likelihood ratio. However, it is not true that the numerators and denominators of both approaches are the same. The continuous model gives the probability, in the numerator, that the peak height of allele 8 is what has been observed, and this probability is also needed in the denominator. These cancel out so that the likelihood ratios coincide. Furthermore the expression $p_8^2 + p_8(1 - p_8)\theta$ is the probability for a random person from the population to have genotype $(8,8)$. However, what we need here in the denominator is the probability that a random person has genotype $(8,8)$, given that the victim and the suspect are both $(8,8)$. This evaluates (see Section 7.4) to $(4\theta + (1-\theta)p_8)/(1+3\theta) \times (5\theta + (1-\theta)p_8)/(1+4\theta)$, the inverse of which is the likelihood ratio.

The SWGDAM report contains many examples of this type, explaining in a number of concrete situations how a suitable likelihood ratio can be computed. However, regrettably the calculations in the report are incorrect at certain places.

For instance, in Example 4B.6.1 of the report, the same situation as in the example above is considered, the only difference being that there is a "reasonable assumption of dropout of the minor contributor's entire genotype at this locus." The report now claims that:

"Since complete genotype dropout of the unknown contributor is considered reasonable, the unknown contributor could have any genotype at this locus. As such, the denominator for both the unrestricted and restricted likelihood ratio would be 1 (the probability of observing this evidence if the contributors are the victim and an unknown contributor is equal to 1)."

This is incorrect. The fact that dropout is considered reasonable does not imply that dropout is certain, which would be needed in order to be certain to only detect allele 8.

A few pages later, in Example 4B.7.1, the mixture at a given locus consists of allele 7 with height 150 rfu, allele 8 with height 1,500 rfu, and allele 11 with height 150 rfu. It cannot be excluded that allele 7 is a stutter of allele 8. The victim has genotype $(8,8)$ at this locus and the POI has genotype $(8,11)$ at this locus. The report considers the likelihood ratio for the hypotheses that the mixture is comprised of the victim and the POI as opposed to the victim and an unknown individual.

The numerator of the ensuing likelihood ratio would assume the presence of both the victim and the POI, and obviously the only way to explain allele 7 in that case would be to say that 7 is stutter. The report now states:

"The numerator of the likelihood ratio would assume the presence of both the victim and the POI and assume the peak in bin 7 is stutter. The probability of observing this electropherogram would be 1 if this hypothesis is true. The numerator equals 1."

But this is, again, unwarranted. The fact that one needs to interpret allele 7 as stutter to make the evidence explainable under the inclusionary hypothesis does not imply that under this hypothesis the evidence has probability 1. Clearly the probability to see this evidence under the first hypothesis cannot be 1, unless one claims that the peak at allele 7 is certainly a stutter, which was not the initial assumption.

The report continues with the description of a mixture in which certain alleles are "major," and others are "minor." In Example 4B.8, the alleles 7, 8, and 9 have peak heights ranging from 2,500 to 2,750 rfu, while alleles 11, 12, and 13 have heights below 250 rfu. The total number of contributors is unknown in this example. The report says the following:

"Since a finite number of total contributors cannot be assumed, the likelihood ratio cannot be applied to the mixture as a whole. However, since the major mixture was defined as being only two contributors, the likelihood ratio can be applied to only alleles 7, 8, and 9. The actual likelihood ratio will be dependent upon the propositions utilized to formulate the likelihood ratio."

This recommendation to only look at the major part of the profile is in itself sound, and has been discussed at length in Chapter 8. The top-down approach explained in that chapter opens the way for a more systematic and less ad hoc treatment of situations of this type.

Finally, we draw attention to a statement made on page 71 of the report, in which it is claimed that:

"The likelihood ratio can be applied to mixtures of 3 or more contributors. It is requisite that a finite number of contributors be assumed in the mixture since the likelihood ratio cannot be applied to an interpretation that assumes only a minimum number of contributors."

Here, a "finite" number of contributors simply means a given definite number. We disagree with this quote for at least two reasons. First of all, even if one cannot or does not want to make a specific statement about the number of contributors, one can in principle use a probability distribution for that number. Of course, this requires a reasonable probability distribution which may be difficult to defend, but it is, in principle, certainly possible. Second, many of the used implementations for the calculations of likelihood ratios use a fixed number, but that does not mean that assuming only a minimum is principally impossible. Again, we refer to the top-down method of calculating likelihood ratios in Section 8.5.

We conclude that the SWGDAM report contains a number of interesting and useful examples of likelihood ratio calculations in the context of DNA mixtures. However, the report also contains a number of statements that seem incorrect, and we fear that this has impact on the overall helpfulness of the report.

14.6 A Guideline for Validation

In this book, we have not touched upon the extensive and important topic of validation. We have mostly treated situations where the model to be applied is quite clear (perhaps up to details, which were not very important in most cases), such as for forensic DNA calculations investigating kinship. For DNA mixtures, where a variety of models has been proposed, we have discussed the extent to which the obtained results depend on the applied models. That discussion could start a more general one, namely how one should decide whether a given statistical model is satisfactory for casework.

If we consider a general framework where traces are compared to possible sources (for instance, fingerprints to fingers, glass fragments to windows, etc.), then one can obtain certain measurements on these (for instance, finding minutiae for fingerprints, obtaining the chemical composition of glass fragments). The outcomes of these measurements are the obtained data, and we want to find the likelihood ratio for the hypotheses that a trace comes from, respectively does not come from a possible source; or for the hypotheses that two items are of common origin or not. For example, the question may be whether a fingerprint was left by a certain finger from which reference prints are available, or whether two prints come from the same but unknown finger. In order to set up a statistical model, one tries to obtain a probabilistic description of the measurements using (laboratory created) source samples and trace samples of known origin. If this is too difficult, for instance because of the high dimensionality of the features compared to the sample size, one may instead define a distance metric that expresses how much the trace profile differs from that of the possible source. In that case, one tries to obtain the evidential value of the observation that a trace profile has a certain distance from a possible source profile. Likelihood ratios thus defined are sometimes called *score-based*, whereas those that process the measured multivariate data are called *feature-based*.

In both cases densities (or probability mass functions) must be defined, which may involve actual modeling, smoothing of density estimates, or a combination of both. Let us call these densities f_p and f_d respectively. The question is whether these defined densities are good enough in the sense that $f(E) := f_p(E)/f_d(E)$ provides the (or rather, an) evidential value of the observations E. The question is, in other words, whether the defined f_p and f_d are a good enough description of the randomness giving rise to measurements under either hypothesis. One aspect of the validation is then to determine the types of samples for which this is the case, for instance, for which minimum quality of obtained fingerprint traces one can still use the model.

This is, of course, a large topic which is not covered in this book. However, what we can do, is consider proposals for validation criteria and consider likelihood ratio distributions that are obtained in situations where there is no doubt about the model. That is, we can consider likelihood ratios that are produced within the applied statistical model. Those likelihood ratios should of course satisfy all validation criteria, whatever they are. As an example, we may consider kinship calculations for forensic DNA profiles. Of course, the model is never completely obvious. Indeed, mutation probabilities and allele probabilities are never completely free from subjective choices. The impact of these is, however, so minimal in many cases, that for practical purposes we may apply the model as if it were completely undisputed.

In the paper "A guideline for validation of likelihood ratio methods used for forensic evidence evaluation"[105], the authors propose "a protocol for the validation of forensic evaluation models at the source level." The aim of the paper is to give criteria that can be tested for any method that aims to derive likelihood ratios. According to [105], "the Guideline proposed is general and can be applied to any forensic method producing likelihood ratio values, whether it is biometric or not, and whether it is score-based or feature-based." Thus indeed the guidelines also are intended to apply to likelihood ratios where there the model is clear, such as for DNA kinship.

Validation is defined as (page 143) "the process followed in order to determine the scope of validity of a method used to compute likelihood ratio values." The authors add that validation entails "that we allow the method to be used in forensic casework in the future." The definition leaves open what validity itself means, but on page 143 the authors define validation criteria as verifying whether certain "performance characteristics" are met by computing statistics, called "performance metrics" that are related to these characteristics.

The guidelines [105] have as objective to give recommendations about performance characteristics and metrics to choose. The choice of these is inspired by validation criteria for physical and chemical measurements, as is clear from the following quote:

"The definitions of these performance characteristics can be found in the International Vocabulary of Metrology (VIM). The performance characteristics proposed in this Guideline for the forensic evaluation methods [...] have been chosen based on their similarity with the original performance characteristics defined for the validation of analytical methods, but have a different meaning."

We now see that the perspective the authors have is very different from ours. The authors seem to see likelihood ratios as some kind of measurement. For measurements, one assumes that the quantity to be measured physically exists, and that we have an apparatus for measuring that quantity. Then one is naturally interested in the precision of that apparatus, in its bias, and similar properties. A device for producing likelihood ratio could be viewed in a similar fashion, if we view it as measuring the strength of the evidence as if it were a truly (perhaps not physically, but with the same objectivity) existing quantity that we aim to measure.

In this book, however, we have argued that such is not the nature of the likelihood ratio. Instead, the likelihood ratio is the quotient of two probabilities that have a subjective-epistemic interpretation. In Chapter 3 we have argued that from our point of view, uncertainty on the model or the measurements does not lead to uncertainty on the likelihood ratio, but to another likelihood ratio. We are in a different epistemic position depending on whether or not we have such uncertainty, and different epistemic positions (can) lead to different likelihood ratios. The point of view that a likelihood ratio is always a measurement of an objectively existing quantity then, not surprisingly, leads to conclusions that we disagree with. In the uncertainty case, it leads to the conclusion that uncertainty on measurements or parameters leads to intervals around the likelihood ratio, and in this case we also think that the point of view reflected by the above quote is not an optimal basis.

In order to view the likelihood ratio as a measurement, the philosophy of [105] seems to be that it measures the ground truth. For example, whereas the definition of accuracy in the metrological sense is "closeness of agreement between a measured quantity value and a true quantity value of a measure," the definition of accuracy, defined as a performance characteristic in [105], is "closeness of agreement between a likelihood ratio computed by a given method and the ground truth status of the proposition in a decision-theoretical inference model."

We again see a divergence between the interpretation the authors have and the theory in this book. In Chapters 2 and 3 we have explained that the likelihood ratio is not a statement about the ground truth. It is a statement about the explanations two hypotheses have for the data. The distribution of the likelihood ratio depends on which hypothesis is true, but that does not make the likelihood ratio a statement about the ground truth. Given the data, the likelihood ratio does not depend on the ground truth, but only on those data. For that reason, we think that criteria that do not reflect this are unlikely to be helpful for validation purposes.

The performance characteristic called *calibration* in [105] is a notable exception to this. The authors call a likelihood ratio system calibrated if it satisfies "the likelihood ratio of the likelihood ratio is the likelihood ratio." The authors note that "The concept of calibration used in the context of analytical methods has nothing to do with the definition of calibration used in statistics," and indeed their definition of calibration is a probabilistic property. This property is automatically satisfied by likelihood ratios if the data come from the distributions we have defined, and can in this book be found in Proposition 2.4.1 and in equation (2.18). We agree therefore, that if the problem is to verify whether the computed number $f(E)$ is a likelihood ratio of the data E, that a violation of calibration characteristic would show that this is not the case.

Our opinion on the performance metrics that are introduced is similar to those of the characteristics they are defined for. The most important performance metric for accuracy is the so-called log-likelihood ratio cost $Cllr$, defined as

$$Cllr = \frac{1}{2}\left(E\left(\log_2\left(1 + \frac{1}{LR}\right) \mid H_p\right) + E(\log_2(1 + LR) \mid H_d) \right). \qquad (14.1)$$

In this equation, LR is what is computed by the system to be validated. The trivial system which always returns $LR = 1$ will yield $Cllr = 1$, whereas the lower bound is zero.

However, this number, although providing some summary of the distribution of likelihood ratios, cannot reveal whether or not the computed likelihood ratios actually behave as likelihood ratios. Likelihood ratios, as we have defined them, may give rise to any $Cllr$ between 0 and 1, and hence from the computation of it one cannot infer whether or not the system actually produces likelihood ratios.

On the other hand, calibration is measured by a quantity called $Cllr^{cal}$. Its definition is not needed here, since what is important is that only for calibrated systems we have $Cllr = Cllr^{cal}$. Thus, verifying whether $Cllr = Cllr^{cal}$ may help validating the system, in the sense of ascertaining that the numbers outputted as likelihood ratios are interpretable as such, whereas $Cllr$ alone cannot do that.

We would like to point out that the calibration property *alone* suffices for checking whether or not $f(E)$ may be interpreted as a likelihood ratio. Indeed, if $f(E)$ is calibrated, we may use $f(E)$ *itself* as feature derived from E and compute the likelihood ratio $P(f(E) \mid H_p)/P(f(E) \mid H_d)$, which by the calibration property is equal to $f(E)$. Hence any such function $f(E)$ can be used as a likelihood ratio for H_p versus H_d of the evidence E, and different choices of f simply lead to different likelihood ratios, all of which are valid in the sense of [105].

The other performance characteristics introduced in [105] are related to the *usefulness* of the obtained likelihood ratio distributions, in the sense of being informative about how often strong evidence may be obtained with it. As an example, we read that "likelihood ratio values should be discriminating in order to be valid." However, a likelihood ratio can be valid without being discriminating, and being useful is something different than being valid. A proposal for a validation criterion is given a few lines later:

"A *validation criterion* presents a condition related to the performance characteristics that has to be met as a necessary condition for the likelihood ratio method to be deemed as valid. For instance, a validation criterion can be formulated as follows: *only methods producing rates of misleading evidence smaller than 1% can be considered as valid.* Note that a single validation criterion is not sufficient in general, and therefore several validation criteria might be necessary in order to determine the validity of the method." (emphasis original)

It would be a serious problem if the condition mentioned as example here would indeed be a necessary condition for validity. Consider as an example the likelihood ratio in favor of two persons being related as (say) first cousins, using linked markers. As we have seen in Chapter 7, if the evaluated persons are indeed first cousins, then there is a relative small probability (about 0.25) that the likelihood ratio is very large, and otherwise it is 0.75. For unrelated individuals, it is almost always 0.75, but occasionally very large. Thus, for related individuals the evidence is misleading in the majority of cases. This is a consequence of using linked markers, but it does not follow in any way that the likelihood ratios obtained from them should be treated differently from likelihood ratios obtained from other types of evidence.

The proposed criterion seems to view misleading evidence, regardless of its magnitude, as some kind of error that should be avoided. That point of view does not recognize that the likelihood ratio does not make statements about the ground truth itself. It makes a statement about which hypothesis provides a better explanation, and how much better. It is a general fact, discussed in Section 2.4, that when data are drawn from the densities that the likelihood ratio uses, the likelihood ratio cannot be misleading both strongly and often, in either direction. If these densities accurately describe the data, as in the example we just gave, then on actual data this is also the case. It is perfectly possible that very many cases give misleading evidence, but most of the time that misleading evidence will be weak. The fact that misleading evidence may be obtained is inevitable. Therefore, whatever notion of validity one endorses, we must reject the condition in the example as being inappropriate.

14.7 Summary and Conclusions

In this chapter we have discussed six guideline documents that intend to assist the forensic scientist or the judiciary in their task of interpreting forensic evidence. Our assessment of the various documents varies. The ENFSI report is generally speaking correct and quite useful, although we have certain points of criticism. The same can be said about the *Twelve Guiding Principles and Recommendations* ensuing from the meeting of forensic scientists in Cambridge 2017. We find the PCAST report, on the other hand, very disappointing from a probabilistic and statistical point of view. The report of the DNA commission of the International Society for Forensic Genetics contains interesting observations, but should be read with some care in places. This remark also applies to the SWGDAM report: it contains useful, interesting and instructive examples of DNA mixture evaluations, but is not free of mistakes. The guidelines about validation in [105] are based on the philosophical position in which the likelihood ratio is a measurement rather than an assignment. Their notion of being calibrated is useful, but other notions of validation confound being valid with being useful, where the latter means that in practice the method often yields strong enough evidence, and the former only means that the method indeed computes a likelihood ratio.

14.8 Bibliographical Notes

Some of our criticism on the PCAST report can also be found in [61] and [109]. For a excellent discussion about the difference between match and identification we refer to [36]. For a discussion of score- versus feature-based likelihood ratios see [25]. The *Cllr* was introduced in [29].

References

[1] C. Aitken and F. Taroni. *Statistics and the Evaluation of Evidence for Forensic Scientists*. Wiley, 2004.

[2] M. Aitkin. *Statistical Inference: An Integrated Bayesian/Likelihood Approach*. Chapman and Hall, 2010.

[3] T. J. Anderson, D. A. Schum, and W. L. Twining. *Analysis of Evidence*. Cambridge Universiy Press, 2005.

[4] I. Ayres and B. Nalebuff. The rule of probabilities: A practical approach for applying Bayes' rule to the analysis of DNA evidence. *Stanford Law Review*, 67:1447–1503, 2015.

[5] D. J. Balding. *Weight-of-evidence for Forensic DNA Profiles*. Wiley, 2005.

[6] D. J. Balding. The DNA database controversy. *Biometrics*, 58:241–244, 2002.

[7] D. J. Balding. Evaluation of mixed-source, low-template DNA profiles in forensic science. *Proceedings of the National Academy of Sciences of the United States of America*, 110(30):12241–12246, 2013.

[8] D. J. Balding and P. Donnelly. Inference in Forensic Identification. *Journal of the Royal Statistical Society, Series A*, 158(1):21–53, 1995.

[9] D. J. Balding and P. Donnelly. Inferring identity from DNA profile evidence. *Proceedings of the National Academy of Sciences USA*, 92:11741–11745, 1995.

[10] D. J. Balding and P. Donnelly. Evaluating DNA profile evidence when the suspect is found through a database search. *Journal of Forensic Sciences*, 41:603–607, 1996.

[11] D. J. Balding, M. Krawczak, J. S. Buckleton, and J. M. Curran. Decision-making in familial database searching: KI alone or not alone? *Forensic Science International: Genetics*, 7(1):52–54, 2013.

[12] D.J. Balding and R.A. Nichols. DNA profile match probability calculation: how to allow for population stratification, relatedness, database selection and single bands. *Forensic Science International*, 64:125–140, 1994.

[13] D. J. Balding and R. A. Nichols. A method for quantifying differentiation between populations at multi-allelic loci and its implications for investigating identity and paternity. *Genetica*, 96:3–12, 1995.

[14] G. W. Beecham and B. S. Weir. Confidence interval of the likelihood ratio associated with mixed stain DNA evidence. *Journal of Forensic Science*, 56:S166–S171, 2011.

[15] M. D. Bello. Trail by statistics: Is a high probability of guilt enough to convict? *Mind*, 128:1045–1084, 2019.

[16] C. C. G. Benschop, A. Nijveld, F. E. Duijs, and T. Sijen. An assessment of the performance of the probabilistic genotyping software EuroForMix: Trends in

likelihood ratios and analysis of Type I & II errors. *Forensic Science International: Genetics*, 42:31–38, 2019.

[17] C. E. H. Berger and K. Slooten. The LR does not exist. *Science and Justice*, 56:388–391, 2016.

[18] C. E. H. Berger, P. Vergeer, and J. S. Buckleton. A more straightforward derivation of the LR for a database search. *Forensic Science International: Genetics*, 14:156–160, 2015.

[19] A. Biedermann, S. Bozza, F. Taroni, and C. Aitken. The consequences of understanding expert probability reporting as a decision. *Science and Justice*, 57:80–85, 2016.

[20] A. Biedermann, S. Bozza, F. Taroni, and C. Aitken. Reframing the debate: A question of probability, not likelihood ratio. *Science and Justice*, 56:392–396, 2016.

[21] A. Biedermann, S. Gittelson, and F. Taroni. Recent misconceptions about the "database search problem": A probabilistic analysis using Bayesian networks. *Forensic Science International*, 212:51–60, 2011.

[22] T. Bille, S. Weitz, J. S. Buckleton, and J.-A. Bright. Interpreting a major component from a mixed DNA profile with an unknown number of minor contributors. *Forensic Science International: Genetics*, 40:150–159, 2019.

[23] Ø. Bleka, C. G. Benschop, G. Storvik, and P. Gill. A comparative study of qualitative and quantitative models used to interpret complex STR DNA profiles. *Forensic Science International: Genetics*, 25:85–96, 2016.

[24] Ø. Bleka, G. Storvik, and P. Gill. EuroForMix: An open source software based on a continuous model to evaluate STR DNA profiles from a mixture of contributors with artefacts. *Forensic Science International: Genetics*, 21:35–44, 2016.

[25] A. Bolck, H. Ni, and M. Lopatka. Evaluating score- and feature-based likelihood ratio models for multivariate continuous data: Applied to forensic MDMA comparison. *Law, Probability and Risk*, 14:243–266, 2015.

[26] W. Bosma, S. Dalm, E. Van Dijk, R. E. Harchaoui, E. Rijgersberg, H. T. Tops, A. Veenstra, and Ypma R. Establishing phone-pair co-usage by comparing mobility patterns. *Science and Justice*, 2019.

[27] W. Briggs. *Uncertainty, the Soul of Modeling, Probability and Statistics*. Springer, 2016.

[28] I. Van Den Brink. Belief functies: theorie en een toepassing in een forensische context. *Bachelor Thesis VU Amsterdam*, 2017.

[29] N. Brümmer and J. de Preez. Application-independent evaluation of speaker detection. *Computer Speech and Language*, 20(2-3):230–275, 2006.

[30] J. Buckleton, C. M. Triggs, and S. J. Walsh (eds.). *Forensic DNA Evidence Interpretation*. CRC Press, 2005.

[31] J. S. Buckleton, J.-A. Bright, K. Cheng, H. Kelly, and D. Taylor. The effect of varying the number of contributors in the prosecution and alternate propositions. *Forensic Science International: Genetics*, 38:225–231, 2019.

[32] J. Butler. *Advanced Topics in Forensic DNA Typing: Methodology*. Elsevier, 2012.

[33] Gomez Case. *No. 99CF0391 Tr. Trans. (Cal. Superior Ct. Orange Cty.)*, 2002.

[34] Y.-K. Chung, Y.-Q. Hu, and W. K. Fung. Familial database search on two-person mixture. *Computational Statistics and Data Analysis*, 54:2046–2051, 2010.

[35] L. J. Cohen. *The Probable and the Provable*. Clarendon Press, 1977.

[36] R. Cole. Forensics without uniqueness, conclusions without individualization: The new epistemology of forensic identification. *Law, Probability and Risk*, 8:233–255, 2009.

[37] A. Collins and N. E. Morton. Likelihood ratios for DNA identification. *Proceedings of the National Academy of Sciences USA*, 91:6007–6011, 1994.

[38] R. Cooke. *Experts in Uncertainty – Opinion and Subjective Probability in Science.* Oxford University Press, 1991.

[39] R. G. Cowell. Computation of marginal distributions of peak-heights in electropherogramsfor analysing single source and mixture STR DNA samples. *Forensic Science International: Genetics*, 35:164–168, 2018.

[40] R. G. Cowell. A unifying framework for the modelling and analysis of STR DNA samples arising in forensic casework. Arxiv.org/abs/1802.03063, 2018

[41] R. G. Cowell, A. P. Dawid, S. L. Lauritzen, and D. J. Spiegelhalter. *Probabilistic Networks and Expert Systems.* Springer, 1999.

[42] R. G. Cowell, T. Graversen, S. L. Lauritzen, and J. Mortera. Analysis of forensic DNA mixtures with artefacts. *Journal of the Royal Statistical Society Series C (with discussion)*, 64(1):1–48, 2014.

[43] R. G. Cowell, T. Graversen, S. L. Lauritzen, and J. Mortera. Analysis of forensic DNA mixtures with artefacts. *Journal of the Royal Statistical Society. Series C: Applied Statistics*, 64(1):1–48, 2015.

[44] S. Cowen and J. Thomson. A likelihood ratio approach to familial searching of large DNA databases. *Forensic Science International: Genetics Supplementary Series*, 1:643–645, 2008.

[45] J. M. Curran. Statistics in forensic science. *WIREs Computational Statistics*, 1:141–156, 2009.

[46] J. M. Curran and J. S. Buckleton. Effectiveness of familial searches. *Science and Justice*, 84:164–167, 2008.

[47] F. Cuzzolin. *Visions of a Generalized Probability Theory.* Lambert Academic Publishing, 2014.

[48] F. Cuzzolin. *The Geometry of Uncertainty.* Springer, 2016.

[49] C. Dahlman. The felony fallacy. *Law, Probability and Risk*, 14:229–241, 2015.

[50] C. Dahlman. De-biasing legal fact-finders with Bayesian thinking. *Topics in Cognitive Science*, 2019.

[51] A. P. Dawid. Comment on Stockmarr's "likelihood ratios for evaluating DNA evidence when the suspect is found through a database search." *Biometrics*, 57:976–980, 2001.

[52] A. P. Dawid. Beware of the DAG! *JMLR: Workshop and Conference Proceedings*, (6), 2008.

[53] A. P. Dawid. Probability and proof. www.cambridge.org, 2008.

[54] A. P. Dawid and J. Mortera. Forensic identification with imperfect evidence. *Biometrika*, 85(4):835–849, 1998.

[55] B. de Finetti. *Theory of Probability.* John Wiley & Sons, 1975.

[56] J. DeKoeijer. Combining evidence in complex cases – a comprehensive approach to interdisciplinary casework. *Science and Justice*, 2019.

[57] P. Donnely and R. D. Friedman. DNA database searches and the legal consumption of scientific evidence. *Michigan Law Review*, 97:931–984, 1999.

[58] G. Dørum, Ø. Bleka, P. Gill, H. Haned, and T. Egeland. Exact computation of the distribution of likelihood ratios with forensic applications. *Forensic Science International: Genetics*, 9:93–101, 2014.

[59] D. Dubois and H. Prade. Evidence, knowledge and belief functions. *Journal of Approximate Reasoning*, 6:295–319, 1992.

[60] *ENFSI Guideline for Evaluative Reporting in Forensic Science.* Available online: http://enfsi.eu/wp-content/uploads/2016/09/m1_guideline.pdf. ENFSI, 2015.

[61] I. W. Evett, C. E. H. Berger, J. S. Buckleton, C. Champod, and G. Jackson. Finding the way forward for forensic science in the US – a commentary on the PCAST report. *Forensic Science International*, 2017.

[62] I. W. Evett, L. A. Foreman, and B. S. Weir. Letter to the Editor. *Biometrics*, 56:1274–1275, 2000.

[63] I. W. Evett and B. S. Weir. *Interpreting DNA Evidence: Statistical Genetics for Forensic Scientists*. Sinauer Associates, Sunderland, 1998.

[64] R. Fagin and J. Y. Halpern. Uncertainty, belief and probability. *Computational Intelligence*, 6:160–173, 1989.

[65] N. Fenton and M. Neil. The Jury Fallacy and the use of Bayesian nets to simplify probabilistic legal arguments. *Mathematics Today (Bulletin of the IMA)*, 36, 2000.

[66] N. Fenton, M. Neil, D. Lagnado, W. Marsh, and B. Yet. How to model mutually exclusive events based on independent causal pathways in Bayesian network models. *Knowledge-Based Systems*, 113:39–50, 2016.

[67] N. Fenton, M. Neil, B. Yet, and D. Lagnado. Analyzing the Simonshaven case using Bayesian networks. *Topics in Cognitive Science*, 2019.

[68] R. A. Fisher. *Statistical Methods for Research Workers*. Oliver and Boyd, 1925.

[69] J. Ge, R. Chakraborty, A. Eisenberg, and B. Budowle. Comparisons of familial DNA database searching strategies. *Journal of Forensic Science*, 56:1448–1456, 2011.

[70] P. Gill and H. Haned. A new methodological framework to interpret complex DNA profiles using likelihood ratios. *Forensic Science International: Genetics*, 7:251–263, 2013.

[71] P. Gill, T. Hicks, J. M. Butler, E. Connolly, L. Gusmao, B. Kokshoorn, N. Morling, R. A. H. Van Oorschot, W. Parson, M. Prinz, P. M. Schneider, T. Sijen, and D. Taylor. DNA commission of the International society of forensic genetics: Assessing the value of forensic biological evidence – Guidelines highlighting the importance of propositions. *Forensic Science International: Genetics*, 36(36):189–202, 2018.

[72] I. J. Good. Studies in the history of probability and statistics. XXXVII A.M. Turing's statistical work in World War II. *Biometrika*, 66(2):393–396, 1979.

[73] S. Goodman. A Dirty Dozen: Twelve P-Value Misconceptions. *Seminars in Hematology*, 45:135–140, 2008.

[74] I. Hacking. *Logic of Statistical Inference*. Cambridge University Press, 1965.

[75] M. Hall. *Combinatorial Theory*. Wiley, 1998.

[76] H. Haned, L. Pène, J. R. Lobry, A. B. Dufour, and D. Pontier. Estimating the number of contributors to forensic DNA mixtures: Does maximum likelihood perform better than maximum allele count? *Journal of Forensic Sciences*, 56(1):23–28, 2011.

[77] H. Haned, K. Slooten, and P. Gill. Exploratory data analysis for the interpretation of low template DNA mixtures. *Forensic Science International: Genetics*, 6(6):762–774, 2012.

[78] H. Haned, G. Dørum, T. Egeland, and P. Gill. On the meaning of the likelihood ratio: Is a large number always an indication of strength of evidence? *Forensic Science International: Genetics Supplement Series*, 4(1):e176–e177, 2013.

[79] T. Hicks, F. Taroni, J. Curran, J. Buckleton, V. Castella, and O. Ribaux. Use of DNA profiles for investigation using a simulated national DNA database: Part II. Statistical and ethical considerations on familial searching. *Forensic Science International: Genetics*, 4(5):316–322, 2010.

[80] A. Van Den Hout and I. Alberink. Posterior distributions for likelihood ratios in forensic science. *Science and Justice*, 56:397–401, 2016.

[81] R. Hubbard and R. M. Lindsay. Why P-values are not a useful measure of evidence in statistical significance testing. *Theory and Psychology*, 18:69–88, 2008.

[82] K. Hummel. On the theory and practice of Essen-Möller's W value and Gürtler's paternity index (PI). *Forensic Science International*, 1984.

[83] T. Kerkvliet and R. Meester. Assessing forensic evidence by computing belief functions. *Law, Probability and Risk*, 15:127–153, 2016.

[84] T. Kerkvliet and R. Meester. A behavioral interpretation of belief functions. *Journal of Theoretical Probability*, 31:2112–2128, 2017.

[85] T. Kerkvliet and R. Meester. Finding persons with special features using belief functions. *Preprint*, 2019.

[86] T. Kerkvliet and R. Meester. A new look at conditional belief functions. *Statistica Neerlandica*, pages 1–18, 2019.

[87] J. Kim, D. Mammo, M. B. Siegel, and S. H. Katsanis. Policy implications for familial searching. *Investigative Genetics*, 2:22, 2011.

[88] J. J. Koehler. One in millions, billions, and trillions: Lessons from People v. Collins (1968) for People v. Simpson. *Journal of Legal Education*, 47:214–223, 1997.

[89] P. J. Van Koppen. De Tengelhamer en het Schedeldak. *Nederlands Juristenblad*, 21:1444–1452, 2017.

[90] M. Kruijver. Characterizing the genetic structure of a forensic DNA database using a latent variable apporach. *Forensic Science International: Genetics*, 23:130–149, 2016.

[91] M. Kruijver, R. Meester, and K. Slooten. P-values should not be used for evaluating the strength of DNA evidence. *Forensic Science International: Genetics*, 16: 226–231, 2015.

[92] M. V. Kruijver, R. Meester, and K. Slooten. Optimal strategies for familial searching. *Forensic Science International: Genetics*, 13:90–103, 2014.

[93] S. L. Lauritzen, A. P. Dawid, B. N. Larsen, and H. G. Leimer. Independence properties of directed Markov fields. *Networks*, 20:491–505, 1990.

[94] D. Lindley. *Understanding Uncertainty*. John Wiley & Sons, 2014.

[95] D. Lucy. *Introduction to Statistics for Forensic Scientists*. Wiley, 2005.

[96] D. Lucy and C. Aitken. A review of role of roster data and evidence of attendance in cases of suspected excess death in a medical context. *Law, Probability and Risk*, 1:141–160, 2002.

[97] C. N. Maguire, L. A. McCallum, C. Storey, and J. P. Whitaker. Familial searching: A specialist forensic DNA profiling service utilising the National DNA Database to identify unknown offenders via their relatives – the UK experience. *Forensic Science International: Genetics*, 8:1–9, 2014.

[98] S. Manabe, C. Morimoto, Y. Hamano, S. Fujimoto, and K. Tamaki. Development and validation of open-source software for DNA mixture interpretation based on a quantitative continuous model. *PLoS ONE*, 12:1–18, 2017.

[99] K. A. Martire, G. Edmond, D. N. Navarro, and B. R. Newell. On the likelihood of "encapsulating all uncertainty." *Science and Justice*, 57:76–79, 2016.

[100] R. Meester. Classical probabilities and belief functions in legal cases. *Law, Probability and Risk*, 2020.

[101] R. Meester, M. Collins, R. Gill, and M. Van Lambalgen. On the (ab)use of statistics in the legal case against the nurse Lucia de B. *Law, Probability and Risk*, 5:233–250, 2007.

[102] R. Meester and M. Sjerps. The evidential value in the DNA database search controversy and the two-stain problem. *Biometrics*, 59:727–732, 2003.

[103] R. Meester and M. Sjerps. Why the effect of prior odds should accompany the likelihood ratio when reporting DNA evidence. *Law, Probability and Risk*, 3:51–62, 2004.

[104] R. Meester and K. Slooten. DNA database matches: A *p* versus *np* problem. *Forensic Science Internatonal: Genetics*, 46, 2020.

[105] D. Meuwly, D. Ramos, and R. Haraksim. A guideline for the validation of likelihood ratio methods used for forensic evidence evaluation. *Forensic Science International*, 276: 142–153, 2017.

[106] G. Miller. Familial DNA testing scores a win in serial killer case. *Science*, 329:262, 2010.

[107] A. Mitchell, L. Ostojic, F. Lucero, M. Prinz, and T. Caragine. Using simulation to improve understanding of likelihood ratio results. *Proceedings of the 66th Annual Scientific Meeting of the American Academy of Forensic Sciences*, 2014.

[108] G. S. Morrison. Special issue on measuring and reporing the precision of forensic likelihood ratios: Introduction to the debate. *Science and Justice*, 56:371–373, 2016.

[109] G. S. Morrison, D. H. Balding, D. J. Taylor, P. Dawid, C. Aitken, S. Gittelson, G. Zadora, B. Robertson, S. M. Willis, S. Pope, M. Neil, K. A. Martire, A. Hepler, R. D. Gill, A. Jamieson, J. De Zoete, R. B. Ostrum, and A. Caliebe. A comment on the PCAST report: Skip the "match"/"non-match" stage. *Forensic Science International*, 272:e7–e9, 2017.

[110] S. Myers, M. D. Tinken, M. L. Piucci, G. A. Sims, M. A. Greenwald, J. J. Weigand, K. C. Konzak, and M. R. Buoncristiani. Searching for first-degree familial relationships in California's offender DNA database: Validation of a likelihood ratio-based approach. *Forensic Science International: Genetics*, 5(5):493–500, 2011.

[111] D. A. Nance. Belief functions and burdens of proof. *Law, Probability and Risk*, 18:53–76, 2018.

[112] M. Neil, N. Fenton, D. Lagnado, and R. Gill. Modelling competing legal arguments using Bayesian model comparison and averaging. *Artificial Intelligence and Law*, 27, 2019.

[113] C. R. Nesson. Reasonable doubt and permissive inferences: The value of complexity. *Harvard Law Review*, 92:1187–1225, 1979.

[114] J. Neyman. *First Course in Probability and Statistics*. Holt, 1950.

[115] P. Nieuwbeerta and G. Leistra. *Dodelijk gewels: moord en doodslag in Nederland*. Amsterdam: Balans, 2007.

[116] A. Nordgaard and B. Rasmusson. The likelihood ratio as value of evidence – more than a question of numbers. *Law, Probability and Risk*, 11:303–315, 2012.

[117] G. A. Nunn. The incompatibility of due process and naked statistical evidence. *Vanderbilt Law Review*, 68:1407–1433, 2015.

[118] PCAST report: *Forensic Science in the Criminal Courts: Ensuring Scientific Validity of Feature-Comparison Methods*. Available online: www.justice.gov/archives/ncfs/page/file/933476/download. PCAST, 2016.

[119] J. Pearl and D. Mackenzie. *The Book of Why: The New Science of Cause and Effect*. Basic Books, 2018.

[120] M. W. Perlin. *Genotype Likelihood Ratio Distributions and Random Match Probability: Generalization, Calculation and Application*. Cybergenetics report (online), July 2017.

[121] M. W. Perlin, M. M. Legler, C. E. Spencer, J. L. Smith, W. P. Allan, J. L. Belrose, and B. W. Duceman. Validating true allele DNA mixture interpretation. *Journal of Forensic Sciences*, 56(6):1430–1447, 2011.

[122] J. Poincaré. *Science and Hypothesis*. The Walter Scott Publishing Co., 1905.

[123] R. Puch-Solis, L. Rodgers, A. Mazumder, S. Pope, I. Evett, J. Curran, and D. Balding. Evaluating forensic DNA profiles using peak heights, allowing for multiple donors, allelic dropout and stutters. *Forensic Science International: Genetics*, 7:555–563, 2013.

[124] National Research Council. *DNA Technology in Forensic Science*. National Academy Press, 1992.

[125] National Research Council. *The Evaluation of Forensic DNA Evidence*. National Academy Press, 1996.

[126] H. Robbins. Statistical methods related to the law of the iterated logarithm. *The Annals of Mathematical Statistics*, 41:1397–1409, 1970.

[127] B. Robertson, G. A. Vignaux, and C. H. Berger. *Interpreting Evidence: Evaluating Forensic Science in the Courtroom*. Wiley, 2016.

[128] R. V. Rohlfs, S. M. Fullerton, and B. S. Weir. Familial identification: Population structure and relationship distinguishability. *PloS Genetics*, 8(2):e1002469, 2012.

[129] R. Royall. *Statistical Evidence*. CRC Press, 1996.

[130] F. F. Schauer. *Profiles, Probabilities and Stereotypes*. Harvard University Press, 2003.

[131] P. M. Schneider et al. Allgemeine Empfehlungen der Spurenkommission zur statistischen Bewertung von DNA-Datenbank Treffern. *Rechtsmedizin*, 20:111–115, 2010.

[132] G. Shafer. *A Mathematical Theory of Evidence*. Princeton University Press, 1976.

[133] G. Shafer. Constructive Probability. *Synthese*, 48(1):1–60, 1981.

[134] G. Shafer. Non-additive probabilities in the work of Bernoulli and Lambert. In Yager, Ronald R. and Liu, Liping (eds.), *Classic Works of the Dempster–Shafer Theory of Belief Functions*, pages 117–181. Springer, 2008.

[135] M. Sjerps. The role of statistics in forensic science casework and research. *Problems of Forensic Sciences*, LXV:82–90, 2006.

[136] M. Sjerps and R. Meester. Selection effects and database screening in forensic science. *Forensic Science International*, 192:56–61, 2009.

[137] M. J. Sjerps, I. Alberink, A. Bolck, R. D. Stoel, P. Vergeer, and J. H. Van Zanten. Uncertainty and LR: To integrate or not to integrate, that's the question. *Law, Probability and Risk*, 15:23–29, 2015.

[138] K. Slooten. Familial searching on DNA mixtures with dropout. *Forensic Science International: Genetics*, 22:128–138, 2016.

[139] K. Slooten. Accurate assessment of the weight of evidence for DNA mixtures by integrating the likelihood ratio. *Forensic Science International: Genetics*, 27:1–16, 2017.

[140] K. Slooten. The information gain from peak height data in DNA mixtures. *Forensic Science International: Genetics*, 36:119–123, 2018.

[141] K. Slooten. A top-down approach to DNA mixtures. *Forensic Science International: Genetics*, 46:1–14, 2020.

[142] K. Slooten and C. E. H. Berger. Response paper to "The likelihood of encapsulating all uncertainty": the relevance of additional information for the LR. *Science and Justice*, 57:468–471, 2017.

[143] K. Slooten and A. Caliebe. Contributors are a nuisance (parameter) for DNA mixture evidence evaluation. *Forensic Science International: Genetics*, 37:116–125, 2018.

[144] K. Slooten and T. Egeland. Exclusion probabilities and likelihood ratios with applications to kinship problems. *International Journal of Legal Medicine*, 128(3):415–425, 2014.

[145] K. Slooten and T. Egeland. The likelihood ratio as a random variable for linked markers in kinship analysis. *International Journal of Legal Medicine*, 130(6):1445–1456, 2016.

[146] K. Slooten and R. Meester. Forensic identification: The island problem and its generalizations. *Statistica Neerlandica*, 65:202–237, 2011.

[147] K. Slooten and R. Meester. Statistical aspects of familial searching. *Forensic Science International: Genetics Supplement Series*, 3:e617–e619, 2011.

[148] K. Slooten and R. Meester. Probabilistic strategies for familial DNA searching. *Journal of the Royal Statistical Society: Series C (Applied Statistics)*, 63(3):361–384, 2014.

[149] M. Smith. When does evidence suffice for conviction? *Mind*, 127:1193–1218, 2018.

[150] C. D. Steele, M. Greenhalgh, and D. J. Balding. Evaluation of low-template DNA profiles using peak heights. *Statistical Applications of Genetics and Molecular Biology*, 15(5):431–445, 2016.

[151] A. Stockmarr. Likelihood ratios for evaluating DNA evidence when the suspect is found through a database search. *Biometrics*, 55(3): 671–677, 1999.

[152] G. Storvik and T. Egeland. The DNA database search controversy revisited: Bridging the Bayesian–Frequentist gap. *Biometrics*, 63:922–925, 2007.

[153] S. Suter. All in the family: Privacy and DNA familial searching. *Harvard Journal of Law & Technology*, 23(2):309–399, 2010.

[154] H. Swaminathan, A. Garg, C. M. Grgicak, M. Medard, and D. S. Lun. CEESIt: A computational tool for the interpretation of STR mixtures. *Forensic Science International: Genetics*, 22:149–160, 2016.

[155] *SWGDAM Interpretation Guidelines for Autosomal STR Typing by Forensic DNA Testing Laboratories*. Available online: `www.swgdam.org/publications`. SWGDAM, 2017.

[156] R. Swinburne. *An Introduction to Confirmation Theory*. Methuen, 1973.

[157] F. Taroni, A. Biedermann, P. Garbolino, and S. Bozza. Reconciliation of subjective probabilities and frequencies in forensic science. *Law, Probability and Risk*, 17:243–262, 2018.

[158] F. Taroni, S. Bozza, A. Biedermann, and C. Aitken. Dismissal of the illusion of uncertainty in the assessment of a likelihood ratio. *Law, Probability and Risk*, (15):1–16, 2015.

[159] F. Taroni, J. A. Lambert, L. Fereday, and D. J. Werrett. Evaluation and presentation of forensic DNA evidence in European laboratories. *Science and Justice*, 42:21–28, 2002.

[160] D. Taylor, J. Bright, and J. Buckleton. The interpretation of single source and mixed DNA profiles. *Forensic Science International: Genetics*, 7(5):516–528, 2013.

[161] D. Taylor, T. Hicks, and C. Champod. Using sensitivity analysis in Bayesian networks to highlight the impact of data paucity and direct future analysis: A contribution to the debate on measuring and reporting the precision of likelihood ratios. *Science and Justice*, 56:402–410, 2016.

[162] A. O. Tillmar and P. Mostad. Choosing supplementary markers in forensic casework. *Forensic Science International: Genetics*, 13:128–133, 2014.

[163] H. L. Van Trees. *Detection, Estimation, and Modulation Theory, Part I*. Wiley, 2001.

[164] C. M. Triggs and J. S. Buckleton. The two trace transfer problem re-examined. *Science and Justice*, 43:127–134, 2003.

[165] *Twelve Guiding Principles and Recommendations for Dealing with Quantitative Evidence in Criminal Law*. Available online: `www.newton.ac.uk/files/preprints/ni16061.pdf`. Isaac Newton Institute for Mathematical Sciences, 2017.

[166] T. Verma and J. Pearl. Causal networks: Semantics and expressiveness. *Uncertainty in Arificial Intelligence*, 9:69–76, 1990.

[167] T. Verma and J. Pearl. Equivalence and synthesis of causal models. *UAI '90: Proceedings of the Sixth Annual Conference on Uncertainty in Artificial intelligence*, pages 255–268, 1990.

[168] J. Ville. *Etude Critique de la Notion de Collectif*. Gauthier-Villers, 1939.

[169] C. Vlek, H. Prakken, H. Renooij, and B. Verheij. Modeling crime scenarios in a Bayesian network. *ICAIL. ACM, Rome*, 2013.

[170] C. Vlek, H. Prakken, H. Renooij, and B. Verheij. Representing the quality of crime scenarios in a Bayesian network. *JURIX: The 28th Annual Conference*, 2015.

[171] C. Vlek, H. Prakken, and B. Verheij. A method for explaining Bayesian networks for legal evidence with scenarios. *Artificial Intelligence and Law*, 24:285–324, 2016.

[172] P. Walley. *Statistical Reasoning with Imprecise Probabilities*. Chapman and Hall, 1991.

[173] D. T. Wasserman. The morality of statistical proof and the risk of mistaken liability. *Cardozo Law Review*, 13:935–976, 1991.

[174] B. S. Weir. The second National Research Council report on forensic DNA evidence. *The American Journal of Human Genetics*, 59:497–500, 1996.

[175] B. S. Weir. The consequence of defending DNA statistics. In Gastwirth, J. (ed.), *Statistical Science in the Courtroom: Statistics for Social Science and Public Policy*, pages 87–97, Springer, 2000.

[176] B. S. Weir and C. C. Cockerham. Estimating F-Statistics for the analysis of population structure. *Evolution*, 38(6):1358–1370, 1984.

[177] A. Westen et al. Comparing six commercial autosomal STR kits in a large Dutch population sample. *Forensic Science International: Genetics*, 10:55–23, 2014.

[178] J. T. Wixted, N. J. S. Christenfeld, and J. N. Rouder. Calculating the posterior odds from a single-match DNA database search. *Law, Probability and Risk*, 18:1–23, 2019.

[179] J. Yellin. Review of Evidence, proof and probability (by Richard Eggleston). *Journal of Economic Literature*, 17(2):583–584, 1979.

Index

CPSIA information can be obtained
at www.ICGtesting.com
Printed in the USA
LVHW062327260421
685675LV00011B/543

9 781108 449